Lecture Notes in Computer Sci

Edited by G. Goos, J. Hartmanis, and J. va

Springer
Berlin
Heidelberg
New York
Barcelona
Hong Kong
London
Milan
Paris
Tokyo

Riccardo Focardi   Roberto Gorrieri (Eds.)

Foundations
of Security Analysis
and Design

Tutorial Lectures

 Springer

Series Editors

Gerhard Goos, Karlsruhe University, Germany
Juris Hartmanis, Cornell University, NY, USA
Jan van Leeuwen, Utrecht University, The Netherlands

Volume Editors

Riccardo Focardi
Università Ca' Foscari di Venezia
Dipartimento di Matematica Applicata e Informatica
Via Torino 155, 30173 Mestre (Ve), Italy
E-mail:focardi@dsi.unive.it

Roberto Gorrieri
Università di Bologna
Dipartimento di Scienze dell'Informazione
Mura Anteo Zamboni 7, 40127 Bologna, Italy
E-mail: gorrieri@cs.unibo.it

Cataloging-in-Publication Data applied for

Die Deutsche Bibliothek - CIP-Einheitsaufnahme

Foundations of security analysis and design : tutorial lectures /
Riccardo Focardi ; Roberto Gorrieri (ed.). - Berlin ; Heidelberg ; New York ;
Barcelona ; Hong Kong ; London ; Milan ; Paris ; Tokyo : Springer, 2002
    (Lecture notes in computer science ; Vol. 2171)
    ISBN 3-540-42896-8

Die Deutsche Bibliothek - CIP-Einheitsaufnahme

CR Subject Classification (1998):D.4.6, C.2, K.6.5, K.4, D.3, F.3, E.3

ISSN 0302-9743
ISBN 3-540-42896-8 Springer-Verlag Berlin Heidelberg New York

Springer-Verlag Berlin Heidelberg New York
a member of BertelsmannSpringer Science+Business Media GmbH

http://www.springer.de

© Springer-Verlag Berlin Heidelberg 2001
Printed in Germany

Typesetting: Camera-ready by author, data conversion by DA-TeX Gerd Blumenstein
Printed on acid-free paper   SPIN 10840402   06/3142   5 4 3 2 1 0

International School on
Foundations of Security Analysis and Design

18-30 September 2000, Bertinoro, Italy

Security is a fast growing area of Computer Science, with increasing relevance to real life applications such as Internet transactions and electronic commerce. Foundations for the analysis and the design of security aspects of these applications are badly needed in order to validate and prove (or guarantee) their correctness. Recently an IFIP Working Group on "Theoretical Foundations of Security Analysis and Design" has been established (see http://www.dsi.unive.it/IFIPWG1_7/ for more details) in order to pursue a number objectives, which include the following:

- to investigate the theoretical foundations of security as an independent discipline with firm grounds in logic, semantics, and complexity;
- to discover and promote new areas of application of theoretical techniques in computer security;
- to make formal methods amenable to the security practitioners, hence increasing awareness of formal verification techniques for security in the computer science community at large.

Hence, the scope of the IFIP Working Group 1.7 encompasses all aspects of the fundamental mathematical theory of system specification and verification, which shares with IFIP TC1 the basic fields of logic (first-order logic, temporal logic, epistemic logic), semantics (static analysis, type theory), formal methods and related approaches (model-checking, theorem-proving, process algebra), and complexity.

Among the many initiatives promoted and partly founded by the WG 1.7, there is also the "International School on Foundations of Security Analysis and Design" (FOSAD) held at the Residential Center of the University of Bologna in Bertinoro, with the goal of disseminating knowledge in this critical area, especially for participants coming from less-favored and non-leading countries. The Residential Center is an ex-convent and Episcopal fortress that has been transformed into a modern conference facility with computing services and Internet access. Bertinoro lies approximately half-way between Bologna and the Adriatic coast town of Rimini. Bertinoro is perched on the foothills of the Appenine Mountains overlooking the Po Valley to the North and the Tuscan-Emilian hills to the South.

The topics covered by the school (see http://www.cs.unibo.it/ aldini/fosad/ for more details) included: Security in Programming Languages and Process Calculi; Mathematical Models of Computer Security (e.g. non interference); Logics and Models for Security Protocols Specification (e.g. belief logic, strand spaces); Cryptographic Protocol Analysis (e.g. by model checking or theorem proving);

Cryptographic Protocols at Work (e.g. in electronic commerce); Access Control and Personal Identification. The school was composed of eight main courses, each one lasting six or eight hours. Additionally, four further courses, lasting two hours each, were offered.

This volume collects six tutorial lectures given at the school. More precisely:

- Andrew D. Gordon, Microsoft, Cambridge (Nominal Calculi for Security and Mobility);
- Roberto Gorrieri, University of Bologna, and Riccardo Forcardi, University of Venice (Classification of Security Properties);
- Joshua Guttman, Mitre, Bedford, (Security Goals: Packet Trajectories, and Strand Spaces);
- Peter Ryan, CMU, Pittsburgh, (Mathematical Models of Computer Security);
- Pierangela Samarati, University of Milan (Access Control: Policies, Models, Architectures, and Mechanisms);
- Paul Syverson, Naval Research Lab, Washington, (The Logic of Security Protocols).

The school attracted a lot of people. We received almost 100 applications from all over the world. Typical applicants were PhD students, young researchers, a few senior researchers in different areas, some industrial researchers, a few governmental institution members. We selected 60 participants from 4 continents (47 European, 5 Asian, 6 American, 2 African participants), a few more than initially planned, due to the enormous pressure of the applicants that firmly wanted to take part in the event. All participants will receive this special volume of the Springer-Verlag Lecture Notes of Computer Science series.

We would like to thank all the institutions that have supported the initiative: EU (High Level Scientific Conferences programme), UNESCO Venice Office, Ser.In.Ar., University of Bologna, Fondazione Cassa di Risparmio di Forli'. Moreover, the school was held under the auspices of the European Association of Theoretical Computer Science (EATCS – Italian Chapter), International Federation for Information Processing (IFIP – WG 1.7), European Educational Forum. Finally, we would like to warmly thank the local organizers of the school, especially Alessandro Aldini, Andrea Bandini, Mario Bravetti, and Roberta Poggi.

September 2001   Riccardo Focardi
                                                        Roberto Gorrieri

Table of Contents

Mathematical Models of Computer Security

Peter Y. A. Ryan

The Software Engineering Institute, Carnegie Mellon University
Pittsburgh, PA 15213
pryan@cert.org

Abstract. In this chapter I present a process algebraic approach to the modelling of security properties and policies. I will concentrate on the concept of *secrecy*, also known as *confidentiality*, and in particular on the notion of non-interference. Non-interference seeks to characterise the absence of information flows through a system and, as such, is a fundamental concept in information security.

A central thesis of these lectures is that, viewed from a process algebraic point of view, the problem of characterising non-interference is essentially equivalent to that of characterising the equivalence of processes. The latter is itself a fundamental and delicate question at the heart of process algebra and indeed theoretical computer science: the semantics of a process is intimately linked to the question of which processes should be regarded as equivalent.

We start, by way of motivation and to set the context, with a brief historical background. A much fuller exposition of security policies in the wider sense, embracing properties other than secrecy, can be found in the chapter by Pierangela Samarati in this volume. We then cover some elements of process algebra, in particular CSP (Communicating Sequential Processes), that we need and present a formulation of non-interference, along with some more operational presentations of process algebra, including the idea of bi-simulation. I argue that the classical notion of *unwinding* found in the security literature is really just bi-simulation in another guise.

Finally, I propose some generalisations of the process algebraic formulations designed to encompass a richer class of policies and examples.

1 Background

This chapter presents a process algebra based framework in which we can express and analyze security requirements at an abstract level. I hope that the reader will come away with the impression that such an approach is well suited to formulating security properties. Many issues that have proved problematic in the formulation of, for example, secrecy in information processing systems, become much clearer when viewed in a process algebraic style. Many insights and results from the process algebra community turn out to be highly relevant in the context of information security. On the other hand, information security presents a number of challenges to current theory and so should help stimulate advances in theory.

R. Focardi and R. Gorrieri (Eds.): FOSAD 2000, LNCS 2171, pp. 1–62, 2001.

The term *security* is often used to cover a multitude of requirements, in particular:

- Secrecy (confidentiality)

- Integrity

- Availability (e.g., resilience to denial-of-service attacks).

By *secrecy* or *confidentiality* I mean, informally, that information can only be acquired by agents or processes entitled to such access. By and large I will regard the task of a policy to be to define when access should be allowed or denied. Integrity, roughly speaking, will mean that the *correctness* of data is ensured: i.e., it can only be established or modified by agents or processes entitled to influence the values of the data. Availability typically means that access to information and services to agents with the right to them is maintained in a timely and dependable manner.

Pierangela has given the background to these concepts in her chapter of this volume so we will not dwell on the various flavours that exist in the security literature. For the most part I will concentrate on secrecy for these lectures but I will touch on the other requirements. Indeed, to some extent at least, other requirements can be captured in a rather similar framework as variants of non-interference.

There has been much debate in the security literature as to what exactly is meant by the terms *security model* or *security policy* and indeed what, if any, is the distinction. I do not propose to enter such debate in these lectures, but refer the interested reader to the excellent and lucid writings of McLean, for example [57], on this and the subject area in general. For the purposes of these lectures I will take the attitude that the purpose of a *policy* is to state what information flows are to be allowed and which are to be prevented. More generally a policy will state what privileges are accorded to which agents. I will regard a *model* as being a mathematical framework in which we can precisely characterise the properties of interest, in particular that of secrecy, i.e., the absence of certain information flows.

Another much debated question is that of whether a "correct," Platonic notion of security, or at least secrecy, exists. Again I will avoid being drawn into the rather philosophical aspects of such discussions. We will see later, however, that even the apparently rather well focussed question of characterising information flows, and in particular their absence, in a system is surprisingly delicate, but for precise mathematical reasons rather than philosophical ones.

In these lectures I am principally concerned with presenting definitions security properties such as secrecy. Such definitions are of little use if we do not have ways to demonstrate that actual designs and systems meet the defintions. I will discuss some of the issues involved in going from the high-level definitions towards implementations. This turns out to be distinctly non-trivial. Step-wise development techniques are well established for so-called *safety* properties but it is well known that security properties tend not to be preserved by such techniques. Safety properties typically amount to assertions that a system will not perform such and such an undesirable behaviour. As we will see later, security properties are far more subtle and cannot be captured by simply outlawing certain behaviours.

The next two sections provide some motivation for the use of mathematical models. Section 4 gives a brief overview of the historical development of models of computer security. This will help to put the central theme, the concept of *non-interference*, in context. Section 5 presents the Goguen-Meseguer formulation of non-interference along with some discussions of the limitations of this formulation. This is usually cited as the primary reference for non-interference although there is some prior work due to Cohen and Feiertag. This is followed by a brief introduction to process algebra, in particular CSP, which will be used to give more up-to-date formulations of non-interference. Finally I present some generalisations of these formulations and topics for further research.

2   Mathematical Models

Before we launch into descriptions of mathematical models, a few words are in order on why such models are needed at all. The purpose of (mathematical) models is to provide abstract descriptions of a more complex reality. The models will typically ignore many details of the real artifact in order to render them understandable and amenable to analysis. Care has to be taken to ensure that such abstractions are not so drastic as to remove any semblance of reality.

Usually we are only interested in certain aspects of the real artifact that are wholly or largely independent of many of the details. For example, in thermodynamics physicists study the behaviour of a gas in a box. Suppose that the gas comprises n molecules, then the state of the gas is represented by a point in a $6n$ dimensional phase space. However we are not remotely interested in the exact point in the phase space the gas actually occupies. Even if we could accurately determine this point it would actually tell us nothing of interest. It is enough for most purposes just to consider the state of the gas to be a function of three parameters: temperature, volume and pressure and to study the relationship between these. The equations of motion on the phase space lift to relations between these parameters.

Similarly in computer science we are dealing with extremely complex artifacts, many of whose details are of no interest to us or are unobservable. Again we use mathematical models which, by their very nature, abstract much of the extraneous detail or are suitably constructed to allow us to make abstractions as appropriate. In these lectures we will be concentrating on process algebras as our mathematical framework and we will see that these give rise rather naturally to a representation of systems that corresponds to what is observable by some outside observer. Process algebras also lead to a number of very natural and powerful abstraction operators. We will see, for example, how the notion of secrecy leads to equivalences on the state space of a system rather analogous to the way a thermodynamical system is factored by equivalences of temperature, pressure and volume.

In short, the use of mathematical models allows us to *introduce simplicity*, to borrow a phrase from Abrial [76]. We can then deploy all the usual mathematician's tricks of abstraction, modularisation, symmetry, etc. to reduce the problem to mind-sized chunks. All the while we have to be careful that we have not simplified too much. This is an ever present danger, especially for security, where the old dictum: "the devil is in the detail," is particularly true.

Another beauty of mathematical models is that they are completely at your mercy: you can do what you like with them, up to requirements of consistency. You can change parameters with an ease that would be impossible with the real thing or even a physical mock up. You can perform *Gedankenexperimente*: thought experiments that would be impossible in reality, along the lines of Einstein's riding a light beam.

Another motivation for models is that they allow us to move from an abstract representation gradually, in a step-wise fashion towards an implementation. The hope is that by making the steps reasonably modest we ensure that the complexity of our manipulations and proofs is kept manageable throughout. This tends to be rather easier said than done, especially for security, but it is nonetheless a worthy and sensible goal.

We also need to bear in mind that absolute security is probably a theoretical impossibility and certainly a practical impossibility. Ultimately we need to aim to provide adequate levels of security against probable threats, enough for to ensure that the cost to the attacker of launching an attack outweighs the benefits. In the world of physical security people have long known how to rate safes in terms of the time they can resist certain types of attack. So, you choose the appropriate safe in terms of its resistance to attack and in terms of the likely value of its contents. Such ratings can be blown away by a new mode of attack and the history of safe design has been a game of cat and mouse between the safe designers and the safe crackers. When a new style of attack is invented, a few safes get blown, and new designs are deployed.

The story is rather similar in the information security world, but there are differences. The game is a far more complex one: the systems in question are vastly complex and the styles of attack vastly more diverse. Often the stakes are much higher. If we are concerned with critical infrastructures for example, we can't just insure everything with Lloyd's of London and upgrade our defences after a cyber terrorist has taken the whole system out.

3   Formal Models and Methods

A few words are also in order on the nature and utility of formal models and formal methods. The idea of formality in mathematics goes back a long way, to around the time of Hilbert. The motivation was to flush out implicit and unstated assumptions in proofs. Most rigorous, journal-style proofs will involve quite large steps whose justification involves understanding and insight into the problem domain. Typically, the detailed justification of such steps can be readily filled in by a competent mathematician. Occasionally errors show up later or, more usually, it is found that the justification actually requires some additional assumption not explicitly stated in the original proof. The delightful book "Proofs and Refutations", [42], by Lakatos illustrates this process beautifully by tracing "proofs" of the Euler formula relating the number of edges, vertices and faces of polyhedra. Early "proofs" were published only for counter-examples to be found later. Closer examination revealed that the "proofs" actually depended on certain unstated assumptions, assumptions that were violated by the counter-examples. Thus, for example, it had unwittingly been assumed that the polyhedra were convex and had a simple topology, i.e., genus zero. The counter-examples, Kepler stars or toroidal polyhedra, etc., violated these conditions.

This is rather troubling and raises the question: when is a proof a proof? The notion of a formal system and a formal proof is an attempt to answer this question. A formal system comprises a finite set of axioms along with a finite set of inference rules. A theorem is a statement that can be reached from the axioms by finite application of the rules. No further insight or creativity is admitted other perhaps than some ingenuity in discovering the right sequence of application of rules. In principle, then, any theorem is checkable in a purely mechanical fashion and there is no way for implicit assumptions to slip into the process.

Why is all this of interest in systems engineering? Why is it not enough just to use rigorous pen-and-paper proofs, for example? There seem to be two motivations: again, the urge to flush out all unstated assumptions and, secondly, to introduce the possibility of mechanised proofs using automated tools. Are these valid motivations? The answer seems to be: *sometimes yes*. Sometimes the design of a system or component is so critical that it really is crucial to eliminate the possibility that unrecognised and flawed assumptions could creep in. Sometimes having an automated tool really does help, in the sense that it reduces the amount of work and/or increases the resulting level of assurance. But it is essential to use the right tool in the right place. The essential question is, as Bob Morris Sr., has phrased it: "Where do I put my extra five bucks of verification money?"

Unfortunately, the history of formal methods is littered with instances of a compulsion to perform a mechanised proof even where this has been vastly expensive and has added little or nothing of benefit. You really have to ask yourself why you are attempting to prove something and, in particular, why with a mechanised proof. The validity of the result has to matter. If you are after insight into why the result holds, you are probably better off with a rigorous, pen-and-paper proof. Often the kinds of theorems that crop when performing a refinement as *proof obligations* (or *opportunities* as Jim Woodcock prefers to call them) involve rather tedious and error-prone case enumeration. This is the kind of thing theorem-provers or model-checkers are actually rather good at. For the more interesting theorems the tools can all too easily get in the way. Mackenzie, for example, discusses such issues in depth [50]. Often the mere process of thinking about how to cast a design in a form ripe for analysis reveals ambiguities, flaws and insights long before any proofs are actually attempted.

We hasten to reassure the reader that none of the results presented here have been subjected to the ignominy of mechanical proof.

4   A Brief History of Security Models

I will concentrate on the concept of non-interference and related models of security, but to help put this in context I give a very swift overview of the early evolution of computer security models in this chapter.

The topic of security models goes back some 30 years, starting with papers by Lampson, for example, that presented ways of formalizing access controls [43]. These models comprised a set of subjects S, objects O and access modes A. From a security point of view each state of the system corresponds to an access control matrix M whose rows correspond to the subjects, and columns to objects. Entries in the matrix are subsets of A and represent the allowed access of the subject to the object. Various rules constrain how states can evolve, i.e., how the entries of the matrix can be updated.

Such early work was based on analogies with the existing policies and mechanisms for the pen-and-paper world. The early work was also very much inspired by (or perhaps more accurately, funded by) the military/government environment.

In the pen and paper world, we traditionally have the notions of classified files and cleared individuals. A simple access control policy is then formulated in terms of these classifications and clearances. Thus a file might be classified *secret* and so only accessible to someone with *secret* clearance or higher. The traditional mechanisms for enforcing such policy might be a trusted registrar who would check the clearance of anyone requesting a particular file and who will only hand it over after the clearance has been verified.

Classification and clearances, that we will refer to collectively as *security levels*, are typically organised in a lattice structure. A particularly simple example is a linear hierarchy:

Top secret

—

Secret

—

Confidential

—

Unclassified

Each element of this hierarchy is said to dominate those below it, as well as itself. You are allowed to view a file if your clearance dominates the classification of the file. Thus someone with *Secret* clearance is allowed to view *Secret*, *Confidential* or *Unclassified* files but not *Top secret*, for example.

More elaborate, non-linear lattices representing partial orders are possible and indeed common, at least in the military world. These correspond to the notion of compartmentalized information and the *need to know* principle. Thus a file might carry not only a classification but also a so-called *caveat*. For example, NATO-Secret, UK-Secret etc.

The lattice might then take the form:

Top secret

—

NATO Secret – UK Secret

—

Confidential

—

Unclassified

NATO-Secret and UK-Secret are incompatible and so someone with UK-Secret would not be entitled to view a NATO-secret file and vice versa. Someone with *Top Secret* could view both. Such lattices form the basis of the so-called Multi-Level-Secure (MLS) policies that were prevalent in the early work in computer security and provide a convenient way to define which information flows are deemed acceptable and which unacceptable.

Early models of computer security sought to map such policies and mechanisms across into the information technology world. The policies map across reasonably cleanly, though even here some subtleties do arise which we will return to shortly. Mapping the mechanisms proves to be distinctly tricky. In the pen-and-paper world the means of access to files was pretty simple: you wandered over to a registry and persuaded Miss Moneypenny that you had the appropriate clearance to view a particular file. For distributed information processing systems there is a far richer set of modes and mechanisms for accessing data and the controls on such access are quite different. Also, access may not be so direct but might be mediated by various intermediate programs.

4.1   The Bell and LaPadula Model

The model proposed by Bell and LaPadula, (BLP), is one of the earliest and best known models [2]. It is embodied in the famous *Orange Book* put out by the NCSC (National Computer Security Centre), a branch of the NSA (National Security Agency) [15]. The Orange Book was the first attempt to establish systematic criteria for the evaluation of secure systems and products.

BLP is fairly straightforward and intuitive and is a rather natural analogue of MLS policies of the pen-and-paper world. I give a somewhat simplified version here; more formal and complete descriptions can be found in [29], for example.

The model comprises a set of subjects S and objects O. Subjects are thought of as active, either principals or processes acting on behalf of principals, whilst objects are passive, e.g., files. We suppose that a lattice L of security levels has been defined along with a mapping C from $S \cup O$ into L that assigns a clearance/classification to each subject/object. For simplicity we will suppose that there are just two modes of access: *read* and *write*. The information-flow policy is now captured by enforcing two rules:

The Simple Security Property :

A subject s is allowed read access to an object o if and only if $C(s)$ dominates $C(o)$.

That is, a subject is allowed to read only objects whose classification is dominated by its clearance. In particular a subject cannot read an object of higher classification, a requirement often referred to as *no read up*.

The * Property :

A subject s is allowed write access to an object o if and only if $C(o)$ dominates $C(s)$.

That is a subject is not allowed to write to an object whose classification is lower than its clearance, i.e., *no write down*.

Assuming that read and write really are the only modes of access to objects and, furthermore, that they really are one-way information flows in the direction we would intuitively expect, then we see that together these rules ensure that information cannot flow downwards through the lattice. Information can flow upwards.

Such a policy is referred to as a *mandatory access control* (MAC) policy. Subjects are not allowed any discretion with respect to these rules or to the classifications assigned to objects. Another class of access policies, in which subjects are accorded some discretion, can be constructed. Such policies are referred to as *discretionary access control* (DAC) policies. They might permit, for example, the owner or creator of a file some discretion as to what classification to assign it or to whom he wishes to grant access. A more elaborate version of BLP can be used to formulate DAC policies but this will not concern us. See Pierangela's chapter for more on this.

In practice the MLS model above is too rigid for real environments. In the pen-and-paper world there are typically rules and mechanisms allowing exceptions to the strict MLS access rules. You might, in some operational circumstances, want to allow a certain agent access to a file to which he would not ordinarily have access according to the MLS rules. Alternatively there may be reasons to lower the classification of a file, perhaps after some period has elapsed after which its contents are no longer deemed sensitive. Such exceptions would typically be handled by a security officer.

In the BLP model the handling of such exceptions are assigned to so-called *trusted subjects*. Exactly how such trusted subjects are implemented and indeed exactly what the term *trusted* means here has been the subject of much debate. The issue will crop up again when we come discuss intransitive non-interference.

4.2   The Harrison-Ruzzo-Ullman Model

The model proposed by Harrison, Ruzzo and Ullman (HRU) is also based on Lampson's access-control-matrix framework, but allows a far richer set of primitives for updating the state than for BLP [32]. In particular, subject to preconditions on the state, entries in the matrix can be added or removed, and indeed rows and columns can be added or deleted (corresponding to the creation or deletion of subject and objects). In effect we have an elaborate, conditional rewriting system. Rather unsurprisingly then we rapidly hit against various undecidablity results: in general establishing whether a certain state can be reached, i.e., whether a certain access can be granted, is undecidable.

BLP sacrifices flexibility and genericity for simplicity and decidability. Questions of whether a flow from a particular object to a particular subject is permitted can be immediately answered by simple comparison of their classification and clearance, ignoring for the moment the actions of trusted subjects.

4.3   Chinese Walls

Chinese walls policies arise naturally in a commercial setting, for example, in a consultancy firm. The firm will consult to various clients. We want to ensure that any given consultant, C say, does not gain access to sensitive information of two competing clients, A and B say. This is enforced by stipulating that should C get access to $A's$ files he should subsequently be barred from access to $B's$ files and vice versa. In effect we need to enforce appropriate mutual exclusion rules for clients with potentially conflicting interests.

Such policies can be formulated in the HRU model and can be modelled in the MLS framework as long as we allow for dynamic clearances, see [22,81]. Here accesses evolve: initially C has access rights to A or B but as soon as he exercises his right to $A's$ files, say, then his right to $B's$ is deleted, or vice versa. Notice, however, that rights are monotonically non-increasing.

Brewer and Nash proposed introducing such policies and models into computer security [5]. They are an instance of a more general class of policies known as *dynamic separation of duties* policies. Here a principal can take on certain roles, but there are certain mutual exclusions between roles. Thus if he takes on a role as a bank teller he cannot also countersign cheques, for example. The purpose of such rules are to try to prevent abuse of privilege by ensuring that a misdemeanor cannot be performed by a single individual and would require collusion.

4.4   The Clark Wilson Model

Clark and Wilson propose a significantly more elaborate framework designed to capture policies of relevance in a commercial environment [9]. This embraces not only confidentiality and integrity requirements but also notions of separation of duties and well-formed transactions. Rather than the access-control lists or matrices of the previous models they use *access-triples*. These define the programs (well-formed transactions) that a user may invoke to access certain data objects. Good references for further reading are: [46,86,23].

4.5   The Biba Model

Thus far we have only considered secrecy, or if you prefer, confidentiality. In some applications, ensuring the *integrity* of data is also often of concern. A simple form of integrity policy was proposed by Biba which is really just a dual of BLP [4]. The elements of the model are identical to BLP except that we invert the *simple* and * properties and think of the lattice as representing integrity levels rather than security levels. The effect then is to ensure that information cannot flow up in terms of the integrity lattice. In other words a low-integrity subject cannot alter an object whose integrity level is higher.

4.6   Drawbacks of BLP

BLP has the advantage of being intuitively appealing and simple to understand. The fact that it is so simple and intuitive, however, conceals a number of subtleties and problems.

Firstly it relies heavily on our intuition as to the meaning of the terms *read* and *write*. These are not given precise, let alone formal, definitions but it is clear that it is being assumed that they constitute one-way flows of information. Thus if Anne reads a file X we are assuming that information only flows from X to Anne and that there is no flow from Anne to X. Similarly if Anne writes to X we are assuming that there is no flow from X to Anne. This sounds plausible and in line with our intuitive undestanding of the terms. However, interactions are rarely one-way, particularly in a distributed context. Communication usually involves protocols with messages passing back and forth to establish and maintain channels.

Let us take an extreme example: devices like the CESG One-Way-Regulator or the NRL Pump, [40], were developed to enforce one way flow of information, from L to H, say. Even these devices require some regulatory signals flowing from H to L to avoid buffer overflows and other problems. Thus, even here, there is two way flow of information, albeit of a very low bandwidth in one direction.

Our intuitions can be deceptive. Consider an even more extreme example. We could completely invert the usual semantics of *read* and *write*. This would give an entirely consistent BLP-style model but systems that satisfied it would be the antithesis of what we had in mind for a system that maintains secrecy. In fact, essentially this occurs when we try to define the notion of integrity as in the Biba model above. The saying "people in glass houses shouldn't throw stones" makes good sense, but then so does: "people who live in stone houses shouldn't throw glasses."

A further difficulty stems from the fact that when we come to map the model down onto a real system we have to try to identify *all* the channels by which subjects can access objects. In a complex system it is clearly difficult to be sure that all such channels have been identified. This, along with the issue raised earlier-that even supposing that we have identified all the channels we may still have failed to model them accurately-makes analysis very difficult. Thus there may easily be information flows in the system that we fail to identify and that might then allow illegal information flows to go undetected. Arguably things are better in an object-oriented framework in that the methods should constitute the full set of access modes to an object. In fact, closer examination of implementations reveals other access channels not explicitly represented at the object-oriented level of abstraction.

Consider a further example: suppose that a user with a low clearance requests to create a file of a given name and suppose that a highly classified file of the same name already exists. The system might well reply to the request with a "request denied" or, arguably worse still: "request denied, file of that name already exists." This results in an information flow from H to L. It may not be a particularly useful flow as it stands but it does represent a channel that could potentially be exploited by some malicious code executing at the high level to signal to a low process. Such malicious code is referred to as a *trojan horse*.

Such channels are well known and standard solutions to this particular problem have been proposed-for example, using poly-instantiation: allowing a file of a given name to have instantiations at several security levels. However, it is also clear that the system may well harbour many other, possibly far more subtle flows of this kind. Such channels are known as covert channels and they typically arise from the sharing of resources.

The traditional reaction to such problems is to perform *covert channel analysis*. Conceptually, the known channels are severed and the system is then studied to see what channels across security-relevant boundaries remain, [41,54,55]. These can either be eliminated or, if they are difficult or impossible to eliminate, then their channel capacity can be limited to an acceptable level. Thus, for example, random delays could be introduced on response signals to introduce noise and so lower the channel capacity, see [65] for example. This tends to have a tradeoff in terms of performance but such tradeoffs are all too familiar in security in any case.

Further objections to BLP have been raised, for example McLean's *System Z* but these need not concern us here [58]. BLP stands as an important and seminal work in the area of security models and indeed continues to play a useful role in the design and evaluation of secure systems. In the next section we will present a radically different approach to modelling computer security that attempts to address some of these objections: the notion of non-interference.

5   Non-interference

5.1   Goguen Meseguer

In response to the concerns raised about BLP and access control style models in general, Goguen and Meseguer in, based on some earlier work of Feiertag and

Cohen, proposed the idea of *non-interference* [26,27,18,11]. It can be thought of as an attempt to get to the essence of what constitutes an information flow in a system and, more to the point, how to characterise the absence of any flow. In this sense it resides at a more abstract level than the access-control models and can be thought of as providing a formal semantics to the one-way-flow intuition behind terms like *read* and *write*. In particular, it abstracts completely from the inner workings of the system in question and formulates the property purely in terms of user interactions with the system interfaces.

The underlying idea will be familiar to anyone with a mathematics background as it is really a reworking in the context of simple model of computation of the standard device for characterising a function's independence with respect to a particular variable.

The model of computation assumed, at least in the original formulation, is a rather simple one. In particular it assumes that all computations are deterministic. In particular the outputs are a simple function of the state and the input. That is, given a state along with an input the resulting output is unique and well defined. We will come to non-deterministic systems a little later. Non-interference seeks to formalise the intuition that the interaction of high-level users with a system S should not influence the interactions of low-level users. We will paraphrase the original formulation to make the transition to later material a little smoother.

Histories of user interactions with the system will be recorded as traces, i.e., sequences of actions. We suppose that the set of users of the system is partitioned into two sets: high users and low users. We suppose further that the high and low users interact via separate interfaces and, in particular, low users cannot directly observe high actions. The whole point is to examine how much a Low user can infer about High actions purely from his (low's) interactions with the system. Clearly if he can directly observe the High actions the whole exercise becomes rather futile.

Notice that we will be assuming that we know the exact design of the system and, perhaps more importantly, that any hostile agents have a complete understanding of the system design. In practice neither we nor the hostile agents will have such a full understanding but it is a safe assumption to make: the less hostile agents know about the system design the less precise the inferences they can make. As with cryptography, we should not seek security through obscurity.

In accordance with the original formulation we will also assume that actions are partitioned into *inputs* and *outputs*. For the moment we will put aside the question of what the semantics behind this distinction might be. Intuitively we are thinking of inputs as being wholly under the control of the user, and outputs as wholly under the control of the system. This is similar to the BLP use of *read* and *write*.

We now think of the system as a finite state machine described by a function that, given a state and an input, returns a transition to a new state and an output. Given that we are assuming the system to be deterministic this really is a function, i.e., the state transition and output associated with an initial state and input are uniquely defined. Furthermore, assuming a unique starting state of the system, we have a one-to-one correspondence between traces and states and so we can identify states with traces.

We now restrict the range of the output function to just outputs visible to Low. Thus:

$$Output_L(S, tr, i)$$

gives the Low output from system S when input i is applied to the state corresponding to trace tr.

The final piece of plumbing that we need is the notion of the *purge* of a trace. Informally, $purge_{HI}$ takes a trace and returns a trace with all High inputs, denoted HI, removed.

A system S is said to be non-interfering from High to Low iff:

$$\forall\, tr \in I^*, c \in I \bullet Output_L(S, tr, c) = Output_L(S, purge_{HI}(tr), c) \qquad (1)$$

In other words, for any possible history of inputs to the system and next input, the output visible to Low will be the same as if we had stripped out all the High inputs. Thus, changing High inputs leaves Low's view of the system unchanged. This is analogous to the standard way of defining a function's independence with respect to one of its variables.

It might seem that we have lost generality by assuming that the alphabet of the system is partitioned into High and Low. In fact we can deal with more general MLS-style policy with a lattice of classifications by a set of non-interference constraints corresponding to the various lattice points. For each lattice point l we define High to be the union of the interfaces of agents whose clearance dominates that of l. Low will be the complement, i.e., the union of the interfaces of all agents whose clearance does not dominate that of l. Notice also that we are assuming that we can clump all the high-level users together and similarly all the low-level users. There is nothing to stop all the low users from colluding. Similarly any high-level user potentially has access to the inputs of all other high users. We are thus again making a worst-case assumption.

Non-interference takes a very abstract view of the system, effectively treating it as a black box and formulating the property purely in terms of its external behaviours. This has advantages and disadvantages. It means that the definition is wholly independent of the details of the system, so, for example, we don't have to worry about what exactly are the internal information-flow channels. On the other hand its abstractness means that it is very remote from real implementations.

A further aspect of reality that has been abstracted away is time. Time simply does not appear in the definition or the underlying model of computation. We are, in effect, assuming that any adversaries have no way of observing the timing of actions. Similarly we have abstracted away from any issues of probability and are really just thinking in terms of what events are possible. We are thus working in what is sometimes referred to as a *possibilistic* framework. This is, of course, wholly unrealistic, but we have to start somewhere. We will discuss later how one might extend the work presented here to address questions of time and probability.

Notice that non-interference is asymmetrical: we are saying nothing about how Low events might influence High outputs. Thus information is allowed to flow from Low to High. This is typically what we want for an MLS style policy.

Non-interference side steps the problems that BLP and other models have with covert channels, but does so at the expense of working at a very high level of abstraction. Leaving aside questions about input/output distinctions, non-interference will capture covert channels. Indeed the motivation for the approach was in large part to address the covert channel problem. In particular it addresses the possibility that a high user or process may deliberately try to signal to a low user.

Note that non-interference is really about characterizing the absence of causal flows rather than information flows. Absence of causal flow implies absence of information flow but there may be situations in which we have a causal flow without an associated flow of information. The canonical example of this is an encrypted channel. Here a secret plaintext will influence a ciphertext that is communicated over open channels: altering the plaintext input will alter the corresponding ciphertext output and so, naivly at least, non-interference is violated. However if the encryption algorithm is sufficiently strong, keys are not compromised etc, then we can think of this as not representing any information flow from classified to unclassified. We are ignoring for the moment questions of traffic analysis. Being sure that such a causal flow doesn't harbour some subtle information flow is very delicate and brings in considerations of cryptanalysis amongst other things. There are a number of delicate issues here and we will return to this point later.

5.2   Unwinding

Goguen and Meseguer also introduce the notion of *unwinding* a non-interference property. As it stands, non-interference is not very useful from a verification point of view as it involves quantification over all possible histories of the system. It is defined purely in terms of the system's interactions with the environment and without any reference to its internal construction etc. It thus constitutes an elegant and abstract definition is not easy to verify directly. Given a black box system, to determine if it obeys the non-interference property we would be reduced to attempting exhaustive testing, clearly an impossibility. In order to render the verification tractable we are forced to assume some (minimal) structure on the state of the system.

The idea of unwinding is to replace the original formulation with conditions on state transitions. It is analogous to the standard technique of defining an invariant that can then be used to prove a property of all reachable states via a structural-induction-style argument.

A few remarks are in order: it is necessary to introduce an equivalence relation over the states of the system. This is the relation induced by the purge function along with the correspondence between traces and states. Two traces are regarded as equivalent if they have the same purges, i.e., are identical in their low-level actions and high outputs.

Unwinding is now stated as a pair of rules. A system S is non-interfering if:

$$\forall S_1, S_2 \in traces(S), a_1, a_2 \in A$$
$$\bullet \ purge_{HI}(a_1) = purge_{HI}(a_2) \wedge S_1 \approx S_2 \Rightarrow S_1' \approx S_2' \qquad (2)$$

where S_1' denotes a state reached from S_1 after the action a_1 and similarly for S_2'. A denotes the full alphabet of S, i.e., inputs and outputs. Thus $A = I \cup O$ and:

$$\forall S_1 \approx S_2 \, and \, \forall \, a \in I \bullet Output_L(S_1, a) = Output_L(S_2, a) \qquad (3)$$

The effect of the first rule is to ensure that the equivalence on the state space of S is exactly that induced by the purge of the traces. A simple induction on the length of traces along with the one-to-one correspondence between traces and states (given that S is deterministic) establishes this. That these together imply the original property now follows from this observation along with the second rule. In this simple context of a deterministic system it is also straightforward to show that these rules are necessary. Things become much more interesting when we extend such results to the non-deterministic context later.

5.3   Non-interference Is Not a Trace Property

An important observation is that non-interference is not a trace property, that is, it cannot be framed simply as a predicate on traces. More precisely, in order to determine whether a system satisfies non-interference we cannot examine it trace by trace to determine whether each trace satisfies a certain predicate. Many useful system properties can be stated as such predicates, so-called *safety* properties. These often arise in specifying safety-critical systems where we are asserting that certain undesirable behaviours should not be allowed, in which case we can formulate a predicate whose characteristic class is equal to, or perhaps is a subset of, the set of acceptable behaviours.

Non-interference is a property of the space of behaviours. It is really asserting that if certain behaviours can occur then it must be the case that other, related behaviours must also be possible. Take a trivial example. Suppose that an allowed behaviour is h followed by l, with h a High action, l a Low action. If the system is to be non-interfering then it must also be possible for just the l to occur without the prior h event. Whereas a trace property can be expressed as a set of *acceptable* behaviours, non-interference must be expressed as a set of sets of behaviours.

Conventional refinement techniques are designed to handle safety-style properties. A system Q is said to refine P, roughly speaking, if the allowed behaviours of Q are contained in P. A consequence of this observation is that non-interference tends not to be preserved by (conventional) refinement. This will be discussed more fully later.

5.4   Relationship to Bell LaPadula

It has been claimed that BLP and non-interference are equivalent, [31] for example. The proof depends on some rather strong assumptions about the system's commands and their correspondence with the access modes of the model. In general it is difficult to establish such a firm correspondence. On the other hand there is a sense in which BLP can be viewed as a mapping of a non-interference property to an implementation architecure. This mapping is necessarily rather informal, given the lack of precise semantics of BLP and the difficulty in identifying all internal channels of information flow in the actual architecture.

There are some interesting issues here: in moving from a non-interference formulation to an access-control formulation like Bell LaPadula we are somehow moving from a non-trace property to a trace property. The step involves introducing assumptions about the architecture and the access modes, etc. In effect we are mapping the abstract state space and equivalence relations onto the architecture in question. In particular, equivalences at the abstract level will typically correspond to states of the system that are indistinguishable under certain projections, for example, in certain pieces of memory. This is discussed in some detail by Rushby [74]. Certain issues remain however. For example in [21] it is shown that an access monitor that obeys the BLP rules can still leak information as a result of deadlocks. We will not discuss these issues further here as they would take us too far from the main thrust of the lectures.

5.5   Generalisations to Non-deterministic Systems

The fact that the original Goguen Meseguer formulation was restricted to deterministic systems is a serious limitation. Most systems of interest will manifest non-determinism, either because it is deliberately introduced for, say, cryptographic reasons, or because it arises as a result of abstracting internal details of the system. The first person to investigate how the Goguen and Meseguer formulation could be extended to deal with non-deterministic systems was McCullough [52,53]. He proposed a generalized version of non-interference but found that this, at least with respect to the definition of composition he proposed, failed to be compositional. Compositionality is widely regarded as a desirable feature of a security property: i.e., given two systems that each satisfy non-interference, then some suitable composition of them should also automatically satisfy it. Whether it is reasonable to assume that a *valid* definition of non-interference should be compositional is still a matter for debate. We will return to the question of compositionality later.

Problems of compositionality, non-determinism and the semantics of inputs and outputs have prompted a proliferation of variations on the original non-intereference formulation. These include: generalised non-interference [52], non-deducibility [88], non-inference [66], restrictiveness [53], forward correctability [39], non-deducibility on strategies [90], trace closure properties [45] and McLean's selective interleavings [59]. We will not go into the details of all of these as this would involve presenting a whole raft of models of computation and would take us off the main thrust of these lectures. We will see a little later how several of these can be related when viewed in a process algebraic framework.

6   The Process Algebraic Approach

A central message that we want to convey in these lectures is that process algebras provide very effective frameworks in which to specify and analyse security properties, especially of distributed systems. There are a number of reasons for this. Process algebras are specifically designed for reasoning about systems interacting via the exchange of messages. They deal carefully with issues that we will see shortly are crucial to the study of security: non-determinism, composition, abstraction and the equivalence of systems. Added to these theoretical considerations is the fact that over the past decade or so the tool support for process algebras has improved dramatically: both theorem-proving and model-checking verification tools are now available.

6.1   Introduction to CSP and Process Algebra

We will base most of our discussion around the process algebra CSP. However, we will find that concepts from other algebras such as CCS and the pi-calculus are also useful, [61] and [63]. We start with a simple introduction to those aspects of CSP that we require.

Communicating Sequential Processes (CSP) was originally developed by Hoare to reason about concurrent systems interacting via hand-shake communications [36]. This was developed further by Roscoe and Brookes [7], and others. Timed CSP was originally proposed by Reed and Roscoe in [70] and further developed by Davies and Schneider [13]. For more up-to-date expositions, Roscoe [73] or, with more about Timed CSP, Schneider [82].

The interface of a process P is represented by its alphabet, denoted by αP, which is a collection of externally visible events (or actions) through which it can interact with the environment. Interaction takes the form of synchronisation on events. Thus, in order to interact, two processes simultaneously participate in some event, a say, and both move together onto the next state. This is an abstraction of the notion of a handshake communication and is well suited to many situations. Sometimes we really want to represent interaction in a more asynchronous fashion in which a process outputs some signal into the ether that might or might not be received by some other remote process at some later time. Typically this situation can be modelled within the CSP framework by introducing a medium with which the processes interact synchronously but which may delay or even lose messages, thus mimicking the effect of asynchronous communication between the end-points.

6.2   CSP Syntax

The basic syntactic constructs that will be of interest to us are as follows:

Prefix:

$$a \to P$$

Prefix choice:

$$a : A \to P(a)$$

Communication (input):

$$c?x \to P(x)$$

External choice:

$$P \square Q$$

Non-deterministic (internal) choice

$$P \sqcap Q$$

Parallel composition over the alphabet A:

$$P \parallel_A Q$$

Interleave

$$P \parallel\mathbin{\vert} Q$$

Hide events from the set A:

$$P \setminus A$$

Rename:

$$P[a/b]$$

P after trace tr:

$$P/tr$$

Let us explain these more fully:

Prefix The process term $a \to P$ can initially participate in the action a after which it behaves as the term P.

Prefix Choice This is similar to prefix except that we provide a set of events A from which the choice of prefix event must be drawn. Note that the continuation after the event a may be dependent on a.

Communication It is sometimes convenient to think in *value-passing* terms in which values can be communicated over channels rather than simply synchronisation on events. Channels will have types assigned to them. Let us denote the type of c by $T(c)$. Thus the term $c?x \rightarrow P(x)$ can accept a value, $x : T(c)$, over the channel c after which it behaves as the term P with appropriate internal variables bound to the value x. It is thus very similar to prefix choice but provides a syntactic sugar. In particular we can have channels with compund types.

External Choice $P \,\square\, Q$ represents a choice of the two processes P and Q. If the initial events of P and Q are distinct the choice can be made by the environment, hence the name. Thus suppose that:

$$P := a \rightarrow P'$$

and

$$Q := b \rightarrow Q'$$

If the environment offers a to $P \,\square\, Q$ then a will occur and $P \,\square\, Q$ will thence behave like P'. Similarly if the environment offers b, then b will occur and $P \,\square\, Q$ will subsequently behave like Q'. If the environment offers both a and b the choice will be made arbitrarily. Also if the intersection of the alphabets of P and Q is non-empty and the environment offers an event in this intersection then again the choice of continuation will be arbitrary.

Internal Choice Like $P \,\square\, Q$ the term $P \,\sqcap\, Q$ represents a choice between P and Q but this time the choice is made internally and the environment has no influence over this choice. Consider P and Q above and suppose that the environment offers the event a to $P \,\sqcap\, Q$. It may be that the internal choice goes for the right-hand branch, i.e., $b \rightarrow Q'$ and so the event a is refused. As long as the environment insists on offering a there will be deadlock.

Parallel Composition In the alphabetised parallel composition of two processes $P \,\|_A\, Q$, P and Q synchronise on all events from the set A, with $A \subseteq \alpha P \cap \alpha Q$. Thus, for any event from A both P and Q must simultaneously be prepared to participate for the event to occur. When such an event does occur both P and Q move together to their next states. Any events outside the set A can occur quite independently in either P or Q.

Interleave In the interleaved composition of P and Q, $P \parallel\!\parallel Q$, both processes can make progress entirely independently of the other. There is no synchronisation and hence no interaction between them. In fact we have:

$$P \parallel\!\parallel Q = P \parallel_{\{\}} Q$$

i.e., interleave can be thought of as parallel composition over the empty alphabet.

Hiding Hiding over a set C simply removes events from C from view of the environment. Such hidden events are internalised: the environment cannot (directly) see or influence their occurrence. It is usual to refer to such internal, hidden events as τ events.

Renaming Renaming alters the identity of events. In general we can perform a renaming with respect to a relation on the events. More typically we will rename with respect to a one-to-one function. Sometimes also we will find it useful to rename several distinct names to a single name. We will refer to this last as *projection*.

Renaming is useful when writing CSP specifications as an alternative to parametrised specifications where, for example, the specification involves replicated components. In the context of security we will see that it is a rather useful abstraction operator that allows us to neatly capture a number of requirements.

After P/tr, where P is a process term and tr a trace, denotes the process P after it has performed the trace tr. For a non-deterministic system, P/tr will correspond to a set of states reachable by the trace tr. We will explain this more fully when we introduce the notion of a Labelled Transition System (LTS).

Constructs also exist for (mutual) recursive definitions of processes but these will not concern us.

6.3   Semantics

The semantics of CSP processes is traditionally presented in a denotational style, that is, a denotational space is constructed along with a mapping from the language to this space. In fact a number of denotation spaces, or models, have been constructed for CSP and which is appropriate for a given application depends on the kinds of property of interest and the kinds of distinctions between processes that are relevant. The simplest model is the traces model. A trace is simply a sequence of (visible) events representing a possible behaviour. In this model a process is mapped into the set of traces that correspond to its possible behaviours. Such a trace set must always contain the empty trace: for any process not having done anything must be a possible behaviour. Furthermore such a set must be prefix closed: if a certain behaviour is possible for a process S then any behaviour leading to that behaviour must also be possible:

$$\langle\rangle \in \mathit{traces}(S)$$

and

$$s \,^\frown t \in \mathit{traces}(S) \Rightarrow s \in \mathit{traces}(S)$$

Consider a simple example:

$$P := a \rightarrow b \rightarrow c \rightarrow STOP$$

Where $STOP$ is the process that does nothing (so $\mathit{traces}(STOP) = \{\langle\rangle\}$). The traces of P are:

$$\{\langle\rangle, \langle a\rangle\langle a, b\rangle, \langle a, b, c\rangle\}$$

We can calculate the traces set for a process term P, denoted $\mathit{traces}(P)$, by structural induction on the syntax. Details can be found in [73] or [82]. Trace sets are thus much like the acceptance languages associated with finite automata. The traces model is well suited to reasoning about *safety* properties, that is, where we want to specify and check that certain undesirable behaviours are not possible. For deterministic processes the traces model is sufficiently rich to fully characterise processes. A process P is said to be deterministic if, for any possible trace, the set of events it is next prepared to participate in is well defined. Thus there is no trace tr after which in one run event a is offered by S whilst in another run which is identical as far as the visible trace tr is concerned, a is refused by S. Branching can occur, but it is controlled by the environment.

Where we are concerned with non-deterministic behaviour the trace model is not rich enough, indeed it is not rich enough to characterize when a system is deterministic. A simple example illustrates this. Consider the two processes P and Q (different to those earlier) defined by:

$$P = a \rightarrow (b \rightarrow STOP \;\square\; c \rightarrow STOP)$$

$$Q = a \rightarrow (b \rightarrow STOP \;\sqcap\; c \rightarrow STOP)$$

These have the same trace sets:

$$\{\langle\rangle, \langle a\rangle, \langle a, b\rangle, \langle a, c\rangle\}$$

But a system trying to interact with them will typically be able to distinguish between them: in particular $Q \parallel_c STOP$ could deadlock after a (if Q internally decides on the right-hand branch of the choice), whilst $P \parallel_c STOP$ can't, it must continue to offer b. Thus, although the space of potential behaviours is identical a user's experience of interacting with these two processes could be completely different. If the user is set on Q doing b, say, but Q has chosen the RHS of the

$\sqcap$ and so is only prepared to offer c, then the user will probably end up kicking Q in frustration. This could not happen with P.

To reason about, and indeed distinguish, non-deterministic behaviours and liveness we need a richer model: we need to look at what a process may choose to refuse (or conversely, accept) as its behaviours unfold. To achieve this we now introduce the notion of a *refusal set*.

Suppose that the environment E initially offers the process P a set of events X, if $P \parallel E$ can deadlock immediately then X is said to be a *refusal* of P. Thus $\{a\}$ is a refusal of $a \to STOP \sqcap b \to STOP$. So is $\{b\}$ but $\{a, b\}$ isn't. Note that if X is a refusal for P then any subset of X will also be a refusal. The set of such refusal sets is denoted by *refusals*(P).

This gives us information about what P may choose to refuse at the outset. We now extend this idea to give us refusal information as the behaviours of P unfold by introducing the *failures* of P.

A *failure* is a trace along with a refusal set. Thus:

$$failures(P) = \{(tr, X) \mid tr \in traces(P) \wedge X \in refusals(P/tr)\}$$

Consider a simple example:

$$P = a \to STOP \,\square\, b \to STOP$$

$$Q = a \to STOP \sqcap b \to STOP$$

Thus

$$failures(P) = \{(\langle\rangle, \{\}), (\langle a\rangle, \{a, b\}), (\langle b\rangle, \{a, b\})\}$$

Whilst:

$$failures(Q) = \{(\langle\rangle, \{a\}), (\langle\rangle, \{b\}), (\langle a\rangle, \{a, b\}), (\langle b\rangle, \{a, b\})\}$$

And so we see that the failures sets for P and Q are distinct in the failures model. Here for brevity we have just given the maximal refusals. The sets should be filled out with the subset closures of the refusal sets. We find that the failures of Q include the elements:

$$(\langle\rangle, \{a\}) \, and \, (\langle\rangle, \{b\})$$

These are absent in the failures of P. This precisely reflects the fact that Q could, at the outset, decide to refuse a or to refuse b. P by contrast cannot refuse either.

Given the failures model we can state formally what it means for a process to be deterministic:

Definition S is deterministic iff:

$$\forall s \in traces(S) \wedge a \in \alpha S \neg (s \frown a \in traces(S) \wedge (s, \{a\}) \in failures(S))$$

In other words, we should not be able to find a trace after which some event might, in one run, be accepted, whilst in another, be refused by S, i.e., a behaviour after which the process can internally choose either to accept or refuse a.

An important point to note is that refusals, and hence failures, are defined on stable states. Stable states are ones in which no internal progress is possible. A stable state is one from which there are no outgoing τ transitions. The reason for this is that it is difficult to meaningfully assign refusals to unstable states as any internal transitions (invisible to the environment) may change these. Refusals are thought of as sets of events that, if offered to the process will never be accepted, at least before any external process has occurred. For unstable states such a definition is inappropriate.

Non-determinism can arise in three ways: explicitly from the internal choice operator, from hiding, or from ambiguous external events, e.g.:

$$(a \rightarrow b \rightarrow STOP \,\square\, a \rightarrow c \rightarrow STOP)$$

Other semantic models exist, for example, the failures/divergence model designed to reason about internal thrashing, i.e., situations in which infinite sequences of internal events are possible without any external progress taking place. We will not need these for what follows.

Refinement Refinement, denoted $\sqsubseteq$ with a subscript to indicate in which model it is defined, is defined as set containment in the appropriate denotational model.

In the traces model:

$$P \sqsubseteq_T Q \Rightarrow traces(Q) \subseteq traces(P)$$

In the failures model:

$$P \sqsubseteq_F Q \Rightarrow failures(Q) \subseteq failures(P)$$

Refinement can be thought of as making processes more predictable. In the traces model we are simply asserting that a refinement cannot introduce new behaviours. In the failures model we are asserting this but also asserting that the refined process will never refuse events that were not refusable by the specification. This allows us to make assertions about the liveness or availability of the system to the environment (e.g., the users of the system). In particular, refinement should not introduce new ways for the system to deadlock. Refinement is monotonic with respect to the CSP operators, e.g.:

$$P \sqsubseteq_T P' \wedge Q \sqsubseteq_T Q' \Rightarrow P \parallel Q \sqsubseteq_T P' \parallel Q'$$

$$P \sqsubseteq_T P' \Rightarrow P \setminus C \sqsubseteq_T P' \setminus C$$

Some Useful Processes A few useful processes that we will need include:
$STOP$, that refuses to do anything:

$$traces(STOP) = \{\langle\rangle\}$$

RUN_A, always prepared to do any event drawn from A. Thus:

$$RUN_A = x \in A \rightarrow RUN_A$$

and

$$traces(RUN_A) = A^*$$

Where A^* is the set of all finite sequences with elements drawn from A.

The process $CHAOS_A$ may at any time choose to accept or reject any event from A. Thus:

$$CHAOS_A = STOP \sqcap ((x \in A \rightarrow CHAOS_A)$$

and

$$failures(CHAOS_A) = \{(tr, X) \mid tr \in A^* \wedge X \subseteq A\}$$

6.4   Labelled Transition Systems

In what follows it will often be useful to think in terms of an underlying labelled transition system (LTS). This is somewhat alien to the usual spirit of CSP, which is to concentrate on the external observations that can be performed on the system and abstract from all internal details. However, in the context of security, these internal details will often include the high-level user and so we have to be careful how we treat them. In particular we can't simply abstract them away.

In an LTS representation a process is thought of a collection of nodes, some of which are linked by labelled, directed arcs. A pair of nodes that are linked by a directed arc with label μ will represent the possibility of a transition between them associated with the event μ in the direction of the arc, where μ can be an internal τ event.

In general, a process term will correspond to a set of nodes of the underlying LTS. For example, P/tr will in general correspond to a set of (stable) states reachable by P executing the visible trace tr.

6.5   Acceptances and Ready Sets

The standard way to capture non-determinism in CSP is to use refusals. At first glance this may seem a little counter-intuitive and begs the question: why not think in terms of what the process will accept rather than what it will refuse? There are good technical reasons to use refusals for CSP rather than acceptances

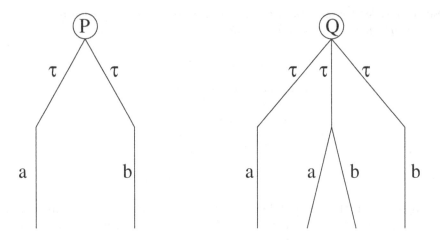

Fig. 1. Refusals vs ReadySets

as explained in [73]. For our purposes it is more intuitive to think in terms of what the system will accept. In particular this sits more comfortably with the bi-simulation approach to defining process equivalence that we will see shortly.

Acceptance sets are defined in a fashion dual to the defintion of refusal sets: X is an acceptance set of P if, when the environment offers the set X to P, an event in X will be accepted. Acceptance sets are defined to be superset closed, where closure is taken with respect to the universal alphabet Σ. The idea is that if an element of a set A will be accepted then if a larger set is offered then something from this larger set should again be accepted.

We will also need to define the idea of a *ready set*. This is defined in terms of the underlying LTS. Each node of the LTS has associated with it a ready set: the set of events that the system offers to the environment when in this state. It is thus the set of labels on the outgoing arcs from the node.

The distinction between acceptances and ready sets is that in the case of ready sets we do not take superset closure. Ready sets allow us to draw finer distinctions between processes than is possible with either acceptances or refusals. The subset or superset closure associated with the acceptances wipes out certain distinctions that are preserved when working purely with the ready sets. Figure 1 serves to illustrate this: the refusals of P and Q are identical, i.e., $\{\{a\}, \{b\}, \{\}\}$, whilst the ready sets of P are $\{\{a\}, \{b\}\}$ and for Q they are $\{\{a\}, \{b\}\}, \{a, b\}\}$.

In the context of security the ready sets model seems the most appropriate. It is slightly more discriminating than either the failures or acceptances, i.e., it draws finer distinctions between processes and so allows hostile agents to draw more inferences about the state of the system. Thus, from a security point of view, it is a safer model to work with.

Usually refusals, acceptances and ready sets are defined only over stable states. This corresponds to assuming that internal events occur *eagerly* as soon as they are available. However for our purposes we will not want to treat all internal events as eager as we will want to think of some of them as under the control of the High user. Consequently we regard ready sets as being defined on unstable states as well as stable. In some contexts we want to include τ's in the ready sets.

Where we need to consider a process term corresponding to sets of nodes of the LTS we need to consider the corresponding sets of ready sets. Let $Nodes(P)$ denote the set of nodes, both stable and unstable, corresponding to the term P. Then

$$ReadySets(P) = \{Ready(p) \mid p \in Nodes(P)\}$$

Often we will want to restrict the ready sets to some subset of the alphabet and we use a subscript to indicate this. Thus $Ready_L$ denotes the acceptance set restricted to L. $Ready_{L\tau}$ will denote the ready set restricted to $L \cup \{\tau\}$.

One final piece of notation we will need is that of *initials*. The initials of a process term P are the events P might be prepared to participate in next, ignoring non-determinism:

$$initials(P) = \{a \mid \langle a \rangle \in traces(P)\}$$

We have now set up all the necessary machinery to introduce various process algebraic definitions of non-interference.

7   CSP Formulations of Non-interference

We now present a formulation of non-interference in CSP, originally presented in [75], that stays close to the spirit of the original Goguen-Meseguer formulation but takes account of non-determinism and dispenses with any distinction between inputs and outputs.

$$\forall\, tr \in traces(S) \bullet ReadySets_L(S/tr) = ReadySets_L(S/(tr \restriction L)) \qquad (4)$$

$tr \restriction L$ projects the trace tr down onto the event set L. It thus has much the same effect as $purge_{HI}(tr)$ except that here we do not draw any input/output distinction and so we in effect "purge" all high events. The ready sets projected onto Low's alphabet encode the non-determinism visible to Low. This formulation therefore seems to be the natural way to extend the Goguen-Meseguer formulation into a CSP framework in a way that accounts for non-determinism.

The same reference also gives a more symmetric formulation:

$$\forall\, tr, tr' \in traces(S) \bullet tr \approx tr' \Rightarrow ReadySets_L(S/tr) = ReadySets_L(S/tr')) \quad (5)$$

Where

$$tr \approx tr' \Leftrightarrow tr \restriction L = tr' \restriction L$$

These are closely related but differ in some subtle ways that we will discuss shortly. Where the system S is known to be deterministic we can get away with just using *initials* in place of *ReadySets*.

Both of these look a little inelegant as they involve quantification over traces and we would like to give an algebraic formulation. An obvious formulation to try is:

$$S \setminus H =_{ReadySets} (S \parallel_H STOP_H) \setminus H \qquad (6)$$

The idea here is that composing S in parallel with $STOP$ over the H alphabet has the effect of preventing the occurrence of any H events in the RHS of the equality. The RHS thus represents the system with all H events prevented. On the LHS of the equality S's interactions with H can proceed unhindered. At first glance this seems as though it should give us what we want: that the original system from Low's point of view is indistinguishable from the system with no High activity.

It actually turns out to be a weaker property for rather subtle reasons to do with the standard semantics of CSP. As remarked earlier, the standard failures semantics of CSP only applies to stable states, i.e., states from which no τ transitions are possible. The H's have been hidden and so are abstracted eagerly and so Equation 6 only constrains the ready sets on stable states. The quantification over all traces in Equation 4, on the other hand, ensures that this definition also constrains states from which High can perform an action. Clearly the latter is appropriate: such H actions could potentially influence the events available to Low.

One way to rectify this, proposed by Roscoe [72], is by using the $CHAOS_H$ process in place of $STOP_H$:

$$S \setminus H =_{ReadySets} (S \parallel_H CHAOS_H) \setminus H \qquad (7)$$

$CHAOS_H$ can choose to deadlock on an event from H at any time, including at any state from which S would accept an H event, and so this formulation, in effect, gives quantification over all traces.

Alternatively we can give a formulation that mirrors the symmetric formulation of Equation 5 with:

$$\forall\, U, U' \in Process_H \; \bullet (S \parallel_H U) =_{ReadySets} (S \parallel_H U') \qquad (8)$$

This is actually a very intuitively appealing formulation as it is really saying that Low has no way to distinguish between users who are interacting with the system through the high-level interface.

These formulations raise a number of points that deserve further discussion. Firstly, CSP draws no distinction between inputs and outputs. We deal simply with events. The act of interaction between processes is thought of as a symmetric, co-operative activity. Both processes must agree to participate in an event for it to occur. If either refuses the event then it will not occur. As soon as both agree, it can occur. There is no concept of one of the processes causing or controlling the occurrence of an event. We will discuss later some elaborations of the usual CSP framework to allow us to draw causal distinctions if and when appropriate.

Not drawing any input/output distinctions is a safe option: we won't make errors as a result of incorrectly categorising events. On the other hand, it may be overly strong in some cases and we may find ourselves rejecting systems that would seem to be secure.

A related point is that the formulations of Equations 4 and 7 imply that the purge of any trace is itself a valid trace. At first glance this would seem right: we are, in effect, saying that to Low the system always looks as though High has done nothing. However, we have to be careful. Consider a system in which an activity of Low triggers an alert message on High's screen and let us suppose that High cannot prevent or delay this message. Here Low will know when such an alert event will occur at the High level (because he caused it) but we would not usually regard this as representing a flow from High to Low. The point is that the occurrence of the alert event cannot be influenced by High and therefore cannot be used by him to signal to Low.

To illustrate this further consider the simple process:

$$S = l \rightarrow h \rightarrow l_2 \rightarrow STOP$$

Low can deduce that h has occurred when he sees l_2. The purge formulation would reject S as insecure. If h is a signal event (e.g., an alarm) over which High has no control we really should regard this process as secure.

If h is not refusable or delayable by High, i.e., High can only passively observe its occurrence, then, for the purge formulation, we should use the process S':

$$S' = l \rightarrow ((h \rightarrow l_2 \rightarrow STOP) \,\square\, (l_2 \rightarrow STOP))$$

H refusing h does not deadlock S. Or, equivalently, we could use the original S with the symmetric formulation. Of course, if the occurrence of h can be influenced by High then we would be right to regard S as insecure. Thus, by suitable formulation of our models, we can capture distinctions between signal and refusable events. We will discuss later how, using the framework of testing equivalence, we can do this in a more systematic and general way.

Another difficulty with the formulations above is that they suffer from what is sometimes referred to as the *refinement paradox*. That is, we can define a process that satisfies them but for which a conventional refinement is insecure. Consider the process defined by:

$$S = (h_1 \rightarrow (l_1 \rightarrow STOP \,\sqcap\, l_2 \rightarrow STOP)) \,\square\, (h_2 \rightarrow (l_1 \rightarrow STOP \,\sqcap\, l_2 \rightarrow STOP))$$

S satisfies our definitions of non-interference but is refined by:

$$S = (h_1 \rightarrow l_1 \rightarrow STOP) \,\square\, (h_2 \rightarrow l_2 \rightarrow STOP)$$

This clearly leaks information. We will discuss this problem in more detail later. It is not unique to the formulations given above. The refinement problem was noted long ago by McLean [59] and, in a different setting, by Jacob [37]. Intuitively the problem arises from the fact that conventional refinements reduce non-determinism, i.e., make the system more predictable. This is entirely appropriate for safety-critical systems but can be disastrous for information security: making a system more predictable potentially allows hostile agents to make more precise inferences on the basis of limited information. A stream cipher with predictable output is not one in which we should have much confidence, to paraphrase Tom Stoppard in "Arcadia."

We should also comment on our use of ready sets rather than refusal sets. By using ready sets we are again making a worst-case assumption: that Low may be able to directly observe exactly which events are on offer. Whether this is appropriate really depends on the system in question. If, for example, the system has a display of lights that indicate at each point which events it will accept then the ready sets formulation is appropriate.

For other systems it may be appropriate to think in terms of Low performing experiments by offering an event or set of events to the system and seeing if anything is accepted. If it is accepted then the system moves on to the next state and, having moved on, Low can obtain no further information about what other events might have been accepted in the previous state. Thus typically the information available to Low is much less in this model, hence his inability to make such fine distinctions between processes. The subset closure of the refusal sets (or alternatively the superset closure of the acceptance sets) encodes this: certain distinctions that could be made working only with ready sets are masked by the closure. There is a sort of *Heisenberg uncertainty principle* at play here: observing certain parameters of the system tends to disturb it and so disrupt the observation of other parameters.

On the other hand, if the environment can back-track to the initial state after an event has been accepted and continue testing then it will be able to identify the exact ready set for that state.

8   Abstraction

Process algebras provide elegant ways of abstracting away details and encoding different views of a system. The most obvious way of abstracting is to hide a set of events, C say:

$$P \setminus C$$

However, as previously remarked, the standard CSP semantics assumes that hidden, internal events occur eagerly. As a result this form of abstraction works fine for signal events, e.g., messages to the screen. In some situations, notably security, we want to abstract certain events but not force them to be eager, they may be under the control of High and so refusable or delayable. Here it is appropriate to use *lazy* abstraction:

$$Lazy_C(S) := (S \parallel_C CHAOS_C) \setminus C$$

Another, closely related, way to abstract events but without hiding them is to camouflage them:

$$Cmflg_C(S) := (S \parallel\mid RUN_C)$$

Here the environment can still see the events from C but cannot tell if they are associated with S or are just spurious C events from RUN_C.

Variants of these are possible, reflecting certain subtleties of the semantics of CSP. A full discussion can be found in chapter 12 of [73].

Renaming can also be a useful abstraction operator. We can use it in two principal ways: permuting a set of event names or renaming a set of events to a single name. We can think of the latter as a sort of projection: Low knows an event from the set in question has occurred but not which.

There are two main ways of using the permutation of a set of events: applying the same permutation throughout an execution or using a fresh permutation at each step of the execution. The latter really gives the same effect as the projection. The former is potentially more interesting as it allows for Low to correlate events. We will see later how these are useful for coding anonymity and encrypted channels.

Mixes of these are also possible and, using certain coding tricks, it is, to some extent at least, possible in CSP to allow for the abstractions to vary dynamically. This kind of modelling works rather better in a process algebra like Milner's π-calculus, which is specifically designed to handle dynamic networks of processes.

9 Unwinding the CSP Formulation

The formulations above all involved quantifications over traces or processes. We would prefer a more convenient definition for verification. In [27] the idea of *unwinding* is introduced. The idea is to replace the original definitions by conditions on individual transitions. Assuming that the class of possible transitions is essentially finite this should give a more tractable formulation set to check. [75] gives such conditions for the formulation of Equations 4 and 5. Let us consider the latter, more symmetric version, as it will prove more suitable for what follows.

Unwinding (Symmetric Version)

– Rule 1:

$$\forall\, Y_i, Y_j \in States(S) \bullet Y_i \approx Y_j \Rightarrow ReadySets_L(Y_i) = ReadySets_L(Y_j)$$

– Rule 2:

$$\forall\, Y_i,\, Y_j \in States(S) \bullet Y_i \approx Y_j \Rightarrow \forall\, e \in Initials(Y_i), \exists\, tr \in traces(Y_j) \bullet$$
$$e \upharpoonright L = tr \upharpoonright L \wedge Y_i/e \approx Y_j/tr$$

Note that we have introduced an (abstract) state space and an equivalence relation $\approx$ on it. Rule 1 has the effect of ensuring that equivalent states give rise to the same *ready sets* when restricted to Low's interface. Rule 2 ensures that $\approx$ is exactly that induced by the purge of H events. That is, states reached by traces with the same purge are regarded as equivalent. A straightforward induction argument on the length of traces establishes this correspondence. With this we can readily proof that:

$$Rule1 \wedge Rule2 \Rightarrow NI_{CSP}$$

The implication in the other direction is more delicate however, i.e., to show that the rules are necessary as well as sufficient. [75] gives a rather clumsy proof of this by arguing that any process that satisfies the non-interference property can be implemented as a machine that satisfies the rules.

In fact a far more elegant and insightful proof is possible when one observes that the unwinding rules actually bear a striking resemblance to the notion of bi-simulation, allowing us to borrow some results from the process algebra literature. First we need to introduce a few ideas from the operation style of process semantics.

10   Operational Semantics

An operational semantics is typically presented in the form of transition rules. Thus $P \xrightarrow{\mu} P'$ indicates that the process term P can make a transition labelled μ to the process term P'. The semantics can then be presented in terms of transition rules corresponding to the various syntactic operators. Simple examples, with empty antecedents include:

$$(a \rightarrow P) \xrightarrow{a} P$$

or

$$(a \rightarrow P \,\square\, b \rightarrow Q) \xrightarrow{a} P$$

and

$$(a \rightarrow P \,\square\, b \rightarrow Q) \xrightarrow{b} Q$$

The first simply asserts that a process term $a \rightarrow P$ can first perform the action a and then behaves like the process P. The latter two simply assert that the term $a \rightarrow P \,\square\, b \rightarrow Q$ can perform an a in which case it subsequently behaves as P or a b in which case it then behaves as Q.

Notice that there are two different kinds of arrows here: inside the brackets the arrows are CSP prefix arrows. The longer, labelled arrows denote labelled transitions between process terms and are not part of the CSP notation but are part of the notation needed to present the operational semantics.

10.1   Strong Bi-simulation

Given a denotational semantics, equivalence is simply that induced by the mapping into the denotational space: two processes are deemed equal if they map to the same object in the space. In an operational style of semantics this device is not available to us and we need alternative ways to characterise the equality of terms of the algebra. The semantics is given purely in terms of what actions a process term can perform, hence we need to define equality in these terms. The usual approach is to use the notion of bi-simulation; intuitively that two terms are equal if each is able to match the others actions.

More formally: processes P and Q are strongly bi-similar if $\exists$ a symmetric relation R on the space of process terms such that:

$$PRQ \wedge P \xrightarrow{\mu} P' \Rightarrow \exists\, Q' \bullet (Q \xrightarrow{\mu} Q' \wedge P'RQ')$$

Here μ is any transition label drawn from the set of actions of P, including τ's.

In other words, assuming that they start off in equivalent states, if one can perform an action μ then the other must also be able to perform the μ action and, furthermore, after these actions they can end up in equivalent states. The latter clause ensures that we can unfold this condition to ensure that they can continue to simulate each other indefinitely. Thus each can mimic the other. Notice that they will not necessarily end up in equivalent states. The condition only requires that it is *possible* for them to reach equivalent states. Thus in general there may be other transitions from Q also labelled μ but that end up in states that are not related to P'.

10.2   Weak Bi-simulation

Strong bi-simulation insists that the processes stay in step on all actions including the hidden τ actions. Given that the τ actions are not observable by the environment this tends to be too strong a criterion. We can have processes that are observationally indistinguishable and yet are not strongly bi-similar. Strong bi-similarity is thus drawing distinctions dependent on internal, unobservable differences between implementations. This is not really in the spirit of the abstract, implementation-independent, viewpoint of process algebra. The natural weakening of this condition is to relax the requirement that the processes stay in step on the τ's.

Weak bi-simlarity is defined in a similar way except that for visible events we allow for arbitrary interleavings of τ events with the matching event to reach equivalent states. A *tau* transition in one process can be matched by an arbitrary sequence of tau's, possibly of length zero. Where μ is a visible event we take $P \stackrel{\hat{\mu}}{\Longrightarrow} P'$ to indicate that P can transition to P' with a visible event μ interleaved with arbitrary τ's, that is, an element of $\hat{\mu} \in \tau^* . \mu . \tau^*$, or where μ is a tau event $\hat{\tau}$ is taken to denote a sequence τ^n of tau's, where n could equal 0. We can now define the weak-bisimulation relation on process terms.

Two process terms P and Q are weakly bi-similar if $\exists$ a symmetric relation R such that:

$$PRQ \wedge P \stackrel{\mu}{\longrightarrow} P' \Rightarrow \exists\, Q' \bullet Q \stackrel{\hat{\mu}}{\Longrightarrow} Q' \wedge P'RQ'$$

Thus, if one process performs a visible event, we require that the other process be able to match this but allow for interleaving with τ events to reach equivalent states. If one process performs a hidden τ event, we require that the other be able to perform some sequence of τ's, possibly none, to arrive at an equivalent state.

10.3   Unwinding and Bi-simulation

There is a clear similarity between unwinding rules and (weak) bi-simulation. Both introduce an equivalence on states and both require the possibility that matching transitions from equivalent states lead to equivalent states.

The point about this analogy is that it potentially gives us a way of viewing unwinding results in a process algebraic context. If we can frame the unwinding rules in a bi-simulation style it also potentially gives us a more elegant and insightful proof of completeness. Furthermore it could give us access to established results and algorithms for establishing bi-simulation relations and for verifying equivalences of processes.

There are, however, some differences: bi-simulation does not have an immediate analogy of rule 1 of the unwinding conditions, i.e., the matching of the ready sets of equivalent states. In fact we will see how this follows from the requirement for a bi-simulation that the processes be able to match visible transitions.

Another difference is that the unwinding rules work with ready sets. It is well known that weak bi-similarity is stronger than failures equivalence and, as discussed earlier, ready sets equivalence is stronger than failures.

Bi-simulation differs from failures equivalence in that it makes distinctions according to where non-determinism is resolved, i.e., at what point internal choices are made. Consider the following simple example that illustrates this:

$$P = (a \rightarrow b \rightarrow STOP) \,\square\, (a \rightarrow c \rightarrow STOP)$$

$$Q = a \rightarrow (b \rightarrow STOP \sqcap c \rightarrow STOP)$$

In the first the branching occurs before the visible a event whilst in the second it occurs after the a. They can easily be shown to be failures and testing equivalent. These two processes are actually also ready sets equivalent as it

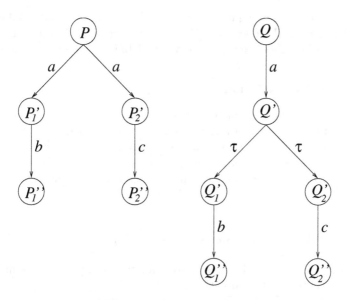

Fig. 2. Processes P and Q

happens. Any process interacting with them but with no visibility of the internal mechanisms would be unable to distinguish them. It can easily be shown, however, that no bi-simulation relation between them can be constructed.

At this point we could adopt the position that because bi-simulation gives a stronger and therefore, arguably, a safer definition of secrecy and we could simply adopt a bi-simulation definition of security. This would give a formulation of secrecy along the lines of those proposed by Gorrieri et al, [19] and described in the chapter by R.Focardi, R.Gorrieri of this volume.

In fact bi-simulation-style definitions of process equivalences have been formulated that are precisely equivalent to the failures equivalence, and indeed which, with a minor change, can also capture ready sets equivalence. We can therefore utilise these to produce a bi-simulation-style formulation that is exactly equivalent to our unwinding rules.

In the theory of automata it has long been known that a non-deterministic finite state automaton can be converted into one that is deterministic and equivalent with respect to the acceptance language model. The construction involves lifting the model to the power set of the state space and working with sets of nodes and transitions rather than single nodes. This is not quite what we want as the accepting language model ignores non-determinism. It does, however, give an indication of how to proceed.

Gardiner introduces a formulation of simulation that is equivalent to failures refinement of CSP [24]. In a more recent paper this is extended to provide a construction of bi-simulation that corresponds to failures equivalence and indeed, by a slight tweak of the construction, also provides a construction that corresponds to the ready sets equivalence [25]. The details are quite elaborate and beyond the scope of these lectures. We will try to give the intuition and provide a construction for processes that satisfy our definitions of non-interference.

10.4   Power Bi-simulation

The problem with the example earlier was the insistence on relating individual states. If instead we think in terms of sets of states we can abstract away from the details of where exactly internal choices are made. The key idea then is to construct a bi-simulation relation on the power set of the state space: $\mathbb{P}\,States$.

For a process S, set of states ϕ and visible event a define the *spray* of ϕ, $\langle[\phi]\rangle_a$, by:

$$\langle[\phi]\rangle_a = \{\phi' \in States(\phi) \mid \exists\, \tilde{a} \in \tau^*.a.\tau^* \bullet \phi \stackrel{\tilde{a}}{\Longrightarrow} \phi'\} \qquad (9)$$

That is, $\langle[\phi]\rangle_a$ gives all states reachable starting from a state in ϕ with a visible a, possibly interleaved with τ's.

A relation $\approx$ on $\mathbb{P}(S) \times \mathbb{P}(S)$ is a power bi-simulation relation for an LTS of S if:

$$S_1 \approx S_2 \Rightarrow \langle[S_1]\rangle_a \approx \langle[S_2]\rangle_a \qquad (10)$$

This in itself is not so useful: trivial solutions for $\approx$ exist. In particular the top relation that relates everything to everything satisfies this so the usual device of taking the largest relation satisfying the property is singularly uninteresting in this case. To get interesting solutions we need to impose additional constraints on $\approx$.

The intuition behind Gardiner's construction is to find the largest symmetric equivalence relation $\approx$ satisfying 10 and such that for any pair of related elements (sets of states) ϕ, ϕ' and any subset $s \in \phi$ we can find a subset s' of ϕ' such that:

$$initials(s) \subseteq initials(s')$$

Thus, refering to figure 2 again, the node Q' must be matched up with the pair of nodes $\{P_1', P_2'\}$, whilst P_1' can be matched with just Q'.

This gives a characterisation of equivalence that is exactly as discriminating as failures equivalence. Alternatively we can obtain ready sets equivalence using the slightly stronger requirement of $=$ of initials rather than $\subseteq$. It also turns out that for the ready sets model the bound has to act on stable states rather than arbitrary states as was the case for the failures equivalence. Gardiner shows that such constructions give bi-simulation characterisations of equivalence that correspond exactly to traces, failures or ready sets (depending on the choice of bound).

The construction is related to the normalisation performed by FDR, the model-checker for CSP. FDR stands for Failures, Divergences and Refinement. The tool, marketed by Formal Systems Europe Ltd performs refinement check between pairs of CSP specifications [17]. The tool creats an LTS representation of a CSP specification. During normalisation it converts the original LTS to a Generalised LTS (GLTS), whose nodes correspond to sets of nodes of the original with annotations (minimal acceptances) to carry the non-determinism information.

10.5   Loose Bi-simulation

We now introduce a construction for the power bi-simulation relation for systems satisfying the definitions of non-interference given by Equation 5, or equivalently Equation 8.

Once again it is helpful to think in terms of an underlying Labelled State Transition System (LTS) with internal transitions exposed, i.e., with labels drawn from $H \cup L \cup \{\tau\}$.

Define the relation $\sim_S$ on states of S by:

$$\sim_S = \{(S/tr, S/tr') \mid tr, tr' \in traces(S) \wedge tr \restriction L_\tau = tr' \restriction L_\tau\} \qquad (11)$$

where $L_\tau = L \cup \{\tau\}$

In effect this is the equivalence relation induced by *purging* the $H's$ but keeping the $L's$ and τ's visible.

We now define a variant of weak bi-simulation that we call loose bi-simulation: P and Q are loosely bi-similar if $\exists$ a symmetric relation $\sim_S$ such that:

$$P \sim_S Q \wedge P \xrightarrow{\mu} P' \Rightarrow \exists\, Q' \bullet Q \xdoublearrow{\overline{\mu}} Q' \wedge P' \sim_S Q' \qquad (12)$$

Where, for $\mu \in L \cup \{\tau\}$, $\overline{\mu}$ denotes a sequence of events in $H^*.\mu.H^*$, the set of all finite sequences of H actions interleaved with a single μ. For $\mu \in H$ we take $\overline{\mu}$ to denote a sequence of H events, possibly of length zero. It is thus analogous to weak bi-simulation but with τ and L events kept visible whilst the $H's$ are hidden. Thus the $H's$ playing the role of τ's.

10.6   Power Bi-simulation for Non-interference

We now define a power bi-simulation relation on $\mathbb{P}\, States(S) \times \mathbb{P}\, States(S)$:

$$\approx_S := \{(\{S \mid S \xdoublearrow{tr} S'\}, \{S \mid S \xdoublearrow{tr'} S'\}) \mid tr, tr' \in traces(S)$$
$$\wedge\; tr \restriction L = tr' \restriction L\} \qquad (13)$$

i.e., abstracting the τ's and $H's$. Note that this relation acts on the power set of the state space and so relates sets of states to sets of states.

Lemma 1. *If S satisfies the loose bi-simulation w.r.t. $\sim_S$ then it satisfies a power bi-simulation w.r.t. $\approx_S$.*

The proof follows straightforwardly from the definitions.

Lemma 2. *If $S_1 \approx_S S_2$ then for all $s_1 \in S_1$ there exists $s_2 \in S_2$ such that $s_1 \sim_S s_2$, and vice versa.*

Again the proof is a straightforward, if slightly messy, induction argument.

Lemma 3.

$$s_1 \sim_S s_2 \Rightarrow Ready_L(s_1) = Ready_L(s_2)$$

This follows immediately from the definition of loose bi-simulation: states related by $\sim_S$ must be able to match transitions and so they must match ready sets.

Lemmata 2 and 3 together immediately imply:

Lemma 4.

$$S_1 \approx_S S_2 \Rightarrow ReadySets_L(S_1) = ReadySets_L(S_2)$$

Figure 3 may help illustrate what is going on. Here p_1 and p_2 are related by $\sim$ and so have matching ready sets on $L \cup \{\tau\}$. p_1 is an element of the set of nodes Ψ_1 and p_2 is an element of Ψ_2 with $\Psi_1 \approx \Psi_2$. The diagram shows both p_1 and p_2 making transitions labelled mu to p_1' and p_2' respectively and, if the system satisfies loose bi-simulation with respect to $\sim$, we have $p_1' \sim p_2'$. Furthermore p_1' and p_2' will be elements of Ψ_1' and Ψ_2' respectively, where $\Psi_1' = \langle [\Phi_1] \rangle_\mu$ and $\Psi_2' = \langle [\Phi_2] \rangle_\mu$, with $\Psi_1' \approx \Psi_2'$. Finally note that $Ready_{L\tau}(p_1') = Ready_{L\tau}(p_2')$.

We have thus established that S satisfies loose bi-simulation w.r.t. $\sim_S$ implies S satisfies power bi-simulation w.r.t. $\approx_S$ and the ready sets bound which in turn is equivalent to S satisfying the non-interference property of Equation 5.

In fact we see that Lemma 4 is really just a restatement of unwinding rule 1 and Lemma 1 is a restatement of rule 2.

We have thus constructed a power bi-simulation formulation equivalent to the original non-interference property. Completeness, i.e., that this formulation is both necessary and sufficient, now follows from Gardiner's results that show that the largest equivalence over the LTS of the CSP language that satisfies the equality of initials bound on stable states gives the same equality of terms as the ready sets model.

It is worth examining this construction more carefully. Although originally designed as a rather formal exercise in recasting certain results in a process algebraic framework and to give a more elegant and insightful proof of the completeness of an unwinding result, it actually has some useful spin-offs. Firstly notice that we have, in effect, divided the hidden events into $H's$ and τ's and are thinking of these as the potential source of any non-determinism that may be observable by Low.

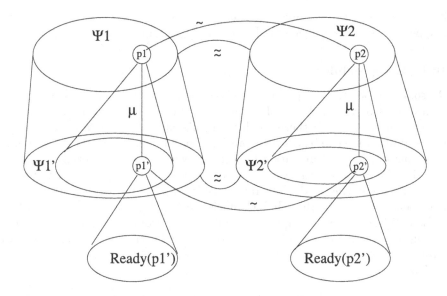

Fig. 3. Loose bi-simulation

Examining the loose bi-simulation property we see that it is asserting that the occurrence of $H's$ cannot influence the availability of τ's. We can think of the τ's as representing internal, system sources of entropy giving rise to the non-determinism visible to L, for example, due to a scheduler or to the output of a stream cipher. For a system satisfying non-interference in this framework the τ's are the sole source of any non-determinism visible to Low. Different τ behaviours can resolve the non-determinism in different ways but differing H behaviours cannot. The fact that $H's$ do not interfere with the τ's ensures that there cannot be an indirect channel from High to Low.

It may be appropriate to disambiguate the τ's. Usually, in CCS for example, τ's are invisible and so can reasonably be regarded as indistinguishable. In our construction above, however, we have, at some stages of the analysis at least, exposed the τ's. Suitable disambiguation of the τ's could allow a closer correspondence to be established between differing τ behaviours and differing non-deterministic behaviours manifest to Low. In effect the τ's are doing the book keeping that ensures that the non-determinism manifest to Low in states equivalent under $\approx$ is consistent.

A pleasing feature of the power-bi-simulation approach is that it connects the denotational, operational and testing formulations of process equivalence, and hence of non-interference. In [33] it is argued that bridging different presentations of semantics should be a major goal of theoretical computer science.

Unwinding results can be interpreted as special forms of bi-simulation and so existing algorithms for constructing bi-simulations may be useful for establishing unwinding rules. Pinsky provides a construction for equivalence classes in a somewhat different, predicate based framework [68]. These results can be mapped across to Gardiner's predicate transformer approach.

10.7   Composability

Reasoning about the composability of various formulations of non-interference with respect to various forms of composition becomes much easier in a process algebraic framework. Furthermore, having a bisimulation formulation appears to help significantly. To illustrate we present a proof of composition for processes satisfying our loose bisimulation formulation with respect to parallel composition. Parallel composition seems to be one of the more interesting operators to consider, interleaving tends to be rather trivial for example. Note that for this to make sense, we assume that High channels are linked to High channels and Low to Low. Without this assumption non-interference would be trivially violated.

Suppose the S and T both satisfy loose bi-simulation w.r.t $\sim_H$ induced by $purge_H$.

Thus

$$S_1 \sim_H S_2 \wedge S_1 \xrightarrow{\mu} S_1' \Rightarrow \exists S_2' \bullet S_2 \xRightarrow{\overline{\mu}} S_2' \wedge S_1' \sim_H S_2'$$

Similarly for T.

Now consider $S \parallel_\Sigma T$ where $\Sigma = H \cup L \cup \{\tau\}$. The Σ subscript on $\parallel$ will be taken as implicit from now on.

and define $\sim_H^*$ on $S \parallel T$ by:

$$S_1 \parallel T_1 \sim_H^* S_2 \parallel T_2 \Leftrightarrow S_1 \sim_H S_2 \wedge T_1 \sim_H T_2$$

Lemma 5.

$$S_1 \parallel T_1 \sim_H^* S_2 \parallel T_2 \Leftrightarrow \exists s_1, s_2 \in traces(S) \bullet S_1 = S/s_1 \wedge S_2 = S/s_2$$

where:

$$purge_H(s_1) = purge_H(s_2)$$

And similarly for T.

That is the $\sim_H^*$ equivalence is the same as would have been induced by purging the traces of the composed process.

Now we need to show:

$$S_1 \parallel T_1 \sim_H^* S_2 \parallel T_2 \wedge S_1 \parallel T_1 \xrightarrow{\mu} S_1' \parallel T_1'$$

implies $\exists S_2' \parallel T_2'$ such that

$$S_2 \parallel T_2 \xRightarrow{\overline{\mu}} S_2' \parallel T_2' \wedge S_1' \parallel T_1' \sim_H^* S_2' \parallel T_2'$$

Now

$$S_1 \parallel T_1 \xrightarrow{\mu} S_1' \parallel T_1' \Rightarrow S_1 \xrightarrow{\mu} S_1' \wedge T_1 \xrightarrow{\mu} T_1'$$

so by Loose bisimulation of S and T we must have S_2' and T_2' such that:

$$S_2 \xoverset{\bar{\mu}}{\Longrightarrow} S_2' \wedge T_2 \xoverset{\bar{\mu}}{\Longrightarrow} T_2'$$

so

$$S_2 \parallel T_2 \xoverset{\bar{\mu}}{\Longrightarrow} S_2' \parallel T_2'$$

but we also have:

$$S_1' \sim_H S_2' \wedge T_1' \sim_H T_2'$$

so indeed:

$$S_1' \parallel T_1' \sim_H^* S_2' \parallel T_2'$$

as required.

The structure of this proof follows largely from the nature of bi-simulation. The only tricky part is in showing that the equivalence used in defining loose bi-simulation for the composition of the processes is the *same* as that used for the processes separately. In this case we had to show that the equivalence $\sim_H^*$ defined above is the same as had we defined it directly from the purge of traces of the composed process. In other words, the key step is to show that the equivalence used in defining the loose bi-simulation *lifts* through composition in the appropriate way. In this case the proof is straightforward but for the subtler forms of non-interference we will meet later it may not necessarily be so straightforward (or even necessarily true). Schneider discusses a variety of compositionality results with respect to a number of styles of composition results in the context of a framework based on testing equivalence [84].

10.8   The Roscoe-Woodcock-Wulf Approach

The fact that the formulations of non-interference given above fail to be preserved under the usual refinement of CSP, or indeed most other styles of refinement, is troubling. Various responses are possible to this: we could conclude that such a formulation is flawed. We could conclude that this is just a fact of life and security is not a property preserved under refinement. This would be a distinctly depressing conclusion as it would deny us the possibility of step-wise development and verification. Another is to accept that conventional refinements will not preserve security and if we want security to be automatically preserved we will need a new formulation of refinement. Yet another response is to conclude that maybe it is unreasonable to expect security to be preserved automatically and that we have no choice but to do further verification as we move down towards the implementation during the design process: i.e., to generate and discharge proof obligations at each refinement step.

We will discuss the latter reactions a little later. First we introduce an alternative CSP formulation of non-interference that is preserved under CSP refinement. The approach is due to Roscoe, Woodcock and Wulf [71].

The key idea here is to assert that a suitable abstraction of the system that represents Low's view be deterministic. In our earlier formulations we sought ways to allow some non-determinism at Low's level but denying High any way to influence the way this is resolved. In the this approach there simply isn't any non-determinism in Low's viewpoint. Such a system is fully under the control of the environment (as far as it's externally observable behaviour is concerned) and so it cannot be the source of any information or entropy. There may be entropy being created and sloshing around internally but it never gets to leak outside.

Definition. A system S satisfies RWW non-interference, denoted $NI_{RWW} S$, iff $Abstract_H(S)$ is deterministic.

Where $Abstract_H$ denotes an appropriate abstraction of the H events giving Low's view of the system.

As remarked earlier, non-determinism is never increased by CSP refinement. Consequently, any system that is deterministic to start will remain deterministic under refinement. Thus any refinement of a system that satisfies the RWW property of non-interference will necessarily also satisfy it. A further advantage is that it can be automatically checked, indeed FRD has a button for this.

This makes the approach very attractive. It is stronger than the previous formulations we have discussed: any system satisfying NI_{RWW} will also satisfy all of the formulations given previously. It also side-steps many of the rather delicate issues that dog other formulations: in particular, what is the right notion of equivalence to use? How can we be sure that there is not some subtle way for High to influence non-determinism that is missed by our models. The latter problem is another manifestation of the refinement problem.

For a system whose security can be formulated as NI_{RWW} it is clearly sensible to use this formulation for the above reasons. The drawback is that it would appear that there is a large class of systems of interest for which this formulation is not appropriate, i.e., for which some residual non-determinism at Low is unavoidable. The classic example is the encrypted channel that we will discuss in greater detail later. Suppose that we consider a stream cipher (essentially a one-time-pad). This is a source of pure entropy and it does leak to the outside. However, a well designed cipher box properly incorporated in a secure architecture should still be secure. In essence the entropy generated by the box cannot be influenced or predicted by High.

Such an example cannot, in any obvious way at least, be formulated in the NI_{RWW} style. Actually it is not trivial to formulate in other weaker formulations either and we will return to this point later.

Another appealing feature is that the definition of determinism is fairly uncontroversial and coincides for most process algebras.

It is possible to combine this approach with the loose bi-simulation approach described earlier: consider an abstraction of the system with the H's abstracted but the τ's kept visible and indeed disambiguated. We now require that this abstraction be deterministic. This is stronger than the loose bi-simulation that we introduced earlier and indeed implies it. The *real* system again has the τ's abstracted and so can manifest non-determinism at Low's interface. Again we know that any non-determinism visible to Low will be entirely due to differing τ behaviours and furthermore we know that High's activity cannot influence the τ's. We thus get the best of both worlds: a simple and easily verifiable and refinable property that still allows for some non-determinism at Low's level.

For this to work we certainly need to disambiguate the τ's as we would otherwise have non-determinism due to ambiguous branching on τ's. There seems no reason not to do this and indeed the identification of all internal events with a single event could itself be regarded as a modelling device, an entirely sensible one for hidden events.

We also need to avoid non-determinism arising from ambiguous Low events. In fact we can always transform a system with ambiguous visible events to one in which such branching is replaced by τ branching.

10.9   The Jacob Security Ordering

A drastically different approach to formalising security was taken by Jacob, [37,38]. Jacob suggests that there is, in fact, no way of saying categorically whether or not a system is secure. In this approach security is considered to be a purely relative property: at best all we can do is establish that one system is at least as secure as another. To this end he introduces a security ordering based on the notion of *infer* functions. Given a Low level projection of a trace the infer function returns the set of system behaviours consistent with this observation. Formally:

Given a trace $tr \in trace(S)$

$$infer_S(tr) := \{s \mid s \in traces(S) \land s \upharpoonright L = tr \upharpoonright L\} \qquad (14)$$

The larger the cardinality of the set returned by *infer* the greater the uncertainty about the system behaviour associated with that observation. The idea now is, for a pair of systems P and Q, to compare the size of the *infer* function for all possible Low observations. We will consider P to be at least as secure as Q if:

$$\forall\, tr \in traces(Q) \bullet infer_Q(tr) \subseteq infer_P(tr) \qquad (15)$$

In other words, for any given Low observation, the set resulting from the infer function applied to P is always a superset of the corresponding infer function for Q. Thus the uncertainty resulting from observations of P is always greater than would be the case for Q.

The idea is very interesting, but it has failed to catch on, presumably because people have tended to feel uncomfortable with not being able to characterise a given system as either secure or insecure. Given that security is never absolute this is really not a valid objection. To return to the safe analogy: it is not meaningful to rate a safe as "secure," but it may be meaningful to claim that one safe is more secure than another, i.e., for all known forms of attack it will withstand for a longer period. The time may be ripe to take a fresh look at this approach.

10.10   Testing Equivalence

Another way of characterising process equivalence is the notion of testing. The idea is highly intuitive: if no experiment that the environment can perform on a pair of systems P and Q can distinguish between them then they are deemed to be equivalent. This is really very compelling in the context of security as we can think of these experiments as representing the efforts by Low to infer something about High's activity.

Schneider shows that several of the existing formulations of non-interference style properties can be cast rather naturally as flavours of testing equivalence [84]. Indeed it seems that in several cases the authors of these were in effect independently reinventing certain flavours of testing equivalence. We will show, for example, how *non-deducibility* and *non-deducibility on strategies* emerge naturally from thinking in terms of testing equivalences. First we give a formal definition of testing equivalence.

A test is a process T with a distinguished *success* event ω. We allow the system P to run in parallel with T and observe whether the resulting process can reach a state in which the ω event is possible. We can then characterise processes in terms of the set of tests they pass, which provides us with an alternative way to assign meaning to process terms. In particular, we regard two processes that, for all possible tests, pass the same set of tests as equivalent. We have to make precise what we mean by *all possible tests*. Typically this will simply be the space of tests that can be expressed in the process algebra. In some circumstances we may want to constrain the space of possible tests to reflect limitations on the capabilities of the environment (or hostile agents in the case of security).

To formally define the notion of a test we need to introduce a special $SUCCESS$ process which satisfies the transition rule: $SUCCESS \xrightarrow{\omega} STOP$. Thus, $SUCCESS$ is a simple process that performs a success event ω and then stops. ω is a special event that is introduced purely as a device to define the success of a test and will not be part of the universal alphabet Σ.

Success of a test is now characterised by whether the process:

$$(P \parallel_\Sigma T) \setminus \Sigma$$

can perform ω. Where T is constructed from the CSP operators along with the $SUCCESS$ process. Thus the occurrence of the ω event signals that P has agreed to perform some behaviour offered by T. You can think of T as representing some abstract test harness that is attached to P.

10.11   May Testing Equivalence

There are three possible outcomes of such a test when applied to a particular process: it might always succeed, always fail or sometimes succeed.

If $(P \parallel_\Sigma T) \setminus \Sigma$ can perform ω then we will say that P *may pass* T, written $PmayT$. That is, $\exists$ an execution of $(P \parallel_\Sigma T) \setminus \Sigma$ that results in ω. It is possible that there are executions of P that do not result in ω so success is not guaranteed, hence the name *may testing*.

P and Q are now deemed to be may testing equivalent, written $P =_{may} Q$, iff:

$$\forall T \bullet PmayT \Leftrightarrow QmayT$$

In other words the set of tests that P may pass is exactly the same as the set that Q may pass. May testing equivalence is known to give the same equivalence as the traces model [10].

An analogous notion of *must testing* can be defined by requiring that all (maximal) executions of $(P \parallel_\Sigma T) \setminus \Sigma$ result in an ω. This gives an equivalence that corresponds to the failures model of CSP. The condition of maximality is required because there will always be the possibility of short runs that have not reached the success state but would if allowed to continue and so should not be regarded as a failure of the test.

10.12   May Testing Non-interference

We can use the form of equivalence given by may testing to give another statement of non-interference.

Definition: S is *mayNI* if for all High processes H_1 and H_2, with $\alpha H_i \subseteq H$:

$$H_1 \parallel_H S \parallel_L T =_{may} H_2 \parallel_H S \parallel_L T \qquad (16)$$

With $\alpha T \subseteq L$

This gives a weaker characterisation than those given above as may testing ignores distinctions that Low may draw based on observations of non-determinism. We can give a formulation similar to, say, Equation 9 by requiring must testing equivalence [84].

10.13   Non-deducibility

Equation 17 is the natural thing to write down in a *may testing* framework. However, by altering this slightly, we can mimic one of the early formulations: *non-deducibility* due to Sutherland, [88]. The essential idea is to stipulate that whatever observations Low may make of the system the space of possible High level *inputs* consistent with those observations is unchanged. Intuitively this is rather appealing and appears to address the encryption problem: whatever ciphertext Low observes he cannot reduce the space of plaintexts compatible with this ciphertext.

We need to partition the High level events into inputs and outputs. We then restrict the high-level processes in the definition to ones with an alphabet drawn only from High *inputs* and we use this in the definition of Equation 17. This is not really a natural thing to do in a process algebraic framework and indeed it and Sutherland's original formulation are found to be flawed, as observed by Johnson and Wittbold [90].

Unsurprisingly, the problem arises from ignoring the High outputs. Wittbold et al, construct a system that satisfies non-deducibility but for which High can modify his behaviour based on observations of High outputs in such a way as to signal to Low. The construction amounts to a stream cipher that High can induce to stutter. This allows him to predict certain bits and so leak plaintext to Low. In fact, as remarked in [77], this is really conceptually this same as High somehow being able to observe the bits of a cipher stream before he submits his plaintext. If he can somehow achieve this he can now exclusive or these into the High inputs (plaintext). The self inverse property of Vernan encryption then results in raw plaintext being visible to Low.

It might seem unlikely that such a flawed installation of a cipher device would be implemented in a secure system but the point is that the non-deducibility formulation fails to detect this problem.

10.14   Non-deducibility on Strategies

The difficulty with non-deduciblity as originally presented is that it takes no account of possible malicious behavious by High, maybe in collusion with Low. Notice that the counter-example provided by Johnson and Wittbold still satisfies non-deducibility in the sense that, assuming that any cipher stream is possible, then any plaintext is consistent with the ciphertext that Low observes.

Having made this observation, Johnson and Wittbold propose a more refined version of non-deducibility: they introduce the notion of High strategies and use this to define *non-deducibility on strategies*. In effect High is allowed to make his choices at run time on the basis of observations he can make on the system. They now require of the system that it satisfy non-deduciblity, whatever strategy High may adopt.

Note that if High had to resolve all his choices ahead of time, for example, had to decide on what text to submit to the cipher box before getting a chance to observe any of its outputs, then he could not communicate with Low.

The strategies of Wittbold et al, are really just instances of High CSP processes. As a result, NDoS turns out to be equivalent to our Equation 17. Thus the CSP testing approach rather naturally shows up the flaw of non-deducibility and leads naturally to the notion of non-deducibility on strategies.

It is also interesting to consider this example in the context of our power-bi-simulation framework. If we think of the τ's as encoding the output of the stream cipher, the loose bi-simulation property ensures that High cannot influence them. High's exclusive-oring of predicted bits into the plaintext is tantamount to tampering with these τ's. There are however some subtle issues here of causality. It is not clear that this has really been precisely captured in the formalism. We would like to show, for example, that predicting and compensating for the bits is equivalent to High forcing the bits to all equal zero and just using the original plaintext. How to capture the act of prediction is rather delicate.

A formulation that is basically equivalent to Equation 17, called non-deduciblity on composition (NDC), can be found in Gorrieri et al, [19] except that they use a conventional bi-simulation, so theirs is slightly stronger. Their formulation predates ours but it is nice to see essentially the same formulation emerging from a different approach.

An elaboration of testing equivalence, due to Schneider [83], allows for non-refusable Low events. In effect we constrain the space of tests to processes that are receptive on the L non-refusable events. We could also consider constraining the space of High processes and we will return to this in the section on generalisations of CSP non-interference.

10.15   The Lowe Approach to Information Flow

Lowe points out some of the limitations of existing formulations of NI [48]. None seem to give just the right characterisation. He traces part of the problem to the way non-determinism can be resolved in CSP. Consider:

$$P = h \rightarrow STOP \parallel\!\parallel (l \rightarrow STOP \sqcap l' \rightarrow STOP)$$

Intuitively this should be secure: the intuition behind the interleave operator is that it allows both processes to execute entirely independently. However if one considers the LTS, figure 4 upper diagram, we see that there appear to be two internal decision points. If these two choices are resolved differently, lower diagram, we get an information flow.

Thus the choice has been resolved differently before and after the occurrence of the h. In fact the original CSP specification only really had one choice but the LTS representation appears to have two. These are really the same and so should really be resolved consistently. The inconsistent resolution has in, effect, introduced a spurious causal relationship between the high and the low events not intended in the original specification.

Lowe's solution is to introduce a demon that ensures that such choices are resolved in a consistent way. He introduces additional labels on the LTS to carry this syntactic information. This allows him to define the notion of consistent refinement and then defines a system to be non-interfering iff any consistent refinement satisfies non-interference in the sense of Equation 5 (except that in this case a formulation suitable for deterministic systems is appropriate and so it is enough to require that the initials match rather than that the ready sets match).

11   Generalisations

Thus far we have dealt with the problem of characterising the complete absence of information flows through a system. We have seen that even in this comparatively simple situation it is remarkably difficult to arrive at a satisfactory

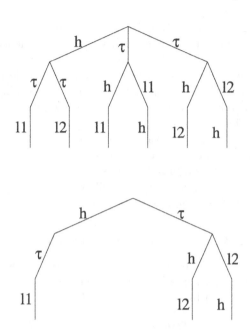

Fig. 4. The Labelled Transition System for P and its "refinement"

characterisation, even where we have abstracted from questions of time or probability. Later we will discuss ways to incorporate these aspects too but in this section we will address generalisations of what we have developed so far.

11.1 Limitations of Non-interference

Up to now we have used the idea of non-interference to characterise the complete absence of information flow or indeed stronger, the absence of any causal flow. Typically this is too strong for practical applications. We have already encountered the encrypted channel example in which we have causal flow but no (significant) information flow. Other situations also call for restricted or controlled flows. Sometimes this will be due to policy requirements. Downgraders are an example in which certain flows are allowed under certain circumstances, i.e., the classification of a previously sensitive file is reduced to unclassified by a security officer or maybe just due to the passage of time. Another example is the downgrading of statistical imformation derived from an otherwise sensitive database.

Sometimes it is more a question of functionality. Typically strict non-interference simply isn't feasible due to clashes of resource demands, etc. A simple example is the One Way Regulator or NRL pump. This is a device intended to allow information flow from Low to High but not from High to Low. In fact some flow from High to Low is necessary to regulate the flow from Low and avoid buffer overflow. For the *NRL Pump* the bandwidth of the High to Low regulating channel is severely restricted.

More generally there is a trend away from simple MLS-style policies to richer styles of policy involving finer granularity and more subtle, dynamic (possibly history- or location-based for example) controls of accesses. A simple example is the Chinese-Walls-style policy, mentioned earlier, in which an access to one class of file denies access to files in a conflicting class.

In this section we investigate to what extent these policies and requirements can be captured in a non-interference framework. There is ,of course, a question as to whether such a framework is the appropriate. It may well be that a large class of such policies simply do not fit naturally or indeed at all into a non-interference framework. It is interesting however to investigate how far we can push things.

The following generalisation of Equation 5 suggests itself:

$$\forall \, tr, tr' \in traces(S) \bullet tr \approx tr' \Rightarrow$$
$$\mathcal{A}_H((S \parallel Constrain)/tr) \equiv \mathcal{A}_H((S \parallel Constrain)/tr') \qquad (17)$$

Firstly observe that $\approx$ can be an arbitrary equivalence on traces, including but not confined to those induced by purge-like functions. We will discuss some of the possibilities that suggest thenselves shortly.

$\mathcal{A}_H$ denotes the operator chosen to abstract parts of the interface to S: eager, lazy, projection or some mixture.

Constrain denotes the envelope of behaviours that we are concerned about (not necessarily itself a process). High behaviours outside this envelope are allowed to interfere with Low under such a definition.

$\equiv$ denotes an appropriate process equivalence.

Alternatively we could seek to generalise Equation 8:

$$U_1 \sim U_2 \Rightarrow \mathcal{A}_H(S \parallel U_1 \parallel Constrain) \equiv \mathcal{A}_H(S \parallel U_2 \parallel Constrain) \qquad (18)$$

where $\sim$ denotes a suitable equivalence over High processes.

Using a testing approach allows us to delimit the space of tests, as in Schneider's work, or indeed to constrain the space of high users that we quantify over. The latter freedom renders redundant the *Constrain* term that we used above.

11.2   Encrypted Channels

As a first example of how such generalised formulations of non-interference might be applied let us return to the encrypted channel in which High feeds a classified plaintext into an encryption device and the resulting ciphertext is transmitted over some open channel c. We will suppose that the encryption algorithm is secure and any keys that might be involved are uncompromised. Indeed we could simply assume that we are dealing with a one-time-pad encryption.

Here we instantiate the equivalence relation $\approx$ in definition 18 by:
$\approx$ is defined by:

$$tr \approx tr' \Leftrightarrow \#(tr \upharpoonright H) = \#(tr' \upharpoonright H)$$

that is, plaintexts of equal length are regarded as equivalent, and define $\mathcal{A}_H$ as projection on the channel c: renaming 0's and 1's to some single symbol, $\bullet$ say.

A secure encryption channel now passes the form of non-interference defined in Equation 17 instantiated with these abstractions and equivalences. Indeed the information flow seems to have been quite accurately encoded: Low can determine the length of a High message transmitted over c but not its contents. It does, however, fail to take account of the fact that Low could detect when identical cipher-texts have been transmitted. Presumably if we really are dealing with a one-time-pad this is not relevant: the occurence of identical cipher-texts is firstly extremely unlikely and secondly signifies nothing. On the other hand, for a block cipher in, say, electronic code book mode it could be highly significant. To capture this situation we can alter the abstraction applied to the c channel. We now allow for process equivalence up to renaming on the alphabet of c. We should now think of the alphabet of c as being the bit strings of length l, where l is the length of the cipher blocks. For electronic code book mode it is appropriate to consider the renaming to be constant on the blocks. This is analogous to our encoding of pseudo-anonymity that will be discussed later.

This last example suggests that it might be useful to consider process equivalence up to isomorphism, where the isomorphism could be more general than simple renaming that we considered above.

11.3 Downgrading Statistical Information from a Sensitive Database

Another situation that can be encoded rather naturally is one in which unclassified statistical information is extracted from an otherwise classified database. Here we simply choose an equivalence over the state space of the database such that states giving rise to the same statistical values are regarded as equivalent.

11.4 File Editing

In general many different editing sequences can lead to the same final text, ignoring mark-up features. Certain edit commands will commute, some will negate others. Thus, editing sequences leading to identical final texts could be classed as equivalent. More generally we could define equivalence under arbitrary rewrite rules on traces, but this might hit decidability problems.

11.5 Operating Systems

The purpose of an operating system can be thought of as maintaining the illusion for each user that they are interacting with their own private system. Thought of this way we see that this kind of requirement is remarkably close to the idea of non-interference: the user's experience of interacting with the system should be largely unaffected by the presence of other users. In fact it is possible to get away with a weaker requirement here as we are not really worried if the user can infer something about the existence and behaviour of other users as long as he still gets the functionality he expects. We will see shortly that this is closely related to fault-tolerance requirements. We thank John McHugh for this observation.

11.6   Intransitive Non-interference

In [74], Rushby discussed what he calls *intransitive non-interference*. The name is actually rather deceptive as it is really about intransitive information flow policies. In some situations it is desirable for information to be allowed to flow in certain circumstances from H to L via some intermediate process, D say, that controls or as least audits the flows. No direct flows from H to L are allowed. At first this seems somewhat bizarre as we are in effect stipulating that $H \Rightarrow D$ and $D \Rightarrow L$ whilst denying $H \Rightarrow L$.

Rushby gives a couple of examples where this kind of requirement arises: downgraders and crypto boxes. Thus, in the case of a down-grader, we allow certain files to flow from a high classification to a lower classification but only if this is controlled by a downgrading device.

What really seems to be asserted here is that any flow from H to L should be regulated or at least audited by D. Rushby deals with this by introducing an *ipurge* function that no longer acts point-wise on individual events but accounts for downgrade events: thus we do not purge events that have been downgraded.

In [28] Goldsmith and Roscoe critique this, pointing out the Rushby's formulation can allow undesired flows. They give an alternative formulation using their determinism approach.

We can use the equivalence induced by *ipurge* to cast Rushby's examples into our generalised formulation. It may be possible to capture more general forms of intransitive information flow policies by suitable choices of traces equivalence.

11.7   Fault-Tolerance

Fault-tolerance and masking can also be encoded as non-interference style properties: roughly speaking, faults should not interfere with users. This idea crops up in [89] and later in [73,87]. For fault-tolerance, however, a weaker version may be acceptable as we are not really concerned with the possibility of information flowing from the faults to the users. It is thus not necessary in the definitions to demand equivalence, refinement is enough: that user functionality is unaffected. We are not really concerned if the errors may be able to resolve some of the non-determinism seen by the users. Indeed we might want information about the error behaviour to flow to the users in the form of warnings, alarms, etc.

We can thus define S to be tolerant of fault behaviours within a certain envelope defined by the process *FAULTS* by:

$$(S \parallel_{faults} FAULTS) \setminus faults \sqsubseteq_F (S \parallel_{faults} STOP) \setminus faults \qquad (19)$$

Thus $FAULTS$ ($\alpha FAULTS = faults$) is a process that encodes the failures behaviours we hope to be able to mask or tolerate. For example, for a Byzantine agreement algorithm, $FAULTS$ might specify the number and type of failures to be tolerated. The RHS of the refinement represents the fault-free behaviour of S. We are thus saying that as long as the fault behaviours stay within the envelope defined by $FAULTS$, the system should continue to be a refinement of the fault-free system, i.e., continues to provide the same functionality. We are assuming that the fault-free system provides the required functionality though strictly speaking this would need to be seperately verified against a suitable requirements specification.

Note the use of refinement in this definition rather than equality as used in the definitions of secrecy.

Alternatively, suppose that $MISSION$ encodes the mission critical functionality, then we could require:

$$S \parallel_{faults} FAULTS \sqsubseteq_F MISSION \qquad (20)$$

Thus, even in the presence of a faults scenario within the envelope defined by $FAULTS$ the mission critical functionality should remain. We could formulate a series of such requirements specifying acceptable degradation of functionality under increasingly severe fault scenarios:

$$S \parallel_{faults} FAULTS_i \sqsubseteq_F MISSION_i \qquad (21)$$

11.8   Intrusion-Tolerance

In principle we could apply this approach to defining intrusion-tolerance with something analogous to $FAULTS$ to encode attack scenarios. It is not really clear that attack scenarios can be so readily modelled. One could, in principle, try to model hostile capabilities (cf security protocols analysis [78]) maybe even including cost factors (which, inter alia, might help reduce the search space). This remains an avenue for research.

11.9   Anonymity

Another property that can be given an elagant non-interference-style formulation is anonymity. It is a sort of converse to authentication: authentication is about a process being assured of the identity of agents or processes with which it is interacting. Anonymity is concerned with preventing identities from being revealed. As with authentication, anonymity comes in many flavours depending on the application and requirements.

It is clear that anonymity has much in common with confidentiality. The latter can be thought of as a kind of anonymity over a message space. Indeed our Equation 8 could be interpreted as a statement of anonymity: Low cannot distinguish which of two possible users are interacting with the system through the High interface. This is actually a little strong for the usual meaning of anonymity as it requires that any user be indistinguishable from no user. More typically anonymity means that you know that an action has been performed but are unable to tell who is associated with it. Process algebraic definitions of various flavours of anonymity can be found in [85].

Pseudo-anonymity can be similarly formulated using a constant permutation in the renaming abstraction rather that just projection. This allows correlation between pseudonyms across time.

11.10   Dynamic Separation of Duty

Earlier we mentioned dynamic separation of duty policies. It turns out that such policies can be remarkably simply stated in a process algebra. As a simple example, suppose that an agent A can choose between two roles, $Role_1$ and $Role_2$, but that these are declared mutually exclusive. Once we have expressed these roles as CSP processes, we can express this in the CSP notation as:

$$A = Role_1 \ \square \ Role_2 \tag{22}$$

This gives a Chinese walls style policy for these two roles. Various generalisations to multiple roles and to situations in which the choices are constrained in certain ways are obvious.

11.11   Dealing with Probability

In principle it seems straightforward to extend the framework presented earlier to deal with probability by asserting that, for example, the probabilities of transitions for related states should be equal. In practice the formalism and verification gets cumbersome. One rather natural way to introduce probability is using the testing framework:

Let

$$S_i^* := Abstract_H(S \ ||_H \ U_i)$$

Then we could assert that S is probabilistically non-interfering if:

$$\forall U1 \approx U2 \wedge T \in Tests \ \bullet$$
$$Prob(Success(S_1^* \ ||_L \ T)) = Prob(Success(S_2^* \ ||_L \ T)) \tag{23}$$

It is far from clear that such a property would be tracable from a verification point of view. However unwinding this definition to some appropriate bi-simulation property might prove more tractable. Here one would be dealing with the deltas in probabilities, in particular asserting that probabilities are unchanged by the occurrence of High events, as the system evolves. Thus we might assert something along the lines of:

$$S_1 \approx S_2 \Rightarrow Prob(S_1 \xrightarrow{h} S_1') = Prob(S_2 \xrightarrow{h'} S_2') \wedge S_1' \approx S_2' \tag{24}$$

where $Prob(S_1 \xrightarrow{h} S_1')$ denoted the probability of a transition labelled h from the state S_1 to S_1'. Note that such probabililites will only really make sense where they arise due to "essential" non-determinism of the system rather than non-determinism that can be resolved by agents or processes interacting with the system. This might sidestep the need to assign absolute probabilities to transitions. We are grateful to Cathy Meadows for pointing this out.

11.12   Dealing with Time

Similarly we could move to a (discrete) timed model, using, for example, the tock dialect of CSP, with assertions that the times at which events become available to Low are independent of High activity. Again things rapidly get very complex- certainly difficult to model-check. Toy examples, for example, encrypted channels and maybe the One-Way-Regulator, can probably be pushed through but real systems seem out of reach for the moment.

12   Future Directions

In this section we outline some directions for future work.

CSP draws a distinction between internal and external non-determinism. These are similar to the *don't know, don't care* style of distinctions drawn in many formal methods. We have seen that these two flavours, although they are fine for investigating safety and liveness properties, are not enough to capture some aspects of information security. In particular, for security, we often need to distinguish *probabilistic* or *essential* non-determinism. We need to be very careful how we refine non-determinism: some non-determinism may be vital to security, for example, that arising from a stream cipher.

We have mentioned a number of approaches to formalising secrecy and hinted at possible connections. These need to be more fully investigated and understood. Besides these a number of other, recent proposals have appeared that appear to be related, for example: Sabelfeld and Sands [79], Mantel [51], and Pinsky [69].

We have illustrated how a few requirements and examples can be encoded in our generalised form of NI_{CSP}. It remains to try to tackle some more realistic examples in this framework: the Java security model, databases, smart cards. It would also be interesting to investigate more fault-tolerance and even intrusion-tolerance examples. It would also appear that a number of non-security applications may be usefully addressed using this kind of framework. Indeed it seems that, although these ideas were developed in a security context, they may turn out to be at least as useful applied in other contexts.

A major challenge is to extend such techniques to address time and probability. In principle this seems straightforward. To extend the models in a way that remains tractable is far from straightforward. Even without time and probability we are straining the limits of what is tractable from a verification point of view. On the other hand some of the subtleties that arise are due to the abstraction that we make of, for example, time. Thus in some respects models that include time may be simpler, at least in a conceptual if not complexity sense.

12.1   Composition Results

We saw earlier how using a bi-simulation formulation of non-interference leads to a very simple and elegant proof of a composition result. It seems likely that using such a bi-simulation formulation of the generalised forms of non-interference could similarly lead to simple proofs of compositionality, or alternatively, where compositionality fails, shed light on exactly why it fails. Indeed it seems likely that one could give a useful characterisation of the class of equivalence relations, i.e policies, that give rise to compositionality.

12.2   Links to Cryptographic Analysis Techniques

To date the cryptographic definitions of secrecy and the formal definitions that we have presented have been developed entirely independently. This is particularly clear in the area of security protocol analysis in which we understand very well how to analyse the strength of the cryptographic algorithms and primitives on the one hand and the protocols on the other. The latter tends however to abstract away from the details of the cryptographic primitives and it is still poorly understood how to link the results of the two styles of analysis. As a result it is possible for subtle interactions between the crypto primitives and the protocol design to slip through analysis. It is quite possible to have a protocol that is perfectly secure inplemented with algorithms that in themselves are secure and yet the whole is seriously flawed. An example of this can be found in [12].

Ideally we would like to be able to tie together the two styles of analysis in a way that remains tractable. An attempt to do this is Lincoln et al [47] but the resulting framework is very elaborate and it is unclear that anything but rather simple examples can be handled. [16] applies the idea of non-interference to the analysis of cryptographic protocols.

Typically the cryptographic definitions and proofs involve reduction arguments and in some cases testing style definitions. The spy is allowed to submit an arbitrary number of plaintexts of his choice to an encryption device and to observe the resulting ciphertexts. His choices can be adaptive: they can depend on the outcomes of previous experiments. He then finally submits a pair of distinct plaintexts and gets the resulting ciphertexts back in an arbitrary order. If he is able to guess which ciphertext corresponds to which plaintext with a significantly greater than 0.5 probability the device is deemed insecure, otherwise it is deemed secure. The details of the definition of *significantly greater than 0.5* is rather technical and need not concern us here. See for, example, [30,3].

The testing style definitions of non-interference that we have presented above may provide a point of contact bewteen the cryptographic and formal methods approaches. This is a topic for future research. One can think of non-deducibility on strategies in terms of the definition of resistance against adaptive chosen plaintext attack: Low is allowed to repeatedly input High behaviours to the system and observe the resulting behaviours through his interface. If eventually he can glean enough insight into the behaviour of the system to be able to make better than evens guesses as to which of a pair of High behaviours has occurred then the system is deemed to be flawed. The analogy is rather subtle and there are some interesting and illuminating differences.

12.3   Subliminal Channels and Information Hiding

Another topic that may be worth investigating using the techniques presented in these lectures is that of subliminal channels and information hiding. An attempt to formally define such channels is given in Desmedt [14]. It would be interesting to see if similar formalisation might be possible using one of the generalised forms of non-interference described here. The idea behind information hiding is to conceal the existence of information in a message or in data. This involves trying to make messages with different hidden information look indistinguishable to an observer lacking some appropriate key. It is clear that this has a similar feel to some of the properties and policies that we have been trying to capture: that behaviours in a given equivalence class be indistinguishable to certain observers.

12.4   Automated Support

Besides the theoretical problems that remain there is still the question of developing suitable tools and techniques to make the verification of significant applications feasible and ideally routine. Significant strides have been made with the usability of theorem provers but they still require specialist expertise to use. Similarly major strides have been made in the application of model-checking to security, see [78]. Model-checking holds out more promise as far as the degree of automation typically achievable but here too highly specialised expertise is still required to keep the state spaces of the model down to managable sizes. Important advances are being made in this area using data independence, for example Lazic et al [44], combining data independence and induction techniques, Broadfoot [6], and using *predicate abstraction*, Saidi [80].

12.5   Links to Other Process Algebras

We have seen that CSP is highly effective at capturing many of the properties of concern but also that we have found ourselves hitting the limits of the framework and having to introduce constructs usually regarded as outside conventional

CSP. CCS has also been applied with great effect to information security, see the chapter by Focardi and Gorrieri in this volume. It seems likely that no single, existing process algebra will provide us with all the machinery we need for information security applications. For example, besides the problems of distinguishing flavours of non-determinism, we need to be able to address mobility. Mobility and dynamic networking is an increasingly pervasive aspect of modern systems and the research community needs to get to grips with it. A number of process algebras have been proposed to address issues of mobility, location etc. These include the pi-calculus [64], the ambient calculus [8]. The chapter by Andy Gordon in this volume provides more on this topic. We need to see what features of these we can adapt or incorporate.

Asynchronous algebras may also prove fruitful to investigate. The asynchronous model of communication is similar to our notion of non-refusable events. We no longer assume a hand-shaking model of communication in which both sides synchronise on an action. Actions are launched into the ether and their reception is not guaranteed. This is in many respects a highly appropriate model for security applications in a distributed environment.

12.6   Static and Typing Analysis

Another rather different approach to defining secrecy is represented by the static analysis and typing analysis techniques of Volpano [91] and others, for example [35]. Here non-interference properties are cast in terms of static or typing conditions on a programming language or process algebra.

13   Conclusions

In these lectures I have sought to give the reader an overview of the evolution of mathematical formulations and frameworks for a number of security requirements and policies. We have concentrated on the notion of secrecy or confidentiality and, in particular, variants of the idea of non-interference as a way to formally characterise the absence of information flows.

The central thesis of these lectures is that characterising non-interference reduces ultimately to characterising the equivalence or indistinguishability of processes. Several corollaries flow from this observation:

Establishing how to characterise the equivalence of processes is itself a fundemental and delicate question. Indeed the whole question of what we mean by a process is intimately related to what processes should be regarded as equal. We should not therefore be too surprised that the problem of what formulation of non-interference is *correct* has remained controversial in the information security community for more than 20 years. Indeed it seems likely that there is no single, Platonic formulation of secrecy. There are no Maxwell's field equations for secrecy, as it were.

Which form of process equivalence is appropriate seems to depend on what model of computation we adopt and what observations and experiments we deem the environment capable of performing on the system. In some cases it will even depend on what computational capabilites we assume of the environment. To some extent this is just the standard problem facing any exercise in mathematical modelling: any model will necessarily be an abstraction of reality. As far as possible we seek to make our models faithful, at least as far as the properties of interest are concerned. Usually in the interests of tractability, we are often forced to make sweeping assumptions and approximations.

On the more positive side, thinking in process algebraic terms and in terms of process equivalence provides many insights and ready-made results. Process algebras deal carefully with questions of non-determinism, process equivalence, composition and so on. We have seen that the idea of unwinding is closely analogous to that of bi-simulation and that many of the historical formulations of non-interference can be cast as flavours of testing equivalence.

We have seen that a process algebraic framework provides an excellent basis from which to explore various generalisations of the original, rather binary concept of non-interference. It also provides an effective framework for reasoning about compositionality.

It should also be acknowledged that we have found ourselves straining the machinery of, for example, CSP to try to capture all the subtleties that information security throws up. Indeed it would appear that no existing process algebra is entirely suited to capturing all the aspects of information security. We have also seen that questions of causality seem not adequately addressed by existing process algebras. This has its plus side: the fact that we are testing the limits of existing theory when trying to apply it to security problems provides new challenges for the theory and stimulates further research.

Significant advances have been made in recent years in the specification and verification of security requirements, protocols, etc,, [78]. I hope at least to have conveyed the point that information security raises some fascinating and fundamental challenges both at the theoretical level and at the practical level of tools and techniques for verification.

The concept of non-interference has been a major preoccupation of the information security community for more than 20 years. We have discussed at length the problems in obtaining a satisfactory definition. Besides this there remains the question of what purpose, if any, non-interference actually serves in the specification and development of secure systems. It has been pointed out that no real security policy ever mentions the notion explicitly and in any case it is, in practice, impossible to realise in any real system: contention for resources means that it can never be fully attained in practice. Add to these concerns the point that non-interference is such an abstract notion that it is generally extremely difficult to map it down to the implementation level. All this might suggest that non-interference is little more than a rather elegant, theoretical debating point.

On the other hand, information security policies are concerned with what information flows are allowed and which are illegal. Thus, information-flows and their absence are central to such policies. It would seem, therefore, that something akin to non-interference, characterising the absence of information flow,

must be a fundamental element of any such policy. If we cannot get the specification and verification of the absence of certain information flows right, then
we really do not understand the foundations of our subject.

It should also be remarked that we are starting to see a number of applications of non-interference-like concepts for a far wider class of applications and
requirements. Maybe the concept will actually prove to be more useful beyond
the realm of information security, in which it was conceived. The proof of the
usefulness of the concept will only really be established when it has found an
effective role in the specification and verification of real applications.

14   Acknowledgements

The author would like to thank the following people who have contributed
to the ideas described here, commented on drafts and with whom I have had
many enjoyable and fruitful discussions: Sven Dietrich, Simon Foley, Paul Gardiner, Michael Goldsmith, Roberto Gorrieri, Joshua Guttman, Gavin Lowe, John
McHugh, John McLean, Cathy Meadows, Sylvan Pinsky, Bill Roscoe, Pierangela
Samarati. A particular thanks to goes Steve Schneider, with whom many of these
ideas were developed. A special thanks also goes to Jeremy Jacob, who was in-
strumental in stirring my interest in applying CSP to the problems of information
assurance.

Thanks also to MSR in Cambridge, UMBC Maryland and NR Oslo for hos-
pitality during the preparation of parts of this material. Finally a thanks goes to
the DERA Strategic Research Programme for support during the development
of many of the ideas presented here.

References

1. Abadi, M. and Gordon, A.: A calculus for Cryptographic Protocols: the Spi Calculus, Information and Computation (1999)
2. Bell, D. E. and LaPadula, L. J.: Secure Computer System: Unified Exposition and
   Multics Interpretation, Tech report ESD-TR-75-306, Mitre Corp, Bedford, Ma.
   (1976) 7
3. Bellare, M. and Rogaway, P.: Entity Authentication and key Distribution, Advances in Cryptography- Proceedings of Crypto (1993) 55
4. Biba, K. J.: Integrity Considerations for Secure Computer Systems, US Airforce
   Electronic Systems Division (1977) 10
5. Brewer, D. F. C., Nash, M. J.: The Chinese Wall security policy, in Proceedings of
   the IEEE Symposium on Security and Privacy, (1989) 206-214 9
6. Broadfoot, P. et al: Automating Data Independence, European Symposium on
   Research in Computer Security, LNCS vol 1895, Springer (2000) 55
7. Brookes, S. D. and Roscoe, A. W.: An Improved Failures Model for Communicating Sequential Processes Springer Verlag, Proceedings NSF-SERC Seminar on
   Concurrency (1985) 17
8. Cardelli, L.: Mobility and Security, Lecture Notes for the Marktoberdorf Summer
   School (1999) 56

9. Clark, D. R. and Wilson, D. R.: A Comparison of commercial and military computer security policies. In Proceedings of the IEEE Symposium on Security and Privacy, (1987) 184-194   9
10. Cleaveland, R. and Hennessy, M.: Testing equivalence as a bisimulation equivalence. Formal Aspects of Computing, Volume 5, (1993) 1-20   44
11. Cohen, E.: Information Transmission in computational Systems. Sixth ACM Symp. on Operating Systems Principles, November (1977) 133-139   12
12. Coppersmith, D. et al.: Low-exponent RSA with related messages. In Advances in Cryptology - EUROCRYPT '96 (Lecture Notes in Computer Science 1070), Springer-Verlag, (1996) 1-9   54
13. Davies, J., Schneider S. A.: A Brief History of Timed CSP, Theoretical Computer Science, 138, (1995)   17
14. Desmedt, Y. and Yung, M.: Minimal cryptosystems and defining subliminal-freeness. In Proceedings 1994 IEEE International Symposium on Information Theory, p. 347, Trondheim, Norway, June 27-July 1, (1994)   55
15. US Department of Defense: DOD Trusted Computer Security System Evaluation Criteria (The Orange Book), DOD 5200.28-STD, (1985)   7
16. Durante, A. et al: A Compiler for Analysing Cryptographic Protocols using Non-Interference, ACM Trans. on Soft.Eng. and Method, 9(4) (2000) 1-9   54
17. http://www.formal.demon.co.uk/   36
18. Feiertag, R. J.: A technique for Proving Specifications are Multi-level Secure Technical report CSL109, CSL, SRI International (1980)   12
19. Focardi, R. and Gorrieri, R.: A Classification of Security Properties, JCS, 3(1): (1995) 5-33   34, 46
20. Focardi, R, Ghelli, A. and Gorrieri, R.: Using noninterference for the analysis of security protocols, DIMACS workshop on Design and Formal Verification of Security protocols (1997)
21. Focardi, R., Gorrieri, R.: The Compositional Security Checker: A Tool for the Verification of Information Flow Security Properties. IEEE Trans. on Soft. Eng., 23(9): (1997) 550-571   16
22. Foley, S. N.: A Taxonomy for Information Flow Policies and Models, in Proceedings of IEEE Symposium on Security and Privacy, IEEE Press (1991)   9
23. Foley, S. N.: The Specification and Implementation of Commercial Security Requirements including Dynamic Segregation of Duties, 4th ACM Conference on Computer and Communications Security, ACM Press, (1997)   10
24. Gardiner, P.: Algebraic Proofs of Consistency and Completeness. Theoretic Computer Science, (1995) 150-161   34
25. Gardiner, P.: Power simulation and its relation to traces and failures refinement, ENTCS, vol 32, URL: http://www.elsevier.nl/locate/entcs/volume32.html   35
26. Goguen, J. A. and Meseguer, J.: Security policies and security models, IEEE Symposium on Security and Privacy, (1982)   12
27. Goguen, J. and Meseguer, J: Inference Control and Unwinding, Proceedings of the IEEE Symposium on Research in Security and Privacy (1984)   12, 30
28. Goldsmith, M. H. and Roscoe, A. W.: What Is Intransitive Noninterference? Proceedings of the Computer Security Foundations Workshop, IEEE Press(1999)   50
29. Gollmann, D.: Computer Security, Wiley (2000)   7
30. Guttman, J. et al: The Faithfulness of Abstract Encryption, to appear   55
31. Haigh, J. T.: A Comparison of Formal Security Models, Proc 7th National Computer Security Conference, Gaithersburg, September (1984) 88-119   16

32. Harrison, M. A. et al: Protection in operating systems. Communications of the ACM, 19(8) , August (1976) 461-471 9
33. He, J. and Hoare, C. A. R.: Unified Theories of programming. Prentice Hall International, (1998) 38
34. Hennessy, M.: Algebraic Theory of Processes, MIT Press (1989)
35. Hennessy, M.: The security pi-calculus and non-interference, Computer Science Technical Report 2000:05, School of Cognitive and Computing Sciences, University of Sussex. 56
36. Hoare, C. A. R.: Communicating Sequential Processes, Prentice Hall (1985) 17
37. Jacob, J. L.: Security Specifications, Proceedings of the IEEE Symposium on Research in Security and Privacy (1988) 29, 42
38. Jacob, J. L.: Basic Theorems about Security Journal of Computer Security, Vol 1 Number 4, (1992) 385-411 42
39. Johnson, D. and Thayer, F.: Security and the Composition of Machines, In Proceedings of the Computer Security Foundations Workshop, IEEE Press, (1988) 16
40. Kang, M. H. et al: Design and Assurance Strategy for the NRL Pump, Computer, Vol. 31, No. 4, April (1998) 56-64 10
41. Kemmerer, D.: Verification Assessment Study Final Report NCSC report (1986) 11
42. Lakatos, I.: Proof and Refutations: The logic of mathematical discovery. Cambridge University Press, (1977) 5
43. Lampson B.: Protection, ACM Operating Systems Reviews, 8, (1974) 6
44. Lazic, R. and Nowak, D.: A Unifying Approach to Data-independence, In Proceedings of the 11th International Conference on Concurrency Theory (CONCUR 2000), Lecture Notes in Computer Science. Springer-Verlag, August (2000) 55
45. Lee, S. and Zakinthinos, A.: A General Theory of Security Properties, Proceedings of the IEEE Symposium on Research in Security and Privacy (1997) 16
46. Lee, T. M. P.: Using Mandatory Integrity to Enforce 'Commerical' Security, Proceedings of the IEEE Symposium on Research in Security and Privacy, (1988) 140-144 10
47. Lincoln, P. et al: Probabilistic polynomial-time equivalence and security analysis, Proceedings of FM'99 (1999) 54
48. Lowe, G.: Probabilities and Priorities in Timed CSP, D.Phil. thesis Oxford University (1993) 46
49. Lowe, G.: Defining Information Flow University of Leicester tech report (1999)
50. MacKenzie, D.: Computers and the Sociology of Mathematical Proof. Prepared for Northern Formal Methods Workshop, Ilkley, September (1998) 5
51. Mantel, H.: Unwinding Possibilistic Security Properties. In Proceedings of ESORICS (2000) 53
52. McCullough, D.: Specifications for Multi-level Security and a Hook-up Property, Proceedings of the IEEE Symposium on Research in Security and Privacy (1987) 16
53. McCullough, D.: Noninterference and the Composition of Security Properties Proceedings of the IEEE Symposium on Research in Security and Privacy (1988) 16
54. McHugh, J.: Covert Channel Analysis. A chapter in the *Handbook for the Computer Security Certification of Trusted Systems*, (An ongoing series published by the Center for High Assurance Computing Systems, Naval research Laboratory, 4555 Overlook Ave, SW, Washington, DC 20375,) November 1994 – Revised December 1995. Available at http://chacs.nrl.navy.mil/publications/handbook/index.html 11

55. McHugh, J.: A Formal Definition for Information Flow in the Gypsy Expression Language. In *Proceedings of The Computer Security Foundations Workshop,* Mitre Corporation, Bedford, MA (1988) 147-165   11
56. McIver, A. et al: Refinement-oriented probability for CSP, Formal Aspects of Computing 8(9) (1996)
57. McLean, J.: Security Models Encyclopedia of Software Engineering (ed. John Marciniak) Wiley & Sons, Inc., (1994)   2
58. McLean, J.: A Comment on the 'Basic Security Theorem' of Bell and LaPadula, Information Processing Letters, vol. 20, no. 2, Feb. (1985)   11
59. McLean, J.: A General Theory of Composition for Trace Sets Closed Under Selective Interleaving Functions, Proceedings of 1994 IEEE Symposium on Research in Security and Privacy, IEEE Press, (1994)   16, 29
60. Menezes, A. J. et al: Handbook of Applied Cryptography. CRC Press (1996)
61. Milner, R.: A Calculus of Communicating Systems. Springer, LNCS 92, (1980)   17
62. Milner, R.: Communication and Concurrency, Prentice-Hall (1989)
63. Milner, R. et al: A calculus of Mobile Processes, I and II. Information and Compution, 100: (1992) 1-77   17
64. Milner, R.: Communicating and Mobile Systems: the Pi-Calculus, CUP (1999)   56
65. Moskowitz, I. and Costich, O.: A classical automata approach to noninterference type problems Proceedings of the Computer Security Foundations Workshop V, (1992)   11
66. O'Halloran, C.: A Calculus of Information Flow, Proceedings of ESORICS (1990)   16
67. Pfitzmann, B. et al: Crptographic security of reactive systems, ENTCS, 32 (2000)
68. Pinsky, S.: Absorbing covers and intransitive non-interference, IEEE Symposium on Research in Security and Privacy (1995)   39
69. Pinsky, S. and Ziegler, E.: Noninterference Equations for Nondeterministic Systems, Proceedings of the Computer Security Foundations Workshop, (2001)   53
70. Reed, M. and Roscoe, A. W.: A Timed Model for Communicating Sequential Processes. In proceedings of the 13th ICALP, LNCS 226, (1986)   17
71. Roscoe, A. W. et al: Non-interference through determinism, Proceedings of ESORICS (1994)   40
72. Roscoe, A. W.: CSP and determinism in security modelling, in proceedings of the IEEE Symposium on Security and Privacy, IEEE Computer Society Press, (1995)   27
73. Roscoe, A. W.: The theory and practice of concurrency, Prentice-Hall (1997)   17, 21, 25, 30, 50
74. Rushby, J.: Noninterference, Transitiivity and Channel-Control Security Policies, SRI Tech Report (1992)   16, 50
75. Ryan, P. Y. A.: A CSP formulation of non-interference and unwinding, Presented at CSFW 1990 and published in Cipher, Winter 1990/1991   26, 30, 31
76. Ryan, P. Y. A. and Sennett C. T. eds: Formal Methods in Systems Engineering Springer Verlag (1993)   4
77. Ryan, P. Y. A. and Schneider, S. A.: Process Algebra and Non-interference, JCS Vol 9, nos 1,2, (2001) 75-103   45
78. P. Y. A. Ryan et al: Modelling and Analysis of Security Protocols, Pearson (2001)   51, 55, 57
79. Sabelfeld, A. and Sands, D.: Probabilistic Non-interference for Multi-threaded Programs. In Proceedings of the IEEE Computer Security Foundations Workshop, Cambridge, July 3-5 2000, IEEE Computer Society, (2000) 200-215   53

80. Saidi, H.: Model Checking Guided Abstraction and Analysis, Proc of the 7th International Static Analysis Symposium (2000) 55
81. Sandhu, R. S.: Lattice Based Access control Models, IEEE Computer, volume 26, number 11, November (1993) 9-19 9
82. Schneider, S. A.: Concurrent and Real time systems: the CSP approach, Wiley (1999) 17, 21
83. Schneider, S. A.: Testing and abstraction, Royal Holloway, University of London Tech Report tr-99-02 (1999) 46
84. Schneider, S. A.: May Testing, Non-interference and Compositionality, Royal Holloway Tech report CSD-TR-00-02, January 2001. 40, 43, 44
85. Schneider, S. A. and Sidiropoulos, A.: CSP and anonymity, Proceedings of ESORICS (2000) 52
86. Shockley, W. R.: Implementing the Clark Wilson Integrity Policy Using Current Technology, in Proceedings of the National Security Conference, (1988) 29-36 10
87. Simpson, A. C.: Safety Through Security, DPhil thesis, Oxford University (1996) 50
88. Sutherland, D.: A model of information, 9th National Computer Security Conference (1986) 16, 44
89. Weber, D.: Specifications for Fault Tolerance. ORA report (1988) 19-3 50
90. Wittbold, J. T. and Johnson, D. M.: Information flow in nondeterministic systems, Proceedings of the Symposium on Research on Security and Privacy (1990) 16, 45
91. Volpano, D and Smith G.: Probablilistic non-interference in a concurrent language. Journal of Computer Security, 7(2, 3): November (1999) 231-253 56

The Logic of Authentication Protocols[*]

Paul Syverson[1] and Iliano Cervesato[2]

[1] Center for High Assurance Computer Systems, Naval Research Laboratory
Washington, DC 20375, USA
syverson@itd.nrl.navy.mil
[2] Advanced Engineering and Sciences Division, ITT Industries, Inc.
2560 Huntington Avenue, Alexandria, VA 22303, USA
iliano@itd.nrl.navy.mil

1 Introduction

The rationale of authentication has been a topic of study for about a decade and a half. First attempts at formal analysis of authentication protocols were not using logics per se, but were certainly logical. Millen's *Interrogator* [Mil84, MCF87] was a Prolog based tool specifically designed for authentication protocol analysis that functioned essentially as a special purpose model checker. Kemmerer used the general purpose formal specification language *Ina Jo* and an accompanying symbolic execution tool *Inatest* to specify and analyze protocols [Kem87].

We will focus on logics of authentication, beginning with BAN [BAN89a]. However, we will not only be discussing logics per se. We will also be looking at the 'rhyme and reason' of authentication, the attempts to formalize and define notions of authentication and to apply these. Thus, we will also be considering the logic of authentication in a broader sense.

We will not discuss (except incidentally) other formal methods that have been applied to authentication. In particular, we will not be describing process algebras, automata, automated tools such as theorem provers or model checkers. Some of these other approaches are discussed elsewhere in this volume. The remainder of this section will provide background on authentication protocols and introduce a running example.

1.1 Background on Authentication Protocols

In this section we present basic background on the concepts of authentication and its building blocks in cryptography. If every device communicating on behalf of a person or other entity shared a secret key with every other such device, and these keys were never compromised, canceled, unsubscribed, or otherwise

---

[*] This paper is based on a course Syverson taught at the 1st International School on Foundations of Security Analysis and Design (FOSAD'00) in Bertinoro, Italy in September 2000. Cervesato was a student there. The work of the first author was supported by ONR. The work of the second author was supported by NSF grant INT98-15731 "Logical Methods for Formal Verification of Software" and by NRL under contract N00173-00-C-2086.

R. Focardi and R. Gorrieri (Eds.): FOSAD 2000, LNCS 2171, pp. 63–137, 2001.

expired, then basic authentication protocols *might* be unnecessary. Clearly this is not even remotely the case. It has thus long been recognized that there must be some mechanism by which principals that do not share such a secret key, and may not even have any knowledge of each other beyond possibly an identifier, can establish a key for a secure communication session.

An *authentication protocol* is an exchange of messages having a specific form for authentication of principals using cryptographic algorithms. They typically have additional goals such as the distribution of session keys. *Symmetric-key cryptography* (also called *secret-key cryptography*) relies on the same key for both encryption and decryption. Classic examples include the data encryption standard, DES, and its recent successor, AES, the advanced encryption standard. (More details about cryptography can be found in any number of books [MvOV97, Sch96, Sti95].) *Public-key cryptography* is encryption and decryption using different keys (also called asymmetric cryptography). The most well known example is RSA. A *public key* is so-called because it is generally available to anyone. Corresponding to the public key is a *private key*, stereotypically known only to one principal. The private key is used to decrypt the message. Because it is uniquely bound to an individual a private key can also be used for a *digital signature* on a message. Typically, different keys and different algorithms are used for decryption and digital signatures. For digital signatures, the public key is used to verify that the signature is that of the principal bound to the public key. Binding is usually accomplished by means of a certificate, typically a message asserting such binding, containing an indicator of timeliness and signed by a well-known trusted principal (server).

Security protocols may have any number of intended purposes. Some exotic examples are voting, fair exchange of goods or contracts, non-repudiation, and anonymous communication. We will focus on authenticated establishment of session keys, which is typically necessary for the running of security protocols for most other purposes. Authentication is essentially assurance of who you are talking to. This can be made more specific in any number of ways: for example, you may want to make sure that those obtaining a session key are who they say they are, make sure that someone who has the key is currently on line, make sure that the principal you think has the key does have it, make sure that the principal with whom you think you share the key also thinks he is sharing it with you, etc. We will go into more detail on these points in Section 4. For now the basic intuition should suffice.

If a protocol is used for some security purpose, this implies an adversary against which the protocol is secure. The standard adversary for formal analysis of security protocols was introduced by Dolev and Yao in 1983 and is commonly known as the Dolev-Yao adversary [DY83]. It is a very strong adversary, much stronger than is typically assumed for secure distributed computation as in, e.g., Byzantine agreement. In the Dolev-Yao case, all messages sent from any honest principal to any other must pass through the adversary. The adversary can read, alter, and redirect any and all messages. However, encryption is treated as a black box. The adversary can only decrypt a message if she has the right keys.

She can only compose new messages from keys and messages that she already possesses. In particular, she cannot perform any statistical or other cryptanalytic attacks. Other common terms for the adversary include: attacker, penetrator, spy, intruder, enemy, and eavesdropper. Eavesdroppers are typically considered as only passive. But, any adversary is often referred to as 'Eve'.

1.2 Running Example

In this section, we introduce an example of an authentication protocol that will also be discussed in later sections. Eve's honest counterparts are traditionally named 'Alice' and 'Bob'. The other main principal in this protocol is the server. Alice and Bob are assumed to share keys (typically called 'long-term keys') with the server. Besides the obvious symbols for Alice (A), Bob (B), the server (S), and the keys they share (k_{AS}, k_{AS}, k_{AB}, etc.), the protocol introduces us to nonces, i.e., random unpredictable values generated by a principal and included in messages so that she can tell any messages later received and containing her nonce must have been produced after she generated and sent the nonce. A nonce generated by Alice is written 'n_A'. The session key that the server generates for Alice and Bob is k_{AB}. Encryption of a message, M, using key k is written '$\{M\}_k$'.

Protocol 1 (Needham-Schroeder Shared-Key) [NS78]

$$\begin{aligned}
&\textit{Message 1} \quad A \rightarrow S: \quad A, B, n_A \\
&\textit{Message 2} \quad S \rightarrow A: \quad \{n_A, B, k_{AB}, \{k_{AB}, A\}_{k_{BS}}\}_{k_{AS}} \\
&\textit{Message 3} \quad A \rightarrow B: \quad \{k_{AB}, A\}_{k_{BS}} \\
&\textit{Message 4} \quad B \rightarrow A: \quad \{n_B\}_{k_{AB}} \\
&\textit{Message 5} \quad A \rightarrow B: \quad \{n_B - 1\}_{k_{AB}}
\end{aligned}$$

In this protocol, Alice indicates to the server that she would like to talk to Bob and includes a nonce, n_A. The server S sends her a message encrypted with the key they share. This message contains her nonce n_A (so that she knows the message is fresh), Bob's identifier (so she knows that this is indeed for a session between her and Bob), the session key k_{AB}, and an encrypted submessage $\{k_{AB}, A\}_{k_{BS}}$ to be forwarded to Bob. Alice decrypts this message and forwards the submessage to Bob. He decrypts it and sends Alice a nonce n_B encrypted with the session key to show that he has the session key and to check that she does. She decrypts the message, subtracts one from the nonce, re-encrypts, and sends it back to Bob, completing the protocol. In the next section, we will set out a logic for analyzing protocols such as this.

1.3 Organization

In Section 2 we will describe BAN logic, its rules and some limitations and revisions. In Section 3 we will describe one of BAN's successors, SVO. Both of those sections will include an analysis of the running example. We will then proceed in Section 4 to the 'rhyme and reason', presenting formal and informal goals of authentication and attempts to define it. We will turn to some of the other aspects of authentication protocols in Section 5, where we will look at design principles and properties that arise from them, such as fail-stop properties. We will also look at ways in which these have been combined with the logical approach described in the earlier sections. Another approach to connecting goals and logics is considered in Section 6, in which a logical language is used to express requirements that are evaluated on a semantic level rather than with a logic for that language. Semantics are further tied to the earlier sections by assigning meanings to BAN constructs in the strand space model of authentication protocols [THG97, THG98b]. Finally, in Section 7 we say a few words about the future of formal analysis of authentication protocols.

2   BAN Logic

In this section we present an overview of BAN logic.[1] Specifically, we introduce the concepts, notation, and rules of BAN, after which, we will give some sample analyses. We will end the section by describing some of the extensions to BAN.

BAN is a logic of belief. The intended use of BAN is to analyze authentication protocols by deriving the beliefs that honest principals correctly executing a protocol can come to as a result of the protocol execution. For example, Alice might come to believe that a key she has received from a server is a good key for a communication session with Bob. What 'good' means here will be discussed below. The approach is to "idealize" the messages in the protocol specification into logical formulae. For example, if a server sends Alice a session key inside an encrypted message, the key might be replace by a formula that means that the key is good. We could then draw inferences based on Alice's ability to decrypt the key and other assumptions that might ultimately lead to the conclusion that she believes that the received key is good for talking with Bob.

BAN has been highly successful in uncovering protocol flaws, needed assumptions, etc., and it is relatively easy to use. A clear motivation in BAN is the math-

---

[1] 'BAN' is derived from the names of its authors, Burrows, Abadi and Needham. It is the first in a family of eponymous authentication logics. Versions of this logic occurred in many places. The first presentation in a public forum was at TARK in March of 1988 [BAN88]. It was also presented at the first CSFW in June of 1988. A revised and expanded version of the logic was given at SOSP in December of 1989 [BAN89b]. Journal versions of this appeared in *ACM TOCS* [BAN90a] and in *Proceedings of the Royal Society of London* [BAN89c]. The *TOCS* paper is an abbreviated version of the same material. The *Proc. Royal Society* paper is the one typically cited by the authors. Our primary source is the the Digital Systems Research Center report [BAN89a], and all descriptions of BAN are drawn from it. This SRC report originated in February 1989 and was revised in February 1990 to include "The Scope of a Logic of Authentication", which first appeared at a DIMACS workshop in October 1989 [BAN90c]. The February 1989 version of the SRC report comprises the *Proc. Royal Society* Paper.

ematician's credo to make only the needed distinctions and no more. Thus for example, the authors simplify reasoning about time by only distinguishing past and present epochs. These are not determined by the ephemeral current instant but are constant, set once and for all. This gives rise to one of BAN's central concepts, freshness. The other central concept is the aforementioned goodness of keys.

2.1 BAN Notation

We note at this point that the notation we will use is not that of [BAN89a]. Rather it is largely the notation introduced in [AT91] (with the public key notation introduced in [vO93]). It is closer to plain English than the original BAN notation, hence a bit more intuitive. For example, compare the following expressions (the first is original BAN notation):

$$P \models Q \hspace{0.2em}\mid\!\sim\hspace{0.2em} \#(X) \quad \text{vs.} \quad P \text{ believes } Q \text{ said fresh}(X)$$

The language of BAN consists of the following expressions:

P believes X :
P received X : message; this may require decryption.
P said X :
P controls X :
fresh(X) : (Read 'X is fresh'.) X has not been sent in any message prior to the current protocol run.
P $\xleftrightarrow{k}$ Q : (Read 'k is a good key for P and Q'.) k will never be discovered by any principal but P, Q, or a principal trusted by P or Q. (The last case is necessary, since the server often sees, indeed generates, k.)
PK(P, k) : (Read 'k is a public key of P'.) The secret key, k^{-1}, corresponding to k will never be discovered by any principal but P or a principal trusted by P.
{X}$_k$: Short for "$\{X\}_k$ from P" (Read 'X encrypted with k (from P)'.) This is the notation for encryption. Principals can recognize their own messages. Encrypted messages are uniquely readable and verifiable as such by holders of the right keys.

In all of these expressions, "X" is either a message or a formula. As we will see, every formula can be a message, but not every message is a formula.

2.2 BAN Rules

In an analysis, the protocol is first idealized into messages containing assertions, then assumptions are stated, and finally conclusions are inferred based on the assertions in the idealized messages and those assumptions. The rules to do so are now given.

The first rule is called "message meaning". It and "nonce verification" are the central rules of BAN.

Message Meaning

$$\frac{P \text{ believes } P \xleftrightarrow{\;k\;} Q \qquad P \text{ received } \{X\}_k}{P \text{ believes } Q \text{ said } X}$$

"If P receives X encrypted with k and if P believes k is a good key for talking with Q, then P believes Q once said X." [BAN89a]

Note that this rule does not tell us anything about what submessage(s) P can extract from an encrypted message. That will come below under **Receiving Rules**. Rather, this rule tells us what P can discern about who sent the message. In applying symmetric keys, there is no explicit distinction between signing and encryption. (In BAN, there is also no distinction when applying public keys. Both signing and encryption are represented by $\{X\}_k$. The distinction is implicit in the notation for the key used: k or k^{-1}.)

There is also a public-key version of message meaning. The implied "*from*" field in the shared-key case would be redundant in the public-key case since it is implicit in the meaning of the notation for binding a public key to a principal who originated the signed message.

$$\frac{P \text{ believes } PK(Q, k) \qquad P \text{ received } \{X\}_{k^{-1}}}{P \text{ believes } Q \text{ said } X}$$

Nonce Verification

$$\frac{P \text{ believes } fresh(X) \qquad P \text{ believes } Q \text{ said } X}{P \text{ believes } Q \text{ believes } X}$$

This rule allows promotion from the past to the present (something said some time in the past to a present belief). In order to be applied, X should not contain any encrypted text. This rule is the only way for such promotion to occur. Since principals are all assumed to be honest and competent with respect to following the protocol, it makes sense that anything that a principal said recently should be something that he believes. That is, it makes sense for assertions, but what if X is a nonce, n? Obviously, it is a stretch of the intuitive meaning of belief to say that Bob believes a nonce. It is not necessary that this technical use respect all of our intuitions. The goal of the logic is to provide something useful for the analysis of authentication protocols, not to formalize reasoning about ordinary belief. Nonetheless, [BAN89a] suggests introducing a "has recently said" operator. This was in fact done by many later authors; although the motivation may have had more to do with making the belief part of the logic conform more closely to traditional modal logics of knowledge and belief.

Jurisdiction

$$\frac{P \ believes \ Q \ controls \ X \qquad P \ believes \ Q \ believes \ X}{P \ believes \ X}$$

The jurisdiction rule is what allows inferences that a principal believes a key is good, even though it is a random string that he has never seen before. An important thing to keep in mind about jurisdiction is the strength of *controls* statements. If P *controls* X, then P cannot make a mistake in asserting X. In BAN, this is somewhat tempered by only allowing inferences , e.g., from Alice's belief that the server controls $A \xleftrightarrow{k_{AB}} B$ to Alice's belief that $A \xleftrightarrow{k_{AB}} B$. In other words, inferences cannot be made about whether a key is actually good, but only about whether a key is believed to be good. Later logics, in particular AT and SVO, by separating off the axioms of belief, lose this tempering in principle. However, in practice this makes little difference.

Note that quantifiers are implicit. So "*A believes S controls $A \xleftrightarrow{k} B$*" is implicit for "*A believes $\forall k.(S$ controls $A \xleftrightarrow{k} B)$*". Of course leaving things implicit leads in principle to some ambiguities. For example, "*A believes $\forall k.(S$ controls B controls $A \xleftrightarrow{k} B)$*" vs. "*A believes S controls $\forall k.(B$ controls $A \xleftrightarrow{k} B)$*".

In practice, these questions do not usually arise in basic authentication protocols because nested assertions of jurisdiction are rarely found. As in other things, the BAN approach is to ignore complications not encountered in practice. If it should become necessary to be explicit, however, then they do so. For example, in [ABKL90], nested *controls* statements occur and the quantifiers in those statements are made explicit.

Belief Conjuncatenation

$$\frac{P \ believes \ X \qquad P \ believes \ Y}{P \ believes \ (X,Y)}$$

$$\frac{P \ believes \ Q \ believes \ (X,Y)}{P \ believes \ Q \ believes \ X} \qquad \frac{P \ believes \ Q \ said \ (X,Y)}{P \ believes \ Q \ said \ X}$$

The obvious rules apply to beliefs concerning concatenations of messages/conjunctions of formulae. We have chosen the neologistic mouthful 'conjuncatenation' to again reinforce the point that BAN makes only the distinctions it needs. In this case, concatenations of messages are not distinguished from conjunctions of formulae: both are represented as (X,Y) in the above rules. Also, following the lead of [BAN89a], we do not list all of the rules; we give only a representative sampling. For example, we will not state versions of the last two rules where the conclusions are replaced by P *believes* Q *believes* Y and P *believes* Q *said* Y.

Freshness Conjuncatenation

$$\frac{P \ believes \ fresh(X)}{P \ believes \ fresh(X,Y)}$$

For some inexplicable reason, this is a commonly misunderstood BAN rule. Some try to deny it; others try to assert the converse rule. Be wary of these mistakes. If X is fresh, then any message containing X is fresh in virtue of having X in it. But, (X, Y) being fresh tell us nothing about the freshness either of X by itself or of Y by itself (because the whole may be fresh in virtue of the other part).

Receiving Rules: Seeing is Receiving

$$\frac{P \text{ believes } P \xleftrightarrow{k} Q \qquad P \text{ received } \{X\}_k}{P \text{ received } X} \qquad \frac{P \text{ received } (X, Y)}{P \text{ received } X}$$

A principal receiving a message also receives submessages he can uncover. Here is another clever BAN fusion, one that is lost a little in our more English-like notation: in BAN the symbol for receiving, '◁', is used to reason about what is visible. Thus, what a principal possesses is not distinguished from what he has received in some message. Virtually all successors to BAN distinguished the two; yet BAN is able to analyze a large number of protocols without this distinction.

This completes our listing of the rules of BAN. We now describe how to use BAN to analyze a protocol.

2.3 BAN Protocol Analysis

There are four steps to a protocol analysis using BAN.

1. Idealize the protocol.
2. Write assumptions about the initial state.
3. Annotate the protocol: For each message transmission "$P \to Q : M$" in the protocol, assert Q received M.
4. Use the logic to derive the beliefs held by protocol principals.

As an example, we will go through a BAN analysis of the Needham-Schroeder Shared-Key protocol of Section 1.2.

Example: Analysis of Needham-Schroeder Shared-Key (NSSK)

The first step is to put the protocol into idealized form.

Idealized Needham-Schroeder Shared-Key [BAN89a]

Message 2 $S \to A : \{n_A, A \xleftrightarrow{k_{AB}} B, fresh(k_{AB}), \{A \xleftrightarrow{k_{AB}} B\}_{k_{BS}}\}_{k_{AS}}$ *from S*

Message 3 $A \to B : \{A \xleftrightarrow{k_{AB}} B\}_{k_{BS}}$ *from S*

Message 4 $B \to A : \{n_B, A \xleftrightarrow{k_{AB}} B\}_{k_{AB}}$ *from B*

Message 5 $A \to B : \{n_B, A \xleftrightarrow{k_{AB}} B\}_{k_{AB}}$ *from A*

Note that the first message of the protocol is omitted in the idealized form. In a BAN idealization, plaintext from the protocol is omitted. Next note the *from* fields. It is always assumed that principals can recognize their own messages. Thus, with a shared key, if a recipient can decrypt a message, she can tell who it is from. As this is often implicitly clear, the *from* field is often omitted from the protocol idealization. What is inside the encrypted messages is also altered. Specifically, the key k_{AB} is replaced by assertions about it. So, Message 2, idealized, is an encrypted message for Alice from the Server that contains a nonce, an assertion that k_{AB} is fresh, an assertion that k_{AB} is good for talking to Bob, and an encrypted message to be forwarded to Bob. Note also that in the last message $n_B - 1$ is changed to just n_B. This is because the purpose of subtracting 1 from the nonce is to differentiate it from Message 4. The differentiation is reflected in the idealization in the *from* field. It would reduce informal interpretation to simply leave $n_B - 1$ in the idealized protocol. But, BAN has no direct rule to infer the freshness of $n_B - 1$ from the freshness of n_B. So, the change is necessary. This was changed in SVO, as we shall see below.

Once the idealization has been made, assumptions are stated.

NSSK Initial State Assumptions

P1. *A believes $A \xleftrightarrow{k_{AS}} S$*
P2. *B believes $B \xleftrightarrow{k_{BS}} S$*

P3. *A believes S controls $A \xleftrightarrow{k} B$*
P4. *B believes S controls $A \xleftrightarrow{k} B$*
P5. *A believes S controls fresh($A \xleftrightarrow{k} B$)*

P6. *A believes fresh(n_A)*
P7. *B believes fresh(n_B)*

Most of the assumptions should be self-explanatory. P1 and P2 express the belief in the quality of the long term keys. (Notice that we make no corresponding assumptions about what S believes. It would be natural to do so, but we have omitted them because, in this case, they are not needed in the derivations that follow.) P3 through P5 give the assertions on which Alice and Bob believe that the server has jurisdiction. P6 and P7 tell us that each principal believes that his/her random value is fresh.

NSSK Annotated Protocol

The annotation states assumptions based on the messages in the idealized protocol. It can be read directly from the idealization.

P8. *A received $\{n_A, A \xleftrightarrow{k_{AB}} B, fresh(k_{AB}), \{A \xleftrightarrow{k_{AB}} B\}_{k_{BS}}\}_{k_{AS}}$*
P9. *B received $\{A \xleftrightarrow{k_{AB}} B\}_{k_{BS}}$ from S*
P10. *A received $\{n_B, A \xleftrightarrow{k_{AB}} B\}_{k_{AB}}$ from B*
P11. *B received $\{n_B - 1, A \xleftrightarrow{k_{AB}} B\}_{k_{AB}}$ from A*

This completes the assumptions needed to analyze the protocol. In the derivations below, every line is followed by a justification, i.e., the rule by which it was derived and the premise(s) and/or derived formula(e) used in its derivation.

NSSK Derivations

1. A *believes* S *said* $(n_A, A \xLeftrightarrow{k_{AB}} B, fresh(A \xLeftrightarrow{k_{AB}} B), \{A \xLeftrightarrow{k_{AB}} B\}_{k_{BS}})$
   By Message Meaning using P1, P8.
2. A *believes* $fresh(n_A, A \xLeftrightarrow{k_{AB}} B, fresh(A \xLeftrightarrow{k_{AB}} B), \{A \xLeftrightarrow{k_{AB}} B\}_{k_{BS}})$
   By Freshness Conjuncatenation using 1, P6.
3. A *believes* S *believes* $(n_A, A \xLeftrightarrow{k_{AB}} B, fresh(A \xLeftrightarrow{k_{AB}} B), \{A \xLeftrightarrow{k_{AB}} B\}_{k_{BS}})$
   By Nonce Verification using 2, 1.
4. A *believes* S *believes* $(A \xLeftrightarrow{k_{AB}} B)$
   By Belief Conjuncatenation using 3.
5. A *believes* S *believes* $(fresh A \xLeftrightarrow{k_{AB}} B)$
   By Belief Conjuncatenation using 3.
6. A *believes* $(A \xLeftrightarrow{k_{AB}} B)$
   By Jurisdiction using 4, P3.
7. A *believes* $fresh(A \xLeftrightarrow{k_{AB}} B)$
   By Jurisdiction using 4, P5.

We have derived Alice's belief in the goodness and in the freshness of k_{AB}. We now turn to Bob.

8. B *believes* S *said* $A \xLeftrightarrow{k_{AB}} B$
   By Message Meaning using P2, P9.

With the assumptions we have made so far this is all we are able to derive with respect to Bob's belief in the goodness of k_{AB}. Unlike Alice, Bob has sent no nonce at this point in the protocol. The only way for us to move further is if we assume that Bob believes something he has received is fresh. We therefore add the assumption that Bob believes that the assertion $A \xLeftrightarrow{k_{AB}} B$ is fresh.

P12. B *believes* $fresh(A \xLeftrightarrow{k_{AB}} B)$

This is different than our earlier freshness assumptions since those were all based on values that the believing principal had herself generated. This one expresses Bob's belief that a random value someone else has generated is fresh. We will return to this odd assumption below after we complete the derivations.

9. B *believes* S *believes* $A \xLeftrightarrow{k_{AB}} B$
   By Nonce Verification using P12, 8.
10. B *believes* $A \xLeftrightarrow{k_{AB}} B$
    By Jurisdiction using P4, 9.

Unlike for A, for B we were forced to assume B *believes* $fresh(A \xLeftrightarrow{k_{AB}} B)$ since we were unable to derive it. We have now derived Alice and Bob's first order beliefs in the goodness and freshness of k_{AB}. We next derive their second order beliefs.

11. A believes B said $(n_B, A \xleftrightarrow{k_{AB}} B)$
    By Message Meaning using 6, P10.

12. A believes $fresh(n_B, A \xleftrightarrow{k_{AB}} B)$
    By Freshness Conjuncatenation using 7.

13. A believes B believes $(n_B, A \xleftrightarrow{k_{AB}} B)$
    By Nonce Verification using 12, 11.

14. A believes B believes $A \xleftrightarrow{k_{AB}} B$
    By Belief Conjuncatenation using 13.

By similar reasoning, we can obtain B believes A believes $A \xleftrightarrow{k_{AB}} B$ but with an important difference. Since Bob believes that $A \xleftrightarrow{k_{AB}} B$ is fresh, there is no need for n_B in order for him to reach this conclusion. The only role n_B plays in the protocol is to differentiate Message 4 from Message 5. It does not need to be fresh for that. This makes the assumption that Bob believes $A \xleftrightarrow{k_{AB}} B$ to be fresh stand out all the more. We now illustrate that the dubious nature of this assumption is not just an artifact of the analysis.

The Denning-Sacco Attack

In 1981, Denning and Sacco showed how the Needham-Schroeder Shared-Key protocol could be attacked if an attacker compromised an old session key [DS81]. In the attack specification 'E_A' is the attacker masquerading as A.

Message 3 $E_A \rightarrow B : \{k_{AB}, A\}_{k_{BS}}$
Message 4 $B \rightarrow E_A : \{n'_B\}_{k_{AB}}$
Message 5 $E_A \rightarrow B : \{n'_B - 1\}_{k_{AB}}$

The attack relies on the fact that Bob has no way to actually be assured that Message 3 is fresh. So, an attacker could spend whatever time is needed to break the session key k_{AB}. As long as she can do so within the lifetime of k_{BS}, then she can run the above attack. Bob will then think he has confirmed sharing k_{AB} with Alice, when in reality Alice is not present and the attacker knows the key. The attack is not directly uncovered by a BAN analysis of the protocol; rather the analysis shows that the protocol cannot achieve any sort of authentication for Bob without making the dubious assumption that underlies the attack.

This concludes our basic introduction to BAN logic and its use in protocol analysis. In the remainder of this section, we will set out some of the issues that led researchers to expand and modify BAN and the analysis technique.

2.4   The Nessett Protocol

In 1990, Nessett introduced the following simple example that "demonstrates that a significant flaw exists in the Burrows, Abadi and Needham logic" [Nes90].

Protocol 2 (Nessett) [Nes90]

    Message 1 $A \rightarrow B$: $\{n_A, k_{AB}\}_{k_A^{-1}}$

    Message 2 $B \rightarrow A$: $\{n_B\}_{k_{AB}}$

In the first message, Alice encrypts a session key using a private key, the public cognate of which is assumed to be widely known. Bob then send her a handshake value encrypted with the session key, k_{AB}. Of course the key is not at all good for communication between Alice and Bob because anyone can extract it from the first message and use it for communication. But, structurally the protocol is the same as one where the first message was encrypted with a good key. Here is Nessett's idealization of the protocol followed by the corresponding annotation, then by the initial state assumptions Nessett presents.

Idealized Nessett Protocol

    Message 1 $A \rightarrow B$: $\{n_A, A \xleftrightarrow{k_{AB}} B\}_{k_A^{-1}}$

    Message 2 $B \rightarrow A$: $\{A \xleftrightarrow{k_{AB}} B\}_{k_{AB}}$

Annotation Premises

P1. B *received* $\{n_A, A \xleftrightarrow{k_{AB}} B\}_{k_A^{-1}}$

P2. A *received* $\{A \xleftrightarrow{k_{AB}} B\}_{k_{AB}}$

Initial State Assumptions

P3. B *believes* $PK(k_A, A)$

P4. A *believes* $A \xleftrightarrow{k_{AB}} B$

P5. A *believes fresh*$(A \xleftrightarrow{k_{AB}} B)$

P6. B *believes fresh*(n_A)

P7. B *believes* A *controls* $(A \xleftrightarrow{k} B)$

Note that Nessett assumes Bob to believe that n_A is fresh. Therefore, it is more naturally thought of as a timestamp than a nonce. We have used this notation to more closely follow Nessett[2]. Based on this idealization and set of assumptions, Nessett is makes the following derivations.

Nessett Protocol Derivations

  1. B *believes* A *said* $(n_A, A \xleftrightarrow{k_{AB}} B)$
        By Message Meaning using P3, P1.

---

[2] Specifically, he used "N_A".

2. B believes fresh$(n_A, A \xleftrightarrow{k_{AB}} B)$
    By Freshness Conjuncatenation using P6.
3. B believes A believes $(n_A, A \xleftrightarrow{k_{AB}} B)$
    By Nonce Verification using 2, 1.
4. B believes A believes $A \xleftrightarrow{k_{AB}} B$
    By Belief Conjuncatenation using 3.
5. B believes $A \xleftrightarrow{k_{AB}} B$
    By Jurisdiction using P7, 4.

This completes the derivations for Bob. We now derive Alice's second order belief in the goodness of k_{AB}. (Her first order belief was assumed.)

6. A believes B said $A \xleftrightarrow{k_{AB}} B$
    By Message Meaning using P4, P2.
7. A believes B believes $A \xleftrightarrow{k_{AB}} B$
    By Nonce Verification using P5, 6.

Nessett's Critique of BAN

Using BAN, one can derive all of the typical BAN authentication goals for both Alice and Bob via the Nessett protocol—as we have just done. This shows that, according to BAN, k_{AB} is a good session key. But, k_{AB} is not a good key. Ergo, BAN is flawed. Nessett traces the source of the "flaw" to the scope of BAN. It addresses who gets and acknowledges a key (authentication), but it does not address who should not get a key (confidentiality).

Burrows et al. respond to Nessett in [BAN90b] by noting that their paper explicitly limits discussion to authentication of honest principals. They explicitly do no attempt to detect unauthorized release of secrets. Since Alice publishes k_{AB} in first message, Nessett's assumption A believes $A \xleftrightarrow{k_{AB}} B$ is inconsistent with these stated restrictions. And, from absurd assumptions come absurd conclusions. The logic does not preclude ridiculous assumptions.

> "This seems fair enough; no logic protects against the assumption of bad premises. All one can reasonably ask is that, if the premises are true, then the conclusion is also true. On the other hand, Nessett could counter that illustrative counterexamples are supposed to be obvious; that's what makes them illustrative. If one wants to demonstrate that an argument form is invalid, one constructs an argument with that form that is clearly invalid. It is hardly fair to say that this shows nothing because it's an obviously invalid argument. That's the point. The danger is that one might use the form to justify an invalid argument that is not obviously so. The question remains: On what (extralogical) basis do we decide what goes into the premise set? For this case, Burrows et al. would no doubt contend that one includes a principal's belief in the goodness of a key only if she has reason to believe that it is good and no reason to think that it is not. Of course that is what we would like to do, but it is also what we are trying to determine how to do." [Syv91]

Certainly it is much too strong to say that the Nessett example shows the logic to be flawed. It does highlight a place where one is expected to rely purely on the intuitive reasonableness of assumptions. However, it has not shown that this results in either a logical error or a practical vulnerability.

Still, it would be nice to have a way to capture either formally or at least rigorously, the difference between Nessett-type protocols and those not flawed in this way. Alice's action is inconsistent with the meaning of A believes $A \xrightarrow{k_{AB}} B$. What is needed is a way to reflect this mathematically [Syv91, Syv92]. Suppose we could derive A believes C has k_{AB} (for arbitrary C). Increasing expressiveness would let us formally demonstrate this.

2.5   Expanding Beyond BAN

In 1990, Gong, Needham, and Yahalom, introduced a new logic [GNY90] that extended BAN. This logic came to be known as *GNY*, following the precedent set by 'BAN'. In it one can represent possession of keys. So A believes C has k_{AB} can be expressed, and possibly derived. GNY also distinguishes available messages from received messages. Other important contributions include formalizing a principal's distinction of his own generated messages from others. Analysis in GNY also leaves cleartext in idealized protocols, rather than assuming that it cannot play a role in authentication. While not specifically formulated as a response to Nessett, this logic allows the expression of key possession and thus can express formally that with which the dubious assumption is supposed to be inconsistent. By itself this does not guarantee that the needed key possession is derivable, nor does it directly express the inconsistency.

Another response to Nessett that comes closer to directly reflecting the inconsistency of meaning was first given by Abadi and Tuttle in [AT91]. Specifically, they presented a BAN-like logic that possessed an independently motivated account of meaning in the form of a model-theoretic semantics. This allows one to rigorously assess the truth of assumptions (consistent with a protocol). Specifically, the *AT* logic was closer to traditional modal logics than BAN, provided a detailed model of computation, had a soundness result with respect to the model, and was also more expressive (e.g., could express key possession). A traditional semantics was much of the motivation for this work. While the published soundness result had a mistaken assumption in it, this was a large step towards putting BAN on a footing both firmer and logically more traditional. We will return to semantics below.

Another important limitation on BAN is the type of protocols to which it can be applied. Diffie-Hellman protocols underly much of modern authenticated key distribution. For example, they underly the IETF standard Internet Key Exchange (IKE) protocol [DH99], as well as both SSL and TLS—what your Web browser uses when it makes a secure connection. Thus, being able to reason about such protocols would be quite useful. Paul van Oorschot's VO logic [vO93] was designed primarily to add this capability. It is an extension of GNY that can be used to reason about Diffie-Hellman type key agreement. In addition, [vO93] extended the lexicon of formally stated authentication properties, and formalized reasoning about confirmed possession of secrets. We will return to those points in Section 4. Right now we turn to a logic that attempts to comprise all of the advantages that VO and the other BAN logics introduce.

3   SVO Logic: Unifying the Predecessors

In the last section, we saw some of the limitations of BAN, and the extensions and variants that were intended to overcome them. Each of the logics, GNY, AT, and VO brought a distinct addition. In response to this diversity, Syverson and van Oorschot devised a logic, SVO, that was intended to unify the above predecessors [SvO94, SvO96]. The intent was not simply to patch on new notation and rules adequately expressive to capture the additional scope of these logics. This would be both inelegant and potentially unsound. Rather, the intent was to produce a model of computation and a logic that was sound with respect to that model while still retaining the expressiveness of the various BAN extensions.

3.1   SVO Notation

SVO uses the notation already introduced for BAN, with the following main additions:

$\neg\varphi$: Negations of formulae are added to the language.
P says X : but P must have said X since the beginning of current epoch.
P has X :
  - Initially available to P,
  - Received by P,
  - Freshly generated by P, and
  - Constructible by P from the above.

The original BAN idea of a public key might be expressed as '$PK(P,k)$', meaning that k is a public key of P — the matching secret key k^{-1} will never be discovered by any principal but P or a principal trusted by P. In SVO, this is refined to cover different types of public key functionality.

$PK_\psi(P,k)$: k is a public ciphering key of P. Only P can read messages encrypted with k.
$PK_\sigma(P,k)$: k is a public signature key of P. The key k verifies that messages signed by k^{-1} are from P.
$PK_\delta(P,k)$: k is a public key-agreement key of P. A Diffie-Hellman key formed with k is shared with P.
$\lfloor X \rfloor_k$: types of public keys, SVO distinguishes signature from encryption.
$\{X\}_k$: This is no longer short for '$\{X\}_k$ from P'. In SVO, it is not assumed that principals can recognize their own messages. But it is still assumed that encrypted messages are uniquely readable and verifiable as such by holders of the right keys.

$\langle X \rangle_{*P}$: of [WK96] and is closer to that than to the notation in [SvO94, SvO96]. This is used for messages that P doesn't know or recognize (e.g., $\{X\}_k$ where P does not know k). P will nonetheless recognize $\langle \{X\}_k \rangle_{*P}$ as the same thing if received again, even if he cannot tie it back to any plaintext.

X *from* P :

3.2   SVO Rules

Like AT, SVO is much more of a traditional axiomatic style logic than BAN, GNY or VO. As such there are only two rules.

Modus Ponens

$$\frac{\varphi \qquad \varphi \rightarrow \psi}{\psi}$$

Necessitation

$$\frac{\vdash \varphi}{\vdash P \; believes \; \varphi}$$

'$\vdash$' is a metalinguistic symbol. '$\Gamma \vdash \varphi$' means that the formula φ is derivable from the set of formulae Γ (and the axioms as stated below) using the above rules. '$\vdash \varphi$' is short for '$\emptyset \vdash \varphi$' and means that φ is a theorem, i.e., derivable from axioms alone without any additional assumptions. We describe derivability (i.e. proofs) below in Section 3.4.

Necessitation is sometimes called by other names, e.g., belief generalization. We have given it the name that reflects its origins in alethic modal logic [Che80]. It applies only to theorems of the logic. Like the Belief Conjuncatenation rule of BAN, this is often misunderstood and misapplied or improperly criticized. If using the assumptions about a protocol it is possible to derive that Q *said* X, it does not follow that P *believes* Q *said* X. This is because Q *said* X is merely derivable given the context of this protocol: it is not a theorem, i.e., derivable using logic alone.

Axioms of the logic are all instances of tautologies of classical propositional calculus [Men87], and all instances of the following axiom schemata.[3]

3.3   SVO Axioms

Belief Axioms

1. $(P \; believes \; \varphi \wedge P \; believes \; (\varphi \rightarrow \psi)) \rightarrow P \; believes \; \psi$
2. $P \; believes \; \varphi \rightarrow \varphi$
3. $P \; believes \; \varphi \rightarrow P \; believes \; (P \; believes \; \varphi)$
4. $\neg(P \; believes \; \varphi) \rightarrow P \; believes \; (\neg P \; believes \; \varphi)$

---

[3] Some of the following are proper axioms, logically. Those containing metavariables for formulae are actually axiom schemata. We will generally ignore this distinction, referring to all as 'axioms'.

These are classic axioms of modal logic [Che80, Gol92] that were thoroughly analyzed in the early and middle part of the last century. (The classic names for them are **K**, **T**, **4**, and **5** respectively.) As in AT, belief is removed from most other axioms, the logic of belief is separated off from the rest of the logic. Readers familiar with modal logic will recognize these as the axioms[4] of the Lewis system **S5** [Che80]. This logical system is usually taken to characterize knowledge rather than belief, so we provide a brief side discussion of the point. It may be skipped without loss of continuity.

Discussion: Knowledge and Belief

Roger Needham has remarked in conversation that perhaps the biggest mistake they made with BAN was calling it a belief logic. We have already seen in the discussion of Nonce Verification in Section 2.2 that BAN-belief does not respect all of the intuitions of ordinary belief. Of course no technical usage could. Intuitions can be helpful, but they can also lead us from the main task of providing a useful analysis of authentication and authentication protocols. More detailed discussion of knowledge and belief in authentication logics can be found in [Syv92, AT91]. Here we cover a few of the main points.

The main question in distinguishing knowledge from belief is: If a principal thinks that φ, is he always right? If the answer is "Yes", then we are talking about knowledge. If the answer is "No", then we are talking about belief. That is overly simplistic, and philosophical counterexamples are thoroughly plumbed in the literature (e.g., look up the Gettier Problem [Mos86]). Nonetheless, it will do for our practical intentions. This translates naturally into the main formal question: Is it a theorem of the logic that (P believes $\varphi \rightarrow \varphi$)?

This is just the **T** axiom introduced above as axiom 2. Faced now with this technical distinction, we can ask the practical question of which do we want. Surprisingly, the answer for our purposes is "I don't care." The reason is that this has played little role in actual analyses. So, if we don't care, how did we come to add it as an axiom?

The answer lies in the semantics of the logic. One of the goals of this logic was that it have an intuitively reasonable model of computation and semantics, and that it be sound with respect to them. Mark Tuttle has noted that we ought to build models not logics in trying to capture our notions of authenticated communication [Tut]. It turns out that in [SvO96], the semantics of the intentional operator is based on an equivalence relation. And, it is a classic result of modal logic, that this is characteristic of the logic **S5**. So, it simply falls out that the above axioms are all valid in our semantics. But, this is not an important practical distinction. In practice, only axioms 1 and 3 seem to play a role.

Source Association Axioms

5. $(P \xrightarrow{k} Q \wedge R \text{ received } \{X \text{ from } Q\}_k) \rightarrow (Q \text{ said } X \wedge Q \text{ has } X)$

---

[4] The **4** axiom (our axiom 3) is actually derivable given the others and is included for tradition and for its intuitive significance.

This replaces the Message Meaning Rule of BAN. Note the absence of the *'believes'* operator, and that the axiom applies when any principal R receives $\{X \text{ from } Q\}_k$. The logical significance of '$P \xleftrightarrow{k} Q$' is now isolated from that of *believes*. As in BAN, there is also a corresponding public-key axiom.

6. $(PK_\sigma(Q, k) \wedge R \text{ received } X \wedge SV(X, k, Y)) \rightarrow Q \text{ said } Y$

We introduce some new notation here. '$SV(X, k, Y)$' means that applying k to X confirms that X is the result of signing Y with a private cognate of k. Note that this axiom separates out key binding (what principal is bound to the key) from key correctness (what key verifies the signature).

Key Agreement Axioms

7. $(PK_\delta(P, k_P) \wedge PK_\delta(Q, k_Q)) \rightarrow P \xleftarrow{F_0(k_P, k_Q)} Q$
8. $\varphi \equiv \varphi[F_0(k, k')/F_0(k', k)]$ $F_0(k', k)$ implicitly names the (Diffie-Hellman) function that combines k' with k^{-1} to form a shared key.

These are the axioms that characterize Diffie-Hellman key agreement. As we mentioned in Section 2.5, this is an important component in widely used authenticated key establishment protocols. We give here a brief account of the mathematics of Diffie-Hellman. For more details consult a standard cryptography text [MvOV97, Sch96].

Protocol 3 (Diffie-Hellman)

1. Assume that Alice and Bob share
   - a large prime p
   - a generator g of the multiplicative group $\mathbb{Z}_p^*$ of integers *modulo p*.
2. Alice chooses large integer x and computes $X = g^x \bmod p$
3. Bob chooses large integer y and computes $Y = g^y \bmod p$
4.   Message 1 $A \rightarrow B : X$

       Message 2 $B \rightarrow A : Y$
5. Alice sets $k_{AB} = X^y \bmod p = g^{xy} \bmod p$ $(= g^{yx} \bmod p)$
6. Bob sets $k_{AB} = Y^x \bmod p = g^{yx} \bmod p$ $(= g^{xy} \bmod p)$

Receiving Axioms

9. $P \text{ received } (X_1, \ldots X_n) \rightarrow P \text{ received } X_i$, for $i = 1, \ldots, n$
10. $(P \text{ received } \{X\}_{k+} \wedge P \text{ has } k^-) \rightarrow P \text{ received } X$
    Here k^+ and $k-$ are used to abstractly represent cognate keys, whether for symmetric or asymmetric cryptography. In the symmetric case, $k^+ = k^- = k$. In the asymmetric case, k^+ is a public key and k^- the associated private key.
11. $(P \text{ received } \lfloor X \rfloor_k) \rightarrow P \text{ received } X$
    Principals are assumed to possess public keys (for convenience).

Possession Axioms

12. P *received* $X \rightarrow P$ *has* X
13. P *has* $(X_1, \ldots, X_n) \rightarrow P$ *has* X_i, for $i = 1, \ldots, n$.
14. $(P$ *has* $X_1 \wedge \ldots \wedge P$ *has* $X_n) \rightarrow P$ *has* $F(X_1, \ldots, X_n)$
    'F' is meta-notation for any function computable in practice by P, e.g., encryption with known keys. The meaning of "computable in practice" is intentionally not formally determined. It could be, e.g., polynomial-time computable but will be treated as a black box, just as "encryption", "signature", etc., are in nearly all formal treatments of cryptographic protocols.

Comprehension Axiom

15. P *believes* $(P$ *has* $F(X)) \rightarrow P$ *believes* $(P$ *has* $X)$
    'F' is meta-notation for any function that is effectively one-one (e.g., collision free hashes) and such that F^+ or F^- is computable in practice by P. Note that this axiom does not imply that F is invertible by P. Note also that the converse of this axiom is a derivable theorem.

Saying Axioms

16. P *said* $(X_1, \ldots, X_n) \rightarrow P$ *said* $X_i \wedge P$ *has* X_i, for $i = 1, \ldots, n$.
17. P *says* $(X_1, \ldots, X_n) \rightarrow (P$ *said* $(X_1, \ldots, X_n) \wedge P$ *says* $X_i)$, for $i = 1, \ldots, n$.

Freshness Axioms

18. $fresh(X_i) \rightarrow fresh(X_1, \ldots, X_n)$, for $i = 1, \ldots, n$.
19. $fresh(X_1, \ldots, X_n) \rightarrow fresh\ F(X_1, \ldots, X_n)$ F must genuinely depend on all component arguments. This means that it is infeasible to compute value of F without value of all the X_i.

Jurisdiction and Nonce-Verification Axioms

20. $(P$ *controls* $\varphi \wedge P$ *says* $\varphi) \rightarrow \varphi$
21. $(fresh(X) \wedge P$ *said* $X) \rightarrow P$ *says* X

Note: Neither axiom refers to belief

Symmetric Goodness Axiom

22. $P \xleftrightarrow{k} Q \equiv Q \xleftrightarrow{k} P$

3.4   Protocol Analysis

We now demonstrate how to do a protocol analysis using SVO. We will continue with our running example of the Needham-Schroeder Shared-Key Protocol 1. A comparison between BAN and SVO analysis is summarized in Figure 1.

BAN Analysis	SVO Analysis
1. Idealize the protocol.	
2. Write assumptions about initial state.	a. Write assumptions about initial state.
3. Annotate protocol. For each message "$P \to Q : M$" of the idealized protocol, assert "Q received M".	b. Annotate protocol. For each message "$P \to Q : M$" of the (not idealized) protocol, assert "Q received M".
	c. Assert comprehensions of received messages.
	d. Assert interpretations of comprehended messages.
4. Use the logic to derive the beliefs held by protocol principals.	e. Use the logic to derive beliefs held by protocol principals.

Fig. 1. Protocol analysis steps

NSSK Initial State Assumptions

As with BAN, the first assumptions to set out are the initial state assumptions. Unlike BAN, we do not idealize the protocol first. The assumptions are virtually the same as the initial state assumptions set out in the above BAN analysis, except that the jurisdiction assumption P5 is about jurisdiction over freshness of keys rather than jurisdiction over freshness of assertions about the goodness of keys.

P1. A believes $A \xleftrightarrow{k_{AS}} S$
P2. B believes $B \xleftrightarrow{k_{BS}} S$

P3. A believes S controls $A \xleftrightarrow{k} B$
P4. B believes S controls $A \xleftrightarrow{k} B$
P5. A believes S controls $fresh(k)$

P6. A believes $fresh(n_A)$
P7. B believes $fresh(n_B)$

P8. B believes $fresh(A \xleftrightarrow{k_{AB}} B)$

NSSK Received Message Assumptions

This step is the same as the annotation assumptions in BAN, except that we here use the specified protocol, not its idealization. Amongst other things, this means that plaintext is not eliminated, and these premises can be read directly from the specification. These premises are not typically used directly in derivations. Rather, they are used in the production of comprehension premises, which are themselves used in producing interpretation premises.

P9. S received (A, B, n_A)
P10. A received $\{n_A, B, k_{AB}, \{k_{AB}, A\}_{k_{BS}}\}_{k_{AS}}$
P11. B received $\{k_{AB}, A\}_{k_{BS}}$
P12. A received $\{n_B\}_{k_{AB}}$
P13. B received $\{n_B - 1\}_{k_{AB}}$

NSSK Comprehension Assumptions

In this step, we express that which a principal comprehends of a received message. The move from the received message assumptions is usually straightforward in practice. In principle, this can be formalized. But a rigorous formalization makes for a very complicated logic and some of the intuitiveness of SVO is lost. Nonetheless, it may be desirable if the intent is to automate as much of the reasoning as possible. (Instances of such a formalization can be found in [WK96, Dek00].)

P14. S believes S received $(A, B, \langle n_A \rangle_{*s})$

P15. A believes A received $\{n_A, B, \langle k_{AB} \rangle_{*A}, \langle \{k_{AB}, A\}_{k_{BS}} \rangle_{*A} \}_{k_{AS}}$

P16. B believes B received $\{\langle k_{AB} \rangle_{*B}, A\}_{k_{BS}}$

P17. A believes A received $\{\langle n_B \rangle_{*A} \text{ from } B\}_{\langle k_{AB} \rangle_{*A}}$

P18. B believes B received $\{n_B - 1\}_{\langle k_{AB} \rangle_{*B}}$

NSSK Interpretation Assumptions

These assumptions are essentially the replacement for idealization. Producing them is inherently an informal process. We are asserting how a principal interprets a received message (as that principal understands it). This is inherently dependent on the protocol design. Idealization is one of the most criticized and/or misapplied aspects of BAN analysis—bad initial state assumptions being the other. While some informality seems necessary in anything like this framework, SVO analysis reduces the potential for problems. First, idealization is split into comprehension and interpretation. Second, and perhaps more important, the interpretational part of the process occurs after annotation rather than before. In idealization, there is a natural and correct tendency to interpret message components using formulae expressing the intent of the sender. BAN annotation then asserts that the receiver receives the intended meaning of the sender. By placing interpretation after annotation and comprehension, the focus naturally shifts to how the intent of the sender is understood by the receiver. That is, focus shifts from the meaning the sender had intended to the meaning that the receiver attaches to a received message.

P19. A believes A received $\{n_A, B, \langle k_{AB} \rangle_{*A}, \langle \{k_{AB}, A\}_{k_{BS}} \rangle_{*A} \}_{k_{AS}} \rightarrow A$ believes A received $\{n_A, B, A \xleftarrow{\langle k_{AB} \rangle_{*A}} B, \text{fresh}(\langle k_{AB} \rangle_{*A}), \langle \{k_{AB}, A\}_{k_{BS}} \rangle_{*A} \}_{k_{AS}}$

P20. B believes B received $\{\langle k_{AB} \rangle_{*B}, A\}_{k_{BS}} \rightarrow$
B believes B received $\{A \xleftarrow{\langle k_{AB} \rangle_{*B}} B, \text{fresh}(\langle k_{AB} \rangle_{*B}), A\}_{k_{BS}}$

P21. $(A$ believes A received $\{\langle n_B \rangle_{*A} \}_{\langle k_{AB} \rangle_{*A}}) \wedge (A$ believes $A \xleftarrow{\langle k_{AB} \rangle_{*A}} B) \rightarrow$
A believes A received $\{\langle n_B \rangle_{*A}, A \xleftarrow{\langle k_{AB} \rangle_{*A}} B\}_{\langle k_{AB} \rangle_{*A}}$

P22. $(B$ believes B received $\{n_B - 1\}_{\langle k_{AB} \rangle_{*B}} \wedge (B$ believes $A \xleftarrow{\langle k_{AB} \rangle_{*B}} B) \rightarrow$
B believes B received $\{n_B - 1, A \xleftarrow{\langle k_{AB} \rangle_{*B}} B\}_{\langle k_{AB} \rangle_{*B}}$

Another point to note about these premises is that they all have conditional form. Often, the conditional is only a formal reminder that the interpretation depends on the comprehension of the actual receipt of the message. But in some cases, e.g., assumption P21, the interpretation depends not just on receipt of a message but also on other things, such as assumptions about good keys.

We have omitted an interpretation premise for the first message because it will play no role in the derivations. (The BAN assumption that plaintext does not affect analysis is not merely capricious.)

NSSK Derivations for Alice

1. A believes A received $\{n_A, B, A \xleftarrow{\langle k_{AB} \rangle_{*A}} B, \text{fresh}(\langle k_{AB} \rangle_{*A}), \langle \{k_{AB}, A\}_{k_{BS}} \rangle_{*A}\}_{k_{AS}}$
   By Modus Ponens using P19, P15

Unlike in BAN, to move from here to Alice believing that the server sent the message she received requires several steps. We would have to apply the necessitation rule to the source association axiom, and also make use of propositional reasoning, axiom 1, modus ponens, etc. We will present here only the highlights, focusing on the authentication reasoning. We will generally omit reference to the rules (modus ponens and necessitation) and will refer to propositional reasoning or reasoning using the belief axioms by saying "by Belief Axioms".

2. A believes S said $\{n_A, B, A \xleftarrow{\langle k_{AB} \rangle_{*A}} B, \text{fresh}(\langle k_{AB} \rangle_{*A}), \langle \{k_{AB}, A\}_{k_{BS}} \rangle_{*A}\}_{k_{AS}}$
   By Source Association, 1, P1, and Belief Axioms

3. A believes S says $\{n_A, B, A \xleftarrow{\langle k_{AB} \rangle_{*A}} B, \text{fresh}(\langle k_{AB} \rangle_{*A}), \langle \{k_{AB}, A\}_{k_{BS}} \rangle_{*A}\}_{k_{AS}}$
   By Freshness, Nonce Verification, 2, P6, and Belief Axioms

4. A believes $A \xleftarrow{\langle k_{AB} \rangle_{*A}} B$
   By Saying, Jurisdiction, 3, P3, and Belief Axioms

5. A believes $\text{fresh}(\langle k_{AB} \rangle_{*A})$
   By Saying, Jurisdiction, 3, P5, and Belief Axioms

6. A believes B said $(\langle n_B \rangle_{*A}, A \xleftarrow{\langle k_{AB} \rangle_{*A}} B)$
   By Source Association, P21, 4, and Belief Axioms

7. A believes B has $\langle k_{AB} \rangle_{*A}$
   By Source Association, P21, 4, and Belief Axioms

8. A believes B says $(\langle n_B \rangle_{*A}, A \xleftarrow{\langle k_{AB} \rangle_{*A}} B)$
   By Freshness, Nonce Verification, 5, 6, and Belief Axioms

We could obtain similar results for Bob (assuming we use the dubious assumption P8, the dubiousity of which is discussed in Section 2.3). This concludes our analysis of the Needham-Schroeder Shared-Key protocol. As noted above, one of the motivations of SVO was to incorporate reasoning about Diffie-Hellman style key agreement. Analyses of two such protocols can be found in [SvO96].

3.5   The Nessett Protocol in SVO

What about the Nessett Protocol? How does it fare in SVO? Since SVO contains both negation and the ability to express possession, it can express who should not get keys. This was Nessett's primary concern about BAN.

More precisely. In SVO, we can state the requirement

$$\neg(E \ has \ k_{AB})$$

where 'E' is the adversary. Now, given our assumption of a Dolev-Yao adversary, it is perfectly reasonable, for every message M of every protocol to add to the annotation assumptions that E received M. It then becomes trivial for the Nessett protocol to derive

$$E \ has \ k_{AB}$$

So, we can prove Nessett Protocol to be insecure. But, what if we could not prove $E \ has \ k_{AB}$? What if this were merely consistent with the protocol not provable from it? As has been observed, failed proofs sometimes reveal attacks. But sometimes they simply reveal our inability to produce a proof. An independent semantics would allow us to evaluate the truth of assumptions and requirements. SVO was given, indeed based on, such a semantics. We defer discussion of it to Section 6. Another question that arises from this discussion is: just what are the goals of an authentication protocol? We now turn to this question.

4   Authentication Goals

In the previous sections, we have described the syntax of BAN logic [BAN89a] and its descendents, most notably SVO [SvO96], and demonstrated how their axioms and inference rules can be used to derive new information from the factual knowledge specifying a given protocol. For example, this allowed us in Section 2 to construct a formal argument in support of the idea that, by the end of a run of the Needham-Schroeder Shared-Key protocol, the involved parties believe that they share a good key for secure mutual communication. As a matter of fact, this was one of the intended functionalities of this protocol. In general, we will be particularly interested in those derivations that relate the specification of a protocol to its intended goals or requirements.

In the present section, we will be concerned with identifying the authentication goals that a given protocol may be expected to fulfill. Rather than directly attacking this general problem, we will trace the historical development of this quest. We start in Section 4.1 by examining which requirements can be expressed in BAN and then, in Section 4.2, we outline the contributions made by its successors, most notably VO [vO93]. Limitations in these approaches triggered the study of authentication goals per se, independently from their expressibility in any given specification language. Replays, i.e. unwanted behaviors due to the interferences of multiple runs of a protocol, were soon identified as a major cause of unsatisfiable authentication goals, which opened the door to subtle attacks.

We examine them in Section 4.3. One of the results that emerged from this study is that specification languages such as BAN and SVO are not expressive enough to capture some of the authentication goals aimed at avoiding replays. The study of the notion of authentication continued, sometimes to tragi-comic extremes for most of the 1990's. We conclude in Section 4.4 by listing some of the problems that emerged and the proposed solutions.

4.1   BAN Authentication Goals

We have already outlined the way BAN goes about establishing authentication properties: given assumptions about the beliefs held by a principal before running a given protocol, it allows deducing beliefs that this principal must hold at the end of a run. This formal derivation is guided by the idealized protocol, which enriches the original specification with explicit descriptions of the intended functionality of selected message components, e.g. that a key is fresh or is good for communication between two principals. Although idealization is an essentially manual process and the logical status of the resulting annotations is dubious, the end-product is the vehicle that allows mapping what a principal believes before running a protocol to what he believes afterward, as described by the following diagram.

$$\text{Idealized protocol}$$
$$\downarrow$$

$$\text{Pre-run beliefs} \longrightarrow \boxed{\vdash_{\text{BAN}}} \longrightarrow \text{Post-run beliefs}$$

In the case of the Needham-Schroeder Shared-Key protocol examined in Section 2, from assumptions such as that principal A possesses a good key to communicate with a server S ("A believes $A \xleftrightarrow{k_{AS}} S$" in symbols) and that the nonce n_A is fresh ("A believes $fresh(n_A)$"), we deduced that she can legitimately think that she is handed a good key k_{AB} to communicate with a receiver B (i.e. "A believes $A \xleftrightarrow{k_{AB}} B$"). The derivation relies on protocol idealizations such as "$A \xleftrightarrow{k_{AB}} B$". We can indeed instantiate the above schema in the following partial diagram:

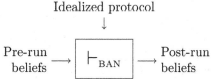

$$\cdots, A \xleftrightarrow{k_{AB}} B, \cdots$$
$$\downarrow$$

$$\begin{array}{c} A \text{ believes } A \xleftrightarrow{k_{AS}} S \\ A \text{ believes } fresh(n_A) \end{array} \longrightarrow \boxed{\vdash_{\text{BAN}}} \longrightarrow A \text{ believes } A \xleftrightarrow{k_{AB}} B$$

BAN logic does not define the notion of authentication. Instead, it offers means to express the fact that certain properties, clearly related to authentication, should be valid at the end of a message exchange, assuming certain premises hold. We call them *authentication goals*, and use the phrasing *authentication assumptions* for the premises they depend upon. BAN logic views authentication as a protocol dependent notion: therefore, different protocols will generally require different authentication assumptions and achieve different authentication goals. We schematically describe BAN's approach to authentication in the following diagram, a final evolution of pictures above:

Idealization of protocol $\mathcal{P}$

$\downarrow$

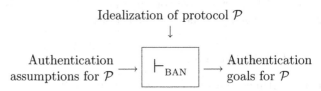

$$\begin{array}{ccc} \text{Authentication} & & \text{Authentication} \\ \text{assumptions for } \mathcal{P} & & \text{goals for } \mathcal{P} \end{array}$$

The realization that authentication is a protocol dependent notion leads to our first *observation on authentication*:

> 1. *There is not a unique definition of authentication that all secure protocols satisfy.*

Although authentication goals depend on the protocol at hands (and on its assumptions), certain goals recur fairly often. In particular, all BAN analyses of key distribution protocols have some of the following formulae as conclusions:

- A *believes* $A \xleftrightarrow{k_{AB}} B$
- B *believes* $A \xleftrightarrow{k_{AB}} B$
- A *believes* B *believes* $A \xleftrightarrow{k_{AB}} B$
- B *believes* A *believes* $A \xleftrightarrow{k_{AB}} B$

Clearly, other goals are possible, e.g. about beliefs concerning public keys. But they do not arise in the examples considered in [BAN89a], in which public keys are always a means to produce session keys in the form of shared keys, rather than the objects about which one would try to establish goals.

On the other hand, there are good key distribution protocols[5] for which some of the above goals are not applicable. Consider for example, the Wide-Mouthed Frog Protocol [BAN89a, CJ97], described below:

Protocol 4 (Wide-Mouthed Frog) [BAN89a, CJ97]

Message 1 $A \to S$: $\{T_A, B, k_{AB}\}_{k_{AS}}$
Message 2 $S \to B$: $\{T_S, A, k_{AB}\}_{k_{BS}}$

The initiator A wants to communicate securely with another party B. She achieves this by generating a key k_{AB} and sending it to a trusted server S together with her intention to communicate with B. The server simply forwards this key to B, together with the identity of the generator. The components T_A and T_S are timestamps. The first message is encrypted with a key k_{AS} that

---
[5] See the end of Section 4.4 below.

A shares with S, which ensures that its contents are not accessible to any other party. Similarly, the second message is encrypted with key k_{BS} that B shares with S. By the end of a run, only A, B and S are expected to know k_{AB}.

Since A generates the key k_{AB}, she has jurisdiction over its freshness and intended use. Therefore

$$A \text{ believes } A \xleftrightarrow{k_{AB}} B$$

is an assumption as well as a goal for the protocol. We leave it to the interested reader to devise the other relevant assumptions of the Wide-Mouthed Frog Protocol 4 as well as the form of its idealization. Provable goals of this protocol include

$$B \text{ believes } A \xleftrightarrow{k_{AB}} B \qquad \text{and} \qquad B \text{ believes } A \text{ believes } A \xleftrightarrow{k_{AB}} B$$

(again, the formal derivation is left to the reader). It should however be observed that the formula

$$A \text{ believes } B \text{ believes } A \xleftrightarrow{k_{AB}} B$$

although taken from the above list of typical goals, is not provable. Indeed A cannot hold any belief about B's beliefs since she is not the recipient of any message in this protocol.

4.2 VO Authentication Goals

As reported in Section 2, BAN was shown to have a number of shortcomings, soon to be fixed by a succession of proposals. While early extensions such as GNY [GNY90] and AT [AT91] concentrated on providing a finer modeling language for protocol actions, the logic VO [vO93] also enriched the lexicon of formally stated authentication goals. At the same time, it exposed nuances of the still vague notion of authentication that BAN and its early successors were unable to express. Altogether, VO provided a better understanding of what authentication actually is.

In this section, we present the various forms of authentication available in VO. Rather than trying to be completely faithful to [vO93], we will incorporate some of the adjustments made in later proposals. For simplicity, we will formalize the notions in this section using the syntax of SVO [SvO96], already introduced in Section 3.

We first need to introduce some syntax. VO expresses the fact that a key k is an *unconfirmed secret* for a principal P to communicate with another principal Q as

$$P \xleftrightarrow{k-} Q$$

Similarly to BAN's key goodness, this expression means that only P and Q (and third parties trusted by both) know k. It also implies that P has access to this key (e.g. by having received it in a message), but does not enforce a similar requirement on Q: this principal may not be aware of k. It was later observed [SvO96] that this expression can be given the following simple definition:

$$P \xleftrightarrow{k-} Q \;\; \equiv \;\; (P \xleftrightarrow{k} Q \land P \text{ has } k)^6$$

It should be observed that key confirmation is not symmetric. Indeed, $P \xleftrightarrow{k-} Q$ is not equivalent to $Q \xleftrightarrow{k-} P$.

Given this definition, VO distinguishes the following six forms of authentication:

Ping authentication captures situations where a principal P wants to know whether an interlocutor Q is alive. It is expressed as the following formula, where X can be any message.

$$P \text{ believes } Q \text{ says } X$$

Observe that not only should Q have uttered something (X), but he should have done so recently, as enforced by the use of *says* as opposed to *said*.

Entity authentication further requires that P's interlocutor Q said something relevant to their present conversation. Given some information Y_P known to be fresh to P (e.g. a nonce), entity authentication mandates that Q recently sent a message $F(X, Y_P)$ from which it is manifest that Q has seen Y_P and has processed it. This is captured by the following formula:

$$P \text{ believes } (Q \text{ says } F(X, Y_P) \land \text{fresh}(Y_P))$$

Suitable message transformation functions F must possess the following properties:

- F is effectively one-to-one, by which we mean that for any choice of the arguments X and Y, if $F(X, Y) = Z$, it is computationally infeasible to find values X' and Y' different from X and Y such that $F(X', Y') = Z$. As in [MvOV97], p. 324, the meaning of 'computationally infeasible' is "intentionally left without formal definition", to be interpreted relative to an understood frame of reference. For example it might mean that there is no algorithm that terminates in a time polynomial in the size of the argument of F that computes such X' and Y'. But this is only one possibility.
  This definition also indicates that F genuinely depends on Y_P, in the sense that it is computationally infeasible for an adversary to produce an alteration Y'_P of Y_P that yields the same result, even if he controls the choice of the first argument of F.
- F is computable in practice by Q. This too is left without precise definition. One example would be, given X and Y_P, Q can compute $F(X, Y_P)$ in polynomial time.

---

[6] In BAN, a principal A could only refer to a key k by believing some property of it, most notably its goodness, or by receiving it in a message. GNY [GNY90] remedied to this deficiency by allowing one to talk about entities possessed by a principal. Here we adopt the AT syntax "A has k" introduced in Section 3.

- P can effectively verify that the received value $F(X, Y_P)$ has actually been constructed by using Y_P. This can be achieved in two different ways:
  - P can in practice compute enough of the inverse of F to expose the use of Y_P. This is the case, for example, if $F(X, Y_P) = \{Y_P\}_X$ and X is P's public key.
  - P has access to X (and Y_P), can effectively compute $F(X, Y_P)$, and can verify whether the result corresponds to the value transmitted by Q. An example of this situation is when F is a hash function and X is known to P.

Secure key establishment indicates that a principal P believes that he has a good key k to communicate with a counterpart Q. Given the above notion of unconfirmed secret, this goal is easily expressed by the following formula:

$$P \text{ believes } P \xleftrightarrow{k-} Q$$

Key freshness simply requires that a principal P believes a key k to be fresh:

$$P \text{ believes } fresh(k)$$

Mutual understanding of shared keys applies to situations where a principal P can establish that an interlocutor Q has sent a key k as an unconfirmed secret between the two of them (from Q's point of view). This is formalized by the following formula:

$$P \text{ believes } Q \text{ says } (Q \xleftrightarrow{k-} P)$$

Key Confirmation is intended to describe scenarios in which a principal P believes that an interlocutor Q has proved to have received and successfully processed a previously unconfirmed secret key k between the two of them. Similarly to the case of entity authentication, we capture the "confirmation" aspect of this definition by requiring Q to return k to P, modulo the application of a function F that is effectively one-to-one, computable in practice by Q, and effectively verifiable by P. We have the following formal definition:

$$P \text{ believes } (P \xleftrightarrow{k-} Q \wedge Q \text{ says } F(k))$$

It should be observed that key confirmation is not the same as the BAN-style second-order belief "P believes Q believes $P \xleftrightarrow{k} Q$", which may wrongly imply that Q believes that k is a good key for them to communicate. For a similar reason, it differs from mutual understanding of shared keys "P believes Q says $Q \xleftrightarrow{k-} P$".

These definition shed substantial light on the notion of authentication. However, they also raise further questions, a clear indication that VO has moved our understanding of authentication forward, but also that it has not exhausted the subject. A closer look at entity authentication and mutual understanding of shared keys will reveal some problems, that will be addressed in the rest of this section.

Given actual principals A and B, the intended meaning of the entity authentication goal

$$A \text{ believes } (B \text{ says } F(X, Y_A) \wedge \text{fresh}(Y_A))$$

is that A is engaged in a protocol run with B and she thinks that B said something in response to the nonce Y_A she generated for this run. Observe however that this goal does not impose any constraint on B's assumptions; an intruder could indeed have rerouted messages in such a way that Y_A entered a conversation B was having with a third principal, C say; B may then have freshly sent $F(X, Y_A)$ to C, but the intruder altered the intended course of this message so that it reached A instead. This undesirable behavior passes the above entity authentication test.

Consider now the following goal, an instance of the mutual understanding of shared keys:

$$A \text{ believes } B \text{ says } (B \xleftrightarrow{k-} A)$$

The concern raised above for entity authentication does not apply here since the presence of the unconfirmed secret expression $B \xleftrightarrow{k-} A$ indicates that B is aware of the fact that k is intended to communicate with A. There is however room for attacks: again, an intruder may have rerouted messages so that B thinks that the key k is being used in a run r he is conducting with A, while A believes she is using it in a different run r', although with B. Again, this potentially harmful behavior satisfies the above notion of mutual understanding of shared keys goal.

Both scenarios arise as (intruder-assisted) misunderstandings: the involved principals are participating in an apparently legal run of the protocol, but not in the same run and not necessarily with each other. Both situations involve an interleaving of at least two protocol runs, with the intruder altering the message routes to unduly connect these otherwise independent runs. Such situations are called replays and will be examined in detail in the next section.

4.3   Replay Attacks

As we just discussed, a *replay attack* is characterized by an intruder opportunistically bending the path of messages belonging to different runs of a protocol, possibly after making minor changes to the messages themselves. An in-depth study of the different incarnations of the notion of replay was undertaken in [Syv94]. We present this analysis and use it to measure the expressiveness of the authentication logics from Sections 2 and 3. Two attempts at covering more replay attacks, one that refines the BAN model of time and one that introduces the notion of role, are then discussed.

A. Run external attacks	B. Run internal attacks

A. Run external attacks

B. Run internal attacks

1. Interleavings
    (a) Deflections
        i. Reflections
        ii. Deflections to a third party
    (b) Straight replays

                                (a) Deflections
                                      i. Reflections
                                      ii. Deflections to a third party
                                (b) Straight replays

2. Classic Replays
    (a) Deflections
        i. Reflections
        ii. Deflections to a third party
    (b) Straight replays

Fig. 2. A full taxonomy of replays [Syv94]

A Taxonomy of Replays

Syverson, in [Syv94], proposes two orthogonal classifications of replays, which formalize the observations that these misbehaviors derive from the interleaving of multiple protocol runs, and that the intruder redirects messages among them, respectively. We will now examine them in detail. The overall combined taxonomy is displayed in Figure 2.

A first way to approach replay attacks is to distinguish them on the basis of which runs the replayed messages are taken from. This materializes in a *run taxonomy* [Syv94], which immediately branches into the following two classes:

A. In a *run external attack*, the replayed message comes from outside the current protocol run. This option involves the execution of at least two runs, which can be either concurrent or sequential, as indicated by the next branching point in this taxonomy:
  (1) An *interleaving attack* requires two or more runs to take place contemporaneously. The intruder uses the different runs in turn as oracles to answer the challenges set forth by the others. A popular example of this form of replays is given by Lowe's attack [Low96] on the Needham-Schroeder Public-Key Authentication Protocol 7, which we will examine in Section 4.4.
  (2) An attack that involves external runs but without the requirement that they should be contemporaneous is called a *classic replay*. The intruder remembers messages sent back and forth during previous runs, and opportunistically replays them to mount an attack on the current run. We have seen an example of classic replay in Section 2 as the Denning-Sacco attack [DS81] on the Needham-Schroeder Shared-Key Authentication Protocol 1.

B. An attack can also result from opportunistically replaying messages from the current protocol run. These are known as *run internal attacks*. An example involving the Neuman-Stubblebine repeated authentication protocol [NS93, CJ97] has been exposed by Syverson in [Syv93b] and by Carlsen in [Car93].

Another way to look at replay attacks examines which messages are rerouted by the intruder, and how this is done. The resulting classification is known as the *destination taxonomy* [Syv94]. Let us first consider who the replayed message was intended for:

a. The first situation, called *deflection*, redirects the replayed message to a principal different from its intended recipient. This situation can be further refined in the following subcases:

    (i) First, the replayed message can be sent back to its sender. This is called a *reflection attack*.

    (ii) We can also have a *deflection to a third party*, in which the message in question is redirected to a principal that is neither the intended recipient or the originator.

b. An intruder can mount an attack by channeling a message to its intended destination, but with some delay and possibly in a different run of the protocols. This is known as a *straight replay*.

We will now demonstrate the various forms of destination attacks by examining a well-known disruption on the a variant of a draft protocol due to Yahalom, a version of which was ultimately published in [Yah93]. The variant we consider here was first presented in [BAN89a]. By virtue of this iterated genesis, we call it the BAN-Yahalom protocol. It is specified as follows:

Protocol 5 (BAN-Yahalom) [BAN89a]

Message 1 $A \to B$: A, n_A

Message 2 $B \to S$: $B, n_B, \{A, n_A\}_{k_{BS}}$

Message 3 $S \to A$: $n_B, \{B, k_{AB}, n_A\}_{k_{AS}}, \{A, k_{AB}, n_B\}_{k_{BS}}$

Message 4 $A \to B$: $\{A, k_{AB}, n_B\}_{k_{BS}}, \{n_B\}_{k_{AB}}$

The initiator A and the responder B rely on a server S to generate a key k_{AB} that would allow them to communicate securely. The long term keys k_{AS} and k_{BS} guarantee the mutual authentication of the server and the principals A and B, respectively. Intentionally, the third message indirectly authenticates B to A by having the server encapsulate both B's identity and A's fresh nonce n_A in the message $\{B, k_{AB}, n_A\}_{k_{AS}}$. The fourth message authenticates A to B by encrypting B's nonce n_B with the newly acquired (and supposedly secure) key k_{AB}.

This protocol is subject to the following attack, first presented in [Syv94], which makes use of three protocol runs, which we distinguish by using different numerals and indentations. The intruder is given the name E (the Eavesdropper), and we write E_P to indicate an action of the attacker while impersonating principal P. The attack unfolds as follows:

$$
\begin{array}{lll}
1. & & A \rightarrow E_B: \ A, n_A \\
I. & & E_B \rightarrow A \ : \ B, n_A \\
II. & & A \rightarrow E_S: \ A, n'_A, \{B, n_A\}_{k_{AS}} \\
& ii. & E_A \rightarrow S \ : \ A, n_A, \{B, n_A\}_{k_{AS}} \\
& iii. & S \rightarrow E_B: \ n_A, \{A, k_{AB}, n_A\}_{k_{BS}}, \{B, k_{AB}, n_A\}_{k_{AS}} \\
3. & & E_S \rightarrow A \ : \ n_E, \{B, k_{AB}, n_A\}_{k_{AS}}, \{A, k_{AB}, n_A\}_{k_{BS}} \\
4. & & A \rightarrow E_B: \ \{A, k_{AB}, n_A\}_{k_{BS}}, \{n_E\}_{k_{AB}}
\end{array}
$$

In line (1), A generates the nonce n_A to communicate with B. The outgoing message is intercepted by E and replayed to A in line (I) after altering its postulated originator to B. In A's view, this is the first message of a different run, with B as its originator, and therefore she responds as expected by generating a nonce n'_A and forwarding the message $(A, n'_A, \{B, n_A\}_{k_{AS}})$ to the server in line (II). The intruder alters this message *en route* by replacing the nonce n'_A with n_A in line (ii). Logically this is part of a third run of the protocol (the server has no reason to suspect that this run lacks its first message). The server performs its task on line (iii) by generating the message $(n_A, \{A, k_{AB}, n_A\}_{k_{BS}}, \{B, k_{AB}, n_A\}_{k_{AS}})$. These two inner runs are left dangling. We return instead to the outer run, where A is expecting a reply from S to her indirect request of line (1) via B. In line (3), the intruder replays the message captured in line (iii) after substituting a nonce n_E of his own in place of the outermost occurrence of n_A. This message has the expected form, and therefore A replies in line (4) as dictated by the text of the protocol.

Although no key is revealed to the intruder E, an attack has taken place since A believes she has been talking to B without this principal even participating in any run. This is clearly a failure of authentication. In order to mount the attack, the intruder makes use of three replay techniques:

- Going from lines (1) to (I), we first have a reflection of the nonce n_A back to A.
- Going from lines (II) to (ii), we have a straight replay of the message components A and $\{B, n_A\}_{k_{AS}}$ across two different runs of the protocol.
- Finally, going from lines (iii) to (3), we have a third party deflection of the encrypted components $\{A, k_{AB}, n_A\}_{k_{BS}}$ and $\{B, k_{AB}, n_A\}_{k_{AS}}$ from S to A and away from B.

Figure 2 integrates the run and destination taxonomies of replays, showing in this way all possibilities for a replay attack. This is therefore a complete classification.

Gauging Expressiveness

The above taxonomy of replays gives a clear view of the different ways an intruder can take advantage of the messages exchanged in one or more runs of a protocol to mount an authentication attack. This minute classification is also an excellent basis to measure the expressive power of various protocol analysis formalisms: an ideal system would successfully apply to all points in Figure 2. Most proposals cover instead a more spotty spectrum. In this section, we will make use of this taxonomy to outline the strengths and weaknesses of the authentication logics discussed in Sections 2 and 3. The results of this analysis should be taken with a grain of salt: there are cases where a formalism does not have mechanisms to systematically expose a certain class of attacks and yet has tackled specific instances of this class.

We shall first consider BAN logic [BAN89a] introduced in Section 2. Freshness is the only mechanism available in BAN to distinguish a run from another. This is a very weak mechanism indeed, since its effect is limited to temporally partitioning protocol actions into recent (i.e. provably fresh) and old. Therefore, freshness alone cannot hope to reveal run internal attacks, nor any form of interleaving attack. It instead focuses on the portion of the run taxonomy [Syv94] that we have called classic replays.

Although by assumption rather than by analysis, BAN captures a similarly small fragment of the destination taxonomy [Syv94]. First, recall that BAN expects a principal to recognize messages he/she has said. This is equivalent to limiting the scope of the verification process to protocols that are immune to reflection attacks. Second, the notion of a (shared) key k being good for two principals A and B to communicate, '$A \xleftrightarrow{k} B$', similarly circumvents deflection-to-third-party attacks. What is left of the destination taxonomy is the category of straight replays and some deflection-to-third-party situations that involve public keys.

In summary, the expressiveness of BAN relative to Figure 2 is limited to the zones marked "straight replays", and the area pertaining to "classic replays" among the run external attacks. In spite of this restricted scope, BAN has been successfully used to perform a large number of analyses.

The logic GNY [GNY90] corrects the inability of BAN to talk about reflection attacks by providing syntax (an asterisk "∗") to flag a message as "not originated here". The other limitations of BAN remain. Surprisingly they are not addressed by the successors of GNY, namely AT [AT91], VO [vO93], and SVO [SvO96].

We can sum up these observations as follows: none of the discussed logics exhausts or fully expresses the notion of authentication. In particular, since all of them, starting with BAN, are equipped to reason about freshness, we deduce that, in general, authentication problems cannot be reduced to enquiries about freshness. This leads to our second observation on authentication:

---

2. *Freshness is not rich enough to express all the kinds of authentication.*

Adding Time to Increase Expressiveness

As mentioned above, BAN and its successors rely on a simplicistic view of time that only distinguishes "recent" events from "old" actions. Freshness declarations draws the temporal line separating them, although recent messages almost always pertain to the current run. A finer use of time in protocol analysis was proposed in [Syv93a] with the introduction of the modality $\diamondsuit$, read "previously". This allows not only breaking the time-line in more than two segments, but also expressing the fact that event occurrences should have happened according to a certain order. For example, a requirement such as

$$A \ received \ \{B, k_{AB}, n_A\}_{k_{AS}} \ \rightarrow \ \diamondsuit(B \ said \ \{A, n_A\}_{k_{BS}})$$

means that if A receives the message on the left-hand side of the implication, then B has previously sent the message on the right-hand side. The added temporal operator has therefore the additional effect of capturing a form of causality between events.

A natural question to ask is whether the addition of the above modality to BAN or SVO is sufficient to address all forms of replay in the taxonomy in Figure 2. The answer is unfortunately negative: at least straight replays are not covered.

In order to demonstrate this point, we will rely on the protocol below, first presented in [Sne91]. The system it models consists of a master computer M and a collection of sensors $S_1, \ldots, S_n$, each controlled by a microprocessor. The master computer periodically queries the sensors. The protocol is aimed at authenticating the order and timeliness of their reports.

Protocol 6 (Snekkenes) [Sne91]

Message 1 $M \rightarrow S_i$: $\mathsf{Query}(i, j)$

Message 2 $S_i \rightarrow M$: $\lfloor n_{ij}, \mathsf{Query}(i, j), \mathsf{Answer}(i, j)\rfloor_{k_i^{-1}}$

Message 3 $M \rightarrow S_i$: $\lfloor n_{ij}\rfloor_{k_M^{-1}}$

In the first message, M sends a query $\mathsf{Query}(i, j)$ to sensor S_i, where j is a progressive number. In the second message, the invoked sensor, S_i returns an answer $\mathsf{Answer}(i, j)$ together with the original query and a nonce n_{ij} aimed at ensuring the freshness of the reply. The origin of this composite message is guaranteed by having S_i sign it with its private key k_i^{-1}. Upon receiving this message, M responds by signing the nonce n_{ij} with his own key k_M^{-1}.

This protocol is not immune to straight replay attacks, even if M keeps track of all used n_{ij} and (correctly) assumes these values are fresh. An intruder can indeed subvert the result of this protocol by intercepting a query $\mathsf{Query}(i, j)$ on its way from M to S_i, forwarding it multiple times to S_i, and letting through to M the most desirable answer.

This attack can be neutralized by reversing the order of the last two messages of this protocol. Consequently, the nonce n_{ij} is now generated by M rather than by S_i. Moreover, it is now the sensor's duty to memorize the nonces, verify their freshness, and limits its answers to one per nonce, to preclude replays. The master computer shall maintain an association between nonces and queries to prevent the subversive rerouting of signed nonces to sensors different from the one they were intended for.

Snekkenes observed in [Sne91] the rather unsettling fact that the BAN analysis of both variants of this protocol is same. He furthermore proved that a similar limitation holds for any two variants of a given protocol that differ only by the order of the exchanged messages:

Theorem 1. *(Snekkenes '91)*

1. *Let $\mathcal{P}$ and $\mathcal{P}'$ be protocols composed of the same messages, although not necessarily in the same order.*
2. *Assume that $\mathcal{P}$ can be shown to satisfy some goal G given certain assumptions $\mathcal{A}$.*
3. *Furthermore, assume that $\mathcal{P}'$ is demonstrably insecure.*

Then, $\mathcal{P}'$ can also be shown to satisfy the goal G given the assumptions $\mathcal{A}$.

This result was rigorously proved in the context of an annotated sequent calculus for BAN logic.

The above theorem states that extending BAN queries to faithfully account for the causal ordering of protocol actions is not sufficient to prevent all forms of replay attacks. This leads to our third observations on authentication:

> 3. *Correct causal order and source of a message are not strong enough for all authentications.*

Roles in Cryptographic Protocols

The most visible effect of the introduction of the temporal operator $\diamondsuit$ in the previous section was to extend the language used to express and validate protocol requirement. A similar proposal in [Bie90] focused instead on the language used to specify a protocol.

In [Bie90], protocols are described in the logic of knowledge and time CKT5, which enriches a fragment of first-order logic with the modal operator $K_{A,t}$ and a suitable set of axioms. The intended meaning of a formula of the form $K_{A,t}\,\varphi$ is that at time t principal A knows that φ holds. The use of proper quantifiers over time variables allows capturing the relative temporal ordering of events, similarly to what we have observed with $\diamondsuit$.

The introduction of this modality makes it possible to put strict temporal constraints on the actions that a principal participating in a protocol is allowed to perform. This permits expressing scenarios where, for example, if A sent m_1 and A received m_2, then the next action of A is to send m_3. In this proposal, the protocol actions available to a principal are organized in a *role*, given as the sequences of message transmissions that this principal is going to perform, possibly in response to the reception of some well-defined messages. A protocol specification is then presented as a set of roles, one for each participating principal. It should be observed that this approach constitutes a radical change of course with respect to the BAN-like specification methodology discussed so far: in these languages, a protocol was described by listing the messages exchanged during an expected run, while roles focus on the individual view of each principal, independently from any run.

The CTK5 specifications given in [Bie90] allowed each honest principal participating in a protocol to play exactly one role. It was shown in [Sne92] that this restriction could give an incorrectly clean bill of health: attacks that relied on having the same principal act both as an initiator and a responder, for example, were missed. This same paper corrected this limitation by upgrading the one-to-one relation between roles and principal proposed in [Bie90] to a many-to-one correspondence. Therefore, a given principal was now associated with a set of roles, an entity also known as a *multi-role*. Differently from roles, multi-roles could, for example, express the necessary conditions to set up the attack on the BAN-Yahalom protocol discussed in Section 4.3.

The CKT5 formalization of roles and multi-roles used in [Sne92] was later simplified in [Car94], which also gave an algorithm to generate CKT5 role specifications from the BAN-like "standard notation" of a protocol.

Clearly, if the protocol at hand is constrained in such a way that every honest principal can play at most one role, then no multi-role flaws can be uncovered. Even in this limited setting, the use of CTK5 as a specification language does not prevent the possibility of all attack. The Snekkenes Protocol 6 from Section 4.3 is subject to the same attack even when expressed in this language. We can therefore strengthen our last observation on authentication as follows:

> 4. *Correct causal order and message source, and freedom from multi-role flaws are not strong enough for all authentications.*

4.4   A Child's Garden of Authentications

Starting with the most common authentication objectives of BAN logic [BAN89a], the previous section has described the contributions made by various researchers to the formalization and understanding of the notion of authentication. We saw how these original goals were extended in languages such as VO [vO93] and SVO [SvO96]. We then categorized attacks relative to the taxonomy of replays defined in [Syv94] and finally discussed a series of proposal aimed at repairing specification [Bie90, Sne92, Car94] and requirement [Syv93a] deficiencies of the BAN family of logics. Yet, not all attacks could be nailed down.

By this time, we were in the mid 1990s and the notion of authentication was looking like a more and more distant chimera. The research toward this holy grail intensified, and considerable effort was spent trying to answer the following basic question:

Is there an adequately strong criterion for freedom from replay?

In this section, we will report on some of the progresses that were made toward this elusive goal. We shall anticipate that this question is still open. As we will see in Section 5, this quest is not however as popular as it once was, mainly because several researchers have now given guidelines aimed at constructing protocols that are free from attacks by design.

What Do We Mean by Entity Authentication?

Gollmann raised the question in the title of this section in the homonymous paper [Gol96]. The notion of *entity authentication* had been used liberally, often abused, in the security literature (we gave one of the many definitions in Section 4.2). Gollmann's paper discusses various meanings attributed to this phrase, and crystallizes some of these definitions in the context they ought to be used.

One of the strongest meanings of "entity authentication" requires that all the communications that constitute a session be accessible only to the involved parties, or to some entity in whose integrity they can put a reasonable amount of confidence. This degree of authentication is usually attained by encrypting all the communications between two principals by means of a *session key* freshly generated in a secure manner by a trusted third party. This constitutes the essence of Gollmann's first authentication goal:

G1: The protocol establishes a fresh session key, known only to the session parties and possibly to a trusted server.

While this goal is sufficient when considering protocol runs in isolation, situations that may involve several runs require reinforcing this requirement with the following clause:

G1': Furthermore, compromising old sessions keys does not lead to the compromise of new session keys.

In particular, new session keys should not be transmitted encrypted with old session keys.

A second meaning of "entity authentication" requires that a principal A can ascertain that an interlocutor B has received and successfully interpreted a message sent by A to B. Gollmann expresses this requirement as follows, modulo minor editing:

G2: A key associated with a principal B was used in a message received by another principal A in the protocol run, in a response to a challenge issued by A in the form of a nonce or a timestamp.

This is what we called "entity authentication" in Section 4.2.

A yet weaker form of "entity authentication" simply requires a principal to be able to ascertain that an intended interlocutor was active during a protocol run. This is expressed as the following goal:

G3: A key associated with a principal B was used during the protocol run, in a response to a challenge issued by another principal A in the form of a nonce or a timestamp. However, A did not need to receive a message where this key was used.

This is essentially what we called "ping authentication" in Section 4.2.

Agreements

In [Low97], Lowe observed that all definitions used to talk about authentication have the following form:

A protocol $\mathcal{P}$ guarantees property X to initiator A for another principal B,

$$iff$$

whenever A completes a run of the protocol, apparently with responder B, then a certain requirement ψ holds.

We denote the condition "whenever A completes a run of the protocol, apparently with responder B" as φ_{AB}. Then, all the definitions can be seen as implications of the following form:

$$\varphi_{AB} \rightarrow \psi.$$

Here, A and B are parameters rather than specific principals. Therefore, although these goals may appear to be bound to the principals, they are actually more general.

It should be observed that these goals are validated once a run is completed. Therefore, they are intended to authenticate runs, rather than individual messages as in the case of the requirements for BAN examined in Section 4.1.

We will now examine some of the property-requirement pairs (X, ψ) considered in [Low97]. These definitions refine and give a more precise meaning to notions such as ping or entity authentications discussed above.

Aliveness: $\psi =$ "B has been running the protocol".

This requirement extends ping authentication to protocol runs. When satisfied, it guarantees that A's interlocutor, B, has been active some time in the past. Situations in which the run proceeds smoothly from A's point of view without B taking part in any action represent a failure of aliveness. We have observed such a situation in the attack to the BAN-Yahalom Protocol 5 in Section 4.3.

Like every requirement discussed in [Low97], there is a *recent* version of aliveness: $\psi =$ "B has been running the protocol *recently*". Recent aliveness requires B to have been active during the current run. Notice that B does not need to have been running the same protocol as A, and even if he did he may have run it with a different party.

It should be noted that recent aliveness is not only stronger than ping authentication, but it also subsumes VO's entity authentication discussed in Section 4.2. Indeed, recent aliveness is manifested in a run of a cryptographic protocol by witnessing precisely the transformations required by this form of authentication. From that point of view, recent aliveness possibly gives a meaning to the notion of entity authentication.

Weak agreement: ψ = "B has previously been running the protocol, *apparently with A*".

Weak agreement strengthens aliveness by requiring not only that A's interlocutor B was active, but that A had evidence that he participated in a very direct manner by decrypting or signing messages that he only could have processed (unless the relevant keys were compromised). Observe that weak agreement does not require B to be running the protocol with A, nor can it he assumed to don the expected role (e.g. if A acts as the initiator, B may not necessarily be playing the responder role).

In [Low96, Low97], the difference between (recent) aliveness and weak agreement was illustrated by the attack below, which has achieved world fame and has become a major test bed, sometimes even a rite of passage, for every new protocol verification tool. Lowe's attack operates on the following fragment of a protocol due to Needham and Schroeder [NS78], the public-key version of the Needham-Schroeder Shared-Key Protocol 1 analyzed in Section 2.3.

Protocol 7 (Abridged Needham-Schroeder Public-Key) [NS78]

> *Message 1* $\quad A \to B: \quad \{n_A, A\}_{k_B}$
>
> *Message 2* $\quad B \to A: \quad \{n_A, n_B\}_{k_A}$
>
> *Message 3* $\quad A \to B: \quad \{n_B\}_{k_B}$

In this protocol, the initiator A sends her identity and a freshly generated nonce n_A to B, protecting this message by encrypting it with B's public key k_B. Upon receiving it, B generates a nonce of his own, n_B, and sends it to A together with n_A, encrypted with A's public key. In the last message, A sends n_B back to B, encoded with k_B. The protocol originally described in [BAN89a] had an initial key distribution phase in which A and B requested and received the keys k_A and k_B from a trusted server.

Upon completing a run of this protocol, A can be confident that she has been talking with B. Lowe's attack [Low96] shows that this protocol does not provide the reverse assurance. The trace of this attack is as follows:

$$
\begin{aligned}
1. & \quad A \to E \ \{n_A, A\}_{k_E} \\
i. & \quad E_A \to B \ \{n_A, A\}_{k_B} \\
ii. & \quad B \to E_A \ \{n_B, n_A\}_{k_A} \\
2. & \quad E \to A \ \{n_B, n_A\}_{k_A} \\
3. & \quad A \to E \ \{n_B\}_{k_E} \\
iii. & \quad E_A \to B \ \{n_B\}_{k_B}
\end{aligned}
$$

On line (1), A starts the protocol with the intruder E, who accesses the contents of the first message, re-encrypts it with B's public key and forwards it to this principal in line (i). On line (ii), B replies as if the message had come directly from A. The attacker intercepts it and directs it to A in lines (ii) and (2). The initiator A completes the protocol with E by encrypting the nonce n_B she received with E's public key. Finally, E forwards this nonce encrypted with k_B to B. In the end, A (correctly) believes that she has been running the protocol with E, but B is fooled into assuming that he has been talking to A.

It is clear that this attack proves that the Needham-Schroeder Public-Key protocol does not satisfy weak agreement from B's point of view (i.e. after swapping A and B in the above definition). However, it is proved in [Low97] that this protocol satisfies (recent) aliveness.

This attack is routinely used in courses and lectures to support the idea that protocol analysis is difficult, and in seminars and papers to motivate new proposals in this area. It is indeed true that it revealed a novel vulnerability to a protocol published 18 years earlier, and proved correct by a number methods, most notably using the BAN logic [BAN89a]. However, the Needham-Schroeder Public-Key Protocol was never deployed in any real-life setting. More importantly, a careful reading of [NS78] indicates that Lowe's weak agreement for the responder was not among the goals of this protocol.

Among the authors who challenged the legitimacy of this attack, Gollmann [Gol00] observed that it does not reveal any flaw if B's objective in this protocol was to have a communication with A. This corresponds to the notion of ping authentication (Gollmann calls it "authenticating packets"). However, if this protocol was used to establish a secure channel between the two parties, then Lowe's attack is a clear manifestation of a violation. Gollmann called this situation "authenticating circuits".

Non-injective agreement (with respect to data set ds): ψ = "B has previously been running the protocol, apparently with A, *and B was acting as the responder in his run, and both agree on values of variables in ds*".
   A yet stronger form of authentication is given by non-injective agreement. Here, A's interlocutor, B, is required to play the expected role, and their runs need to be synchronized to the extent that their respective variables among ds contain the same values. Observe however that this goal does not guaranteed a one-to-one relationship between A's and B's runs (hence the name).
   The Needham-Schroeder Public-Key Protocol 7 does clearly not satisfy this requirement. There are however protocols that pass the weak agreement test, but fail non-injective agreement. Examples include the Andrew Secure RPC Handshake [Sat89, CJ97], and Snekkenes Protocol 6 analyzed in Section 4.3.

Agreement: This goal, sometimes called *injective* agreement, reinforces non-injective agreement with the requirement that there is a *one-to-one correspondence between runs*. This last goal in [Low97] forces the runs of each involved party to by fully synchronized, and therefore may appear as the ultimate authentication requirement.
   The Wide-Mouthed Frog Protocol 4 presented in Section 4.1 can be proved to satisfy non-injective agreement, but does not pass the stronger agreement

test. An attack that exemplifies this situation is presented in [CJ97]: the adversary replays the server's message to B within the lifetime of the timestamp, essentially acquiring a new timestamp from the server, and repeats this game until A tries to run a legitimate session of the protocol with B, at which point he can replay the appropriate message to B. This attack can be formally expressed in a logic that includes time. A formal analysis in CSP using PVS is given in [ES00].

Intensional Specification

Lowe's hierarchy of authentication goals discussed in the previous section was essentially a response to *intensional specification*, a perhaps overly strict notion of protocol correctness defined by Roscoe in [Ros96]. The definition of intensional specification is as follows:

> A party cannot believe that a run has completed successfully unless a series of messages that agree on all parameters has occurred, up to and including the last message communicated by the given party.

In [Low97], Lowe observes that intensional specification is such a strong requirement that only the most inconsequential behaviors could violated it and yet satisfy agreement. Examples of such failures of intensional specification are:

– Assume that, in response to a request, a server sends a pair of messages (m_A, m_B) to principal A. This party can decrypt m_A, but not m_B, and is expected to forward this component to another principal B, who is able to interpret it. We have seen an instance of this scenario in the BAN-Yahalom Protocol 5 discussed in Section 4.3. Lowe's first example of an intensional specification "attack" that passes the agreement test relies on an adversary that substitutes m_B with some random value X in the message from the server to A. Then, it reinstalls m_B in place of X in the second message from A to B.
– Lowe's second "attack" example takes place in a situation where a server sends messages m_A and m_B to principals A and B, respectively, and in that precise order. An intruder delays the first message so that m_B reaches B before m_A reaches A.

It has been debated whether these failures can reasonably be seen as attacks, in any even remotely practical meaning of the term. In particular, it is not clear whether there are "real" attacks that satisfy agreement but not intensional specification. These doubts are highlighted by analyzing the following previously unpublished protocol.

Protocol 8 (Unpublished)

$Message\ 1$ $A \to B:$ $\{n_A, A, B\}_{k_{AB}}$

$Message\ 2$ $B \to A:$ $\{n_B, n_A, A, B\}_{k_{AB}}$

$Message\ 3$ $A \to C:$ $\{A, C, (n'_A \oplus n_B)\}_{k_{AC}}$

$Message\ 4$ $C \to A:$ $\{n_C, A, C, (n'_A \oplus n_B)\}_{k_{AC}}$

$Message\ 5$ $A \to B:$ $\{n_B, (n''_A \oplus n_C), A, B\}_{k_{AB}}$

Principals A and B set up a mutual challenge involving nonces n_A and n_B in line (1) and (2). In line (3) and (4), a similar process occurs between A and C, but the fresh value in the third message is not properly a nonce, but the result of taking the X-OR of B's nonce n_B from line (2) and some newly generated nonce n'_A. In the last message, A answers B's challenge from line (2), but also includes one of these pseudo-nonces, which is obtained by taking the X-OR of C's nonce n_C and yet another nonce n''_A generated by A.

Although we did not conduct a formal proof, this protocol seems to satisfy Lowe's notion of agreement. There are however situations in which it violates Roscoe's intentional specification:

- Suppose that A sends the message in line (3) before receiving the nonce n_B in line (2): she could for example use $n'_A = n^*_A$ to form this message without taking any X-OR. While the one-to-one correspondence between runs is not affected, intensional specification is violated since C would receive the nonce n'_A rather than the pseudo-nonce $(n'_A \oplus n_B)$. This may be potentially harmful since the causal relation of messages appears to be affected.

- Suppose now that A generates a nonce n^*_A before receiving B's nonce in line (2), waits for n_B, and only then calculates $n'_A = n^*_A \oplus n_B$ and sends the message in line (3). Now intensional specification seems to be satisfied. However, the end-result is identical since, being X-OR associative and idempotent, $(n^*_A \oplus n_B) \oplus n_B = n^*_A$. Indeed, the value sent to C has been decided before receiving B's message.

- Last, consider an identical scenario, but in which A generates n^*_A *after* receiving B's message in line (2), but without using n_B. Now, the causal relation between the messages is clearly respected, yet C will receive a value that is independent from the nonce n_B.

Similar "attacks" can be constructed with respect the the messages on lines (4) and (5).

Matching Histories

Matching histories [DvOW92] is an older proposal whose strength fits between Lowe's (injective) agreement and weak agreement. This characterization of authentication is particularly interesting because its definition was developed by industrial specialists in secure system design and cryptography rather than by formal methods experts, as for the proposals discussed so far. In particular, their focus was likely to be on a more practical articulation of the notion of "authentication" geared toward actual applications rather than on mapping out the theoretical terrain.

A protocol satisfies matching histories if the following condition can be proved to hold:

> When a principal A accepts the other party's identity (before receiving or sending further messages), the other party's record of the partial or full run matches A's (with the same values for all message variables).

This requirement is as strong as Lowe's (injective) agreement insofar as the number of runs and all variables must match between A and B. It is however not as powerful as weak agreement since B does not need to have been running the protocol with A. It can however be shown that matching histories and agreement are equivalent if every message exchanged in a protocol includes the identities of the apparent sender and of the intended recipient.

It is interesting to observe that matching histories is motivationally similar to VO's key confirmation (see Section 4.2),

$$P \text{ believes } (P \xleftrightarrow{k-} Q \wedge Q \text{ says } F(k))$$

while Lowe's various "agreements" goals are motivationally similar to VO's mutual understanding of shared keys (see Section 4.2) and to BAN's second-order belief (see Section 4.1),

$$P \text{ believes } Q \text{ says } (Q \xleftrightarrow{k-} P) \qquad\qquad P \text{ believes } Q \text{ believes } (Q \xleftrightarrow{k} P).$$

Cautionary Note

By the end of the 1990s, the research on issues related to authentication had proliferated to the point that some practitioners started noticing a dichotomy between the problems addressed in the academic literature on security, and the solutions sought in real world scenarios. Gollmann, again, voiced these concerns in the paper [Gol00]. He observed that the research in this area was often fueled by a perceived informality in protocol analysis, and, putting it in his own words,

> [this] motivates the presentation of a new formalism for the analysis of authentication protocols, and the biggest prize to be won is the detection of an attack hitherto unreported. We will argue that such exercises in formal analysis more often add to the problem than help in its resolution.

Furthermore:

> Perceived problems with authentication are caused by intuitive but imprecise interpretations of the objective of "authentication", and by neglecting to take into account the environment a protocol is intended to operate in. In many cases, new attacks do not expose subtle flaws in protocols but differences in assumption about protocol goals.

However, sometimes they do expose subtle flaws. Furthermore, new theories sometimes do turn out to be practically useful. Clearly, this is not always the case, but even then, they often have an impact on our understanding of the various concepts that contribute to what we call security. In these cases (and many other), it is essential not to mistake theoretical results for applied ones, or vice versa.

5   Design Principles and Protocol Logics

At this point we take a brief holiday from formal characterizations of authentication to consider protocols from a more informal and more applied perspective.

5.1   Protocol Design Principles

Abadi and Needham set out "prudent engineering practices for cryptographic protocols" in [AN94, AN96]. These are rules of thumb for good protocol design. They are not meant to apply to every protocol in every instance, but they do provide a laundry list of things that should be considered when designing a protocol. The paper contains useful examples and discussion of the principles. We quote from [AN96] just the principles here and then briefly comment on them below.

PRINCIPLE 1.   Every message should say what it means: The interpretation of the message should depend only on its content. It should be possible to write down a straightforward English sentence describing the content—though if there is a suitable formalism available, that is good too.

PRINCIPLE 2.   The conditions for a message to be acted upon should be clearly set out so that someone reviewing the design may see whether they are acceptable or not.

PRINCIPLE 3.   If the identity of a principal is essential to the meaning of a message, it is prudent to mention the principal's name explicitly in the message.

PRINCIPLE 4.   Be clear as to why encryption is being done. Encryption is not wholly cheap, and not asking precisely why it is being done can lead to redundancy. Encryption is not synonymous with security, and its improper use can lead to errors.

PRINCIPLE 5.   When a principal signs material that has already been encrypted, it should not be inferred that the principal knows the content of the message. On the other hand, it is proper to infer that the principal that signs a message and then encrypts it for privacy knows the content of the message.

PRINCIPLE 6.   Be clear about what properties you are assuming about nonces. What may do for ensuring temporal succession may not do for ensuring association—and perhaps association is best established by other means.

PRINCIPLE 7.   The use of a predictable quantity (such as the value of a counter) can serve in guaranteeing newness, through a challenge-response exchange. But if a predictable quantity is to be effective, it should be protected so that an intruder cannot simulate a challenge and later replay a response.

PRINCIPLE 8.   If timestamps are used as freshness guarantees by reference to
   absolute time, then the difference between local clocks at various machines
   must be much less than the allowable age of a message deemed to be valid.
   Furthermore, the time maintenance mechanism everywhere becomes part of
   the trusted computing base.

PRINCIPLE 9.   A key may have been used recently, for example to encrypt
   a nonce, yet be quite old, and possibly compromised. Recent use does not
   make the key look any better than it would otherwise.

PRINCIPLE 10.   If an encoding is used to present the meaning of a message, then
   it should be possible to tell which encoding is being used. In the common case
   where the encoding is protocol dependent, it should be possible to deduce
   that the message belongs to this protocol, and in fact to a particular run of
   the protocol, and to know its number in the protocol.

PRINCIPLE 11.   The protocol designer should know which trust relations his
   protocol depends on, and why the dependence is necessary. The reasons for
   particular trust relations being acceptable should be explicit though they will
   be founded on judgment and policy rather than on logic.

5.2   Design Principle Comments

Such rules of thumb should always be considered when designing a protocol and
only violated when the violation is consciously done for a superseding reason.
Since the rules are generally quite compelling, we focus on some of the ways
in which they might not apply, as a caution against applying them blindly.
(Comments in this section are mostly drawn from [Syv96].)

Building on the above principles, Anderson and Needham set out further
principles specifically focused on public-key protocols. Their first principle is an
expansion of PRINCIPLE 5 above.

> Sign before encrypting. If a signature is affixed to encrypted data, then
> one cannot assume that the signer has any knowledge of the data. A third
> party certainly cannot assume that the signature is authentic, so non-
> repudiation[7] is lost. ([AN95], p. 237, Principle 1)

This is a nice principle for illustrating limitations: there are many places
where non-repudiation may not be of paramount concern; thus the principle may
be too narrow. For example, anonymity may take priority over non-repudiation.
This would occur in voting protocols, and in digital cash. Digital cash often
makes use of a blind signature, in which the authority issuing the cash signs
a 'coin' that has been 'blinded' so that the authority cannot recognize the specific
coin and thus tie it to the principal to whom it was issued. After signing the
blinded coin, the principal unblinds it so that anyone can recognize it as a coin
authentically signed by the issuer.[8]

---

[7] The goal of non-repudiation is to prevent a principal from denying some action s/he
   has taken, such as sending or receiving a message.

[8] This is a very simple description. Blinding was invented by Chaum [Cha83]. More
   on digital cash and other applications of blinding can be found in [Sch96].

This principle may also be too broad: signing encrypted data may be necessary for non-repudiation. One place this can be seen is in a coin-flip protocol. A principal signs encryptions of "Heads" and "Tails" and later reveals the encryption key. Part of the reason is so that she cannot deny the choices offered and also so that the opposing principal cannot deny the choice made. A simple coin-flip protocol protocol demonstrating this point was given in [Syv96]. What follows is an even more simple version of this (without, e.g., replay protection). Other similar protocols were discussed in [Tou92].

Protocol 9 (Simple Coin Flip)

$Message\ 1\quad A \to B: \quad \lfloor \{Heads\}_k, \{Tails\}_k \rfloor_{k_A^{-1}}$

$Message\ 2\quad B \to A: \quad \lfloor X \rfloor_{k_B^{-1}} \quad (\text{where } X \text{ is one of } \{Heads\}_k \text{ or } \{Tails\}_k)$

$Message\ 3\quad A \to B: \quad \lfloor k \rfloor_{k_A^{-1}}$

$Message\ 4\quad B \to A: \quad \lfloor k \rfloor_{k_B^{-1}}$

Non-repudiation is a fairly subtle requirement. It may be unsurprising that principles such as the one under discussion are subject to the cautionary remarks we have been making. Explicitness, however, would seem to be paramount in all security protocols, and especially in authentication protocols. Indeed, Abadi and Needham regard it (as embodied in PRINCIPLES 1 and 2 above) as the overarching principle in the design of secure cryptographic protocols. It is therefore surprising that there are authenticated key distribution protocols that can only function in the absence of explicitness (especially explicitness as in PRINCIPLE 10). We now present such a protocol.

Protocol 10 (EKE — Encrypted Key Exchange) [BM92, BM93]

$Message\ 1\quad A \to B: \quad A, \{k_A\}_P$

$Message\ 2\quad B \to A: \quad \{\{k_{AB}\}_{k_A}\}_P$

$Message\ 3\quad A \to B: \quad \{n_A\}_{k_{AB}}$

$Message\ 4\quad B \to A: \quad \{n_A, n_B\}_{k_{AB}}$

$Message\ 5\quad A \to B: \quad \{n_B\}_{k_{AB}}$

The idea of the EKE protocol is to function as a privacy multiplier. Let Alice be some client and Bob a server for which Alice has password P. P is thus a secret shared between A and B, and the only means of authentication A possesses. She encrypts a public key k_A with P and sends it to Bob. Bob generates a session key k_{AB} and encrypts this with k_A and then encrypts the result with P. There is then a handshake that shows fresh possession of the session key. The important thing to observe about this protocol is that the content of messages cannot be confirmed upon receipt since the recipient of a message cannot tie its content to any known values until s/he completes the protocol. In particular, principals cannot tell if received messages have the correct form for them to take the next step. It is only when a recipient gets his last message that he can confirm that the preceding messages had the correct content and acting upon them was appropriate. If any of the messages contained adequate redundancy in content or coding for a principal to know what s/he is receiving (or sending) before the end of the protocol, then the protocol would be vulnerable to guessing attacks since P is a weak secret.

Even if this protocol is a counterexample to the complete generality of explicitness, it is also an example for another of the design principles; Anderson and Needham warn

> Be careful when signing or decrypting data that you never let yourself be used as an oracle by your opponent. ([AN95], p. 240, Principle 3)

EKE puts a spin on that principle; instead of preventing use of principals as oracles it ensures that the output of such oracles is of no use to the attacker.

Despite such unusual examples, explicitness is very often exactly what is required. We now delve deeper into its implications.

5.3   Fail-Stop Protocols

For any definition of authentication, almost all of the failures in the literature are due to active attacks in which a message is somehow altered or substituted for another in a way it was not intended. Thus, stopping such attacks would go a long way towards a general guarantee of protocol security. Fail-stop protocols [GS98] are designed to meet this goal.

Using Lamport's definition of causality [Lam78], we can organize the messages of a protocol into an acyclic directed graph where each arc represents a message and each directed path represents a sequence of messages. In a fail-stop protocol, if a message actually sent is in any way inconsistent with the protocol specification, then all those messages that come after this altered message on some path in the graph (i.e., they are causally after the altered message) will not be sent. Obviously conditions to act upon all protocol messages must be explicit in the content and format of each message in order for the protocol to be fail-stop.

A protocol is said to be *fail-stop* if any attack interfering with a message in one step will cause all causally-after message in the next step or later not to be sent [GS98].

No definition of authentication given so far is sufficient for fail-stop. The main reason is that the definitions we have discussed are focussed on properties that must hold if and when a principal has completed a protocol run. But, fail-stop is a requirement that must hold as the protocol executes. For example, consider the EKE protocol of the last section. This is quintessentially not fail-stop. A principal cannot confirm anything about the content or possibly even encoding of any message until s/he has received the last message of the protocol run.

Claim 1 *Active attacks cannot cause the release of secrets within the run of a fail-stop protocol.*

Claim 1 follows immediately from the definition of a fail-stop protocol, because active attacks do not cause more (or different) messages to be sent; so an attacker using active attacks cannot obtain more secrets than one using passive eavesdropping.

One of the desirable features of a fail-stop protocol is this form of immunity to active attacks. More generally, since an active attack will cause a fail-stop protocol to halt, in a fail-stop protocol no principal will ever produce encryptions or any other computations on data from a message that was not entirely legitimate. Therefore, we need to consider only passive attacks in which an adversary records messages and tries to compute secrets from them. Such passive attacks (and protection measures against them) are much better understood than active attacks and easier to analyze. And, as already noted, they are substantially less common in the attack literature.

This shows us the beginnings of a synergy between design principles and formal analysis, except that fail-stop is not quite a design principle. But the synergy can be strengthened via explicitness based on the principles of Abadi and Needham.

One of the ways to make a protocol fail-stop is to design it in accordance with the following criteria:

1. The content of each message has a header containing the identity of its sender, the identity of its intended recipient, the protocol identifier and its version number, a message sequence number, and a freshness identifier.
2. Each message is encrypted under a key shared between its sender and intended recipient.
3. An honest principal follows the protocol and ignores all unexpected messages.
4. A principal halts any protocol run in which an expected message does not arrive within a specified timeout period.

Here a freshness identifier can be a timestamp (if clocks are assumed to be securely and reliably synchronized) or a nonce issued by the intended recipient. But, the freshness identifier in the first message of the protocol cannot be a nonce since the recipient must be able to determine if the protocol should proceed based on it. So, it must be a sequence number, timestamp, or something that will meaningfully indicate freshness to the recipient. When a freshness identifier takes on a more complicated form, the rules for reasoning about freshness in sections 2 and 3 can be used to determine if the identifier is fresh with regard to the recipient. Basically, these rules say that, if x is deemed fresh and y cannot be computed (in a computationally feasible way) by someone without the knowledge of x, then y is also deemed fresh. Encryption with a shared key in item 2 of this claim can be replaced by the use of an encryption using the recipient's public key of a signature using the sender's private key. We can offer no formal proof of the claim, but it should be clear by inspection.

It might seem that fail-stop protocols automatically guarantee authentication.

Protocol 11 (Simple Fail-Stop Example)

Message 1 $A \rightarrow B$: $\{A, B, Prot\_name, version, seq.= 1, T_A, Query\}_{k_{AB}}$

Message 2 $B \rightarrow A$:   *Response.*

In the first message T_A is a timestamp, and other fields have their obvious meaning. This message clearly follows the format of above design criteria. The second message is not of that format, but since it is the last one in the protocol, there are no causally-after messages. Thus, the protocol is fail-stop. However, the second message is not authenticated (according to virtually any definition).

Extensible Fail-Stop Protocols

A protocol can be fail-stop even if it contains messages that could have come from any principal at any time. In this section we explore a strengthening of the fail-stop concept.

A message in a protocol is *last* if no protocol message is causally after it. A protocol is *extensible fail-stop* (EFS) if adding any last message to the protocol results in a fail-stop protocol.

Note that limiting to "ping-pong" protocols (where each message is followed by a single successor) implies a unique last message. This is the typical case for two party authentication protocols. The example of Protocol 11 is not EFS because adding a another message after Message 2 would result in a protocol that is not fail-stop. For EFS protocols, authentication is in fact automatically guaranteed—but only message authentication. An example of an EFS protocol is as follows:

Protocol 12 (Simple EFS Example)

Message 1 $A \rightarrow S$: $\{A, S, Prot., vers., seq.= 1, T_1, request(A, B)\}_{k_{AS}}$

Message 2 $S \rightarrow A$: $\{S, A, Prot., vers., seq.= 2, T_2, (k, A, B)\}_{k_{AS}}$

Message 3 $A \rightarrow S$: $\{A, S, Prot., vers., seq.= 3, T_3, (k, A, B)\}_{k_{AS}}$

Message 4 $S \rightarrow B$: $\{S, B, Prot., vers., seq.= 4, T_4, (k, B)\}_{k_{BS}}$

Message 5 $B \rightarrow S$: $\{B, S, Prot., vers., seq.= 5, T_5, (k, B)\}_{k_{BS}}$

This example demonstrates that fail-stop, even extensible-fail-stop, does not imply that the protocol satisfies all kinds of authentication. In the example, all messages are authenticated, but Bob does not know with whom he shares a key. Even a protocol in which Bob is given the wrong name for the principal meant to share the key could still be EFS.

Roughly, most of the authentication properties discussed in Section 4 are properties established by a complete protocol run about messages and the content of messages sent during that run. But, (extensible) fail-stop properties are authentication properties established by messages about the complete protocol run. For example, the following claim is immediate.

Claim 2 *Extensible fail-stop protocols are immune to replay.*

There is another, potentially more interesting property of EFS protocols.

Claim 3 *The sequential and parallel composition of EFS protocols is extensible fail-stop.*

The claim is justified by cases. For parallel composition: a message inserted causally before a last message of a fail-stop protocol will be ignored or cause a halt. Thus, it will not cause an EFS protocol to cease to be EFS. For sequential composition: let Pr_1 and Pr_2 be two EFS protocols. Suppose that some or all of the messages of Pr_1 are received after a last message of PR_2. If the first message of Pr_1 causes the result to be non-EFS, then Pr_2 was not EFS. (Contradiction.) And, if any later message causes the result to be non-EFS, then Pr_1 was not EFS.

We have already seen that fail-stop protocols need only to be examined for secrecy in the context of passive attacks (because active attacks cannot cause the release of secrets). In addition to its inherent interest, Claim 3 provides another design advantage of EFS protocols. Even analyses that consider interleaving typically assume only one protocol is running. If protocols are EFS, we are free to run multiple protocols in one environment without concern for interleaving attacks.[9]

As noted above, EFS protocols can be simply designed using basic explicitness rules. EFS protocols more flexible wrt composability, and EFS rules simplify the analysis task by removing replay considerations. How else might design rules synergize with protocol analysis logics?

5.4   Design Rules and Protocol Logics

A straightforward way for design rules to synergize with protocol logics is to build design checks directly into the logic. Brackin did precisely that in [Bra00]: he designed the logic BGNY [Bra96], based on GNY. He later developed an associated automated HOL tool, AAPA (Automated Authentication Protocol Analyzer) [Bra98], and a specification language similar to Millen's CAPSL [DM00, Mil]. The resulting system appears to be easy to use. Brackin has analyzed the entire Clark-Jacob library[10] using AAPA. He has also analyzed large commercial protocols such as the Cybercash main sequence protocol [Bra97]. This alone makes his a significant body of work, although we are not primarily concerned with automated tools in this paper.

---

[9] See Section 7 for a cautionary note.

[10] The Clark-Jacob library is a fairly comprehensive list of known attacks on published authentication protocols [CJ97].

Wedel and Kessler devised another BAN logic we will call 'WK' [WK96]. WK works with an automated tool AUTLOG based on Prolog. One advantages of the WK approach is that no formulae occur in messages. This is another step in solving the problem of the informal nature of idealization. Of course there is still the need for interpretation assumptions (as they were called in Section 3.4). That part cannot be automated. However, analysis in WK automates derivation of the comprehension assumptions. Recall that these were the assumptions that allowed us to express what a principal understands of received messages even though some of the message may be unfamiliar or not decryptable by the principal. In fact, the WK notation for not-understood messages motivated the notation given above in Section 3, although the use by Wedel and Kessler is not exactly the same. Another automated tool in the BAN family is the recent C3PO of Anthony Dekker [Dek00]. This is a GUI tool based on the Isabelle theorem-prover. The logic associated with this tool is called 'SVD', and, like WK, it is a variant on SVO. Neither of these has the published track record of analyses of Brackin's work, however.

A different approach to automation that again combines logics and design is that taken by Clark and Jacob in [CJ00]. In some sense the idea of this approach is to not do design at all. Rather goals are stated and then protocols are synthesized that meet these goals. Clark and Jacob automatically generate protocols from basic BAN logic goals (as described in Section 4.1) using genetic algorithms and simulated annealing. Another automated synthesis, but based on Song's Athena model checker rather than on BAN, was presented by Perrig and Song in [PS00]. Related ideas can be found in [Gut]. This no-design approach may have great long term potential, but it is still early. As we have seen, even simple protocols are subtle and the contribution of such approaches may be to produce protocols with desirable features that no person would be likely to design.

Buttyán, Staamann, and Wilhelm also synthesize protocols from a BAN-like logic [BSW98]. However, unlike the previously mentioned approaches that effectively generate random protocols and then prune to the results that meet desired goals, they directly synthesize protocol designs from goals. Their protocol designs are slightly more abstract than we have been considering. They specify and reason about protocols on the more abstract level of channels. The encryption mechanism used to secure the channel is regarded as an implementation issue. The result is thus somewhat similar to spi calculus [AG99] but is closer to Needham-Schroeder style specifications. Roughly speaking, their design logic synthesis rules work by running an abstracted version of BAN in reverse. For example, if C is a channel, then the following is a synthesis rule.

$$\frac{P \; believes \; P \; received \; X \; on \; C}{P \; sees \; X \; on \; C \qquad P \; can \; read \; C}$$

A protocol that would satisfy the goal above the line would need to have P receiving X on channel C, where C might be, e.g., encryption using P's public key or a key P shares with another principal.

These rules give articulated goals, not conclusions. In some cases they yield intermediate goals that require further applications of rules before the protocol can be synthesized.

A common theme of this design logic and the synthesis tools is that one first specifies what is wanted then looks at the protocol. That means that one must state generic requirements in a formal language. The intuitive expression of requirements is thus a strong advantage of the logical approach. This also suggests another way of combining formal requirements statements with existing formal analysis techniques: Give the semantics of requirements language in the language of the formal analysis method. Then, use the formal analysis method to evaluate the truth of requirements statements in models of the protocol.

6   Semantic Approaches

We have seen in the previous section that it is often advantageous to use distinct languages to express a protocol under investigation and the goals it is expected to meet. The protocol specification language typically has an operational flavor that makes it particularly adequate for analyses based on simulation, such as model checking. Requirements are more easily stated in declarative formalisms, preferably with strong logical foundations. In order to be usable, requirements need to be mapped down to the execution model supported by the protocol specification language. We do so by endowing the requirement logic with an operational semantics in terms of the formalism used to express the protocol.

In this section, we will briefly examine two instances of this symbiosis. First, in Section 6.1, we look at the successful NRL Protocol Analyzer [Mea94, Mea96] together with the NPATRL requirements logic [SM96]. Then, in Section 6.2, we discuss a recently proposed synergy that adopts the popular strand formalism [THG97, THG98b] as an operational model and a BAN-like logic as the specification formalism [Syv00].

6.1   NPATRL

Our first case study will consist of the established synergy between the NRL Protocol Analyzer [Mea94, Mea96] and the NPATRL requirement language [SM96]. We first sketch relevant aspects of the NRL Protocol Analyzer and then introduce NPATRL.

The NRL Protocol Analyzer Model

The NRL Protocol Analyzer, or NPA for short, is a computer-assisted verification tool for security protocols which combines model checking and theorem-proving techniques to establish authentication and secrecy properties. We will limit the presentation of this system to the aspects that will be relevant to our discussion of the NPATRL language. The interested reader is invited to consult [Mea94, Mea96] for further details.

A protocol is modeled as a number of communicating state machines, each associated with a different roles. Their transitions correspond to the actions that comprise the corresponding role. At run time, roles are executed by *honest principals* who faithfully follow the protocol. Several instances can be executing at the same time, and they are distinguished by means of a unique round number.

The intruder is modeled after the Dolev-Yao adversary, described in Section 1.1. *Dishonest principals* share their keys and other confidential information with the adversary.

The messages in transit, the information held by each principal and the intruder, the runs currently being executed, and the point that each of them has reached constitute the global *state* of the NRL Protocol Analyzer. A protocol action implements a local transformation with global effects on the state. The initial state is implicit in the protocol specification.

In order to verify a protocol, a specification is fed into the run-time system of the NRL Protocol Analyzer together with the description of a family of states that correspond to attack situations. The system applies protocol actions backwards from these target states until it either reaches the initial state, or it exhausts all possibilities for doing so. In the first case, it reports the sequence of transitions that link these two states: this tracks a possible attack. The second case establishes that an attacker cannot produce the target scenario. Although the search space is in general infinite, the NRL Protocol Analyzer incorporates techniques based on theorem proving that have the effect of soundly restricting the search to a finite abstraction, in most cases. We can pictorially describe the operations of the NRL Protocol Analyzer by means of the following diagram, where we have kept the fairly stable intruder model implicit:

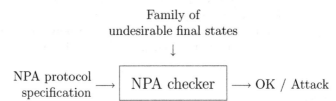

As it regresses back towards the initial state, the NRL Protocol Analyzer maintains a *trace* of the sequence of actions that, when executed, lead to the target state. If the initial state is ever reached, the sequence constructed in this manner is returned as a description of the attack it has found. When a path is abandoned, the corresponding trace fragment is discarded. Traces are sequences of *events* of the following form:

$$event(P, Q, T, L, N)$$

In general, any protocol or intruder state transition may be assigned an event. The arguments are interpreted as follows: P is the principal executing the transition, Q is the set of the other parties involved in it, T is a name that identifies the transition, L is a set of relevant words, and N is the local round number of the transition. There are three categories of events which correspond to receiving a message (predicate "receive"), accepting data as valid as a result of performing certain checks (predicate "accept"), and sending a message (predicate "send"). Here are two examples:

$$\text{accept}(\text{user}(A, \text{honest}), [\text{user}(B, H)], \text{initiator\_accept\_key}, [K], N)$$

$$\text{send}(\text{server}, [\text{user}(A, \text{honest}), \text{user}(B, \text{honest})], \text{server\_send\_key}, [K], N)$$

The first event describes the execution of a transition called "initiator_accept_key" by honest principal A that involves a key K and some other principal B who may or may not be honest. The second event records a server's application of rule "server_send_key" relative to honest principals A and B, and key K.

Any principal can perform a "send" or a "receive" event, but only the honest principals are entitled to do an "accept" event. As we will see below, events are the building blocks of the NPATRL language.

A Requirement Language for the NRL Protocol Analyzer

The NRL Protocol Analyzer model described above has successfully been used to verify a number of protocols, sometimes uncovering previously unknown flaws [Mea94, Mea96]. This is all the more laudable once we acknowledge the implicit and rudimentary manner in which requirements are entered in this system: secrecy and authentication goals are expressed as states that should not be reachable from the initial state. This unintuitive and occasionally error prone way of writing requirements would have made it very difficult to use the NRL Protocol Analyzer for large protocols.

The *NRL Protocol Analyzer Temporal Requirements Language*, better known as NPATRL (and pronounced "N Patrol"), was designed to address these shortcomings [SM96]. This formalism makes available the abstract expressiveness of a logical language to specify requirements at a high enough level to capture intuitive goals precisely, and yet it can be interpreted in the NRL Protocol Analyzer search engine.

NPATRL requirements are logical expressions whose atomic formulas are *event statements*: they include the "receive", "accept" and "send" events that can be found in the trace of an NRL Protocol Analyzer search, and the special "learn" event that indicates the acquisition of information by the adversary. The logical infrastructure of NPATRL consists of the usual connectives $\neg$, $\wedge$, $\rightarrow$, etc, and the temporal modality $\diamondsuit$ which, similarly to what we saw in Section 4.3, is interpreted as "happens before" or "previously".

For example, we may have the following requirement:

If an honest principal A accepts a key K for communicating with another honest principal B, then a server must have previously generated and sent this key with the idea that it should be used for communications between A and B, and that both are expected to be honest.

We can use the NRL Protocol Analyzer events given in the previous section to construct an NPATRL formula that expresses it:

$$\text{accept}(\text{user}(A, \text{honest}), [\text{user}(B, H)], \text{initiator\_accept\_key}, [K], N)$$
$$\rightarrow \; \diamond \; \text{send}(\text{server}, [\text{user}(A, \text{honest}), \text{user}(B, \text{honest})], \text{server\_send\_key}, [K], N)$$

This formula is a simple expression of the above requirement. A direct encoding in terms of final states is tricky, in particular if we want to faithfully express the temporal meaning of the operator "$\diamond$".

Intuitively, the protocol verification process changes from what we discussed in the previous section by using NPATRL requirements where the final state appeared. More precisely, we first need to map every NPATRL event statement to an actual event in the NRL Protocol Analyzer specification of the protocol. Then, we take the negation of each NPATRL requirement as a way to characterize the states that should be unreachable if and only if that requirement is satisfied. At this point, we perform the analysis as in the previous section: if the NRL Protocol Analyzer proves that this goal is unreachable, the protocol satisfies the original requirement. Otherwise, it returns a trace corresponding to a attack on the protocol that potentially invalidates the requirement.

Abstractly, the verification process of the NRL Protocol Analyzer enhanced with the NPATRL language can be expressed by the following diagram:

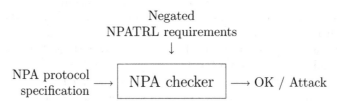

NPATRL has been extensively used in the last few years to analyze protocols with various characteristics. Among these, generic requirements have been given for two-party key distribution protocols [SM93, SM94] and two-party key agreement protocols [SM96]. The most ambitious specification undertaken using NPATRL has involved the requirements of the credit card payment transaction protocol SET (Secure Electronic Transactions) [MS98]. SET proved particularly difficult to specify for several reasons. First, nowhere in its hefty documentation (indeed, about 50cm thick) [SET97] are the requirements of this protocol stated, even informally. Second, it relies on some unfamiliar constructs such as dual signatures. Finally, the objects to be authenticated are dynamic: unlike keys, what is agreed upon changes as it passes from one principal to another. This exercise revealed several ambiguities [MS98].

6.2   Strand Semantics for BAN Languages

In the last section, we presented a case study that separated the syntax in which requirements are best stated (NPATRL) from the semantics in which the protocol is best specified and evaluated (NPA). In this section we explore the possibility of a similar strategy for BAN-style languages. (The content of this section is largely taken from [Syv00].)

Some BAN-like logics already have a model-theoretic semantics, for example, AT and SVO. Such a semantics can provide assurance in the reasoning embodied in a logic, via a soundness result. However, as illustrated in the last section, it can also provide another level on which to reason. These points were alluded to in Sections 2.4 and 3.5. And, providing an independently motivated model-theoretic semantics for BAN was a central design idea underlying the development of both AT and SVO. But, the model of computation in the semantics for each of these was adapted from general models underlying epistemic logics to reason about distributed computing. Their primary focus was not authentication or even cryptographic protocols generally. It is perhaps not surprising, therefore, that previous analysis showed AT and SVO computational models not easily compatible with those of NPA [Mea94, Syv98].

Perhaps what is needed is a model of computation that is more directly intended to represent authentication protocols. One such model is strand spaces [THG97, THG98b]. (See also [Gut] in this volume. Related to strands is the multiset rewriting (MSR) approach [CDL$^+$].) Besides being a model specifically directed at this problem area and having a growing base of theoretical literature, it seems to fit somewhat naturally to NPA and similar tools, e.g., Athena [Son99]. The question that naturally arises is then whether we can effectively repeat the above NPATRL idea using something like BAN for the requirements language and strands as the model. In other words, could we have a process as expressed in the following diagram?

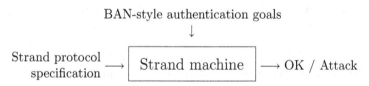

An affirmative answer would require a strand semantics for a BAN-style language. We will present a proposal for one below. We shall first provide a brief overview of the relevant strand space concepts.

Overview of Strands

A strand is basically a local history of sent and received messages in a protocol run. A strand space is a collection of strands, and a bundle is a graph that reflects a causally meaningful way that a set of strands might be connected.

The messages sent between principals are taken from an algebra A of terms. We will say more about the algebra shortly. Terms can be signed, e.g., $+t$ or $-t$, to indicate sending and receiving of messages respectively. We will give definitions for all the relevant concepts below. First, here is a picture of a bundle for Protocol 7, the (abridged) Needham-Schroeder Public-Key Protocol.

$$+\{n_A, A\}_{k_B} \qquad \longrightarrow \qquad -\{n_A, A\}_{k_B}$$

$$\Downarrow \qquad\qquad\qquad\qquad \Downarrow$$

$$-\{n_A, n_B\}_{k_A} \qquad \longrightarrow \qquad +\{n_A, n_B\}_{k_A}$$

$$\Downarrow$$

$$+\{n_B\}_{k_B}$$

The vertical sequences of double arrows are the strands, the local traces of messages sent to and from a given principal (in a given run). The horizontal (single) arrows link one strand to another by connecting the transmission and the reception of the same message. We now give more precise definitions, all of which are taken from [THG99b].

Let Σ be a set of strands and $(\pm A)^*$ be the set of all finite sequences of signed terms. A *strand space* over A is a set Σ together with a trace mapping $tr : \Sigma \to (\pm A)^*$.

Fix a strand space Σ

1. A *node* is a pair $\langle s, i \rangle$, with $s \in \Sigma$ and i an integer satisying $1 \leq i \leq$ length(tr(s)). The set of nodes is denoted by $\mathcal{N}$. We will say the node $\langle s, i \rangle$ belongs to the strand s. Clearly, every node belongs to a unique strand.
2. If $n = \langle s, i \rangle \in \mathcal{N}$ then index(n) = i and strand(n) = s. Define term(n) to be $(\text{tr}(s))_i$, i.e. the ith signed term in the trace of s. Similarly, uns_term(n) is $((\text{tr}(s))_i)_2$, i.e. the unsigned part of the ith signed term in the trace of s.
3. There is an edge $n_1 \to n_2$ if and only if term(n_1) = $+a$ and term(n_2) = $-a$ for some $a \in A$. Intuitively, the edge means that node n_1 sends the message a, which is received by n_2, recording a potential causal link between those strands.
4. When $n_1 = \langle s, i \rangle$ and $n_2 = \langle s, i+1 \rangle$ are members of $\mathcal{N}$, there is an edge $n_1 \Rightarrow n_2$. Intuitively, the edge expresses that n_1 is an immediate causal predecessor of n_2 on the strand s. We write $n' \Rightarrow^+ n$ to mean that n' precedes n (not necessarily immediately) on the same strand.
5. $\mathcal{N}$ together with both sets of edges $n_1 \to n_2$ and $n_1 \Rightarrow n_2$ is a directed graph $\langle \mathcal{N}, (\to \cup \Rightarrow) \rangle$.

Suppose $\to_\mathcal{C} \subseteq \to$; suppose $\Rightarrow_\mathcal{C} \subseteq \Rightarrow$; and suppose $\mathcal{C} = \langle \mathcal{N}_\mathcal{C}, (\to_\mathcal{C} \cup \Rightarrow_\mathcal{C}) \rangle$ is a subgraph of $\langle \mathcal{N}, (\to \cup \Rightarrow) \rangle$. $\mathcal{C}$ is a *bundle* if:

1. $\mathcal{C}$ is finite.
2. If $n_2 \in \mathcal{N}_\mathcal{C}$ and term(n_2) is negative, then there is a unique $n_1 \in \mathcal{N}_\mathcal{C}$ such that $n_1 \to_\mathcal{C} n_2$.
3. If $n_2 \in \mathcal{N}_\mathcal{C}$ and $n_1 \Rightarrow n_2$ then $n_1 \Rightarrow_\mathcal{C} n_2$.
4. $\mathcal{C}$ is acyclic.

If $\mathcal{S}$ is a set of edges, i.e. $\mathcal{S} \subseteq (\to \cup \Rightarrow)$, then $\prec_\mathcal{S}$ is the transitive closure of $\mathcal{S}$, and $\preceq_\mathcal{S}$ is the reflexive and transitive closure of $\mathcal{S}$. The relations $\prec_\mathcal{S}$ and

$\preceq_\mathcal{S}$ are each subsets of $\mathcal{N}_\mathcal{S} \times \mathcal{N}_\mathcal{S}$, where $\mathcal{N}_\mathcal{S}$ is the set of nodes incident with any edge in $\mathcal{S}$.

These are all of the definitions that we need to set out a possible worlds model and semantics for sending, receiving, and knowledge. We will provide below more details about the term algebra that will allow us to express, e.g., that a principal who receives a ciphertext (encrypted message) and has the decryption key has also got the unencrypted message.

Possible Worlds from Strand Spaces

We now describe a possible world semantics of epistemic logics for distributed computing in general and for security protocols in particular, for example, as presented in [AT91, SvO94, SvO96].

In a traditional system model and knowledge semantics for distributed computing, computation is performed by a finite set of principals, $P_1, \ldots, P_n$, who send messages to one another. In addition there is a principal P_e representing the environment. This allows modeling of any penetrator actions as well as reflecting messages in transit.

Each principal P_i has a local state s_i. A global state is thus an $(n+1)$-tuple of local states.

A run is a sequence of global states indexed by integers to represent time. The first state of a given run r is assigned a time $t_r \leq 0$. The initial state of the current authentication is at $t = 0$. The global state at time t in run r determines a possible world (sometimes also called nodes or points). We assume that global states are unique wrt runs and times. Thus, they can be referred to by, e.g., '$\langle r, t \rangle$'. At any given global state, various things will be true, e.g., that principal Q has previously sent the message $\{X\}_k$. What a principal P then knows (believes) at a given point $\langle r, t \rangle$ is precisely that which is true at all possible worlds with the same local state $r_P(t)$ for P as $\langle r, t \rangle$. This is typically captured by means of an accessibility relation on global states $\leadsto_P$ for a principal P. When the relation is an equivalence, it is also called an indistinguishability relation $\sim_P$ for a principal P. This allows for a simple intuitive definition, without even having to describe in any way properties of local states, viz:

- $\langle r, t \rangle \sim_P \langle r', t' \rangle$ iff P is in the same local state at both points, i.e., $r_P(t) = r'_P(t')$.

Given an indistinguishability relation, we can then go on to define principal P's knowledge in terms of the worlds that are P-indistinguishable.

- $\langle r, t \rangle \models P$ knows φ iff $\langle r', t' \rangle \models \varphi$ for all $\langle r', t' \rangle$ such that $\langle r, t \rangle \sim_P \langle r', t' \rangle$

The above system model and characterization of knowledge (belief) is essentially what is found in [AT91, SvO94, SvO96]. It is largely based on similar models and characterizations of knowledge in distributed computing; see for example [FHMV95]. Note that the relation just given is an equivalence relation, as is the strand-based relation to be given presently. For this reason, and to be consistent with earlier literature such as [FHMV95], we refer to the associated modality as knowledge rather than belief, but no great significance should be attached to this choice, as we saw in Section 3.3. We now turn specifically to strand spaces as a basis for knowledge semantics.

Strand Semantics for Knowledge

In the conclusion of [THG97] it was suggested that,

> "[what] a protocol participant knows, in virtue of his experience in executing a protocol, is that he has performed the actions lying on some strand s. Thus, the real world must include some bundle C such that s is contained in C. The beliefs that the participant may justifiably hold are those that are true in every bundle C containing s." [THG97]

Thus, a possible world on this approach is simply a bundle. This is a reasonable approach for reasoning about some protocol features. However, we found it also worthwhile to include in the definition of possible worlds the nodes within bundles. We did this in order to capture temporal aspects of the above authentication logics, specifically freshness. This will also facilitate the addition of richer temporal formulae to the logic, as in [Syv93a].

Neither strand spaces nor bundles have a notion of global time. Thus we cannot have an indistinguishability relation that corresponds directly to the above. However, $\langle C, s, i \rangle$ picks a unique point $\langle s, i \rangle$ in bundle C and partitions $\mathcal{N}_C$ into $\{\langle t, j \rangle : \langle t, j \rangle \preceq_C \langle s, i \rangle\}$ and $\{\langle t, j \rangle : \langle t, j \rangle \npreceq_C \langle s, i \rangle\}$. This partition allows us to define an accessibility relation on nodes in bundles based on local time.

1. Given a strand s, let princ(s) refer to the principal whose strand s is.
2. Given a node $\langle s, i \rangle$ and a strand t in a bundle C, let the *restriction of t to* $\langle s, i \rangle$ *in* C be tr(t) $\upharpoonright \langle s, i \rangle = \langle \text{tr}(t)_1, \ldots, \text{tr}(t)_j \rangle$, where $\langle t, j \rangle$ is the greatest node on t s.t. $\langle t, j \rangle \preceq_C \langle s, i \rangle$.

With this notation in place we can now define an indistinguishability relation. Assume bundles C, C', and strands s, s', and indices i, i' such that $\langle s, i \rangle \in \mathcal{N}_C$ and, $\langle s', i' \rangle \in \mathcal{N}_{C'}$. A natural definition, analogous to the runs-and-times definition of the traditional literature would be to have $\langle C, s, i \rangle \sim_P \langle C', s', i' \rangle$ (i.e., $\langle C, s, i \rangle$ is *P-indistinguishable* from $\langle C', s', i' \rangle$) just in case P's history in C up to $\langle s, i \rangle$ matches P's history in C' up to $\langle s', i' \rangle$. This is exactly right. However, just as there is no global time in a bundle, there may also be multiple strands associated with one principal. The resulting definition is thus:

$\langle C, s, i \rangle$ is *P-indistinguishable* from $\langle C', s', i' \rangle$ (written as $\langle C, s, i \rangle \sim_P \langle C', s', i' \rangle$) iff

1. for any t in C s.t. princ(t) $= P$ there exists t' in C' s.t. tr(t) $\upharpoonright \langle s, i \rangle = $ tr(t') $\upharpoonright (s', i')$ and princ(t') $= P$, and
2. the number of strands satisfying clause 1 is the same in C and C'.

Truth Conditions for BAN-Style Formulae

The purpose of this section, is to present truth conditions for basic formulae of a BAN-style language. The basic notions we cover are freshness, key goodness, said and received (got) messages, and jurisdiction.

Given our definition of $\sim_P$ above we can now present truth conditions for knowledge in this semantics. Let φ be some formula in our language. We will define $\models$ inductively; however the presentation is organized pedagogically rather than to respect the inductive construction. We assume the usual truth conditions for logical connectives; although we will not discuss compound formulae here.

$$\langle \mathcal{C}, s, i \rangle \models P \; knows \; \varphi$$

iff $\langle \mathcal{C}', s', i' \rangle \models \varphi$ at all $\langle \mathcal{C}', s', i' \rangle$ s.t. $\langle \mathcal{C}, s, i \rangle \sim_P \langle \mathcal{C}', s', i' \rangle$

This definition gives a strand semantics for knowledge in a distributed environment. However, we have not yet described what specific types of things φ might express. Giving truth conditions for the various possibilities is the focus of the remainder of this section.

We can give semantics for formulae expressing the sending and receiving of messages without giving any more details about the model. Let M be an arbitrary message from our term algebra A. Then,

$$\langle \mathcal{C}, s, i \rangle \models P \; sent \; M$$

iff there is a node $\langle t, j \rangle$ in $\mathcal{C}$ s.t. (i) $\mathrm{princ}(t) = P$, (ii) $\langle t, j \rangle \preceq \langle s, i \rangle$, and (iii) $\mathrm{term}(\langle t, j \rangle) = +M$. Moreover,

$$\langle \mathcal{C}, s, i \rangle \models P \; received \; M$$

iff there is a node $\langle t, j \rangle$ in $\mathcal{C}$ s.t. (i) $\mathrm{princ}(t) = P$, (ii) $\langle t, j \rangle \preceq \langle s, i \rangle$, and (iii) $\mathrm{term}(\langle t, j \rangle) = -M$.

To give the truth conditions for other formulae, we must first spell out some of the structure of the term algebra and define a notion of submessage. The following definitions are taken from [THG99b] and can also be found in the preceding strand space papers.

Assume the following:

- A set $\mathbf{T} \subseteq \mathsf{A}$ of texts (representing the atomic messages).
- A set $\mathbf{K} \subseteq \mathsf{A}$ of cryptographic keys disjoint from $\mathbf{T}$, equipped with a unary operator $\mathsf{inv} : \mathbf{K} \to \mathbf{K}$.
  inv is injective; i.e., that it maps each member of a key pair for an asymmetric cryptosystem to the other; and that it maps a symmetric key to itself.
- Two binary operators

$$\mathsf{encr} : \mathbf{K} \times \mathsf{A} \to \mathsf{A}$$
$$\mathsf{join} : \mathsf{A} \times \mathsf{A} \to \mathsf{A}$$

We will follow notational conventions, some of which have already been mentioned, and write $\mathsf{inv}(k)$ as k^{-1}, $\mathsf{encr}(k, M)$ as $\{M\}_k$, and $\mathsf{join}(a, b)$ as $(a\,b)$. If K is a set of keys, K^{-1} denotes the set of inverses of elements of K.

The next assumption we make is that A is the algebra freely generated from $\mathbf{T}$ and $\mathbf{K}$ by the two operators encr and join. As noted in [THG99b], this assumption has been commonly made in this area of research going back to [DY83]. As in [THG99b] it is probably stronger than what we ultimately need but is pedagogically convenient. Amongst other things, it implies that encryptions and concatenations are unique and always distinct from each other and from $\mathbf{T}$ and $\mathbf{K}$.

Central to the semantics of *said* formulae is the concept of an ideal. Interestingly, in the strand space papers, it was introduced to formulate general facts about the penetrator's capabilities; while, for this discussion, we will say virtually nothing about the nature of the penetrator.

If $K \subseteq \mathbf{K}$, a K-ideal of A is a subset I of A such that for all $h \in I$, $g \in \mathsf{A}$ and $k \in K$

1. $h\,g, g\,h \in I$.
2. $\{h\}_k \in I$.

The smallest K-ideal containing h is denoted $I_K[h]$.

The notion of ideal can be used to define a subterm relation $\sqsubset$ as follows [THG98a].

Let $K \subseteq \mathbf{K}$. $s \in \mathsf{A}$ is a K-*subterm of* $t \in \mathsf{A}$, $(s \sqsubset_K t)$ iff $t \in I_K[s]$.

If $K = \mathbf{K}$ in this definition, then we say simply that s *is a subterm of* t, and write $s \sqsubset t$.

We now give truth conditions for *said* formulae

$$\langle \mathcal{C}, s, i \rangle \models P \ said \ M$$

iff there is a message M' s.t. $\langle \mathcal{C}, s, i \rangle \models P \ sent \ M'$ and $M \sqsubset_K M'$ where K is the set of keys possessed by P at $\langle s, i \rangle$.

Notice that P is held accountable, e.g., for saying M at n, if he sends $\{M\}_k$ at $n' \preceq n$ and he has k at n, even if k was not in his key set until some n'' s.t. $n' \prec n'' \preceq n$.

A definition that does not occur in any of the strand space papers is that of a filter. In many contexts, filters are the duals of ideals. In our case, they are useful for giving semantics to *got* formulae, those that express the understood messages contained in received messages. (Millen and Rueß introduce the same idea in [MR00] to reason about secrecy invariants. They call it a "coideal".)

If $K \subseteq \mathbf{K}$, a K-filter of A is a subset F of A such that for all $h, g \in \mathsf{A}$ and $k \in K$

1. $h\,g \in F$ implies $h \in F$ and $g \in F$
2. $\{h\}_k \in F$ implies $h \in F$ for $k^{-1} \in K$

The smallest K-filter containing h is denoted $F_K[h]$.

In general, the relation between filters and ideals is not so simple because, in public-key cryptography, one may have k and not have k^{-1}, or vice versa.

However, in this section we are limiting discussion to the symmetric key case, $k = k^{-1}$—for which there is a simple relation. (This relation also holds when both cognates of a public/private key pair are known.) It is easy to show that

Claim 4 *For all sets of keys K' of the form $K \cup K^{-1}$*

$$g \in F_{K'}[h] \ \textit{iff} \ h \in I_{K'}[g].$$

Thus, for key sets K' of this form, by definition 6.2, $s \sqsubseteq_{K'} t$ iff $s \in F_{K'}[t]$. We can now give the truth conditions for *got* formulae. (We present them for the general case.)

$$\langle \mathcal{C}, s, i \rangle \models P \ got \ M$$

iff there is a message M' s.t. $\langle \mathcal{C}, s, i \rangle \models P \ received \ M'$ and $M \in F_K[M']$ where K is the set of keys possessed by P at $\langle s, i \rangle$.

We can use the truth conditions for *said* and *got* formulae to further give the truth conditions for key goodness.

$$\langle \mathcal{C}, s, i \rangle \models P \xleftrightarrow{k} Q$$

iff, for all $\langle s', i' \rangle \in \mathcal{N}_{\mathcal{C}}$, $\langle \mathcal{C}, s', i' \rangle \models R \ said \ \{M \ from \ Q\}_k$ implies either $\langle \mathcal{C}, s', i' \rangle \models R \ received \ \{M \ from \ Q\}_k$, or $R = Q$ and $\langle \mathcal{C}, s', i' \rangle \models R \ said \ M$. Moreover, if $\langle \mathcal{C}, s', i' \rangle \models R \ said \ \{M\}_k$ (instead of the stronger $\langle \mathcal{C}, s', i' \rangle \models R \ said \ \{M \ from \ Q\}_k$), then $R \in \{P, Q\}$ (instead of the stronger $R = P$).

Note that these are the truth conditions from [SvO96] with $\langle \mathcal{C}, s, i \rangle$ replacing $\langle r, t \rangle$ and $\langle \mathcal{C}, s', i' \rangle$ replacing $\langle r, t' \rangle$ throughout. This was itself based on the truth conditions for goodness given in [AT91].

Once we have a mechanism to express the beginning of the current epoch, we will be able to similarly dispatch the freshness and jurisdiction formulae. In order to do that, we must again confront the absence of a global concept of time. In the system models for possible world semantics of BAN-like logics, it was trivial to stipulate a global time t_0 and then define something as fresh if it was not said (by anyone) prior to t_0. We instead define a concept now as follows.

For any bundle $\mathcal{C}$, $\text{now}_{\mathcal{C}} \subseteq \mathcal{N}_{\mathcal{C}}$, is a nonempty set of incomparable nodes (i.e., a nonempty set of nodes s.t. $n, n' \in \text{now}_{\mathcal{C}}$ implies $n \npreceq n'$ and $n' \npreceq n$). For $n \in \mathcal{N}_{\mathcal{C}}$, we may write '$\text{now}_{\mathcal{C}} \preceq n$' just in case there exists $n' \in \text{now}_{\mathcal{C}}$ s.t. $n' \preceq n$. When it is clear from context which bundle is relevant, we will write simply 'now'.

Thus,

$$\langle \mathcal{C}, s, i \rangle \models \textit{fresh}(M)$$

iff for all principals P, $\langle \mathcal{C}, s', i' \rangle \models P \ said \ M$ implies $\text{now} \preceq \langle s', i' \rangle$.

The truth conditions for jurisdiction assume truth conditions for *says* formulae, which the definition of $\text{now}_{\mathcal{C}}$ allows us to formulate.

$$\langle \mathcal{C}, s, i \rangle \models P \ says \ M$$

iff   there is a message M' and a node $\langle t, j \rangle$ in $\mathcal{C}$ s.t. (i) princ(t) = P, (ii) now $\preceq \langle t, j \rangle \preceq \langle s, i \rangle$, (iii) term($\langle t, j \rangle$) = $+M'$, and (iv) $M \sqsubseteq_K M'$ where K is the key set possessed by P at $\langle s, i \rangle$.

If φ is a formula.

$$\langle \mathcal{C}, s, i \rangle \models P \text{ controls } \varphi$$

iff $\langle \mathcal{C}, s, i \rangle \models P$ says φ implies $\langle \mathcal{C}, s', i' \rangle \models \varphi$ for any $\langle s', i' \rangle$ s.t. now $\preceq \langle s', i' \rangle$.

These conditions are similar to those in [AT91] and [SvO94, SvO96], *mutatis mutandis*. Notice that goodness is a condition that is constant across all points in the same bundle. And, jurisdiction and freshness are constant across all points in the present epoch. Notice also that jurisdiction is restricted to those messages that are formulae, rather than messages in general.

This completes our presentation of truth conditions. Strand based truth conditions for public keys, Diffie-Hellman, and other aspects of SVO have yet to be developed. What we have done is to provide a means by which BAN-style requirements can be mapped to strand-style protocol specifications. Something like this is necessary for the protocol analysis approach characterized by the diagram at the beginning of this section. For the "strand machine" to process its inputs there must be some means for it to combine them. The mapping provides such a means. To completely develop the semantic approach using BAN-style requirements for a strand-style model, the strand machine itself must be built. We conclude with a description of some of other areas where there is still much work to be done.

7   The Future

In [Mea00b], Meadows sets out a number of open areas in the application of formal methods to cryptographic protocols. The primary focus is beyond simple two-party authentication protocols, and that paper is a good place to get an idea of where much of the cutting edge research is or soon will be. We finish up with a discussion of these open areas, but with a slant towards the kinds of formalisms and ideas that have been discussed above. We also try to mention some of the recent work which has not been alluded to elsewhere above. Indeed, such a large amount of work has been done in formal analysis of authentication and other security protocols that, despite the number of references cited herein, far more work has gone unmentioned, much of it quite good.

Appropriately, one of the open areas is in *open-ended protocols*. The two major ways in which a protocol can be open-ended is in what data is sent and in who is sending or receiving. We address these in order.

A protocol may be open-ended in virtue of the data sent. For example, the Internet Key Exchange Protocol (IKE) that is part of IPSEC [DH99], includes an agreement on a Security Association (SA). The SA includes such things as a choice of algorithms and other parameters. But, there is no defined (upper) limit on what can be included in an SA. This sort of open-endedness has not been formally analyzed as far as we know. Another aspect of IKE is that the SA has a more elaborate, indeed open-ended, data structure than a simple cryptographic key. In classic authentication protocols, the data about which we prove authentication and secrecy properties is simply a key. In Diffie-Hellman exchange, there may be parts contributed by the principals that make up the key, but Diffie-Hellman based protocols have been analyzed using VO and SVO [vO93, SvO96].

Protocols can also be open-ended in the participants involved. An obvious example is in various kinds of group protocols. These can be for both group authentication and group confidentiality properties. One example of such a group protocol is a group signature protocol, in which a signature can identify only that the signer was from a group unless an additional protocol is run (typically with a trusted authority) to reveal the individual responsible for the given signature. As introduced in [CvH91], these were perhaps only open-ended in principle since there was no efficient means to add members to an existing group. The first significant advance on that problem was made in [CS97], and others have since followed. There has not been any formal methods work that we know of directly on this area. More positive results have been seen in the area of group Diffie-Hellman [AST98]. These are essentially Diffie-Hellman type establishments for open-ended groups. Meadows was able to analyze these protocols after expanding NPA [Mea00a]. More recently, Meadows has presented evaluations of secure multicast to the IETF and the IRTF Secure Multicast Group. We have begun specification and examination of secure multicast protocols using NPA-TRL. Other formal methods work involving groups of arbitrary size can be found in [Pau97, BS97]. Both of these papers make use of theorem proving, Isabelle and PVS respectively to examine the same protocol.

Another important open are is *denial of service*. Meadows has devised a framework [Mea01] for reasoning about denial of service in cryptographic protocols, although not a formal method per se. The problem with authentication is that it is not only a protection against but a great source of denial-of-service attacks. If only authenticated principals are allowed to perform any actions, then unauthenticated principals cannot deny service. But, verifying authentication typically involves computationally intensive cryptographic operations. Thus, initiating many authentic connections can be an even more effective denial-of-service attack than simply initiating many connections. Meadows builds on the fail-stop concept set out in Section 5.3. The idea is to have the amount of work expended to defend a protocol against denial of service increase as the protocol progresses. The protocol is analyzed to show that it is fail-stop against an attacker whose capabilities are within a specified constraint. Note that this is a diversion from the Dolev-Yao intruder model that we have assumed throughout, up to this point. Obviously a Dolev-Yao intruder can arbitrarily deny service. Much of the open work involves backing off from such an unrealistically strong attacker to consider properties that can be established in the face of a different attacker.

Electronic commerce, in particular non-repudiation and fair exchange, is an area that has seen an explosion of protocols and also some formal work in the last several years. In fair exchange, there is no adversary per se. Rather, the idea is to make sure that each party gets his goods, signed contract, etc. just in case the other does as well. In non-repudiation, the goal is to have evidence that a principal cannot repudiate. This can be evidence of messages sent (evidence of origin) or messages received (evidence of receipt). Obviously fair exchange and non-repudiation are closely related. The first attempt to reason about this area formally was by Kailar using a BAN-like logic [Kai95, Kai96]. The central logical construct is CanProve as in "A CanProve B says X". Zhou and Gollman also used SVO to reason about non-repudiation properties [ZG98]. We have already mentioned Brackin's verification of the Cybercash main sequence protocol using BGNY [Bra97]. A more recent approach to non-repudiation, using temporal logic with a game semantics can be found in [KR00].

The SET protocol is a good illustrator of several of the complexities we have introduced in this section. Like IKE, it is not a single protocol but a collection of subprotocols. As mentioned in Section 6.1, the protocol is very large and complex with many options, yet its specification lacks even an informal statement of requirements. It has a more elaborate structure than just a key on which principals must agree: there is a transaction on which the customer, merchant, and bank must agree, but parts of the transaction are hidden from some of the principals and parts are added to it as the protocol progresses. And, the reason that parts of the transaction are hidden is because the principals are mutually mistrusting and attempting some sort of non-repudiable fair exchange. Nonetheless, NPATRL was adapted to express requirements for payments in SET and related protocols by adding abstract structures for which some of the components are not revealed [MS98]. Also, the cardholder registration subprotocol has been verified using Isabelle and HOL [BMPT00]. Recall that in SVO and the AUTLOG based logic of [WK96] one can reason about principals' beliefs concerning messages in which not all the parts are recognizable. This would seem naturally generalizable to SET. In [KN98], Kessler and Neuman devised a logic for reasoning about payment in SET that combine elements from these logics, from Kailar's logic of accountability, and from the Stubblebine-Wright logic of recent security [SW96].

These large protocol suites raise still another open issue: *protocol composability*. The fail-stop protocols of Section 5.3 constitute one answer to this problem. But are there less onerous design restrictions that can be imposed (similar constraints on composition are given in [HT96])? It might seem that protocol composability is completely guaranteed by having only EFS protocols. However, even when the protocols are all EFS, the application environment generally will not be. Thus, there are still oracles available for active attacks.

Suppose that principals are willing to use keys obtained through a key-distribution protocol before the protocol completes. This is sometimes called "eager" use of keys in the literature. Only if the authentication protocol does not complete within some reasonable timeout is there an alarm or noting of anomaly in the logs. This eagerness might be all the more reasonable if the protocol distributing the keys is EFS. In this case, there would seem to be no possibility of mistake about who the session key is for, who the relevant principals are, or the roles they each play (i.e., initiator or responder). But, allowing eager use of keys in an application that authenticates a random challenge by encryption using the session key could be used to attack the protocol. (This could be a variant of the sensor example of Protocol 6.)

Specifically, suppose Alice begins NSSK (Protocol 1) for a session with Bob, the attacker prevents the third message from arriving. Then, for the application challenge-response he produces:

Application Message 1 $E_B \to A : n_B$

Application Message 2 $A \to E_B : \{n_B\}_{K_{ab}}$

The attacker uses the response from Alice for the fourth message in NSSK, and intercepts the final message from Alice to Bob. Alice will now be spoofed into thinking she has completed a handshake with Bob when Bob was never present.

This attack is even possible if NSSK is strengthened to be made EFS. The point is to show that the applications that use keys established in an authentication protocol must also be considered. This aspect of protocol composability has received only a little attention. A version of this attack and related issues are discussed in [CMS01]. Besides general composable protocol design, there has also been a little work done into showing that particular protocols are composable [Mea99a, THG99a].

Another type of composability is between protocols and the cryptographic algorithms they employ. Protocol analysis as we have described it herein has treated cryptography as a black box, but some protocols and algorithms are secure if used in one combination while they are insecure in different combinations. Formal work going beyond black box treatments of cryptography in protocol analysis is just beginning [AR00, Can00, Jür00].

We mentioned the inappropriateness of Dolev-Yao adversaries for modeling denial-of-service attacks. They are also clearly inadequate for exchange protocols involving mutually mistrusting parties. Another area in which a Dolev-Yao adversary is simply too strong is anonymity. *Anonymity* services that have either been designed to be practical for most applications or that have actually been fielded are simply broken against a Dolev-Yao adversary [Oni, Ano, Cro, Fre]. One reason is that anonymity for all of these involves passing messages through an intermediate point so as to obscure identity of an originator from anyone observing a transmission. Some involve hopping through several points and some change the appearance of messages at each point so that parts of the transmission cannot be compared and seen to *be* parts of the same transmission. No matter how many of these precautions are taken, in a system where all messages pass through the intruder, the intruder will know exactly who is talking to whom (and possibly what is being said unless confidentiality is also protected). There are communication mechanisms that are secure against a Dolev-Yao intruder, e.g., dining cryptographer (DC) nets [Cha88]. However, nothing that is practical for widely used email, Web browsing, remote login, etc. is secure against a Dolev-Yao intruder. In [SS99], an epistemic model and logic was introduced for reasoning about group principals. This built on ideas in [FHMV95]. Recall from Section 6.2 that the usual model of computation associated with these logics has a single principal to represent the environment/penetrator. This is in perfect keeping with the Dolev-Yao model. However, in [SS99], all communication principals, including the environment must be specified. And, there is in fact no single environment. Rather, there are many environment principals that have various capabilities and properties and that can be assembled in a variety of ways, i.e., into various sorts of group principals. One can then reason about various properties associated with a group of principals (the 'good guys') that another group of principals (the intruder) can actively or passively determine. For example, a particular distributed intruder may be able to determine that some (atomic) subprincipal of a group principal of cardinality n was the source of a message, but cannot narrow the cardinality lower than n. Work is underway to combine this approach, which has an intuitive yet formal expressiveness, with a CSP based approach [SS96]. The intent is to use the CSP as a semantics, much as the strand semantics for BAN described in Section 6.2. The language in [SS99] includes threshold-group principals and other primitives that should make it applicable to other areas besides anonymity.

Childhood's End

Specification and analysis of basic authentication protocols has been the focus of much of the above discussion—and much of the work in the last dozen years of formal methods in application to cryptographic protocols. The main concepts have been extensively explored and both intuitive and fully automated techniques have been developed, techniques that now do a thorough job and require no great sophistication. It has been several years since merely documenting a new attack on such protocols or devising a new formal method for reasoning about them was sufficient for publication in even small workshops. This is a positive sign. More complex protocols and protocols to accomplish more ambitious and subtle goals continue to come along. Formal methods are increasingly employed in the specification and analysis of protocols that are more than academic exercises: commercial products, complex protocol suites, international standards, etc. And, they have begun to have an impact in the real-world protocols that are being deployed. At the same time there has been a resurgence in theoretical models of both the new and the classic concepts, and these have in turn influenced the development and refinement of formal methods for protocol analysis and even design. It's an exciting time to be in the field.

References

[ABKL90] M. Abadi, M. Burrows, C. Kaufman, and B. Lampson. Authentication and delegation with smart-cards. Research Report 67, Digital Systems Research Center, October 1990. Revised July, 1992. 69

[AG97] Martín Abadi and Andrew D. Gordon. A calculus for cryptographic protocols: the spi calculus. In *Proceedings of the Fourth ACM Conference on Computer and Communications Security*, pages 36–47. ACM Press, April 1997. 130

[AG99] Martín Abadi and Andrew D. Gordon. A calculus for cryptographic protocols: the spi calculus. *Information and Computation*, 143:1–70, 1999. An extended version of this paper appears as Research Report 149, Digital Equipment Corporation Systems Research Center, January 1998. An early presentation appears in [AG97]. 113

[AN94]   Martín Abadi and Roger Needham. Prudent engineering practices for cryptographic protocols. In *Proceedings of the IEEE Computer Society Symposium on Research in Security and Privacy*, pages 122–136. IEEE CS Press, May 1994. 106, 130

[AN95]   Ross Anderson and Roger Needham. Robustness principles for public key protocols. In D. Coppersmith, editor, *Advances in Cryptology — CRYPTO '95*, pages 236–247. Springer-Verlag, LNCS 963, August 1995. 107, 109

[AN96]   Martín Abadi and Roger Needham. Prudent engineering practices for cryptographic protocols. *IEEE Transactions on Software Engineering*, 22(1):6–15, January 1996. A preliminary version appeared as [AN94]. 106

[Ano]   The anonymizer. http://www.anonymizer.com/. 128

[AR00]   Martín Abadi and Phillip Rogaway. Reconciling two views of cryptographic protocols (the compuational soundness of formal encryption. In *IFIP International Conference on Theoretical Computer Science (IFIP TCS2000)*. Springer-Verlag, LNCS, 2000. 128

[AST98] Giuseppe Ateniese, Michael Steiner, and Gene Tsudik. Authenticated group key agreement and friends. In *5th ACM Conference on Computer and Communications Security (CCS'98)*, pages 17–26. ACM Press, November 1998. 126

[AT91]   Martín Abadi and Mark R. Tuttle. A semantics for a logic of authentication. In *Proceedings of the Tenth Annual ACM Symposium on Principles of Distributed Computing*, pages 201–216. ACM Press, August 1991. 67, 76, 79, 88, 95, 120, 124, 125

[BAN88] Michael Burrows, Martín Abadi, and Roger Needham. Authentication: A practical study of belief in action. In M. Vardi, editor, *Proceedings of the Second Conference on Theoretical Aspects of Reasoning About Knowledge (Tark)*, pages 325–342. Morgan Kaufmann, March 1988. Also presented at The Computer Security Foundations Workshop, Franconia, NH, June 1988. 66

[BAN89a] Michael Burrows, Martín Abadi, and Roger Needham. A logic of authentication. Research Report 39, Digital Systems Research Center, February 1989. Revised Feb. 22, 1990. 63, 66, 67, 68, 69, 70, 85, 87, 93, 95, 98, 101, 102

[BAN89b] Michael Burrows, Martín Abadi, and Roger Needham. A logic of authentication. *Operating Systems Review*, 23(5):1–13, December 1989. This issue of *OSR*: Proceedings of the Twelfth ACM Symposium on Operating Systems Principles (SOSP), Litchfield Park, Arizona, December 1989. 66

[BAN89c] Michael Burrows, Martín Abadi, and Roger Needham. A logic of authentication. *Proceedings of the Royal Society of London. Series A, Mathematical and Physical Sciences*, 426(1871):233–271, December 1989. 66

[BAN90a] Michael Burrows, Martín Abadi, and Roger Needham. A logic of authentication. *ACM Transactions on Computer Systems*, 8(1):18–36, Feb 1990. 66

[BAN90b] Michael Burrows, Martín Abadi, and Roger Needham. Rejoinder to nessett. *Operating Systems Review*, 24(2):39–40, April 1990. 75

[BAN90c] Michael Burrows, Martín Abadi, and Roger Needham. The scope of a logic of authentication. In J. Feigenbaum and M. Merritt, editors, *Distributed*

Computing and Cryptography, volume 2 of *DIMACS Series in Discrete Mathematics and Theoretical Computer Science*, pages 119–126. AMS and ACM, 1990. Proceedings of a DIMACS workshop, October 1989. 66

[Bie90]   Pierre Bieber. A logic of communication in hostile environment. In *Proceedings of the Computer Security Foundations Workshop III*, pages 14–22. IEEE CS Press, June 1990. 97, 98

[BM92]   Steven M. Bellovin and Michael Merritt. Encrypted key exchange: Password-based protocols secure against dictionary attacks. In *Proceedings of the IEEE Computer Society Symposium on Research in Security and Privacy*, pages 72–84. IEEE CS Press, May 1992. 108

[BM93]   Steve Bellovin and Michael Merritt. Augmented encrypted key exchange: a password-based protocol secure against dictionary attacks and password file compromise. In *Proceedings of the 1st ACM Conference on Computer and Communications Security*, pages 244–250. ACM Press, November 1993. 108

[BMPT00] Giampaolo Bella, Fabio Massacci, Lawrence C. Paulson, and Piero Tramontano. Formal verification of cardholder registration in SET. In F. Cuppens, Y. Deswarte, D. Gollmann, and M. Waidner, editors, *Computer Security – ESORICS 2000*, pages 159–174. Springer-Verlag, LNCS 1895, October 2000. 127

[Bra96]   Stephen H. Brackin. A HOL extension of GNY for automatically analyzing cryptographic protocols. In *9th IEEE Computer Security Foundations Workshop*, pages 62–76. IEEE CS Press, June 1996. 112

[Bra97]   Stephen H. Brackin. Automatic formal analyses of two large commercial protocols. In *DIMACS Workshop on Design and Formal Verification of Security Protocols*, September 1997. Available at http://dimacs.rutgers.edu/Workshops/Security/program2/brackin.html. 112, 127

[Bra98]   Stephen H. Brackin. Evaluating and improving protocol analysis by automatic proof. In *11th IEEE Computer Security Foundations Workshop*, pages 138–152. IEEE CS Press, 1998. 112

[Bra00]   Stephen H. Brackin. Automatically detecting most vulnerabilities in cryptographic protocols. In *DISCEX 2000: Proceedings of the DARPA Information Survivability Conference and Exposition*, volume I, pages 222–236. IEEE CS Press, January 2000. 112

[BS97]   Jeremy Bryans and Steve Schneider. CSP, PVS and a recursive authentication protocol. In *DIMACS Workshop on Design and Formal Verification of Security Protocols*, September 1997. Available at http://dimacs.rutgers.edu/Workshops/Security/program2/program.html. 126

[BSW98] Levente Buttyán, Sebastian Staamann, and Uwe Wilhelm. A simple logic for authentication protocol design. In *11th IEEE Computer Security Foundations Workshop*, pages 153–162. IEEE CS Press, June 1998. 113

[Can00]   Ran Canetti. A unified framework for analyzing security of protocols. Cryptology ePrint Archive, Report 2000/067, 2000. http://eprint.iacr.org/. 128

[Car93]   Ulf Carlsen. Using Logics to Detect Implementation-Dependent Flaws. In *Proceedings of the Ninth Annual Computer Security Applications Conference*, pages 64–73. IEEE Computer Society Press, December 1993. 93

[Car94]   Ulf Carlsen. Generating formal cryptographic protocol specifications. In *Proceedings of the IEEE Computer Society Symposium on Research in Security and Privacy*, pages 137–146. IEEE CS Press, May 1994. 98

[CDL⁺]   Iliano Cervesato, Nancy Durgin, Patrick Lincoln, John Mitchell, and Andre
          Scedrov. A comparison between strand spaces and transition systems for the
          specification of security protocols. To appear as a technical report, Depart-
          ment of Computer Science, Stanford University. 118

[Cha83]   David Chaum. Blind signatures for untraceable payments. In D. Chaum, R.
          L. Rivest, and A. T. Sherman, editors, *Advances in Cryptology – Proceedings
          of Crypto 82*, pages 199–203, 1983. 107

[Cha88]   David Chaum. The dining cryptographers problem: Unconditional sender
          and receiver untraceability. *Journal of Cryptology*, 1(1):65–75, 1988. 128

[Che80]   Brian F. Chellas. *Modal Logic: An Introduction.* Cambridge University Press,
          1980. 78, 79

[CJ97]   John Clark and Jeremy Jacob. A survey of authentication protocol literature:
          Version 1.0, nov 1997. Available at www-users.cs.york.ac.uk/~jac/ under
          the link "Security Protocols Review". 87, 93, 102, 103, 112

[CJ00]   John Clark and Jeremy Jacob. Searching for a solution: Engineering tradeoffs
          and the evolution of provably secure protocols. In *Proceedings of the IEEE
          Symposium on Security and Privacy*, pages 82–95. IEEE CS Press, May 2000.
          113

[CMS01]   Ran Canetti, Catherine Meadows, and Paul Syverson. Environmental re-
          quirements and authentication protocols. In *Proceedings of the Symposium
          on Requirements Engineering for Information Security (SREIS)*, March 2001.
          A version of this paper has been invited for a special issue of *Requirements
          Engineering*. 128

[Cro]   Crowds. http://www.research.att.com/projects/crowds/. 128

[CS97]   Jan L. Camenisch and Markus A. Stadler. Efficient group signature schemes
          for large groups. In B. Kaliski, editor, *Advances in Cryptology – CRYPTO
          '97*, pages 410–424. Springer-Verlag, LNCS 1294, 1997. 126

[CvH91]   David Chaum and Eugène van Heyst. Group signature. In D. W. Davies,
          editor, *Advances in Cryptology – EUROCRYPT '91*, pages 257–265. Springer-
          Verlag, LNCS 547, 1991. 126

[Dek00]   Anthony H. Dekker. C3po: a tool for automatic sound cryptographic protocol
          analysis. In *13th IEEE Computer Security Foundations Workshop*, pages 77–
          87. IEEE CS Press, June 2000. 83, 113

[DH99]   Naganand Doraswamy and Dan Harkins. *IPSEC: The New Security Standard
          for the Internet, Intranets, and Virtual Private Networks.* Prentice Hall, 1999.
          76, 125

[DM00]   G. Denker and J. Millen. Capsl integrated protocol environment. In *DISCEX
          2000: Proceedings of the DARPA Information Survivability Conference and
          Exposition*, volume I, pages 207–221. IEEE CS Press, January 2000. 112

[DS81]   Dorothy E. Denning and Giovanni Maria Sacco. Timestamps in key distri-
          bution protocols. *Communications of the ACM*, 24(8):533–536, August 1981.
          73, 92

[DvOW92] Whitfield Diffie, Paul C. van Oorschot, and Michael J. Wiener. Authenti-
          cation and authenticated key exchanges. *Designs, Codes, and Cryptography*,
          2:107–125, 1992. 104

[DY83]   Danny Dolev and Andrew C. Yao. On the security of public-key protocols.
          IEEE Transactions on Information Theory, 2(29):198–208, March 1983. 64,
          123

[ES00]   Neil Evans and Steve Schneider. Analysing time dependent security prop-
          erties in CSP using PVS. In F. Cuppens, Y. Deswarte, D. Gollmann, and

M. Waidner, editors, *Computer Security – ESORICS 2000*, pages 222–237. Springer-Verlag, LNCS 1895, October 2000. 103

[FHMV95] Ronald Fagin, Joseph Y. Halpern, Yoram Moses, and Moshe Y. Vardi. *Reasoning About Knowledge*. MIT Press, 1995. 120, 121, 128

[Fre] Freedom. http://www.freedom.net/. 128

[GNY90] Li Gong, Roger Needham, and Raphael Yahalom. Reasoning about Belief in Cryptographic Protocols. In *Proceedings of the IEEE Computer Society Symposium on Research in Security and Privacy*, pages 234–248. IEEE Computer Society Press, 1990. 76, 88, 89, 95

[Gol92] Robert Goldblatt. *Logics of Time and Computation, 2nd edition*, volume 7 of *CSLI Lecture Notes*. CSLI Publications, 1992. 79

[Gol96] Dieter Gollmann. What do we mean by entity authentication? In *Proceedings of the IEEE Symposium on Security and Privacy*, pages 46–54. IEEE CS Press, May 1996. 99

[Gol00] Dieter Gollmann. On the verification of cryptographic protocols - a tale of two committees. In Steve Schneider and Peter Ryan, editors, *Electronic Notes in Theoretical Computer Science*, volume 32. Elsevier Science Publishers, 2000. 102, 105

[GS98] Li Gong and Paul Syverson. Fail-stop protocols: An approach to designing secure protocols. In R. K. Iyer, M. Morganti, W. K. Fuchs, and V. Gligor, editors, *Dependable Computing for Critical Applications 5*, pages 79–100. IEEE Computer Society Press, 1998. 109

[Gut] Joshua D. Guttman. Security goals: Packet trajectories and strand spaces. This volume. 113, 118

[HT96] N. Heintze and J. D. Tygar. A model for secure protocols and their composition. *IEEE Transactions on Software Engineering*, 22(1):16–30, January 1996. 127

[Jür00] Jan Jürjens. Bridging the gap: Formal vs. complexity-theoretical reasoning about cryptography, December 2000. Presentation at the Schloss Dagstuhl Seminar on Security through Analysis and Verification. 128

[Kai95] Rajashekar Kailar. Reasoning about accountability in protocols for electronic commerce. In *Proceedings of the IEEE Symposium on Security and Privacy*, pages 236–250. IEEE CS Press, May 1995. 127

[Kai96] Rajashekar Kailar. Accountability in electronic commerce protocols. *IEEE Transactions on Software Engineering*, 5(22), May 1996. 127

[Kem87] Richard A. Kemmerer. Using formal verification techniques to analyze cryptographic protocols. In *Proceedings of the 1987 IEEE Symposium on Security and Privacy*, pages 134–139. IEEE CS Press, May 1987. 63

[KN98] Volker Kessler and Heike Neumann. A sound logic for analysing electronic commerce protocols. In J.-J. Quisquater, Y. Deswarte, C. Meadows, and D. Gollmann, editors, *Computer Security – ESORICS 98*, pages 345–360. Springer-Verlag, LNCS 1485, September 1998. 127

[KR00] Steve Kremer and Jean-François Raskin. A game approach to the verification of exchange protocols: Application to non-repudiation protocols. In P. Degano, editor, *First Workshop on Issues in the Theory of Security – WITS'00*, pages 93–98, July 2000. 127

[Lam78] Leslie Lamport. Time, clocks, and the ordering of events in a distributed system. *Communications of the ACM*, 21(7):558–565, July 1978. 109

[Low96] G. Lowe. Breaking and fixing the Needham-Schroeder public-key protocol using FDR. *Software - Concepts and Tools*, 17:93–102, 1996. 92, 101

[Low97]   Gavin Lowe. A herarchy of authentication specifications. In *Proceedings of the 10th IEEE Computer Security Foundations Workshop (CSFW9)*, pages 31–43. IEEE Computer Society Press, June 1997. 100, 101, 102, 103

[MCF87]   Jonathan K. Millen, Sidney C. Clark, and Sheryl B. Freedman. The Interrogator: Protocol security analysis. *IEEE Transactions on Software Engineering*, 13(2):274–288, 1987. 63

[Mea94]   Catherine Meadows. A model of computation for the NRL Protocol Analyzer. In *Proceedings of the 7th Computer Security Foundations Workshop*, pages 84–89. IEEE CS Press, June 1994. 114, 116, 118

[Mea96]   Catherine Meadows. The NRL Protocol Analyzer: An overview. *Journal of Logic Programming*, 26(2):113–131, February 1996. 114, 116

[Mea99a] C. Meadows. Analysis of the Internet Key Exchange protocol using the NRL Protocol Analyzer. In *Proceedings of the IEEE Symposium on Security and Privacy*. IEEE Computer Society Press, May 1999. 128

[Mea99b] Catherine Meadows. A formal framework and evaluation method for network denial of service. In *Proceedings of the 12th IEEE Computer Security Foundations Workshop (CSFW12)*, pages 4–13. IEEE CS Press, June 1999. 134

[Mea00a] Catherine Meadows. Extending formal cryptographic protocol analysis techniques for group protocols and low-level cryptographic primitives. In P. Degano, editor, *First Workshop on Issues in the Theory of Security – WITS'00*, pages 87–92, July 2000. 126

[Mea00b] Catherine Meadows. Open issues in formal methods for cryptographic protocol analysis. In *DISCEX 2000: Proceedings of the DARPA Information Survivability Conference and Exposition*, volume I, pages 237–250. IEEE Computer Society Press, January 2000. 125

[Mea01]   Catherine Meadows. A cost-based framework for analysis of denial of service in networks. *Journal of Computer Security*, 2001. Forthcoming. A preliminary version of portions of this work appeared in [Mea99b]. 126

[Men87]   Elliott Mendelson. *Introduction to Mathematical Logic*. Wadsworth Publishing Co., 1987. 78

[Mil]   J. Millen. Capsl Web site. www.csl.sri.com/~millen/capsl. 112

[Mil84]   Jonathan K. Millen. The Interrogator: A tool for cryptographic protocol security. In *Proceedings of the 1984 IEEE Symposium on Security and Privacy*, pages 134–141, Oakland, CA, April 1984. IEEE Computer Society Press. 63

[Mos86]   Paul K. Moser, editor. *Empirical Knowledge: Readings in Contemporary Epistemology*. Rowman & Littlefield, 1986. 79

[MR00]   Jon Millen and Harald Rueß. Protocol-independent secrecy. In *Proceedings of the IEEE Symposium on Security and Privacy*, pages 110–119, May 2000. 123

[MS98]   C. Meadows and P. Syverson. A formal specification of requirements for payment trnasactions in the SET protocol. In R. Hirschfeld, editor, *Financial Cryptography, FC'98*, pages 122–140. Springer-Verlag, LNCS 1465, 1998. 117, 127

[MvOV97] Alfred J. Menezes, Paul C. van Oorschot, and Scott A. Vanstone. *Handbook of Applied Cryptography*. CRC Press, 1997. 64, 80, 89

[Nes90]   D. M. Nessett. A critique of the burrows, abadi, and needham logic. *Operating Systems Review*, 24(2):35–38, April 1990. 73, 74

[NS78]   R. M. Needham and M. D. Schroeder. Using encryption for authentication in large networks of computers. *Communications of the ACM*, 21(12):993–999, 1978. 65, 101, 102

[NS93]   B. Clifford Neuman and Stuart G. Stubblebine. A Note on the Use of Times-
          tamps as Nonces. *Operating Systems Review*, 27(2):10–14, April 1993. 93
[Oni]   Onion routing. http://www.onion-router.net/. 128
[Pau97]   Lawrence C. Paulson. Mechanized proofs for a recursive authentication pro-
          tocol. In *Proceedings of the 10th IEEE Computer Security Foundations Work-
          shop (CSFW10)*, pages 84–94. IEEE CS Press, June 1997. 126
[PS00]   Adrian Perrig and Dawn Song. Looking for diamonds in the desert — ex-
          tending automatic protocol generation to three-party authentication and key
          agreement. In *13th IEEE Computer Security Foundations Workshop*, pages
          64–76. IEEE CS Press, June 2000. 113
[Ros96]   A. W. Roscoe. Intensional specification of security protocols. In *Proceedings
          of the 9th IEEE Computer Security Foundations Workshop (CSFW9)*, pages
          28–36. IEEE CS Press, June 1996. 103
[Sat89]   M. Satyanarayanan. Integrating security in a large distributed system. *ACM
          Transactions on Computer Systems*, 15(3):247–280, August 1989. 102
[Sch96]   Bruce Schneier. *Applied Cryptography, Second Edition: Protocols, Algorithms,
          and Source Code in C*. John Wiley & Sons, 1996. 64, 80, 107
[SET97]   Secure Electronic Transaction Specification, Version 1.0, May 1997.
          http://www.visa.com/set/. 117
[SM93]   P. Syverson and C. Meadows. A logical language for specifying cryptographic
          protocol requirements. In *Proceedings of the IEEE Computer Society Sym-
          posium on Research in Security and Privacy*, pages 165–177. IEEE CS Press,
          May 1993. 117
[SM94]   P. Syverson and C. Meadows. Formal requirements for key distribution pro-
          tocols. In A. De Santis, editor, *Advances in Cryptology — EUROCRYPT '94*,
          pages 32–331. Springer-Verlag, LNCS 950, 1994. 117
[SM96]   P. Syverson and C. Meadows. A formal language for cryptographic protocol
          requirements. *Designs, Codes, and Cryptography*, 7(1 and 2):27–59, January
          1996. 114, 116, 117
[Sne91]   Einar Snekkenes. Exploring the BAN approach to protocol analysis. In *Pro-
          ceedings of the IEEE Computer Society Symposium on Research in Security
          and Privacy*, pages 171–181. IEEE CS Press, May 1991. 96, 97
[Sne92]   Einar Snekkenes. Roles in cryptographic protocols. In *Proceedings of the
          IEEE Computer Society Symposium on Research in Security and Privacy*,
          pages 105–119. IEEE CS Press, May 1992. 98
[Son99]   Dawn Song. Athena: a new efficient automatic checker for security protocol
          analysis. In *Proceedings of the Twelth IEEE Computer Security Foundations
          Workshop*, pages 192–202, Mordano, Italy, June 1999. IEEE Computer Soci-
          ety Press. 118
[SS96]   Steve Schneider and Abraham Sidiropoulos. CSP and anonymity. In
          E. Bertino, H. Kurth, G. Martella, and E. Montolivio, editors, *Computer
          Security – ESORICS 96*, pages 198–218. Springer Verlag, LNCS 1146, 1996.
          129
[SS99]   Paul Syverson and Stuart Stubblebine. Group principals and the formaliza-
          tion of anonymity. In J. M. Wing, J. Woodcock, and J. Davies, editors, *FM'99
          – Formal Methods, Vol. I*, pages 814–833. Springer-Verlag, LNCS 1708, 1999.
          128, 129
[Sti95]   Douglas R. Stinson. *Cryptography: Theory and Practice*. CRC Press, 1995.
          64

[SvO94] Paul F. Syverson and Paul C. van Oorschot. On unifying some cryptographic protocols. In *Proceedings of the IEEE Computer Society Symposium on Research in Security and Privacy*, pages 14–28. IEEE CS Press, May 1994. 77, 78, 120, 125

[SvO96] Paul F. Syverson and Paul C. van Oorschot. A unified cryptographic protocol logic. NRL Publication 5540-227, Naval Research Lab, 1996. 77, 78, 79, 84, 85, 88, 95, 98, 120, 124, 125, 126

[SW96] Stuart Stubblebine and Rebecca Wright. An authentication logic supporting synchronization, revocation, and recency. In *3rd ACM Conference on Computer and Communications Security (CCS'96)*, pages 95–105. ACM Press, March 1996. 127

[Syv91] Paul F. Syverson. The use of logic in the analysis of cryptographic protocols. In *Proceedings of the IEEE Computer Society Symposium on Research in Security and Privacy*, pages 156–170. IEEE CS Press, May 1991. 75, 76

[Syv92] Paul F. Syverson. Knowledge, belief, and semantics in the analysis of cryptographic protocols. *Journal of Computer Security*, 1(3,4):317–334, 1992. 76, 79

[Syv93a] Paul F. Syverson. Adding time to a logic of authentication. In *Proceedings of the First ACM Conference on Computer and Communications Security*, pages 97–101, November, 1993. ACM Press. 96, 98, 121

[Syv93b] Paul F. Syverson. On Key Distribution Protocols for Repeated Authentication. *Operating Systems Review*, 27(4):24–30, October 1993. 93

[Syv94] Paul Syverson. A taxonomy of replay attacks. In *Proceedings of the Computer Security Foundations Workshop (CSFW7)*, pages 187–191. IEEE CS Press, June 1994. 91, 92, 93, 95, 98

[Syv96] Paul Syverson. Limitations on design principles for public key protocols. In *Proceedings of the IEEE Symposium on Security and Privacy*, pages 62–72. IEEE Computer Society Press, May 1996. 107, 108

[Syv98] Paul F. Syverson. Relating two models of computation for security protocols. In *Workshop on Formal Methods and Security Protocols*, Indianapolis, Indiana, June 1998. Available at `http://www.cs.bell-labs.com/who/nch/fmsp/program.html`. 118

[Syv00] Paul F. Syverson. Towards a strand semantics for authentication logic. *Electronic Notes in Theoretical Computer Science*, 20, 2000. Proceedings of MFPS XV (S. Brookes, A. Jung, M. Mislove and A. Scedrov, eds.), New Orleans, LA, April 1999. 114, 118

[THG97] F. Javier Thayer Fábrega, Jonathan C. Herzog, and Joshua D. Guttman. Strand spaces. Technical report, The MITRE Corporation, November 1997. 66, 114, 118, 121

[THG98a] F. Javier Thayer Fábrega, Jonathan C. Herzog, and Joshua D. Guttman. Honest ideals on strand spaces. In *Proceedings of the 1998 IEEE Computer Security Foundations Workshop — CSFW'11*, pages 66–77. IEEE Computer Society Press, 1998. 123

[THG98b] F. Javier Thayer Fábrega, Jonathan C. Herzog, and Joshua D. Guttman. Strand spaces: Why is a security protocol correct? In *Proceedings of the 1998 IEEE Symposium on Security and Privacy*, pages 160–171, Oakland, CA, May 1998. IEEE Computer Society Press. 66, 114, 118

[THG99a] F. Javier Thayer Fábrega, Jonathan C. Herzog, and Joshua D. Guttman. Mixed strand spaces. In P. Syverson, editor, *Proceedings of the 12th IEEE Computer Security Foundations Workshop — CSFW'99*, pages 72–82, Mordano, Italy, June 1999. IEEE Computer Society Press. 128

[THG99b] F. Javier Thayer Fábrega, Jonathan C. Herzog, and Joshua D. Guttman. Strand spaces: Proving security protocols correct. *Journal of Computer Security*, 7(2,3):191–230, 1999. 119, 122, 123

[Tou92] Marie-Jeanne Toussaint. Separating the specification and implementation phases in cryptology. In Y. Deswarte, G. Eizenberg, and J.-J. Quisquater, editors, *Computer Security – ESORICS 92*, pages 77–102. Springer-Verlag, LNCS 648, November 1992. 108

[Tut] Mark Tuttle. Flaming in Franconia. Remarks made in a panel discussion on the use of formal methods in the analysis of cryptographic protocols at the IEEE Computer Security Foundations Workshop in Franconia, New Hampshire, June 1992. 79

[vO93] Paul C. van Oorschot. Extending cryptographic logics of belief to key agreement protocols. In *Proceedings of the 1st ACM Conference on Computer and Communications Security*, pages 233–243. ACM Press, November 1993. 67, 76, 85, 88, 95, 98, 126

[WK96] Gabriele Wedel and Volker Kessler. Formal semantics for authentication logics. In E. Bertino, H. Kurth, G. Martella, and E. Montolivo, editors, *Computer Security – ESORICS 96*, pages 219–241. Springer-Verlag, LNCS 1146, September 1996. 78, 83, 113, 127

[Yah93] Raphael Yahalom. Optimality of asynchronous two-party secure data-exchange protocol. *Journal of Computer Security*, 2(2–3):191–209, 1993. 93

[ZG98] Jianying Zhou and Dieter Gollmann. Towards verification of non-repudiation protocols. In T. Vickers J. Grundy, M. Schwenke, editor, *International Refinement Workshop and Formal Methods Pacific 1998*, pages 370–380. Springer-Verlag, 1998. 127

Access Control: Policies, Models, and Mechanisms

Pierangela Samarati[1] and Sabrina de Capitani di Vimercati[2]

[1] Dipartimento di Tecnologie dell'Informazione, Università di Milano
Via Bramante 65, 26013 Crema (CR), Italy
samarati@dsi.unimi.it
http://homes.dsi.unimi.it/~samarati
[2] Dip. di Elettronica per l'Automazione, Università di Brescia
Via Branze 38, 25123 Brescia, Italy
decapita@ing.unibs.it
http://www.ing.unibs.it/~decapita

Abstract. Access control is the process of mediating every request to resources and data maintained by a system and determining whether the request should be granted or denied. The access control decision is enforced by a mechanism implementing regulations established by a security policy. Different access control policies can be applied, corresponding to different criteria for defining what should, and what should not, be allowed, and, in some sense, to different definitions of what ensuring security means. In this chapter we investigate the basic concepts behind access control design and enforcement, and point out different security requirements that may need to be taken into consideration. We discuss several access control policies, and models formalizing them, that have been proposed in the literature or that are currently under investigation.

1 Introduction

An important requirement of any information management system is to *protect data and resources* against unauthorized disclosure (*secrecy*) and unauthorized or improper modifications (*integrity*), while at the same time ensuring their availability to legitimate users (*no denials-of-service*). Enforcing protection therefore requires that *every access to a system and its resources be controlled and that all and only authorized accesses can take place*. This process goes under the name of *access control*. The development of an access control system requires the definition of the regulations according to which access is to be controlled and their implementation as functions executable by a computer system. The development process is usually carried out with a multi-phase approach based on the following concepts:

Security policy: it defines the (high-level) rules according to which access control must be regulated.[1]

---

[1] Often, the term policy is also used to refer to particular instances of a policy, that is, actual authorizations and access restrictions to be enforced (e.g., Employees can read bulletin-board).

R. Focardi and R. Gorrieri (Eds.): FOSAD 2000, LNCS 2171, pp. 137–196, 2001.
© Springer-Verlag Berlin Heidelberg 2001

Security model: it provides a *formal* representation of the access control security policy and its working. The formalization allows the proof of properties on the security provided by the access control system being designed.

Security mechanism: it defines the low level (software and hardware) functions that implement the controls imposed by the policy and formally stated in the model.

The three concepts above correspond to a conceptual separation between different levels of abstraction of the design, and provides the traditional advantages of multi-phase software development. In particular, the separation between policies and mechanisms introduces an independence between protection requirements to be enforced on the one side, and mechanisms enforcing them on the other. It is then possible to: *i)* discuss protection requirements independently of their implementation, *ii)* compare different access control policies as well as different mechanisms that enforce the same policy, and *iii)* design mechanisms able to enforce multiple policies. This latter aspect is particularly important: if a mechanism is tied to a specific policy, a change in the policy would require changing the whole access control system; mechanisms able to enforce multiple policies avoid this drawback. The formalization phase between the policy definition and its implementation as a mechanism allows the definition of a formal model representing the policy and its working, making it possible to define and prove security properties that systems enforcing the model will enjoy [54]. Therefore, by proving that the model is "secure" and that the mechanism *correctly implements* the model, we can argue that the system is "secure" (w.r.t. the definition of security considered). The implementation of a correct mechanism is far from being trivial and is complicated by the need to cope with possible security weaknesses due to the implementation itself and by the difficulty of mapping the access control primitives to a computer system. The access control mechanism must work as a *reference monitor*, that is, a trusted component intercepting each and every request to the system [5]. It must also enjoy the following properties:

- *tamper-proof*: it should not be possible to alter it (or at least it should not be possible for alterations to go undetected);
- *non-bypassable*: it must mediate all accesses to the system and its resources;
- *security kernel*: it must be confined in a limited part of the system (scattering security functions all over the system implies that all the code must be verified);
- *small*: it must be of limited size to be susceptible of rigorous verification methods.

Even the definition of access control policies (and their corresponding models) is far from being a trivial process. One of the major difficulty lies in the interpretation of, often complex and sometimes ambiguous, real world security policies and in their translation in well defined and unambiguous rules enforceable by a computer system. Many real world situations have complex policies, where access decisions depend on the application of different rules coming, for example, from laws, practices, and organizational regulations. A security policy must capture all the different regulations to be enforced and, in addition, must also consider possible additional threats due to the use of a computer system. Access control policies can be grouped into three main classes:

Discretionary (DAC) (authorization-based) policies control access based on the identity of the requestor and on access rules stating what requestors are (or are not) allowed to do.

Mandatory (MAC) policies control access based on mandated regulations determined by a central authority.

Role-based (RBAC) policies control access depending on the roles that users have within the system and on rules stating what accesses are allowed to users in given roles.

Discretionary and role-based policies are usually coupled with (or include) an *administrative* policy that defines who can specify authorizations/rules governing access control.

In this chapter we illustrate different access control policies and models that have been proposed in the literature, also investigating their low level implementation in terms of security mechanisms. In illustrating the literature and the current status of access control systems, of course, the chapter does not pretend to be exhaustive. However, by discussing different approaches with their advantages and limitations, this chapter hopes to give an idea of the different issues to be tackled in the development of an access control system, and of good security principles that should be taken into account in the design.

The chapter is structured as follows. Section 2 introduces the basic concepts of discretionary policies and authorization-based models. Section 3 shows the limitation of authorization-based controls to introduce the basis for the need of mandatory policies, which are then discussed in Section 4. Section 5 illustrates approaches combining mandatory and discretionary principles to the goal of achieving mandatory information flow protection without loosing the flexibility of discretionary authorizations. Section 6 illustrates several discretionary policies and models that have been proposed. Section 7 illustrates role-based access control policies. Finally, Section 8 discusses advanced approaches and directions in the specification and enforcement of access control regulations.

2   Basic Concepts of Discretionary Policies

Discretionary policies enforce access control on the basis of the identity of the requestors and explicit access rules that establish who can, or cannot, execute which actions on which resources. They are called discretionary as users can be given the ability of passing on their privileges to other users, where granting and revocation of privileges is regulated by an administrative policy. Different discretionary access control policies and models have been proposed in the literature. We start in this section with the early discretionary models, to convey the basic ideas of authorization specifications and their enforcement. We will come back to discretionary policies after having dealt with mandatory controls. We base the discussion of the "primitive" discretionary policies on the access matrix model.

2.1   The Access Matrix Model

The access matrix model provides a framework for describing discretionary access control. First proposed by Lampson [53] for the protection of resources within the context of operating systems, and later refined by Graham and Denning [41], the model was subsequently formalized by Harrison, Ruzzo, and Ullmann (HRU model) [44], who developed the access control model proposed by Lampson to the goal of analyzing the complexity of determining an access control policy. The original model is called access matrix since the authorization state, meaning the authorizations holding at a given time in the system, is represented as a matrix. The matrix therefore gives an abstract representation of protection systems. Although the model may seem primitive, as richer policies and languages have been investigated subsequently (see Section 6), its treatment is useful to illustrate some aspects to be taken into account in the formalization of an access control system.

A first step in the development of an access control system is the identification of the *objects* to be protected, the *subjects* that execute activities and request access to objects, and the *actions* that can be executed on the objects, and that must be controlled. Subjects, objects, and actions may be different in different systems or application contexts. For instance, in the protection of operating systems, objects are typically files, directories, or programs; in database systems, objects can be relations, views, stored procedures, and so on. It is interesting to note that subjects can be themselves objects (this is the case, for example, of executable code and stored procedures). A subject can create additional subjects (e.g., children processes) in order to accomplish its task. The creator subject acquires control privileges on the created processes (e.g., to be able to suspend or terminate its children).

In the access matrix model, the state of the system is defined by a triple (S, O, A), where S is the set of subjects, who can exercise privileges; O is the set of objects, on which privileges can be exercised (subjects may be considered as objects, in which case $S \subseteq O$); and A is the access matrix, where rows correspond to subjects, columns correspond to objects, and entry $A[s, o]$ reports the privileges of s on o. The type of the objects and the actions executable on them depend on the system. By simply providing a framework where authorizations can be specified, the model can accommodate different privileges. For instance, in addition to the traditional read, write, and execute actions, *ownership* (i.e., property of objects by subjects), and *control* (to model father-children relationships between processes) can be considered. Figure 1 illustrates an example of access matrix.

Changes to the state of a system is carried out through *commands* that can execute *primitive* operations on the authorization state, possibly depending on some conditions. The HRU formalization identified six primitive operations that

File 1	File 2	File 3	Program 1

	File 1	File 2	File 3	Program 1
Ann	own read write	read write		execute
Bob	read		read write	
Carl		read		execute read

Fig. 1. An example of access matrix

describe changes to the state of a system. These operations, whose effect on the authorization state is illustrated in Figure 2, correspond to adding and removing a subject, adding and removing an object, and adding and removing a privilege. Each command has a conditional part and a body and has the form

command $c(x_1, \ldots, x_k)$
    if r_1 in $A[x_{s_1}, x_{o_1}]$ and
    r_2 in $A[x_{s_2}, x_{o_2}]$ and
    .
    .
    r_m in $A[x_{s_m}, x_{o_m}]$
    then op_1
      op_2
      .
      .
      op_n
end.

with $n > 0, m \geq 0$. Here $r_1, \ldots, r_m$ are actions, $op_1, \ldots, op_n$ are primitive operations, while $s_1, \ldots, s_m$ and $o_1, \ldots, o_m$ are integers between 1 and k. If $m=0$, the command has no conditional part.

For example, the following command creates a file and gives the creating subject ownership privilege on it.

command CREATE(creator,file)
    create object file
    enter Own *into* A[creator,file] **end.**

The following commands allow an owner to grant to others, and revoke ¿from others, a privilege to execute an action on her files.

command CONFER$_a$(owner,friend,file)
    if Own in A[owner,file]
      then *enter a into* A[friend,file] **end.**

OPERATION (op)	CONDITIONS	NEW STATE ($Q \vdash_{op} Q'$)
enter r into $A[s,o]$	$s \in S$ $o \in O$	$S' = S$ $O' = O$ $A'[s,o] = A[s,o] \cup \{r\}$ $A'[s_i,o_j] = A[s_i,o_j] \quad \forall(s_i,o_j) \neq (s,o)$
delete r from $A[s,o]$	$s \in S$ $o \in O$	$S' = S$ $O' = O$ $A'[s,o] = A[s,o] \setminus \{r\}$ $A'[s_i,o_j] = A[s_i,o_j] \quad \forall(s_i,o_j) \neq (s,o)$
create subject s'	$s' \notin S$	$S' = S \cup \{s'\}$ $O' = O \cup \{s'\}$ $A'[s,o] = A[s,o] \quad \forall s \in S, o \in O$ $A'[s',o] = \emptyset \quad \forall o \in O'$ $A'[s,s'] = \emptyset \quad \forall s \in S'$
create object o'	$o' \notin O$	$S' = S$ $O' = O \cup \{o'\}$ $A'[s,o] = A[s,o] \quad \forall s \in S, o \in O$ $A'[s,o'] = \emptyset \quad \forall s \in S'$
destroy subject s'	$s' \in S$	$S' = S \setminus \{s'\}$ $O' = O \setminus \{s'\}$ $A'[s,o] = A[s,o] \quad \forall s \in S', o \in O'$
destroy object o'	$o' \in O$ $o' \notin S$	$S' = S$ $O' = O \setminus \{o'\}$ $A'[s,o] = A[s,o] \quad \forall s \in S', o \in O'$

Fig. 2. Primitive operations of the HRU model

command REVOKE$_a$(owner,ex-friend,file)
      if Own in A[owner,file]
          then *delete a from* A[ex-friend,file] **end.**

Note that here a is not a parameter, but an abbreviation for defining many similar commands, one for each value that a can take (e.g., CONFER$_{\text{read}}$, REVOKE$_{\text{write}}$). Since commands are not parametric w.r.t. actions, a different command needs to be specified for each action that can be granted/revoked.

Let $Q \vdash_{op} Q'$ denote the execution of operation op on state Q, resulting in state Q'. The execution of command $c(a_1, ..., a_k)$ on a system state $Q = (S, O, A)$ causes the *transition* from state Q to state Q' such that $\exists Q_1, ..., Q_n$ for which $Q \vdash_{op_1^*} Q_1 \vdash_{op_2^*} ... \vdash_{op_n^*} Q_n = Q'$, where $op_1^* ... op_n^*$ are the primitive operations $op_1 ... op_n$ in the body (operational part) of command c, in which actual parameters a_i are substituted for each formal parameters x_i, $i := 1, ..., k$. If the conditional part of the command is not verified, then the command has no effect and $Q = Q'$.

Although the HRU model does not include any buil-in administrative policies, the possibility of defining commands allows their formulation. Administrative authorizations can be specified by attaching flags to access privileges.

For instance, a *copy flag*, denoted ∗, attached to a privilege may indicate that the privilege can be transferred to others. Granting of authorizations can then be accomplished by the execution of commands like the one below (again here TRANSFER$_a$ is an abbreviation for as many commands as there are actions).

command TRANSFER$_a$(subj,friend,file)
      if a^* in A[subj,file]
          then *enter a into* A[friend,file] **end.**

The ability of specifying commands of this type clearly provides flexibility as different administrative policies can be taken into account by defining appropriate commands. For instance, an alternative administrative flag (called *transfer only* and denoted +) can be supported, which gives the subject the ability of passing on the privilege to others but for which, so doing, the subject looses the privilege. Such a flexibility introduces an interesting problem referred to as *safety*, and concerned with the propagation of privileges to subjects in the system. Intuitively, given a system with initial configuration Q, the *safety* problem is concerned with determining whether or not a given subject s can ever acquire a given access a on an object o, that is, if there exists a sequence of requests that executed on Q can produce a state Q' where a appears in a cell $A[s,o]$ that did not have it in Q. (Note that, of course, not all leakages of privileges are bad and subjects may intentionally transfer their privileges to "trusworthy" subjects. Trustworthy subjects are therefore ignored in the analysis.) It turns out that the safety problem is undecidable in general (it can be reduced to the halting problem of a Turing machine) [4]. It remains instead decidable for cases where subjects and objects are finite, and in *mono-operational* systems, that is, systems where the body of commands can have at most one operation (while the conditional part can still be arbitrarily complex). However, as noted in [81], mono-operational systems have the limitation of making create operations pretty useless: a single create command cannot do more than adding an empty row/column (it cannot write anything in it). It is therefore not possible to support ownership or control relationships between subjects. Progresses in safety analysis were made in a later extension of the HRU model by Sandhu [81], who proposed the *TAM* (Typed Access Matrix) model. TAM extends HRU with strong typing: each subject and object has a type; the type is associated with the subjects/objects when they are created and thereafter does not change. Safety results decidable in polynomial time for cases where the system is monotonic (privileges cannot be deleted), commands are limited to three parameters, and there are no cyclic creates. Safety remains undecidable otherwise.

2.2   Implementation of the Access Matrix

Although the matrix represents a good conceptualization of authorizations, it is not appropriate for implementation. In a general system, the access matrix will be usually enormous in size and sparse (most of its cells are likely to be empty). Storing the matrix as a two-dimensional array is therefore a waste of memory space. There are three approaches to implementing the access matrix in a practical way:

Authorization Table Non empty entries of the matrix are reported in a table with three columns, corresponding to subjects, actions, and objects, respectively. Each tuple in the table corresponds to an authorization. The authorization table approach is generally used in DBMS systems, where authorizations are stored as catalogs (relational tables) of the database.

Access Control List (ACL) The matrix is stored by column. Each object is associated with a list indicating, for each subject, the actions that the subject can exercise on the object.

Capability The matrix is stored by row. Each user has associated a list, called capability list, indicating, for each object, the accesses that the user is allowed to exercise on the object.

Figure 3 illustrates the authorization table, ACLs, and capabilities, respectively, corresponding to the access matrix in Figure 1.

Capabilities and ACLs present advantages and disadvantages with respect to authorization control and management. In particular, with ACLs it is immediate to check the authorizations holding on an object, while retrieving all the authorizations of a subject requires the examination of the ACLs for all the objects. Analogously, with capabilities, it is immediate to determine the privileges of a subject, while retrieving all the accesses executable on an object requires the examination of all the different capabilities. These aspects affect the efficiency of authorization revocation upon deletion of either subjects or objects.

In a system supporting capabilities, it is sufficient for a subject to present the appropriate capability to gain access to an object. This represents an advantage in distributed systems since it permits to avoid repeated authentication of a subject: a user can be authenticated at a host, acquire the appropriate capabilities and present them to obtain accesses at the various servers of the system. However, capabilities are vulnerable to *forgery* (they can be copied and reused by an unauthorized third party). Another problem in the use of capability is the enforcement of revocation, meaning invalidation of capabilities that have been released.

A number of capability-based computer systems were developed in the 1970s, but did not prove to be commercially successful. Modern operating systems typically take the ACL-based approach. Some systems implement an abbreviated form of ACL by restricting the assignment of authorizations to a limited number (usually one or two) of named groups of users, while individual authorizations are not allowed. The advantage of this is that ACLs can be efficiently represented as small bit-vectors. For instance, in the popular Unix operating system, each user in the system belongs to exactly one group and each file has an owner (generally the user who created it), and is associated with a group (usually the group of its owner). Authorizations for each file can be specified for the file's owner, for the group to which the file belongs, and for "the rest of the world" (meaning all the remaining users). No explicit reference to users or groups is allowed.

USER	ACCESS MODE	OBJECT
Ann	own	File 1
Ann	read	File 1
Ann	write	File 1
Ann	read	File 2
Ann	write	File 2
Ann	execute	Program 1
Bob	read	File 1
Bob	read	File 3
Bob	write	File 3
Carl	read	File 2
Carl	execute	Program 1
Carl	read	Program 1

Fig. 3. Authorization table, ACLs, and capabilities for the matrix in Figure 1

Authorizations are represented by associating with each object an access control list of 9 bits: bits 1 through 3 reflect the privileges of the file's owner, bits 4 through 6 those of the user group to which the file belongs, and bits 7 through 9 those of all the other users. The three bits correspond to the read (r), write (w), and execute (x) privilege, respectively. For instance, ACL rwxr-x--x associated with a file indicates that the file can be read, written, and executed by its owner, read and executed by users belonging to the group associated with the file, and executed by all the other users.

3   Vulnerabilities of the Discretionary Policies

In defining the basic concepts of discretionary policies, we have referred to access requests on objects submitted by users, which are then checked against the users' authorizations. Although it is true that each request is originated because of some user's actions, a more precise examination of the access control problem shows the utility of separating *users* from *subjects*. Users are passive entities for whom authorizations can be specified and who can connect to the system. Once connected to the system, users originate processes (subjects) that execute on their behalf and, accordingly, submit requests to the system. Discretionary policies ignore this distinction and evaluate all requests submitted by a process running on behalf of some user against the authorizations of the user. This aspect makes discretionary policies vulnerable from processes executing malicious programs exploiting the authorizations of the user on behalf of whom they are executing. In particular, the access control system can be bypassed by Trojan Horses embedded in programs. A *Trojan Horse* is a computer program with an apparently or actually useful function, which contains additional *hidden* functions that surreptitiously exploit the legitimate authorizations of the invoking process. (Viruses and logic bombs are usually transmitted as Trojan Horses.) A Trojan Horse can improperly use any authorizations of the invoking user, for example, it could even delete all files of the user (this destructive behavior is not uncommon in the case of viruses). This vulnerability to Trojan Horses, together with the fact that *discretionary policies do not enforce any control on the flow of information once this information is acquired by a process,* makes it possible for processes to leak information to users not allowed to read it. All this can happen without the cognizance of the data administrator/owner, and despite the fact that each single access request is controlled against the authorizations. To understand how a Trojan Horse can leak information to unauthorized users despite the discretionary access control, consider the following example. Assume that within an organization, Vicky, a top-level manager, creates a file Market containing important information about releases of new products. This information is very sensitive for the organization and, according to the organization's policy, should not be disclosed to anybody besides Vicky. Consider now John, one of Vicky's subordinates, who wants to acquire this sensitive information to sell it to a competitor organization. To achieve this, John creates a file, let's call it Stolen, and gives Vicky the authorization to write the file. Note that Vicky may not even know about the existence of Stolen, or about the fact that she has the write authorization on it. Moreover, John modifies an application generally used by Vicky, to include two hidden operations, a read operation on file Market and a write operation on file Stolen (Figure 4(a)). Then, he gives the new application to his manager. Suppose now that Vicky executes the application. Since the application executes on behalf of Vicky, every access is checked against Vicky's authorizations, and the read and write operations above are allowed. As a result, during execution, sensitive information in Market is transferred to Stolen and thus made readable to the dishonest employee John, who can then sell it to the competitor (Figure 4(b)). The reader may object that there is little point in

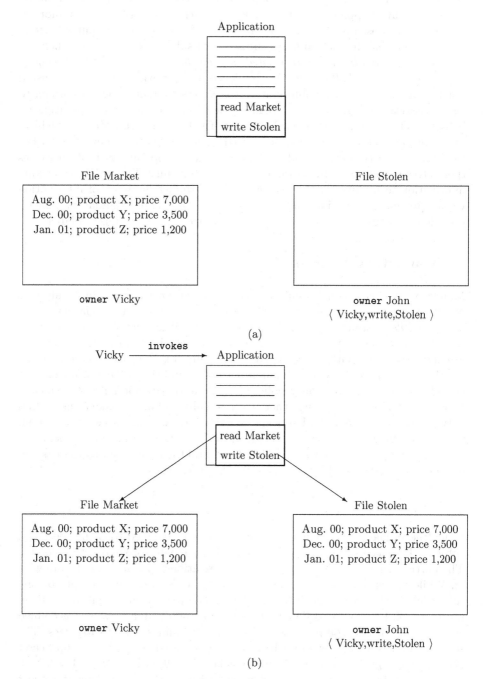

Fig. 4. An example of Trojan Horse improperly leaking information

defending against Trojan Horses leaking information flow: such an information flow could have happened anyway, by having Vicky explicitly tell this information to John, possibly even off-line, without the use of the computer system. Here is where the distinction between users and subjects operating on their behalf comes in. *While users are trusted to obey the access restrictions, subjects operating on their behalf are not.* With reference to our example, Vicky is trusted not to release the sensitive information she knows to John, since, according to the authorizations, John cannot read it. However, the processes operating on behalf of Vicky cannot be given the same trust. Processes run programs which, unless properly certified, cannot be trusted for the operations they execute. For this reason, restrictions should be enforced on the operations that processes themselves can execute. In particular, protection against Trojan Horses leaking information to unauthorized users requires controlling the flows of information within processes execution and possibly restricting them. Mandatory policies provide a way to enforce information flow control through the use of labels.

4 Mandatory Policies

Mandatory security policies enforce access control on the basis of regulations mandated by a central authority. The most common form of mandatory policy is the *multilevel security policy*, based on the classifications of *subjects* and *objects* in the system. Objects are passive entities storing information. Subjects are active entities that request access to the objects. Note that there is a distinction between *subjects* of the mandatory policy and the *authorization subjects* considered in the discretionary policies. While authorization subjects typically correspond to users (or groups thereof), mandatory policies make a distinction between *users* and *subjects*. Users are human beings who can access the system, while subjects are processes (i.e., programs in execution) operating on behalf of users. This distinction allows the policy to control the indirect accesses (leakages or modifications) caused by the execution of processes.

4.1 Security Classifications

In multilevel mandatory policies, an access class is assigned to each object and subject. The access class is one element of a partially ordered set of classes. The partial order is defined by a *dominance* relationship, which we denote with $\geq$. While in the most general case, the set of access classes can simply be any set of labels that together with the dominance relationship defined on them form a POSET (partially ordered set), most commonly an access class is defined as consisting of two components: a *security level* and a *set of categories*. The security level is an element of a hierarchically ordered set, such as Top Secret (TS), Secret (S), Confidential (C), and Unclassified (U), where $TS > S > C > U$. The set of categories is a subset of an unordered set, whose elements reflect functional, or competence, areas (e.g., NATO, Nuclear, and Army, for military systems; Financial, Administration, and Research, for commercial systems). The

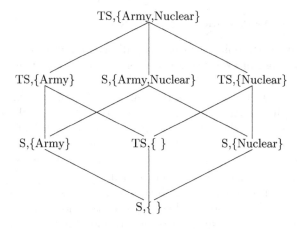

Fig. 5. An example of security lattice

dominance relationship $\geq$ is then defined as follows: an access class c_1 *dominates* ($\geq$) an access class c_2 iff the security level of c_1 is greater than or equal to that of c_2 and the categories of c_1 include those of c_2. Formally, given a totally ordered set of security levels $\mathcal{L}$, and a set of categories $\mathcal{C}$, the set of access classes is $\mathcal{AC} = \mathcal{L} \times \wp(\mathcal{C})^2$, and $\forall c_1 = (L_1, C_1), c_2 = (L_2, C_2) : c_1 \geq c_2 \iff L_1 \geq L_2 \wedge C_1 \supseteq C_2$. Two classes c_1 and c_2 such that neither $c_1 \geq c_2$ nor $c_2 \geq c_1$ holds are said to be *incomparable*.

It is easy to see that the dominance relationship so defined on a set of access classes $\mathcal{AC}$ satisfies the following properties.

- *Reflexivity:* $\quad \forall x \in \mathcal{AC} : x \geq x$
- *Transitivity:* $\quad \forall x, y, z \in \mathcal{AC} : x \geq y, y \geq z \Longrightarrow x \geq z$
- *Antisymmetry:* $\quad \forall x, y \in \mathcal{AC} : x \geq y, y \geq x \Longrightarrow x = y$
- *Existence of a least upper bound:* $\quad \forall x, y \in \mathcal{AC} : \exists \, !z \in \mathcal{AC}$
    - $z \geq x$ and $z \geq y$
    - $\forall t \in \mathcal{AC} : t \geq x$ and $t \geq y \Longrightarrow t \geq z$.
- *Existence of a greatest lower bound:* $\quad \forall x, y \in \mathcal{AC} : \exists \, !z \in \mathcal{AC}$
    - $x \geq z$ and $y \geq z$
    - $\forall t \in \mathcal{AC} : x \geq t$ and $y \geq t \Longrightarrow z \geq t$.

Access classes defined as above together with the dominance relationship between them therefore form a lattice [31]. Figure 5 illustrates the security lattice obtained considering security levels TS and S, with TS>S and the set of categories {Nuclear,Army}.

The semantics and use of the classifications assigned to objects and subjects within the application of a multilevel mandatory policy is different depending on whether the classification is intended for a *secrecy* or an *integrity* policy. We next examine secrecy-based and integrity-based mandatory policies.

---

[2] $\wp(\mathcal{C})$ denotes the powerset of $\mathcal{C}$.

4.2   Secrecy-Based Mandatory Policies

A secrecy mandatory policy controls the direct and *indirect* flows of information to the purpose of preventing leakages to unauthorized subjects. Here, the semantics of the classification is as follows. The security level of the access class associated with an object reflects the sensitivity of the information contained in the object, that is, the potential damage that could result from the unauthorized disclosure of the information. The security level of the access class associated with a user, also called *clearance*, reflects the user's trustworthiness not to disclose sensitive information to users not cleared to see it. Categories define the area of competence of users and data and are used to provide finer grained security classifications of subjects and objects than classifications provided by security levels alone. They are the basis for enforcing *need-to-know* restrictions (i.e., confining subjects to access information they actually need to know to perform their job).

Users can connect to the system at any access class dominated by their clearance. A user connecting to the system at a given access class originates a subject at that access class. For instance, with reference to the lattice in Figure 5, a user cleared (TS, {Nuclear}) can connect to the system as a (S, {Nuclear}), (TS, ∅), or (TS, ∅) subject. Requests by a subject to access an object are controlled with respect to the access class of the subject and the object and granted only if some relationship, depending on the requested access, is satisfied. In particular, two principles, first formulated by Bell and LaPadula [12], must be satisfied to protect information confidentiality:

No-read-up A subject is allowed a read access to an object only if the access class of the subject dominates the access class of the object.

No-write-down A subject is allowed a write access to an object only if the access class of the subject is dominated by the access class of the object.

Satisfaction of these two principles prevents information to flow from high level subjects/objects to subjects/objects at lower (or incomparable) levels, thereby ensuring the satisfaction of the protection requirements (i.e., no process will be able to make sensitive information available to users not cleared for it). This is illustrated in Figure 6, where four accesses classes composed only of a security level (TS, S, C, and U) are taken as example. Note the importance of controlling both read and write operations, since both can be improperly used to leak information. Consider the example on the Trojan Horse illustrated in Section 3. Possible classifications reflecting the access restrictions to be enforced could be: Secret for Vicky and Market, and Unclassified for John and Stolen. In the respect of the no-read-up and no-write-down principles, the Trojan Horse will never be able to complete successfully. If Vicky connects to the system as a Secret (or Confidential) subject, and thus the application runs with a Secret (or Confidential) access class, the write operation will be blocked. If Vicky invokes the application as an Unclassified subject, the read operation will be blocked instead.

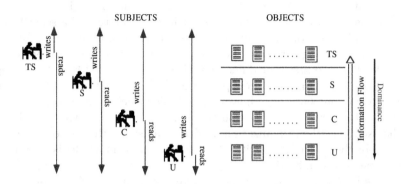

Fig. 6. Information flow for secrecy

Given the no-write-down principle, it is clear now why users are allowed to connect to the system at different access classes, so that they are able to access information at different levels (provided that they are cleared for it). For instance, Vicky has to connect to the system at a level below her clearance if she wants to write some Unclassified information, such as working instructions for John. Note that a lower class does not mean "less" privileges in absolute terms, but only less reading privileges (see Figure 6).

Although users can connect to the system at any level below their clearance, the strict application of the no-read-up and the no-write-down principles may result too rigid. Real world situations often require exceptions to the mandatory restrictions. For instance, data may need to be downgraded (e.g., data subject to embargoes that can be released after some time). Also, information released by a process may be less sensitive than the information the process has read. For instance, a procedure may access personal information regarding the employees of an organization and return the benefits to be granted to each employee. While the personal information can be considered Secret, the benefits can be considered Confidential. To respond to situations like these, multilevel systems should then allow for exceptions, loosening or waiving restrictions, in a controlled way, to processes that are *trusted* and ensure that information is *sanitized* (meaning the sensitivity of the original information is lost).

Note also that DAC and MAC policies are not mutually exclusive, but can be applied jointly. In this case, an access to be granted needs both *i)* the existence of the necessary authorization for it, and *ii)* to satisfy the mandatory policy. Intuitively, the discretionary policy operates *within the boundaries* of the mandatory policy: it can only restrict the set of accesses that would be allowed by MAC alone.

4.3   The Bell-LaPadula Model (Some History)

The secrecy based control principles just illustrated summarize the basic axioms of the security model proposed by David Bell and Leonard LaPadula [12]. Here, we illustrate some concepts of the model formalization to give an idea of the different aspects to be taken into account in the definition of a security model. This little bit of history is useful to understand the complications of formalizing a policy and making sure that the policy' axioms actually ensure protection as intended. We note first that different versions of the model have been proposed (due to the formalization of new properties [10,12,55], or related to specific application environments [11]), however the basic principles remain the same (and are those illustrated in the previous section). Also, here we will be looking only at the aspects of the formalization needed to illustrate the concepts we want to convey: for the sake of simplicity, the formulation of the model is simplified and some aspects are omitted.

In the Bell and LaPadula model a system is composed of a set of subjects S, objects O, and actions A, which includes read and write[3]. The model also assumes a lattice L of access classes and a function $\lambda : S \cup O \rightarrow L$ that, when applied to a subject (object, resp.) in a given state, returns the classification of the subject (object, resp.) in that state. A state $v \in V$ is defined as a triple (b, M, λ), where $b \in \wp(S \times O \times A)$ is the set of current accesses (s, o, a), M is the access matrix expressing discretionary permissions (as in the HRU model), and λ is the association of access classes with subjects and objects. A system consists of an initial state v_0, a set of requests R, and a state transition function $T : V \times R \rightarrow V$ that transforms a system state into another state resulting from the execution of a request. Intuitively, requests capture acquisition and release of accesses, granting and revocation of authorizations, as well as changes of levels. The model then defines a set of axioms stating properties that the system must satisfy and that express the constraints imposed by the mandatory policy. The first version of the Bell and LaPadula model stated the following criteria.

simple property A state v satisfies the simple security property iff for every
$s \in S$, $o \in O$: $(s, o, \mathtt{read}) \in b \Longrightarrow \lambda(s) \geq \lambda(o)$.
*-property A state v satisfies the *-security property iff for every $s \in S$, $o \in O$:
$(s, o, \mathtt{write}) \in b \Longrightarrow \lambda(o) \geq \lambda(s)$.

The two axioms above correspond to the no-read-up and no-write-down principles we have illustrated in Section 4.2. A state is then defined to be secure if it satisfies both the simple security property and the *-property. A system (v_0, R, T) is secure if and only if every state reachable from v_0 by executing one or more finite sequences of requests from R is *state secure*.

In the first formulation of their model, Bell and LaPadula provide a *Basic Security Theorem (BST)*, which states that a system is secure if *i)* its initial

---

[3] For uniformity of the discussion, we use the term "write" here to denote the "write-only" (or "append") action.

state v_0 is secure, and *ii)* the state transition T is security preserving, that is, it transforms a secure state into another secure state.

As noticed by McLean in his example called "System Z" [63], the BST theorem does not actually guarantee security. The problem lies in the fact that no restriction, but to be preserving of state security, is put on transitions. In his System Z example, McLean shows how failing to control transitions can compromise security. Consider a system Z whose initial state is secure and that has only one type of transition: when a subject requests any type of access to an object o, every subject and object in the system are downgraded to the lowest possible access class and the access is granted. System Z satisfies the Bell and LaPadula notion of security, but it is obviously not secure in any meaningful sense. The problem pointed out by System Z is that transitions need to be controlled. Accordingly, McLean proposes extending the model with a new function $C : S \cup O \rightarrow \wp(S)$, which returns the set of subjects allowed to change the level of its argument. A transition is secure if it allows changes to the level of a subject/object x only by subjects in $C(x)$; intuitively, these are subjects trusted for downgrading. A system (v_0, R, T) is *secure* if and only if *i)* v_0 is secure, *ii)* every state reachable from v_0 by executing a finite sequence of one or more requests from R is (BLP) secure, and *iii)* T *is transition secure*.

The problem with changing the security level of subjects and objects was not captured formally as an axiom or property in the Bell and LaPadula, but as an informal design guidance called *tranquility* principle. The tranquility principle states that the classification of active objects should not be changed during normal operation [55]. A subsequent revision of the model [10] introduced a distinction between the level assigned to a subject (*clearance*) and its current level (which could be any level dominated by the clearance), which also implied changing the formulation of the axioms, introducing more flexibility in the control.

Another property included in the Bell and LaPadula model is the *discretionary property* which constraints the set of current accesses b to be a subset of the access matrix M. Intuitively, it enforces discretionary controls.

4.4 Integrity-based Mandatory Policies: The Biba Model

The mandatory policy that we have discussed above protects only the confidentiality of the information; no control is enforced on its integrity. Low classified subjects could still be able to enforce improper indirect modifications to objects they cannot write. With reference to our organization example, for instance, integrity could be compromised if the Trojan Horse implanted by John in the application would write data in file Market (this operation would not be blocked by the secrecy policy). Starting from the principles of the Bell and LaPadula model, Biba [16] proposed a dual policy for safeguarding integrity, which controls the flow of information and prevents subjects to *indirectly* modify information they cannot write. Like for secrecy, each subject and object in the system is assigned an integrity classification. The classifications and the dominance relationship between them are defined as before. Example of integrity levels can be: Crucial (C), Important (I), and Unknown (U). The semantics of integrity

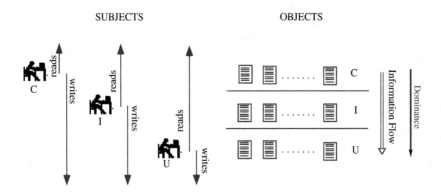

Fig. 7. Information flow for integrity

classifications is as follows. The integrity level associated with a user reflects the user's trustworthiness for inserting, modifying, or deleting information. The integrity level associated with an object reflects both the degree of trust that can be placed on the information stored in the object and the potential damage that could result from unauthorized modifications of the information. Again, categories define the area of competence of users and data. Access control is enforced according to the following two principles:

No-read-down A subject is allowed a read access to an object only if the access class of the object dominates the access class of the subject.

No-write-up A subject is allowed a write access to an object only if the access class of the subject is dominated by the access class of the object.

Satisfaction of these principles safeguard integrity by preventing information stored in low objects (and therefore less reliable) to flow to higher, or incomparable, objects. This is illustrated in Figure 7, where classes composed only of integrity levels (C,I, and U) are taken as example.

The two principles above are the dual of the two principles formulated by Bell and LaPadula. Biba's proposal also investigated alternative criteria for safeguarding integrity, allowing for more dynamic controls. These included the following two policies.

Low-water mark for subjects It constraints write operations according to the no-write-up principle. No restriction is imposed on read operations. However, a subject s that reads an object o has its classification downgraded to the greatest lower bound of the classification of the two, that is, $\lambda'(s) = \mathsf{glb}(\lambda(s), \lambda(o))$.

Low-water mark for objects It constraints read operations according to the no-read-down principle. No restriction is imposed on write operations. However, if a subject s writes an object o, the object has its classification downgraded to the greatest lower bound of the classification of the two, that is, $\lambda'(o) = \mathsf{glb}(\lambda(s), \lambda(o))$.

Intuitively, the two policies attempt to apply a more dynamic behavior in the enforcement of the constraints. The two approaches suffer however of drawbacks. In the low-water mark for subjects approach, the ability of a subject to execute a procedure may depend on the order with which operations are requested: a subject may be denied the execution of a procedure because of read operations executed before. The latter policy cannot actually be considered as safeguarding integrity: given that subjects are allowed to write above their level, integrity compromises can certainly occur; by downgrading the level of the object the policy simply signals this fact.

As it is visible from Figures 6 and 7, secrecy policies allow the flow of information only from lower to higher (secrecy) classes while integrity policies allow the flow of information only from higher to lower (integrity) classes. If both secrecy and integrity have to be controlled, objects and subjects have to be assigned two access classes, one for secrecy control and one for integrity control.

A major limitation of the policies proposed by Biba is that they only capture integrity compromises due to impoproper information flows. However, integrity is a much broader concept and additional aspects should be taken into account (see Section 6.5).

4.5   Applying Mandatory Policies to Databases

The first formulation of the multilevel mandatory policies, and the Bell LaPadula model, simply assumed the existence of objects (information container) to which a classification is assigned. This assumption works well in the operating system context, where objects to be protected are essentially files containing the data. Later studies investigated the extension of mandatory policies to database systems. While in operating systems access classes are assigned to files, database systems can afford a finer-grained classification. Classification can in fact be considered at the level of relations (equivalent to file-level classification in OS), at the level of columns (different properties can have a different classification), at the level of rows (properties referred to a given real world entity or association have the same classification), or at the level of single cells (each data element, meaning the value assigned to a property for a given entity or association, can have a different classification), this latter being the finest possible classification. Early efforts to classifying information in database systems, considered classification at the level of each single element [50,61]. Element-level classification is clearly appealing since it allows the assignment of a security class to each single real world fact that needs to be represented. For instance, an employee's name can be labeled Unclassified, while his salary can be labeled Secret; also the salary of different employees can take on different classifications. However, the support of fine-grained classifications together with the obvious constraint of maintaining secrecy in the system operation introduces complications. The major complication is represented by the so called *polyinstantiation* problem [49,60], which is

Name	λ_N	Dept	λ_D	Salary	λ_S
Bob	U	Dept1	U	100K	U
Jim	U	Dept1	U	100K	U
Ann	S	Dept2	S	200K	S
Sam	U	Dept1	U	150K	S

(a)

Name	λ_N	Dept	λ_D	Salary	λ_S
Bob	U	Dept1	U	100K	U
Jim	U	Dept1	U	100K	U
Sam	U	Dept1	U	–	U

(b)

Fig. 8. An example of multilevel relation (a) and the unclassified view on it (b)

probably one of the main reasons why multilevel databases did not have much success. Generally speaking, polyinstantiation is the presence in the system of multiple instances of the same real world fact or entity, where the instances differ for the access class associated with them.

To illustrate the problem, let us start giving the definition of multilevel relational database. A relational database is composed of a finite set of relations, each defined over a set of attributes $A_1, \ldots, A_n$ (columns of the relation). Each relation is composed of a set of tuples $t_1, \ldots, t_k$ (rows of the relation) mapping attributes to values over their domain. A subset of the attributes, called key attributes, are used to uniquely identify each tuple in the relation, and the following *key constraints* are imposed: *i)* no two tuples can have the same values for the key attributes, and *ii)* key attributes cannot be null. In a multilevel relational database supporting element-level labeling, an access class $\lambda(t[A])$ is associated with each element $t[A]$ in a relation. An example of multilevel relation is illustrated in Figure 8(a). Note that the classification associated with a value does not represent the absolute sensitivity of the value as such, but rather the sensitivity of the fact that the attribute takes on that value for a specific entity in the real world. For instance, classification Secret associated with value 150K of the last tuple is not the classification of value 150K by itself, but of the fact that it is the salary of Sam.[4]

Access control in multilevel DBMSs applies the two basic principles discussed in Section 4.2, although the no-write-up restriction is usually reduced to the principle of "write at their own level". In fact, while write-up operations can make sense in operating systems, where a file is seen as an information container and subjects may need to append low-level data in a high-level container, element-level classification nullifies this reasoning.

Subjects at different levels have different views on a relation, which is the view composed only of elements they are cleared to see (i.e., whose classification they dominate). For instance, the view of an Unclassified subject on the multilevel relation in Figure 8(a) is the table in Figure 8(b). Note that, in principle, to not convey information, the Unclassified subject should see no difference between values that are actually null in the database and those that are null since they

---

[4] Note that this is not meant to say that the classification of an element is independent of its value. As a matter of fact it can depend on the value; for instance a classification rule may state that all salaries above 100K must be classified as Secret [30].

Name	λ_N	Dept	λ_D	Salary	λ_S
Bob	U	Dept1	U	100K	U
Jim	U	Dept1	U	100K	U
Ann	S	Dept2	S	200K	S
Sam	U	Dept1	U	150K	S
Ann	U	Dept1	U	100K	U
Sam	U	Dept1	U	100K	U

Name	λ_N	Dept	λ_D	Salary	λ_S
Bob	U	Dept1	U	100K	U
Jim	U	Dept1	U	100K	U
Ann	U	Dept1	U	100K	U
Sam	U	Dept1	U	100K	U

(a)   (b)

Fig. 9. An example of a relation with polyinstantiation (a) and the unclassified view on it (b)

have a higher classification.[5] To produce a view consistent with the relational database constraints the classification needs to satisfy at least the following two basic constraints: *i)* the key attributes must be uniformly classified, and *ii)* the classifications of nonkey attributes must dominate that of key attributes. If it were not so, the view at some levels would contain a null value for some or all key attributes (and therefore would not satisfy the key constraints).

To see how polyinstantiation can arise, suppose that an Unclassified subject, whose view on the table in Figure 8(a) is as illustrated in Figure 8(b), requests insertion of tuple ⟨Ann, Dept1, 100K⟩. According to the key constraints imposed by the relational model, no two tuples can have the same value for the key attributes. Therefore if classifications were not taken into account, the insertion could have not been accepted. The database could have two alternative choices: *i)* tell the subject that a tuple with the same key already exists, or *ii)* replace the old tuple with the new one. The first solution introduces a *covert channel*[6], since by rejecting the request the system would be revealing protected information (meaning the existence of a Secret entity named Ann), and clearly compromises secrecy. On the other hand, the second solution compromises integrity, since high classified data would be lost, being overridden by the newly inserted tuple. Both solutions are therefore inapplicable. The only remaining solution would then be to accept the insertion and manage the presence of both tuples (see Figure 9(a)). Two tuples would then exist with the same value, but different classification, for their key (*polyinstantiated tuples*). A similar situation happens if the unclassified subject requests to update the salary of Sam to value 100K. Again, telling the subject that a value already exists would compromise secrecy (if the subject is not suppose to distinguish between real nulls and values for which it does not have sufficient clearance), while overwriting the existing Secret value would compromise integrity (as the Secret salary would be lost).

---

[5] Some proposals do not adopt this assumption. For instance, in LDV [43], a special value "restricted" appears in a subject's view to denote the existence of values not visible to the subject.

[6] We will talk more about covert channels in Section 4.6.

Name	λ_N	Dept	λ_D	Salary	λ_S
Bob	U	Dept1	U	100K	U
Jim	U	Dept1	U	100K	U
Ann	S	Dept2	S	200K	S
Sam	U	Dept1	U	150K	S
Bob	S	Dept2	S	200K	S
Jim	U	Dept1	U	150K	S

Name	λ_N	Dept	λ_D	Salary	λ_S
Bob	U	Dept1	U	100K	U
Jim	U	Dept1	U	100K	U
Sam	U	Dept1	U	–	U

(a)   (b)

Fig. 10. An example of a relation with polyinstantiation (a) and the unclassified view on it (b)

The only remaining solution would therefore seem to be to accept the insertion (Figure 9(a)), implying then the existence of two tuples with the same value and classification for their key, but with different value and classification for one of their attributes (*polyinstantiated elements*). Note that, when producing the view visible to a subject in the presence of polyinstantiation, the DBMS must completely hide those tuples with high polyinstiated values that the subject cannot see. For instance, an unclassified subject querying the relation in Figure 9(a) will see only one tuple for Ann and Sam (see Figure 9(b)).

Polyinstantiation can also occur because of requests by high level subjects. For instance, consider again the relation in Figure 8(a) and assume a Secret subject requests to insert tuple (Bob, Dept2, 200K). A tuple with key Bob already exists at level Unclassified. If key uniqueness is to be preserved, the system can either *i)* inform the subject of the conflict and refuse the insertion, or *ii)* overwrite the existing tuple. Again, the solution of refusing insertion is not advisable: although it would not leak protected information, it introduces *denials-of-service*, since high level subjects would not be allowed to insert data. The second solution also is not viable since it would introduce a covert channel due to the effect that the overwriting would have on the view of lower level subjects (which would see the Unclassified tuple disappear). Again, the only possible solution seems to be to accept the insertion and have the two (polyinstantiated) tuples coexist (see Figure 10(a)). A similar problem would arise at the attribute level, for update operations. For instance, if a secret subject requires updating Jim's salary to 150K, polyinstantiated elements would be introduced (see Figure 10(a)).

Earlier work in multilevel database systems accepted polyinstantiation as an inevitable consequence of fine-grained classification and attempted to clarify the semantics of the database states in the presence of polyinstantiation [50,61]. For instance, the presence of two tuples with the same value, but different classification, for the primary key (tuple polyinstantiation) can be interpreted as the existence of *two different entities* of the real world (one of which is known only at a higher level). The presence of two tuples with the same key and same key classification but that differ for the value and classification of some of its attributes can be interpreted as a *single* real world entity for which different values are recorded (corresponding to the different beliefs at different levels). However, unfortunately, polyinstantiation quickly goes out of hand, and the execution of few operations could result in a database whose semantics does not appear clear anymore. Subsequent work tried to establish constraints to maintain semantic integrity of the database status [69,75,90]. However, probably because of all the complications and semantics confusion that polyinstantiation bears, fine-grained multilevel databases did not have much success, and current DBMSs do not support element-level classification. Commercial systems (e.g., Trusted Oracle [66] and SYBASE Secure SQL Server) support tuple level classification.

It is worth noticing that, although polyinstantiation is often blamed to be the reason why multilevel relational databases did not have success, polyinstantiation is not necessarily always bad. Controlled polyinstantiation may, for example, be useful to support *cover stories* [38,49], meaning non-true data whose presence in the database is meant to hide the existence of the actual value. Cover stories are useful when the fact that a given data is not released is by itself a cause of information leakage. For instance, suppose that a subject requires access to a hospital's data and the hospital returns, for all its patients, but for few of them, the illness for which they are being cured. Suppose also that HIV never appears as an illness value. Observing this, the recipient may infer that it is probably the case that the patients for which illness is not disclosed suffer from HIV. The hospital could have avoided exposure to such an inference by simply releasing a non-true alternative value (*cover story*) for these patients. Intuitively, cover stories are "lies" that the DBMS says to uncleared subjects not to disclose (directly or indirectly) the actual values to be protected. We do note that, while cover stories are useful for protection, they have raise objections for the possible integrity compromises which they may indirectly cause, as low level subjects can base their actions on cover stories they believe true.

A complicating aspects in the support of a mandatory policy at a fine-grained level is that the definition of the access class to be associated with each piece of data is not always easy [30]. This is the case, for example, of *association* and *aggregation* requirements, where the classification of a set of values (properties, resp.) is higher than the classification of each of the values singularly taken. As an example, while names and salaries in an organization may be considered Unclassified, the association of a specific salary with an employee's name can be considered Secret (association constraint). Similarly, while the location of a single military ship can be Unclassified, the location of all the ships of a fleet can be Secret (aggregation constraint), as by knowing it one could infer that some operations are being planned. Proper data classification assignment is also complicated by the need to take into account possible inference channels [30,47,59]. There is an inference channel between a set of data x and a set of data y if, by knowing x a user can infer some information on y (e.g., an inference channel can exist between an employee's taxes and her salary). Inference-aware classification requires that no information x be classified at a level lower (or incomparable) than the level of the information y that can be inferred from it. Capturing and

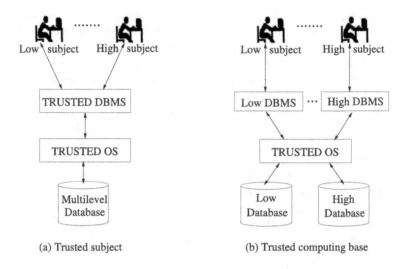

(a) Trusted subject   (b) Trusted computing base

Fig. 11. Multilevel DBMSs architectures

blocking all inference channels is a complex process, also because of the intrinsic difficulty of detecting all the semantics relationships between the data that can cause inference channels.

An interesting point that must be taken into account in multilevel database systems is the system architecture, which is concerned with the need of confining subjects accessing a multilevel database to the data that can be made visible to them. This problem comes out in any data system where classification has a finer granularity than the stored objects (e.g., multilevel object-oriented systems). Two possible approaches are [68]:

- *Trusted subject:* data at different levels are stored in a single database (Figure 11(a)). The DBMS itself must be *trusted* to ensure obedience of the mandatory policy (i.e., subjects will not gain access to data whose classification they do not dominate).
- *Trusted computing base:* data are partitioned in different databases, one for each level (Figure 11(b)). In this case only the operating system needs to be trusted since every DBMS will be confined to data which subjects using that DBMS can access. Decomposition and recovery algorithms must be carefully constructed to be correct and efficient [33].

4.6   Limitations of Mandatory Policies

Although mandatory policies, unlike discretionary ones, provide protection against indirect information leakages they do not guarantee complete secrecy of the information. In fact, secrecy mandatory policies (even with tranquility) control only *overt* channels of information (i.e., flow through *legitimate* channels);

they still remain vulnerable to *covert channels*. Covert channels are channels that are not intended for normal communication, but still can be exploited to infer information. For instance, consider the request of a low level subject to write a non-existent high level file (the operation is legitimate since write-up operations are allowed). Now, if the system returns the error, it exposes itself to improper leakages due to malicious high level processes creating and destroying the high level file to signal information to low processes. However, if the low process is not informed of the error, or the system automatically creates the file, subjects may not be signalled possible errors made in legitimate attempts to write. As another example, consider a low level subject that requires a resource (e.g., CPU or lock) that is busy by a high level subject. The system, by not allocating the resource because it is busy, can again be exploited to signal information at lower levels (high level processes can module the signal by requiring or releasing resources). If a low process can see any different result due to a high process operation, there is a channel between them. Channels may also be enacted without modifying the system's response to processes. This is, for example, the case of *timing channels*, that can be enacted when it is possible for a high process to affect the system's response time to a low process. With timing channels the response that the low process receives is always the same, it is the time at which the low process receives the response that communicates information. Therefore, in principle, any *common resource or observable property* of the system state can be used to leak information. Consideration of covert channels requires particular care in the design of the enforcement mechanism. For instance, locking and concurrency mechanisms must be revised and be properly designed [7]. A complication in their design is that care must be taken to avoid the policy for blocking covert channels to introduce denials-of-service. For instance, a trivial solution to avoid covert channels between high and low level processes competing over common resources could be to always give priority to low level processes (possibly terminating high level processes). This approach, however, exposes the systems to denials-of-service attacks whereby low level processes can impede high level (and therefore, presumably, more important) processes to complete their activity.

Covert channels are difficult to control also because of the difficulty of mapping an access control model's primitive to a computer system [64]. For this reason, covert channels analysis is usually carried out in the implementation phase, to make sure that the implementation of the model's primitive is not too weak. Covert channel analysis can be based on tracing the information flows in programs [31], checking programs for shared resources that can be used to transfer information [52], or checking the system clock for timing channels [92]. Beside the complexity, the limitation of such solutions is that covert channels are found out at the end of the development process, where system changes are much more expensive to correct. Interface models have been proposed which attempt to rule out covert channels analysis in the modeling phase [64,37]. Rather than specifying a particular method to enforce security, interface models specify restrictions on a system's input/output that must be obeyed to avoid covert channels. It is then task of the implementor to determine a method for satisfying the specifications. A well known principle which formed the basis of interface models is the *non-interference* principle proposed by Goguen and Meseguer [40]. Intuitively, non-interference requires that high-level input cannot interfere with low-level output. Non-interference constraints enhance the security properties that can be formalized and proved in the model; it is however important to note that security models do not establish complete security of the system, they merely establish security with respect to a model, they can prove only properties that have been captured into the model.

5   Enriching DAC with Mandatory Restrictions

As we have discussed in the previous section, mandatory policies guarantee better security than discretionary policies, since they can also control indirect information flows. However, their application may result too rigid. Several proposals have attempted a combination of mandatory flow control and discretionary authorizations. We illustrate some of them in this section.

5.1   The Chinese Wall Policy

The Chinese Wall [22] policy was introduced as an attempt to balance commercial discretion with mandatory controls. The goal is to prevent information flows which cause conflict of interest for individual consultants (e.g., an individual consultant should not have information about two banks or two oil companies). However, unlike in the Bell and LaPadula model, access to data is not constrained by the data classifications but by what data the subjects have already accessed. The model is based on a hierarchical organization of data objects as follows:

- *basic objects* are individual items of information (e.g., files), each concerning a single corporation;
- *company datasets* define groups of objects that refer to a same corporation;
- *conflict of interest classes* define company datasets that refer to competing corporations.

Figure 12 illustrates an example of data organization where nine objects of four different corporations, namely A,B,C, and D, are maintained. Correspondingly four company datasets are defined. The two conflict of interest classes depicted define the conflicts between A and B, and between C and D.

Given the object organization as above, the Chinese Wall policy restricts access according to the following two properties [22]:

Simple security rule A subject s can be granted access to an object o only if the object o:
- is in the same company datasets as the objects already accessed by s, that is, "within the Wall", or

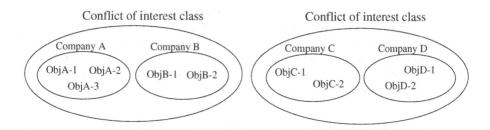

Fig. 12. An example of object organization

- belongs to an entirely different conflict of interest class.

*-property Write access is only permitted if
- access is permitted by the simple security rule, and
- no object can be read which *i)* is in a different company dataset than the one for which write access is requested, and *ii)* contains unsanitized information.

The term subject used in the properties is to be interpreted as user (meaning access restrictions are referred to users). The reason for this is that, unlike mandatory policies that control processes, the Chinese Wall policy controls users. It would therefore not make sense to enforce restrictions on processes as a user could be able to acquire information about organizations that are in conflict of interest simply running two different processes.

Intuitively, the simple security rule blocks direct information leakages that can be attempted by a single user, while the *-property blocks indirect information leakages that can occur with the collusion of two or more users. For instance, with reference to Figure 12, an indirect improper flow could happen if, *i)* a user reads information from object ObjA-1 and writes it into ObjC-1, and subsequently *ii)* a different user reads information from ObjC-1 and writes it into ObjB-1.

Clearly, the application of the Chinese Wall policy still has some limitations. In particular, strict enforcement of the properties may result too rigid and, like for the mandatory policy, there will be the need for exceptions and support of sanitization (which is mentioned, but not investigated, in [22]). Also, the enforcement of the policies requires keeping and querying the history of the accesses. A further point to take into consideration is to ensure that the enforcement of the properties will not block the system working. For instance, if in a system composed of ten users there are eleven company datasets in a conflict of interest class, then one dataset will remain inaccessible. This aspect was noticed in [22], where the authors point out that there must be at least as many users as the maximum number of datasets which appear together in a conflict of interest class. However, while this condition makes the system operation possible, it cannot ensure it when users are left completely free choice on the datasets they access. For instance, in a system with ten users and ten datasets, again one dataset may remain inaccessible if two users access the same dataset.

Although the model does have some limitations and drawbacks, the Chinese Wall policy represents a good example of *dynamic separation of duty* constraints present in the real world, and has been taken as a reference in the development of several subsequent policies and models (see Section 7).

5.2   Authorization-Based Information Flow Policies

Other proposals that tried to overcome the vulnerability of discretionary policies have worked on complementing authorization control with information flow restrictions, interpreting the mandatory and information flow policies [31,55] in a discretionary context.

The work in [19,51] proposes interposing, between programs and the actual file system, a protected system imposing further restrictions. In particular, Boebert and Ferguson [19] forces all files to go through a dynamic linker that compares the name of the user who invoked the program, the name of the originator of the program, and the name of the owner of any data files. If a user invokes a program owned by someone else and the program attempts to write the user's files, the dynamic linker will recognize the name mismatch and raise an alarm. Karger [51] proposes instead the specification of name restrictions on the files that programs can access, and the refusal by the system of all access requests not satisfying the given patterns (e.g., a FORTRAN compiler may be restricted to read only files with suffix ".for" and to create only files with suffix ".obj" and ".lis").

McCollum et al. [62] point out data protection requirements that neither the discretionary nor the mandatory policies can effectively handle. They propose a dissemination control system that maintains access control over one's data by attaching to the data object an access control list (imposing access restrictions) that propagates, through subject and object labels, to all objects into which its content may flow. Examples of restrictions can be: NOCONTRACT (meaning no access to contractors) or NOFORN (no releasable to foreign nationals). By propagating restrictions and enforcing the control, intuitively, the approach behaves like a dynamic mandatory policy; however, explicit restrictions in the access list give more flexibility than mandatory security labels. The model also provides support for exceptions (the originator of an ACL can allow restrictions to be waived) and downgrading (trusted subjects can remove restrictions imposed on objects).

A similar approach appears in [85], which, intuitively, interprets the information flow model of Denning [31] in the discretionary context. In [85] each object has two protection attributes: the *current access* and the *potential access*. The current access attribute describes what operations each user can apply on the object (like traditional ACLs). It is a subset of the potential access attribute. The potential access attribute describes what operations which users can potentially apply to the information contained in that object, information that, in the future, may be contained in any object and may be of any type. The potential access attributes therefore control information flow. When a new value of some object y is produced as a function of objects in $x_1, \ldots, x_n$, then the potential access attribute of y is set to be the intersection of the potential access attributes of $x_1, \ldots, x_n$.

Walter et al. [87] propose an interpretation of the mandatory controls within the discretionary context. Intuitively, the policy behind this approach, which we call *strict* policy, is based on the same principles as the mandatory policy. Access control lists are used in place of labels, and the inclusion relationship between sets is used in place of the dominance relationship between labels. Information flow restrictions impose that a process can write an object o only if o is protected in reading at least as all the objects read by the process up to that point. (An object o is at least as protected in reading as another object o' if the set of subjects allowed to read o is contained in the set of subjects allowed to read o'.) Although the discretionary flexibility of specifying accesses is not lost, the overall flexibility is definitely reduced by the application of the strict policy. After having read an object o, a process is completely unable to write any object less protected in reading than o, even if the write operation would not result in any improper information leakage.

Bertino et al. [14] present an enhancement of the strict policy to introduce more flexibility in the policy enforcement. The proposal bases on the observation that whether or not some information can be released also depends on the procedure enacting the release. A process may access sensitive data and yet not release any sensitive information. Such a process should be allowed to bypass the restrictions of the strict policy, thus representing an *exception*. On the other side, the information produced by a process may be more sensitive than the information the process has read. An exception should in this case restrict the write actions otherwise allowed by the strict policy. Starting from these observations, Bertino et al. [14] allow procedures to be granted exceptions to the strict policy. The proposal is developed in the context of object-oriented systems, where the modularity provided by methods associated with objects allows users to identify specific pieces of *trusted* code for which exceptions can be allowed, and therefore provide flexibility in the application of the control. Exceptions can be positive or negative. A positive exception overrides a restriction imposed by the strict policy, permitting an information flow which would otherwise be blocked. A negative exception overrides a permission stated by the strict policy forbidding an information flow which would otherwise be allowed. Two kinds of exceptions are supported by the model: *reply-exceptions* and *invoke-exceptions*. Reply exceptions apply to the information returned by a method. Intuitively, positive reply exceptions apply when the information returned by a method is less sensitive than the information the method has read. Reply exceptions can waive the strict policy restrictions and allow information returned by a method to be disclosed to users not authorized to read the objects that the method has read. Invoke exceptions apply during a method's execution, for write operations that the method requests. Intuitively, positive invoke exceptions apply to methods that are trusted not to leak (through write operations or method invocations) the information they have acquired. The mechanism enforcing the control is based on the notion of *message filter* first introduced by Jajodia and Kogan [46] for the enforcement of mandatory policies in object-oriented systems. The *message filter* is a trusted system component that acts as a reference monitor, intercepting every message exchanged among the objects in a transaction execution to guarantee that no unsafe flow takes place. To check whether a write or create operation should be blocked, the message filter in [14] keeps track of the information transmitted between executions and of the users who are allowed to know (read) it. A write operation on object *o* is allowed if, based on the ACLs of the objects read and on the exceptions encountered, the information can be released to all users who have read privileges on *o*.

6 Discretionary Access Control Policies

In Section 2 we introduced the basic concepts of the discretionary policy by illustrating the access matrix (or HRU) model. Although the access matrix still remains a framework for reasoning about accesses permitted by a discretionary policy, discretionary policies have developed considerably since the access matrix was proposed.

6.1 Expanding Authorizations

Even early approaches to authorization specifications allowed *conditions* to be associated with authorizations to restrict their validity. Conditions can make the authorization validity dependent on the satisfaction of some system predicates (*system-dependent* conditions) like the time or location of access. For instance, a condition can be associated with the bank-clerks' authorization to access accounts, restricting its application only from machines within the bank building and in working hours. Conditions can also constraint access depending on the content of objects on which the authorization is defined (*content-dependent* conditions). Content-dependent conditions can be used simply as way to determine whether or not an access to the object should be granted or as way to restrict the portion of the object that can be accessed (e.g., a subset of the tuples in a relation). This latter option is useful when the authorization object has a coarser granularity than the one supported by the data model [29]. Other possible conditions that can be enforced can make an access decision depend on accesses previously executed (*history dependent* conditions).

Another feature usually supported even by early approaches is the concept of *user groups* (e.g., Employees, Programmers, Consultants). Groups can be nested and need not be disjoint. Figure 13 illustrates an example of user-group hierarchy. Support of groups greatly simplifies management of authorizations, since a single authorization granted to a group can be enjoyed by all its members. Later efforts moved to the support of groups on all the elements of the authorization triple (i.e., subject, object, and action), where, typically, groups are abstractions hierarchically organized. For instance, in an operating system the hierarchy can

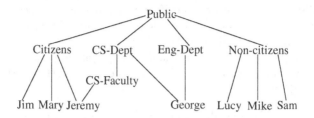

Fig. 13. An example of user-group hierarchy

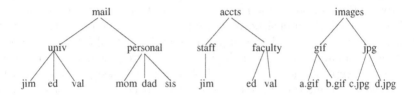

Fig. 14. An example of object hierarchy

reflect the logical file system tree structure, while in object-oriented system it can reflect the class (is-a) hierarchy. Figure 14 illustrates an example of object hierarchy. Even actions can be organized hierarchically, where the hierarchy may reflect an implication of privileges (e.g., write is more powerful than read [70]) or a grouping of sets of privileges (e.g., a "writing privileges" group can be defined containing write, append, and undo [84]). These hierarchical relationships can be exploited *i)* to support preconditions on accesses (e.g., in Unix a subject needs the execute, x, privilege on a directory in order to access the files within it), or *ii)* to support authorization implication, that is, authorizations specified on an abstraction apply to all its members. Support of abstractions with implications provides a short hand way to specify authorizations, clearly simplifying authorization management. As a matter of fact, in most situations the ability to execute privileges depends on the membership of users into groups or objects into collections: translating these requirements into basic triples of the form (user,object,action) that then have to be singularly managed is a considerable administrative burden, and makes it difficult to maintain both satisfactory security and administrative efficiency. However, although there are cases where abstractions can work just fine, many will be the cases where exceptions (i.e., authorizations applicable to all members of a group but few) will need to be supported. This observation has brought to the combined support of both *positive* and *negative* authorizations. Traditionally, positive and negative authorizations have been used in mutual exclusion corresponding to two classical approaches to access control, namely:

Closed policy: authorizations specify permissions for an access (like in the HRU model). The closed policy allows an access if there exists a positive authorization for it, and denies it otherwise.

Open policy: (negative) authorizations specify denials for an access. The open policy denies an access if there exists a negative authorization for it, and allows it otherwise.

The open policy has usually found application only in those scenarios where the need for protection is not strong and by default access is to be granted. Most systems adopt the closed policy, which, denying access by default, ensures better protection; cases where information is public by default are enforced with a positive authorization on the root of the subject hierarchy (e.g., Public).

The combined use of positive and negative authorizations was therefore considered as a way to conveniently support exceptions. To illustrate, suppose we wish to grant an authorization to all members of a group composed of one thousand users, except to one specific member Bob. In a closed policy approach, we would have to express the above requirement by specifying a positive authorization for each member of the group except Bob.[7] However, if we combine positive and negative authorizations we can specify the same requirement by granting a positive authorization to the group and a negative authorization to Bob.

The combined use of positive and negative authorizations brings now to the problem of how the two specifications should be treated:

- what if for an access no authorization is specified? (*incompleteness*)
- what if for an access there are both a negative and a positive authorization? (*inconsistency*)

Completeness can be easily achieved by assuming that one of either the open or closed policy operates as a *default*, and accordingly access is granted or denied if no authorization is found for it. Note that the alternative of explicitly requiring completeness of the authorizations is too heavy and complicates administration.

Conflict resolution is a more complex matter and does not usually have a unique answer [48,58]. Rather, different decision criteria could be adopted, each applicable in specific situations, corresponding to different policies that can be implemented. A natural and straightforward policy is the one stating that "the most specific authorization should be the one that prevails"; after all this is what we had in mind when we introduced negative authorizations in the first place (our example about Bob). Although the most-specific-takes-precedence principle is intuitive and natural and likely to fit in many situations, it is not enough. As a matter of fact, even if we adopt the argument that the most specific authorization always wins (and this may not always be the case) it is not always clear what more specific is:

- what if two authorizations are specified on non-disjoint, but non-hierarchically related groups (e.g., Citizens and CS-Dept in Figure 13)?

---

[7] In an open policy scenario, the dual example of all users, but a few, who have to be denied an access can be considered.

− what if for two authorizations the most specific relationship appear reversed over different domains? For instance, consider authorizations (CS-Faculty, read+, mail) and (CS-Dept, read−, personal); the first has a more specific subject, while the second has a more specific object (see Figures 13 and 14).

A slightly alternative policy on the same line as the most specific policy is what in [48] is called *most-specific-along-a-path-takes-precedence*. This policy considers an authorization specified on an element x as overriding an authorization specified on a more general element y only for those elements that are members of y because of x. Intuitively, this policy takes into account the fact that, even in the presence of a more specific authorization, the more general authorization can still be applicable because of other paths in the hierarchy. For instance, consider the group hierarchy in Figure 13 and suppose that for an access a positive authorization is granted to Public while a negative authorization is granted to CS-Dept. What should we decide for George? On the one side, it is true that CS-Dept is more specific than Public; on the other side, however, George belongs to Eng-Dept, and for Eng-Dept members the positive authorization is not overridden. While the most-specific-takes-precedence policy would consider the authorization granted to Public as being overridden for George, the most-specific-along-a-path considers both authorizations as applicable to George. Intuitively, in the most-specific-along-a-path policy, an authorization propagates down the hierarchy until overridden by a more specific authorization [35].

The most specific argument does not always apply. For instance, an organization may want to be able to state that consultants should not be given access to private projects, *no exceptions allowed*. However, if the most specific policy is applied, any authorization explicitly granted to a single consultant will override the denial specified by the organization. To address situations like this, some approaches proposed adopting *explicit priorities*. In ORION [70], authorizations are classified as *strong* or *weak*: weak authorizations override each other based on the most-specific policy, and strong authorizations override weak authorizations (no matter their specificity) and *cannot be overridden*. Given that strong authorizations must be certainly obeyed, they are required to be consistent. However, this requirement may be not always be enforceable. This is, for example, the case where groupings are not explicitly defined but depend on the evaluation of some conditions (e.g., "all objects owned by Tom", "all objects created before 1/1/01"). Also, while the distinction between strong and weak authorizations is convenient in many situations and, for example, allows us to express the organizational requirement just mentioned, it is limited to two levels of priority, which may not be enough. Many other conflict resolution policies can be applied. Some approaches, extending the strong and weak paradigm, proposed adopting *explicit priorities*; however, these solutions do not appear viable as the authorization specifications may result not always clear. Other approaches (e.g., [84]) proposed making authorization priority dependent on the *order in which authorizations are listed* (i.e., the authorizations that is encountered first applies). This approach, however, has the drawback that granting or removing an au-

- *Denials-take-precedence:* negative authorizations take precedence (satisfies the "fail safe principle")
- *Most-specific-takes-precedence* the authorization that is "more specific" w.r.t. a partial order (i.e., hierarchy) wins
- *Most-specific-along-a-path-takes-precedence:* the authorization that is "more specific" wins only on the paths passing through it. Intuitively, an authorization propagates down a hierarchy until overridden by a more specific authorization.
- *Strong/weak:* authorizations are classified as strong or weak: weak authorizations override each other based on the most-specific policy, and strong authorizations override weak authorizations (no matter their specificity). Strong authorizations are therefore required to be consistent.
- *Priority level:* each authorization is associated with a priority level, the authorization with the highest priority wins.
- *Positional:* the priority of the authorizations depends on the order in which they appear in the authorization list.
- *Grantor-dependent:* the priority of the authorizations depends on who granted them.
- *Time-dependent* the priority of the authorizations depends on the time at they have been granted (e.g., more recent wins)

Fig. 15. Examples of conflict resolution policies

thorization requires inserting the authorization in the proper place in the list. Beside the administrative burden put on the administrator (who, essentially, has to explicitly solve the conflicts when deciding the order), specifying authorizations implies explicitly writing the ACL associated with the object, and may impede delegation of administrative privileges. Other possible ways of defining priorities, and therefore solving conflicts, can make the authorization's priority dependent on the *time* at which the authorizations was granted (e.g., more recent authorizations prevails) or on priorities between the *grantors*. For instance, authorizations specified by an employee may be overridden by those specified by his supervisor; the authorizations specified by an object's owner may override those specified by other users to whom the owner has delegated administrative authority.

As it is clear from this discussion, different approaches can be taken to deal with positive and negative authorizations. Also, if it is true that some solutions may appear more natural than others, none of them represents "the perfect solution". Whichever approach we take, we will always find one situation for which it does not fit. Also, note that different conflict resolution policies are not mutually exclusive. For instance, one can decide to try solving conflicts with the most-specific-takes-precedence policy first, and apply the denials-take-precedence principle on the remaining conflicts (i.e., conflicting authorizations that are not hierarchically related).

The support of negative authorizations does not come for free, and there is a price to pay in terms of authorization management and less clarity of the specifications. However, the complications brought by negative authorizations are not due to negative authorizations themselves, but to the different semantics that the presence of permissions and denials can have, that is, to the complexity of the different real world scenarios and requirements that may need to be captured. There is therefore a trade-off between expressiveness and simplicity. For this reason, most current systems adopting negative authorizations for exception support impose specific conflict resolution policies, or support a limited form of conflict resolution. For instance, in the Apache server [6], authorizations can be positive and negative and an ordering ("deny,allow" or "allow,deny") can be specified dictating how negative and positive authorizations are to be interpreted. In the "deny,allow" order, negative authorizations are evaluated first and access is allowed by default (open policy). Any client that does not match a negative authorization or matches a positive authorization is allowed access. In the "allow,deny" order, the positive authorizations are evaluated first and access is denied by default (closed policy). Any client that does not match a positive authorization *or* does match a negative authorization will be denied access.

More recent approaches are moving towards the development of flexible frameworks with the support of multiple conflict resolution and decision policies. We will examine them in Section 8.

Other advancements in authorization specification and enforcement have been carried out with reference to specific applications and data models. For instance, authorization models proposed for object-oriented systems (e.g., [2,35,71]) exploit the *encapsulation* concept, meaning the fact that access to objects is always carried out through methods (read and write operations being primitive methods). In particular, users granted authorizations to invoke methods can be given the ability to successfully complete them, without need to have the authorizations for all the accesses that the method execution entails. For instance, in OSQL, each derived function (i.e., method) can be specified as supporting *static* or *dynamic* authorizations [2]. A dynamic authorization allows the user to invoke the function, but its successful completion requires the user to have the authorization for all the calls the function makes during its execution. With a *static* authorization, calls made by the function are checked against the creator of the function, instead of those of the calling user. Intuitively, static authorizations behave like the setuid (set user id) option, provided by the Unix operating system that, attached to a program (e.g., lpr) implies that all access control checks are to be performed against the authorizations of the program's owner (instead of those of the caller as it would otherwise be). A similar feature is also proposed in [71], where each method is associated with a principal, and accesses requested during a method execution are checked against the authorization of the method's principal. Encapsulation is also exploited by the Java 2 security model [83] where authorizations can be granted to code, and requests to access resources are checked against the authorizations of the code directly attempting the access.

6.2 Temporal Authorizations

Bertino et al. [13] propose extending authorizations with temporal constraints and extending authorization implication with time-based reasoning. Authorizations have associated a validity specified by a temporal expression identifying the instants in which the authorization applies. The temporal expression is formed by a *periodic expression* (e.g., 9 a.m. to 1 p.m. on Working-days, identifying the periods from 9a.m. to 1p.m. in all days excluding weekends and vacations), and a *temporal interval* bounding the scope of the periodic expression (e.g., [2/1997,8/1997], restricting the specified periods to those between February and August 1997). The model allows also the specification of derivation rules, expressing temporal dependencies among authorizations, that allow the derivation of new authorizations based on the presence or absence of other authorizations in specific periods of time. For instance, it is possible to specify that two users, working on the same project, must receive the same authorizations on given objects, or that a user should receive the authorization to access an object in certain periods, only if nobody else was ever authorized to access the same object in any instant within those periods. Like authorizations, derivation rules are associated with a temporal expression identifying the instants in which the rule applies. A derivation rule is a triple ($[t_b, t_e]$, P, A $\langle$OP$\rangle$ $\mathcal{A}$), where interval $[t_b, t_e]$ and period P represent the temporal expression, A is the authorization to be derived, $\mathcal{A}$ a is boolean formula of authorizations on which derivation is based, and OP is one of the following operators: WHENEVER, ASLONGAS, UPON. The three operators correspond to different temporal relationships between authorizations on which derivation can work, and have the following semantics:

- WHENEVER derives A for each instant in ($[t_b, t_e]$,P) for which $\mathcal{A}$ is valid.
- ASLONGAS derives A for each instant in ($[t_b, t_e]$,P) such that $\mathcal{A}$ has been "continuously" valid in ($[t_b, t_e]$,P).
- UPON derives A from the first instant in ($[t_b, t_e]$,P) for which $\mathcal{A}$ is valid up to t_e.

A graphical representation of the semantics of the different temporal operators is given in Figure 16. Intuitively, WHENEVER captures the usual implication of authorizations. For instance, a rule can state that summer-staff can read a document for every instance (i.e., WHENEVER) in the summer of year 2000 in which regular-staff can read it. ASLONGAS works in a similar way but stops the derivation at the first instant in which the boolean formula on which derivation works is not satisfied. For instance, a rule can state that regular-staff can read a document every working day in year 2000 until the first working day in which (i.e., ASLONGAS) summer-staff is allowed for that. Finally, UPON works like a trigger. For instance, a rule can state that Ann can read pay-checks each working day starting from the first working day in year 2000 in which (i.e., UPON) Tom can write pay-checks.

The enforcement mechanism is based on a translation of temporal authorizations and derivation rules into logic programs (Datalog programs with negation and periodicity and order constraints). The materialization of the logic program

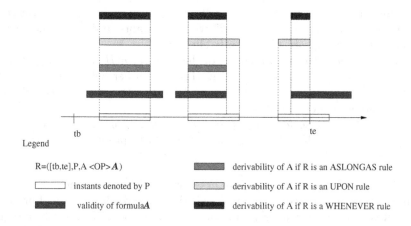

Legend

R=([tb,te],P,A <OP>**A**)   ████████ derivability of A if R is an ASLONGAS rule

[   ] instants denoted by P   ████████ derivability of A if R is an UPON rule

████████ validity of formula**A**   ████████ derivability of A if R is a WHENEVER rule

Fig. 16. Semantics of the different temporal operators [13]

guarantees efficient access. The model is focussed on time-based constraints and reasoning and allows expressing authorization relationships and derivation not covered in other models. However, it does not address the enforcement of different implication and conflict resolution policies (conflicts between permissions and denials are solved according to the denials-take-precedence policy).

6.3   A Calculus for Access Control

Abadi et al. [1] present a calculus for access control that combines authentication (i.e., identity check) and authorization control, taking also into account possible delegation of privileges among parties. The calculus is based on the notion of *principals*. Principals are sources of requests and make statements (e.g., "read file tmp"). Principals can be either simple (e.g., users, machines, and communication channels) or composite. Composite principals are obtained combining principals by means of constructors that allow to capture groups and delegations.a Principals can be as follows [1]:

- *Users* and *machines*.
- *Channels*, such as input devices and cryptographic channels.
- *Conjunction of principals*, of the form $A \wedge B$. A request ¿from $A \wedge B$ is a request that both A and B make (it is not necessary that the request be made in concert).
- *Groups*, define groups of principals, membership of principal P_i in group G_i is written $P_i \Longrightarrow G_i$. Disjunction $A \vee B$ denotes a group composed only of A and B.

- Principals in *roles*, of the form *A as R*. The principal *A* may adopt the role *R* and act under the name "*A as R*" when she wants to diminish her powers, in particular as protection against blunders.[8]
- Principals *on behalf* of principals, of the form *A for B*. The principal *A* may delegate authority to *B*, and *B* can then act on her behalf, using the identity *B for A*. In most cases, *A* is a user delegating to a machine *B*; delegation can also occur between machines.
- Principals *speaking for* other principals, of the form *A ∘ B*, denoting that *B* speaks on behalf of *A*, but not necessarily with a proof that *A* has delegated authority to *B*.

The process of determining whether a request from a principal should be granted or denied is based on a modal logic that extends the algebra of principals and serves as a basis for different algorithms and protocols. Intuitively, a request on an object will be granted if it is authorized according to the authorizations stated in the ACL of the object and the implication relationships and delegations holding among principals.

6.4 Administrative Policies

Administrative policies determine who is authorized to modify the allowed accesses. This is one of the most important, and probably least understood, aspect of access controls. In multilevel mandatory access control the allowed accesses are determined entirely on basis of the security classification of subjects and objects. Security levels are assigned to users by the security administrator. Security levels of objects are determined by the system on the basis of the levels of the users creating them. The security administrator is typically the only one who can change security levels of subjects and objects. The administrative policy is therefore very simple. Discretionary access control permits a wide range of administrative policies. Some of these are described below.

- *Centralized:* A single authorizer (or group) is allowed to grant and revoke authorizations to the users.
- *Hierarchical:* A central authorizer is responsible for assigning administrative responsibilities to other administrators. The administrators can then grant and revoke access authorizations to the users of the system. Hierarchical administration can be applied, for example, according to the organization chart.
- *Cooperative:* Special authorizations on given resources cannot be granted by a single authorizer but need cooperation of several authorizers.

---

[8] Note that there is a difference in the semantics assigned to roles in [1] and in role-based access control model (see Section 7). In [1] a principal's privileges always diminish when the principal takes on some role; also an implication relationship is enforced allowing a principal *P* to use authorizations granted to any principal of the form *P as R*.

- *Ownership:* Each object is associated with an owner, who generally coincides with the user who created the object. Users can grant and revoke authorizations on the objects they own.
- *Decentralized:* Extending the previous approaches, the owner of an object (or its administrators) can delegate other users the privilege of specifying authorizations, possibly with the ability of further delegating it.

Decentralized administration is convenient since it allows users to delegate administrative privileges to others. Delegation, however, complicates the authorization management. In particular, it becomes more difficult for users to keep track of who can access their objects. Furthermore, revocation of authorizations becomes more complex. There are many possible variations on the way decentralized administration works, which may differ in the way the following questions are answered.

- what is the granularity of administrative authorizations?
- can delegation be restricted, that is, can the grantor of an administrative authorization impose restrictions on the subjects to which the recipient can further grant the authorization?
- who can revoke authorizations?
- what about authorizations granted by the revokee?

In general, existing decentralized policies allow users to grant administration for a specific privilege (meaning a given access on a given object). They do not allow, however, to put constraints on the subjects to which the recipient receiving administrative authority can grant the access. This feature could, however, result useful. For instance, an organization could delegate one of its employees to granting access to some resources constraining the authorizations she can grant to employees working within her laboratory. Usually, authorizations can be revoked only by the user who granted them (or, possibly, by the object's owner). When an administrative authorization is revoked, the problem arises of dealing with the authorizations specified by the users from whom the administrative privilege is being revoked. For instance, suppose that Ann gives Bob the authorization to read File1 and gives him the privilege of granting this authorization to others (in some systems, such capability of delegation is called *grant option* [42]). Suppose then that Bob grants the authorization to Chris, and susequently Ann revokes the authorization from Bob. The question now is: what should happen to the authorization that Chris has received? To illustrate how revocation can work it is useful to look at the history of System R [42]. In the System R authorization model, users creating a table can grant other users access privileges on it. Authorizations can be granted with the *grant-option*. If a user receives the authorization for an access with the grant-option she can grant the access (and the grant option on it) to others. Intuitively, this introduces a chain of authorizations. The original System R policy, which we call *(time-based) cascade* revocation, adopted the following semantics for revocation: when a user is revoked the grant option on an access, all authorizations that

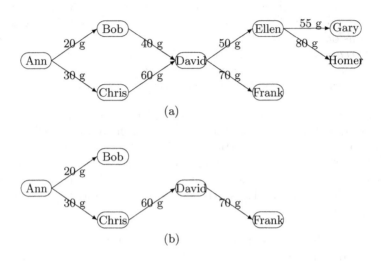

(a)

(b)

Fig. 17. Example of the original System-R, time-based cascade revocation

she granted and could not have been granted had the revoked authorization not been present, should also be (recursively) deleted. The revocation is recursive since it may, in turn, cause other authorizations to be deleted. More precisely, let $AUTH$ be the initial authorization state and $G_1, \ldots, G_n$ be a sequence of grant requests (history) that produced authorization state $AUTH'$. The revocation of a grant G_k should result in authorization state $AUTH''$ as if G_k had never been granted, that is, resulting from history $G_1, \ldots, G_{k-1}, G_{k+1}, \ldots, G_n$. Enforcement of this revocation semantics requires to keep track of *i)* who granted which authorization, and *ii)* the time at which the authorization was granted. To illustrate, consider the sequence of grant operations pictured in Figure 17(a), referred to the delegation of a specific privilege. Here, nodes represent users, and arcs represent the granting of a specific access from one user to another. The label associated with the arc states the time at which the authorization was granted and whether the grant option was granted as well. For instance, Ann granted the authorization, with the grant option, to Bob at time 20, and to Chris at time 30. Suppose now that Bob revokes the authorization he granted to David. According to the revocation semantics to be enforced, the authorization that David granted to Ellen must be deleted as well, since it was granted at time 50 when, had David not hold the authorizations being revoked, the grant request would have been denied. Consequently, and for the same reasoning, the two authorizations granted by Ellen also need to be deleted, resulting in the authorization state of Figure 17(b).

   Although the time-based cascade revocation has a clean semantics, it is not always accepted. Deleting all authorizations granted in virtue of an authorization that is being revoked is not always wanted. In many organizations, the authorizations that users possess are related to their particular tasks or functions within the organization. Suppose there is a change in the task or function of a user (say, because of a job promotion). This change may imply a change in the responsibilities of the user and therefore in her privileges. New authorizations will be granted to the user and some of her previous authorizations will be revoked. Applying a recursive revocation will result in the undesirable effect of deleting all authorizations the revokee granted and, recursively, all the authorizations granted through them, which then will need to be re-issued. Moreover, all application programs depending on the revoked authorizations will be invalidated. An alternative form of revocation was proposed in [15], where *non-cascade* revocation is introduced. Instead of deleting all the authorizations granted by the revokee in virtue of the authorizations being revoked, non-recursive revocation re-specifies them to be under the authority of the revoker, which can then retain or selectively delete them. The original time-based revocation policy of System R, was changed to not consider time anymore. In SQL:1999 [28] revocation can be requested *with* or *without cascade*. Cascade revocation recursively deletes authorizations if the revokee does not hold anymore the grant option for the access. However, if the revokee still holds the grant option for the access, the authorizations she granted are not deleted (regardless of time they were granted). For instance, with reference to Figure 17(a), the revocation by Bob of the authorization granted to David, would only delete the authorization granted to David by Bob. Ellen's authorization would still remain valid since David still holds the grant option of the access (because of the authorization from Chris). With the non cascade option the system rejects the revoke operation if its enforcement would entail deletion of other authorizations beside the one for which revocation is requested.

6.5   Integrity Policies

In Section 4.4 we illustrated a mandatory policy (namely Biba's model) for protecting information integrity. Biba's approach, however, suffers of two major drawbacks: *i)* the constraints imposed on the information flow may result too restrictive, and *ii)* it only controls integrity intended as the prevention of a flow of information from low integrity objects to high integrity objects. However, this notion of one-directional information flow in a lattice captures only a small part of the data integrity problem [74].

Integrity is concerned with ensuring that no resource (including data and programs[9]) has been modified in an *unauthorized* or *improper* way and that the data stored in the system correctly reflect the real world they are intended to represent (i.e., that users expect). Integrity preservation requires prevention of frauds and errors, as the term "improper" used above suggests: violations to data integrity are often enacted by legitimate users executing authorized actions but misusing their privileges.

Any data management system today has functionalities for ensuring integrity [8]. Basic integrity services are, for example, *concurrency control* (to

---

[9] Programs improperly modified can fool the access control and bypass the system restrictions, thus violating the secrecy and/or integrity of the data (see Section 3).

ensure correctness in case of multiple processes concurrently accessing data)
and *recovery* techniques (to reconstruct the state of the system in the case of
violations or errors occur). Database systems also support the definition and
enforcement of integrity constraints, that define the valid states of the database
constraining the values that it can contain. Also, database systems support the
notion of *transaction*, which is a sequence of actions for which the *ACID* properties must be ensured, where the acronym stands for: *Atomicity* (a transaction
is either performed in its entirety or not performed at all); *Consistency* (a transaction must preserve the consistency of the database); *Isolation* (a transaction
should not make its updates visible to other transactions until it is committed);
and *Durability* (changes made by a transaction that has committed must never
be lost because of subsequent failures).

Although rich, the integrity features provided by database management systems are not enough: they are only specified with respect to the data and their
semantics, and do not take into account the subjects operating on them. Therefore, they can only protect against obvious errors in the data or in the system
operation, and not against misuses by subjects [23]. The task of a security policy for integrity is therefore to fill this gap and control data modifications and
procedure executions with respect to the subjects performing them. An attempt
in this respect is represented by the Clark and Wilson's proposal [25], where the
following four basic criteria for achieving data integrity are defined.

1. *Authentication*. The identity of all users accessing the system must be properly authenticated (this is an obvious prerequisite for correctness of the control, as well as for establishing accountability).
2. *Audit*. Modifications should be logged for the purpose of maintaining an
   audit log that records every program executed and the user who executed
   it, so that changes could be undone.
3. **Well-formed transactions** Users should not manipulate data arbitrarily
   but only in constrained ways that ensure data integrity (e.g., double entry bookkeeping in accounting systems). A system in which transactions are
   well-formed ensures that only legitimate actions can be executed. In addition, well-formed transactions should provide logging and serializability of
   resulting subtransactions in a way that concurrency and recovery mechanisms can be established.
4. **Separation of duty** The system must associate with each user a valid set
   of programs to be run. The privileges given to each user must satisfy the
   separation of duty principle. Separation of duty prevents authorized users
   from making improper modifications, thus preserving the consistency of data
   by ensuring that data in the system reflect the real world they represent.

While authentication and audit are two common mechanisms for any access
control system, the latter two aspects are peculiar to the Clark and Wilson
proposal.

The definition of well-formed transaction and the enforcement of separation
of duty constraints is based on the following concepts.

C1: All IVPs must ensure that all CDIs are in a valid state when the IVP is run.
C2: All TPs must be certified to be valid (i.e., preserve validity of CDIs' state)
C3: Assignment of TPs to users must satisfy separation of duty
C4: The operations of TPs must be logged
C5: TPs execute on UDIs must result in valid CDIs
E1: Only certified TPs can manipulate CDIs
E2: Users must only access CDIs by means of TPs for which they are authorized
E3: The identity of each user attempting to execute a TP must be authenticated
E4: Only the agent permitted to certify entities can change the list of such entities associated with other entities

Fig. 18. Clark and Wilson integrity rules

- *Constrained Data Items.* CDIs are the objects whose integrity must be safeguarded.
- *Unconstrained Data Items.* UDIs are objects that are not covered by the integrity policy (e.g., information typed by the user on the keyboard).
- *Integrity Verification Procedures.* IVPs are procedures meant to verify that CDIs are in a valid state, that is, the IVPs confirm that the data conforms to the integrity specifications at the time the verification is performed.
- *Transformation Procedures.* TPs are the only procedures (well-formed procedures) that are allowed to modify CDIs or to take arbitrary user input and create new CDIs. TPs are designed to take the system from one valid state to the next

Intuitively, IVPs and TPs are the means for enforcing the well-formed transaction requirement: all data modifications must be carried out through TPs, and the result must satisfy the conditions imposed by the IVPs.

Separation of duty must be taken care of in the definition of authorized operations. In the context of the Clark and Wilson's model, authorized operations are specified by assigning to each user a set of well-formed transactions that she can execute (which have access to constraint data items). Separation of duty requires the assignment to be defined in a way that makes it impossible for a user to violate the integrity of the system. Intuitively, separation of duty is enforced by splitting operations in subparts, each to be executed by a different person (to make frauds difficult). For instance, any person permitted to create or certify a well-formed transaction should not be able to execute it (against production data).

Figure 18 summarizes the nine rules that Clark and Wilson presented for the enforcement of system integrity. The rules are partitioned into two types: certification (C) and enforcement (E). Certification rules involve the evaluation of transactions by an administrator, whereas enforcement is performed by the system.

The Clark and Wilson's proposal outlines good principles for controlling integrity. However, it has limitations due to the fact that it is far from formal and it is unclear how to formalize it in a general setting.

7   Role-Based Access Control Policies

Role-based access control (RBAC) is an alternative to traditional discretionary (DAC) and mandatory access control (MAC) policies that is attracting increasing attention, particularly for commercial applications. The main motivation behind RBAC is the necessity to specify and enforce enterprise-specific security policies in a way that maps naturally to an organization's structure. In fact, in a large number of business activities a user's identity is relevant only ¿from the point of view of accountability. For access control purposes it is much more important to know what a user's organizational responsibilities are, rather than who the user is. The conventional discretionary access controls, in which individual user ownership of data plays such an important part, are not a good fit. Neither are the full mandatory access controls, in which users have security clearances and objects have security classifications. Role-based access control tries to fill in this gap by merging the flexibility of explicit authorizations with additionally imposed organizational constraints.

7.1   Named Protection Domain

The idea behind role-based access control is grouping privileges (i.e., authorizations). The first work proposing collecting privileges for authorization assignment is probably the work by Baldwin [9], where the concept of *named protection domain* (NPD) is introduced as a way to simplify security management in an SQL-based framework. Intuitively, a named protection domain identifies a set of privileges (those granted to the NPD) needed to accomplish a well-defined task. For instance, in a bank organization, an NPD `Accounts_Receivable` can be defined to which all the privileges needed to perform the account-receivable task are granted. NPD can be granted to users as well as to other NPDs, thus forming a chain of privileges. The authorization state can be graphically represented as a directed acyclic graph where nodes correspond to privileges, NPDs, and users, while arcs denote authorization assignments. An example of privilege graph is illustrated in Figure 19, where three NPDs (`Accounts_Receivable`, `Accounts_Payable`, and `Accounts_Supervisor`) and the corresponding privileges are depicted. Users can access objects only by activating NPDs holding privileges on them. Users can only activate NPDs that have been directly or indirectly assigned to them. For instance, with reference to Figure 19, `Bob` can activate any of three NPDs, thus acquiring the corresponding privileges. To enforce *least privilege*, users are restricted to activate only one NPD at the time. NPDs can also be used to group users. For instance, a NPD named `Employees` can be defined which corresponds to the set of employees of an organization. NPDs correspond to the current concept of *roles* in SQL:1999 [28].

7.2   Role-Based Policies

Role-based policies regulate the access of users to the information on the basis of the organizational activities and responsibility that users have in a system.

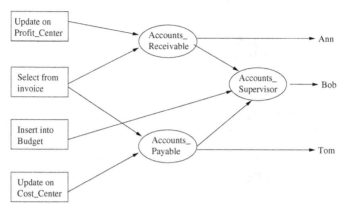

Fig. 19. An example of NPD privilege graph [9]

Although different proposals have been made (e.g., [3,36,45,56,67,76,80]), the basic concepts are common to all approaches. Essentially, role based policies require the identification of *roles* in the system, where a role can be defined as a set of actions and responsibilities associated with a particular working activity. The role can be widely scoped, reflecting a user's job title (e.g., `secretary`), or it can be more specific, reflecting, for example, a task that the user needs to perform (e.g., `order_processing`). Then, instead of specifying all the accesses each users is allowed to execute, access authorizations on objects are specified for roles. Users are then given authorizations to adopt roles (see Figure 20). The user playing a role is allowed to execute all accesses for which the role is authorized. In general, a user can take on different roles on different occasions. Also the same role can be played by several users, perhaps simultaneously. Some proposals for role-based access control (e.g., [76,80]) allow a user to exercise multiple roles at the same time. Other proposals (e.g., [28,48]) limit the user to only one role at a time, or recognize that some roles can be jointly exercised while others must be adopted in exclusion to one another. It is important to note the difference between groups (see Section 6) and roles: groups define sets of users while roles define sets of privileges. There is a semantic difference between them: roles can be "activated" and "deactivated" by users at their discretion, while group membership always applies, that is, users cannot enable and disable group memberships (and corresponding authorizations) at their will. However, since roles can be defined which correspond to organizational figures (e.g., `secretary`, `chair`, and `faculty`), a same "concept" can be seen both as a group and as a role.

The role-based approach has several advantages. Some of these are discussed below.

Authorization management Role-based policies benefit from a logical independence in specifying user authorizations by breaking this task into two parts: *i)* assignment of roles to users, and *ii)* assignment of authorizations to access objects to roles. This greatly simplifies the management of the

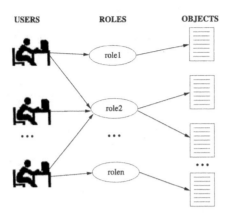

Fig. 20. Role-based access control

security policy: when a new user joins the organization, the administrator only needs to grant her the roles corresponding to her job; when a user's job changes, the administrator simply has to change the roles associated with that user; when a new application or task is added to the system, the administrator needs only to decide which roles are permitted to execute it.

Hierarchical roles In many applications there is a natural hierarchy of roles, based on the familiar principles of generalization and specialization. Figure 21 illustrates an example of role hierarchy: each role is represented as a node and there is an arc between a specialized role and its generalization. The role hierarchy can be exploited for authorization implication. For instance, authorizations granted to roles can be propagated to their specializations (e.g., the secretary role can be allowed all accesses granted to adm_staff). Authorization implication can also be enforced on role assignments, by allowing users to activate all generalizations of the roles assigned to them (e.g., a user allowed to activate secretary will also be allowed to activate role adm_staff). Authorization implication has the advantage of further simplifying authorization management. Note however that not always implication may be wanted, as propagating all authorizations is contrary to the least privilege principle. The hierarchy has also been exploited in [77] for the definition of administrative privileges: beside the hierarchy of organizational roles, an additional hierarchy of administrative roles is defined; each administrative role can be given authority over a portion of the role hierarchy.

Least privilege Roles allow a user to sign on with the least privilege required for the particular task she needs to perform. Users authorized to powerful roles do not need to exercise them until those privileges are actually needed. This minimizes the danger of damage due to inadvertent errors, Trojan Horses, or intruders masquerading as legitimate users.

Separation of duties Separation of duties refer to the principle that no user should be given enough privileges to misuse the system on their own. For

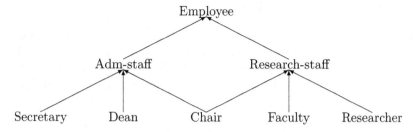

Fig. 21. An example of role hierarchy

instance, the person authorizing a paycheck should not be the same person who can prepare them. Separation of duties can be enforced either statically (by defining conflicting roles, that is, roles which cannot be executed by the same user) or dynamically (by enforcing the control at access time). An example of dynamic separation of duty restriction is the two-person rule. The first user to execute a two-person operation can be any authorized user, whereas the second user can be any authorized user different ¿from the first [79].

Constraints enforcement Roles provide a basis for the specification and enforcement of further protection requirements that real world policies may need to express. For instance, cardinality constraints can be specified, that restrict the number of users allowed to activate a role or the number of roles allowed to exercise a given privilege. The constraints can also be dynamic, that is, be imposed on roles activation rather than on their assignment. For instance, while several users may be allowed to activate role `chair`, a further constraint can require that at most one user at a time can activate it.

Role-based policies represent a promising direction and a useful paradigm for many commercial and government organizations. However, there is still some work to be done to cover all the different requirements that real world scenarios may present. For instance, the simple hierarchical relationship as intended in current proposals may not be sufficient to model the different kinds of relationships that can occur. For example, a secretary may need to be allowed to write specific documents *on behalf* of her manager, but neither role is a specialization of the other. Different ways of propagating privileges (delegation) should then be supported. Similarly, administrative policies should be enriched. For instance, the traditional concept of ownership may not apply anymore: a user does not necessarily own the objects she created when in a given role. Also, users' identities should not be forgotten. If it true that in most organizations, the role (and not the identity) identifies the privileges that one may execute, it is also true that in some cases the requestor's identity needs to be considered even when a role-based policy is adopted. For instance, a doctor may be allowed to specify treatments and access files but she may be restricted to treatments and files for her own patients, where the doctor-patient relationships is defined based on their identity.

8   Advanced Access Control Models

Throughout the chapter we investigated different issues concerning the development of an access control system, discussing security principles, policies, and models proposed in the literature. In this section we illustrate recent proposals and ongoing work addressing access control in emerging applications and new scenarios.

8.1   Logic-Based Authorization Languages

As discussed in Section 6, access control systems based only on the closed policy clearly have limitations. The support of abstractions and authorization implications along them and the support of positive and negative authorizations provide more flexibility in the authorization specifications. As we have seen, several access control policies can be applied in this context (e.g., denials-take-precedence, most-specific-takes-precedence, strong and weak) and have been proposed in the literature. Correspondingly, several authorization models have been formalized and access control mechanisms enforcing them implemented. However, each model, and its corresponding enforcement mechanism, implements a single specified policy, which is in fact built into the mechanism. As a consequence, although different policy choices are possible in theory, each access control system is in practice bound to a specific policy. The major drawback of this approach is that a single policy simply cannot capture all the protection requirements that may arise over time. As a matter of fact, even within a single system:

- different users may have different protection requirements;
- a single user may have different protection requirements on different objects;
- protection requirements may change over time.

When a system imposes a specific policy on users, they have to work within the confines imposed by the policy. When the protection requirements of an application are different from the policy built into the system, in most cases, the only solution is to implement the policy as part of the application code. This solution, however, is dangerous from a security viewpoint since it makes the tasks of verification, modification, and adequate enforcement of the policy difficult.

Recent proposals have worked towards languages and models able to express, in a single framework, different access control policies, to the goal of providing a single mechanism able to enforce multiple policies. Logic-based languages, for their expressive power and formal foundations, represent a good candidate. The first work investigating logic-languages for the specification of authorizations is the work by Woo and Lam [91]. Their proposal makes the point for the need of flexibility and extensibility in access specifications and illustrates how these advantages can be achieved by abstracting from the low level authorization triples and adopting a high level authorization language. Their language is essentially a many-sorted first-order language with a rule construct, useful to express authorization derivations and therefore model authorization implications and default decisions (e.g., closed or open policy). The use of a very general language, which has almost the same expressive power of first order logic, allows the expression of different kinds of authorization implications, constraints on authorizations, and access control policies. However, as a drawback, authorization specifications may result difficult to understand and manage. Also, the trade-off between expressiveness and efficiency seems to be strongly unbalanced: the lack of restrictions on the language results in the specification of models which may not even be decidable and therefore will not be implementable. As noted in [48], Woo and Lam's approach is based on truth in extensions of arbitrary default theories, which is known, even in the propositional case to be NP-complete, and in the first order case, is worse than undecidable.

Starting from these observations, Jajodia et al. [48] worked on a proposal for a logic-based language that attempted to balance flexibility and expressiveness on the one side, and easy management and performance on the other. The language allows the representation of different policies and protection requirements, while at the same time providing understandable specifications, clear semantics (guaranteeing therefore the behavior of the specifications), and bearable data complexity. Their proposal for a Flexible Authorization Framework (FAF) identifies a polynomial time (in fact quadratic time) data complexity fragment of default logic; thus resulting effectively implementable. The language identifies the following predicates for the specification of authorizations. (Below s, o, and a denote a subject, object, and action term, respectively, where a term is either a constant value in the corresponding domain or a variable ranging over it).

cando(o,s,⟨*sign*⟩a) represents authorizations explicitly inserted by the security administrator. They represent the accesses that the administrator wishes to allow or deny (depending on the sign associated with the action).

dercando(o,s,⟨*sign*⟩a) represents authorizations derived by the system using logical rules of inference (modus ponens plus rules for stratified negation). Logical rules can express hierarchy-based authorization derivation (e.g., propagation of authorizations from groups to their members) as well as different implication relationships that may need to be represented.

do(o,s,⟨*sign*⟩a) definitely represents the accesses that must be granted or denied. Intuitively, do enforces the conflict resolution and access decision policies, that is, it decides whether to grant or deny the access possibly solving existing conflicts and enforcing default decisions (in the case where no authorization has been specified for an access).

done(o,s,r,a,t) keeps the history of the accesses executed. A fact of the form done(o,s,r,a,t) indicates that s operating in role r executed action a on object o at time t.

error signals errors in the specification or use of authorizations; it can be used to enforce static and dynamic constraints on the specifications.

In addition, the language considers predicates, called hie-predicates, for the evaluation of hierarchical relationships between the elements of the data system (e.g., user's membership in groups, inclusion relationships between objects). The language also allows the inclusion of additional application-specific predicates, called `rel-` predicates. These predicates can capture the possible different relationships, existing between the elements of the data system, that may need to be taken into account by the access control system. Examples of these predicates can be `owner(user,object)`, which models ownership of objects by users, or `supervisor(user1,user2)`, which models responsibilities and controls between users according to the organizational structure.

Authorization specifications are stated as logic rules defined on the predicates of the language. To ensure clean semantics and implementability, the format of the rules is restricted to guarantee (local) stratification of the resulting program (see Figure 22).[10] The stratification also reflects the different semantics given to the predicates: `cando` will be used to specify basic authorizations, `dercando` to enforce implication relationships and produce derived authorizations, and `do` to take the final access decision. Stratification ensures that the logic program corresponding to the rules has a unique stable model, which coincides with the well founded semantics. Also, this model can be effectively computed in polynomial time. The authors also present a materialization technique for producing and storing the model corresponding to a set of logical rules. Materialization has been usually coupled with logic-based authorization languages. Indeed, given a logic program whose rules correspond to an authorization specification in the given language, one can assess a request to execute a particular action on an object by checking if it is true in the unique stable model of the logic program. If so, the request is authorized, otherwise it is denied. However, when implementing an algorithm to support this kind of evaluation, one needs to consider the following facts:

- the request should be either authorized or denied very fast, and
- changes to the specifications are far less frequent than access requests.

Indeed, since access requests happen all the time, the security architecture should optimize the processing of these requests. Therefore, Jajodia et al. [48] propose implementing their FAF with a *materialized view architecture*, which maintains the model corresponding to the authorization specifications. The model is computed on the initial specifications and updated with incremental maintenance strategies.

8.2   Composition of Access Control Policies

In many real world situations, access control needs to combine restrictions independently stated that should be enforced as one, while retaining their independence and administrative autonomy. For instance, the global policy of a large organization can be the combination of the policies of its different departments and divisions as well as of externally imposed constraints (e.g., privacy regulations); each of these policies should be taken into account while remaining

---

[10] A program is locally stratified if there is no recursion among predicates going through negation.

Stratum	Predicate	Rules defining predicate
0	hie-predicates	base relations.
	rel-predicates	base relations.
	done	base relation.
1	cando	body may contain done, hie- and rel-literals.
2	dercando	body may contain cando, dercando, done, hie-, and rel- literals. Occurrences of dercando literals must be positive.
3	do	in the case when head is of the form do(_, _, +a) body may contain cando, dercando, done, hie- and rel- literals.
4	do	in the case when head is of the form do(o, s, −a) body contains just one literal ¬do(o, s, +a).
5	error	body may contain do, cando, dercando, done, hie-, and rel- literals.

Fig. 22. Rule composition and stratification of the proposal in [48]

independent and autonomously managed. Another example is represented by the emerging dynamic coalition scenarios where different parties, coming together for a common goal for a limited time, need to merge their security requirements in a controlled way while retaining their autonomy. Since existing frameworks assume a single monolithic specification of the entire access control policy, the situations above would require translating and merging the different component policies into a single "program" in the adopted access control language. While existing languages are flexible enough to obtain the desired combined behavior, this method has several drawbacks. First, the translation process is far from being trivial; it must be done very carefully to avoid undesirable side effects due to interference between the component policies. Interference may result in the combined specifications not reflecting correctly the intended restrictions. Second, after translation it is not possible anymore to operate on the individual components and maintain them autonomously. Third, existing approaches cannot take into account incomplete policies, where some components are not (completely) known a priori (e.g., when somebody else is to provide that component). Starting from these observations, Bonatti et al. [20] make the point for the need of a policy composition framework by which different component policies can be integrated while retaining their independence. They propose an algebra for combining security policies. Compound policies are formulated as expressions of the algebra, constructed by using the following operators.

Addition merges two policies by returning their union. For instance, in an organization composed of different divisions, access to the main gate can be authorized by any of the administrator of the divisions (each of them knows which users need access to reach their division). The totality of the accesses through the main gate to be authorized should then be the union of the statements of each division. Intuitively, additions can be applied in any situation where accesses can be authorized if allowed by any of the component policies.

Conjunction merges two policies by returning their intersection. For instance, consider an organization in which divisions share certain documents (e.g., clinical folders of patients). An access to a document may be allowed only if all the authorities that have a say on the document agree on it. That is, if the corresponding authorization triple belongs to the intersection of their policies.

Subtraction restricts a policy by eliminating all the accesses in a second policy. Intuitively, subtraction specifies exceptions to statements made by a policy, and encompasses the functionality of negative authorizations in existing approaches.

Closure closes a policy under a set of derivation (i.e., implication) rules, w.r.t. which the algebra is parametric. Rules can be, for example, expressed with a logic-based language (e.g., [48]).

Scoping restriction restricts the application of a policy to a given set of subjects, objects, and actions that satisfy certain properties (i.e., belong to a given class). It is useful to enforce authority confinement (e.g., authorizations specified in a given component can be referred only to specific subjects and objects).

Overriding replaces portion of a policy with another. For instance, a laboratory policy may impose authorizations granted by the lab tutors to be overridden by the department policy (which can either confirm the authorization or not) for students appearing in a blacklist for infraction to rules.

Template defines a partially specified (i.e., parametric) policy that can be completed by supplying the parameters. Templates are useful for representing policies where some components are to be specified at a later stage. For instance, the components might be the result of further policy refinement, or might be specified by a different authority.

Enforcement of compound policies is based on a translation from policy expressions into logic programs, which provide executable specifications compatible with different evaluation strategies (e.g., run time, materialized view, partial evaluation). The logic program simply provides an enforcement mechanism and is transparent to the users, who can therefore enjoy the simplicity of algebra expressions. The modularity of the algebra, where each policy can be seen as a different component, provides a convenient way for reasoning about policies at different levels of abstractions. Also, it allows for the support of heterogeneous policies and policies that are unknown a priori and can only be queried at access control time.

8.3   Certificate-Based Access Control

Today's Globally Internetworked Infrastructure connects remote parties through the use of large scale networks, such as the World Wide Web. Execution of activities at various levels is based on the use of remote resources and services, and on the interaction between different, remotely located, parties that may know little about each other. In such a scenario, traditional assumptions for establishing and enforcing access control regulations do not hold anymore. For instance, a server may receive requests not just from the local community of users, but also from remote, previously unknown users. The server may not be able to authenticate these users or to specify authorizations for them (with respect to their identity). The traditional separation between *authentication* and *access control* cannot be applied in this context, and alternative access control solutions should be devised. A possible solution to this problem is represented by the use of digital certificates (or credentials), representing statements certified by given entities (e.g., certification authorities), which can be used to establish properties of their holder (such as identity, accreditation, or authorizations) [39]. Trust-management systems (e.g., PolicyMaker [18], Keynote [17], REFEREE [24], and DL [57]) use credentials to describe specific delegation of trusts among keys and to bind public keys to authorizations. They therefore depart from the traditional separation between authentication and authorizations by granting authorizations directly to keys (bypassing identities). Trust management systems provide an interesting framework for reasoning about trust between unknown parties; however, assigning authorizations to keys, may result limiting and make authorization specifications difficult to manage. A promising direction exploiting digital certificates to regulate access control is represented by new authorization models making the access decision of whether or not a party may execute an access dependent on properties that the party may have, and can prove by presenting one or more certificates (authorization certificates in [18] being a specific kind of them). Besides a more complex authorization language and model, there is however a further complication arising in this new scenario, due to the fact that the access control paradigm is changing. On the one side, the server may not have all the information it needs in order to decide whether or not an access should be granted (and exploits certificates to take the decision). On the other side, however, the requestor may not know which certificates she needs to present to a (possibly just encountered) server in order to get access. Therefore, the server itself should, upon reception of the request, return the user with the information of what she should do (if possible) to get access. In other words the system cannot simply return a "yes/no" access decision anymore. Rather, it should return the information of the requisites that it requires be satisfied for the access to be allowed. The certificates mentioned above are one type of access requisites. In addition, other uncertified declarations (i.e., not signed by any authority) may be required. For instance, we may be requested our credit card number to perform an electronic purchase; we may be requested to fill in a profile when using public or semipublic services (e.g., browsing for flight schedules). The access control decision is therefore a more complex process and completing a service may require communicating information not related to the access itself, but related to additional restrictions on its execution, possibly introducing a form of negotiation [21,72,89]. Such information communication

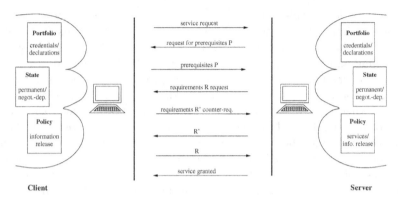

Fig. 23. Client/server interplay in [21]

makes the picture even more complex, since it introduces two new protection requirements (in addition to the obvious need of protecting resources managed by the server from unauthorized or improper access):

Client portfolio protection: the client (requestor) may not be always willing to release information and digital certificates to other parties [65], and may therefore impose restrictions on their communication. For this purpose, a client may—like a server—require the counterpart to fulfill some requirements. For instance, a client may be willing to release a AAA membership number only to servers supplying a credential stating that the travel agent is approved by AAA.

Server's state protection: the server, when communicating requisites for access to a client, wants to be sure that possible sensitive information about its access control policy is not disclosed. For instance, a server may require a digitally signed guarantee to specific customers (who appear blacklisted for bad credit in some database it has access to); the server should simply ask this signed document, it should not tell the customer that she appears blacklisted.

The first proposals investigating the application of credential-based access control regulating access to a server, were made by Winslett et al. [82,89]. Access control rules are expressed in a logic language and rules applicable to an access can be communicated by the server to clients. The work was also extended in [88,93] investigating trust negotiation issues and strategies that a party can apply to select credentials to submit to the opponent party in a negotiation. In particular, [88] distinguishes between *eager* and *parsimonious* credential release strategies. Parties applying the first strategy turn over all their credentials if the release policy for them is satisfied, without waiting for the credentials to be requested. Parsimonious parties only release credentials upon explicit request by the server (avoiding unnecessary releases). Yu et al. [93] present a prudent negotiation strategy to the goal of establishing trust among parties, while avoiding disclosure of irrelevant credentials.

A credential-based access control is also presented by Bonatti and Samarati in [21]. They propose a uniform framework for regulating service access and information disclosure in an open, distributed network system like the Web. Like in previous proposals, access regulations are specified as logical rules, where some predicates are explicitly identified. Besides credentials, the proposal also allows to reason about declarations (i.e., unsigned statements) and user-profiles that the server can maintain and exploit for taking the access decision. Communication of requisites to be satisfied by the requestor is based on a filtering and renaming process applied on the server's policy, which exploits partial evaluation techniques in logic programs. The filtering process allows the server to communicate to the client the requisites for an access, without disclosing possible sensitive information on which the access decision is taken. The proposal allows also clients to control the release of their credentials, possibly making counter-requests to the server, and releasing certain credentials only if their counter-requests are satisfied (see Figure 23). Client-server interplay is limited to two interactions to allow clients to apply a parsimonious strategy (i.e., minimizing the set of information and credentials released) when deciding which set credentials/declarations release among possible alternative choices they may have.

While all these approaches assume access control rules to be expressed in logic form, often the people specifying the security policies are unfamiliar with logic based languages. An interesting aspect to be investigated concerns the definition of a language for expressing and exchanging policies based on a high level formulation that, while powerful, can be easily interchangeable and both human and machine readable. Insights in this respect can be taken from recent proposals expressing access control policies as XML documents [26,27].

All the proposals above open new interesting directions in the access control area.

References

1. M. Abadi, M. Burrows, B. Lampson, and G. Plotkin. A calculus for access control in distributed systems. *ACM Transactions on Programming Languages and Systems*, 15:706–734, 1993. 173, 174
2. R. Ahad, J. David, S. Gower, P. Lyngbaek, A. Marynowski, and E. Onuebge. Supporting access control in an object-oriented database language. In *Proc. of the Int. Conference on Extending Database Technology (EDBT)*, Vienna, Austria, 1992. 171
3. G. Ahn and R. Sandhu. The RSL99 language for role-based separation of duty constraints. In *Proc. of the fourth ACM Workshop on Role-based Access Control*, pages 43–54, Fairfax, VA, USA, October 1999. 181
4. A. Aho, J. Hoperoft, and J. Ullman. *The Design and Analysis of Computer Algorithms*. Addison-Wesley, 1974. 143
5. J. P. Anderson. Computer security technology planning study. Technical Report ESD-TR-73-51, Electronic System Division/AFSC, Bedford, MA, October 1972. 138

6. Apache http server version 2.0. `http://www.apache.org/docs-2.0/misc/tutorials.html`. 171

7. V. Atluri, S. Jajodia, and B. George. *Multilevel Secure Transaction Processing*. Kluwer Academic Publishers, 1999. 161

8. P. Atzeni, S. Ceri, S. Paraboschi, and R. Torlone. *Database Systems*. McGraw-Hill, 1999. 177

9. Robert W. Baldwin. Naming and grouping privileges to simplify security management in large database. In *Proceedings IEEE Computer Society Symposium on Research in Security and Privacy*, pages 61–70, Oakland, CA, April 1990. 180, 181

10. D. E. Bell. Secure computer systems: A refinement of the mathematical model. Technical Report ESD-TR-278, vol. 3, The Mitre Corp., Bedford, MA, 1973. 152, 153

11. D. E. Bell and L. J. LaPadula. Secure computer system: Unified exposition and multics interpretation. Technical Report ESD-TR-278, vol. 4, The Mitre Corp., Bedford, MA, 1973. 152

12. D. E. Bell and L. J. LaPadula. Secure computer systems: Mathematical foundations. Technical Report ESD-TR-278, vol. 1, The Mitre Corp., Bedford, MA, 1973. 150, 152

13. E. Bertino, C. Bettini, E. Ferrari, and P. Samarati. An access control model supporting periodicity constraints and temporal reasoning. *ACM Transactions on Database Systems*, 23(3):231–285, September 1998. 172, 173

14. E. Bertino, S. de Capitani di Vimercati, E. Ferrari, and P. Samarati. Exception-based information flow control in object-oriented systems. *ACM Transactions on Information and System Security (TISSEC)*, 1(1):26–65, 1998. 165, 166

15. E. Bertino, P. Samarati, and S. Jajodia. An extended authorization model for relational databases. *IEEE-TKDE*, 9(1):85–101, January-February 1997. 177

16. K. J. Biba. Integrity considerations for secure computer systems. Technical Report TR-3153, The Mitre Corporation, Bedford, MA, April 1977. 153

17. M. Blaze, J. Feigenbaum, J. Ioannidis, and A. D. Keromytis. The role of trust management in distributed systems security. In *Secure Internet Programming: Issues in Distributed and Mobile Object Systems*. Springer Verlag – LNCS State-of-the-Art series, 1998. 189

18. M. Blaze, J. Feigenbaum, and J. Lacy. Decentralized trust management. In *Proc. of 1996 IEEE Symposium on Security and Privacy*, pages 164–173, Oakland, CA, May 1996. 189

19. W. E. Boebert and C. T. Ferguson. A partial solution to the discretionary Trojan horse problem. In *Proc. of the 8th Nat. Computer Security Conf.*, pages 141–144, Gaithersburg, MD, 1985. 164

20. P. Bonatti, S. de Capitani di Vimercati, and P. Samarati. A modular approach to composing access control policies. In *Proc. of the Seventh ACM Conference on Computer and Communications Security*, Athens, Greece, 2000. 187

21. P. Bonatti and P. Samarati. Regulating service access and information release on the web. In *Proc. of the Seventh ACM Conference on Computer and Communications Security*, Athens, Greece, 2000. 189, 190, 191

22. D. F. C. Brewer and M. J. Nash. The Chinese Wall security policy. In *Proc. IEEE Symposium on Security and Privacy*, pages 215–228, Oakland, CA, 1989. 162, 163

23. S. Castano, M. G. Fugini, G. Martella, and P. Samarati. *Database Security*. Addison-Wesley, 1995. 178

24. Y.-H. Chu, J. Feigenbaum, B. LaMacchia, P. Resnick, and M. Strauss. REFEREE: Trust management for Web applications. *Computer Networks and ISDN Systems*, 29(8–13):953–964, 1997. 189

25. D. D. Clark and D. R. Wilson. A comparison of commercial and military computer security policies. In *Proceedings IEEE Computer Society Symposium on Security and Privacy*, pages 184–194, Oakland, CA, May 1987. 178

26. E. Damiani, S. de Capitani di Vimercati, S. Paraboschi, and P. Samarati. Design and implementation of an access control processor for XML documents. *Computer Networks*, 33(1–6):59–75, June 2000. 191

27. E. Damiani, S. de Capitani di Vimercati, S. Paraboschi, and P. Samarati. Fine grained access control for SOAP e-services. In *Tenth International World Wide Web Conference*, Hong Kong, China, May 2001. 191

28. Database language SQL – part 2: Foundation (SQL/foundation). ISO International Standard, ISo/IEC 9075:1999, 1999. 177, 180, 181

29. C. J. Date. *An Introduction to Database Systems*. Addison-Wesley, 6th edition, 1995. 166

30. S. Dawson, S. de Capitani di Vimercati, P. Lincoln, and P. Samarati. Minimal data upgrading to prevent inference and association attacks. In *Proc. of the 18th ACM SIGMOD-SIGACT-SIGART Symposium on Principles of Database Systems (PODS)*, Philadelphia, CA, 1999. 156, 159

31. D. E. Denning. A lattice model of secure information flow. *Communications of the ACM*, 19(5):236–243, May 1976. 149, 161, 164

32. D. E. Denning. *Cryptography and Data Security*. Addison-Wesley, Reading, MA, 1982.

33. D. E. Denning. Commutative filters for reducing inference threats in multilevel database systems. In *Proc. of the 1985 IEEE Symposium on Security and Privacy*, pages 134–146, April 1985. 160

34. S. de Capitani di Vimercati, P. Samarati, and S. Jajodia. Hardware and software data security. In *Encyclopedia of Life Support Systems*. EOLSS publishers, 2001. To appear.

35. E. B. Fernandez, E. Gudes, and H. Song. A model for evaluation and administration of security in object-oriented databases. *IEEE Transaction on Knowledge and Data Engineering*, 6(2):275–292, 1994. 169, 171

36. D. Ferraiolo and R. Kuhn. Role-based access controls. In *Proc. of the 15th NIST-NCSC Naional Computer Security Conference*, pages 554–563, Baltimore, MD, October 1992. 181

37. R. Focardi and R. Gorrieri. The compositional security checker: A tool for the verification of information flow security properties. *IEEE Transactions on Software Engineering*, 23(9), September 1997. 161

38. T. D. Garvey and T. F. Lunt. Cover stories for database security. In C. E. Landwehr and S. Jajodia, editors, *Database Security, V: Status and Prospects*, North-Holland, 1992. Elsevier Science Publishers. 159

39. B. Gladman, C. Ellison, and N. Bohm. Digital signatures, certificates and electronic commerce. http://jya.com/bg/digsig.pdf. 189

40. J.A Goguen and J. Meseguer. Unwinding and inference control. In *Proc. of the 1984 Symposium on Research in Security and Privacy*, pages 75–86, 1984. 162

41. G. S. Graham and P. J. Denning. Protection – principles and practice. In AFIPS Press, editor, *Proc. Spring Jt. Computer Conference*, volume 40, pages 417–429, Montvale, N. J., 1972. 140

42. P. P. Griffiths and B. W. Wade. An authorization mechanism for a relational database system. *ACM Transactions on Database Systems*, 1(3):242–255, 1976. 175

43. J. T. Haigh, R. C. O'Brien, and D. J. Thomsen. The LDV secure relational DBMS model. In S. Jajodia and C. E. Landwehr, editors, *Database Security, IV: Status and Prospects*, pages 265–279, North-Holland, 1991. Elsevier Science Publishers. 157

44. M. H. Harrison, W. L. Ruzzo, and J. D. Ullman. Protection in operating systems. *Communications of the ACM*, 19(8):461–471, 1976. 140

45. T. Jaeger and A. Prakash. Requirements of role-based access control for collaborative systems. In *Proc. of the first ACM Workshop on Role-Based Access Control*, Gaithersburg, MD, USA, November 1995. 181

46. S. Jajodia and B. Kogan. Integrating an object-oriented data model with multilevel security. In *Proc. of the IEEE Symposium on Security and Privacy*, pages 76–85, Oakland, CA, 1990. 166

47. S. Jajodia and C. Meadows. Inference problems in multilevel secure database management systems. In M. D. Abrams, S. Jajodia, and H. J. Podell, editors, *Information Security: An Integrated Collection of Essays*, pages 570–584. IEEE Computer Society Press, 1995. 159

48. S. Jajodia, P. Samarati, M. L. Sapino, and V. S. Subrahmanian. Flexible supporting for multiple access control policies. *ACM Transactions on Database Systems*, 2000. To appear. 168, 169, 181, 185, 186, 187, 188

49. S. Jajodia and R. Sandhu. Polyinstantiation for cover stories. In *Proc. of the Second European Symposium on Research in Computer Security*, pages 307–328, Toulouse, France, November 1992. 155, 159

50. S. Jajodia and Ravi S. Sandhu. Toward a multilevel secure relational data model. In *Proc. CM SIGMOD International Conference on Management of Data*, pages 50–59, Denver, CO, May 1991. 155, 158

51. P. A. Karger. Limiting the damage potential of discretionary Trojan Horses. In *Proc. IEEE Symposium on Security and Privacy*, pages 32–37, Oakland, CA, 1987. 164

52. R. Kemmerer. Share resource matrix methodology: an approach to identifying storage and timing channels. *ACM Transactions on Computer Systems*, 1(3):256–277, April 1983. 161

53. B. W. Lampson. Protection. In *5th Princeton Symposium on Information Science and Systems*, pages 437–443, 1971. Reprinted in *ACM Operating Systems Review* 8(1):18–24, 1974. 140

54. C. E. Landwehr. Formal models for computer security. *ACM Computing Surveys*, 13(3):247–278, 1981. 138

55. L. J. LaPadula and D. E. Bell. Secure computer systems: A mathematical model. Technical Report ESD-TR-278, vol. 2, The Mitre Corp., Bedford, MA, 1973. 152, 153, 164

56. G. Lawrence. The role of roles. *Computers and Security*, 12(1), 1993. 181

57. N. Li, B. N. Grosof, and J. Feigenbaum. A practically implementable and tractable delegation logic. In *Proc. of the IEEE Symposium on Security and Privacy*, pages 27–42, Oakland, CA, 2000. 189

58. Teresa Lunt. Access control policies: Some unanswered questions. In *IEEE Computer Security Foundations Workshop II*, pages 227–245, Franconia, NH, June 1988. 168

59. T. F. Lunt. Aggregation and inference: Facts and fallacies. In *Proc. IEEE Symposium on Security and Privacy*, pages 102–109, Oakland, CA, 1989. 159

60. T. F. Lunt. Polyinstantiation: an inevitable part of a multilevel world. In *Proc. Of the IEEE Workshop on computer Security Foundations*, pages 236–238, Franconia, New Hampshire, June 1991. 155

61. T. F. Lunt, D. E. Denning, R. R. Schell, M. Heckman, and W. R. Shockley. The SeaView security model. *IEEE Transactions on Software Engineering*, 16(6):593–607, June 1990. 155, 158

62. C. J. McCollum, J. R. Messing, and L. Notargiacomo. Beyond the pale of MAC and DAC - Defining new forms of access control. In *Proc. of the IEEE Symposium on Security and Privacy*, pages 190–200, Oakland, CA, 1990. 164

63. J. McLean. The specification and modeling of computer security. *Computer*, 23(1):9–16, January 1990. 153

64. J. McLean. Security models. In *Encyclopedia of Software Engineering*. Wiley Press, 1994. 161

65. Communication of the ACM. Special issue on internet privacy. *CACM*, February 1999. 190

66. Oracle Corporation, Redwood City, CA. *Trusted Oracle7 Server Administration Guide, Version 7.0*, January 1993. 159

67. S. Osborn, R. Sandhu, and Q. Munawer. Configuring role-based access control to enforce mandatory and discretionary access control policies. *ACM Transactions on Information and System Security*, 3(2):85–106, 2000. 181

68. W. R. Polk and L. E. Bassham. Security issues in the database language SQL. Technical Report NIST special publication 800-8, Institute of Standards and Technology, 1993. 160

69. X. Qian and T. F. Lunt. A MAC policy framework for multilevel relational databases. *IEEE Transactions on Knowledge and Data Engineering*, 8(1):1–14, February 1996. 159

70. F. Rabitti, E. Bertino, W. Kim, and D. Woelk. A model of authorization for next-generation database systems. *ACM TODS*, 16(1):89–131, March 1991. 167, 169

71. J. Richardson, P. Schwarz, and L. Cabrera. CACL: Efficient fine-grained protection for objects. In *Proceedings of OOPSLA*, 1992. 171

72. M. Roscheisen and T. Winograd. A communication agreement framework for access/action control. In *Proc. of 1996 IEEE Symposium on Security and Privacy*, pages 154–163, Oakland, CA, May 1996. 189

73. P. Samarati and S. Jajodia. Data security. In J. G. Webster, editor, *Wiley Encyclopedia of Electrical and Electronics Engineering*. John Wiley & Sons, 1999.

74. R. Sandhu. On five definitions of data integrity. In *Proc. of the IFIP WG 11.3 Workshop on Database Security*, Lake Guntersville, Alabama, September 1993. 177

75. R. Sandhu and F. Chen. The multilevel relational (MLR) data model. *ACM Transactions on Information and System Security (TISSEC)*, 2000. 159

76. R. Sandhu, D. Ferraiolo, and R. Kuhn. The NIST model for role-based access control: Towards a unified standard. In *Proc. of the fifth ACM Workshop on Role-based Access Control*, pages 47–63, Berlin Germany, July 2000. 181

77. R. Sandhu and Q. Munawer. The ARBAC99 model for administration of roles. In *Proc. of the 15th Annual Computer Security Applications Conference*, Phoenix, Arizona, December 1999. 182

78. R. Sandhu and P. Samarati. Authentication, access control and intrusion detection. In A. Tucker, editor, *CRC Handbook of Computer Science and Engineering*, pages 1929–1948. CRC Press Inc., 1997.

79. Ravi S. Sandhu. Transaction control expressions for separation of duties. In *Fourth Annual Computer Security Application Conference*, pages 282–286, Orlando, FL, December 1988. 183

80. Ravi S. Sandhu, Edward J. Coyne, Hal L. Feinstein, and Charles E. Youman. Role-based access control models. *IEEE Computer*, 29(2):38–47, February 1996. 181

81. R. S. Sandhu. The typed access matrix model. In *Proc. of 1992 IEEE Symposium on Security and Privacy*, pages 122–136, Oakland, CA, May 1992. 143

82. K. E. Seamons, W. Winsborough, and M. Winslett. Internet credential acceptance policies. In *Proceedings of the Workshop on Logic Programming for Internet Applications*, Leuven, Belgium, July 1997. 190

83. Security. http://java.sun.com/products/jdk/1.2/docs/guide/security/index.html. 171

84. H. Shen and P. Dewan. Access control for collaborative environments. In *Proc. Int. Conf. on Computer Supported Cooperative Work*, pages 51–58, November 1992. 167, 169

85. A. Stoughton. Access flow: A protection model which integrates access control and information flow. In *Proc. of the IEEE Symposium on Security and Privacy*, pages 9–18, Oakland, CA, 1981. 164

86. R. C. Summers. *Secure Computing: Threats and Safeguard*. McGraw-Hill, 1997.

87. K. G. Walter, W. F. Ogden, W. C. Rounds, F. T. Bradshaw, S. R. Ames, and D. G. Sumaway. Primitive models for computer security. Technical Report TR ESD-TR-4-117, Case Western Reserve University, 1974. 165

88. W. Winsborough, K. E. Seamons, and V. Jones. Automated trust negotiation. In *Proc. of the DARPA Information Survivability Conf. & Exposition*, Hilton Head Island, SC, USA, January 25-27 2000. IEEE-CS. 190

89. M. Winslett, N. Ching, V. Jones, and I. Slepchin. Assuring security and privacy for digital library transactions on the web: Client and server security policies. In *Proceedings of ADL '97 — Forum on Research and Tech. Advances in Digital Libraries*, Washington, DC, May 1997. 189, 190

90. M. Winslett, K. Smith, and X. Qian. Formal query languages for secure relational databases. *ACM Transactions on Database Systems*, 19(4):626–662, December 1994. 159

91. T. Y. C. Woo and S. S. Lam. Authorizations in distributed systems: A new approach. *Journal of Computer Security*, 2(2,3):107–136, 1993. 184

92. J. Wray. An analysis of covert timing channels. In *Proc. IEEE Symposium on Security and Privacy*, Oakland, CA, 1991. 161

93. T. Yu, X. Ma, and M. Winslett. An efficient complete strategy for automated trust negotiation over the internet. In *Proceedings of 7th ACM Computer and Communication Security*, Athens, Greece, November 2000. 190

Security Goals: Packet Trajectories and Strand Spaces*

Joshua D. Guttman

The MITRE Corporation
Bedford, MA 01730 USA
guttman@mitre.org

Abstract. This material was presented in a series of lectures at FOSAD, a summer school on Foundations of Security Analysis and Design, at the University of Bologna Center at Bertinoro in September 2000. It has two main purposes.

The first purpose is to explain how to model and analyze two important security problems, and how to derive systematic solutions to them. One problem area is the "packet protection problem," concerning how to use the security services provided by routers—services such as packet filtering and the IP security protocols—to achieve useful protection in complex networks. The other problem area, the "Dolev-Yao" problem, concerns how to determine, given a cryptographic protocol, what authentication and confidentiality properties it achieves, assuming that the cryptographic primitives it uses are ideal.

Our secondary purpose is to argue in favor of an overall approach to modeling and then solving information security problems. We argue in favor of discovering security goals for specific domains by examining the threats and enforcement mechanisms available in those domains. Mathematical modeling allows us to develop algorithms and proof methods to ensure that the mechanisms achieve particular security goals. This leads to a systematic approach to trust management, often a more pressing information security problem than inventing new and improved security mechanisms.

1 Introduction

We summarize here a series of lectures at FOSAD, a summer school on Foundations of Security Analysis and Design, at the University of Bologna Center at Bertinoro, in September 2000.

1.1 The Purpose of These Lectures

This series of lectures has two main goals. The first goal is to explain how to model and analyze two important security problems, and how to design reliable solutions to them, namely:

---

* Work reported here was supported by the National Security Agency through US Army CECOM contract DAAB07-99-C-C201. Work was in collaboration with Amy L. Herzog, Jonathan C. Herzog, and F. Javier Thayer.

R. Focardi and R. Gorrieri (Eds.): FOSAD 2000, LNCS 2171, pp. 197–261, 2001.

1. How to use the security services provided by routers—services such as packet filtering and the IP security protocols—to achieve useful protection in complex networks; and
2. How to determine, given a cryptographic protocol, what authentication and confidentiality properties it achieves, assuming that the cryptographic primitives it uses are ideal.

We refer to these two problems as the packet protection problem and the Dolev-Yao [9] problem respectively.

The second goal is to argue in favor of an overall approach to modeling and solving information security problems, based around three ideas:

1. There does not exist any single property, which if we achieve it, will provide the information security we need in every situation.

    Instead, in each application area we must analyze the kinds of threat we face. From this, we can abstract a class of properties that capture the different meaningful protections in this type of situation. We call each property in the class a "security goal," and we regard the class itself as defining the range of security that may need to be provided in this application area.

    Different application areas will lead to different classes of security goals, formulated in terms of different modeling ideas.
2. Security goals need to be expressed using a simple, well-understood vocabulary of mathematical notions, and we will use the same vocabulary to model systems, the systems that we want to ensure will meet these security goals. In this series of lectures, the mathematical vocabulary we use will include boolean algebras and freely generated algebras of terms, as well as graphs. The graphs will include directed and undirected graphs, and at various stages we will need to partition either the nodes or the edges into distinct classes. Needless to say, this vocabulary is very familiar and very easy to reason about.
3. These mathematical notions themselves suggest algorithms and proof methods that are useful for *security management*. The mathematical notions lead to flexible and efficient ways to resolve problems, such as:
   (a) Does a given system meet a particular security goal?
   (b) Given a system, what security goals does it meet?
   (c) Given a security goal, how can we configure (or modify) a system to meet it?
   (d) Given a real-world system, how can we construct the abstraction that models it?
   (e) Given a real-world system, what automated tests (or manual analysis) will check whether a given abstraction models it faithfully? Whether a given security goal has been violated?
   (f) If two given systems each meet a security goal, does each continue to meet that security goal if they are combined in a particular way?

   These questions are the core of the crucial real-world problem of security management.

1.2   The Structure of These Lectures

We divide the remainder of our report into five sections.

Section 2 *Packet Trajectories*: Derived from [11,13]. Coauthors: A. Herzog and J. Thayer.
Contents: Introduce the packet protection problem. Define a class of security goals that filtering routers can achieve. Network model. Algorithms to determine whether given filtering behavior achieves a goal, and to assign filtering behavior that will achieve a given goal. Abstraction from router configuration files.

Section 3 *Strand Spaces and Protocol Security Goals*: Material derived from [47]. Coauthors: J. Herzog and J. Thayer. Also from [14,16]. Coauthor: J. Thayer.
Contents: Cryptographic protocols and the Dolev-Yao problem. Why cryptographic protocols fail: Unintended services. Powers of the penetrator. Strand space definitions. Authentication and secrecy goals.

Section 4 *Well-Behaved Bundles and Paths through Them*: Material derived from [16]. Coauthor: J. Thayer.
Contents: Bundle equivalence. Redundancies and redundancy elimination. Paths. The normal form lemma. Rising and falling paths, bridges, efficiency. Proof of the secrecy theorem.

Section 5 *Authentication Tests*: Material derived from [14,16]. Coauthor: J. Thayer.
Authentication tests: proving authentication and secrecy. Proofs of the authentication test results. Application to examples.

Section 6 *Protocol Independence via Disjoint Encryption*: Material derived from [15]. Coauthor: J. Thayer.
Contents: Multiprotocol strand spaces, independence. Disjoint encryption. Applications of protocol independence.

Copies of the papers cited above are available at URL

> http://www.ccs.neu.edu/home/guttman/.

Acknowledgements I am grateful to my coauthors Amy L. Herzog, Jonathan C. Herzog, and F. Javier Thayer. Dan Klain made numerous suggestions. Sylvan Pinsky and Grant Wagner provided stimulus, support, and discussion.

2   The Packet Protection Problem

In this section, we explore one security mechanism, namely filtering routers (and firewalls of related kinds). They are widely used to protect enterprises or their parts from attacks that could be launched from outside them. Wide practical experience exists as to the types of packets (identified by the IP, TCP and UDP headers) that are most capable of causing harm to their recipients, and firewall administrators configure their enforcement mechanisms to trade the danger of incoming datagrams off against the value of the network services that they provide and the level of trust in those that may have crafted the datagrams. We will describe a systematic method to ensure that security policies of this kind are faithfully implemented, despite the topological complexity of the networks. Most of this material is contained in [11] in a more systematic style, although the material on abstraction is previously unpublished.

We have carried out a similar study of how to use the IP security protocols (IPSEC) to achieve genuine confidentiality, authentication, and integrity. The IP security protocols apply cryptographic operations to individual datagrams, and they may be active either at the end systems (source and destination) exchanging the datagrams, or else at intermediate routers ("security gateways") that provide cryptographic services on behalf of nearby end systems. Indeed, IPSEC is currently used predominantly at security gateways, and there are large potential advantages of management in doing so. A systematic way to be sure of reaping those benefits is needed. That material is instead available in [13].

We start by considering the security goals that we would like to achieve. From those, we infer a way of modeling the goals (and the systems that should meet those goals) using simple mathematical notions. They in turn suggest algorithms to solve our security management problems.

2.1 Packet Filtering

The purpose of packet filtering is to prevent the delivery of packets that may harm the recipient, or occasionally to prevent the transmission of packets considered inappropriate (e.g. http requests to unwholesome servers). The filtering point must typically decide what action to take without examining the payload; only the headers are typically examined by the devices we are concerned with. Thus, aspects of the headers must be used as a clue to which packets ought to be discarded.

2.2 An Example

For instance, ICMP *destination unreachable* packets may be used to map an organization's network, to the extent of determining what IP addresses are in use and which routers are nearby. The attacker sends unsolicited ICMP *destination unreachable* messages with source IP address s into the organization. If the destination address d for that message is not in use, then a router r near the network on which d would lie sends back an outbound ICMP *destination unreachable* packet, with destination s. The source address for this packet is an IP address r for the router itself. In this way, the attacker learns which addresses are not in use (because an ICMP packet is returned); the rest are in use. He also learns which router r serves each missing IP address.

The scheme works because most firewalls permit ICMP *destination unreachable* packets to pass, because they are a useful part of the network infrastructure.

If an organization would like to prevent this sort of probing, then its administrators need to configure their routers (or firewall) to prevent it. They would prefer to allow as many ICMP packets as possible to pass around the network, so long as the attack is prevented. To prevent the attack with the least loss of service, the administrators would like to select a small number of filtering routers. Those routers will be the enforcement points. Each path should traverse an enforcement point, if that path leads from a network area where the attack might be launched to a network area whose contents should not be disclosed.

The enforcement point could discard inbound ICMP probes; indeed, it would suffice to discard inbound probes with destination addresses d that are not in use. The outbound replies are generated only for these addresses, so filtering these probes will ensure that no information is returned. Of course, this finer strategy can be used only if this set is known when the router configuration is chosen. Alternatively, the router could discard the outbound ICMP response, although in this case the packet source address is r, so that we cannot fine-tune the behavior depending on which addresses are in use.

2.3   Types of Information in Our Security Goals

There were two phases to the reasoning we have just described. One was to determine a potential kind of attack, and to infer from it a kind of packet that should be discarded, depending where that packet had come from. In the second phase, we looked for enforcement points, and attempted to assign filtering behavior to each enforcement point with the consequence that every harmful packet's path would be disrupted. We try to do so without disrupting the paths of too many other packets.

The security goal here is to prevent the delivery of certain packets, and the definition of *which* packets involves two different types of information. First, it concerns what the header of the packet says. In our example, we were concerned with the following IP header fields or protocol-specific header fields:

– The protocol header field in the IP header, which must indicate ICMP for this concern to be relevant;
– The ICMP-specific fields for message type and message code, which jointly indicate a *destination unreachable* message;
– The IP destination address, in case we wish to filter only inbound probes destined for addresses not in use.

In other examples, we would be concerned with the IP source address, or other protocols such as TCP or UDP, or with the protocol-specific fields for those protocols, such as source or destination port number, and the TCP syn and ack bits. All this information is contained in the datagrams, and available to any router inspecting it.

The other kind of information concerns the path that the packet has taken through the network. If the packet has never been on the public Internet, then we do not have to worry whether it is an attempt to map our networks. That is, assuming that we trust our employees not to attack us, or we acknowledge that they have other ways to obtain mapping information if they intend to carry out an attack.

The path information is not contained in the packet itself (certainly not in any reliable form, given the ways that packets can be spoofed). Indeed, no individual router can observe the whole path, but different routers observe different small pieces of the path. The behavior of a router for a packet it receives is sensitive to which interface the router received it over; and the behavior of a router for a packet to be transmitted is sensitive to which interface it will be transmitted over. The access lists governing filtering are specified on an interface-by-interface basis. Thus, they are sensitive to a portion of the path. The art of achieving the desired network-wide security therefore requires us to do different filtering at different points in the network, thereby disrupting the paths that worry us. A typical example network, containing enough information to represent the paths of concern to us, may take the form shown in Figure 1.

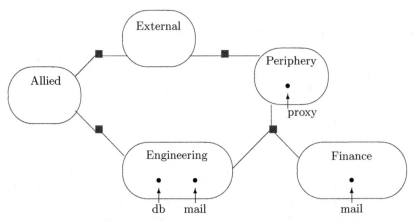

Fig. 1. Corporate protection example

The task of deciding on a security policy is simplified by the fact that information we care about is a limited portion of the path information: We care only whether the datagram was previously in a network region we do not trust, and whether the datagram has reached a region we would like to protect. A firewall policy can also enforce a confidentiality policy, thereby restricting the flow of packets from a vulnerable (internal) area to an untrusted (external) area. The strategy of filtering the outbound return ICMP packets in our example is a case of enforcing confidentiality (with regard to network information) via a firewall. Naturally, more inclusive kinds of confidentiality are likely to be harder to enforce reliably using a firewall.

2.4   The Logical Form of Our Security Goals

From our intuitive analysis, we can now stipulate the logical form of the security goals we would like to achieve. They integrate information about path with information about header in a specific way. A security goal always concerns two network areas a and a', with one (say, a) traversed earlier and the other a' traversed later. If a packet has followed any path from a to a', then its header fields should have some property φ. Thus, a "policy statement" for pair of areas a, a' is a statement of the form:

If p was in a and later reaches a',
then p's header fields satisfy φ.

Thus, for our firewall analysis, we have identified a class of security goals. Each goal describes a class of paths—those that traverse the areas a and a' in that order—and says which packets, defined in terms of header fields, are permitted to travel along those paths in the network. These firewall security goals are characterized by this logical form, namely an implication in which the antecedent mentions two areas in a particular order, and the consequent gives a constraint on the packets traversing those areas.

A *security policy*, in this context, will mean a security goal for every pair of areas. Given a graph in which the areas belong to a set A, a policy is a function $\Pi \colon A \times A \to B$, where B is some suitable collection of sets of packets.

In other contexts, other security goals will be needed. For instance, the security goals we can achieve using IPSEC, as have discussed in [13], may take different logical forms or require different real world ingredients to be modeled.

2.5   Some Security Goals

We have already mentioned two candidate security goals, each a possible way to prevent the ICMP *destination unreachable* network mapping attack. First, we may prevent the attack by pruning the incoming probe. We assume that the attack is possible only if the probe packet has passed through the External area (in the terminology of Figure 1), and we assume that we are concerned only about an attacker mapping our internal networks, labelled Engineering and Financial. The Periphery network, being more exposed, may well be vulnerable to mapping in any case. Thus, one security goal would be:

If p was in External and later reaches Engineering,
then p's header fields satisfy φ,

where φ stipulates

Either $p.destination \notin$ Engineering,
or $p.protocol \neq$ ICMP,
or $p.message\_type \neq$ destination unreachable.

Another example security goal in this network (assuming that most TCP connections are proxied at the application level on the Proxy host on the Periphery network) may be to ensure that no TCP packet travels from External to Engineering unless it is an SMTP packet, and its destination is the email server Eng_mail. In this case, the antecedent of the policy statement is unchanged, since we are still concerned with what packets reach Engineering from External; the choice of φ is then:

$$p.destination = \text{Eng\_mail},$$
and $p.protocol = \text{TCP},$
and $p.dest\_port = 25.$

2.6   Security Modeling

Our analysis of the security goals we would like to achieve also suggests some modeling decisions. We must model the paths of packets as they pass from a network area across an interface to a router and then across another interface to some other network area. Thus, we may regard the system as forming a graph. The edges represent the interfaces, and since packets may flow in either direction over an interface we may regard the edges as undirected. The nodes are of two different kinds, namely the router at one end of an edge and the network area at the other end. Thus, we represent the system by a bipartite graph with undirected edges. A diagram like Figure 1 summarizes this view of the topology of the system.

Now, at each edge, for each direction, we have a filter that will be used to discard some packets that would otherwise flow in that direction. The filter divides all packets into two sets, those that are permitted to flow over the interface in that direction and those that will be discarded. Since different characteristics of packet headers will be used to make these decisions, but presumably not every set of packets will be relevant, we will regard the relevant sets of packets as forming a boolean algebra, always a vastly smaller boolean algebra than the boolean algebra of all sets of packet headers.

Since there are thirty-two bits of source address, thirty-two bits of destination address, and eight bits for selecting protocols, there are at least 2^{72} different IP headers, so at least $2^{2^{72}}$ different sets of IP headers. For ICMP there are sixteen bits of protocol specific message type and message code; for TCP there are sixteen bits of source port and sixteen bits of destination ports, and likewise for UDP. Thus, we have many more sets considering these protocol specific header fields. Naturally, many of these sets are ridiculously ragged, and play no role in any meaningful network protection. The "practically useful" sets are comparatively few and far between, and have smoother edges.

In our example above, there are just a few distinctions we need among IP addresses. The special hosts have IP addresses that must be distinguished from all others, since filters will need to permit packets through specially, if those hosts are source or destination. Then the workstations in a particular network area may need to be distinguished from those in any other area. Finally, for our

ICMP example, we might want to distinguish the unused IP addresses in the three internal corporate networks. This leads to a total of twelve relevantly different IP addresses, far less than the 2^{32} different addresses a priori. There is a big advantage to taking a special-purpose representation of the boolean algebra of relevant packet sets, rather than using a representation that could express all the addresses and all the sets of addresses, and all the sets of packet headers.

Thus, our modeling process leads us to two ideas, the idea of a undirected bipartite graph to represent the network, and the idea of a boolean algebra to represent the constraints, both the sets permitted at the various filtering points and also the φs used in the consequents of security goals. Let us see now what problems we can solve using these two modeling ideas.

2.7   Localization

The core issue with our packet filtering security policies concerns localization. Although our security properties are global properties about all paths from a to a', even when these areas are distant from each other, our enforcement mechanism consists of routers each of which must make its own decision. It has only local information about what interface a packet has been received over, and what interface it will be transmitted over. Localization is the problem of achieving global security goals using this local information.

Localization may be used in two different ways. First, we may know what security goals we want to achieve, and also the filtering that will be applied on each interface to packets flowing in each direction. Then the problem is to decide whether each security goal is enforced by those filters. When they are not satisfied, one would like to exhibit the undesirable packets and the paths by which they may reach their targets.

Alternatively, we may decide on the security goals, and wish to discover an assignment of filtering to interfaces that will achieve them. Each of these two problems is a matter of localization, because the problem is to interrelate security policies stated in terms of network-wide paths, with an enforcement mechanism that must act locally at specific interfaces.

We will use the word *posture* to mean a specification of filtering behavior. Filtering routers allow a different set of packets to be filtered at each interface, and in each direction of flow, into the router or out of the router. Thus, a filtering posture will mean an assignment of a filter to each interface/direction pair. A filter just means a set of packets, namely those permitted to traverse the interface in that direction. The sets of packets are the members of some boolean algebra that will be far smaller than the boolean algebra of all sets of packet headers.

2.8   Two Algorithms

We have mentioned two problems, namely

1. Given a security policy and a filtering posture, to determine whether the posture faithfully enforces the policy, and if not, to enumerate the counterexamples; and
2. Given a security policy, to construct a filtering posture guaranteed to enforce the policy.

We will describe an algorithm to resolve each problem, for which we need some auxiliary notions. Let $p = \langle \ell_0, \ldots, \ell_n \rangle$ be a path p. Here, each ℓ_i is either an area or a router in a bipartite graph such as the one in Figure 1, and p is a path only if ℓ_i and ℓ_{i+1} are adjacent for each i from 0 to $n - 1$. We will write p_i for the ith entry in p; we will write $|p|$ for the length of p; and we will write $p_{|p|}$ for the last entry in p. We use $p \frown p'$ to mean the concatenation of p with p', which is well-defined only if $p_{|p|} = p'_0$, and is the path consisting of p followed by p', omitting the second occurrence of the common location at the end of p and beginning of p'.

We also assume to simplify notation that each router has at most one interface on any area. Thus, we regard a filtering posture as a function $f : R \times A \times D \to B$, where

R is the set of routers;
A is the set of areas;
D is the set containing the two directions *in* and *out*, meaning into the router and out of the router, respectively; and
B is a boolean algebra of sets of packets.

We adopt the convention that $f(r, a, d) = \emptyset$ when r lacks an interface on a. Let $\phi(\ell_i, \ell_j) = f(\ell_i, \ell_j, out)$ when ℓ_i is a router and ℓ_j is a network area, and $f(\ell_j, \ell_i, in)$ otherwise. Thus, in either case it is the set of packets allowed to traverse the interface from ℓ_i to ℓ_j.

We define $\mathcal{F}(p)$, the feasibility set for p, inductively:

1. $\mathcal{F}(\langle \rangle) = \mathcal{F}(\langle \ell_0 \rangle) = \top$, the top member of the boolean algebra;
2. $\mathcal{F}(p \frown \langle \ell_i, \ell_{i+1} \rangle) = \mathcal{F}(p) \cap \phi(\ell_i, \ell_{i+1})$.

Thus, the feasibility set for a path p is the set of packets that survive all of the filters that are traversed while following p. Observe that if the range of a filtering posture f is in the boolean algebra B, then $\mathcal{F}(p)$ is also in B, for any p. Also, by the laws of boolean algebra, $\mathcal{F}(p \frown p') = \mathcal{F}(p) \cap \mathcal{F}(p')$.

2.9   Posture Checking

Suppose given a posture f and a security policy $\Pi \colon A \times A \to B$, we would like to know whether f enforces Π. What does this mean?

It means that whatever path a packet may take from area a_0 to a_n, if that packet survives every filter it traverses, then it satisfies the policy constraint $\mathcal{F}(p) \subset \Pi(p_0, p_{|p|})$.

Note also that we may ignore any cyclic path $p = \langle \ell_0, \ldots, \ell_i, \ldots, \ell_i, \ldots \ell_n \rangle$, because

$$\begin{aligned}
\mathcal{F}(p) &= \mathcal{F}(\langle \ell_0, \ldots, \ell_i \rangle) \cap \mathcal{F}(\langle \ell_i, \ldots, \ell_i \rangle) \cap \mathcal{F}(\langle \ell_i, \ldots, \ell_n \rangle) \\
&\subset \mathcal{F}(\langle \ell_0, \ldots, \ell_i \rangle) \cap \mathcal{F}(\langle \ell_i, \ldots, \ell_n \rangle) \\
&= \mathcal{F}(\langle \ell_0, \ldots, \ell_i \rangle ^\frown \langle \ell_i, \ldots, \ell_n \rangle)
\end{aligned}$$

So p cannot cause more violations than its cycle-free part $\langle \ell_0, \ldots, \ell_i \rangle ^\frown \langle \ell_i, \ldots, \ell_n \rangle$.

Therefore, to find all violations, we need only enumerate, starting at each area a, each cycle-free path p leading to another area $a' = p_{|p|}$. We test $\mathcal{F}(p) \subset \Pi(a, a')$. If this is false, we report as violations all packets in the set-difference $\mathcal{F}(p) \setminus \Pi(a, a')$, noting that the path p permits them to pass. If no cycle-free path starting at any area a leads to violations, then f correctly enforces Π.

Doubtless, this algorithm could be made more efficient in several ways were it necessary to handle large graphs.

2.10   Posture Generation

Suppose next that we have a security policy Π that we want to enforce, and the task is to construct a filtering posture f that does so. The idea of this algorithm is this: We start with a simple but useful initial posture f_0, and we correct it successively to eliminate all violations.

The correction process enumerates all cycle-free paths p that start and end at distinct areas a_0 and a_n. The next-to-last entry in p is a router r, because the underlying graph is bipartite. Using the current approximation f_i, we calculate $\mathcal{F}(p)$. If $\mathcal{F}(p) \subset \Pi(a_0, a_n)$, then $f_{i+1} = f_i$. Otherwise, we correct the violations V, which are the packets in the set difference $V = \mathcal{F}(p) \setminus \Pi(a_0, a_n)$, those packets that may feasibly traverse the path p but are not permissible. The corrected posture f_{i+1} differs from f_i only for the arguments (r, a_n, out), where we have $f_{i+1}(r, a_n, out) = f_i(r, a_n, out) \setminus V$. Observe that this algorithm modifies only the outbound filters, not the inbound ones.

There are different strategies for constructing the initial posture f_0. A useful choice is the following.

1. $f_0(r, a_n, out) = \top$, the top member of the boolean algebra;
2. For any datagram δ, $\delta \in f_0(r, a, in)$ if $\delta.src \in a$, or else if, every a' adjacent to r, $\delta.src \notin a'$.

This choice of f_0 uses the inbound filters to protect against spoofing: If a datagram δ claims a source in some adjacent area a', but is observed entering r from some different adjacent area a, then δ must be lying. If it were really from a', it would reach r off its interface on area a'. This reasoning assumes that the packet has not been routed along on odd path because some network resources are currently down, but it matches an assumption that security-attuned network administrators frequently want to make.

This algorithm is not guaranteed to be ideal. The correction process discards packets only at the last step, immediately before they would finally cause a violation. It may be preferable instead, in a particular case, to discard the packet earlier, as it embarks on a path that will eventually lead to violations. Similarly, the choice of an anti-spoofing initial posture f_0 may not be ideal. For instance, a packet arriving at the External/Periphery router in Figure 1, inbound on its External interface, which claims to be from Finance, is doubtless lying, but our initial posture f_0 does not discard it. The reason is that Finance is not adjacent to this router. We know something about the way that packets from Finance should travel, but it would be hard to generalize that knowledge and incorporate it into our algorithm.

A reasonable implementation, such as the one described in [11] or its successor, the current Network Policy Tool (NPT) software available from the author, will combine this posture generation algorithm with the posture checking algorithm described previously. Then a human user can edit the posture output by the generation algorithm to make local improvements. The checking algorithm may then be used to ensure that these "improvements" have not in fact introduced violations. Alternatively, to understand why NPT has done something apparently unnecessarily complex, it is interesting to edit the output to the simpler, expected form. The checking algorithm will then show what would have gone wrong.

If one is given a posture f, it is also possible to calculate a security policy that describes what f permits; it is the policy Π_f inferred from f. It is defined by:

$$\Pi_f(a, a') = \bigcup_p \mathcal{F}(p)$$

where the union is taken over all p of the form $p = \langle a, \ldots, a' \rangle$.

2.11   Implementing Boolean Algebras

Any such piece of software needs to select a suitable data structure to represent the members of the boolean algebra. Different possibilities may be tried, although it is natural to regard each packet as a triple, consisting of a source IP address, a destination IP address, and "the rest."

The rest consists of information about the network service that the packet provides. It includes the packet's protocol field (possible values being TCP, UDP, ICMP, and so on), together with a variety of protocol specific fields. For instance, for UDP and TCP, the source port and destination port are important. If the destination port is a well-known value like 25, then this packet is headed toward a server (in this case an SMTP server); if its source port is 25, then it is headed from an SMTP server to a client.

For TCP, so are the syn and ack bits that say whether the packet belongs to the set-up phase of a connection, or to a connection that has already been negotiated. For ICMP, the message type and code are relevant.

Since each packet is characterized by the three dimensions of source, destination, and service, a boolean algebra of sets of packets may be regarded as consisting of regions of a three dimensional space. Although it is a large space, we are in fact interested only in rather coarse regions. For instance, looking at a diagram such as Figure 1, we can see that the number of relevantly different addresses is quite low, nine in fact:

- There are four specific systems mentioned, that will need special treatment in defining policy and implementing a suitable posture. They are `engineering db`, `engineering mail`, `finance mail`, and `periphery proxy`.
- Hosts other than these are treated uniformly according to the area in which they are located. Thus, we have `engineering other`, `finance other`, `periphery other`, `external any`, and `allied any`.

We also call these "relevantly different" addresses *abstract addresses.*

A similar consideration of the protocols and services that the network supports, and of the policy for permitting them from area to area, might lead to a short list of relevantly different services, for instance,

- ICMP, distinguishing *destination unreachable* messages from all others;
- TCP, distinguishing `ftp`, `smtp`, and `http` by their well-known ports;
- UDP, distinguishing messages to a particular port on the `engineering db` machine, on which a data base server is listening;
- all other protocols.

In addition, for the distinguished TCP and UDP services, one will want to treat packets differently depending whether the packet is traveling from client to server or *vice versa*; this doubles the number of distinguished TCP and UDP services. There is one additional service grouping together all others, the "undistinguished" services. On our example, we have thirteen relevantly different services:

- Two ICMP services;
- Seven $(= 3 \cdot 2 + 1)$ TCP services;
- Three $(= 1 \cdot 2 + 1)$ UDP services;
- One for the others.

We also call these relevantly different services *abstract services.*

All in all, there are $9 \cdot 9 \cdot 13 = 1053$ relevantly different packets in this example, leading to 2^{1053} sets in the boolean algebra. Naturally, far fewer sets will come up in any relevant computation. Observe that these "relevantly different packets," called "abstract packets" in [11], are the *atoms* of the boolean algebra, in the sense that any two atoms have a null intersection, and any set in the algebra is a union of atoms. Thus, an abstract packet is a triple, consisting of two abstract addresses (source and destination) together with an abstract service. Examples of these abstract packets, shown as triples of abstract source, destination, and service, would be:

```
(external any,  engineering any,   ICMP dest unreachable)
(engineering db,  allied any,  UDP db from server)
(engineering mail,   external any, TCP smtp to server)
```

Each of these represents a set of possible concrete (real) packets, namely all those with IP addresses matching the source and destination, and protocol specific header fields matching the service. It thus represents a cube in the three dimensional space of real datagrams, being the intersection of the sets of packets matching each of the three dimensions individually.[1] There are different ways to represent the algebra with these atoms. In NPT, we represent any set as a list of cubes, although we treat the source and destination dimensions specially. The lists are maintained in a form such that no source destination pair lies in the projection of two different cubes. For this reason, we described the lists as lists of colored rectangles, where the source-destination rectangles were always disjoint, and the permissible services for the packets with those sources and destinations were regarded as a coloring.

Wool and his colleagues [34] follow [11] in representing sets of packets as lists of disjoint colored rectangles, although in their work the relevantly different sources and destinations are not inferred at the start. Instead, they are constructed by examining real configuration files, and splitting IP addresses into ranges according to the access list lines contained in the configuration files.

One might alternatively dispense with lists of rectangles and instead represent the sets more directly, for instance using Binary Decision Diagrams (BDDs) [3]. In our next section, we will instead consider how BDDs can be used as an auxiliary structure to discover the set of atoms that naturally describe existing configuration files.

2.12   The Abstraction Problem

We have described how to use a boolean algebra in which the atoms are abstract packets as a way to represent problems about distributed packet filtering. But, how can we construct a boolean algebra that is faithful to the distinctions made in a particular set of configuration files? That is, we would like to take the configuration files for a given set of filtering routers, and deduce from them a set of abstract addresses and abstract services, such that the filtering posture determined by these configuration files can be represented in the resulting three dimensional boolean algebra. Indeed, we would prefer to choose the coarsest such boolean algebra, so that our abstract addresses and services make the minimum number of distinctions compatible with the files themselves. This is the problem addressed in [12], for which the binary decision diagram is an ideal data structure.

An abstract address is a set s of concrete IP addresses such that $i, j \in s$ implies that replacing i by j as the source or destination of a packet never transforms a packet rejected by a filter into a packet accepted by it, or *vice versa*. A set of IP addresses is an atom for a filtering posture is this holds for all of the filters specified by its configuration files.

---

[1] If there were some natural sense of adjacency for the points on the axes, this would amount to a finite union of cubes. Since we do not recognize any natural notion of adjacency, we collect together the matching intervals along any one axis, and regard the region as a single cube.

The problem is the more pressing because the router configurations of real organizations evolve over time as hosts and routers are added to the network or removed; as users clamor for additional services or administrators worry about new attacks; and as staff comes and goes with an increasingly hazy understanding of the contributions of their predecessors. Indeed, their decisions are typically documented only in the configuration file itself, with its low-level, procedural notation and inflexible syntax.

From our point of view, a configuration file such as for a Cisco router, contains *interface declarations* and *access lists*. An interface declaration may specify a particular access list to apply to packets arriving inbound over the interface or being transmitted outbound over the interface.

An access list is a list of lines. Each line specifies that certain matching packets should be accepted ("permitted") or discarded ("denied"). When a packet traverses the interface in the appropriate direction, the router examines each line in turn. If the first line that matches is a "deny" line, then the packet is discarded. If the first line that matches is a "permit" line, then the packet is permitted to pass. If no line matches, then the default action (with Cisco routers) is to discard the packet.

For instance, the lines in Figure 2 permit two hosts (at IP addresses 129.83.10.1 and 11.1) to talk to the network 129.83.114.*. They also permit the other hosts on the networks 129.83.10.* and 129.83.11.* to talk to the network 129.83.115.*. The asterisks are expressed using a netmask 0.0.0.255, meaning that the last octet is a wildcard.

```
!   (comments start with !)
!
! keyword    num action prot source              destination
access-list 101 permit ip   host 129.83.10.1     129.83.114.0 0.0.0.255
access-list 101 permit ip   host 129.83.11.1     129.83.114.0 0.0.0.255
access-list 101 deny ip     host 129.83.10.1     any
access-list 101 deny ip     host 129.83.11.1     any
access-list 101 permit ip   129.83.10.0 0.0.0.255 129.83.115.0 0.0.0.255
access-list 101 permit ip   129.83.11.0 0.0.0.255 129.83.115.0 0.0.0.255
```

Fig. 2. A cisco-style access list

2.13   The Logic of Access Lists

Each line of an access list defines a set of sources φ_s, destinations φ_d, and service characteristics φ_v, and stipulates whether matching packets should be discarded or passed. A datagram δ matches a line if $\delta.src \in \varphi_s \wedge \delta.dst \in \varphi_d \wedge \delta.svc \in \varphi_v$.

At any stage in processing, a packet that has not yet been accepted or rejected is tested against the first remaining line of the list. If the line is a "permit" line, the packet has two chances to be permitted: it may match the specification for the first line, or it may be permitted somehow later in the list. If the line is a "deny" line, the packet has to meet two tests to be permitted: it must not match the specification for the first line, and it must be permitted somehow later in the list. Since the default is to deny packets, the empty list corresponds to the null set of permissible packets. Thus, we have a recursive function η of the access list:

$$\eta([\,]) = \emptyset$$
$$\eta((\text{permit}, \varphi_s, \varphi_d, \varphi_v) :: r) = (\varphi_s \cap \varphi_d \cap \varphi_v) \cup \eta(r)$$
$$\eta((\text{deny}, \varphi_s, \varphi_d, \varphi_v) :: r) = \eta(r) \setminus (\varphi_s \cap \varphi_d \cap \varphi_v)$$

The function η allows us to transform a parser for the individual configuration file lines (emitting sets describing the matching conditions) into a parser that emits a set describing the meaning of the whole access list.

2.14   Binary Decision Diagrams

Again we face the question how to implement the boolean algebra of sets in this context, and for our current purpose of solving the abstraction problem, the binary decision diagram [3] fits our needs perfectly.

A binary decision diagram (BDD) is a finite directed acyclic graph with two sinks, labelled *true* and *false*. Each interior node has out-degree two, and is labeled with a propositional (bit-valued) variable. One out-arrow is associated with the variable taking the value *true* and the other with the variable taking the value *false*. One node is distinguished as the root.

A BDD n represents a propositional function; that is, it yields a truth value as a function of a number of truth-valued variables: to evaluate it for an assignment of values to the variables, we start at the root and follow a path determined as follows:

1. If we have reached a sink, its label is the result.
2. If the current node is labeled with variable v, and the assignment associates $v \mapsto b$, then we traverse the arrow associated with the value b.

Observe that any node n' accessible from a BDD n is itself a BDD. If α is an assignment of truth values to the variables, then we write $\alpha(n)$ for the truth value that results from evaluating n at α, i.e. traversing n as described above.

An example is shown in Figure 3, page 214. Each node represents a choice for the truth value of the variable shown at the right margin. The line marked + represents the result if that variable is true; the other line represents the result if that variable is false.

A BDD n is *ordered* if there exists an ordering $\prec$ on the variables such that $v \prec v'$ if any traversal starting at n encounters v before v'. A BDD n is *reduced* if, whenever n_0 and n_1 are accessible from n and $n_0 \neq n_1$, then there is some variable assignment α such that $\alpha(n_0) \neq \alpha(n_1)$. Thus, a BDD is reduced if its nodes obey the extensionality principle that different nodes represent different propositional functions. Algorithms for maintaining BDDs in ordered, reduced form are found in [2].

In our case, we are interested in using BDDs to represent sets of packets. Since a packet is determined by source address, destination address, and protocol-specific information, the propositional variables are the thirty-two bits of the source address (for IP Version 4), the thirty-two bits of the destination address, and a number of bits representing the protocol-specific information (sixty-four bits is enough). Thus, any protocol header may be summarized, to the extent we need to model how filter routers treat it, as a sequence of 128 bits. Any filter (set of packets) may therefore be represented as a reduced, ordered binary decision diagram where each internal node is labeled with one of these 128 propositional variables.

An example BDD is shown in Figure 3; in this diagram, we have assumed that IP addresses are only three bits, and that protocol-specific information may be summarized in four bits. The nodes are thus labeled $s_1, s_2, s_3,\ d_1, d_2, d_3$, and p_1, p_2, p_3, p_4. The variables are grouped into three sections representing source information, destination information, and protocol information.

2.15 Finding Atoms in BDDs

Suppose that we are given a BDD like the one in Figure 3, in which the variables have been divided into sections. We would like to identify the sets of values in each section that are treated as atoms. For instance, we will identify the sets of IP addresses that are treated the same as packet source addresses, so that if two addresses i, j belong to the same atom, then a packet with source address i and the identical packet with source address j will necessarily receive the same treatment from the packet filter. Two concrete addresses belong to the same abstract addresses if they are treated the same as sources and also as destinations.

To find the source atoms, we will enumerate the *outcomes*, meaning those nodes that are not labeled by source variables, but lie at the end of an arc starting at a node labeled by a source variable. In our example (Figure 3), one of these nodes is enclosed in a small box. If two paths lead to the same outcome, then those paths can make no difference: in combination with any assignment to the remaining variables, either both paths evaluate to *true* or else both paths evaluate to *false*. For instance, let p_1 be the path that assigns T to s_1 and s_2, and F to s_3; let p_2 be the path that assigns F to s_1 and s_2, and T to s_3. Then both p_1 and p_2 lead to the boxed outcome. Therefore they must belong to the same source outcome.

On the other hand, if two paths through the source variables lead to different outcomes, then because the BDD is in reduced form, there must be at least one assignment to the remaining variables that leads to different outcomes. Therefore, the paths do not belong to the same source atom.

This way of thinking suggests some definitions and an algorithm. First, let us call a sequence of variable/value pairs a *path* if the variables occur in an order compatible with $\prec$. Some examples of paths involving only source variables are:

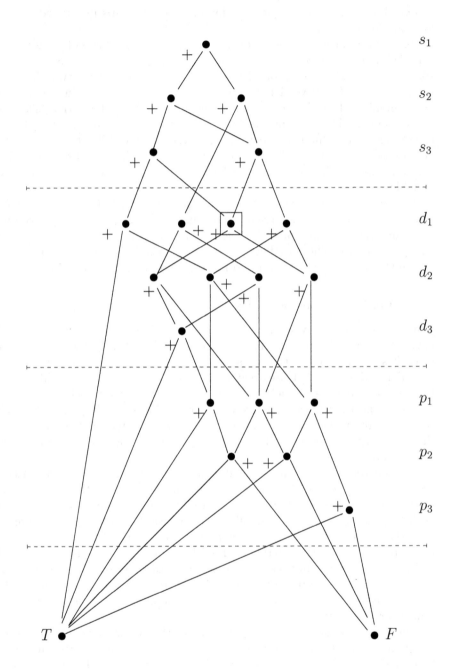

Fig. 3. An example BDD

$$(s_1, \mathit{true}), \quad (s_2, \mathit{true}), \quad (s_3, \mathit{false})$$
$$(s_1, \mathit{false}), \quad (s_2, \mathit{false}), \quad (s_3, \mathit{true})$$
$$(s_1, \mathit{false}), \quad (s_3, \mathit{true})$$

We say that a path p leads from n_0 to n_k, and write $n_0 \xrightarrow{p} n_k$, if there is a sequence of arcs leading from n_0 to n_k, and each node n_i for $i < k$ is labeled by a variable v_i mentioned in p, and the arc from n_i to n_{i+1} is labeled by the truth value paired with v_i in p. There may be several paths leading from n_0 to n_k. On the other hand, a particular path may not lead anywhere in a given BDD: the third path just mentioned does not lead anywhere in the BDD of Figure 3. In that BDD, each path involving s_1 and s_3 needs also to specify a value for s_2.

We may interpret each path as a formula in the obvious way, namely as a conjunction in which each variable in the path occurs negated if the associated value is *false* and unnegated if it is *true*. For convenience, we write the interpretation of a path p as $[\![p]\!]$. With this notation, we have the following interpretations for our example paths:

$$[\![(s_1, \mathit{true}), \quad (s_2, \mathit{true}), \quad (s_3, \mathit{false})]\!] \quad = \quad s_1 \wedge s_2 \wedge \neg s_3$$
$$[\![(s_1, \mathit{false}), \quad (s_2, \mathit{false}), \quad (s_3, \mathit{true})]\!] \quad = \quad \neg s_1 \wedge \neg s_2 \wedge s_3$$
$$[\![(s_1, \mathit{false}), \quad (s_3, \mathit{true})]\!] \quad = \quad \neg s_1 \wedge s_3$$

If s is a set of paths, we use $[\![s]\!]$ to mean the disjunction $\bigvee_{p \in s}[\![p]\!]$. Thus, for instance, if s contains the three paths mentioned above, then

$$[\![s]\!] \quad = \quad (s_1 \wedge s_2 \wedge \neg s_3) \vee (\neg s_2 \wedge \neg s_3) \vee (\neg s_1 \wedge s_3)$$

We also say that m is an *outcome* for n if for some path p, $n \xrightarrow{p} m$, and m does not lie in the same section as n, but if p' is any proper subpath of p and $n \xrightarrow{p'} n'$, then n' lies in the same section as n.

We can now see that each atom rooted at n_0 is of the form $[\![\{p \colon n \xrightarrow{p} m\}]\!]$ where m is an outcome for n. For if p, p' are two paths such that $n \xrightarrow{p} m$ and $n \xrightarrow{p'} m$, then they surely belong to the same atom. Since they re-join at m, no assignment to the remaining variables can cause p and p' to lead to different results. Moreover, if two paths lead to different outcomes, then by the extensionality principle for reduced BDDs, there must be some assignment to the remaining variables that separates them.

2.16   An Algorithm for Finding Atoms

The analysis we have just carried out motivates an algorithm for finding atoms in a BDD that has been divided into sections like Figure 3, where the sections consist of the source address variables, the destination address variables, and the protocol-specific variables. The two sinks lie below all three sections.

The algorithm maintains a hash table h that associates each outcome with the paths that lead to it. The algorithm has two phases. Phase one traverses the BDD rooted at n_0, and phase two traverses the hash table. In phase one, we recursively descend the BDD. If the node n at the end of the current path p is an outcome for n_0, then:

If h contains an entry s for n, then the new entry for n in h is $\{p\} \cup s$;
Otherwise the initial entry for n in h is the singleton $\{p\}$.

If n is not yet an outcome, recursively consider both extensions of the path p.

In phase two, we walk the hash table h. Each entry associates an outcome node n with the set s of paths leading from n_0 to n. Each entry determines an atom with value $[\![s]\!]$. Since every path from n_0 must eventually leave the section, each path reaches some outcome, which entails that the union of all the atoms is exhaustive. The atoms are mutually exclusive because any path reaches at most one outcome. Thus, we have derived a partition of the set of source addresses.

As described, this algorithm discovers the source atoms, those sets of source addresses that are treated the same by a single filter, when appearing as IP packet sources. The destination atoms may be calculated in the same way, starting from each outcome n that arose in finding the source atoms. Each outcome n leads to a list of destination atoms, containing those destination addresses that are treated the same starting from n. The algorithm is executed once starting for each source outcome n, each time yielding some destination outcomes. Finally, service atoms may be discovered starting from each of these destination-atom outcomes; in calculating the service atoms, the remaining outcomes can only be the two sinks *true* and *false*.

2.17   Source and Destination Addresses, Multiple Filters

So far, we have computed a partition of the set of source addresses; a family of partitions of the set of destination addresses, starting from various source-atom outcomes; and a similar family of partitions of services. This calculation analyzes a single filter. Several filters may be defined for different interfaces (and opposite directions of traversal) within the same configuration file, and several configuration files for different routers may need to be analyzed. How do we put all of these pieces together? Let us concentrate on constructing the right abstract addresses, the treatment of abstract services being essentially the same.

In essence, we have a number of partitions $\mathcal{F}_i$ of the IP addresses. Each partition is a congruence with respect to one condition, such as the source addresses of packets passing through a particular filter, or the destination addresses, assuming that the source led to a particular outcome. We call each of these families a *family of pre-atoms*. We want to construct a single partition of the IP addresses which is a congruence with respect to all of the conditions. It will thus be the coarsest common refinement of the $\mathcal{F}_i$.

To do so we must split the pre-atoms of $\mathcal{F}_i$ wherever the pre-atoms of $\mathcal{F}_j$ overlap with them. Let $s_i \in \mathcal{F}_i$ and $s_j \in \mathcal{F}_j$, and define superimpose(s_i, s_j) to be either the tag None or the tag Some applied to a triple of sets:

– None, if $s_i \cap s_j = \emptyset$;

- Some$((s_i \cap s_j), (s_i \setminus s_j), (s_j \setminus s_i))$, otherwise.

To add a single pre-atom s_i to a list f representing a family of pre-atoms we recursively apply the following procedure:

- If f is the empty list $[\,]$, then the result is the singleton list $[s_i]$.
- Otherwise, f is of the form $s_j :: rest$. If the result of superimposing s_i on s_j is None, recursively add s_i to $rest$, obtaining f', and return $s_j :: f'$.
- If the result of superimposing s_i on s_j is Some(c, s'_i, s'_j), then recursively add s'_i to $rest$, obtaining f', and return $c :: s'_j :: f'$.

Finally, if we have two families, represented as lists f_1 and f_2, then to combine them:

- If f_1 is the empty list $[\,]$, then return f_2.
- Otherwise, f_1 is of the form $s_1 :: rest$. Recursively, combine $rest$ with f_2, and then add the single pre-atom s_1 to the result (as defined above).

2.18 Atomizer Results

The Atomizer has been implemented as a rather large program written in OCaml, an implementation of ML developed at INRIA/Rocquencourt [25]. When run against a set of three unusually large configuration files in actual use, containing 1380 lines of access lists, it constructs about a hundred atoms. Computation takes 29 seconds on a 550MHz Pentium III with 700MB of store. The maximum process size is 58MB of store. The bulk of the space seems to be devoted to storing the BDDs, so that re-implementing that data structure in C (which is accessible from OCaml) would probably reduce the space used significantly.

When run against even larger but artificially generated configuration files, containing 5,575 lines of access lists, it completes in 20.5 seconds, having occupied 45MB of store.

The Atomizer generates abstract addresses and abstract services to be used in NPT, thus providing a method for analyzing actual router configurations to discover the security goals that they jointly achieve in use.

2.19 Packet Trajectories and Security Management

In this section, we have modeled the trajectories that packets may take through networks. We regard the networks as bipartite graphs, in which a node is either a router (used as an enforcement point) or a network area. Edges represent a router's interface on a network area. The packets that can survive all of the filters on a particular path form the *feasibility set* for that path. Given an implementation for boolean algebras and their fundamental operations, we can calculate feasibility sets, and use them to answer questions. We described an algorithm to determine whether a given posture meets a security policy. Another algorithm constructs a posture that will meet a security policy. We also described an algorithm that uses binary decision diagrams to determine (from a number of actual configuration files) the atoms that will be needed in the boolean algebra for these computations.

Thus, this approach to modeling allows us to answer a number of different *security management* questions about our networks. In the introduction, we enumerated some crucial security management questions. Let us return to that list, and comment on the extent to which our methods, as described in this section, give answers to them, in the specific context of packet filtering.

1. Does a given system meet a particular security goal?
   If the system is described in terms of the abstract packets passed or discarded at the different filtering points, then NPT answers this question.
2. Given a system, what security goals does it meet?
   We use the Atomizer to construct a suitable boolean algebra and representations of the filters. Then, given any two areas a, a', we can calculate the union of the feasibility sets $\bigcup_p \mathcal{F}(p)$ for all p such that $p_0 = a$ and $p_{|p|} = a'$. This union is the most inclusive security policy enforced by these filters.
3. Given a security goal, how can we configure (or modify) a system to meet it?
   We have described how to use NPT to calculate a posture to enforce the policy. We have not, however, described an algorithm to construct a (procedural, Cisco-style) configuration file from a list-of-rectangles specification for a filter, or from a BDD representing it, although work has been done in this direction.
4. Given a real-world system, how can we construct the abstraction that models it?
   Network mapping tools may be used to construct the bipartite graph for the system, after which the Atomizer designs the necessary abstractions for the filters.
5. Given a real-world system, what automated tests (or manual analysis) will check whether a given abstraction models it faithfully? Whether a given security goal has been violated?
   Our methods can be used to discover what packets are expected to emerge from a given interface; by sniffing the network and sampling the headers, we can raise an alarm if an unexpected packet is found. See also [22], in which specifications are used to generate test cases systematically.
6. If two given systems each meet a security goal, does each continue to meet that security goal if they are combined in a particular way?
   NPT can be used to determine the security consequence of adding direct network connections between previously distant areas.

Thus, we have illustrated in some breadth how to specify and reason about network-wide security policies for filtering routers, providing an instance of the rigorous approach to security management.

3   Strand Spaces and Protocol Security Goals

In the remainder of this series of lectures, we will discuss cryptographic protocols. We would like to define a particular type of failure, and the class of security goals that rule out these failures. We will explain our modeling for cryptographic protocols and their security goals in this section, and illustrate how to use the modeling ideas to detect flaws in protocols that have them. In Section 4 we will give a more rigorous treatment, leading to a simple method for proving that keys are not disclosed. Section 5 focuses on how to prove authentication goals. Finally, in Section 6, we will explain how to determine whether mixing two protocols will cause interactions that will undermine their (separate) security guarantees.

3.1 What is a Cryptographic Protocol?

A cryptographic protocol is a short, convention-bound sequence of messages. It uses cryptography to aim at security services such as authentication and key distribution (or key agreement) for session keys.

Despite their simplicity, cryptographic protocols are frequently wrong. Lowe estimates that about half the protocols published fail to achieve their goals in some respect [28]. Since this comment concerns only published, peer-reviewed protocols, one may imagine that the success rate for proprietary protocols would be lower. However, as a consequence of intense work on this problem, including apparently hundreds of published papers,[2] the quality of newer protocols such as SSH [50] and TLS [8] seems much better.

The problem is tricky because an attacker ("the penetrator") can be an active participant on the network itself. The attacker can start sessions with other principals, or wait for them to start sessions with each other or with the attacker (not realizing that the attacker is malicious). The penetrator can encrypt or decrypt using public keys, or legitimately obtained secret keys, or stolen keys, or keys extracted from messages. The penetrator can prevent the regular participants from receiving messages, and can substitute messages of his own.

3.2 The Dolev-Yao Problem

Because of this collection of potential tricks, it is difficult to see what the penetrator can accomplish. Indeed, the penetrator can sometimes undermine the goals of a protocol without any cryptanalysis. The attacks would succeed even if the protocol was implemented with ideal cryptography. The idea of studying protocol correctness without regard to cryptographic flaws is due to Dolev and Yao [9].

The terminology of correctness and flaws is, however, too crude. The question is really what security goals a cryptographic protocol can achieve. A "flaw" is a counterexample that shows that a protocol does not achieve some goal that we thought it should meet. A correct protocol is one that achieves specific goals that we find useful.

---

[2] See [6] for an extensive bibliography through the mid-nineties. Indeed, the present chapter has 50 citations, despite not citing large numbers of papers in the literature. For instance, we do not even cite [4], let alone the hordes of papers derived from it.

Thus, a more nuanced way to state the Dolev-Yao problem is, to determine, given a cryptographic protocol, what security goals it achieves, and to find counterexamples showing why it does not meet other goals. In doing so, one assumes that the cryptography in use is ideal, meaning that one cannot determine anything about plaintext from ciphertext, or anything about ciphertext from plaintext, without possessing the decryption or encryption key (respectively).

The problem is important, because cryptographic protocols are a central part of the infrastructure for secure communications and networking, and for distributed systems and electronic commerce. Their importance applies equally to military and civil systems. The Dolev-Yao approach of separating cryptographic issues from structural protocol flaws is valuable for two main reasons. First, it allows us to discover this class of flaws unencumbered by the complexity of cryptographic issues. Second, the same protocol can be implemented using a variety of different cryptographic algorithms; the Dolev-Yao approach tells us whether even the best adapted implementation can achieve its goals.

3.3   An Example: The Needham-Schroeder Public Key Protocol

The famous Needham-Schroeder article [37] introduced the idea of using cryptographic protocols to achieve authentication for networked systems. It discusses both secret-key and public-key protocols, and proposed one of each, both of which were problematic. Let us examine the public-key protocol. In this protocol (as presented here) each participant has the other's public key, guaranteed using some public-key infrastructure assumed reliable. The initiator A constructs a nonce—a randomly chosen bitstring—N_a and transmits it to the recipient B accompanied by A's name, encrypted in B's public key. B, if willing to have a conversation with A, replies with a nonce N_b of his own construction, accompanied by N_a and encrypted with A's public key. Finally, A replies with N_b, translated now into B's public key. This is summarized in Figure 4. We write

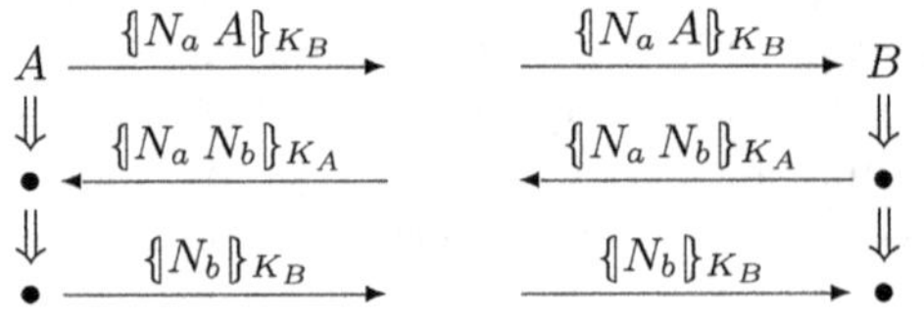

$$A \xrightarrow{\{\!|N_a\,A|\!\}_{K_B}} \qquad \xrightarrow{\{\!|N_a\,A|\!\}_{K_B}} B$$

$$\Downarrow \xleftarrow{\{\!|N_a\,N_b|\!\}_{K_A}} \qquad \xleftarrow{\{\!|N_a\,N_b|\!\}_{K_A}} \Downarrow$$

$$\Downarrow \xrightarrow{\{\!|N_b|\!\}_{K_B}} \qquad \xrightarrow{\{\!|N_b|\!\}_{K_B}} \Downarrow$$

Fig. 4. The Needham-Schroeder protocol

$\{\!|t|\!\}_K$ to mean the encryption of t by K, and $t\,t'$ to mean the concatenation of t and t'. The protocol is intended to authenticate A and B to each other, and to assure them that they share the secret values N_a and N_b. These values may be combined (for instance, using exclusive-or) for a symmetric session key.

One of the most important parts of Figure 4 is the whitespace that separates the left side from the right side. The initiator A knows that on a particular occasion he sent $\{\!|N_a\,A|\!\}_{K_B}$ and then received $\{\!|N_a\,N_b|\!\}_{K_A}$, but he certainly does not know that B received the outgoing message and sent the reply. Otherwise, there would be no need for authentication. On the contrary, A needs to deduce from the way that the protocol is constructed, that if $\{\!|N_a\,N_b|\!\}_{K_A}$ came back, only B can have sent it, assuming that B's private key, K_B^{-1}, is uncompromised.

Protocol analysis is the art of inferring what others have done, knowing only what one has done oneself, and the laws of the protocol.

Unfortunately, in this protocol, we cannot simply ignore the whitespace. There is another way that things can fit together, if a malicious penetrator is present, shown in Figure 5. The attack is due to Lowe [27], and was discovered a decade and a half after the protocol was published. A has initiated a session

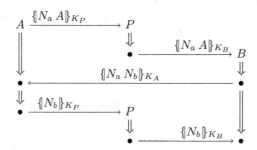

Fig. 5. A bundle: penetrated run of Needham-Schroeder

with a participant P who has decided to misbehave, possibly in response to this opportunity. As a consequence of A's bad luck, B is duped. B believes that he shares the confidential values N_a, N_b with A, whereas messages encrypted with the resulting session key will come from P.

A is not duped, because A intended to communicate with P and has done so. B is duped, because B believes that A is sending messages to B using the resulting session key, whereas P is doing so. Secrecy has failed, because the nonces and session key are known to P, and authentication has failed, because A has no run of the protocol intended for B, whereas B has a run apparently with A. How has this situation come about?

3.4   Unintended Services

The protocol itself imposes an obligation on A, when A starts a run as initiator, with responder P. A transmits a value N_a, and then undertakes to provide a service. If a value of the form $\{\!|N_a\,N|\!\}_{K_A}$ is presented (for any N), then A will perform a translation. A will translate N into the form $\{\!|N|\!\}_{K_P}$. Thus, N is retransmitted in a form that P can read. We call this an unintended service, because the protocol requires initiators to perform it, despite its being potentially useful to penetrators.

Indeed, getting N in a readable form is particularly useful to a penetrator, and the reason for this becomes clear when we consider how the responder B gets his authentication guarantee. B can get a guarantee that A is executing his matching run only by receiving some message from B that only A can produce, and only in a matching run.

If we look at B's behavior, he receives only two messages. The first message is of the form $\{\!| N\, A |\!\}_{K_B}$. Since K_B is public, anyone can create a nonce N, concatenate it with A's name, and encode it with the public key. Therefore, from the point of view of its authenticating force, this message is mere junk. It contributes to no guarantee. Thus, any authenticating force is concentrated in the last message $\{\!| N_b |\!\}_{K_B}$.

Thus, we may examine a principal's incoming messages to determine which are junk. Discarding the junk messages, we are left with the other messages, those capable of providing authenticating force. We then examine the protocol to see what unintended services it provides, and whether these unintended services suffice to counterfeit the non-junk messages. This is a practical recipe for informal protocol analysis.

3.5   Another Example: An ISO Candidate

The protocol shown in Figure 6 was a candidate considered by an ISO committee as a *pure* authentication protocol. No shared secret is achieved. It was intended merely to assure each principal that the expected partner was initiating communications. In this protocol A uses his private key K_A^{-1} to sign nonces passed to B,

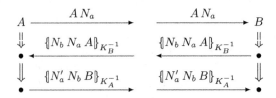

Fig. 6. An ISO candidate protocol

and conversely. Considering how A may authenticate itself to B, clearly the first, unsigned message is junk. Thus, the last message $\{\!| N'_a\, N_b\, B |\!\}_{K_A^{-1}}$ contains any authenticating force. Thus, we want to look for unintended services that would create a value of this form.

The possible services are the two transformations shown in Figure 7. In these services, any variables originating in incoming messages may be freely renamed.

Those originating on outgoing messages, by contrast, are created by the principal, and therefore cannot be manipulated by the penetrator. Now if A is active as a responder, and is presented with the values $B\,N_b$ in the incoming message, then the target term $\{\!|N_a'\,N_b\,B|\!\}_{K_A^{-1}}$ will be the result.

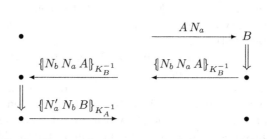

Fig. 7. Unintended services in the ISO candidate

The resulting attack is shown in Figure 8. Since it was discovered by the Canadian representatives to the committee, it is sometimes called the Canadian attack. To discover this attack, we discarded junk messages and focused on the

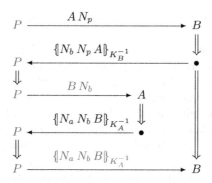

Fig. 8. The canadian attack

remaining non-junk target. The unintended services provided by the protocol then give us a recipe for generating our target message. In fact, it is easy to multiply examples in which this method of junk messages and unintended services lead us to attacks.

3.6 Types of Unintended Service

There are effectively four types of unintended service that a protocol can offer to the penetrator.

Signature In a signature service, a protocol entity is required to sign messages containing an incoming ingredient.

The transformation is $N_a \mapsto \{\!|\ N_a\ |\!\}_{K^{-1}}$. The Canadian attack of Section 3.5 is an example.

Encryption In an encryption service, a protocol entity is required to encrypt messages containing an incoming ingredient.

The transformation is $N_a \mapsto \{\!|\ N_a\ |\!\}_K$. It frequently occurs in protocols in which the ability to encrypt using a symmetric key is used as an authenticating characteristic.

Decryption In a decryption service, a protocol entity is required to decrypt messages containing an incoming ingredient.

The transformation is $\{\!|\ N_a\ |\!\}_K \mapsto N_a$. This one does not occur in nature as far as I know; presumably it is too obviously a problem.

Translation In a translation service, a protocol entity receives encrypted messages and transmits some ingredients encrypted under a different key.

The transformation is $\{\!|\ N_a\ |\!\}_K \mapsto \{\!|\ N_a\ |\!\}_{K'}$. Lowe's attack on the Needham-Schroeder protocol is an example.

3.7 The Dolev-Yao Problem Defined

The Dolev-Yao problem is the following challenge. The player is presented with a cryptographic protocol. The player must then state the secrecy properties and authentication properties that the protocol achieves. He must also give counter-examples to any secrecy or authentication properties that he believes it does not achieve.

In playing this game, the player is allowed to assume that cryptographic primitives will be chosen to be perfect. The primitives will never have collisions. The penetrator can infer nothing about plaintext, given a ciphertext, without using the key. Conversely, the penetrator can infer nothing about ciphertext, given a plaintext, without using the key. Moreover, the penetrator cannot learn a key, unless the key is contained in a message that the penetrator can decrypt.

We have already explained how to play the second part of the game, the part where counter-examples must be given. The next section is devoted to explaining how to find and prove the secrecy and authentication properties protocols achieve. The remainder of this section will be devoted to defining our model of protocol execution, called the strand space model, and to defining what secrecy and authentication properties mean in this model.

3.8 Strand Space Ideas

We very briefly summarize the ideas behind the strand space model [47,16]; see also the definitions given in Section 3.14, which is an appendix to Section 3.

A is the set of messages that can be sent between principals. We call elements of A *terms*. A is freely generated from two disjoint sets, T (representing texts such as nonces or names) and K (representing keys) by means of concatenation and encryption. The concatenation of terms g and h is denoted $g\,h$, and the encryption of h using key K is denoted $\{\!|h|\!\}_K$. (See Section 3.14.)

A term t is a *subterm* of another term t', written $t \sqsubset t'$, if starting with t we can reach t' by repeatedly concatenating with arbitrary terms and encrypting with arbitrary keys. Hence, $K \not\sqsubset \{\!|t|\!\}_K$, except in case $K \sqsubset t$. The subterms of t are the values that are uttered when t is sent; in $\{\!|t|\!\}_K$, K is not uttered but used. (See Definition 6.)

A *strand* is a sequence of message transmissions and receptions, where transmission of a term t is represented as $+t$ and reception of term t is represented as $-t$. A strand element is called a *node*. If s is a strand, $\langle s, i \rangle$ is the ith node on s. The relation $n \Rightarrow n'$ holds between nodes n and n' if $n = \langle s, i \rangle$ and $n' = \langle s, i+1 \rangle$. Hence, $n \Rightarrow^{+} n'$ means that $n = \langle s, i \rangle$ and $n' = \langle s, j \rangle$ for some $j > i$. Each column of nodes connected by vertical arrows $\Rightarrow$ in Figures 4–8 is a strand.

The relation $n \rightarrow n'$ represents inter-strand communication; it means that term$(n_1) = +t$ and node term$(n_2) = -t$. Inter-strand communication is shown by horizontal arrows $\rightarrow$ in Figures 5–8.

A *strand space* Σ is a set of strands. The two relations $\Rightarrow$ and $\rightarrow$ jointly impose a graph structure on the nodes of Σ. The vertices of this graph are the nodes, and the edges are the union of $\Rightarrow$ and $\rightarrow$.

We say that a term t *originates* at a node $n = \langle s, i \rangle$ if the sign of n is positive; $t \sqsubset$ term(n); and $t \not\sqsubset$ term$(\langle s, i' \rangle)$ for every $i' < i$. Thus, n represents a message transmission that includes t, and it is the first node in s including t. For instance, A and N_p originate at the top left node of Figure 8. If a value originates on only one node in the strand space, we call it *uniquely originating*; uniquely originating values are desirable as nonces and session keys.

A bundle is a finite, causally well-founded collection of nodes and arrows of both kinds. In a bundle, when a strand receives a message m, there is a unique node transmitting m from which the message was immediately received. By contrast, when a strand transmits a message m, many strands (or none) may immediately receive m. (See Definition 3.) Figures 5 and 8 are examples of bundles; those examples happen to be undesirable.

Since a bundle $\mathcal{C}$ is an acyclic directed graph, the reflexive, transitive closure of the arrows ($\rightarrow$ together with $\Rightarrow$) form a partial order $\preceq_\mathcal{C}$. The statement $m \preceq_\mathcal{C} n$ means that there is a path from m to n traversing 0 or more arrows, in which both $\rightarrow$ and $\Rightarrow$ may appear. Because $\mathcal{C}$ is finite, $\preceq_\mathcal{C}$ is a well-ordering, meaning that every non-empty set of nodes contains a $\preceq_\mathcal{C}$-minimal element. This is an induction principle, used extensively in [47].

The height of a strand in a bundle is the number of nodes on the strand that are in the bundle. Authentication theorems generally assert that a strand has at least a given height in some bundle, meaning that the principal must have engaged in at least that many steps of its run.

A strand represents the local view of a participant in a run of a protocol. For a legitimate participant, it represents the messages that participant would send or receive as part of one particular run of his side of the protocol. We call a strand representing a legitimate participant a *regular* strand.

3.9   The Powers of the Penetrator

For the penetrator, the strand represents an atomic deduction. More complex actions can be formed by connecting several penetrator strands. While regular principals are represented only by what they say and hear, the behavior of the penetrator is represented more explicitly, because the values he deduces are treated as if they had been said publicly.

We partition penetrator strands according to the operations they exemplify. E-strands encrypt when given a key and a plaintext; D-strands decrypt when given a decryption key and matching ciphertext; C-strands and S-strands concatenate and separate terms, respectively; K-strands emit keys from a set of known keys; and M-strands emit known atomic texts or guesses. A parameter to the model is the set $K_\mathcal{P}$ of keys known initially to the penetrator. It represents an assumption about what keys the penetrator may emit on K-strands, as opposed to getting them indirectly, for instance by decrypting a message containing a new session key. (See Definition 8.)

As an example of how the penetrator can hook together several atomic strands to achieve a harmful compound effect, let us consider how the penetrator carries out his attack in Figure 5. To get from the incoming value $\{\!|N_a\,A|\!\}_{K_P}$ to the outgoing value $\{\!|N_a\,A|\!\}_{K_B}$, the penetrator must decrypt and then encrypt. To decrypt $\{\!|N_a\,A|\!\}_{K_P}$, the penetrator must apply his (private) decryption key K_P^{-1}. He obtains this directly, as it is assumed a member of the set $K_\mathcal{P}$ that he possesses from the start. In the encryption that produces $\{\!|N_a\,A|\!\}_{K_B}$, the penetrator applies B's public key. We my also assume that it is a member of the set $K_\mathcal{P}$, because it is public knowledge. Thus, we may diagram the penetrator's activity as shown in Figure 9. The lower column of penetrator activity in Figure 5 may be expanded similarly.

3.10   Representing Protocols

We turn now to the regular participants. Unlike the powers of the penetrator, which are the same regardless of the protocol, the behavior of the regular principals is dictated by the protocol. We may assume that we already have a diagram describing the protocol, in the style of Figure 4. To define a protocol, we take three steps. We will illustrate these steps starting with the Carlsen protocol [5], the diagram for which is shown in Figure 10.

Auxiliary Functions A public-key protocol typically requires a function associating a public key with each principal. A symmetric-key protocol typically requires a function associating a long-term key, shared with a key server, with each principal. We typically write such functions using subscripts, with K_A being the key associated with A, and refer to it as the "key-of" function. In the

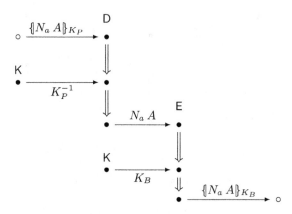

Fig. 9. Penetrator activity in figure 5

case of the Carlsen protocol, K_A represents the long-term key of A, shared with the key server.

If a protocol uses a key server as Carlsen's protocol does, then we will require that the session keys it chooses must be disjoint from the range of "key-of" function.

Occasionally a protocol requires a different function, such as a function associating a long-term shared secret with each pair of principals.

Parametric Strands Next we define the strands for the protocol. To do this, we start from the columns shown in the diagram. Each separate column represents a different role. In the Carlsen protocol, they are initiator, responder, and key server.

In some cases, there may be message components received a principal that it cannot check, because they are encrypted using a key that the recipient does not possess. These terms are simply forwarded to another principal. They will be represented simply by variables. The component (presumably) of the form $\{\!|N_a\, B\, K|\!\}_{K_A}$ cannot be checked when it is received by B. B can only forward it to A. We will represent this component using the variable H. Other messages are represented by terms of the obvious form.

By collecting the variables occurring in any term sent or received by that column, we find the parameters for that role. The parameters for the recipient are $A, B, N_a, N_b, K, N_b', H$, while those for the initiator are A, B, N_a, K, N_b'. The initiator never sees N_b, and never interprets an encrypted unit as H. The parameters for the key server are A, B, N_a, N_b, K, since it never sees N_b' and never interprets an encrypted unit as H. We write:

- CInit$[A, B, N_a, K, N_b']$ is the set of strands with trace (behavior):

$$+A\, N_a, \quad -\{\!|N_a\, B\, K|\!\}_{K_A}\, \{\!|N_a|\!\}_K\, N_b', \quad +\{\!|N_b'|\!\}_K$$

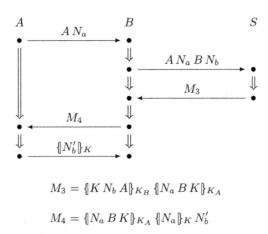

$$M_3 = \{\!| K \, N_b \, A |\!\}_{K_B} \, \{\!| N_a \, B \, K |\!\}_{K_A}$$

$$M_4 = \{\!| N_a \, B \, K |\!\}_{K_A} \, \{\!| N_a |\!\}_K \, N_b'$$

Fig. 10. Carlsen's protocol

This means that first a message is sent containing A and N_a, and then a message is received containing the nonce N_a again, encrypted in A's long-term key, and so on.

- CResp$[A, B, N_a, N_b, K, N_b', H]$ is the set of strands with trace

$$-A \, N_a, \quad +A \, N_a \, B \, N_b, \quad -\{\!| K \, N_b \, A |\!\}_{K_B} \, H, \quad +H \, \{\!| N_a |\!\}_K \, N_b', \quad -\{\!| N_b' |\!\}_K$$

- CServ$[A, B, N_a, N_b, K]$ is the set of strands with trace

$$-A \, N_a \, B \, N_b, \quad +\{\!| K \, N_b \, A |\!\}_{K_B} \, \{\!| N_a \, B \, K |\!\}_{K_A}$$

We write $*$ in particular argument positions to indicate a union. For instance,

$$\text{CInit}[A, B, *, *, *] = \bigcup_{N_a, K, N_b'} \text{CInit}[A, B, N_a, K, N_b']$$

is the set of all initiator strands involving A and B, with any nonces and session keys. We also use $**$ to indicate that multiple adjacent arguments have been projected, writing e.g. CInit$[A, B, **]$ for CInit$[A, B, *, *, *]$.

The regular strands are generated by filling in the parameters with appropriate values. Instantiations may be limited to subtypes of the message algebra. For instance, the parameters A and B may be instantiated with any value that names a principal (perhaps these are IP addresses or X.509 Distinguished Names); N_a may be instantiated with any bitstring of length 128; and so on. We assume that there is some association D of variables with sets of terms in A. Very often it is convenient to assume some of these sets are disjoint, for instance the sets $D(N_a), D(K), D(A)$ of nonces, keys, and names (respectively).

Often, a strand space contains strands belonging to a parametric strand whenever the instantiation is type-correct. For instance, in the case of a parametric strand such as CServ$[A, B, N_a, N_b, K]$, if $a \in D(A)$, $b \in D(B)$, $n_a \in$

$D(N_a)$, $n_b \in D(N_b)$, and $k \in D(K)$, then $\text{CServ}[a, b, n_a, n_b, k]$ is non-empty. Sometimes it is convenient to stipulate that variables get distinct instantiations. For instance, in our formalization of the Needham-Schroeder-Lowe responder's guarantee (see below, Section 3.12 and [47,16]) we assume that the responder's nonce N_b is different from the initiator's nonce N_a. This may be encoded into the strand space itself by stipulating that $\text{NSLResp}[a, b, n_a, n_b]$ is non-empty whenever $a \in D(A)$, $b \in D(B)$, $n_a \in D(N_a)$, $n_b \in D(N_b)$, and $n_a \neq n_b$.

Restricted Values There are also some additional restrictions on the way that the values are used. For instance, in the case of the Carlsen protocol, the values N_a, N_b, and N_b' are nonces. This means that they are intended to originate uniquely. The session keys K are also intended to originate uniquely, as well as to be disjoint from the long-term keys. Correctness goals may also depend on the assumption that the player's long-term keys are not in $\mathsf{K}_{\mathcal{P}}$, the penetrator's initial knowledge, compromised through nefarious means or lucky guessing. This assumption is unavoidable, in that, when $K_A \in \mathsf{K}_{\mathcal{P}}$, the key server and B can have no assurance that A has done anything, or that session keys destined for A remain secret.

In this protocol, the assumption that $K_A \notin \mathsf{K}_{\mathcal{P}}$ is also an origination assumption. It amounts to the assumption that K_A will originate nowhere. It entails that K_A does not originate on a penetrator K-strand. No key originates on an initiator or responder strand in this protocol. And we have assumed that the session keys originating at the key server are disjoint from the long-term keys.

Origination restrictions are of course implemented using probabilistic mechanisms in reality, and some work has been done on quantifying the extent to which a particular implementation is reliable [17].

3.11   Unique Origination and Non-origination

The value N_a *originates* on the first node of any strand $s \in \text{CInit}[*, *, N_a, *, *]$. What we mean by this is that a message is sent on that node, and the message contains N_a, and that this is the first node on the strand containing N_a. By contrast, N_b' does not originate on the third node of any $s \in \text{CInit}[**, N_b']$, because although a message is sent on that node and that message contains N_b', the previous (receiving) node also contained N_b'.

We say that a term t originates uniquely in a bundle $\mathcal{C}$ if there is exactly one node n in $\mathcal{C}$ such that t originates on n. When there is no node on which t originates, we say that t is non-originating in $\mathcal{C}$.

In particular, K_A does not originate on $s \in \text{CServ}[A, **]$, because although a term encrypted with K_A is sent on the second node of s, and K_A has not been used previously, K_A is not a subterm of the message. It contributes to *how* the term is constructed, but not what the term contains, and this is the intuition formalized in our definition of *subterm* (Definition 6).

Assumptions about unique origination and non-origination are a way of restricting what attacks on a protocol we are willing to worry about. For instance, in Figure 11 we illustrate an "attack" on the Needham-Schroeder protocol in which the penetrator simply somehow knows what the responder's nonce N_b is. While this could conceivably happen, it is not a strategy likely to succeed for

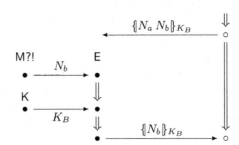

Fig. 11. An improbable attack: guessing a Needham-Schroeder nonce

the penetrator. Protocol design, therefore, does not need to concern itself systematically with how to prevent it.

A bundle describes what happens when a protocol runs, and in this we follow Robert Lowell's maxim, "Why not say what happened?" A bundle may contain some regular strands and some penetrator strands. The events of sending and receiving messages are connected in a causally well-founded way. We are concerned with a particular bundle only if it satisfies some unique origination conditions and some non-origination assumptions; otherwise, things may go wrong, but it is too implausible an attack.

3.12   What Is an Authentication Goal?

Strands are a suggestive formalism for understanding authentication and authentication failures. A strand represents one principal's experience of a protocol execution. The strand includes the information that the principal knows directly, namely that it sent certain messages and received other messages, in a particular order. Security goals for protocols concern what else must also have happened. Authentication goals are about what another regular principal must have done. Secrecy goals are inferences about what the penetrator cannot have done.

Let us return to the Needham-Schroeder protocol to consider what authentication goals are, in the light of the failure illustrated in Figure 5. One of the goals of the protocol is to assure the responder B,

For every B-strand (apparently with A),
there is an A-strand (apparently with B),
and they agree on the nonces N_a, N_b.[3]

---

[3] It is sometimes said that this was not a goal of the protocol as originally described, but that the protocol was intended only to establish that A was active. That is,

The attack shows that there can be a B-strand, apparently with A, without any A-strand apparently with B.

This example is typical. An authentication result justifies a sound inference, and a counterexample to an authentication property shows that the inference is unsound. From B's local experience, a conclusion about A's behavior should follow. Naturally, there are assumptions that must be met for the inference to hold good, and protocol analysis is informative because it identifies exactly what the assumptions are.

When we consider the epistemology of authentication protocols, that is, the theory of knowledge that applies to them, there are four ingredients. First, there are the facts that a principal knows, which is to say the message sends and receives belonging to a single strand. Second, there are the conventions of the protocol, which dictate that the behavior of other regular participants will be described by the strands of the protocol. Third, there is the model of the penetrator embodied in Definition 8. Finally, there assumptions about origination: the unique origination of nonces and session keys, and the non-origination of long-term secrets.

From these elements, we try to infer what other events have occurred. The real world (the bundle) must contain events that causally explain what we saw. To find out what these events could be, we use the causal laws embodied in the definition of bundle (Definition 3). We may use these principles:

- What is heard was said, i.e. every negative node has a unique in-arrow in the bundle $\mathcal{C}$;
- Every principal starts at the beginning, i.e. if $n \in \mathcal{C}$, and $m \Rightarrow n$ precedes it on the same strand, then $m \in \mathcal{C}$;
- Causality is acyclic, and bundles are finite.

From the last of these, an induction principle follows. Namely, if $\preceq_\mathcal{C}$ is defined as the reflexive, transitive closure of the union of the two kinds of arrows, $\rightarrow$ and $\Rightarrow$, then every non-empty set S of nodes in $\mathcal{C}$ has a $preceq_\mathcal{C}$-minimal member. If S is a set of nodes at which the penetrator possesses some dangerous value, then a minimal member of S pinpoints how the penetrator learnt it. The maxim here, as in Watergate, is, "What did he know and when did he know it?"

To illustrate an authentication goal, let us switch now to a protocol that achieves its goals, such as the Needham-Schroeder-Lowe protocol [27] as shown in Figure 12. The only difference from the Needham-Schroeder protocol is in the second message $\{\!|N_a\,N_b\,B|\!\}_{K_A}$, in which the responder includes his name. This prevents the attack shown in Figure 5. We use NSLInit$[A, B, N_a, N_b]$ to refer to the set of all strands having the behavior shown in the left column of Figure 12,

---

there should be an A-strand with *some* partner. The protocol does in fact achieve this.

However, unless the goal of the protocol is the stronger assertion we have given, and the nonces are intended to become a shared secret between A and B, it is hard to see why the last message should be the encrypted value $\{\!|N_b|\!\}_{K_B}$. The plaintext message N_b would also achieve the weaker goal.

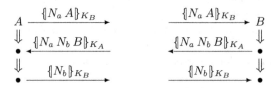

Fig. 12. Needham-Schroeder-Lowe protocol

while NSLResp$[A, B, N_a, N_b]$ refers to the set of all strands having the behavior shown in the right column.

In the revised Needham-Schroeder-Lowe, the responder B can in fact be sure that the initiator A wanted to execute a run with B. This means that in any bundle $\mathcal{C}$ containing a responder strand $s_r \in$ NSLResp$[A, B, N_a, N_b]$, there is an initiator strand $s_i \in$ NSLInit$[A, B, N_a, N_b]$ contained in $\mathcal{C}$ (subject to some origination assumptions). In fact [47], the assumptions needed are

- N_b is uniquely originating in $\mathcal{C}$ and $N_b \neq N_a$; and
- K_A^{-1} is non-originating in $\mathcal{C}$ (or alternatively, $K_A^{-1} \notin \mathsf{K}_\mathcal{P}$).

In the case of the initiator's guarantee, the situation is slightly different. Since the initiator sends the last message, the initiator can certainly never know whether the responder receives it. Thus, the only reasonable goal is to show that the first two nodes of the responder's strand are in the bundle $\mathcal{C}$. We express this by saying that the strand has $\mathcal{C}$-height at least 2 (see Definition 4). The initiator's guarantee states that if

- N_a is uniquely originating in $\mathcal{C}$; and
- K_A^{-1} and K_B^{-1} are non-originating in $\mathcal{C}$
  (or alternatively, $K_A^{-1}, K_B^{-1} \notin \mathsf{K}_\mathcal{P}$)

and $s_i \in$ NSLInit$[A, B, N_a, N_b]$ has $\mathcal{C}$-height 2,
then some $s_r \in$ NSLResp$[A, B, N_a, N_b]$ has $\mathcal{C}$-height 2.

It is an unexpected asymmetry of the Needham-Schroeder-Lowe protocol that the initiator's guarantee depends on both participants' private keys being uncompromised, while the responder's guarantee depends only on one private key being uncompromised.

In some cases, not all data values are authenticated between the principals. For instance, in the Carlsen protocol (Figure 10), the initiator never sees the responder's first nonce N_b. Thus, the conclusion of the initiator's guarantee can specify only that $s_r \in$ CResp$[A, B, N_a, *, K, \ldots]$.

We can now give the logical form of an authentication goal. Authentication goals always take the form: for all bundles $\mathcal{C}$ and all strands s, there exists a strand s' such that

If some origination assumptions hold,
and $s \in R$ has $\mathcal{C}$-height i,

then $s' \in R'$ and s' has $\mathcal{C}$-height j.

In this, R and R' are role predicates (or "asterisked" unions over role predicates), such as NSLInit$[A, B, N_a, N_b]$ and CResp$[A, B, N_a, *, K, N'_b, *]$. An origination assumption always concerns either a parameter X mentioned in R, or else K_X where X is a parameter mentioned in R.

Analyzing the authentication properties of a protocol means finding the right choices for R and R', for i and j, and the necessary origination assumptions.

Many different goals can be stated and proved (or refuted) within our framework. For instance, Gollmann has said that Lowe's attack does not undermine the claims made by Needham and Schroeder themselves, because they were working in a context where they assumed that all the principals with whom one might want to talk are trustworthy. Of course, in a world of open networks and widespread electronic commerce, this would not be a reasonable assumption, but such a world was remote in 1978 when their article was published.

Their authentication goal may be stated as follows. Let us say that X is an *interlocutor* in a bundle $\mathcal{C}$ if there exists a strand $s \in \mathcal{C}$ such that $s \in$ NSInit$[*, X, **]$ or $s \in$ NSResp$[X, **]$. Then the intended Needham-Schroeder authentication result simply has the additional assumption that for every interlocutor X, K_X^{-1} is non-originating in $\mathcal{C}$. The responder's authentication goal is sound with this additional assumption.

3.13   What Is a Secrecy Goal?

Secrecy goals are loosely dual to authentication goals. While authentication goals assert that j nodes of some strand $s' \in R'$ have happened in the bundle $\mathcal{C}$, secrecy goals say that nodes of a certain form do not occur in the bundle. Like authentication goals, they may depend on assumptions about origination. For instance, in the Needham-Schroeder-Lowe protocol, we want to ensure that there is no node in the bundle (even a penetrator node) where the message is N_a or N_b. The result takes the form: For all bundles $\mathcal{C}$, strands s_i, s_r, and nodes $n \in \mathcal{C}$

If $s_i \in$ NSLInit$[A, B, N_a, N_b]$ and $s_r \in$ NSLResp$[A, B, N_a, N_b]$ have $\mathcal{C}$-height at least 1 and 2 respectively,
and N_a and N_b are uniquely originating in $\mathcal{C}$, and
and K_A^{-1} and K_B^{-1} are non-originating in $\mathcal{C}$,
then term$(n) \neq N_a$ and term$(n) \neq N_b$.

Naturally, if we prove that N_a and N_b are not said in public in any bundle $\mathcal{C}$, then it follows that the penetrator cannot derive them from what he sees. If he could derive them, then there would exist a bundle in which he also (perhaps imprudently) utters them.

Secrecy goals always take the form: for all bundles $\mathcal{C}$ and all strands s

If some origination assumptions hold,
and $s \in R$ has $\mathcal{C}$-height i,
then there is no node $n \in \mathcal{C}$ such that term$(n) = t$.

Again, the origination assumptions concern parameters to R or values K_X where X is a parameter to R. The term t is a parameter to R, or a term constructed from parameters to R.

We can call the role R in a secrecy or authentication goal the *core* role of the goal, since the principal playing role R receives the assurance that the peer is active, or that the secret has not been disclosed. Thus, the origination assumptions always concern parameters to the core role.

Summary of this Section In this section, we have studied cryptographic protocols. We started by explaining the Dolev-Yao problem. We illustrated how to find flaws in protocols, even assuming that the cryptography by which they are implemented is perfect. One important insight for finding flaws is that we may ignore junk messages; the other one is that we want to examine the protocol to find the unintended services that may allow the penetrator to construct the non-junk messages that are intended to provide authenticating force to the regular principals. We then described how to formalize protocol behaviors using strand spaces; possible executions are bundles. Finally, we defined the logical forms of authentication and secrecy goals. We have thus illustrated two of the themes mentioned in the introduction, namely modeling security problems using simple mathematical materials, and defining specific classes of security properties to formalize real-world security goals.

3.14   Appendix: Strand Space Definitions

In this appendix to Section 3, we will define the basic strand space notions. This material is derived from [47,16]. The definitions of unique origination and non-origination (Definition 2, Clause 8) have been relativized to a bundle here, however. We also stipulate that a strand space has all the penetrator strands that it can (Definition 8).

Strand Spaces Consider a set A, the elements of which are the possible messages that can be exchanged between principals in a protocol. We will refer to the elements of A as *terms*. We assume that a *subterm* relation is defined on A. $t_0 \sqsubset t_1$ means t_0 is a subterm of t_1. We constrain the set A further below in Section 3.14, and define a subterm relation there.

In a protocol, principals can either send or receive terms. We represent transmission of a term as the occurrence of that term with positive sign, and reception of a term as its occurrence with negative sign.

Definition 1. *A signed term is a pair* $\langle \sigma, a \rangle$ *with* $a \in$ A *and* σ *one of the symbols* $+, -$. *We will write a signed term as* $+t$ *or* $-t$. $(\pm$A$)^*$ *is the set of finite sequences of signed terms. We will denote a typical element of* $(\pm$A$)^*$ *by* $\langle\, \langle \sigma_1, a_1 \rangle,\ \ldots,\ \langle \sigma_n, a_n \rangle\, \rangle$.

A strand space over A *is a set* Σ *with a trace mapping* tr $: \Sigma \rightarrow (\pm$A$)^*$.

By abuse of language, we will still treat signed terms as ordinary terms. For instance, we shall refer to subterms of signed terms. We will usually represent a strand space by its underlying set of strands Σ.

Definition 2. *Fix a strand space Σ.*

1. *A* node *is a pair $\langle s, i \rangle$, with $s \in \Sigma$ and i an integer satisfying $1 \leq i \leq length(tr(s))$. The set of nodes is denoted by $\mathcal{N}$. We will say the node $\langle s, i \rangle$ belongs to the strand s. Clearly, every node belongs to a unique strand.*
2. *If $n = \langle s, i \rangle \in \mathcal{N}$ then $index(n) = i$ and $strand(n) = s$. Define $term(n)$ to be $(tr(s))_i$, i.e. the ith signed term in the trace of s. Similarly, $uns\_term(n)$ is $((tr(s))_i)_2$, i.e. the unsigned part of the ith signed term in the trace of s.*
3. *There is an edge $n_1 \rightarrow n_2$ if and only if $term(n_1) = +a$ and $term(n_2) = -a$ for some $a \in \mathsf{A}$. Intuitively, the edge means that node n_1 sends the message a, which is received by n_2, recording a potential causal link between those strands.*
4. *When $n_1 = \langle s, i \rangle$ and $n_2 = \langle s, i+1 \rangle$ are members of $\mathcal{N}$, there is an edge $n_1 \Rightarrow n_2$. Intuitively, the edge expresses that n_1 is an immediate causal predecessor of n_2 on the strand s. We write $n' \Rightarrow^+ n$ to mean that n' precedes n (not necessarily immediately) on the same strand.*
5. *An unsigned term t occurs in $n \in \mathcal{N}$ iff $t \sqsubseteq term(n)$.*
6. *Suppose I is a set of unsigned terms. The node $n \in \mathcal{N}$ is an* entry point *for I iff $term(n) = +t$ for some $t \in I$, and whenever $n' \Rightarrow^+ n$, $term(n') \notin I$.*
7. *An unsigned term t* originates *on $n \in \mathcal{N}$ iff n is an entry point for the set $I = \{t' : t \sqsubseteq t'\}$.*
8. *An unsigned term t is* uniquely originating *in a set of nodes $S \subset \mathcal{N}$ iff there is a unique $n \in S$ such that t originates on n.*
9. *An unsigned term t is* non-originating *in a set of nodes $S \subset \mathcal{N}$ iff there is no $n \in S$ such that t originates on n.*

If a term t originates uniquely in a suitable set of nodes, then it can play the role of a nonce or session key, assuming that everything that the penetrator does in some scenario is in that set of nodes.

$\mathcal{N}$ together with both sets of edges $n_1 \rightarrow n_2$ and $n_1 \Rightarrow n_2$ is a directed graph $\langle \mathcal{N}, (\rightarrow \cup \Rightarrow) \rangle$.

Bundles and Causal Precedence A *bundle* is a finite subgraph of $\langle \mathcal{N}, (\rightarrow \cup \Rightarrow) \rangle$, for which we can regard the edges as expressing the causal dependencies of the nodes.

Definition 3. *Suppose $\rightarrow_{\mathcal{C}} \subset \rightarrow$; suppose $\Rightarrow_{\mathcal{C}} \subset \Rightarrow$; and suppose $\mathcal{C} = \langle \mathcal{N}_{\mathcal{C}}, (\rightarrow_{\mathcal{C}} \cup \Rightarrow_{\mathcal{C}}) \rangle$ is a subgraph of $\langle \mathcal{N}, (\rightarrow \cup \Rightarrow) \rangle$. $\mathcal{C}$ is a* bundle *if:*

1. *$\mathcal{N}_{\mathcal{C}}$ and $\rightarrow_{\mathcal{C}} \cup \Rightarrow_{\mathcal{C}}$ are finite.*
2. *If $n_2 \in \mathcal{N}_{\mathcal{C}}$ and $term(n_2)$ is negative, then there is a unique n_1 such that $n_1 \rightarrow_{\mathcal{C}} n_2$.*
3. *If $n_2 \in \mathcal{N}_{\mathcal{C}}$ and $n_1 \Rightarrow n_2$ then $n_1 \Rightarrow_{\mathcal{C}} n_2$.*

4. C is acyclic.

In conditions 2 and 3, it follows that $n_1 \in \mathcal{N}_{\mathcal{C}}$, because $\mathcal{C}$ is a graph.

For our purposes, it does not matter whether communication is regarded as a synchronizing event or as an asynchronous activity. The definition of bundle formalizes a process communication model with three properties:

- A strand (process) may send and receive messages, but not both at the same time;
- When a strand receives a message t, there is a unique node transmitting t from which the message was immediately received;
- If a strand transmits a message t, many strands may immediately receive t.

Definition 4. *A node n is in a bundle $\mathcal{C} = \langle \mathcal{N}_{\mathcal{C}}, \to_{\mathcal{C}} \cup \Rightarrow_{\mathcal{C}} \rangle$, written $n \in \mathcal{C}$, if $n \in \mathcal{N}_{\mathcal{C}}$; a strand s is in $\mathcal{C}$ if all of its nodes are in $\mathcal{N}_{\mathcal{C}}$.*

If $\mathcal{C}$ is a bundle, then the $\mathcal{C}$-height of a strand s is the largest i such that $\langle s, i \rangle \in \mathcal{C}$. $\mathcal{C}$-trace$(s) = \langle tr(s)(1), \ldots, tr(s)(m) \rangle$, where $m = \mathcal{C}$-height(s). We say that $s \in \mathcal{C}$ if the $\mathcal{C}$-height of s equals length(s).

Definition 5. *If $\mathcal{S}$ is a set of edges, i.e. $\mathcal{S} \subset \to \cup \Rightarrow$, then $\prec_{\mathcal{S}}$ is the transitive closure of $\mathcal{S}$, and $\preceq_{\mathcal{S}}$ is the reflexive, transitive closure of $\mathcal{S}$.*

The relations $\prec_{\mathcal{S}}$ and $\preceq_{\mathcal{S}}$ are each subsets of $\mathcal{N}_{\mathcal{S}} \times \mathcal{N}_{\mathcal{S}}$, where $\mathcal{N}_{\mathcal{S}}$ is the set of nodes incident with any edge in $\mathcal{S}$.

Proposition 1 *Suppose $\mathcal{C}$ is a bundle. Then $\preceq_{\mathcal{C}}$ is a partial order, i.e. a reflexive, antisymmetric, transitive relation. Every non-empty subset of the nodes in $\mathcal{C}$ has $\preceq_{\mathcal{C}}$-minimal members.*

We regard $\preceq_{\mathcal{C}}$ as expressing causal precedence, because $n \prec_{\mathcal{S}} n'$ holds only when n's occurrence causally contributes to the occurrence of n'. When a bundle $\mathcal{C}$ is understood, we will simply write $\preceq$. Similarly, "minimal" will mean $\preceq_{\mathcal{C}}$-minimal.

Terms, Encryption, and Freeness Assumptions We will now specialize the set of terms A. In particular we will assume given:

- A set $\mathsf{T} \subseteq \mathsf{A}$ of texts (representing the atomic messages).
- A set $\mathsf{K} \subseteq \mathsf{A}$ of cryptographic keys disjoint from T, equipped with a unary operator **inv** : $\mathsf{K} \to \mathsf{K}$. We assume that **inv** is an inverse mapping each member of a key pair for an asymmetric cryptosystem to the other, and each symmetric key to itself.
- Two binary operators **encr** : $\mathsf{K} \times \mathsf{A} \to \mathsf{A}$ and **join** : $\mathsf{A} \times \mathsf{A} \to \mathsf{A}$.

We follow custom and write **inv**(K) as K^{-1}, **encr**(K, m) as $\{\!|m|\!\}_K$, and **join**(a, b) as $a\,b$. If $\mathfrak{K}$ is a set of keys, $\mathfrak{K}^{-1}$ denotes the set of inverses of elements of $\mathfrak{K}$. We assume, like many others (e.g. [29,32,39]), that A is freely generated, which is crucial for the results in this paper.

Axiom 1 A *is freely generated from* T *and* K *by* **encr** *and* **join**.

Definition 6. *The subterm relation* $\sqsubseteq$ *is defined inductively, as the smallest relation such that* $a \sqsubseteq a$; $a \sqsubseteq \{\!|g|\!\}_K$ *if* $a \sqsubseteq g$; *and* $a \sqsubseteq g\,h$ *if* $a \sqsubseteq g$ *or* $a \sqsubseteq h$.

By this definition, for $K \in$ K, we have $K \sqsubseteq \{\!|g|\!\}_K$ only if $K \sqsubseteq g$ already.

Definition 7.   *1. If* $\mathfrak{K} \subset$ K, *then* $t_0 \sqsubseteq_\mathfrak{K} t$ *if* t *is in the smallest set containing* t_0 *and closed under encryption with* $K \in \mathfrak{K}$ *and concatenation with arbitrary terms* t_1.
   2. *A term* t *is* simple *if it is not of the form* $g\,h$.
   3. *A term* t_0 *is a* component *of* t *if* t_0 *is simple and* $t_0 \sqsubseteq_\emptyset t$.

Penetrator Strands The atomic actions available to the penetrator are encoded in a set of *penetrator traces*. They summarize his ability to discard messages, generate well known messages, piece messages together, and apply cryptographic operations using keys that become available to him. A protocol attack typically requires hooking together several of these atomic actions.

The actions available to the penetrator are relative to the set of keys that the penetrator knows initially. We encode this in a parameter, the set of penetrator keys $K_\mathcal{P}$.

Definition 8. *A* penetrator trace *relative to* $K_\mathcal{P}$ *is one of the following:*

$\mathbf{M}_t$ *Text message:* $\langle +t \rangle$ *where* $t \in$ T.
$\mathbf{K}_K$ *Key:* $\langle +K \rangle$ *where* $K \in K_\mathcal{P}$.
$\mathbf{C}_{g,h}$ *Concatenation:* $\langle -g, -h, +g\,h \rangle$
$\mathbf{S}_{g,h}$ *Separation:* $\langle -g\,h, +g, +h \rangle$
$\mathbf{E}_{h,K}$ *Encryption:* $\langle -K, -h, +\{\!|h|\!\}_K \rangle$.
$\mathbf{D}_{h,K}$ *Decryption:* $\langle -K^{-1}, -\{\!|h|\!\}_K, +h \rangle$.

$\mathcal{P}_\Sigma$ *is the set of all strands* $s \in \Sigma$ *such that* $\mathrm{tr}(s)$ *is a penetrator trace.*

We assume that $\mathcal{P}_\Sigma$ contains instances of a penetrator strand type, whenever the instantiation is type-correct, and (in the case of a K-strand) the key $K \in K_\mathcal{P}$.

A strand $s \in \Sigma$ is a *penetrator strand* if it belongs to $\mathcal{P}_\Sigma$, and a node is a *penetrator node* if the strand it lies on is a penetrator strand. Otherwise we will call it a *non-penetrator* or *regular* strand or node. A node n is M, C, etc. node if n lies on a penetrator strand with a trace of kind M, C, etc.

4   Paths and Well-Behaved Bundles

In this section we will study the notion of bundle, focusing on a particular equivalence relation on them, and on the paths that messages and their constituents take through bundles. In certain "well-behaved" bundles, the paths are especially predictable, and in fact every bundle has an equivalent well-behaved bundle. This section will illustrate the advantages of the strand space model over closely related alternatives [40,43], at least as a heuristic for discovering results about cryptographic protocols.

4.1   Bundle Equivalence

Definition 9. *Bundles C, C' on a strand space Σ are equivalent iff*

1. *they have the same regular nodes;*
2. *for all a, a originates uniquely and on a regular node in C if and only if a originates uniquely and on a regular node in C';*
3. *for all a, a is non-originating in C iff a is non-originating in C'.*

A set ϕ *of bundles is* invariant under bundle equivalences *if whenever bundles C and C' are equivalent, $C \in \phi \Rightarrow C' \in \phi$.*

The penetrator's behavior may differ arbitrarily between two bundles that are equivalent in this sense, and the orderings $\preceq_C$ and $\preceq_{C'}$ may also differ freely.

Authentication goals as defined in Section 3.12 are invariant under bundle equivalences in this sense (see also [30,47,49]). As such, it always concerns what nodes, representing regular activity of the protocol, must be present in bundles. Penetrator activity may or may not be present.

Secrecy properties may also be expressed in a form that is invariant under bundle equivalences. We say (temporarily) that a value t is uncompromised in C if for every C' equivalent to C, there is no node $n \in C'$ such that $\text{term}(n) = t$. In this form, a value is uncompromised if the penetrator cannot extract it in explicit form without further cooperation of regular strands. When stated in this form, the assertion that a value is uncompromised is invariant under bundle equivalences.

4.2   Redundancies

Some portions of the penetrator behavior in a bundle may be redundant in the sense that they may be excised locally. Removing them leads to a simpler yet equivalent bundle. We identify here two kinds of redundancy. First are cased where the penetrator encrypts a value with a key K, and then decrypts with the corresponding decryption key K^{-1}. This is illustrated in the upper portion of Figure 13, and may be eliminated by omitting nodes and adding the dotted arrow shown in the lower portion. Something very similar arises if the penetrator concatenates two values and then promptly separates the concatenated unit into its two immediate subterms. Since these operations introduce no cycles, the resulting graph is a bundle. They remove only penetrator nodes, so the new bundle is equivalent to the original one. Finally, since each bundle is finite, the process of removing redundancies must finally terminate with an equivalent bundle containing no redundancies.

As a consequence, we may assume that the penetrator's behavior always follows a specific pattern:

First take messages apart;
then put messages together;
finally deliver the resulting messages to a regular principal.

In order to formalize this pattern, we introduce the notion of a path.

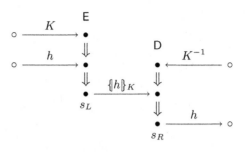

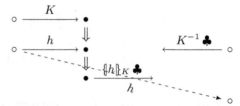

♣ Discarded message

Fig. 13. E-D redundancies, and how to eliminate them

4.3 Paths

$m \Rightarrow^+ n$ means that m, n are nodes on the same strand with n occuring after m (Definition 2, Clause 4). The notation $m \longmapsto n$ means:

Either $m \Rightarrow^+ n$ with term(m) negative and term(n) positive,
or else $m \rightarrow n$.

A *path* p through $\mathcal{C}$ is any finite sequence of nodes and edges $n_1 \longmapsto n_2 \longmapsto \cdots \longmapsto n_k$. We refer to the ith node of the path p as p_i. The length of p will be $|p|$, and we will write $\ell(p)$ to mean $p_{|p|}$, i.e. the last node in p. A penetrator path is one in which all nodes other than possibly the first or the last node are penetrator nodes. As an example of a penetrator path, in which the first and last nodes are in fact regular, consider again the partial bundle shown in Figure 14. The path $\pi =$

$$\pi_1 \rightarrow \pi_2 \Rightarrow^+ \pi_3 \rightarrow \pi_4 \Rightarrow^+ \pi_5 \rightarrow \pi_6$$

is a path that traverses penetrator nodes, connecting A's first transmission $\{\!|N_a\, A|\!\}_{K_P}$ to B's first reception $\{\!|N_a\, A|\!\}_{K_B}$. In contrast to π, the path $\psi =$

$$\psi_1 \rightarrow \psi_2 \Rightarrow^+ \pi_5 \rightarrow \pi_6$$

starts on a penetrator node and ends on a regular node. Observe that by our conventions, ψ_3 and ψ_4 are well-defined (and equal to π_5 and π_6 respectively).

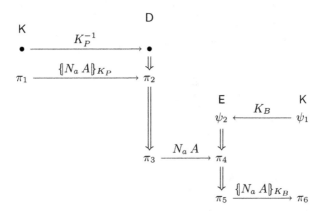

Fig. 14. Penetrator strands for Lowe's attack on Needham-Schroeder

4.4   Constructive and Destructive Edges, Normal Bundles

Definition 10. *A $\Rightarrow^{+}$-edge is constructive if it is part of a E or C strand. It is destructive if it is part of a D or if it is part of a S strand.*

A penetrator node n is initial if it is a K or M node.

Any penetrator path that begins at a regular node contains only constructive and destructive $\Rightarrow^{+}$-edges, because initial nodes can occur only at the beginning of a path.

Proposition 2 *In a bundle, a constructive edge immediately followed by a destructive edge has one of the following two forms:*

1. *Part of a $E_{h,K}$ immediately followed by part of a $D_{h,K}$ strand for some h, K.*
2. *Part of a $C_{g,h}$ immediately followed by part of a $S_{g,h}$ strand for some g, h.*

This result requires the freeness of the message algebra.

Proposition 3 (Penetrator Normal Form Lemma) *If the bundle C has no redundancies of type C-S and E-D, then for any penetrator path of C, every destructive edge precedes every constructive edge.*

Every bundle is equivalent to a bundle with no redundancies of type C-S and E-D.

We call a bundle *normal* if it has no redundancies of type C-S and E-D, by analogy with Prawitz's normal deductions [42]. Many others have noted related properties, including [7,40,20].

We may also assume another property of the bundle C.

Definition 11. *C is directed if for every node $n \in C$, there is a regular node $m \in C$ such that $n \preceq_C m$.*

Every bundle $\mathcal{C}$ is equivalent to some directed bundle $\mathcal{C}'$. Define the graph $\mathcal{C}'$ to contain those nodes n of $\mathcal{C}$ such that $n \preceq_{\mathcal{C}} m$ for some regular node m; the arrows of $\mathcal{C}'$ are those arrows of $\mathcal{C}$ that connect nodes in $\mathcal{C}'$. $\mathcal{C}'$ is easily seen to be a bundle by enumerating the clauses in Definition 3. Moreover, $\mathcal{C}'$ is equivalent to $\mathcal{C}$, just by the reflexiveness of $\preceq_{\mathcal{C}}$.

4.5   Rising and Falling Paths

We will call a path p *rising* if $\mathrm{term}(p_i) \sqsubseteq \mathrm{term}(p_{i+1})$ whenever $1 \le i$ and $i + 1 \le |p|$. This means that each term is a subterm of the next, and ultimately the first is a subterm of the last. Moving in the other direction, we will call a path p *falling* if $\mathrm{term}(p_{i+1}) \sqsubseteq \mathrm{term}(p_i)$ whenever $1 \le i$ and $i + 1 \le |p|$. In this case, each term includes the next, so that the last is a subterm of the first.

A destructive $\Rightarrow$-edge may not be part of a falling path, because the path may traverse the key edge of a D-strand, as shown in left diagram of Figure 15. K^{-1} will typically have no relation to h. As we see in the right side, a E-strand

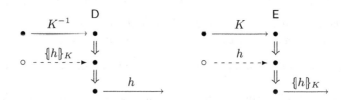

Fig. 15. Key edges into D and E-strands

is similar, since with our definitions, $K \not\sqsubseteq \{\!|h|\!\}_K$ unless by chance $K \sqsubseteq h$. However, as long as a path p does not traverse a key edge, it will be falling while traversing destructive penetrator strands and rising while traversing constructive penetrator strands.

Falling Paths, Rising Paths, and Subterms Falling paths have a property we need to explain; rising paths have a dual property. As we follow a falling path, we traverse a number of S-strands, which select a subterm from a concatenation, and a number of D-strands which select a plaintext from an encryption. If the encryption is of the form $\{\!|h|\!\}_K$, then the key used on this D-strand is K^{-1}.

Suppose that p is a falling path and $\mathfrak{K}$ is a set of keys, and suppose that p traverses a D-strand only when the key used is of the form K^{-1} for some $K \in \mathfrak{K}$. So the ciphertext is always of the form $\{\!|h|\!\}_K$ with $K \in \mathfrak{K}$. That means that the term p_1 at the start of p is of the form

$$\cdots \{\!| \cdots \mathrm{term}(\ell(p)) \cdots |\!\}_K \cdots$$

in the sense that it can be constructed from $\text{term}(\ell(p))$ by concatenating (with anything) and encrypting using only keys $K \in \mathfrak{K}$. This is what in Definition 7 we wrote $\text{term}(\ell(p)) \sqsubset_{\mathfrak{K}} p_1$.

The case of a rising path is similar except that we may omit the inverses. Suppose that p is a rising path and $\mathfrak{K}$ is a set of keys, and suppose that p traverses an E-strand only when the key used is some $K \in \mathfrak{K}$. Then $p_1 \sqsubset_{\mathfrak{K}} \text{term}(\ell(p))$.

4.6   A Catalog of Penetrator Paths

This suggests that we separate penetrator activity into paths which do not traverse key edges; we end a path p at the node before it traverses a key edge. In this case, $\text{term}(\ell(p)) = K$ for some key K. The ciphertext is of the form $\{\!|h|\!\}_K$ if we stopped before an E-strand, and of the form $\{\!|h|\!\}_{K^{-1}}$ if we stopped before a D-strand.

In cataloging penetrator paths, we may assume that the bundle is normal, since otherwise there is an equivalent bundle that is. We may also assume that the bundle is directed. From this, we may infer that a penetrator path terminates only when it reaches either a key edge or a regular node.

Thus, the purpose of a penetrator path is always either:

- To make a key available for a D or E-strand, or
- To construct some message to deliver to a regular node.

The first type of path terminates before a key edge, and the second terminates at a regular node.

In our catalog of paths p that never traverse a key edge, we will also distinguish possibilities depending whether p begins on a penetrator node or on a regular node.

1. p begins on a penetrator node and ends before a key edge. Then $\text{term}(\ell(p)) = K$, and since p_1 is an initial penetrator node, it must be a K node with $|p| = 1$.
2. p begins on a regular node and ends before a key edge. So $\text{term}(\ell(p)) = K$. Because p never traverses a key edge and ends with an atomic term, p is falling. So $K \sqsubset \text{term}(p_1)$. In other words, the penetrator has extracted a key from a message sent by a regular principal. By our remark at the beginning of Section 4.6, if every occurrence of K in $\text{term}(p_1)$ is encrypted using some other key K_1, then K_1^{-1} is a key edge joining p at some D-strand. There must be an earlier path p' furnishing this key K_1^{-1}.
3. p begins on a penetrator node and ends at a regular node. Then p_1 is either a K node or a M node, and in either case $\text{term}(p_1)$ is atomic. Therefore p is a rising path and $\text{term}(p_1) \sqsubset \text{term}(\ell(p))$. In this path, the penetrator makes up a value, and after possibly combining it with other ingredients, delivers it to a regular participant at $\ell(p)$.
4. p begins at a positive regular node and ends at a negative regular node. In this case, p consists of a falling portion followed by a rising portion, either (or both) of which can be trivial in the sense that it consists of a single node and no arrows.

Thus, there is a falling path q ending at a positive node $\ell(q)$, and a rising path q' beginning at a negative node q'_1, where $\text{term}(\ell(q)) = \text{term}(q'_1)$. We call this common term the *path bridge term* of p, writing it as $\text{pbt}(p)$. The whole path p is of the form $q \to q'$.

We know that $\text{pbt}(p) \sqsubset \text{term}(p_1)$, and $\text{pbt}(p) \sqsubset \text{term}(\ell(p))$. So the effect of the whole path p is to extract the term $\text{pbt}(p)$ via the falling part q, and compose it with other ingredients in the rising part q', delivering the result to a regular participant.

This is a complete listing of what the penetrator can achieve by means of any path.

4.7   New Components and Efficient Bundles

According to Definition 7, a component of t is a subterm t_0 such that t_0 is either an atom or an encryption, and such that there are no encryptions hiding t_0 in t. Thus, given a term t, we generate the set of its components by repeatedly separating concatenations, stopping whenever we reach an atom or an encryption. Components are important in cryptographic protocols, because the penetrator can always undo concatenations and redo them in whatever form is desired. Only the cryptographic work required to change components can provide authentication or confidentiality. We write $\boxed{t_0} \sqsubset t$ to mean that t_0 is a component of t.

A term t_0 is a new component of a node n if $\boxed{t_0} \sqsubset \text{term}(n)$, and whenever $m \Rightarrow^+ n$ it is not the case that $\boxed{t_0} \sqsubset \text{term}(m)$. That is, it should not have been a component of an earlier node on the same strand. We are interested in the new components of a node, because they summarize what cryptographic work has been done at that point on the strand.

To simplify reasoning about bundles, it is convenient to assume that when a penetrator gets a component from the regular participants, he gets it from the earliest point possible. We call such a bundle *efficient*.

Definition 12. *A bundle is* efficient *if and only if, for every node m and negative penetrator node n, if every component of n is a component of m, then there is no regular node m' such that $m \prec m' \prec n$.*

We call a bundle of this kind efficient because the penetrator does the most with what he has rather than making use of additional regular nodes.

All of the bundles we have shown in earlier figures are efficient. Whenever the penetrator node handles a term, there is no earlier node that has all the same components, and a regular node has been traversed in between. However, in the case of the nonsensical variant of the Needham-Schroeder protocol shown in Figure 16, the edge marked ♣ would need to be removed, and replaced with the dashed diagonal. The negative penetrator node n must not receive its term from the third initiator node, when it can be obtained directly from the first initiator node.

Every bundle $\mathcal{C}$ may be replaced by an equivalent efficient bundle $\mathcal{C}'$, and $\mathcal{C}'$ will be normal or directed assuming that $\mathcal{C}$ was.

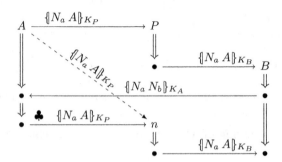

Fig. 16. An inefficient bundle for a fictitious protocol

4.8   Penetrable Keys

We may use the ideas we have developed to give an easy way to determine whether the secrecy of a key is preserved by a protocol. Let us suppose that $\mathcal{C}$ is a bundle in which some key K is disclosed, meaning that there exists a node $n \in \mathcal{C}$ such that $\boxed{K} \sqsubset \text{term}(n)$. We may assume that $\mathcal{C}$ is normal, directed, and efficient. By the bundle induction principle, we may assume that n has been chosen minimal in the ordering $\preceq_C$ with component K. We want to determine when a key is penetrable.

There are only three cases:

- n may be a K node, in which case $K \in \mathsf{K}_\mathcal{P}$;
- n may be a regular node, in which case (by minimality), K is a new component of n;
- n lies on a penetrator path p at node p_i with $1 < i$. We may assume that p traverses no key edges.

In the last case, the path $\langle p_1, \dots, p_i \rangle$ is falling, as it ends with an atomic value, so p_1 is a regular node. We know from Section 4.5 that $K \sqsubset_{\mathfrak{K}} \text{term}(p_1)$, where $\mathfrak{K}$ contains K_1 whenever K_1^{-1} was used in a D-strand along p.

So a collection of previously penetrable keys, namely the K_1^{-1}s for $K_1 \in \mathfrak{K}$, suffice to extract K from some component $\boxed{t_0} \sqsubset \text{term}(p_1)$. By the efficiency of $\mathcal{C}$, t_0 is a *new* component of the regular node p_1.

Letting $\mathfrak{K} = \emptyset$, this also covers the second case. Therefore, for every penetrable key K, either:

1. $K \in \mathsf{K}_\mathcal{P}$, or
2. There is a regular node $m \in \mathcal{C}$ and a new component t_0 of m such that $K \sqsubset_{\mathfrak{K}} t_0$, where for every $K \in \mathfrak{K}$, K_1^{-1} is already penetrable.

So every key that the penetrator learns, he either starts off knowing in $\mathsf{K}_\mathcal{P}$, or else some regular participant puts K into a new component, where it is protected only by keys that the penetrator can already learn to undo. In this construction, we are primarily interested in paths of type 2 in our list of possible types of penetrator path in Section 4.6.

We may therefore define $P(\mathcal{C})$ to be the smallest set of keys such that $K_{\mathcal{P}} \subset P(\mathcal{C})$ and closed under Clause 2 as just given. We have just proved that if $K = \text{term}(n)$ for any $n \in \mathcal{C}$, then $K \in P(\mathcal{C})$.

Why is this useful? Because we can define a set of *safe* keys such that it is very easy to see when a key is safe, and the safe keys are disjoint from the penetrable keys.

4.9   Safe Keys

Let $S_0(\mathcal{C})$ be the set of keys K such that:

- $K \notin K_{\mathcal{P}}$, and
- for every positive regular node $n \in \mathcal{C}$ and every new component $\boxed{t_0} \sqsubseteq \text{term}(n)$, $K \not\sqsubseteq t_0$.

These keys are patently safe. No regular principal will ever utter them in a component, unless given that component earlier. So, no one is ever the first to spill the beans.

Let $S_{i+1}(\mathcal{C})$ be the set of keys K such that:

- $K \notin K_{\mathcal{P}}$, and
- for every positive regular node $n \in \mathcal{C}$ and every new component $\boxed{t_0} \sqsubseteq \text{term}(n)$, every occurrence of K in t_0 lies within an encryption using some key K_0 where $K_0^{-1} \in S_i(\mathcal{C})$:

$$\cdots \{\!| \cdots K \cdots |\!\}_{K_0} \cdots$$

These keys are derivatively safe, since they can never be penetrated unless the penetrator gets K_0^{-1}, which is already known to be safe.

In practice, protocol secrecy goals frequently amount to showing that certain keys are in either S_0 or S_1. Larger values of i seem rarely to occur in these protocols. Showing that a private key or a long-term symmetric key is in S_0 typically reduces to checking that it is assumed not to be in $K_{\mathcal{P}}$, because protocols generally avoid emitting terms containing these keys.

For instance, in the Needham-Schroeder protocol, if n is a regular node, then $K \not\sqsubseteq \text{term}(n)$. Hence, $S_0 = K \setminus K_{\mathcal{P}}$, which says that any key not initially known to the penetrator is permanently safe.

Many protocols expect session keys to be generated by a key server, which sends them encrypted in the long-term keys of two principals, and no principal ever re-encrypts a session key under a new key. In a particular session, a session key K may be sent encrypted with long-term keys not in $K_{\mathcal{P}}$ (or, if they are asymmetric, their inverses are not in $K_{\mathcal{P}}$). If the server never re-sends the same session key K in a different session, then $K \in S_1$. This method is an easy way to establish secrecy.

5 Proving Authentication

We focus now on protocols in which a regular participant authenticates its peer by sending a fresh value a (typically a nonce N), expecting to receive it back in a cryptographically altered form. If only the intended peer can perform the right cryptographic operation, then this pattern will authenticate the peer. The treatment of authentication tests in this section differs from that in [16], and is indebted to [41].

Consider some arbitrary bundle $\mathcal{C}$.

5.1 The Outgoing Authentication Test

Let us say that $n_0 \Rightarrow^+ n_1$ is an *outgoing test edge* for a if

- a originates uniquely on n_0;
- There is only one component $t_0 = \boxed{\{\!|h|\!\}_K} \sqsubset \text{term}(n_0)$ such that $a \sqsubset t_0$;
- $t_0 \not\sqsubset \text{term}(n_1)$ but $a \sqsubset \text{term}(n_1)$; and
- $K^{-1} \notin \mathsf{P}$.

Consider the set $S = \{m \in \mathcal{C} : a \sqsubset \text{term}(m) \wedge t_0 \not\sqsubset \text{term}(m)\}$. S is non-empty, because $n_1 \in S$. So by the bundle induction principle, S has minimal members m_1.

We claim that no such m_1 is a penetrator node. Clearly such an m_1 is positive, since if it were negative, it must receive its message from another node with the same property. If m_1 is an initial penetrator node, this contradicts the assumption that a originates uniquely at n_0. Thus, if it is a penetrator node at all, m_1 lies on an edge $m_0 \Rightarrow^+ m_1$ where $t_0 \sqsubset \text{term}(m_0)$ but $t_0 \not\sqsubset \text{term}(m_1)$. Since $t_0 = \{\!|h|\!\}_K$, $m_0 \Rightarrow^+ m_1$ lies on a D-strand, with key edge K^{-1}. But this contradicts the assumption that $K^{-1} \notin \mathsf{P}$. Therefore, every minimal member of S is regular.

Let us call a regular edge $m_0 \Rightarrow^+ m_1$ a *transforming edge for* $n_0 \Rightarrow^+ n_1$ if $t_0 \sqsubset \text{term}(m_0)$ and m_1 is a minimal member of S.

The outgoing test authentication principle states that if $\mathcal{C}$ contains an outgoing test edge, then it also contains a (regular) transforming edge for it.

The meaning of this assertion is illustrated in Figure 17. The two bulleted nodes in the figure represent m_0 and m_1.

The Outgoing Test in Needham-Schroeder We may illustrate the outgoing authentication tests by Needham-Schroeder (see Figure 4). Assume that $\mathcal{C}$ is a bundle, and the $\mathcal{C}$-height of $s_r \in \text{NSResp}[A, B, N_a, N_b]$ is 3, which means that all three nodes of s_r belong to $\mathcal{C}$. Assume that $K_A^{-1} \notin K_{\mathcal{P}}$. Finally, assume that N_b originates uniquely, and $N_b \neq N_a$ (which together mean that N_b originates uniquely at the second node of s_r).

Hence, the edge from the seocnd node of s_r to its third node is an outgoing test edge for N_b. By the Outgoing Authentication Test principle, there exist regular nodes $m_0, m_1 \in \mathcal{C}$ such that $m_0 \Rightarrow^+ m_1$ is a transforming edge for it. So

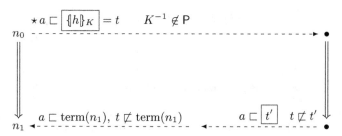

• means this regular node must exist
$\star a$ means a originates uniquely here

Fig. 17. Authentication provided by an outgoing test

$\{N_a\, N_b\}_{K_A} \sqsubset (m_0)$. The only negative regular node containing a subterm of this form is the second node of an initiator strand s_i for $s_i \in \mathrm{NSInit}[A, B', N_a, N_b]$ and some responder B'. Thus, the transforming edge $m_0 \Rightarrow^+ m_1$ must be the edge from the second node of s_i to its third node, and s_i has $\mathcal{C}$-height 3.

Unfortunately, we have not proved that $s_i \in \mathrm{NSInit}[A, B, N_a, N_b]$ for the expected responder B, rather than some other responder B'. And Figure 5 is a counterexample in which $B' = P \neq B$. Hence we have uncovered a limitation in the authentication achieved by Needham-Schroeder, first noted by Lowe [26,27], which led Lowe to amend the protocol to contain the responder's name B in the second message $\{N_a\, N_b\, B\}_{K_A}$.

The Outgoing Test in Needham-Schroeder-Lowe Consider now the corrected Needham-Schroeder-Lowe protocol as shown in Figure 12. As before, assume that $\mathcal{C}$ is a bundle, and the $\mathcal{C}$-height of $s_r \in \mathrm{NSResp}[A, B, N_a, N_b]$ is 3. Assume again that $K_A^{-1} \notin \mathsf{K}_{\mathcal{P}}$; that N_b originates uniquely; and that $N_b \neq N_a$.

We again infer that there exist regular nodes $m_0, m_1 \in \mathcal{C}$ such that $m_0 \Rightarrow^+ m_1$ is a transforming edge for it. So $\{N_a\, N_b\, B\}_{K_A} \sqsubset (m_0)$. The only negative regular node containing a subterm of this form is the second node of an initiator strand s_i for $s_i \in \mathrm{NSInit}[A, B, N_a, N_b]$. Hence, the desired s_i has $\mathcal{C}$-height 3.

5.2   The Incoming Authentication Test

Let us say that $n_0 \Rightarrow^+ n_1$ is an *incoming test edge* for a if

- a originates uniquely on n_0, and $t_1 = \{h\}_K \not\sqsubset \mathrm{term}(n_0)$;
- $a \sqsubset t_1$, and $t_1 \sqsubset \mathrm{term}(n_1)$; and
- $K \notin \mathsf{P}$.

We call a regular edge $m_0 \Rightarrow^+ m_1$ a *transforming edge* for $n_0 \Rightarrow^+ n_1$ if m_0 contains a as a subterm and m_1 is a minimal node such that $t_1 \sqsubset \mathrm{term}(m_1)$.

As before, only a regular edge can have this property. This assertion is illustrated in Figure 18 using the same conventions as in Figure 17. Carlsen's

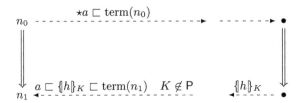

Fig. 18. Authentication provided by an incoming test

protocol (see Figure 10) is designed around incoming authentication tests. So is the Neuman-Stubblebine protocol, as we will illustrate in Section 5.4.

5.3 The Unsolicited Test

One other authentication test is important especially in the case of a key server, but in some other instances too. This is the unsolicited test. If $\{\!|h|\!\}_K \sqsubset \mathrm{term}(n)$ and $K \notin \mathsf{P}$, then we may infer that there is a node m such that:

- m is regular;
- $\{\!|h|\!\}_K$ originates at m.

This is valid because $\{\!|h|\!\}_K$ certainly originates at some node m, and m cannot be a penetrator node: If it were, it would be the positive node of a D-strand. And then the preceding key node would have the term K, contrary to the assumption $K \notin \mathsf{P}$.

5.4 Neuman-Stubblebine

The Neuman-Stubblebine protocol [38] contains two sub-protocols. We will call the first sub-protocol the authentication protocol and the second sub-protocol the re-authentication protocol. In the authentication sub-protocol, a key distribution center generates a session key for an initiator (a network client) and a responder (a network server); the message exchange is shown in Figure 19. This session key is embedded in encrypted form in a re-usable ticket of the form $\{\!|A\,K\,T|\!\}_{K_B}$. In the re-authentication protocol the client presents the same ticket again to the network server to use the same key for another session. The value T is an expiration date, after which the network server should no longer accept the ticket, although we will not bother to model this aspect of the behavior.

We consider the authentication protocol alone first. Strands of the form shown in the columns labelled A, B, and S in Figure 19 will be called

- Init$[A, B, N_a, N_b, t_b, K, H]$,
- Resp$[A, B, N_a, N_b, t_b, K]$, and
- Serv$[A, B, N_a, N_b, t_b, K]$,

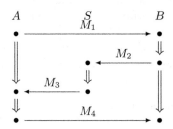

$$M_1 = A\,N_a$$
$$M_2 = B\,\{\!|A\,N_a\,t_b|\!\}_{K_B}\,N_b$$
$$M_3 = \{\!|B\,N_a\,K\,t_b|\!\}_{K_A}\,\{\!|A\,K\,t_b|\!\}_{K_B}\,N_b$$
$$M_4 = \{\!|A\,K\,t_b|\!\}_{K_B}\,\{\!|N_b|\!\}_K$$

Fig. 19. Neuman-Stubblebine part I (Authentication)

respectively.

We define LT to be the set of long-term keys, i.e. the range of the injective function K_A for $A \in \mathsf{T}_{\text{name}}$. All long-terms keys are symmetrical: $K \in \mathsf{LT}$ implies $K = K^{-1}$.

We likewise assume that the key server generates keys in a reasonable way, meaning that that $\mathrm{Serv}[**, K] \cap \mathcal{C} = \emptyset$ unless:

- $K \notin \mathsf{K}_\mathcal{P}$;
- $K = K^{-1}$;
- K is uniquely originating in $\mathcal{C}$;
- $K \notin \mathsf{LT}$.

Because of the unique origination assumption, it follows that the cardinality $|\mathrm{Serv}[**, K] \cap \mathcal{C}| \leq 1$ for every K. We say that $\mathcal{C}$ has a *reasonable server* when these conditions are met.

The overall strategy for showing the responder's guarantee, assuming given a bundle $\mathcal{C}$ such that $\mathcal{C}$ has a reasonable server and $\mathcal{C}$ contains a strand $s_r \in \mathrm{Resp}[A, B, N_a, N_b, t_b, K]$ with $K_A, K_B \notin \mathsf{K}_\mathcal{P}$, is the following:

1. Observe that $\mathsf{LT} \subset \mathsf{S}_0 \cup \mathsf{K}_\mathcal{P}$, as the protocol never transmits a long-term key. For any key K', if $\mathrm{Serv}[A, B, *, *, *, K'] \neq \emptyset$, then K' is transmitted protected by K_A and K_B, but it will never be transmitted with any different protection (with a reasonable key server). Since $K_A, K_B \in \mathsf{S}_0$, $K' \in \mathsf{S}_1$ whenever $\mathrm{Serv}[A, B, *, *, *, K'] \neq \emptyset$.
2. $\{\!|A\,K\,t_b|\!\}_{K_B}$ is an unsolicited test, originating on a regular strand. This can only be a server strand $s_s \in \mathrm{Serv}[A, B, *, *, t_b, K]$. Therefore, $K \in \mathsf{S}_1$.
3. $M_2 \Rightarrow M_4$ is an incoming test for N_b in $\{\!|N_b|\!\}_K$. Hence, there is a regular transforming edge producing $\{\!|N_b|\!\}_K$. This can lie only on the second and third nodes of an initiator strand $s_i \in \mathrm{Init}[A', B', N_a', N_b, t_b', K, *]$.

4. The first and second nodes of s_i form an incoming test for N'_a. Therefore, there is a regular transforming edge producing $\{\!| B'\, N'_a\, K\, t'_b |\!\}_{K_{A'}}$. This can only be $s'_s \in \mathrm{Serv}[A', B', *, *, t'_b, K]$.
5. By the assumption that $\mathcal{C}$ has a reasonable key server, K is uniquely originating in $\mathcal{C}$. Therefore, $s'_s = s_s$, and $A' = A$, $B' = B$, $t'_b = t_b$. Thus, $s_i \in \mathrm{Init}[A, B, *, N_b, t_b, K, *]$.

The initiator's guarantee is simpler to establish. The edge $M_1 \Rightarrow M_3$ on an initiator strand is an incoming test for N_a in $\{\!| B\, N_a\, K\, t_b |\!\}_{K_A}$. It shows there is a server strand $s_s \in \mathrm{Serv}[A, B, N_a, *, t_b, K]$. The first node of s_s is an unsolicited test, showing the existence of a responder strand $s_r \in \mathrm{Resp}[A, B, N_a, *, t_b, *]$.

In the re-authentication sub-protocol, the key distribution center no longer needs to be involved; the initiator again presents the same ticket to the responder, as shown in Figure 20. In this diagram, the first arrow inbound to the initiator

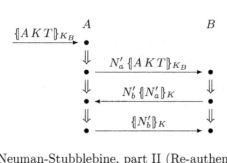

Fig. 20. Neuman-Stubblebine, part II (Re-authentication)

strand does not represent a real message; it represents the state stored in the initiator that preserves the ticket for later re-use.

In the presence of this additional sub-protocol, step 3 in the responder's guarantee can no longer be completed. There must certainly still be a transforming edge producing $\{\!| N_b |\!\}_K$, but this edge may lie either on an initiator strand for Part I of the protocol, or on (conceivably) either type of strand for Part II. By contrast, the initiator's guarantee for Part I is unaffected, because we have not added any strand with a transforming edge producing a term of the form $\{\!| B\, N_a\, K\, t_b |\!\}_{K_A}$.

This example illustrates the need for a systematic way to understand protocol mixing, as for instance the mixing of part I and part II of Neuman-Stubblebine. We undertake that task in the next section.

6   Protocol Independence via Disjoint Encryption

Whether a cryptographic protocol achieves a security goal depends on what cannot happen. To authenticate a regular principal engaging in a protocol run, we

must observe a pattern of messages that can only be constructed by that principal
in that run, regardless of how the penetrator combines his own actions with those
of principals engaging in other runs, as codified in the Dolev-Yao model [9].
When several cryptographic protocols are combined, the penetrator has new
opportunities to obtain the messages which ought to authenticate principals to
their peers. The penetrator has more unintended services to draw on.

Indeed, because protocol mixing has shown itself to be a significant cause of
protocol failure, and makes protocol analysis more difficult [6,10,23,35,46,48], it
has been identified [36] as a key problem in applying formal methods to cryptographic protocols.

Moreover, in practice, different protocols using cryptography are usually combined. A key distribution protocol is useful only if the session key it delivers is
used for encryption. That later use may involve constructing messages similar
to messages used in the key distribution protocol itself. Does this make replay
attacks possible? Does the use of a key undermine the guarantees provided by
the protocol distributing that key? Or conversely, can the penetrator manipulate
messages from the key distribution protocol to spoof the later use of the key?

There are other reasons why protocol mixture is prevalent. Many recent protocols have large numbers of different options, and therefore have large numbers
of different sub-protocols [33,18,8,35]. Each of these protocols may be easy to
analyze on its own. But the same principal is required to be able to engage in
any sub-protocol. Can the penetrator manipulate this willingness for his own
purposes?

When protocols are mixed together, and we want to appraise whether the
security of one is affected by the others, we will refer to the protocol under study
as the *primary* protocol. We will refer to the others as *secondary* protocols.

6.1   Avoiding Conflict

Common sense suggests a rule of thumb when protocols are to be mixed together.
This rule is that if the primary protocol uses a particular form of encrypted
message as a test to authenticate a peer [14], then the secondary protocols should
not construct a message of that form. If the primary protocol uses a particular
form of encrypted component to protect some private value, then the secondary
protocol should not receive messages of that form and retransmit their contents
in other (potentially less secure) forms. Putting these two ideas together, the
sets of encrypted messages that the different protocols manipulate should be
disjoint.

In the case of Neuman-Stubblebine, for instance, the ticket $\{\!|A\,K\,T|\!\}_{K_B}$ origi-
nates on the primary protocol; it is stored by the initiator for use in the secondary
protocol; and it is then manipulated and transformed by the responder in the
secondary protocol. This violates the disjointness we would like to maintain.

One way to arrange for disjoint encryption is to give each protocol some distinguishing value, such as a number; that number may then be included as part
of each plaintext before encipherment. Then no principal can mistake a value as

belonging to the wrong protocol; an encrypted value bearing a different protocol's number must not be transformed. Another way to achieve disjoint encryption is to ensure that different protocols never use the same key, although this may be expensive or difficult to arrange. Although the Abadi-Needham paper on prudent engineering practice for cryptographic protocols [1] does not discuss mixing different protocols, this rule—to try to achieve disjoint encryption—is in the same spirit as those it proposes.

In this section, we will prove that, properly formalized, it suffices. If two protocols have disjoint encryption, then the first protocol is *independent* of the second. By this we mean that if the primary protocol achieves a security goal (whether an authentication goal or a secrecy goal as defined in Sections 3.12–3.13) when the protocol is executed in isolation, then it still achieves the same security goal when executed in combination with the secondary protocol.

One of the advantages of our approach is that the result works for all secrecy and authentication goals; in this it continues a trend visible from several recent papers [31,21,45,44,19]. We have an additional reason for including this material here: It is a good example of the power of the machinery of paths and well-behaved bundles developed in Section 4.

6.2   Multiprotocol Strand Spaces

To represent multiple protocols [46], we select some regular strands as being runs of the primary protocol; we call these strands *primary strands*.

Definition 13. *A* multiprotocol strand space *is a strand space* (Σ, tr) *together with a distinguished subset of the regular strands* $\Sigma_1 \subset \Sigma \setminus \mathcal{P}_\Sigma$ *called the set of* primary strands.

Σ_2 denotes the set of all other regular strands, called *secondary strands*. A node is primary or secondary if the strand it lies on is. From the point of view of a particular analysis, the secondary strands represent runs of other protocols, different from the primary one under analysis.

The notion of *equivalence* needed for our purposes in this section concentrates on primary nodes.

Definition 14. *Two bundles* $\mathcal{C}, \mathcal{C}'$ *in the multiprotocol strand space* (Σ, tr, Σ_1) *are equivalent if and only if*

1. *they have the same primary nodes, meaning* $\mathcal{C} \cap \Sigma_1 = \mathcal{C}' \cap \Sigma_1$*;*
2. *for all* a*,* a *originates uniquely and on a primary node in* $\mathcal{C}$ *if and only if* a *originates uniquely and on a primary node in* $\mathcal{C}'$*;*
3. *for all* a*,* a *is non-originating in* $\mathcal{C}$ *iff* a *is non-originating in* $\mathcal{C}'$*.*

Since this is a more liberal notion of equivalence (it requires fewer nodes and unique origination facts to be unchanged), any existence assertion about equivalent bundles from Section 4 remains true in the present context.

We will also jettison the strand space parameter $\mathsf{K}_\mathcal{P}$ for our current purposes, and express our assumptions about safe keys purely in terms of non-origination.

For our present purposes, this has the advantage of not distinguishing whether a key is disclosed through a K-strand or through a secondary strand. The effect for us is now the same.

6.3   Linking Paths

From Section 4, we also know that every bundle $\mathcal{C}$ is equivalent to a directed bundle $\mathcal{C}'$ (Definition 11), and this remains true with our new definition of equivalent, assuming that in the definition of directed bundles we make the same substitution of "primary" for "regular:"

Definition 15. $\mathcal{C}$ is directed *if for every node* $n \in \mathcal{C}$, *there is a primary node* $m \in \mathcal{C} \cap \Sigma_1$ *such that* $n \preceq_{\mathcal{C}} m$.

Suppose we can show that given any bundle $\mathcal{C}$ involving both protocols, we can find an equivalent bundle in which no path leads from a secondary node to a primary node. Then there is also an equivalent $\mathcal{C}'$ in which there are no secondary nodes at all. Therefore, if $\mathcal{C}$ is a counterexample to some authentication goal, $\mathcal{C}'$ is a counterexample in which the secondary protocol does not occur at all. This will establish protocol independence for authentication goals.

Let us say that a penetrator path p is an *inbound linking path* if $p_0 \in \Sigma_2$ and $\ell(p) \in \Sigma_1$. We thus take the point of view of the primary path, and regard p as linking the secondary node to a primary node. One of the crucial steps in showing protocol independence is showing that we can unlink inbound linking paths.

A penetrator path p is an *outbound linking path* if $p_0 \in \Sigma_1$ and $\ell(p) \in \Sigma_2$. We need not unlink these, but we need to ensure that they do not deliver terms to the secondary protocol from which the secondary protocol will extract a secret.

6.4   Bridges

If $\mathcal{C}$ is a normal bundle and p is a penetrator path through $\mathcal{C}$, then all destructive edges precede constructive edges in p. The edge that separates the destructive portion of a path from the constructive portion is of special interest. We call it a bridge.

Definition 16. *A* bridge *in a bundle* $\mathcal{C}$ *is a message transmission edge* $m \rightarrow n$ *embedded in a subgraph of one the types shown in Figure 21.*
   If $m \rightarrow n$ *is a bridge, then its* bridge term *is* $term(m)$, *which equals* $term(n)$.
   A bridge is simple *iff its bridge term is simple, that is, is not of the form* $g \, h$.

Any edge between regular nodes is an external bridge. The source m of a bridge $m \rightarrow n$ is never on a constructive penetrator strand, and the target n is never on a destructive penetrator strand.

A term is simple if it is an atom or an encryption, not a concatenation (see Definition 7 in Section 3.14).

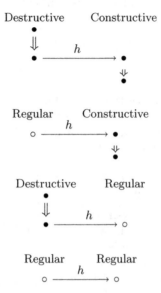

Fig. 21. Four types of bridge: internal, entry, exit, and external bridges

Proposition 4 *Suppose that C is a normal bundle, and p is any penetrator path in C. Then p traverses exactly one bridge.*

Any bundle C can be replaced by an equivalent bundle C' in which the bridge term for every path is simple. Moreover if C is normal or efficient, so is C'.

The proof of the second assertion consists of adding S-strands to separate any concatenated bridge term $g\,h$ and C-strands to reconstruct $g\,h$ after the bridges of the two new sub-paths.

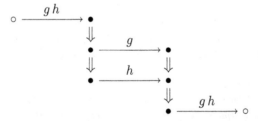

Since every path p has a unique bridge, we can write $\mathrm{pbt}(p)$ for the bridge term occurring on the bridge.

If a path includes penetrator nodes and regular nodes, then it never traverses the same component before and after a regular node:

Proposition 5 *Suppose that C is normal, efficient, and has simple bridges, and p is a path through C that traverses no key edges. If $i < j < k$, p_j is a negative regular node, and p_i, p_k are penetrator nodes with simple terms, then $\mathrm{term}(p_i) \neq \mathrm{term}(p_k)$.*

Suppose moreover that p_k is the first penetrator node after p_j such that p_k has a simple term. Then $p_j \Rightarrow^+ p_{j+1}$ produces a new component $\boxed{t_0} \sqsubset term(p_{j+1})$, and $term(p_k) = t_0$.

The result follows routinely from efficiency.

6.5   Disjoint Encryption

The simplest way to state the disjoint encryption assumption would be to require that the two protocols not use the same ciphertext as a part of any message. That would mean that if $n_1 \in \Sigma_1$ and $n_2 \in \Sigma_2$, and if $\{\!|h|\!\}_K \sqsubset term(n_1)$, then $\{\!|h|\!\}_K \not\sqsubset term(n_2)$.

However, this simple version is unnecessarily restrictive. The secondary protocol would be unable to accept public-key certificates generated in the primary protocol, which is intuitively harmless because the contents are public in any case. The secondary protocol would also be unable to re-use symmetric-key tickets such as those generated by the Kerberos Key Distribution Center [24,38]. These are also intuitively harmless, so long as the secondary protocol does not extract private values from within them, or repackage their private contents, potentially insecurely. Hence, we allow these harmless exceptions to the requirement that no encrypted term be used by both protocols.

Definition 17. $\{\!|h|\!\}_K$ *is a* shared encryption *if there exist $n_1 \in \Sigma_1$ and $n_2 \in \Sigma_2$ such that $\{\!|h|\!\}_K \sqsubset term(n_1)$ and $\{\!|h|\!\}_K \sqsubset term(n_2)$. It is an* outbound shared encryption *if this holds with n_1 positive and n_2 negative. It is an* inbound shared encryption *if this holds with n_1 negative and n_2 positive.*

We want to restrict but not prohibit shared encryptions, and we will do so in slightly different ways for inbound and outbound shared encryptions.

Definition 18. (Disjoint Outbound Encryption) Σ *has* disjoint outbound encryption *if and only if, for every outbound shared encryption $\{\!|h|\!\}_K$, for every atom $a \sqsubset \{\!|h|\!\}_K$, and for every $n_2 \Rightarrow^+ n_2' \in \Sigma_2$,*

if n_2 *is negative and $\{\!|h|\!\}_K \sqsubset term(n_2)$,*
and n_2' *is positive and t_0 is a new component of n_2',*
then $a \not\sqsubset t_0$.

That is, no secondary strand manipulates a into a new component.

This definition has the important property that values originating uniquely on primary nodes cannot "zigzag" to a secondary node, before being disclosed to the penetrator.

Proposition 6 (No Zigzags) *Let Σ have disjoint outbound encryption, and let C be a normal, efficient bundle with simple bridges in Σ. Suppose p is a path such that $term(\ell(p)) = a$ (where $a \in \mathsf{K} \cup \mathsf{T}$), $a \sqsubset term(p_i)$ for all $1 \leq i \leq |p|$, and $p_k \in \Sigma_2$. Then $p_j \notin \Sigma_1$ for any $j < k$.*

PROOF. Suppose otherwise. We may assume that j, k are chosen so that j is the largest index such that $p_j \in \Sigma_1$ and there is some later $p_k \in \Sigma_2$, and k is the smallest value $> j$ such that $p_k \in \Sigma_2$. So the path $\tilde{p} = p_j \longmapsto \cdots \longmapsto p_k$ is a penetrator path.

If $\tilde{p}$ traverses a key edge (see Section 4.6) at $p_i \to p_{i+1}$, then $\mathrm{term}(p_i) = a$ is a key. Therefore $p_i \prec p_k \prec \ell(p)$, contradicting efficiency.

Therefore $\tilde{p}$ begins at a positive regular (primary) node, ends at a negative regular (secondary) node, and never traverses a key edge. It is of type 4 in the catalog of Section 4.6. Therefore it has a bridge term $\mathrm{pbt}(\tilde{p})$ such that $\mathrm{pbt}(\tilde{p}) \sqsubset \mathrm{term}(p_j)$ and $\mathrm{pbt}(\tilde{p}) \sqsubset \mathrm{term}(p_k)$. Since $a \sqsubset \mathrm{pbt}(\tilde{p})$, either a is itself a component of $\mathrm{pbt}(\tilde{p})$, or else $a \sqsubset \boxed{\{\!|h|\!\}_K} \sqsubset \mathrm{pbt}(\tilde{p})$. If a is a component of $\mathrm{pbt}(\tilde{p})$, then we have a contradiction to efficiency as before.

Otherwise, $\{\!|h|\!\}_K$ is an outbound shared encryption. By Proposition 5, $p_k \Rightarrow^+$ p_{k+1} produces a new component t_0, and $a \sqsubset t_0$. But this contradicts the definition of outbound disjoint encryption. $\square$

As a consequence, we may infer that there is never a failure of secrecy where any secondary node touches the secret value.

The condition on inbound shared encryptions is that they should never occur in new components created on secondary nodes.

Definition 19. (Disjoint Encryption) Σ *has* disjoint inbound encryption *if, for every inbound shared encryption $\{\!|h|\!\}_K$ and $n_2 \Rightarrow^+ n_2' \in \Sigma_2$, if $\boxed{t_0} \sqsubset \mathrm{term}(n_2')$ is a new component, then $\{\!|h|\!\}_K \not\sqsubset t_0$.*

Σ *has* disjoint encryption *if it has both disjoint inbound encryption and disjoint outbound encryption.*

6.6   The Protocol Independence Theorem

Definition 20. Σ_1 *is* independent of Σ_2 *if for every bundle $\mathcal{C}$ in Σ, there is a bundle $\mathcal{C}'$ in Σ that is equivalent to $\mathcal{C}$ such that $\mathcal{C}'$ is disjoint from Σ_2.*

Proposition 7 (Protocol Independence) *If Σ has disjoint encryption, then Σ_1 is independent of Σ_2.*

PROOF. We may assume that $\mathcal{C}$ is normal, efficient, and has simple bridges. We want to show that we can remove any inbound linking paths in $\mathcal{C}$.

Let p be an inbound linking path. Suppose first that p traverses an atomic value $a \in \mathsf{T} \cup \mathsf{K}$. This may either be the key edge into a D or E strand, or it may be the bridge of p. In any case, let a be the first atomic value on p. By Proposition 6, a does not originate uniquely on a primary node. Therefore, there is an equivalent bundle $\mathcal{C}'$ in which a is produced by an initial penetrator strand (a K-strand or a M-strand).

Suppose next that p never traverses an atomic value. Then in particular it never traverses a key edge into a D or E strand. Thus, the path bridge term $\mathrm{pbt}(p) \sqsubset \mathrm{term}(p_1)$ and $\mathrm{pbt}(p) \sqsubset \mathrm{term}(\ell(p))$. Since $\mathrm{pbt}(p)$ is not atomic but it is simple, it is of the form $\{\!|h|\!\}_K$. Therefore, by disjoint inbound encryption, it does not occur in a new component of p_1. But by Proposition 5, this contradicts efficiency.

Therefore we may remove any inbound linking path p in a normal, efficient bundle with simple bridges. It follows that there is a $\mathcal{C}'$ equivalent to $\mathcal{C}$ such that $\mathcal{C}' \cap \Sigma_2 = \emptyset$. $\square$

An easy consequence of this theorem shows that if the primary and secondary protocols share no keys whatever, then we have independence.

Corollary 1 *For $i = 1$ and 2, let $\mathfrak{K}_i$ be the set of K such that $K \sqsubset term(n)$ for any $n \in \Sigma_i$ or $\{\!|h|\!\}_K \sqsubset term(n)$ for any h and any $n \in \Sigma_i$.*
If $\mathfrak{K}_1 \cap \mathfrak{K}_2 = \emptyset$, then Σ_1 is independent of Σ_2.

If Σ_1 and Σ_2 involve the activity of different principals, and the keys for the protocols are chosen in an unpredictable way from a large set, then the keys they use will in practice never overlap. Therefore, Σ_1 is independent of Σ_2. The same holds when the same principals may participate in both protocols, but they choose keys independently for each protocol.

Similarly, suppose each ciphertext created in Σ_1 or Σ_2 contains a distinguishing values such as different protocol numbers. If Σ_1 never accepts a ciphertext containing Σ_2's value, then we have disjoint inbound encryption. If Σ_2 never extracts a subterm from a ciphertext containing Σ_1's value, then we have disjoint outbound encryption. Together, they suffice for protocol independence.

6.7   An Application of Protocol Independence

Let us return to the Neuman-Stubblebine protocol, as described in Section 5.4 and summarized in Figures 19 and 20.

We regard the re-authentication protocol as the secondary protocol; the presence of the re-authentication protocol should not undermine any security guarantee offered by the primary protocol. However, terms of the form $\{\!|N|\!\}_K$ are constructed as new components on secondary strands, and accepted on primary strands. Hence the corresponding multiprotocol strand space does not have disjoint inbound encryption. Indeed, the penetrator can use a session of the re-authentication protocol to complete a responder strand in a bundle with no initiator [46].

For this reason, we amend (see [46]) the re-authentication protocol to the form shown in Figure 22. To apply our independence theorem, we check that the corresponding strand space Σ has disjoint encryption. But that is trivial, because tickets $\{\!|A\,K\,T|\!\}_{K_{BS}}$ are the only common encrypted subterms of primary and secondary nodes. The outbound property holds because no private subterm of a ticket is uttered in a new component of a secondary node. The inbound property holds because no new component of a secondary node contains a ticket.

Therefore, if $\mathcal{C}$ is a counterexample to some security property, we may deform $\mathcal{C}$ into an equivalent standard bundle $\mathcal{C}'$, in which there are no secondary nodes. $\mathcal{C}'$ is still a counterexample, assuming that the security property is invariant

Fig. 22. Neuman-Stubblebine, part II modified (Re-authentication)

under bundle equivalences, as authentication and secrecy properties are. Thus, if the primary protocol fails to meet the security goal, that is independent of the presence of the secondary protocol: the corrected Neuman-Stubblebine re-authentication protocol is entirely guiltless in this affair.

6.8   Conclusion

In this report, we have focused on two information security problems. One is the packet protection problem, where we have studied filtering routers and firewall-oriented security goals that they are capable of achieving. The other is the Dolev-Yao problem, where we have studied how to achieve authentication and confidentiality goals in the presence of an active penetrator.

In both areas, we applied essentially the same method. We identified a class of security goals that capture important real-world security services that people need to achieve. We introduced simple mathematical modeling notions, such as directed graphs, boolean algebras, and freely generated algebras. In terms of this vocabulary, we were able to formalize the security goals and develop proof techniques and algorithms to determine what postures or protocols achieve the goals.

We regard these two problems as instances of foundational work in *security management*. Although the phrase sounds prosaic, the problems it covers are fundamental in a world where many mechanisms and systems cooperate to achieve our security objectives. Knowing that they jointly achieve something meaningful is difficult. Yet the problems have enough structure to repay mathematical abstraction, and the abstractions tell us, systematically, how to marshal the mechanisms to achieve practical protection.

References

1. Martín Abadi and Roger Needham. Prudent engineering practice for cryptographic protocols. In *Proceedings, 1994 IEEE Symposium on Research in Security and Privacy*, pages 122–136. IEEE, IEEE Computer Society Press, 1994. 252

2. Karl S. Brace, Richard L. Rudell, and Randal E. Bryant. Efficient implementation of a BDD package. In *27th ACM/IEEE Design Automation Conference*, pages 40–45, 1990. 213

3. Randal E. Bryant. Graph-based algorithms for boolean function manipulation. *IEEE Transactions on Computers*, C-35(8):677–691, August 1986. 210, 212

4. Michael Burrows, Martín Abadi, and Roger Needham. A logic of authentication. *Proceedings of the Royal Society*, Series A, 426(1871):233–271, December 1989. Also appeared as SRC Research Report 39 and, in a shortened form, in ACM Transactions on Computer Systems 8, 1 (February 1990), 18-36. 219

5. Ulf Carlsen. Optimal privacy and authentication on a portable communications system. *Operating Systems Review*, 28(3):16–23, 1994. 226

6. John Clark and Jeremy Jacob. A survey of authentication protocol literature: Version 1.0. University of York, Department of Computer Science, November 1997. 219, 251

7. Edmund Clarke, Somesh Jha, and Will Marrero. Using state space exploration and a natural deduction style message derivation engine to verify security protocols. In *Proceedings, IFIP Working Conference on Programming Concepts and Methods (PROCOMET)*, 1998. 240

8. T. Dierks and C. Allen. The TLS protocol. RFC 2246, January 1999. 219, 251

9. D. Dolev and A. Yao. On the security of public-key protocols. *IEEE Transactions on Information Theory*, 29:198–208, 1983. 198, 219, 251

10. Li Gong and Paul Syverson. Fail-stop protocols: An approach to designing secure protocols. In *5th International Working Conference on Dependable Computing for Critical Applications*, pages 44–55, September 1995. 251

11. Joshua D. Guttman. Filtering postures: Local enforcement for global policies. In *Proceedings, 1997 IEEE Symposium on Security and Privacy*, pages 120–29. IEEE Computer Society Press, May 1997. 199, 200, 208, 209, 210

12. Joshua D. Guttman. Packet filters and their atoms. Lecture at University of Pennsylvania, host C. Gunter, April 1999. 210

13. Joshua D. Guttman, Amy L. Herzog, and F. Javier Thayer. Authentication and confidentiality via IPsec. In D. Gollman, editor, *ESORICS 2000: European Symposium on Research in Computer Security*, LNCS. Springer Verlag, 2000. 199, 200, 203

14. Joshua D. Guttman and F. Javier THAYER Fábrega. Authentication tests. In *Proceedings, 2000 IEEE Symposium on Security and Privacy*. May, IEEE Computer Society Press, 2000. 199, 251

15. Joshua D. Guttman and F. Javier THAYER Fábrega. Protocol independence through disjoint encryption. In *Proceedings, 13th Computer Security Foundations Workshop*. IEEE Computer Society Press, July 2000. 199

16. Joshua D. Guttman and F. Javier THAYER Fábrega. Authentication tests and the structure of bundles. *Theoretical Computer Science*, 2001. To appear. 199, 224, 229, 234, 246

17. Joshua D. Guttman, F. Javier THAYER Fábrega, and Lenore D. Zuck. Faithful to the cryptography. Submitted for publication. Available at http://cs.nyu.edu/zuck. 229

18. D. Harkins and D. Carrel. *The Internet Key Exchange (IKE)*. IETF Network Working Group RFC 2409, November 1998. 251

19. James Heather, Gavin Lowe, and Steve Schneider. How to prevent type flaw attacks on security protocols. In *Proceedings, 13th Computer Security Foundations Workshop*. IEEE Computer Society Press, July 2000. 252

20. James Heather and Steve Schneider. Toward automatic verification of authentication protocols on an unbounded network. In *Proceedings, 13th Computer Security Foundations Workshop*. IEEE Computer Society Press, July 2000. 240

21. Mei Lin Hui and Gavin Lowe. Safe simplifying transformations for security protocols. In *12th Computer Security Foundations Workshop Proceedings*, pages 32–43. IEEE Computer Society Press, June 1999. 252

22. Jan Jürjens and Guido Wimmel. Specification-based testing of firewalls. Submitted for publication, 2001. 218

23. John Kelsey, Bruce Schneier, and David Wagner. Protocol interactions and the chosen protocol attack. In *Security Protocols, International Workshop April 1997 Proceedings*, pages 91–104. Springer-Verlag, 1998. 251

24. J. Kohl and C. Neuman. The Kerberos network authentication service (v5). RFC 1510, September 1993. 255

25. Xavier Leroy, Damien Doligez, Jacques Garrigue, Didier Rémy, and Jérôme Vouillon. *The Objective Caml System*. INRIA, http://caml.inria.fr/, 2000. Version 3.00. 217

26. Gavin Lowe. An attack on the Needham-Schroeder public key authentication protocol. *Information Processing Letters*, 56(3):131–136, November 1995. 247

27. Gavin Lowe. Breaking and fixing the Needham-Schroeder public-key protocol using FDR. In *Proceeedings of* TACAS, volume 1055 of *Lecture Notes in Computer Science*, pages 147–166. Springer Verlag, 1996. 221, 231, 247

28. Gavin Lowe. Some new attacks upon security protocols. In *Proceedings of the Computer Security Foundations Workshop IX*. IEEE Computer Society Press, 1996. 219

29. Gavin Lowe. Casper: A compiler for the analysis of security protocols. In *10th Computer Security Foundations Workshop Proceedings*, pages 18–30. IEEE Computer Society Press, 1997. 236

30. Gavin Lowe. A hierarchy of authentication specifications. In *10th Computer Security Foundations Workshop Proceedings*, pages 31–43. IEEE Computer Society Press, 1997. 238

31. Gavin Lowe. Toward a completeness result for model checking of security protocols. In *11th Computer Security Foundations Workshop Proceedings*, pages 96–105. IEEE Computer Society Press, 1998. 252

32. Will Marrero, Edmund Clarke, and Somesh Jha. A model checker for authentication protocols. In Cathy Meadows and Hilary Orman, editors, *Proceedings of the DIMACS Workshop on Design and Verification of Security Protocols*. DIMACS, Rutgers University, September 1997. 236

33. D. Maughan, M. Schertler, M. Schneider, and J. Turner. *Internet Security Association and Key Management Protocol (ISAKMP)*. IETF Network Working Group RFC 2408, November 1998. 251

34. Alain Mayer, Avishai Wool, and Elisha Ziskind. Fang: A firewall analysis engine. In *Proceedings, IEEE Symposium on Security and Privacy*, 2000. 210

35. Catherine Meadows. Analysis of the Internet Key Exchange protocol using the NRL protocol analyzer. In *Proceedings, 1999 IEEE Symposium on Security and Privacy*. IEEE Computer Society Press, May 1999. 251

36. Catherine Meadows. Open issues in formal methods for cryptographic protocol analysis. In *DISCEX Workshop*. DARPA, January 2000. 251

37. Roger Needham and Michael Schroeder. Using encryption for authentication in large networks of computers. *Communications of the ACM*, 21(12), December 1978. 220

38. B. Clifford Neuman and Stuart G. Stubblebine. A note on the use of timestamps as nonces. *Operating Systems Review*, 27(2):10–14, April 1993. 248, 255

39. Lawrence C. Paulson. Proving properties of security protocols by induction. In *10th IEEE Computer Security Foundations Workshop*, pages 70–83. IEEE Computer Society Press, 1997. 236

40. Lawrence C. Paulson. The inductive approach to verifying cryptographic protocols. *Journal of Computer Security*, 1998. Also Report 443, Cambridge University Computer Lab. 237, 240

41. Adrian Perrig and Dawn Xiaodong Song. Looking for diamonds in the desert: Extending automatic protocol generation to three-party authentication and key agreement protocols. In *Proceedings of the 13th IEEE Computer Security Foundations Workshop*. IEEE Computer Society Press, July 2000. 246

42. Dag Prawitz. *Natural Deduction: A Proof-Theoretic Study*. Almqvist and Wiksel, Stockholm, 1965. 240

43. Steve Schneider. Verifying authentication protocols with CSP. In *Proceedings of the 10th IEEE Computer Security Foundations Workshop*, pages 3–17. IEEE Computer Society Press, 1997. 237

44. Scott Stoller. A bound on attacks on authentication protocols. Available at http://www.cs.indiana.edu/~stoller/, July 1999. 252

45. Scott Stoller. A reduction for automated verification of authentication protocols. In *Workshop on Formal Methods and Security Protocols*, July 1999. Available at http://www.cs.indiana.edu/~stoller/. 252

46. F. Javier THAYER Fábrega, Jonathan C. Herzog, and Joshua D. Guttman. Mixed strand spaces. In *Proceedings of the 12th IEEE Computer Security Foundations Workshop*. IEEE Computer Society Press, June 1999. 251, 252, 257

47. F. Javier THAYER Fábrega, Jonathan C. Herzog, and Joshua D. Guttman. Strand spaces: Proving security protocols correct. *Journal of Computer Security*, 7(2/3):191–230, 1999. 199, 224, 225, 229, 232, 234, 238

48. D. Wagner and B. Schneier. Analysis of the SSL 3.0 protocol. In *Proceedings, Second USENIX Workshop on Electronic Commerce*, pages 29–40, 1996. Available at http://www.counterpane.com/ssl.html. 251

49. Thomas Y. C. Woo and Simon S. Lam. Verifying authentication protocols: Methodology and example. In *Proc. Int. Conference on Network Protocols*, October 1993. 238

50. T. Ylonen, T. Kivinen, and M. Saarinen. SSH prototcol architecture. Internet draft, November 1997. Also named draft-ietf-secsh-architecture-01.txt. 219

Notes on Nominal Calculi for Security and Mobility

Andrew D. Gordon

Microsoft Research

Lecture notes for the FOSAD Summer School 2000, from works co-authored with Martín Abadi, Luca Cardelli, and Giorgio Ghelli

Abstract. There is great interest in applying nominal calculi—computational formalisms that include dynamic name generation—to the problems of programming, specifying, and verifying secure and mobile computations. These notes introduce three nominal calculi—the pi calculus, the spi calculus, and the ambient calculus. We describe some typical techniques, and survey related work.

1 Introduction

Programming a concurrent application is difficult. Deadlocks and race conditions are well known problems in multi-threaded applications on a single machine.

Programming a concurrent application running on a distributed network is more difficult, as we must deal with additional problems such as partial failure of one or more of the host machines. Moreover, if there are untrustworthy hosts on the network, as on the internet, we may need to resort to cryptographic protocols to achieve security, and such protocols are notoriously hard to get right.

Programming a concurrent application running on a network that includes mobile hosts or mobile software is still more difficult. We need to solve the communication problem of supporting reliable interaction between mobile devices or between mobile software agents. We need to solve the security problems induced by untrusted code and untrusted hosts.

These notes introduce an approach to these problems of security and mobility based on three related calculi for concurrency, all of which stress the importance of names. We call these *nominal calculi*. The three calculi are tiny but extremely expressive languages for programming concurrent computations. These calculi have well defined formal semantics upon which sophisticated semantic theories have been constructed. The point of defining the calculi and exploring their theories is to help shed light on the difficulties of programming concurrent, distributed, and mobile computations. The ways in which these calculi and their theories can help include the following. We can program intricate computations—such as protocols for communications or security—within these calculi, and apply their theories directly to try to prove properties or to expose flaws. We can use these calculi as simple settings in which to prototype programming models—such as communication or mobility primitives—that subsequently

R. Focardi and R. Gorrieri (Eds.): FOSAD 2000, LNCS 2171, pp. 262–330, 2001.

can be implemented as new libraries or language extensions in full programming langauges. Similarly, we can develop static checks such as type systems or flow analyses for these simple calculi and subsequently apply them to full languages.

In these notes on nominal calculi, we emphasise the application of equational reasoning and type systems to reasoning about security and mobility. Moreover, we survey other work on implementations and on other formal techniques such as logics and flow analyses.

Pure Names and Nominal Calculi

In his 1989 lecture notes on naming and security in distributed systems, Needham [Nee89] stresses the usefulness of pure names for referring to distributed objects. Needham defines a pure name to be "nothing but a bit pattern that is an identifier, and is only useful for comparing for identity with other bit patterns— which includes looking up in tables in order to find other information". An example of a pure name is the 128-bit GUID (Globally Unique Identifier) that uniquely identifies an interface or an implementation in the COM component model [Box98]. A pure name is atomic. In contrast, an impure name is one with some kind of recognisable structure, such as a file path or a URL containing a path. An impure name does more than simply name a single object. For example, the file name *rmn/animals/pig* may imply the presence of a directory *rmn* and a subdirectory *animals*.

The idea of a pure name is a useful abstraction for referring to many kinds of computational structures, not just distributed objects. All three formalisms described in these notes include an abstract set of pure names and an operator for local generation of fresh, unguessable names. This is what we mean when we say that a formalism is a nominal calculus.

The Pi Calculus—Programming with Names

The pi calculus [MPW92, Mil99, SW01] is a small but extremely expressive programming language. It is the original example of a nominal calculus, and is the archetype for many others. It was originally designed to be a foundation for concurrent computation, in the same way as the λ-calculus is a foundation for sequential computation. First published in the same year as Needham's lecture notes, it places a still greater emphasis on pure names. The pi calculus embodies the view that in principle most, if not all, distributed computation may usefully be explained in terms of exchanges of names on named communication channels.

Programs in the pi calculus are systems of independent, parallel processes that synchronise via message-passing handshakes on named channels. The channels a process knows about determine the communication possibilities of the process. Channels may be *restricted*, so that only certain processes may communicate on them. In this respect the pi calculus is similar to earlier process calculi such as CSP [Hoa85] and CCS [Mil89].

What sets the pi calculus apart from earlier calculi is that the scope of a restriction—the program text in which a channel may be used—may change during computation. When a process sends a restricted name as a message to a process outside the scope of the restriction, the scope is said to *extrude*, that is, it enlarges to embrace the process receiving the channel. The communication possibilities of a process may change over time; a process may learn the names of new channels via scope extrusion. Thus, a channel is a transferable capability for communication.

A central technical idea of these notes is to use the restriction operator and scope extrusion from the pi calculus as a formal model of the possession and communication of secrets, such as cryptographic keys. These features of the pi calculus and other nominal calculi are essential in our descriptions of security protocols. At the formal level, we can guarantee freshness absolutely by treating a fresh name as a bound variable, distinct from all others. At the implementation level, there are several strategies to guarantee freshness; a common one in a distributed setting is to do so probabilistically by treating a fresh name as a random bitstring of sufficiently many bits to make collisions implausible.

The pi calculus enjoys a broad mathematical theory—including observational equivalences, program logics, and type systems—that addresses the difficulty of programming concurrent applications. Remarkably, a wide variety of data structures—from bits, tuples, and lists, through to objects—and procedural abstractions—such as functions and methods—can all be reduced to interactions on named channels. Hence, the pi calculus is a basis for semantic accounts of functional, imperative, and object-oriented programming, and for the design of several concurrent languages [FG96, PT00, Ode00], as well as other applications. In Part I of these notes, we introduce the pi calculus informally, as a simple programming notation for describing abstract versions of security protocols.

The Spi Calculus—Programming with Cryptography

Security protocols accomplish goals such as establishing the authenticity of one principal to another or preserving the secrecy of information during an interaction. Cryptographic protocols are security protocols implemented over a public network using cryptographic primitives such as encryption, digital signatures, and hashing. Widely-deployed examples include Kerberos and SSL. Designing cryptographic protocols is difficult, in part because they must work correctly even in the presence of an active adversary on the network, who may replay or modify messages. Even if we rule out cryptanalysis, that is, assume perfectly secure cryptographic primitives, cryptographic protocols are notorious for containing flaws, or being brittle in the sense that apparently innocuous changes in operating assumptions may cause failure. For example, Denning and Sacco [DS81] and Lowe [Low96] point out such brittleness in protocols proposed by Needham and Schroeder [NS78].

The spi calculus [AG99] is a version of the pi calculus equipped with abstract cryptographic primitives, in particular, with primitives for perfect encryption and decryption. In this nominal calculus, names represent encryption keys as well as communication channels. The idea is that to analyse a protocol, we begin by modelling it as a spi calculus program. We can then apply techniques from the theory of the pi calculus such as equational reasoning or type systems to either show the protocol correct or identify a defect. In Part II of these notes, we introduce the spi calculus and explain how to apply equational reasoning to a series of example protocols.

The Ambient Calculus—Programming with Mobility

It is becoming more common for networks to include mobile devices or mobile software. When programming such networks, one area of difficulty is mobility: not so much how to move objects themselves, but how to specify which objects to move. This is a lesson reported by pioneers of mobile computation such as the designers of Telescript [Whi96] or Obliq [Car95]: in those systems, it is easy to move a single object or the whole running computation, but harder to specify a cluster of logically related objects that is to be moved. Another area of difficulty is security: this arises not so much from mobility itself, but from the careless or malicious crossing of administrative domains.

An *ambient* is an abstract collection or group of running processes and objects that functions both as a unit of mobility—of either software and hardware—and as a unit of security—an administrative domain or a security perimeter. An ambient is a bounded place where computation happens, with an inside and an outside. An ambient may contain other ambients, to model related clusters of object or to model hierarchical administrative domains. An ambient has an unforgeable name. An ambient's security rests on the controlled distribution of suitable credentials, or *capabilities*, derived from its name. A capability embodies the right to move a whole running ambient inside another, or the right to move one outside another, or the right to dissolve an ambient boundary.

The ambient calculus [CG00b, Car99] formalizes ambients by adopting the extreme position that everything is an ambient. Its purpose is to provide a formal model for describing mobility, and to be a prototypical programming language for mobile applications. Processes have a spatial structure induced by ambient nesting. Computations are series of re-arrangements of this spatial structures, representing ambient mobility. In this nominal calculus, names are the names of ambients rather than communication channels as in the pi calculus. Ambients are explicit boundaries: in the pi calculus, interaction depends on shared names— parties need to know the same communication channel to interact; in the ambient calculus, interaction depends on shared position—parties need to be inside the same ambient to interact. In this way, the ambient hierarchy regulates who may communicate with who.

In Part III of these notes, we introduce the ambient calculus, show how it can model a programming language for mobile computation with features akin to Telescript, describe a series of type systems for ambients, and show how we can type aspects of mobile computation.

Scope of These Notes

The goal of these notes is to introduce nominal calculi and their applications to security and mobility. The bulk of the notes consists of abridged versions of earlier articles [AG99, CG00b, CG99, CGG00a] concerning aspects of the three calculi we have discussed. Proof techniques and proofs omitted from these notes may be found in the full versions of the original articles.

Many nominal calculi that have been applied to security or mobility are of course not covered. Two prominent examples are the join calculus and the seal calculus. The join calculus [FG96] is a variant of the pi calculus based on asynchronous communications; a distributed implementation [FGL+96] has been used to implement the ambient calculus [FLS00], amongst other things. The seal calculus [VC99] is a calculus of mobile agents, akin to the ambient calculus, but with a richer set of primitive operations; it forms the basis of the JavaSeal platform for mobile agents [BV01].

Part I: The Pi Calculus

This part of the notes introduces the pi calculus as a programming notation for studying security protocols. Section 2 introduces the syntax and informal semantics of the pi calculus. In Section 3 we explain an application of the pi calculus to the study of abstract security protocols. Section 4 ends this part with pointers to some of the main works on the pi calculus.

Since the spi calculus of Part II is in fact an extension of the pi calculus of this part, we postpone formal definitions of operational semantics and equivalence until Part II.

2   Outline of the Pi Calculus

There are in fact several versions of the pi calculus. Here we review the syntax and semantics of a particular version. The differences with other versions are mostly orthogonal to our concerns.

We assume an infinite set of *names*, to be used for communication channels, and an infinite set of *variables*. We let m, n, p, q, and r range over names, and let x, y, and z range over variables. The set of *terms* is defined by the grammar:

Syntax of Terms:

$L, M, N ::=$	terms
n	name
(M, N)	pair
0	zero
$suc(M)$	successor
x	variable

In the standard pi calculus, names are the only terms. For convenience we have added constructs for pairing and numbers, (M, N), 0, and $suc(M)$. We have also distinguished variables from names.

The set of *processes* is defined by the grammar:

Syntax of Processes:

$P, Q, R ::=$	processes
$\overline{M}\langle N\rangle.P$	output
$M(x).P$	input
$P \mid Q$	composition
$(\nu n)P$	restriction
$!P$	replication
$[M \text{ is } N]\, P$	match
$\mathbf{0}$	nil
$let\ (x, y) = M\ in\ P$	pair splitting
$case\ M\ of\ 0 : P\ suc(x) : Q$	integer case

In $(\nu n)P$, the name n is bound in P. In $M(x).P$, the variable x is bound in P. In $let\ (x, y) = M\ in\ P$, the variables x and y are bound in P. In $case\ M\ of\ 0 : P\ suc(x) : Q$, the variable x is bound in the second branch, Q. We write $P\{M\}x$ for the outcome of replacing each free occurrence of x in process P with the term M, and identify processes up to renaming of bound variables and names. We adopt the abbreviation $\overline{M}\langle N\rangle$ for $\overline{M}\langle N\rangle.\mathbf{0}$.

Intuitively, the constructs of the pi calculus have the following meanings:

- The basic computation and synchronisation mechanism in the pi calculus is *interaction*, in which a term N is communicated from an output process to an input process via a named channel, m.
  - An *output process* $\overline{m}\langle N\rangle.P$ is ready to output on channel m. If an interaction occurs, term N is communicated on m and then process P runs.
  - An *input process* $m(x).P$ is ready to input from channel m. If an interaction occurs in which N is communicated on m, then process $P\{N\}x$ runs.

  (The general forms $\overline{M}\langle N\rangle.P$ and $M(x).P$ of output and input allow for the channel to be an arbitrary term M. The only useful cases are for M to be a name, or a variable that gets instantiated to a name.)
- A *composition* $P \mid Q$ behaves as processes P and Q running in parallel. Each may interact with the other on channels known to both, or with the outside world, independently of the other.
- A *restriction* $(\nu n)P$ is a process that makes a new, private name n, which may occur in P, and then behaves as P.
- A *replication* $!P$ behaves as an infinite number of copies of P running in parallel.
- A *match* $[M \text{ is } N]\, P$ behaves as P provided that terms M and N are the same; otherwise it is stuck, that is, it does nothing.

– The *nil* process **0** does nothing.

Since we added pairs and integers, we have two new process forms:

– A *pair splitting* process *let* $(x, y) = M$ *in* P behaves as $P\{N\}x\{L\}y$ if term M is the pair (N, L), and otherwise it is stuck.
– An *integer case* process *case* M *of* $0 : P$ $suc(x) : Q$ behaves as P if term M is 0, as $Q\{N\}x$ if M is $suc(N)$, and otherwise is stuck.

We write $P \simeq Q$ to mean that the behaviours of the processes P and Q are indistinguishable. In other words, a third process R cannot distinguish running in parallel with P from running in parallel with Q; as far as R can tell, P and Q have the same properties (more precisely, the same safety properties). We define the relation $\simeq$ in Part II as a form of testing equivalence. For now, it suffices to understand $\simeq$ informally.

3   Security Examples Using Restricted Channels

Next we show how to express some abstract security protocols in the pi calculus. In security protocols, it is common to find channels on which only a given set of principals is allowed to send data or listen. The set of principals may expand in the course of a protocol run, for example as the result of channel establishment. Remarkably, it is easy to model this property of channels in the pi calculus, via the restriction operation; the expansion of the set of principals that can access a channel corresponds to scope extrusion.

3.1   A First Example

Our first example is extremely basic. In this example, there are two principals A and B that share a channel, c_{AB}; only A and B can send data or listen on this channel. The protocol is simply that A uses c_{AB} for sending a single message M to B. In informal notation, we may write this protocol as follows:

$$\text{Message } 1 \ A \rightarrow B : M \text{ on } c_{AB}$$

A first pi calculus description of this protocol is:

$$A(M) \triangleq \overline{c_{AB}}\langle M \rangle$$
$$B \triangleq c_{AB}(x).\mathbf{0}$$
$$Inst(M) \triangleq (\nu c_{AB})(A(M) \mid B)$$

The processes $A(M)$ and B describe the two principals, and $Inst(M)$ describes (one instance of) the whole protocol. The channel c_{AB} is restricted; intuitively, this achieves the effect that only A and B have access to c_{AB}.

In these definitions, $A(M)$ and $Inst(M)$ are processes parameterised by M. More formally, we view A and $Inst$ as functions that map terms to processes, called abstractions, and treat the M's on the left of $\triangleq$ as bound parameters. Abstractions can of course be instantiated (applied); for example, the instantiation $A(0)$ yields $\overline{c_{AB}}\langle 0 \rangle$. The standard rules of substitution govern application, forbidding parameter captures; for example, expanding $Inst(c_{AB})$ would require a renaming of the bound occurrence of c_{AB} in the definition of $Inst$.

The first pi calculus description of the protocol may seem a little futile because, according to it, B does nothing with its input. A more useful and general description says that B runs a process F with its input. We revise our definitions as follows:

$$A(M) \triangleq \overline{c_{AB}}\langle M \rangle$$
$$B \triangleq c_{AB}(x).F(x)$$
$$Inst(M) \triangleq (\nu c_{AB})(A(M) \mid B)$$

Informally, $F(x)$ is simply the result of applying F to x. More formally, F is an abstraction, and $F(x)$ is an instantiation of the abstraction. We adopt the convention that the bound parameters of the protocol (in this case, M, c_{AB}, and x) cannot occur free in F.

This protocol has two important properties:

- Authenticity (or integrity): B always applies F to the message M that A sends; an attacker cannot cause B to apply F to some other message.
- Secrecy: The message M cannot be read in transit from A to B: if F does not reveal M, then the whole protocol does not reveal M.

The secrecy property can be stated in terms of equivalences: if $F(M) \simeq F(M')$, for any M, M', then $Inst(M) \simeq Inst(M')$. This means that if $F(M)$ is indistinguishable from $F(M')$, then the protocol with message M is indistinguishable from the protocol with message M'.

There are many sensible ways of formalising the authenticity property. In particular, it may be possible to use notions of refinement or a suitable program logic. However, we choose to write authenticity as an equivalence, for economy. This equivalence compares the protocol with another protocol. Our intent is that the latter protocol serves as a specification. In this case, the specification is:

$$A(M) \triangleq \overline{c_{AB}}\langle M \rangle$$
$$B_{spec}(M) \triangleq c_{AB}(x).F(M)$$
$$Inst_{spec}(M) \triangleq (\nu c_{AB})(A(M) \mid B_{spec}(M))$$

The principal A is as usual, but the principal B is replaced with a variant $B_{spec}(M)$; this variant receives an input from A and then acts like B when B receives M. We may say that $B_{spec}(M)$ is a "magical" version of B that knows the message M sent by A, and similarly $Inst_{spec}$ is a "magical" version of $Inst$.

Although the specification and the protocol are similar in structure, the specification is more evidently "correct" than the protocol. Therefore, we take the

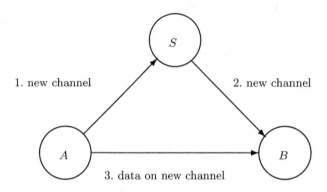

Fig. 1. Structure of the Wide Mouthed Frog protocol

following equivalence as our authenticity property: $Inst(M) \simeq Inst_{spec}(M)$, for any M.

In summary, we have:

Authenticity: $Inst(M) \simeq Inst_{spec}(M)$,
for any M.

Secrecy: $Inst(M) \simeq Inst(M')$ if $F(M) \simeq F(M')$,
for any M, M'.

Each of these equivalences means that two processes being equated are indistinguishable, even when an active attacker is their environment. Neither of these equivalences would hold without the restriction of channel c_{AB}.

3.2   An Example with Channel Establishment

A more interesting variant of our first example is obtained by adding a channel establishment phase. In this phase, before communication of data, the principals A and B obtain a new channel with the help of a server S.

There are many different ways of establishing a channel, even at the abstract level at which we work here. The one we describe is inspired by the Wide Mouthed Frog protocol [BAN89], which has the basic structure shown in Figure 1.

We consider an abstract and simplified version of the Wide Mouthed Frog protocol. Our version is abstract in that we deal with channels instead of keys; it is simplified in that channel establishment and data communication happen only once (so there is no need for timestamps). In the next section we show how to treat keys and how to allow many instances of the protocol, with an arbitrary number of messages.

Informally, our version is:

$$\text{Message 1 } A \rightarrow S : c_{AB} \text{ on } c_{AS}$$
$$\text{Message 2 } S \rightarrow B : c_{AB} \text{ on } c_{SB}$$
$$\text{Message 3 } A \rightarrow B : M \quad \text{on } c_{AB}$$

Here c_{AS} is a channel that A and S share initially, c_{SB} is a channel that S and B share initially, and c_{AB} is a channel that A creates for communication with B. After passing the channel c_{AB} to B through S, A sends a message M on c_{AB}. Note that S does not use the channel, but only transmits it.

In the pi calculus, we formulate this protocol as follows:

$$A(M) \triangleq (\nu c_{AB})\overline{c_{AS}}\langle c_{AB} \rangle . \overline{c_{AB}}\langle M \rangle$$
$$S \triangleq c_{AS}(x).\overline{c_{SB}}\langle x \rangle$$
$$B \triangleq c_{SB}(x).x(y).F(y)$$
$$Inst(M) \triangleq (\nu c_{AS})(\nu c_{SB})(A(M) \mid S \mid B)$$

Here we write $F(y)$ to represent what B does with the message y that it receives, as in the previous example. The restrictions on the channels c_{AS}, c_{SB}, and c_{AB} reflect the expected privacy guarantees for these channels. The most salient new feature of this specification is the use of scope extrusion: A generates a fresh channel c_{AB}, and then sends it out of scope to B via S. We could not have written this description in formalisms such as CCS or CSP; the use of the pi calculus is important.

For discussing authenticity, we introduce the following specification:

$$A(M) \triangleq (\nu c_{AB})\overline{c_{AS}}\langle c_{AB} \rangle . \overline{c_{AB}}\langle M \rangle$$
$$S \triangleq c_{AS}(x).\overline{c_{SB}}\langle x \rangle$$
$$B_{spec}(M) \triangleq c_{SB}(x).x(y).F(M)$$
$$Inst_{spec}(M) \triangleq (\nu c_{AS})(\nu c_{SB})(A(M) \mid S \mid B_{spec}(M))$$

According to this specification, the message M is communicated "magically": the process F is applied to the message M that A sends independently of whatever happens during the rest of the protocol run.

We obtain the following authenticity and secrecy properties:

Authenticity: $Inst(M) \simeq Inst_{spec}(M)$,
                   for any M.

Secrecy: $Inst(M) \simeq Inst(M')$ if $F(M) \simeq F(M')$,
                   for any M, M'.

Again, these properties hold because of the scoping rules of the pi calculus.

4   Discussion: The Pi Calculus

In this part, we have briefly and informally introduced the pi calculus as a notation for describing and specifying security protocols. In the next part, we extend these ideas to apply to cryptographic protocols.

Starting with the original presentation [MPW92] there is by now an extensive literature on the pi calculus, covered, for instance, by introductory [Mil99] and advanced [SW01] textbooks. A good deal of the theory of the pi calculus concerns equational reasoning; two important works are on testing equivalence [BN95] and barbed bisimulation [MS92]. There are several works on logic [MPW93] and model checking [Dam96] for the pi calculus.

The study of type systems for the pi calculus is a booming research area. We cite just three out of many papers. The simplest type system for the pi calculus is a system of channel sorts proposed by Milner [Mil99]. Pierce and Sangiorgi [PS96] develop a more advanced system supporting subtyping. Igarashi and Kobayashi [IK01] propose a generic framework in which to understand a variety of previous systems.

Most versions of the pi calculus allow only passive data such as names to be transmitted on channels. Sangiorgi's higher-order pi calculus [SW01] is a variant in which processes may be transmitted on channels. Dam [Dam98] uses a second-order pi calculus to study security protocols.

Part II: The Spi Calculus

The spi calculus is an extension of the pi calculus with cryptographic primitives. It is designed for the description and analysis of security protocols, such as those for authentication and for electronic commerce. These protocols rely on cryptography and on communication channels with properties like authenticity and privacy. Accordingly, cryptographic operations and communication through channels are the main ingredients of the spi calculus.

In Part I of these notes, we used the pi calculus (without extension) for describing protocols at an abstract level. The pi calculus primitives for channels are simple but powerful. Channels can be created and passed, for example from authentication servers to clients. The scoping rules of the pi calculus guarantee that the environment of a protocol (the attacker) cannot access a channel that it is not explicitly given; scoping is thus the basis of security. In sum, the pi calculus appears as a fairly convenient calculus of protocols for secure communication.

However, the pi calculus does not express the cryptographic operations that are commonly used for implementing channels in distributed systems: it does not include any constructs for encryption and decryption, and these do not seem easy to represent. Since the use of cryptography is notoriously error-prone, we prefer not to abstract it away. We define the spi calculus in order to permit an explicit representation of the use of cryptography in protocols.

There are many other notations for describing security protocols. Some, which have long been used in the authentication literature, have a fairly clear connection to the intended implementations of those protocols (e.g., [NS78, Lie93]). Their main shortcoming is that they do not provide a precise and solid basis for reasoning about protocols. Other notations (e.g., [BAN89]) are more formal, but their relation to implementations may be more tenuous or subtle. The spi calculus is a middle ground: it is directly executable and it has a precise semantics.

Because the semantics of the spi calculus is not only precise but intelligible, the spi calculus provides a setting for analysing protocols. Specifically, we can express security guarantees as equivalences between spi calculus processes. For example, we can say that a protocol keeps secret a piece of data X by stating that the protocol with X is equivalent to the protocol with X', for any X'. Here, equivalence means equivalence in the eyes of an arbitrary environment. The environment can interact with the protocol, perhaps attempting to create confusion between different messages or sessions. This definition of equivalence yields the desired properties for our security applications. Moreover, in our experience, equivalence is not too hard to prove.

Although the definition of equivalence makes reference to the environment, we do not need to give a model of the environment explicitly. This is one of the main advantages of our approach. Writing such a model can be tedious and can lead to new arbitrariness and error. In particular, it is always difficult to express that the environment can invent random numbers but is not lucky enough to guess the random secrets on which a protocol depends. We resolve this conflict by letting the environment be an arbitrary spi calculus process.

Our approach has some similarities with other recent approaches for reasoning about protocols. Like work based on temporal logics or process algebras (e.g., [FG94, GM95, Low96, Sch96a]), our method builds on a standard concurrency formalism; this has obvious advantages but it also implies that our method is less intuitive than some based on ad hoc formalisms (e.g., [BAN89]). As in some modal logics (e.g., [ABLP93, LABW92]), we emphasise reasoning about channels. As in state-transition models (e.g., [DY83, MCF87, Kem89, Mea92]), we are interested in characterising the knowledge of an environment. The unique features of our approach are its reliance on the powerful scoping constructs of the pi calculus; the radical definition of the environment as an arbitrary spi calculus process; and the representation of security properties, both integrity and secrecy, as equivalences.

Our model of protocols is simpler, but poorer, than some models developed for informal mathematical arguments because the spi calculus does not include any notion of probability or complexity (cf. [BR95]). It would be interesting to bridge the gap between the spi calculus and those models, perhaps by giving a probabilistic interpretation for our results. Recent work [LMMS98, AR00] makes progress in this direction.

Remainder of Part II

The remainder of this part is organised as follows. Section 5 extends the pi calculus with primitives for shared-key cryptography. Section 6 describes a series of protocol examples in the spi calculus. Sections 7 defines the formal semantics of the spi calculus. Section 8 discusses how to add primitives for hashing and public-key cryptography to the pi calculus. Finally, Section 9 offers some conclusions and discusses related work.

5   The Spi Calculus with Shared-Key Cryptography

Just as there are several versions of the pi calculus, there are several versions of the spi calculus. These differ in particular in what cryptographic constructs they include. In this section we introduce a relatively simple spi calculus, namely the pi calculus extended with primitives for shared-key cryptography. We then write several protocols that use shared-key cryptography in this calculus.

Throughout these notes, we often refer to the calculus presented in this section as "the" spi calculus; but we define other versions of the spi calculus in Section 8.

The syntax of the spi calculus is an extension of that of the pi calculus. In order to represent encrypted messages, we add a clause to the syntax of terms:

Syntax of Terms:

$L, M, N ::=$	terms
$\ldots$	as in Section 2
$\{M\}_N$	shared-key encryption

In order to represent decryption, we add a clause to the syntax of processes:

Syntax of Processes:

$P, Q ::=$	processes
$\ldots$	as in Section 2
case L *of* $\{x\}_N$ *in* P	shared-key decryption

The variable x is bound in P.

Intuitively, the meaning of the new constructs is as follows:

- The term $\{M\}_N$ represents the ciphertext obtained by encrypting the term M under the key N using a shared-key cryptosystem such as DES [DES77].
- The process *case* L *of* $\{x\}_N$ *in* P attempts to decrypt the term L with the key N. If L is a ciphertext of the form $\{M\}_N$, then the process behaves as $P\{M\}x$. Otherwise the process is stuck.

Implicit in this definition are some standard but significant assumptions about cryptography:

- The only way to decrypt an encrypted packet is to know the corresponding key.
- An encrypted packet does not reveal the key that was used to encrypt it.
- There is sufficient redundancy in messages so that the decryption algorithm can detect whether a ciphertext was encrypted with the expected key.

It is not assumed that all messages contain information that allows each principal to recognise its own messages (cf. [BAN89]).

The semantics of the spi calculus can be formalised in much the same way as the semantics of the pi calculus. We carry out this formalisation in Section 7.

Again, we write $P \simeq Q$ to mean that the behaviours of the processes P and Q are indistinguishable. The notion of indistinguishability is complicated by the presence of cryptography. As an example of these complications, consider the following process:

$$P(M) \triangleq (\nu K)\bar{c}\langle \{M\}_K \rangle$$

This process simply sends M under a new key K on a public channel c; the key K is not transmitted. Intuitively, we would like to equate $P(M)$ and $P(M')$, for any M and M', because an observer cannot discover K and hence cannot tell whether M or M' is sent under K. On the other hand, $P(M)$ and $P(M')$ are clearly different, since they transmit different messages on c. Our equivalence $\simeq$ is coarse-grained enough to equate $P(M)$ and $P(M')$.

6   Security Examples Using Shared-Key Cryptography

The spi calculus enables more detailed descriptions of security protocols than the pi calculus. While the pi calculus enables the representation of channels, the spi calculus also enables the representation of the channel implementations in terms of cryptography. In this section we show a few example cryptographic protocols.

As in the pi calculus, scoping is the basis of security in the spi calculus. In particular, restriction can be used to model the creation of fresh, unguessable cryptographic keys. Restriction can also be used to model the creation of fresh nonces of the sort used in challenge-response exchanges.

Security properties can still be expressed as equivalences, although the notion of equivalence is more delicate, as we have discussed.

6.1   A First Cryptographic Example

Our first example is a cryptographic version of the example of Section 3.1. We consider two principals A and B that share a key K_{AB}; in addition, we assume there is a public channel c_{AB} that A and B can use for communication, but which is in no way secure. The protocol is simply that A sends a message M under K_{AB} to B, on c_{AB}.

Informally, we write this protocol as follows:

$$\text{Message 1 } A \rightarrow B : \{M\}_{K_{AB}} \text{ on } c_{AB}$$

In the spi calculus, we write:

$$A(M) \triangleq \overline{c_{AB}}\langle \{M\}_{K_{AB}} \rangle$$
$$B \triangleq c_{AB}(x).\text{case } x \text{ of } \{y\}_{K_{AB}} \text{ in } F(y)$$
$$Inst(M) \triangleq (\nu K_{AB})(A(M) \mid B)$$

According to this definition, A sends $\{M\}_{K_{AB}}$ on c_{AB} while B listens for a message on c_{AB}. Given such a message, B attempts to decrypt it using K_{AB}; if this decryption succeeds, B applies F to the result. The assumption that A and B share K_{AB} gives rise to the restriction on K_{AB}, which is syntactically legal and meaningful although K_{AB} is not used as a channel. On the other hand, c_{AB} is not restricted, since it is a public channel. Other principals may send messages on c_{AB}, so B may attempt to decrypt a message not encrypted under K_{AB}; in that case, the protocol will get stuck. We are not concerned about this possibility, but it would be easy enough to avoid it by writing a slightly more elaborate program for B.

We use the following specification:

$$A(M) \triangleq \overline{c_{AB}}\langle\{M\}_{K_{AB}}\rangle$$
$$B_{spec}(M) \triangleq c_{AB}(x).case\ x\ of\ \{y\}_{K_{AB}}\ in\ F(M)$$
$$Inst_{spec}(M) \triangleq (\nu K_{AB})(A(M) \mid B_{spec}(M))$$

and we obtain the properties:

Authenticity: $Inst(M) \simeq Inst_{spec}(M)$,
     for any M.

Secrecy: $Inst(M) \simeq Inst(M')$ if $F(M) \simeq F(M')$,
     for any M, M'.

Intuitively, authenticity holds even if the key K_{AB} is somehow compromised after its use. Many factors can contribute to key compromise, for example incompetence on the part of protocol participants, and malice and brute force on the part of attackers. We cannot model all these factors, but we can model deliberate key publication, which is in a sense the most extreme of them. It suffices to make a small change in the definitions of B and B_{spec}, so that they send K_{AB} on a public channel after receiving $\{M\}_{K_{AB}}$. This change preserves the authenticity equation, but clearly not the secrecy equation.

6.2   An Example with Key Establishment

In cryptographic protocols, the establishment of new channels often means the exchange of new keys. There are many methods (most of them flawed) for key exchange. The following example is the cryptographic version of that of Section 3.2; it uses a simplified (one-shot) form of the Wide Mouthed Frog key exchange.

In the Wide Mouthed Frog protocol, the principals A and B share keys K_{AS} and K_{SB} respectively with a server S. When A and B want to communicate securely, A creates a new key K_{AB}, sends it to the server under K_{AS}, and the server forwards it to B under K_{SB}. All communication being protected by encryption, it can happen through public channels, which we write c_{AS}, c_{SB}, and c_{AB}. Informally, a simplified version of this protocol is:

$$\text{Message } 1 \ A \rightarrow S : \{K_{AB}\}_{K_{AS}} \text{ on } c_{AS}$$
$$\text{Message } 2 \ S \rightarrow B : \{K_{AB}\}_{K_{SB}} \text{ on } c_{SB}$$
$$\text{Message } 3 \ A \rightarrow B : \{M\}_{K_{AB}} \quad \text{on } c_{AB}$$

In the spi calculus, we can express this message sequence as follows:

$$A(M) \triangleq (\nu K_{AB})(\overline{c_{AS}}\langle \{K_{AB}\}_{K_{AS}}\rangle.\overline{c_{AB}}\langle \{M\}_{K_{AB}}\rangle)$$
$$S \triangleq c_{AS}(x).case\ x\ of\ \{y\}_{K_{AS}}\ in\ \overline{c_{SB}}\langle \{y\}_{K_{SB}}\rangle$$
$$B \triangleq c_{SB}(x).case\ x\ of\ \{y\}_{K_{SB}}\ in$$
$$c_{AB}(z).case\ z\ of\ \{w\}_y\ in\ F(w)$$
$$Inst(M) \triangleq (\nu K_{AS})(\nu K_{SB})(A(M) \mid S \mid B)$$

where $F(w)$ is a process representing the rest of the behaviour of B upon receiving a message w. Notice the essential use of scope extrusion: A generates the key K_{AB} and sends it out of scope to B via S.

In the usual pattern, we introduce a specification for discussing authenticity:

$$A(M) \triangleq (\nu K_{AB})(\overline{c_{AS}}\langle \{K_{AB}\}_{K_{AS}}\rangle.\overline{c_{AB}}\langle \{M\}_{K_{AB}}\rangle)$$
$$S \triangleq c_{AS}(x).case\ x\ of\ \{y\}_{K_{AS}}\ in\ \overline{c_{SB}}\langle \{y\}_{K_{SB}}\rangle$$
$$B_{spec}(M) \triangleq c_{SB}(x).case\ x\ of\ \{y\}_{K_{SB}}\ in$$
$$c_{AB}(z).case\ z\ of\ \{w\}_y\ in\ F(M)$$
$$Inst_{spec}(M) \triangleq (\nu K_{AS})(\nu K_{SB})(A(M) \mid S \mid B_{spec}(M))$$

One may be concerned about the apparent complexity of this specification. On the other hand, despite its complexity, the specification is still more evidently "correct" than the protocol. In particular, it is still evident that $B_{spec}(M)$ applies F to the data M from A, rather than to some other message chosen as the result of error or attack.

We obtain the usual properties of authenticity and secrecy:

Authenticity: $Inst(M) \simeq Inst_{spec}(M)$,
            for any M.

Secrecy: $Inst(M) \simeq Inst(M')$ if $F(M) \simeq F(M')$,
            for any M, M'.

6.3   A Complete Authentication Example (with a Flaw)

In the examples discussed so far, channel establishment and data communication happen only once. As we demonstrate now, it is a simple matter of programming to remove this restriction and to represent more sophisticated examples with many sessions between many principals. However, as the intricacy of our examples increases, so does the opportunity for error. This should not be construed as a limitation of our approach, but rather as the sign of an intrinsic

278 Andrew D. Gordon

difficulty: many of the mistakes in authentication protocols arise from confusion between sessions.

We consider a system with a server S and n other principals. We use the terms $suc(0)$, $suc(suc(0))$, ..., which we abbreviate to $\underline{1}$, $\underline{2}$, ..., as the names of these other principals. We assume that each principal has an input channel; these input channels are public and have the names c_1, c_2, ..., c_n and c_S. We also assume that the server shares a pair of keys with each other principal, one key for each direction: principal i uses key K_{iS} to send to S and key K_{Si} to receive from S, for $1 \leq i \leq n$.

We extend our standard example to this system of $n+1$ principals, with the following message sequence:

$$\begin{array}{llll} \text{Message 1} & A \rightarrow S : & A, \{B, K_{AB}\}_{K_{AS}} & \text{on } c_S \\ \text{Message 2} & S \rightarrow B : & \{A, K_{AB}\}_{K_{SB}} & \text{on } c_B \\ \text{Message 3} & A \rightarrow B : & A, \{M\}_{K_{AB}} & \text{on } c_B \end{array}$$

Here A and B range over the n principals. The names A and B appear in messages in order to avoid ambiguity; when these names appear in clear, they function as hints that help the recipient choose the appropriate key for decryption of the rest of the message. The intent is that the protocol can be used by any pair of principals, arbitrarily often; concurrent runs are allowed. As it stands, the protocol has obvious flaws; we discuss it in order to explain our method for representing it in the spi calculus.

In our spi calculus representation, we use several convenient abbreviations. Firstly, we rely on pair splitting on input and on decryption:

$$c(x_1, x_2).P \triangleq c(y).let\ (x_1, x_2) = y\ in\ P$$

$$case\ L\ of\ \{x_1, x_2\}_N\ in\ P \triangleq case\ L\ of\ \{y\}_N\ in$$
$$let\ (x_1, x_2) = y\ in\ P$$

where variable y is fresh. Secondly, we need the standard notation for the composition of a finite set of processes. Given a finite family of processes $P_1, \ldots, P_k$, we let $\prod_{i \in 1..k} P_i$ be their k-way composition $P_1 \mid \cdots \mid P_k$. Finally, we omit the inner parentheses from an encrypted pair of the form $\{(N, N')\}_{N''}$, and simply write $\{N, N'\}_{N''}$, as is common in informal descriptions.

Informally, an instance of the protocol is determined by a choice of parties (who is A and who is B) and by the message sent after key establishment. More formally, an instance I is a triple (i, j, M) such that i and j are principals and M is a message. We say that i is the source address and j the destination address of the instance. Moreover, we assume that there is an abstraction F representing the behaviour of any principal after receipt of Message 3 of the protocol. For an instance (i, j, M) that runs as intended, the argument to F is the triple $(\underline{i}, \underline{j}, M)$.

Given an instance (i, j, M), the following process corresponds to the role of A:

$$Send(i, j, M) \triangleq (\nu K)(\overline{c_S}\langle(\underline{i}, \{\underline{j}, K\}_{K_{iS}})\rangle \mid \overline{c_j}\langle(\underline{i}, \{M\}_K)\rangle)$$

The sending process creates a key K and sends it to the server, along with the names $\underline{i}$ and $\underline{j}$ of the principals of the instance. The sending process also sends M under K, along with its name i. We have put the two messages in parallel, somewhat arbitrarily; putting them in sequence would have much the same effect.

The following process corresponds to the role of B for principal j:

$$Recv(j) \triangleq c_j(y_{cipher}).case\ y_{cipher}\ of\ \{x_A, x_{key}\}_{K_{Sj}}\ in$$
$$c_j(z_A, z_{cipher}).[x_A\ is\ z_A]$$
$$case\ z_{cipher}\ of\ \{z_{plain}\}_{x_{key}}\ in\ F(x_A, j, z_{plain})$$

The receiving process waits for a message y_{cipher} from the server, extracts a key x_{key} from this message, then waits for a message z_{cipher} under this key, and finally applies F to the name x_A of the presumed sender, to its own name j, and to the contents z_{plain} of the message. The variables x_A and z_A are both intended as the name of the sending process, so they are expected to match.

The server S is the same for all instances:

$$S \triangleq c_S(x_A, x_{cipher}).$$
$$\textstyle\prod_{i \in 1..n}[x_A\ is\ i]\ case\ x_{cipher}\ of\ \{x_B, x_{key}\}_{K_{iS}}\ in$$
$$\textstyle\prod_{j \in 1..n}[x_B\ is\ j]\ \overline{c_j}\langle\{x_A, x_{key}\}_{K_{Sj}}\rangle$$

The variable x_A is intended as the name of the sending process, x_B as the name of the receiving process, x_{key} as the new key, and x_{cipher} as the encrypted part of the first message of the protocol. In the code for the server, we program an n-way branch on the name x_A by using a parallel composition of processes indexed by $i \in 1..n$. We also program an n-way branch on the name x_B, similarly. (This casual use of multiple threads is characteristic of the pi calculus; in practice the branch could be implemented more efficiently, but here we are interested only in the behaviour of the server, not in its efficient implementation.)

Finally we define a whole system, parameterised on a list of instances:

$$Sys(I_1, \ldots, I_m) \triangleq (\nu \boldsymbol{K_{iS}})(\nu \boldsymbol{K_{Sj}})$$
$$(Send(I_1) \mid \cdots \mid Send(I_m) \mid$$
$$!S \mid$$
$$!Recv(1) \mid \cdots \mid !Recv(n))$$

where $(\nu \boldsymbol{K_{iS}})(\nu \boldsymbol{K_{Sj}})$ stands for:

$$(\nu K_{1S}) \ldots (\nu K_{nS})(\nu K_{S1}) \ldots (\nu K_{Sn})$$

The expression $Sys(I_1, \ldots, I_m)$ represents a system with m instances of the protocol. The server is replicated; in addition, the replication of the receiving processes means that each principal is willing to play the role of receiver in any number of runs of the protocol in parallel. Thus, any two runs of the protocol can be simultaneous, even if they involve the same principals.

As before, we write a specification by modifying the protocol. For this specification, we revise the sending and the receiving processes, but not the server:

$$Send_{spec}(i, j, M) \triangleq (\nu p)(Send(i, j, p) \mid p(x).F(\underline{i}, \underline{j}, M))$$

$$Recv_{spec}(j) \triangleq c_j(y_{cipher}).$$
$$\quad case \ y_{cipher} \ of \ \{x_A, x_{key}\}_{K_{Sj}} \ in$$
$$\quad c_j(z_A, z_{cipher}).[x_A \ is \ z_A]$$
$$\quad case \ z_{cipher} \ of \ \{z_{plain}\}_{x_{key}} \ in$$
$$\quad \overline{z_{plain}}\langle * \rangle$$

$$Sys_{spec}(I_1, \ldots, I_m) \triangleq (\nu \boldsymbol{K_{iS}})(\nu \boldsymbol{K_{Sj}})$$
$$\quad (Send_{spec}(I_1) \mid \cdots \mid Send_{spec}(I_m) \mid$$
$$\quad !S \mid$$
$$\quad !Recv_{spec}(1) \mid \cdots \mid !Recv_{spec}(n))$$

In this specification, the sending process for instance (i, j, M) is as in the implementation, except that it sends a fresh channel name p instead of M, and runs $F(\underline{i}, \underline{j}, M)$ when it receives any message on p. The receiving process in the specification is identical to that in the implementation, except that $F(y_A, \underline{j}, z_{plain})$ is replaced with $\overline{z_{plain}}\langle * \rangle$, where the symbol $*$ represents a fixed but arbitrary message. The variable z_{plain} will be bound to the fresh name p for the corresponding instance of the protocol. Thus, the receiving process will signal on p, triggering the execution of the appropriate process $F(\underline{i}, \underline{j}, M)$.

A crucial property of this specification is that the only occurrences of F are bundled into the description of the sending process. There, F is applied to the desired parameters, $(\underline{i}, \underline{j}, M)$. Hence it is obvious that an instance (i, j, M) will cause the execution of $\overline{F}(\underline{i}', \underline{j}', M')$ only if i' is i, j' is j, and M' is M. Therefore, despite its complexity, the specification is more obviously "correct" than the implementation.

Much as in previous examples, we would like the protocol to have the following authenticity property:

$$Sys(I_1, \ldots, I_m) \simeq Sys_{spec}(I_1, \ldots, I_m),$$
$$\text{for any instances } I_1, \ldots, I_m.$$

Unfortunately, the protocol is vulnerable to a replay attack that invalidates the authenticity equation. Consider the system $Sys(I, I')$ where $I = (i, j, M)$ and $I' = (i, j, M')$. An attacker can replay messages of one instance and get them mistaken for messages of the other instance, causing M to be passed twice to F. Thus, $Sys(I, I')$ can be made to execute two copies of $F(\underline{i}, \underline{j}, M)$. In contrast, no matter what an attacker does, $Sys_{spec}(I, I')$ will run each of $F(\underline{i}, \underline{j}, M)$ and $F(\underline{i}, \underline{j}, M')$ at most once. The authenticity equation therefore does not hold. (We can disprove it formally by defining an attacker that distinguishes $Sys(I, I')$ and $Sys_{spec}(I, I')$, within the spi calculus.)

6.4   A Complete Authentication Example (Repaired)

Now we improve the protocol of the previous section by adding nonce handshakes as protection against replay attacks. The Wide Mouthed Frog protocol

$$Send(i, j, M) \triangleq \overline{c_S}\langle \underline{i} \rangle \mid$$
$$c_i(x_{nonce}).(\nu K)(\overline{c_S}\langle (\underline{i}, \{\underline{i}, \underline{i}, \underline{j}, K, x_{nonce}\}_{K_{iS}}) \rangle \mid \overline{c_j}\langle (\underline{i}, \{M\}_K) \rangle)$$

$$S \triangleq c_S(x_A). \prod_{i \in 1..n}[x_A \ is \ \underline{i}] \ (\nu N_S)(\overline{c_i}\langle N_S \rangle \mid$$
$$c_S(x'_A, x_{cipher}).[x'_A \ is \ \underline{i}]$$
$$case \ x_{cipher} \ of \ \{y_A, z_A, x_B, x_{key}, x_{nonce}\}_{K_{iS}} \ in$$
$$\prod_{j \in 1..n}[y_A \ is \ \underline{i}] \ [z_A \ is \ \underline{i}] \ [x_B \ is \ \underline{j}] \ [x_{nonce} \ is \ N_S]$$
$$(\overline{c_j}\langle * \rangle \mid c_S(y_{nonce}).\overline{c_j}\langle \{S, \underline{i}, \underline{j}, x_{key}, y_{nonce}\}_{K_{Sj}} \rangle)))$$

$$Recv(j) \triangleq c_j(w).(\nu N_B)(\overline{c_S}\langle N_B \rangle \mid$$
$$c_j(y_{cipher}).$$
$$case \ y_{cipher} \ of \ \{x_S, x_A, x_B, x_{key}, y_{nonce}\}_{K_{Sj}} \ in$$
$$\prod_{i \in 1..n}[x_S \ is \ S] \ [x_A \ is \ \underline{i}] \ [x_B \ is \ \underline{j}] \ [y_{nonce} \ is \ N_B]$$
$$c_j(z_A, z_{cipher}).[z_A \ is \ x_A]$$
$$case \ z_{cipher} \ of \ \{z_{plain}\}_{x_{key}} \ in \ F(\underline{i}, \underline{j}, z_{plain}))$$

$$Sys(I_1, \ldots, I_m) \triangleq (\nu \mathbf{K_{iS}})(\nu \mathbf{K_{Sj}})$$
$$(Send(I_1) \mid \cdots \mid Send(I_m) \mid$$
$$!S \mid$$
$$!Recv(1) \mid \cdots \mid !Recv(n))$$

Fig. 2. Formalisation of the Seven-Message protocol

uses timestamps instead of handshakes. The treatment of timestamps in the spi calculus is possible, but it requires additional elements, including at least a rudimentary account of clock synchronisation. Protocols that use handshakes are fundamentally more self-contained than protocols that use timestamps; therefore, handshakes make for clearer examples.

Informally, our new protocol is:

Message 1 $A \to S$: A		on c_S
Message 2 $S \to A$: N_S		on c_A
Message 3 $A \to S$: $A, \{A, A, B, K_{AB}, N_S\}_{K_{As}}$		on c_S
Message 4 $S \to B$: $*$		on c_B
Message 5 $B \to S$: N_B		on c_S
Message 6 $S \to B$: $\{S, A, B, K_{AB}, N_B\}_{K_{SB}}$		on c_B
Message 7 $A \to B$: $A, \{M\}_{K_{AB}}$		on c_B

Messages 1 and 2 are the request for a challenge and the challenge, respectively. The challenge is N_S, a nonce created by S; the nonce must not have been used before for this purpose. Obviously the nonce is not secret, but it must be unpredictable (for otherwise an attacker could simulate a challenge and later replay the response [AN96]). In Message 3, A says that A and B can communicate under K_{AB}, sometime after receipt of N_S. All the components A, B, K_{AB}, N_S appear explicitly in the message, for safety [AN96], but A could perhaps be elided. The presence of N_S in Message 3 proves the freshness of the message. In Message 4,

* represents a fixed but arbitrary message; S uses * to signal that it is ready for a nonce challenge N_B from B. In Message 6, S says that A says that A and B can communicate under K_{AB}, sometime after receipt of N_B. The first field of the encrypted portions of Messages 3 and 6 (A or S) is included in order to distinguish these messages; it serves as a "direction bit". Finally, Message 7 is the transmission of data under K_{AB}.

The messages of this protocol have many components. For the spi calculus representation it is therefore convenient to generalise our syntax of pairs and pair splitting to arbitrary tuples. We use the following standard abbreviations:

$$(N_1, \ldots, N_{k+1}) \triangleq ((N_1, \ldots, N_k), N_{k+1})$$
$$let\ (x_1, \ldots, x_{k+1}) = N\ in\ P \triangleq let\ (y, x_{k+1}) = N\ in$$
$$let\ (x_1, \ldots, x_k) = y\ in\ P$$

where variable y is fresh.

In the spi calculus, we represent the nonces of this protocol as newly created names. We obtain the spi calculus expressions given in Figure 2. In those expressions, the names N_S and N_B represent the nonces. The variable subscripts are hints that indicate what the corresponding variables should represent; for example, x_A, x'_A, y_A, and z_A are all expected to be the name of the sending process, and x_{nonce} and y_{nonce} are expected to be the nonces generated by S and B, respectively.

The definition of Sys_{spec} is exactly analogous to that of the previous section, so we omit it. We obtain the authenticity property:

$$Sys(I_1, \ldots, I_m) \simeq Sys_{spec}(I_1, \ldots, I_m),$$
$$\text{for any instances } I_1, \ldots, I_m.$$

This property holds because of the use of nonces. In particular, the replay attack of Section 6.3 can no longer distinguish $Sys(I_1, \ldots, I_m)$ and $Sys_{spec}(I_1, \ldots, I_m)$.

As a secrecy property, we would like to express that there is no way for an external observer to tell apart two executions of the system with identical participants but different messages. The secrecy property should therefore assert that the protocol does not reveal any information about the contents of exchanged messages if none is revealed after the key exchange.

In order to express that no information is revealed after the key exchange, we introduce the following definition. We say that a pair of instances (i, j, M) and (i', j', M') is *indistinguishable* if the two instances have the same source and destination addresses ($i = i'$ and $j = j'$) and if $F(\underline{i, j}, M) \simeq F(i, j, M')$.

Our definition of secrecy is that, if each pair $(I_1, \bar{J}_1), \ldots, (I_m, \bar{J}_m)$ is indistinguishable, then $Sys(I_1, \ldots, I_m) \simeq Sys(J_1, \ldots, J_m)$. This means that an observer cannot distinguish two systems parameterised by two sets of indistinguishable instances. This property holds for our protocol.

In summary, we have:

Authenticity: $Sys(I_1, \ldots, I_m) \simeq Sys_{spec}(I_1, \ldots, I_m)$,
    for any instances $I_1, \ldots, I_m$.

Secrecy: $Sys(I_1, \ldots, I_m) \simeq Sys(J_1, \ldots, J_m)$,
    if each pair $(I_1, J_1), \ldots, (I_m, J_m)$
    is indistinguishable.

We could ask for a further property of anonymity, namely that the source and the destination addresses of instances be protected from eavesdroppers. However, anonymity holds neither for our protocol nor for most current, practical protocols. It would be easy enough to specify anonymity, should it be relevant.

6.5   Discussion of the Examples

As these examples show, writing a protocol in the spi calculus is essentially analogous to writing it in any programming language with suitable communication and encryption libraries. The main advantage of the spi calculus is its formal precision.

Writing a protocol in the spi calculus may be a little harder than writing it in some of the notations common in the literature. On the other hand, the spi calculus versions are more detailed. They make clear not only what messages are sent but how the messages are generated and how they are checked. These aspects of the spi calculus descriptions add complexity, but they enable finer analysis.

7   Formal Semantics of the Spi Calculus

In this section we give a brief formal treatment of the spi calculus. In Section 7.1 we introduce the reaction relation; $P \rightarrow Q$ means there is a reaction amongst the subprocesses of P such that the whole can take a step to process Q. Reaction is the basic notion of computation in both the pi calculus and the spi calculus. In Section 7.2 we give a precise definition of the equivalence relation $\simeq$, which we have used for expressing security properties.

Syntactic Conventions

We write $fn(M)$ and $fn(P)$ for the sets of names free in term M and process P respectively. Similarly, we write $fv(M)$ and $fv(P)$ for the sets of variables free in M and P respectively. We say that a term or process is *closed* to mean that it has no free variables. (To be able to communicate externally, a process must have free names.) The set $Proc = \{P \mid fv(P) = \varnothing\}$ is the set of closed processes.

7.1   The Reaction Relation

The reaction relation is a concise account of computation in the pi calculus introduced by Milner [Mil92], inspired by the Chemical Abstract Machine of

Berry and Boudol [BB90]. One thinks of a process as consisting of a chemical solution of molecules waiting to react. A reaction step arises from the interaction of the adjacent molecules $\overline{m}\langle N\rangle.P$ and $m(x).Q$, as follows:

$$\text{(React Inter)}\quad \overline{m}\langle N\rangle.P \mid m(x).Q \;\rightarrow\; P \mid Q\{N\}x$$

Just as one might stir a chemical solution to allow non-adjacent molecules to react, we define a relation, *structural equivalence*, that allows processes to be rearranged so that the rule above is applicable. We first define the *reduction relation* $>$ on closed processes:

Reduction:

(Red Repl)	$!P > P \mid !P$
(Red Match)	$[M \text{ is } M]\,P > P$
(Red Let)	$\text{let } (x,y) = (M,N) \text{ in } P > P\{M\}x\{N\}y$
(Red Zero)	$\text{case } 0 \text{ of } 0 : P \; suc(x) : Q > P$
(Red Suc)	$\text{case } suc(M) \text{ of } 0 : P \; suc(x) : Q > Q\{M\}x$
(Red Decrypt)	$\text{case } \{M\}_N \text{ of } \{x\}_N \text{ in } P > P\{M\}x$

We let structural equivalence, $\equiv$, be the least relation on closed processes that satisfies the following equations and rules:

Structural Congruence:

(Struct Nil)	$P \mid \mathbf{0} \equiv P$
(Struct Comm)	$P \mid Q \equiv Q \mid P$
(Struct Assoc)	$P \mid (Q \mid R) \equiv (P \mid Q) \mid R$
(Struct Switch)	$(\nu m)(\nu n)P \equiv (\nu n)(\nu m)P$
(Struct Drop)	$(\nu n)\mathbf{0} \equiv \mathbf{0}$
(Struct Extrusion)	$(\nu n)(P \mid Q) \equiv P \mid (\nu n)Q \quad \text{if } n \notin fn(P)$

(Struct Red)   (Struct Refl)   (Struct Symm)

$$\frac{P > Q}{P \equiv Q} \qquad \frac{}{P \equiv P} \qquad \frac{P \equiv Q}{Q \equiv P}$$

(Struct Trans)   (Struct Par)   (Struct Res)

$$\frac{P \equiv Q \quad Q \equiv R}{P \equiv R} \qquad \frac{P \equiv P'}{P \mid Q \equiv P' \mid Q} \qquad \frac{P \equiv P'}{(\nu m)P \equiv (\nu m)P'}$$

Now we can complete the formal description of the reaction relation. We let the *reaction relation*, $\rightarrow$, be the least relation on closed processes that satisfies the rule (React Inter) displayed above and the following rules:

Reaction:

(React Struct)   (React Par)   (React Res)

$$\frac{P \equiv P' \quad P' \rightarrow Q' \quad Q' \equiv Q}{P \rightarrow Q} \qquad \frac{P \rightarrow P'}{P \mid Q \rightarrow P' \mid Q} \qquad \frac{P \rightarrow P'}{(\nu n)P \rightarrow (\nu n)P'}$$

This definition of the reaction relation corresponds to the informal description of process behaviour given in Sections 2 and 5.

As an example, we can use the definition of the reaction relation to show the behaviour of the protocol of Section 6.2:

$$
\begin{aligned}
Inst(M) &\equiv (\nu K_{AS})(\nu K_{SB})(A(M) \mid S \mid B) \\
&\to (\nu K_{AS})(\nu K_{SB})(\nu K_{AB}) \\
&\quad (\overline{c_{AB}}\langle\{M\}_{K_{AB}}\rangle \mid \overline{c_{SB}}\langle\{K_{AB}\}_{K_{SB}}\rangle \mid B) \\
&\to (\nu K_{AS})(\nu K_{SB})(\nu K_{AB}) \\
&\quad (\overline{c_{AB}}\langle\{M\}_{K_{AB}}\rangle \mid \\
&\quad c_{AB}(z).case\ z\ of\ \{w\}_{K_{AB}}\ in\ F(w)) \\
&\to (\nu K_{AS})(\nu K_{SB})(\nu K_{AB})F(M) \\
&\equiv F(M)
\end{aligned}
$$

The last step in this calculation is justified by our general convention that none of the bound parameters of the protocol (including, in this case, K_{AS}, K_{SB}, and K_{AB}) occurs free in F.

7.2   Testing Equivalence

In order to define equivalence, we first define a predicate that describes the channels on which a process can communicate. We let a *barb*, β, be an input or output channel, that is, either a name m (representing input) or a *co-name* $\overline{m}$ (representing output). For a closed process P, we define the predicate P *exhibits barb* β, written $P \downarrow \beta$, by the following rules:

Exhibition of a Barb:

(Barb In)	(Barb Out)	(Barb Par)
		$P \downarrow \beta$
$m(x).P \downarrow m$	$\overline{m}\langle M\rangle.P \downarrow \overline{m}$	$P \mid Q \downarrow \beta$

(Barb Res)	(Barb Struct)
$P \downarrow \beta \quad \beta \notin \{m, \overline{m}\}$	$P \equiv Q \quad Q \downarrow \beta$
$(\nu m)P \downarrow \beta$	$P \downarrow \beta$

Intuitively, $P \downarrow \beta$ holds just if P is a closed process that may input or output immediately on barb β. The *convergence* predicate $P{\Downarrow}\beta$ holds if P is a closed process that exhibits β after some reactions:

Convergence to a Barb:

(Conv Barb)	(Conv React)
$P \downarrow \beta$	$P \to Q \quad Q{\Downarrow}\beta$
$P{\Downarrow}\beta$	$P{\Downarrow}\beta$

We let a *test* consist of any closed process R and any barb β. A closed process P *passes* the test if and only if $(P \mid R)\Downarrow\beta$. The notion of testing gives rise to a testing equivalence on the set *Proc* of closed processes:

$$P \simeq Q \triangleq \text{for any test } (R, \beta),$$
$$(P \mid R)\Downarrow\beta \text{ if and only if } (Q \mid R)\Downarrow\beta$$

The idea of testing equivalence comes from the work of De Nicola and Hennessy [DH84]. Despite superficial differences, we can show that our relation $\simeq$ is a version of De Nicola and Hennessy's may-testing equivalence. As De Nicola and Hennessy have explained, may-testing corresponds to partial correctness (or safety), while must-testing corresponds to total correctness. Like much of the security literature, our work focuses on safety properties, hence our definitions.

A test neatly formalises the idea of a generic experiment or observation another process (such as an attacker) might perform on a process, so testing equivalence captures the concept of equivalence in an arbitrary environment. One possible drawback of testing equivalence is that it is sensitive to the choice of language [BN95]. However, our results appear fairly robust in that they carry over smoothly to some extensions of our calculus.

8   Further Cryptographic Primitives

Although so far we have discussed only shared-key cryptography, other kinds of cryptography are also easy to treat within the spi calculus. In this section we show how to handle cryptographic hashing, public-key encryption, and digital signatures. We add syntax for these operations to the spi calculus and give their semantics. We thus provide evidence that our ideas are applicable to a wide range of security protocols, beyond those that rely on shared-key encryption. We believe that we may be able to deal similarly with Diffie-Hellman techniques and with secret sharing. However, protocols for oblivious transfer and for zero-knowledge proofs, for example, are probably beyond the scope of our approach.

8.1   Hashing

A cryptographic hash function has the properties that it is very expensive to recover an input from its image or to find two inputs with the same image. Functions such as SHA and RIPE-MD are generally believed to have these properties [Sch96b].

When we represent hash functions in the spi calculus, we pretend that operations that are very expensive are altogether impossible. We simply add a construct to the syntax of terms of the spi calculus:

Extension for Hashing:

$L, M, N ::=$	terms
$\ldots$	as in Section 5
$H(M)$	hashing

The syntax of processes is unchanged. Intuitively, $H(M)$ represents the hash of M. The absence of a construct for recovering M from $H(M)$ corresponds to the assumption that H cannot be inverted. The lack of any equations $H(M) = H(M')$ corresponds to the assumption that H is free of collisions.

8.2   Public-Key Encryption and Digital Signatures

Traditional public-key encryption systems are based on key pairs. Normally, one of the keys in each pair is private to one principal, while the other key is public. Any principal can encrypt a message using the public key; only a principal that has the private key can then decrypt the message [DH76, RSA78].

We assume that neither key can be recovered from the other. We could just as easily deal with the case where the public key can be derived from the private one. Much as in Section 5, we also assume that the only way to decrypt an encrypted packet is to know the corresponding private key; that an encrypted packet does not reveal the public key that was used to encrypt it; and that there is sufficient redundancy in messages so that the decryption algorithm can detect whether a ciphertext was encrypted with the expected public key.

We arrive at the following syntax for the spi calculus with public-key encryption. (This syntax is concise, rather than memorable.)

Extensions for Public-Key Cryptography:

$L, M, N ::=$	terms
$\ldots$	as in Section 5
M^+	public part
M^-	private part
$\{\![M]\!\}_N$	public-key encryption
$P, Q ::=$	processes
$\ldots$	as in Section 5
$case\ L\ of\ \{\![x]\!\}_N\ in\ P$	decryption

If M represents a key pair, then M^+ represents its public half and M^- represents its private half. Given a public key N, the term $\{\![M]\!\}_N$ represents the result of the public-key encryption of M with N. In $case\ L\ of\ \{\![x]\!\}_N\ in\ P$, the variable x is bound in P. This construct is useful when N is a private key K^-; then it binds x to the M such that $\{\![M]\!\}_{K^+}$ is L, if such an M exists.

It is also common to use key pairs for digital signatures. Private keys are used for signing, while public keys are used for checking signatures. We can represent digital signatures through the following extended syntax:

Extensions for Digital Signatures:

$L, M, N ::=$	terms
$\ldots$	as above
$[\{M\}]_N$	private-key signature

$P, Q ::=$	processes
$\ldots$	as above
$case\ N\ of\ \lVert x \rVert_M\ in\ P$	signature check

Given a private key N, the term $\lVert M \rVert_N$ represents the result of the signature of M with N. Again, variable x is bound in P in the syntax $case\ N\ of\ \lVert x \rVert_M\ in\,P$. This construct is dual to $case\ L\ of\ \{\lvert x \rvert\}_N\ in\,P$. The new construct is useful when N is a public key K^+; then it binds x to the M such that $\lVert M \rVert_{K^-}$ is L, if such an M exists. (Thus, we are assuming that M can be recovered from the result of signing it; but there is no difficulty in dropping this assumption.)

Formally, the semantics of the new constructs is captured with two new rules for the reduction relation:

(Red Public Decrypt) $case\ \lVert M \rVert_{N^+}\ of\ \lVert x \rVert_{N^-}\ in\ P > P\{M\}x$
(Red Signature Check) $case\ \lVert M \rVert_{N^-}\ of\ \lVert x \rVert_{N^+}\ in\ P > P\{M\}x$

As a small example, we can write the following public-key analogue for the protocol of Section 6.1:

$$A(M) \triangleq \overline{c_{AB}}\langle \{\lvert M, \lVert H(M) \rVert_{K_A^-} \rvert\}_{K_B^+} \rangle$$
$$B \triangleq c_{AB}(x).case\ x\ of\ \{\lvert y \rvert\}_{K_B^-}\ in$$
$$let\ (y_1, y_2) = y\ in$$
$$case\ y_2\ of\ \lVert z \rVert_{K_A^+}\ in$$
$$[H(y_1)\ is\ z]\ F(y_1)$$
$$Inst(M) \triangleq (\nu K_A)(\nu K_B)(A(M) \mid B)$$

In this protocol, A sends M on the channel c_{AB}, signed with A's private key and encrypted under B's public key; the signature is applied to a hash of M rather than to M itself. On receipt of a message on c_{AB}, B decrypts using its private key, checks A's signature using A's public key, checks the hash, and applies F to the body of the message (to M). The key pairs K_A and K_B are restricted; but there would be no harm in sending their public parts K_A^+ and K_B^+ on a public channel.

Other formalisations of public-key cryptography are possible, perhaps even desirable. In particular, we have represented cryptographic operations at an abstract level, and do not attempt to model closely the properties of any one algorithm. We are concerned with public-key encryption and digital signatures in general rather than with their RSA implementations, say. The RSA system satisfies equations that our formalisation does not capture. For example, in the RSA system, $\lVert \{\lvert M \rvert\}_{K^+} \rVert_{K^-}$ equals M. Abadi and Fournet [AF01] investigate a pi calculus in which such equations may be imposed on terms.

9   Discussion: The Spi Calculus

In this part, we have applied the spi calculus to the description and analysis of security protocols. We showed how to represent protocols and how to express their security properties. Our model of protocols takes into account the possibility of attacks, but does not require writing explicit specifications for an attacker. In particular, we express secrecy properties as simple equations that mean indistinguishability from the point of view of an arbitrary attacker. To our knowledge, this sharp treatment of attacks has not been previously possible.

As examples, we chose protocols of the sort commonly found in the authentication literature. Although our examples are small, we have found them instructive and encouraging. In particular, there seems to be no fundamental difficulty in writing other kinds of examples, such as protocols for electronic commerce. Unfortunately, the specifications for those protocols do not yet seem to be fully understood, even in informal terms [Mao96].

Several proof techniques for the spi calculus have been developed since the work reported in this part of the notes was completed. Several researchers have devised proof techniques for equational reasoning in spi and its generalisations [AG98, BNP99, AF01]. A type system due to Abadi [Aba99] can prove equationally-specified secrecy properties including the one stated in Section 6.4. There is no comparable type system for proving equationally-specified authenticity properties. Still, recent work on type systems for the spi calculus [GJ01] allow the proof by type-checking of authenticity properties specified using the correspondence assertions of Woo and Lam [WL93].

Apart from the spi calculus, other nominal calculi to have been applied to cryptographic protocols include the sjoin calculus [AFG98], a version of the join calculus equipped with abstract cryptographic primitives. It is surprisingly difficult to encode encryption within the pi calculus; Amadio and Prasad [AP99] investigate one such encoding.

Part III: The Ambient Calculus

The ambient calculus is a nominal calculus whose basic abstraction, the *ambient*, represents mobile, nested, computational environments, with local communications. Ambients can represent the standard components of distributed systems, such as nodes, channels, messages, and mobile code. They can also represent situations where entire active computational environments are moved, as happens with mobile computing devices, and with multi-threaded mobile agents.

This part of the notes introduces the ambient calculus, and explains how we can regulate aspects of mobility by typing. It is organised as follows. In Section 10, we informally motivate the ambient abstraction, and then in Section 11 we present the basic untyped ambient calculus. Next, in Section 12, we motivate the development of type systems for the ambient calculus. In Section 13 we informally introduce a type system that only tracks communications. In Section 14 we give a precise definition of the same system, and a subject reduction result. Section 15 and 16 enrich this system to regulate the mobility of ambients. In Section 17, to illustrate the expressiveness of the ambient calculus and its type system, we present a typed encoding of a distributed programming language. Section 18 concludes.

10   Motivation for Ambients

There are two distinct areas of work in mobility: mobile computing, concerning computation that is carried out in mobile devices (laptops, personal digital assistants, etc.), and mobile computation, concerning mobile code that moves between devices (applets, agents, etc.). We aim to describe all these aspects of mobility within a single framework that encompasses mobile agents, the ambients where agents interact and the mobility of the ambients themselves.

The inspiration for this work comes from the potential for mobile computation over the World-Wide Web. The geographic distribution of the Web naturally calls for mobility of computation, as a way of flexibly managing latency and bandwidth. Because of recent advances in networking and language technology, the basic tenets of mobile computation are now technologically realizable. The high-level software architecture potential, however, is still largely unexplored, although it is being actively investigated in the coordination and agents communities.

The main difficulty with mobile computation on the Web is not in mobility per se, but in the handling of administrative domains. In the early days of the internet one could rely on a flat name space given by IP addresses; knowing the IP address of a computer would very likely allow one to talk to that computer in some way. This is no longer the case: firewalls partition the internet into administrative domains that are isolated from each other except for rigidly controlled pathways. System administrators enforce policies about what can move through firewalls and how.

Mobility requires more than the traditional notion of authorization to run or to access information in certain domains: it involves the authorization to enter or exit certain domains. In particular, as far as mobile computation is concerned, it is not realistic to imagine that an agent can migrate from any point A to any point B on the internet. Rather, an agent must first exit its administrative domain (obtaining permission to do so), enter someone else's administrative domain (again, obtaining permission to do so) and then enter a protected area of some machine where it is allowed to run (after obtaining permission to do so). Access to information is controlled at many levels, thus multiple levels of authorization may be involved. Among these levels we have: local computer, local area network, regional area network, wide-area intranet and internet. Mobile programs must be equipped to navigate this hierarchy of administrative domains, at every step obtaining authorization to move further. Similarly, laptops must be equipped to access resources depending on their location in the administrative hierarchy. Therefore, at the most fundamental level we need to capture notions of locations, of mobility and of authorization to move.

Today, it is very difficult to transport a working environment between two computers, for example, between a laptop and a desktop, or between home and work computers. The working environment might consist of data that has to be copied, and of running programs in various stages of active or suspended communication with the network that have to be shut down and restarted. Why can't we just say "move this (part of the) environment to that computer" and carry on? When on a trip, why couldn't we transfer a piece of the desktop environment (for example, a forgotten open document along with its editor) to the laptop over a phone line? We would like to discover techniques to achieve all this easily and reliably.

With these motivations, we adopt a paradigm of mobility where computational ambients are hierarchically structured, where agents are confined to ambients and where ambients move under the control of agents. A novelty of this approach is in allowing the movement of self-contained nested environments that include data and live computation, as opposed to the more common techniques that move single agents or individual objects. Our goal is to make mobile computation scale-up to widely distributed, intermittently connected and well administered computational environments.

10.1   Ambients

An ambient, in the sense in which we are going to use this word, has the following main characteristics:

- An ambient is a bounded place where computation happens. The interesting property here is the existence of a boundary around an ambient. If we want to move computations easily we must be able to determine what should move; a boundary determines what is inside and what is outside an ambient. Examples of ambients, in this sense, are: a web page (bounded by a file), a virtual address space (bounded by an addressing range), a Unix file system (bounded within a physical volume), a single data object (bounded by "self") and a laptop (bounded by its case and data ports). Non-examples are: threads (where the boundary of what is "reachable" is difficult to determine) and logically related collections of objects. We can already see that a boundary implies some flexible addressing scheme that can denote entities across the boundary; examples are symbolic links, Uniform Resource Locators and Remote Procedure Call proxies. Flexible addressing is what enables, or at least facilitates, mobility. It is also, of course, a cause of problems when the addressing links are "broken".
- An ambient is something that can be nested within other ambients. As we discussed, administrative domains are (often) organized hierarchically. If we want to move a running application from work to home, the application must be removed from an enclosing (work) ambient and inserted in a different enclosing (home) ambient. A laptop may need a removal pass to leave a workplace, and a government pass to leave or enter a country.
- An ambient is something that can be moved as a whole. If we reconnect a laptop to a different network, all the address spaces and file systems within it move accordingly and automatically. If we move an agent from one computer to another, its local data should move accordingly and automatically.

More precisely, we investigate ambients that have the following structure:

- Each ambient has a name. The name of an ambient is used to control access (entry, exit, communication, etc.). In a realistic situation the true name of an ambient would be guarded very closely, and only specific capabilities would be handed out about how to use the name. In our examples we are usually more liberal in the handling of names, for the sake of simplicity.
- Each ambient has a collection of local agents (also known as threads, processes, etc.). These are the computations that run directly within the ambient and, in a sense, control the ambient. For example, they can instruct the ambient to move.
- Each ambient has a collection of subambients. Each subambient has its own name, agents, subambients, etc.

10.2   Technical Context: Systems

Many software systems have explored and are exploring notions of mobility. Among these are:

- Obliq [Car95]. The Obliq project attacked the problems of distribution and mobility for intranet computing. It was carried out largely before the Web became popular. Within its scope, Obliq works quite well, but is not really suitable for computation and mobility over the Web, just like most other distributed paradigms developed in pre-Web days.
- Telescript [Whi96]. Our ambient model is partially inspired by Telescript, but is almost dual to it. In Telescript, agents move whereas places stay put. Ambients, instead, move whereas agents are confined to ambients. A Telescript agent, however, is itself a little ambient, since it contains a "suitcase" of data. Some nesting of places is allowed in Telescript.
- Java [GJS96]. Java provides a working paradigm for mobile computation, as well as a huge amount of available and expected infrastructure on which to base more ambitious mobility efforts.
- Linda [CG89]. Linda is a "coordination language" where multiple processes interact in a common space (called a tuple space) by dropping and picking up tokens asynchronously. Distributed versions of Linda exist that use multiple tuple spaces and allow remote operations over those. A dialect of Linda [CGZ95] allows nested tuple spaces, but not mobility of the tuple spaces.

10.3   Technical Context: Formalisms

Many existing calculi have provided inspiration for our work. In particular:

- Enrichments of the pi calculus with locations have been studied, with the aim of capturing notions of distributed computation. In the simplest form, a flat space of locations is added, and operations can be indexed by the location where they are executed. Riely and Hennessy [RH98] and Sewell [Sew98] propose versions of the pi calculus extended with primitives to allow computations to migrate between named locations. The emphasis in this work is on developing type systems for mobile computation based on existing type systems for the pi calculus. Riely and Hennessy's type system regulates the usage of channel names according to permissions represented by types. Sewell's type system differentiates between local and remote channels for the sake of efficient implementation of communication.

- The join calculus [FG96] is a reformulation of the pi calculus with a more explicit notion of places of interaction; this greatly helps in building distributed implementations of channel mechanisms. The distributed join calculus [FGL+96] adds a notion of named locations, with essentially the same aims as ours, and a notion of distributed failure. Locations in the distributed join calculus form a tree, and subtrees can migrate from one part of the tree to another. A significant difference from our ambients is that movement may happen directly from any active location to any other known location.

- LLinda [NFP97] is a formalization of Linda using process calculi techniques. As in distributed versions of Linda, LLinda has multiple distributed tuple spaces. Multiple tuple spaces are very similar in spirit to multiple ambients, but Linda's tuple spaces do not nest, and there are no restrictions about accessing a tuple space from any other tuple space.

- A growing body of literature is concentrating on the idea of adding discrete locations to a process calculus and considering failure of those locations [Ama97, FGL+96]. This approach aims to model traditional distributed environments, along with algorithms that tolerate node failures. However, on the internet, node failure is almost irrelevant compared with inability to reach nodes. Web servers do not often fail forever, but they frequently disappear from sight because of network or node overload, and then they come back. Sometimes they come back in a different place, for example, when a Web site changes its internet Service Provider. Moreover, inability to reach a Web site only implies that a certain path is unavailable; it implies neither failure of that site nor global unreachability. In this sense, an observed node failure cannot simply be associated with the node itself, but instead is a property of the whole network, a property that changes over time. Our notion of locality is induced by a non-trivial and dynamic topology of locations. Failure is only represented, in a weak but realistic sense, as becoming forever unreachable.

10.4   Summary of Our Approach

With respect to previous work on process calculi, we can characterize the main differences in the ambient calculus approach as follows. In each of the following points, our emphasis is on boundaries and their effect on computation. The existence of separate locations is represented by a topology of boundaries. This topology induces an abstract notion of distance between locations. Locations are not uniformly accessible, and are not identified by globally unique names. Process mobility is represented as crossing of boundaries. In particular, process mobility is not represented as communication of processes or process names over channels. Security is represented as the ability or inability to cross boundaries. In particular, security is not directly represented by cryptographic primitives or access control lists. Interaction between processes is by shared location within a common boundary. In particular, interaction cannot happen without proper consideration of boundaries and their topology.

11   A Polyadic Ambient Calculus

The ambient calculus of this section is a slight extension of the original untyped ambient calculus [CG00b]. In that calculus, communication is based on the exchange of single values. Here we extend the calculus with communication based on tuples of values (polyadic communication), since this simple extension greatly facilitates the task of providing an expressive type system. We also add objective moves and we annotate bound variables with type information.

The ambient calculus is a derivative of the pi calculus. Four of its process constructions (restriction, inactivity, composition, and replication) are exactly as in the pi calculus. To these we add ambients, capabilities, and a simple form of communication. We briefly discuss these constructions; see [CG00b] for a more detailed introduction.

The restriction operator, $(\nu n{:}W)P$, creates a new (unique) name n of type W within a scope P. The new name can be used to name ambients and to operate on ambients by name. The inactive process, $\mathbf{0}$, does nothing. Parallel composition is denoted by a binary operator, $P \mid Q$, that is commutative and associative. As in the pi calculus, replication is a technically convenient way of representing iteration and recursion: the process $!P$ denotes the unbounded replication of the process P and is equivalent to $P \mid !P$.

An ambient is written $M[P]$, where M is the name of the ambient, and P is the process running inside the ambient.

The process $M.P$ executes an action regulated by the capability M, and then continues as the process P. We consider three kinds of capabilities: one for entering an ambient, one for exiting an ambient, and one for opening up an ambient. (The latter requires special care in the type system.) Capabilities are obtained from names; given a name n, the capability $in\, n$ allows entry into n, the capability $out\, n$ allows exit out of n and the capability $open\, n$ allows the opening of n. Implicitly, the possession of one or all of these capabilities is insufficient to reconstruct the original name n from which they were extracted. Capabilities can also be composed into paths, $M.M'$, with ϵ for the empty path.

Communication is asynchronous and local to an ambient. It is similar to channel communication in the pi calculus, except that the channel has no name: the surrounding ambient provides the context where the communication happens. The process $\langle M_1, \ldots, M_k \rangle$ represents the output of a tuple of values, with no continuation. The process $(x_1{:}W_1, \ldots, x_k{:}W_k).P$ represents the input of a tuple of values, whose components are bound to $x_1, \ldots, x_k$, with continuation P.

Communication is used to exchange both names and capabilities, which share the same syntactic class M of messages. The first task of our type system is to distinguish the messages that are names from the messages that are capabilities, so that each is guaranteed to be used in an appropriate context. In general, the type system might distinguish other kinds of expressions, such as integer and boolean expressions, but we do not include those in our basic calculus.

The process $go\ N.M[P]$ moves the ambient $M[P]$ as specified by the N capability, and has $M[P]$ as its continuation. It is called an *objective move* since the ambient $M[P]$ is moved from the outside, while a movement caused by a process $N.P$ which runs inside an ambient is called a *subjective move*. In the untyped calculus, we can define an objective move $go\ N.M[P]$ to be short for the process $(\nu k)k[N.M[out\ k.P]]$ where k is not free in P. As we will show in Section 16.2, a primitive typing rule for objective moves allows more refined typings than are possible with only subjective moves.

Messages and Processes:

$M ::=$	message
n	name
$in\ M$	can enter into M
$out\ M$	can exit out of M
$open\ M$	can open M
ϵ	null
$M.M'$	path
$P, Q, R ::=$	process
$(\nu n{:}W)P$	restriction
$\mathbf{0}$	inactivity
$P \mid Q$	composition
$!P$	replication
$M[P]$	ambient
$M.P$	action
$(x_1{:}W_1, \ldots, x_k{:}W_k).P$	input action
$\langle M_1, \ldots, M_k \rangle$	output action
$go\ N.M[P]$	objective move

The following table displays the main reduction rules of the calculus (the full set is presented in Section 14). The notation $P\{x_1{\leftarrow}M_1\} \cdots \{x_k{\leftarrow}M_k\}$ in rule (Red I/O) denotes the outcome of a capture-avoiding simultaneous substitution of message M_i for each free occurrence of the corresponding name x_i in the process P, for $i \in 1..k$.

Reduction:

$n[in\ m.P \mid Q] \mid m[R] \rightarrow m[n[P \mid Q] \mid R]$	(Red In)
$m[n[out\ m.P \mid Q] \mid R] \rightarrow n[P \mid Q] \mid m[R]$	(Red Out)

$$open\ n.P \mid n[Q] \rightarrow P \mid Q \qquad \text{(Red Open)}$$

$$\langle M_1, \ldots, M_k \rangle \mid (x_1{:}W_1, \ldots, x_k{:}W_k).P \rightarrow \qquad \text{(Red I/O)}$$
$$\qquad P\{x_1 \leftarrow M_1\} \cdots \{x_k \leftarrow M_k\}$$
$$go(in\ m.N).n[P] \mid m[Q] \rightarrow m[go\ N.n[P] \mid Q] \qquad \text{(Red Go In)}$$
$$m[go(out\ m.N).n[P] \mid Q] \rightarrow go\ N.n[P] \mid m[Q] \qquad \text{(Red Go Out)}$$

We will use the following syntactic conventions:

- parentheses may be used for precedence
- $(\nu n{:}W)P \mid Q$ is read $((\nu n{:}W)P) \mid Q$
- $!P \mid Q$ is read $(!P) \mid Q$
- $M.P \mid Q$ is read $(M.P) \mid Q$
- $(n_1{:}W_1, \ldots, n_k{:}W_k).P \mid Q$ is read $((n_1{:}W_1, \ldots, n_k{:}W_k).P) \mid Q$
- $n[] \triangleq n[\mathbf{0}]$
- $M \triangleq M.\mathbf{0}$ (where appropriate)

As an example, consider the following process:

$$a[p[out\ a.in\ b.\langle c \rangle]] \mid b[open\ p.(x).x[]]$$

Intuitively, this example represents a packet named p being sent from a machine a to a machine b. The process $p[out\ a.in\ b.\langle c \rangle]$ represents the packet, as a subambient of ambient a. The name of the packet ambient is p, and its interior is the process $out\ a.in\ b.\langle c \rangle$. This process consists of three sequential actions: exercise the capability $out\ a$, exercise the capability $in\ b$, and then output the name c. The effect of the two capabilities on the enclosing ambient p is to move p out of a and into b (rules (Red Out), (Red In)), to reach the state:

$$a[] \mid b[p[\langle c \rangle] \mid open\ p.(x).x[]]$$

In this state, the interior of a is empty but the interior of b consists of two running processes, the subambient $p[\langle c \rangle]$ and the process $open\ p.(x).x[]$. This process is attempting to exercise the $open\ p$ capability. Previously it was blocked. Now that the p ambient is present, the capability's effect is to dissolve the ambient's boundary; hence, the interior of b becomes the process $\langle c \rangle \mid (x).x[]$ (Red Open). This is a composition of an output $\langle c \rangle$ with an input $(x).x[]$. The input consumes the output, leaving $c[]$ as the interior of b (Red I/O). Hence, the final state of the whole example is $a[] \mid b[c[]]$.

As an example of objective moves, consider the following variation of the previous process:

$$a[go(out\ a.in\ b).p[\langle c \rangle]] \mid b[open\ p.(x).x[]]$$

In this case, the ambient $p[\langle c \rangle]$ is moved from the outside, out of a and into b (rules (Red Go Out), (Red Go In)), to reach the same state that was reached in the previous version after the (Red Out), (Red In) subjective moves:

$$a[] \mid b[p[\langle c \rangle] \mid open\ p.(x).x[]]$$

See the original paper on the ambient calculus [CG00b] for many more examples, including locks, data structures such as booleans and numerals, Turing Machines, routable packets and active networks, and encodings of the lambda calculus and the pi calculus.

12   Types for the Ambient Calculus

Type systems are, today, a widely applied technique allowing programmers to describe the key properties of their code, and to have these properties mechanically and efficiently checked. Mobile code makes types, and machine-checkable properties in general, useful for security reasons too, as has been demonstrated by the checking performed on Java applets [LY97] and on other mobile code [GS01].

In standard languages, the key invariants that are maintained by type systems have mainly to do with the contents of variables and with the interfaces of functions, procedures, or methods. In the ambient calculus, the basic properties of a piece of code are those related to its mobility, to the possibility of opening an ambient and exposing its content, and to the type of data which may be exchanged inside an ambient. To understand how groups arise in this context, consider a typical static property we may want to express in a type system for the ambient calculus; informally:

The ambient named n can enter the ambient named m.

This could be expressed as a typing $n : CanEnter(m)$ stating that n is a member of the collection $CanEnter(m)$ of names that can enter m. However, this would bring us straight into the domain of dependent types [CH88], since the type $CanEnter(m)$ depends on the name m. Instead, we introduce type-level groups of names, G, H, and restate our property as:

The name m belongs to group G.
The ambient named n can enter any ambient of group G.

This idea leads to typings of the form: $m : G$, $n : CanEnter(G)$ which are akin to standard typings such as $x : Int$, $y : Channel(Int)$.

To appreciate the relevance of groups in the description of distributed systems, consider a programmer coding a typical distributed system composed of nodes and mobile threads moving from one node to another, and where threads communicate by sending input and output packets through typed channels. In these notes, we define a type system where a programmer can:

- define groups such as *Node*, *Thread*, *Channel*, and *Packet*, which match the system structure;
- declare properties such as: this ambient is a *Thread* and it may only cross ambients which are *Nodes*; this ambient is a *Packet* and can enter *Channels*; this ambient is a *Channel* of type T, and it cannot move or be opened, but it may open *Packets* containing data of type T; this ambient is a *Node* and it cannot move or be opened;

– have the system statically verify all these properties.

Our *groups* are similar to *sorts* used in typed versions of the pi calculus [Mil99], but we introduce an operation, $(\nu G)P$, for creating a new group G, which can be used within the process P.

The binders for new groups, (νG), can float outward as long as this adjustment, extrusion, does not introduce name clashes. Because of extrusion, group binders do not impede the mobility of ambients that are enclosed in the initial scope of fresh groups but later move away. On the other hand, even though extrusion enlarges scopes, simple scoping restrictions in the typing rules prevent names belonging to a fresh group from ever being received by a process which has been defined outside the initial scope of the group.

Therefore, we obtain a flexible way of protecting the propagation of names. This is to be contrasted with the situation in most untyped nominal calculi, where names can (intentionally, accidentally, or maliciously) be extruded arbitrarily far, by the automatic and unrestricted application of extrusion rules, and communicated to other parties.

13   Introduction to Exchange Types

An ambient is a place where processes can exchange messages and where other ambients can enter and exit. We introduce here a type system which regulates communication, while mobility will be tackled in the following sections. This system generalizes the one presented in [CG99] by allowing the partitioning of ambients into groups.

13.1   Topics of Conversation

Within an ambient, multiple processes can freely execute input and output actions. Since the messages are undirected, it is easily possible for a process to utter a message that is not appropriate for some receiver. The main idea of the exchange type system is to keep track of the topic of conversation that is permitted within a given ambient, so that talkers and listeners can be certain of exchanging appropriate messages.

The range of topics is described in the following table by message types, W, and exchange types, T. The message types are $G[T]$, the type of names of ambients which belong to the group G and that allow exchanges of type T, and $Cap[T]$, the type of capabilities that when used may cause the unleashing of T exchanges (as a consequence of opening ambients that exchange T). The exchange types are Shh, the absence of exchanges, and $W_1 \times \ldots \times W_k$, the exchange of a tuple of messages with elements of the respective message types. For $k = 0$, the empty tuple type is called $\mathbf{1}$; it allows the exchange of empty tuples, that is, it allows pure synchronization. The case $k = 1$ allows any message type to be an exchange type.

Types:

$W ::=$	message type
$\quad G[T]$	name in group G for ambients allowing T exchanges
$\quad Cap[T]$	capability unleashing T exchanges
$S, T ::=$	exchange type
$\quad Shh$	no exchange
$\quad W_1 \times \cdots \times W_k$	tuple exchange ($\mathbf{1}$ is the null product)

For example, in a scope where the *Agent* and *Place* groups have been defined, we can express the following types:

- An ambient of the *Agent* group where no exchange is allowed (a quiet *Agent*): *Agent*[*Shh*]
- A harmless capability: *Cap*[*Shh*]
- A *Place* where names of quiet *Agent*s may be exchanged:

$$Place[Agent[Shh]]$$

- A *Place* where harmless capabilities may be exchanged:

$$Place[Cap[Shh]]$$

- A capability that may unleash the exchange of names of quiet *Agent*s:

$$Cap[Agent[Shh]]$$

13.2 Intuitions

Before presenting the formal type rules (in Section 14), we discuss the intuitions that lead to them.

Typing of Processes If a message M has message type W, then $\langle M \rangle$ is a process that outputs (exchanges) W messages. Therefore, we will have a rule stating that:

$$M : W \quad \text{implies} \quad \langle M \rangle : W$$

If P is a process that may exchange W messages, then $(x{:}W).P$ is also a process that may exchange W messages. Therefore:

$$P : W \quad \text{implies} \quad (x{:}W).P : W$$

The process $\mathbf{0}$ exchanges nothing, so it naturally has exchange type *Shh*. However, we may also consider $\mathbf{0}$ as a process that may exchange any type. This is useful when we need to place $\mathbf{0}$ in a context that is already expected to exchange some type:

$$\mathbf{0} : T \text{ for any } T$$

Alternatively, we may add a subtype relation among types, give $\mathbf{0}$ a minimal type, and add a rule which allows processes with a type to appear where processes with a supertype are required [Zim00]. We reject this approach here only because we want to explore the ideas of group-based exchange and mobility types in the simplest possible setting.

If P and Q are processes that may exchange T, then $P \mid Q$ is also such a process. Similarly for $!P$:

$$P : T, Q : T \text{ implies } P \mid Q : T$$
$$P : T \qquad \text{implies } !P : T$$

Therefore, by keeping track of the exchange type of a process, T-inputs and T-outputs are tracked so that they match correctly when placed in parallel.

Typing of Ambients An ambient $n[P]$ is a process that exchanges nothing at the current level, so, like $\mathbf{0}$, it can be placed in parallel with any process, hence we allow it to have any exchange type:

$$n[P] : T \text{ for any } T$$

There needs to be, however, a connection between the type of n and the type of P. We give to each ambient name n a type $G[T]$, meaning that n belongs to the group G and that only T exchanges are allowed in any ambient of that name. Hence, a process P can be placed inside an ambient with that name n only if the type of P is T:

$$n : G[T], P : T \text{ implies } n[P] \text{ is well-formed (and can have any type)}$$

By tagging the name of an ambient with the type of exchanges, we know what kind of exchanges to expect in any ambient we enter. Moreover, we can tell what happens when we open an ambient of a given name.

Typing of Open Tracking the type of I/O exchanges is not enough by itself. We also need to worry about *open*, which might open an ambient and unleash its exchanges inside the surrounding ambient.

If ambients named n permit T exchanges, then the capability *open* n may unleash those T exchanges. We then say that *open* n has a capability type $Cap[T]$, meaning that it may unleash T exchanges when used:

$$n : G[T] \text{ implies } open \, n : Cap[T]$$

As a consequence, any process that uses a $Cap[T]$ must be a process that is already willing to participate in exchanges of type T, because further T exchanges may be unleashed:

$$M : Cap[T], P : T \text{ implies } M.P : T$$

Typing of In and Out The exercise of an *in* or *out* capability cannot cause any exchange, hence such capabilities can be prepended to any process. Following the same pattern we used with **0** and ambients, the silent nature of these capabilities is formalized by allowing them to acquire any capability type:

$$in\ n : Cap[T]\ \ \text{for any } T$$
$$out\ n : Cap[T]\ \ \text{for any } T$$

Groups Groups are used in the exchange system to specify which kinds of messages can be exchanged inside an ambient. We add a process construct to create a new group G with scope P:

$$(\nu G)P$$

The type rule of this construct specifies that the process P should have an exchange type T that does not contain G. Then, $(\nu G)P$ can be given type T as well. That is, G is never be allowed to "escape" into the type of $(\nu G)P$:

$$P : T, \quad G \text{ does not occur in } T \text{ implies} \quad (\nu G)P : T$$

14   Typed Ambient Calculus

We are now ready for a formal presentation of the typed calculus which has been informally introduced in the previous section. We first present its syntax, then its typing rules, and finally a subject reduction theorem, which states that types are preserved during computation.

14.1   Types and Processes

We first recall the definition of the types of the exchange system.

Types:

$W ::=$	message type
$G[T]$	name in group G for ambients allowing T exchanges
$Cap[T]$	capability unleashing T exchanges
$S, T ::=$	exchange type
Shh	no exchange
$W_1 \times \cdots \times W_k$	tuple exchange (**1** is the null product)

Messages and processes are the same as in the untyped calculus of Section 11.

Messages and Processes:

$M ::=$	message
n	name

in M	can enter into M
out M	can exit out of M
open M	can open M
ϵ	null
$M.M'$	path

$P, Q, R ::=$	process
$(\nu G)P$	group creation
$(\nu n{:}W)P$	restriction
$\mathbf{0}$	inactivity
$P \mid Q$	composition
$!P$	replication
$M[P]$	ambient
$M.P$	action
$(x_1{:}W_1, \ldots, x_k{:}W_k).P$	input action
$\langle M_1, \ldots, M_k \rangle$	output action
go N.M$[P]$	objective move

We identify processes up to consistent renaming of bound names and groups. In the processes $(\nu G)P$ and $(\nu n{:}W)P$, the group G and the name n, respectively, are bound, with scope P. In the process $(x_1{:}W_1, \ldots, x_k{:}W_k).P$, the names x_1, $\ldots$, x_k are bound, with scope P.

The following table defines the free names of processes and messages, and the free groups of processes and types.

Free Names and Free Groups:

$fn((\nu G)P) \triangleq fn(P)$ $fn(n) \triangleq \{n\}$

$fn((\nu n{:}W)P) \triangleq fn(P) - \{n\}$ $fn(in\, M) \triangleq fn(M)$

$fn(\mathbf{0}) \triangleq \varnothing$ $fn(out\, M) \triangleq fn(M)$

$fn(P \mid Q) \triangleq fn(P) \cup fn(Q)$ $fn(open\, M) \triangleq fn(M)$

$fn(!P) \triangleq fn(P)$ $fn(\epsilon) \triangleq \varnothing$

$fn(M[P]) \triangleq fn(M) \cup fn(P)$ $fn(M.N) \triangleq fn(M) \cup fn(N)$

$fn(M.P) \triangleq fn(M) \cup fn(P)$

$fn((x_1{:}W_1, \ldots, x_k{:}W_k).P) \triangleq fn(P) - \{x_1, \ldots, x_k\}$

$fn(\langle M_1, \ldots, M_k \rangle) \triangleq fn(M_1) \cup \cdots \cup fn(M_k)$

$fn(go\, N.M[P]) \triangleq fn(N) \cup fn(M) \cup fn(P)$

$fg((\nu G)P) \triangleq fg(P) - \{G\}$ $fg(G[T]) \triangleq \{G\} \cup fg(T)$

$fg((\nu n{:}W)P) \triangleq fg(W) \cup fg(P)$ $fg(Cap[T]) \triangleq fg(T)$

$fg(\mathbf{0}) \triangleq \varnothing$ $fg(Shh) \triangleq \varnothing$

$fg(P \mid Q) \triangleq fg(P) \cup fg(Q)$ $fg(W_1 \times \cdots \times W_k) \triangleq$

$fg(!P) \triangleq fg(P)$ $\qquad fg(W_1) \cup \cdots \cup fg(W_k)$

$$fg(M[P]) \triangleq fg(P)$$
$$fg(M.P) \triangleq fg(P)$$
$$fg((x_1:W_1,\ldots,x_k:W_k).P) \triangleq fg(W_1) \cup \cdots \cup fg(W_k) \cup fg(P)$$
$$fg(\langle M_1,\ldots,M_k\rangle) \triangleq \varnothing$$
$$fg(go\ N.M[P]) \triangleq fg(P)$$

The following tables describe the operational semantics of the calculus. The type annotations present in the syntax do not play a role in reduction; they are simply carried along by the reductions.

Processes are identified up to an equivalence relation, $\equiv$, called structural congruence. As in the pi calculus, this relation provides a way of rearranging processes so that interacting parts can be brought together. Then, a reduction relation, $\rightarrow$, acts on the interacting parts to produce computation steps. The core of the calculus is given by the reduction rules (Red In), (Red Out), (Red Go In), (Red Go Out), and (Red Open), for mobility, and (Red I/O), for communication.

The rules of structural congruence are similar to the rules for the pi calculus. The rules (Struct GRes ...) describe the extrusion behaviour of the (νG) binders. Note that (νG) extrudes exactly as (νn) does, hence it does not pose any dynamic restriction on the movement of ambients or messages.

Reduction:

$n[in\ m.P \mid Q] \mid m[R] \rightarrow m[n[P \mid Q] \mid R]$	(Red In)
$m[n[out\ m.P \mid Q] \mid R] \rightarrow n[P \mid Q] \mid m[R]$	(Red Out)
$open\ n.P \mid n[Q] \rightarrow P \mid Q$	(Red Open)
$\langle M_1,\ldots,M_k\rangle \mid (x_1:W_1,\ldots,x_k:W_k).P \rightarrow$	(Red I/O)
$\quad P\{x_1{\leftarrow}M_1\}\cdots\{x_k{\leftarrow}M_k\}$	
$go(in\ m.N).n[P] \mid m[Q] \rightarrow m[go\ N.n[P] \mid Q]$	(Red Go In)
$m[go(out\ m.N).n[P] \mid Q] \rightarrow go\ N.n[P] \mid m[Q]$	(Red Go Out)
$P \rightarrow Q \Rightarrow P \mid R \rightarrow Q \mid R$	(Red Par)
$P \rightarrow Q \Rightarrow (\nu n:W)P \rightarrow (\nu n:W)Q$	(Red Res)
$P \rightarrow Q \Rightarrow (\nu G)P \rightarrow (\nu G)Q$	(Red GRes)
$P \rightarrow Q \Rightarrow n[P] \rightarrow n[Q]$	(Red Amb)
$P' \equiv P, P \rightarrow Q, Q \equiv Q' \Rightarrow P' \rightarrow Q'$	(Red $\equiv$)

Structural Congruence:

$P \equiv P$	(Struct Refl)
$Q \equiv P \Rightarrow P \equiv Q$	(Struct Symm)
$P \equiv Q, Q \equiv R \Rightarrow P \equiv R$	(Struct Trans)
$P \equiv Q \Rightarrow (\nu n:W)P \equiv (\nu n:W)Q$	(Struct Res)
$P \equiv Q \Rightarrow (\nu G)P \equiv (\nu G)Q$	(Struct GRes)
$P \equiv Q \Rightarrow P \mid R \equiv Q \mid R$	(Struct Par)

$P \equiv Q \Rightarrow !P \equiv !Q$	(Struct Repl)
$P \equiv Q \Rightarrow M[P] \equiv M[Q]$	(Struct Amb)
$P \equiv Q \Rightarrow M.P \equiv M.Q$	(Struct Action)
$P \equiv Q \Rightarrow$	(Struct Input)
$\quad (x_1{:}W_1, \ldots, x_k{:}W_k).P \equiv (x_1{:}W_1, \ldots, x_k{:}W_k).Q$	
$P \equiv Q \Rightarrow go\ N.M[P] \equiv go\ N.M[Q]$	(Struct Go)
$P \mid Q \equiv Q \mid P$	(Struct Par Comm)
$(P \mid Q) \mid R \equiv P \mid (Q \mid R)$	(Struct Par Assoc)
$!P \equiv P \mid !P$	(Struct Repl Par)
$n_1 \neq n_2 \Rightarrow$	(Struct Res Res)
$\quad (\nu n_1{:}W_1)(\nu n_2{:}W_2)P \equiv (\nu n_2{:}W_2)(\nu n_1{:}W_1)P$	
$n \notin fn(P) \Rightarrow (\nu n{:}W)(P \mid Q) \equiv P \mid (\nu n{:}W)Q$	(Struct Res Par)
$n \neq m \Rightarrow (\nu n{:}W)m[P] \equiv m[(\nu n{:}W)P]$	(Struct Res Amb)
$(\nu G_1)(\nu G_2)P \equiv (\nu G_2)(\nu G_1)P$	(Struct GRes GRes)
$G \notin fg(W) \Rightarrow (\nu G)(\nu n{:}W)P \equiv (\nu n{:}W)(\nu G)P$	(Struct GRes Res)
$G \notin fg(P) \Rightarrow (\nu G)(P \mid Q) \equiv P \mid (\nu G)Q$	(Struct GRes Par)
$(\nu G)m[P] \equiv m[(\nu G)P]$	(Struct GRes Amb)
$P \mid \mathbf{0} \equiv P$	(Struct Zero Par)
$(\nu n{:}W)\mathbf{0} \equiv \mathbf{0}$	(Struct Zero Res)
$(\nu G)\mathbf{0} \equiv \mathbf{0}$	(Struct Zero GRes)
$!\mathbf{0} \equiv \mathbf{0}$	(Struct Zero Repl)
$\epsilon.P \equiv P$	(Struct ϵ)
$(M.M').P \equiv M.M'.P$	(Struct .)
$go\ \epsilon.M[P] \equiv M[P]$	(Struct Go ϵ)

14.2 Typing Rules

In the tables below, we introduce typing environments, E, the five basic judgments, and the typing rules.

Environments, E, and the Domain, $dom(E)$, of an Environment:

$E ::= \varnothing \mid E, G \mid E, n{:}W$ environment
$dom(\varnothing) \triangleq \varnothing$
$dom(E, G) \triangleq dom(E) \cup \{G\}$
$dom(E, n{:}W) \triangleq dom(E) \cup \{n\}$

Judgments:

$E \vdash \diamond$	good environment
$E \vdash W$	good message type W
$E \vdash T$	good exchange type T
$E \vdash M : W$	good message M of message type W
$E \vdash P : T$	good process P with exchange type T

Good Environments:

(Env $\varnothing$)

$$\overline{\varnothing \vdash \diamond}$$

(Env n)

$$\frac{E \vdash W \quad n \notin dom(E)}{E, n{:}W \vdash \diamond}$$

(Env G)

$$\frac{E \vdash \diamond \quad G \notin dom(E)}{E, G \vdash \diamond}$$

Good Types:

(Type Amb)

$$\frac{G \in dom(E) \quad E \vdash T}{E \vdash G[T]}$$

(Type Cap)

$$\frac{E \vdash T}{E \vdash Cap[T]}$$

(Type Shh)

$$\frac{E \vdash \diamond}{E \vdash Shh}$$

(Type Prod)

$$\frac{E \vdash W_1 \quad \cdots \quad E \vdash W_k}{E \vdash W_1 \times \cdots \times W_k}$$

Good Messages:

(Exp n)

$$\frac{E', n{:}W, E'' \vdash \diamond}{E', n{:}W, E'' \vdash n : W}$$

(Exp .)

$$\frac{E \vdash M : Cap[T] \quad E \vdash M' : Cap[T]}{E \vdash M.M' : Cap[T]}$$

(Exp ϵ)

$$\frac{E \vdash Cap[T]}{E \vdash \epsilon : Cap[T]}$$

(Exp In)

$$\frac{E \vdash n : G[S] \quad E \vdash T}{E \vdash in\ n : Cap[T]}$$

(Exp Out)

$$\frac{E \vdash n : G[S] \quad E \vdash T}{E \vdash out\ n : Cap[T]}$$

(Exp Open)

$$\frac{E \vdash n : G[T]}{E \vdash open\ n : Cap[T]}$$

Good Processes:

(Proc Action)

$$\frac{E \vdash M : Cap[T] \quad E \vdash P : T}{E \vdash M.P : T}$$

(Proc Amb)

$$\frac{E \vdash M : G[S] \quad E \vdash P : S \quad E \vdash T}{E \vdash M[P] : T}$$

(Proc Res)

$$\frac{E, n{:}G[S] \vdash P : T}{E \vdash (\nu n{:}G[S])P : T}$$

(Proc GRes)

$$\frac{E, G \vdash P : T \quad G \notin fg(T)}{E \vdash (\nu G)P : T}$$

(Proc Zero)

$$\frac{E \vdash T}{E \vdash \mathbf{0} : T}$$

(Proc Par)

$$\frac{E \vdash P : T \quad E \vdash Q : T}{E \vdash P \mid Q : T}$$

(Proc Repl)

$$\frac{E \vdash P : T}{E \vdash !P : T}$$

(Proc Input)
$$\frac{E, n_1{:}W_1, \ldots, n_k{:}W_k \vdash P : W_1 \times \cdots \times W_k}{E \vdash (n_1{:}W_1, \ldots, n_k{:}W_k).P : W_1 \times \cdots \times W_k}$$

(Proc Output)
$$\frac{E \vdash M_1 : W_1 \quad \cdots \quad E \vdash M_k : W_k}{E \vdash \langle M_1, \ldots, M_k \rangle : W_1 \times \cdots \times W_k}$$

(Proc Go)
$$\frac{E \vdash N : Cap[S'] \quad E \vdash M : G[S] \quad E \vdash P : S \quad E \vdash T}{E \vdash go\ N.M[P] : T}$$

14.3 Subject Reduction

We obtain a standard subject reduction result. A subtle point, though, is the need to account for the appearance of new groups (G_1, ..., G_k, below) during reduction. This is because reduction is defined up to structural congruence, and structural congruence does not preserve the set of free groups of a process. The culprit is the rule $(\nu n{:}W)\mathbf{0} \equiv \mathbf{0}$, in which groups free in W are not free in $\mathbf{0}$.

Lemma 1 (Subject Congruence). *If $E \vdash P : T$ and $P \equiv Q$ then there are G_1, ..., G_k such that $G_1, \ldots, G_k, E \vdash Q : T$.*

Theorem 1 (Subject Reduction). *If $E \vdash P : T$ and $P \rightarrow Q$ then there are G_1, ..., G_k such that $G_1, \ldots, G_k, E \vdash Q : T$.*

Subject reduction specifies that, if P is well-typed, it will only reduce to well-typed terms. This fact has some practical consequences:

- P will never reduce to meaningless processes allowed by the syntax like $(in\ n)[P]$;
- no process deriving from P will contain an ambient where a process attempts an input or output operation which does not match the ambient type.

Subject reduction has also interesting and subtle connections with secrecy of names. Consider a well-typed process $((\nu G).P) \mid O$, where O is a type-checked "opponent", and a name n is declared inside P with a type $G[T]$. Although (νG) can be extruded arbitrarily far, according to the extrusion rules, no process which derives from the opponent O will ever be able to read n through an input $(x{:}W).Q$. Any process $\langle n \rangle \mid (x{:}W).Q$ which derives from $((\nu G).P) \mid O$ is well-typed, hence $W = G[T]$, but the opponent was not, by assumption, in the initial scope of G, and therefore cannot even mention the type $G[T]$. Therefore, we can guarantee that names of group G can never be communicated to processes outside of the initial scope of G, simply because those processes cannot name G to receive the message.

This situation is in sharp contrast with ordinary name restriction, where a name that is initially held secret (e.g., a key) may accidentally be given away and misused (e.g., to decrypt current or old messages). This is because scoping of names can be extruded too far, inadvertently. Scoping of groups can be extruded as well, but still offers protection against accidental or even malicious leakage.

Of course, we would have even stronger protection if we did not allow (νG) binders to extrude at all. But this would be too rigid. Since (νG) binders can be extruded, they do not impede the mobility of ambients that carry secrets. They just prevent those ambients from giving the secrets away. Consider the following example of travelling agents sharing secrets.

$$a[(\nu G)(\nu k' : G[Shh])(\nu k'' : G[Shh])($$
$$k'[out\ a.in\ b.out\ b.in\ c]\ |$$
$$k''[out\ a.in\ c.in\ k'])$$
$$]\ |\ b[]\ |\ c[]$$

Within an ambient a, two agents share a secret group G and two names k' and k'' belonging to that group. The two agents adopt the names k' and k'' as their respective names, knowing that those names cannot be leaked even by themselves. This way, as they travel, nobody else can interfere with them. If somebody interferes with them, or demonstrates knowledge of the names k' or k'', the agents know that the other party must be (a descendant of) the other agent. In this example, the first agent travels to ambient b and then to c, and the second agent goes to ambient c directly. The scope extrusion rules for groups and names allow this to happen. Inside c, out of the initial scope of (νG), the second agent then interacts with the first by entering it. It can do so because it still holds the shared secret k'.

We omit the proof that structural congruence preserves typing, but we comment here on the crucial case: the preservation of typing by the extrusion rule (Struct GRes Amb). For a well-typed P, $(\nu G)P$ is well-typed if and only if P does not communicate a tuple which names G in its type (rule (Proc GRes)): (νG) must not "see" G-typed names communicated at its own level. This intuition suggests that, referring to the following table, P' should be typeable $((\nu G)$ cannot "see" the output $\langle n \rangle$) while P'' should be not ($\langle n \rangle$ is at the same level as (νG)). However, the two processes are equivalent, modulo extrusion of (νG) (rule (Struct GRes Amb)):

$$P' = (\nu G)m[(\nu n{:}G[Shh])\langle n \rangle]$$
$$P'' = m[(\nu G)(\nu n{:}G[Shh])\langle n \rangle]$$

We go through the example step by step, to solve the apparent paradox. First consider the term

$$(\nu G)(\nu n{:}G[Shh])\langle n \rangle$$

This term cannot be typed, because G attempts to escape the scope of $(\nu G)(\nu n{:}G[Shh])$ as the type of the message n. An attempted typing derivation fails at the last step below:

$$\ldots$$
$$\Rightarrow \quad G, n{:}G[Shh] \vdash n : G[Shh]$$
$$\Rightarrow \quad G, n{:}G[Shh] \vdash \langle n\rangle : G[Shh]$$
$$\Rightarrow \quad G \vdash (\nu n{:}G[Shh])\langle n\rangle : G[Shh]$$
$$\not\Rightarrow \quad \vdash (\nu G)(\nu n{:}G[Shh])\langle n\rangle : G[Shh] \text{ (because } G \in \mathit{fn}(G[Shh]))$$

Similarly, the term

$$(\nu m{:}W)m[(\nu G)(\nu n{:}G[Shh])\langle n\rangle]$$

cannot be typed, because it contains the previous untypeable term. But now consider the following term, which is equivalent to the one above up to structural congruence, by extrusion of (νG) across an ambient boundary:

$$(\nu m{:}W)(\nu G)m[(\nu n{:}G[Shh])\langle n\rangle]$$

This term might appear typeable (contradicting the subject congruence property) because the message $\langle n\rangle{:}G[Shh]$ is confined to the ambient m, and $m[\ldots]$ can be given an arbitrary type, e.g., Shh, which does not contain G. Therefore (νG) would not "see" any occurrence of G escaping from its scope. However, consider the type of m in this term. It must have the form $H[T]$, where H is some group, and T is the type of messages exchanged inside m. But that's $G[Shh]$. So we would have

$$(\nu m{:}H[G[Shh]])(\nu G)m[(\nu n{:}G[Shh])\langle n\rangle]$$

which is not typeable because the first occurrence of G is out of scope.

This example tells us why (νG) *intrusion* (floating inwards) into ambients is not going to break good typing: (νG) cannot enter the scope of the $(\nu m{:}W)$ restriction which creates the name m of an ambient where messages with a G-named type are exchanged. This prevents (νG) from entering such ambients.

Indeed, the following variation (not equivalent to the previous one) is typeable, but (νG) cannot intrude any more:

$$(\nu G)(\nu m{:}H[G[Shh]])m[(\nu n{:}G[Shh])\langle n\rangle]$$

15   Opening Control

Ambient opening is a prerequisite for any communication to happen between processes which did not originate in the same ambient. On the other hand, opening is one of the most delicate operations in the ambient calculus, since the contents of the guest spill inside the host, with two different classes of possible consequences:

– the content of the guest acquires the possibility of performing communications inside the hosts, and of moving the host around;

– the host is now able to examine the content of the guest, mainly in terms of receiving messages sent by the processes inside the guest, and of opening its subambients.

For these reasons, a type system for ambients should support a careful control of the usage of the *open* capability.

15.1   The System

In this section, we enrich the ambient types, $G[T]$, and the capability types, $Cap[T]$, of the previous type system to control usage of the *open* capability.

To control the opening of ambients, we formalize the constraint that the name of any ambient opened by a process is in one of the groups $G_1, \ldots, G_k$, but in no others. To do so, we add an attribute $^{\circ}\{G_1, \ldots, G_k\}$ to ambient types, which now take the form $G[^{\circ}\{G_1, \ldots, G_k\}, T]$. A name of this type is in group G, and names ambients within which processes may exchange messages of type T and may only open ambients in the groups $G_1, \ldots, G_k$. We need to add the same attribute to capability types, which now take the form $Cap[^{\circ}\{G_1, \ldots, G_k\}, T]$. Exercising a capability of this type may unleash exchanges of type T and openings of ambients in groups $G_1, \ldots, G_k$. The typing judgment for processes acquires the form $E \vdash P : ^{\circ}\{G_1, \ldots, G_k\}, T$. The pair $^{\circ}\{G_1, \ldots, G_k\}, T$ constrains both the *opening effects* (what ambients the process opens) and the *exchange effects* (what messages the process exchanges). We call such a pair an *effect*, and introduce the metavariable F to range over effects. It is also convenient to introduce metavariables $\mathbf{G}, \mathbf{H}$ to range over finite sets of groups. The following tables summarize these metavariable conventions and our enhanced syntax for types:

Group Sets:

$\mathbf{G}, \mathbf{H} ::= \{G_1, \ldots, G_k\}$	finite set of groups

Types:

$W ::=$	message type
$\quad G[F]$	name in group G for ambients which contain processes with F effects
$\quad Cap[F]$	capability (unleashes F effects)
$F ::=$	effect
$\quad ^{\circ}\mathbf{H}, T$	may open $\mathbf{H}$, may exchange T
$S, T ::=$	exchange type
$\quad Shh$	no exchange
$\quad W_1 \times \cdots \times W_k$	tuple exchange

The definition of free groups is the same as in Section 14 except that we redefine $fg(W)$ by the equations $fg(G[F]) = \{G\} \cup fg(F)$ and $fg(Cap[F]) = fg(F)$, and we define $fg(F) = \mathbf{H} \cup fg(T)$ where $F = ^{\circ}\mathbf{H}, T$.

The following tables define the type system in detail. There are five basic judgments as before. They have the same format except that the judgment $E \vdash F$, meaning that the effect F is good given environment E, replaces the previous judgment $E \vdash T$. We omit the three rules for deriving good environments; they are exactly as in the previous section. There are two main differences between the other rules below and the rules of the previous section. First, effects, F, replace exchange types, T, throughout. Second, in the rule (Exp Open), the condition $G \in \mathbf{H}$ constrains the opening effect $\mathbf{H}$ of a capability $open\ n$ to include the group G, the group of the name n.

Judgments:

$E \vdash \diamond$	good environment
$E \vdash W$	good message type W
$E \vdash F$	good effect F
$E \vdash M : W$	good message M of message type W
$E \vdash P : F$	good process P with F effects

Good Types:

(Type Amb)
$$\frac{G \in dom(E) \quad E \vdash F}{E \vdash G[F]}$$

(Type Cap)
$$\frac{E \vdash F}{E \vdash Cap[F]}$$

(Effect Shh)
$$\frac{\mathbf{H} \subseteq dom(E) \quad E \vdash \diamond}{E \vdash {}^{\circ}\mathbf{H}, Shh}$$

(Effect Prod)
$$\frac{\mathbf{H} \subseteq dom(E) \quad E \vdash W_1 \quad \cdots \quad E \vdash W_k}{E \vdash {}^{\circ}\mathbf{H}, W_1 \times \cdots \times W_k}$$

Good Messages:

(Exp n)
$$\frac{E', n{:}W, E'' \vdash \diamond}{E', n{:}W, E'' \vdash n : W}$$

(Exp ϵ)
$$\frac{E \vdash Cap[F]}{E \vdash \epsilon : Cap[F]}$$

(Exp .)
$$\frac{E \vdash M : Cap[F] \quad E \vdash M' : Cap[F]}{E \vdash M.M' : Cap[F]}$$

(Exp In)
$$\frac{E \vdash n : G[F] \quad E \vdash {}^{\circ}\mathbf{H}, T}{E \vdash in\ n : Cap[{}^{\circ}\mathbf{H}, T]}$$

(Exp Out)
$$\frac{E \vdash n : G[F] \quad E \vdash {}^{\circ}\mathbf{H}, T}{E \vdash out\ n : Cap[{}^{\circ}\mathbf{H}, T]}$$

(Exp Open)
$$\frac{E \vdash n : G[{}^{\circ}\mathbf{H}, T] \quad G \in \mathbf{H}}{E \vdash open\ n : Cap[{}^{\circ}\mathbf{H}, T]}$$

Good Processes:

(Proc Action)
$$\frac{E \vdash M : Cap[F] \quad E \vdash P : F}{E \vdash M.P : F}$$

(Proc Amb)
$$\frac{E \vdash M : G[F] \quad E \vdash P : F \quad E \vdash F'}{E \vdash M[P] : F'}$$

(Proc Res)

$$\frac{E, n{:}G[F] \vdash P : F'}{E \vdash (\nu n{:}G[F])P : F'}$$

(Proc GRes)

$$\frac{E, G \vdash P : F \quad G \notin fg(F)}{E \vdash (\nu G)P : F}$$

(Proc Zero)

$$\frac{}{E \vdash \mathbf{0} : F}$$

(Proc Par)

$$\frac{E \vdash P : F \quad E \vdash Q : F}{E \vdash P \mid Q : F}$$

(Proc Repl)

$$\frac{E \vdash P : F}{E \vdash {!}P : F}$$

(Proc Input)

$$\frac{E, n_1{:}W_1, \ldots, n_k{:}W_k \vdash P : {}^\circ\mathbf{H}, W_1 \times \cdots \times W_k}{E \vdash (n_1{:}W_1, \ldots, n_k{:}W_k).P : {}^\circ\mathbf{H}, W_1 \times \cdots \times W_k}$$

(Proc Output)

$$\frac{E \vdash M_1 : W_1 \quad \cdots \quad E \vdash M_k : W_k \quad \mathbf{H} \subseteq dom(E)}{E \vdash \langle M_1, \ldots, M_k \rangle : {}^\circ\mathbf{H}, W_1 \times \cdots \times W_k}$$

(Proc Go)

$$\frac{E \vdash N : Cap[{}^\circ\mathbf{H}, T] \quad E \vdash M : G[F] \quad E \vdash P : F \quad E \vdash F'}{E \vdash go\ N.M[P] : F'}$$

15.2 Subject Reduction

We obtain a subject reduction result.

Theorem 2. *If* $E \vdash P : F$ *and* $P \to Q$ *then there are* G_1, ..., G_k *such that* $G_1, \ldots, G_k, E \vdash Q : F$.

Here is a simple example of a typing derivable in this system:

$$G, n{:}G[{}^\circ\{G\}, Shh] \vdash n[\mathbf{0}] \mid open\ n.\mathbf{0} : {}^\circ\{G\}, Shh$$

This asserts that the whole process $n[\mathbf{0}] \mid open\ n.\mathbf{0}$ is well-typed and opens only ambients in the group G.

On the other hand, one might expect the following variant to be derivable, but it is not:

$$G, n{:}G[{}^\circ\{\}, Shh] \vdash n[\mathbf{0}] \mid open\ n.\mathbf{0} : {}^\circ\{G\}, Shh$$

This is because the typing rule (Exp Open) requires the effect unleashed by the *open n* capability to be the same as the effect contained within the ambient n. But the opening effect ${}^\circ\{\}$ specified by the type $G[{}^\circ\{\}, Shh]$ of n cannot be the same as the effect unleashed by *open n*, because (Exp Open) also requires the latter to at least include the group G of n.

This feature of (Exp Open) has a positive side-effect: the type $G[{}^\circ\mathbf{G}, T]$ of an ambient name n not only tells which opening effects may happen inside the ambient, but also tells whether n may be opened from outside: it is openable only if $G \in \mathbf{G}$, since this is the only case when $open\ n.\mathbf{0} \mid n[P]$ may be well-typed. Hence, the presence of G in the set $\mathbf{G}$ may either mean that n is meant to be an ambient within which other ambients in group G may be opened, or that it is meant to be an openable ambient.

More generally, because of the shape of the open rule, the opening effects in the ambient type of n not only record the openings that may take place inside the ambient, but also the opening effects of any ambient m which is going to open n, and, recursively, of any ambient which is going to open m as well. A similar phenomenon occurs with exchange types and with the subjective-crossing effects of the next section.

While this turns out to be unproblematic for the examples we consider in these notes, one may prefer to avoid this "inward propagation" of effects by replacing (Exp Open) with the following rule:

$$\frac{E \vdash n : G[^{\circ}\mathbf{H}, T]}{E \vdash open\ n : Cap[^{\circ}(\{G\} \cup \mathbf{H}), T]}$$

With this rule, we could derive that the example process above, $n[\mathbf{0}] \mid open\ n.\mathbf{0}$, has effect $^{\circ}\{G\}, Shh$, with no need to attribute this effect to processes running inside n itself, but unfortunately, subject reduction fails. To see this, consider the process $open\ n \mid n[open\ m]$, which can be assigned the effect $^{\circ}\{G, H\}, Shh$:

$$G, H, m{:}G[^{\circ}\{\}, Shh], n{:}H[^{\circ}\{G\}, Shh] \vdash open\ n \mid n[open\ m] : {}^{\circ}\{G, H\}, Shh$$

The process reduces in one step to $open\ m$, but we cannot derive the following:

$$G, H, m{:}G[^{\circ}\{\}, Shh], n{:}H[^{\circ}\{G\}, Shh] \vdash open\ m : {}^{\circ}\{G, H\}, Shh$$

To obtain a subject reduction property in the presence of the rule displayed above, we should introduce a notion of subtyping, such that if $\mathbf{G} \subseteq \mathbf{H}$ and a process has type $^{\circ}\mathbf{G}, T$, then the process has type $^{\circ}\mathbf{H}, T$ too. This would complicate the type system, as shown in [Zim00]. Moreover, we would lose the indirect way of declaring ambient openability, so we prefer to stick to the basic approach.

16   Crossing Control

This section presents the third and final type system of these notes. We obtain it by enriching the type system of the previous section with attributes to control the mobility of ambients.

16.1   The System

Movement operators enable an ambient n to cross the boundary of another ambient m either by entering it via an $in\ m$ capability or by exiting it via an $out\ m$ capability. In the type system of this section, the type of n lists those groups that may be crossed; the ambient n may only cross the boundary of another ambient m if the group of m is included in this list. In our typed calculus, there are two kinds of movement, subjective moves and objective moves, for reasons explained in Section 16.2. Therefore, we separately list those groups that may be crossed by objective moves and those groups that may be crossed by subjective moves.

We add new attributes to the syntax of ambient types, effects, and capability types. An ambient type acquires the form $G^\frown \mathbf{G}'[^\frown\mathbf{G},^\circ\mathbf{H}, T]$. An ambient of this type is in group G, may cross ambients in groups $\mathbf{G}'$ by objective moves, may cross ambients in groups $\mathbf{G}$ by subjective moves, may open ambients in groups $\mathbf{H}$, and may contain exchanges of type T. An effect, F, of a process is now of the form $^\frown\mathbf{G},^\circ\mathbf{H}, T$. It asserts that the process may exercise *in* and *out* capabilities to accomplish subjective moves across ambients in groups $\mathbf{G}$, that the process may open ambients in groups $\mathbf{H}$, and that the process may exchange messages of type T. Finally, a capability type retains the form $Cap[F]$, but with the new interpretation of F. Exercising a capability of this type may unleash F effects.

Types:

$W ::=$	message type
$\quad G^\frown\mathbf{G}[F]$	name in group G for ambients which cross $\mathbf{G}$
	objectively and contain processes with F effects
$\quad Cap[F]$	capability (unleashes F effects)
$F ::=$	effect
$\quad ^\frown\mathbf{G},^\circ\mathbf{H}, T$	crosses $\mathbf{G}$, opens $\mathbf{H}$, exchanges T
$S, T ::=$	exchange type
$\quad Shh$	no exchange
$\quad W_1 \times \cdots \times W_k$	tuple exchange

The definition of free groups is the same as in Section 14 except that we redefine $fg(W)$ by the equations $fg(G^\frown\mathbf{G}[F]) = \{G\} \cup \mathbf{G} \cup fg(F)$ and $fg(Cap[F]) = fg(F)$, and we define $fg(F) = \mathbf{G} \cup \mathbf{H} \cup fg(T)$ where $F = {}^\frown\mathbf{G},^\circ\mathbf{H}, T$.

The format of the five judgments making up the system is the same as in Section 15. We omit the three rules defining good environments; they are as in Section 14. There are two main changes to the previous system to control mobility. First, (Exp In) and (Exp Out) change to assign a type $Cap[^\frown\mathbf{G},^\circ\mathbf{H}, T]$ to capabilities *in n* and *out n* only if $G \in \mathbf{G}$ where G is the group of n. Second, (Proc Go) changes to allow an objective move of an ambient of type $G^\frown\mathbf{G}'[F]$ by a capability of type $Cap[^\frown\mathbf{G},^\circ\mathbf{H}, T]$ only if $\mathbf{G} = \mathbf{G}'$.

Good Types:

(Type Amb)
$$\frac{G \in dom(E) \quad \mathbf{G} \subseteq dom(E) \quad E \vdash F}{E \vdash G^\frown\mathbf{G}[F]}$$

(Type Cap)
$$\frac{E \vdash F}{E \vdash Cap[F]}$$

(Effect Shh)
$$\frac{\mathbf{G} \subseteq dom(E) \quad \mathbf{H} \subseteq dom(E) \quad E \vdash \diamond}{E \vdash {}^\frown\mathbf{G},^\circ\mathbf{H}, Shh}$$

(Effect Prod)

$$\frac{\mathbf{G} \subseteq dom(E) \quad \mathbf{H} \subseteq dom(E) \quad E \vdash W_1 \quad \cdots \quad E \vdash W_k}{E \vdash {}^\frown\mathbf{G}, {}^\circ\mathbf{H}, W_1 \times \cdots \times W_k}$$

Good Messages:

(Exp n)

$$\frac{E', n{:}W, E'' \vdash \diamond}{E', n{:}W, E'' \vdash n : W}$$

(Exp ϵ)

$$\frac{E \vdash Cap[F]}{E \vdash \epsilon : Cap[F]}$$

(Exp .)

$$\frac{E \vdash M : Cap[F] \quad E \vdash M' : Cap[F]}{E \vdash M.M' : Cap[F]}$$

(Exp In)

$$\frac{E \vdash n : G {}^\frown\mathbf{G}'[F] \quad E \vdash {}^\frown\mathbf{G}, {}^\circ\mathbf{H}, T \quad G \in \mathbf{G}}{E \vdash in\ n : Cap[{}^\frown\mathbf{G}, {}^\circ\mathbf{H}, T]}$$

(Exp Out)

$$\frac{E \vdash n : G {}^\frown\mathbf{G}'[F] \quad E \vdash {}^\frown\mathbf{G}, {}^\circ\mathbf{H}, T \quad G \in \mathbf{G}}{E \vdash out\ n : Cap[{}^\frown\mathbf{G}, {}^\circ\mathbf{H}, T]}$$

(Exp Open)

$$\frac{E \vdash n : G {}^\frown\mathbf{G}'[{}^\frown\mathbf{G}, {}^\circ\mathbf{H}, T] \quad G \in \mathbf{H}}{E \vdash open\ n : Cap[{}^\frown\mathbf{G}, {}^\circ\mathbf{H}, T]}$$

Good Processes:

(Proc Action)

$$\frac{E \vdash M : Cap[F] \quad E \vdash P : F}{E \vdash M.P : F}$$

(Proc Amb)

$$\frac{E \vdash M : G {}^\frown\mathbf{G}[F] \quad E \vdash P : F \quad E \vdash F'}{E \vdash M[P] : F'}$$

(Proc Res)

$$\frac{E, n{:}G {}^\frown\mathbf{G}[F] \vdash P : F'}{E \vdash (\nu n{:}G {}^\frown\mathbf{G}[F])P : F'}$$

(Proc GRes)

$$\frac{E, G \vdash P : F \quad G \notin fg(F)}{E \vdash (\nu G)P : F}$$

(Proc Zero)

$$\frac{E \vdash F}{E \vdash \mathbf{0} : F}$$

(Proc Par)

$$\frac{E \vdash P : F \quad E \vdash Q : F}{E \vdash P \mid Q : F}$$

(Proc Repl)

$$\frac{E \vdash P : F}{E \vdash {!}P : F}$$

(Proc Input)

$$\frac{E, n_1{:}W_1, \ldots, n_k{:}W_k \vdash P : {}^\frown\mathbf{G}, {}^\circ\mathbf{H}, W_1 \times \cdots \times W_k}{E \vdash (n_1{:}W_1, \ldots, n_k{:}W_k).P : {}^\frown\mathbf{G}, {}^\circ\mathbf{H}, W_1 \times \cdots \times W_k}$$

(Proc Output)

$$\frac{E \vdash M_1 : W_1 \quad \cdots \quad E \vdash M_k : W_k \quad \mathbf{G} \subseteq dom(E) \quad \mathbf{H} \subseteq dom(E)}{E \vdash \langle M_1, \ldots, M_k \rangle : {}^\frown\mathbf{G}, {}^\circ\mathbf{H}, W_1 \times \cdots \times W_k}$$

(Proc Go)

$$\frac{E \vdash N : Cap[{}^\frown\mathbf{G}, {}^\circ\mathbf{H}, T] \quad E \vdash M : G \,{}^\frown\mathbf{G}[F] \quad E \vdash P : F \quad E \vdash F'}{E \vdash go\ N.M[P] : F'}$$

Theorem 3. *If $E \vdash P : F$ and $P \to Q$ then there are $G_1, \ldots, G_k$ such that $G_1, \ldots, G_k, E \vdash Q : F$.*

16.2   The Need for Objective Moves

We can now show how primitive typing rules for objective moves allow us to assign better types in some crucial situations. Recall the untyped example from Section 11. Suppose we have two groups Ch and Pk (for channels and packets). Let W be any well-formed type (where Ch and Pk may appear), and set P to be the example process:

$$P = a[p[out\ a.in\ b.\langle c \rangle]] \mid b[open\ p.(x{:}W).x[]]$$

Let

$$
\begin{aligned}
E = \ & Ch, Pk, \\
& a{:}Ch\ {}^\frown\{\}[{}^\frown\{\},{}^\circ\{\}, Shh], \\
& b{:}Ch\ {}^\frown\{\}[{}^\frown\{Ch\},{}^\circ\{Pk\}, W], \\
& c{:}W, \\
& p{:}Pk\ {}^\frown\{\}[{}^\frown\{Ch\},{}^\circ\{Pk\}, W]
\end{aligned}
$$

and we can derive the typings:

$$
\begin{aligned}
& E \vdash out\ a.in\ b.\langle c \rangle : {}^\frown\{Ch\},{}^\circ\{Pk\}, W \\
& E \vdash open\ p.(x{:}W).x[] : {}^\frown\{Ch\},{}^\circ\{Pk\}, W \\
& E \vdash P : {}^\frown\{\},{}^\circ\{\}, Shh
\end{aligned}
$$

From the typing $a : Ch\ {}^\frown\{\}[{}^\frown\{\},{}^\circ\{\}, Shh]$, we can tell that a is an immobile ambient in which nothing is exchanged and that cannot be opened. From the typings $p{:}Pk\ {}^\frown\{\}[{}^\frown\{Ch\},{}^\circ\{Pk\}, W], b{:}Ch\ {}^\frown\{\}[{}^\frown\{Ch\},{}^\circ\{Pk\}, W]$, we can tell that the ambients b and p cross only Ch ambients, open only Pk ambients, and contain W exchanges; the typing of p also tells us it can be opened. This is not fully satisfactory, since, if b were meant to be immobile, we would like to express this immobility invariant in its type. However, since b opens a subjectively mobile ambient, then b must be typed as if it were subjectively mobile itself. The problem is quite general, as it applies to any immobile ambient wishing to open a subjectively mobile one.

This problem can be solved by replacing the subjective moves by objective moves, since objective moves are less expressive than subjective moves, but they cannot be inherited by opening another ambient. Let Q be the example process with objective instead of subjective moves:

$$Q = a[go(out\ a.in\ b).p[\langle c\rangle]] \mid b[open\ p.(x{:}W).x[]]$$

Let

$$
\begin{aligned}
E = {}&Ch, Pk,\\
&a{:}Ch \,^\frown\{\}[^\frown\{\},^\circ\{\}, Shh],\\
&b{:}Ch \,^\frown\{\}[^\frown\{\},^\circ\{Pk\}, W],\\
&c{:}W,\\
&p{:}Pk \,^\frown\{Ch\}[^\frown\{\},^\circ\{Pk\}, W]
\end{aligned}
$$

and we can derive:

$$
\begin{aligned}
&E \vdash out\ a.in\ b : Cap[^\frown\{Ch\},^\circ\{\}, Shh]\\
&E \vdash go(out\ a.in\ b).p[\langle c\rangle] : \,^\frown\{\},^\circ\{\}, Shh\\
&E \vdash open\ p.(x{:}W).x[] : \,^\frown\{\},^\circ\{Pk\}, W\\
&E \vdash Q : \,^\frown\{\},^\circ\{\}, Shh
\end{aligned}
$$

The typings of a and c are unchanged, but the new typings of p and b are more informative. We can tell from the typing $p{:}Pk \,^\frown\{Ch\}[^\frown\{\},^\circ\{Pk\}, W]$ that movement of p is due to objective rather than subjective moves. Moreover, as desired, we can tell from the typing $b{:}Ch \,^\frown\{\}[^\frown\{\},^\circ\{Pk\}, W]$ that the ambient b is immobile.

This example suggests that in some situations objective moves lead to more informative typings than subjective moves. Still, subjective moves are essential for moving ambients containing running processes. An extended example in the next section illustrates the type system of this section; the treatment of thread mobility makes essential use of subjective moves.

17   Encoding a Distributed Language

In this section, we consider a fragment of a typed, distributed language in which mobile threads can migrate between immobile network nodes. We obtain a semantics for this form of thread mobility via a translation into the ambient calculus. In the translation, ambients model both threads and nodes. The encoding can be typed in all three of the systems presented in these notes; for the sake of brevity we describe the encoding only for the full system of Section 16. The encoding illustrates how groups can be used to partition the set of ambient names according to their intended usage, and how opening and crossing control allows the programmer to state interesting invariants. In particular, the typing of the translation guarantees that an ambient modelling a node moves neither subjectively nor objectively. On the other hand, an ambient modelling a thread is free to move subjectively, but is guaranteed not to move objectively.

17.1   The Distributed Language

The computational model is that there is an unstructured collection of named network nodes, each of which hosts a collection of named communication channels and anonymous threads. This is similar to the computational models underlying various distributed variants of the pi calculus, such as those proposed by Amadio and Prasad [AP94], Riely and Hennessy [RH98], and Sewell [Sew98]. In another paper [CG99], we show how to mimic Telescript's computational model by translation into the ambient calculus. In the language fragment we describe here, communication is based on named communication channels (as in the pi calculus) rather than by direct agent-to-agent communication (as in our stripped down version of Telescript). As in our previous paper, we focus on language constructs for mobility, synchronization, and communication. We omit standard constructs for data processing and control flow. They could easily be added.

To introduce the syntax of our language fragment, here is a simple example:

$$node\ a\ [channel\ a_c\ |\ thread[\overline{a_c}\langle b, b_c\rangle]]\ |\ node\ b\ [channel\ b_c]\ |$$
$$node\ c\ [thread[go\ a.a_c(x{:}Node, y{:}Ch[Node]).go\ x.\overline{y}\langle a\rangle]$$

This program describes a network consisting of three network nodes, named a, b, and c. Node a hosts a channel a_c and a thread running the code $\overline{a_c}\langle b, b_c\rangle$, which simply sends the pair $\langle b, b_c\rangle$ on the channel a_c. Node b hosts a channel b_c. Finally, node c hosts a single thread, running the code:

$$go\ a.a_c(x{:}Node, y{:}Ch[Node]).go\ x.\overline{y}\langle a\rangle$$

The effect of this is to move the thread from node c to node a. There it awaits a message sent on the communication channel a_c. We may assume that it receives the message $\langle b, b_c\rangle$ being sent by the thread already at a. (If there were another thread at node a sending another message, the receiver thread would end up receiving one or other of the messages.) The thread then migrates to node b, where it transmits a message a on the channel b_c.

Messages on communication channels are assigned types, ranged over by Ty. The type $Node$ is the type of names of network nodes. The type $Ch[Ty_1, \ldots, Ty_k]$ is the type of a polyadic communication channel. The messages communicated on such a channel are k-tuples whose components have types $Ty_1, \ldots, Ty_k$. In the setting of the example above, channel a_c has type $Ch[Node, Ch[Node]]$, and channel b_c has type $Ch[Node]$.

Next, we describe the formal grammar of our language fragment. A *network*, *Net*, is a collection of nodes, built up using composition *Net | Net* and restrictions $(\nu n{:}Ty)Net$. A *crowd*, *Cro*, is the group of threads and channels hosted by a node. Like networks, crowds are built up using composition *Cro | Cro* and restriction $(\nu n{:}Ty)Cro$. A *thread*, *Th*, is a mobile thread of control. As well as the constructs illustrated above, a thread may include the constructs *fork(Cro).Th* and *spawn n [Cro].Th*. The first forks a new crowd *Cro* inside the current node, and continues with *Th*. The second spawns a new node *node n [Cro]* outside the current node, at the network level, and continues with *Th*.

A Fragment of a Typed, Distributed Programming Language:

$Ty ::=$	type
$Node$	name of a node
$Ch[Ty_1, \ldots, Ty_k]$	name of a channel
$Net ::=$	network
$(\nu n{:}Ty)Net$	restriction
$Net \mid Net$	network composition
$node\ n\ [Cro]$	node
$Cro ::=$	crowd of channels and threads
$(\nu n{:}Ty)\ Cro$	restriction
$Cro \mid Cro$	crowd composition
$channel\ c$	channel
$thread[Th]$	thread
$Th ::=$	thread
$go\ n.\ Th$	migration
$\bar{c}\langle n_1, \ldots, n_k \rangle$	output to a channel
$c(x_1{:}Ty_1, \ldots, x_k{:}Ty_k).\ Th$	input from a channel
$fork(Cro).\ Th$	fork a crowd
$spawn\ n\ [Cro].\ Th$	spawn a new node

In the phrases $(\nu n{:}Ty)Net$ and $(\nu n{:}Ty)\ Cro$, the name n is bound; its scope is Net and Cro, respectively. In the phrase $c(x_1{:}Ty_1, \ldots, x_k{:}Ty_k).\ Th$, the names x_1, $\ldots, x_k$ are bound; their scope is the phrase Th.

The type system of our language controls the typing of messages on communication channels, much as in previous schemes for the pi calculus [Mil99]. We formalize the type system using five judgments, defined by the following rules.

Judgments:

$E \vdash \diamond$	good environment
$E \vdash n : Ty$	name n has type Ty
$E \vdash Net$	good network
$E \vdash Cro$	good crowd
$E \vdash Th$	good thread

Typing Rules:

$$\frac{}{\varnothing \vdash \diamond} \qquad \frac{E \vdash \diamond \quad n \notin dom(E)}{E, n{:}Ty \vdash \diamond} \qquad \frac{E, n{:}Ty, E' \vdash \diamond}{E, n{:}Ty, E' \vdash n : Ty} \qquad \frac{E, n{:}Ty \vdash Net}{E \vdash (\nu n{:}Ty)Net}$$

$$\frac{E \vdash Net \quad E \vdash Net'}{E \vdash Net \mid Net'} \qquad \frac{E \vdash n : Node \quad E \vdash Cro}{E \vdash node\ n\ [Cro]} \qquad \frac{E, n{:}Ty \vdash Cro}{E \vdash (\nu n{:}Ty)\ Cro}$$

$$\frac{E \vdash Cro \quad E \vdash Cro'}{E \vdash Cro \mid Cro'} \qquad \frac{E \vdash c : Ch[Ty_1, \ldots, Ty_k]}{E \vdash channel\ c} \qquad \frac{E \vdash Th}{E \vdash thread[Th]}$$

$$\frac{E \vdash n : Node \quad E \vdash Th}{E \vdash go\ n.\,Th} \qquad \frac{E \vdash c : Ch[Ty_1, \ldots, Ty_k] \quad E \vdash n_i : Ty_i \quad \forall i \in 1..k}{E \vdash \bar{c}\langle n_1, \ldots, n_k \rangle}$$

$$\frac{E \vdash c : Ch[Ty_1, \ldots, Ty_k] \quad E, x_1 : Ty_1, \ldots, x_k : Ty_k \vdash Th}{E \vdash c(x_1 : Ty_1, \ldots, x_k : Ty_k).\,Th}$$

$$\frac{E \vdash Cro \quad E \vdash Th}{E \vdash fork(Cro).\,Th} \qquad \frac{E \vdash n : Node \quad E \vdash Cro \quad E \vdash Th}{E \vdash spawn\ n\ [Cro].\,Th}$$

17.2 Typed Translation to the Ambient Calculus

In this section, we translate our distributed language to the typed ambient calculus of Section 16.

The basic idea of the translation is that ambients model nodes, channels, and threads. For each channel, there is a name for a buffer ambient, of group Ch^b, and there is a second name, of group Ch^p, for packets exchanged within the channel buffer. Similarly, for each node, there is a name, of group $Node^b$, for the node itself, and a second name, of group $Node^p$, for short-lived ambients that help fork crowds within the node, or to spawn other nodes. Finally, there is a group Thr to classify the names of ambients that model threads. The following table summarizes these five groups:

Global Groups Used in the Translation:

$Node^b$	ambients that model nodes
$Node^p$	ambients to help fork crowds or spawn nodes
Ch^b	ambients that model channel buffers
Ch^p	ambients that model packets on a channel
Thr	ambients that model threads

We begin the translation by giving types in the ambient calculus corresponding to types in the distributed language. Each type Ty gets translated to a pair $[\![Ty]\!]^b$, $[\![Ty]\!]^p$ of ambient calculus types. Throughout this section, we omit the curly braces when writing singleton group sets; for example, we write $^\frown Node^b$ as a shorthand for $^\frown \{Node^b\}$.

First, if Ty is a node type, $[\![Ty]\!]^b$ is the type of an ambient (of group $Node^b$) modelling a node, and $[\![Ty]\!]^p$ is the type of helper ambients (of group $Node^p$). Second, if Ty is a channel type, $[\![Ty]\!]^b$ is the type of an ambient (of group Ch^b) modelling a channel buffer, and $[\![Ty]\!]^p$ is the type of a packet ambient (of group Ch^p).

Translations $[\![Ty]\!]^b$, $[\![Ty]\!]^p$ of a Type Ty:

$[\![Node]\!]^b \triangleq$
    $Node^b\ ^\frown Node^b[^\frown\{\},{}^\circ Node^p, Shh]$

$$[\![Node]\!]^p \triangleq$$
$$\qquad Node^p \frown Thr[\frown\{\}, {}^\circ Node^p, Shh]$$
$$[\![Ch[Ty_1, \ldots, Ty_k]]\!]^b \triangleq$$
$$\qquad Ch^b \frown\{\}[\frown\{\}, {}^\circ Ch^p, [\![Ty_1]\!]^b \times [\![Ty_1]\!]^p \times \cdots \times [\![Ty_k]\!]^b \times [\![Ty_k]\!]^p]$$
$$[\![Ch[Ty_1, \ldots, Ty_k]]\!]^p \triangleq$$
$$\qquad Ch^p \frown\{Thr, Ch\}[\frown\{\}, {}^\circ Ch^p, [\![Ty_1]\!]^b \times [\![Ty_1]\!]^p \times \cdots \times [\![Ty_k]\!]^b \times [\![Ty_k]\!]^p]$$

These typings say a lot about the rest of the translation, because of the presence of five different groups. Nodes and helpers are silent ambients, whereas tuples of ambient names are exchanged within both channel buffers and packets. None of these ambients is subjectively mobile—in this translation only threads are subjectively mobile. On the other hand, nodes and helpers may both objectively cross nodes, while buffers are objectively immobile, and packets objectively cross both threads and buffers. Finally, both nodes and helpers may open only helpers, and both buffers and packets may open only packets (actually, the ${}^\circ Ch^p$ annotation inside the type of a packet c^p of group Ch^p means that c^p can be opened, and similarly for helpers).

Next, we translate networks to typed processes. A restriction of a single name is sent to restrictions of a couple of names: either names for a node and helpers, if the name is a node, or names for a buffer and packets, if the name is a channel. A composition is simply translated to a composition. A network node n is translated to an ambient named n^b representing the node, containing a replicated $open\, n^p$, where n^p is the name of helper ambients for that node.

Translation $[\![Net]\!]$ of a Network Net:

$$[\![(\nu n : Ty)Net]\!] \triangleq (\nu n^b : [\![Ty]\!]^b)(\nu n^p : [\![Ty]\!]^p)[\![Net]\!]$$
$$[\![Net \mid Net]\!] \triangleq [\![Net]\!] \mid [\![Net]\!]$$
$$[\![node\, n\, [Cro]]\!] \triangleq n^b[!open\, n^p \mid [\![Cro]\!]_n]$$

The translation $[\![Cro]\!]_n$ of a crowd is indexed by the name n of the node in which the crowd is located. Restrictions and compositions in crowds are translated like their counterparts at the network level. A channel c is represented by a buffer ambient c^b of group Ch^b. It is initially empty but for a replicated $open\, c^p$, where c^p is the name, of group Ch^p, of packets on the channel. The replication allows inputs and outputs on the channel to meet and exchange messages.

An ambient of the following type models each thread:

$$Thr \frown\{\}[\frown Node^b, {}^\circ Sync, Shh]$$

From the type, we know that a thread ambient is silent, that it crosses node boundaries by subjective moves but crosses nothing by objective moves, and that it may only open ambients in the $Sync$ group. Such ambients help synchronize parallel processes in thread constructs such as receiving on a channel. A fresh group named $Sync$ is created by a $(\nu Sync)$ in the translation of each thread. The existence of a separate lexical scope for $Sync$ in each thread implies there can be no accidental transmission between threads of the names of private synchronization ambients.

Translation $[\![Cro]\!]_n$ of a Crowd Cro Located at Node n:

$$[\![(\nu m : Ty)\, Cro]\!]_n \triangleq (\nu m^b : [\![Ty]\!]^b)(\nu m^p : [\![Ty]\!]^p)[\![Cro]\!]_n$$

$$[\![Cro \mid Cro]\!]_n \triangleq [\![Cro]\!]_n \mid [\![Cro]\!]_n$$

$$[\![channel\ c]\!]_n \triangleq c^b[!open\ c^p]$$

$$[\![thread\ Th]\!]_n \triangleq$$
$$(\nu Sync)(\nu t : Thr\ ^\frown\{\}[^\frown Node^b, {}^\circ Sync, Shh])t[\![Th]\!]_n^t]\quad \text{for } t \notin fn([\![Th]\!]_n^t)$$

The translation $[\![Th]\!]_n^t$ of a thread is indexed by the name t of the thread and by the name n of the node in which the thread is enclosed.

A migration $go\ m.\,Th$ is translated to subjective moves taking the thread t out of the current node n and into the target node m.

An output $\bar{c}\langle n_1, \ldots, n_k \rangle$ is translated to a packet ambient c^p that travels to the channel buffer c^b, where it is opened, and outputs a tuple of names.

An input $c(x_1 : Ty_1, \ldots, x_k : Ty_k).\,Th$ is translated to a packet ambient c^p that travels to the channel buffer c^b, where it is opened, and inputs a tuple of names; the tuple is returned to the host thread t by way of a synchronization ambient s, that exits the buffer and then returns to the thread.

A fork $fork(Cro).\,Th$ is translated to a helper ambient n^p that exits the thread t and gets opened within the enclosing node n. This unleashes the crowd Cro and allows a synchronization ambient s to return to the thread t, where it triggers the continuation Th.

A spawn $spawn\ m\ [Cro].\,Th$ is translated to a helper ambient n^p that exits the thread t and gets opened within the enclosing node n^b. This unleashes an objective move $go(out\ n^b).m^b[!open\ m^p \mid [\![Cro]\!]_m]]$ that travels out of the node to the top, network level, where it starts the fresh node $m^b[!open\ m^p \mid [\![Cro]\!]_m]]$. Concurrently, a synchronization ambient s returns to the thread t, where it triggers the continuation Th.

Translation $[\![Th]\!]_n^t$ of a Thread Th Named t Located at Node n:

$$[\![go\ m.\,Th]\!]_n^t \triangleq out\ n.in\ m.[\![Th]\!]_m^t$$

$$[\![\bar{c}\langle n_1, \ldots, n_k \rangle]\!]_n^t \triangleq go(out\ t.in\ c^b).c^p[\langle n_1, n_1^p, \ldots, n_k, n_k^p \rangle]$$

$$[\![c(x_1 : Ty_1, \ldots, x_k : Ty_k).\,Th]\!]_n^t \triangleq$$
$$(\nu s : Sync\ ^\frown\{Thr, Ch\}[^\frown Node^b, {}^\circ Sync, Shh])$$
$$(go(out\ t.in\ c^b).$$
$$c^p[(x_1^b : [\![Ty_1]\!]^b, x_1^p : [\![Ty_1]\!]^p, \ldots, x_k^b : [\![Ty_k]\!]^b, x_k^p : [\![Ty_k]\!]^p).$$
$$go(out\ c^b.in\ t).s[open\ s.[\![Th]\!]_n^t]] \mid$$
$$open\ s.s[])$$
$$\text{for } s \notin \{t, c^b, c^p\} \cup fn([\![Th]\!]_n^t)$$

$$[\![fork(Cro).Th]\!]_n^t \triangleq$$
$$(\nu s{:}Sync \,^\frown Thr[^\frown Node^b, {}^\circ Sync, Shh])$$
$$(go\ out\ t.n^p[go\ in\ t.s[] \mid [\![Cro]\!]_n] \mid open\ s.[\![Th]\!]_n^t)$$
$$for\ s \notin \{t, n^p\} \cup [\![Cro]\!]_n \cup [\![Th]\!]_n^t$$
$$[\![spawn\ m\ [Cro].Th]\!]_n^t \triangleq$$
$$(\nu s{:}Sync \,^\frown Thr[^\frown Node^b, {}^\circ Sync, Shh])$$
$$(go\ out\ t.n^p[go\ in\ t.s[] \mid go\ out\ n^b.m^b[!open\ m^p \mid [\![Cro]\!]_m]] \mid$$
$$open\ s.[\![Th]\!]_n^t)$$
$$for\ s \notin \{t, n^b, n^p, m^b, m^p\} \cup fn([\![Cro]\!]_m) \cup fn([\![Th]\!]_n^t)$$

Finally, we translate typing environments as follows.

Translation $[\![E]\!]$ of an Environment E:

$$[\![\varnothing]\!] \triangleq Node^b, Node^p, Ch^b, Ch^p, Thr$$
$$[\![E, c{:}Ty]\!] \triangleq [\![E]\!], c^b{:}[\![Ty]\!]^b, c^p{:}[\![Ty]\!]^p$$

Our translation preserves typing judgments:

Proposition 1.

(1) If $E \vdash Net$ then $[\![E]\!] \vdash [\![Net]\!] : \,^\frown\{\}, {}^\circ\{\}, Shh$.
(2) If $E \vdash Cro$ and $E \vdash n : Node$ then $[\![E]\!] \vdash [\![Cro]\!]_n : \,^\frown\{\}, {}^\circ\{\}, Shh$.
(3) If $E \vdash Th$, $E \vdash n : Node$, $t \notin dom(E)$ then
$[\![E]\!], Sync, t{:}Thr \,^\frown\{\}[^\frown Node^b, {}^\circ Sync, Shh] \vdash [\![Th]\!]_n^t : \,^\frown Node^b, {}^\circ Sync, Shh$.

Apart from having more refined types, this translation is the same as a translation to the type system with binary annotations of [CGG99]. The translation shows that ambients can model a variety of concepts arising in mobile computation: nodes, threads, communication packets and buffers. Groups admit more precise typings for this translation than were possible in the system with binary annotations. For example, here we can tell that a thread ambient subjectively crosses only node ambients, but never crosses helpers, buffers, or packets, and that it is objectively immobile; in the binary system, all we could say was that a thread ambient was subjectively mobile and objectively immobile.

18   Discussion: The Ambient Calculus

In this part, we introduced the ambient calculus as an abstract model for the mobility of hardware and software. We explained some of the type systems that have been proposed for ambients. We gave an application of the calculus as a semantic metalanguage for describing distributed computation. Our full type system tracks the communication, mobility, and opening behaviour of ambients, which are classified by *groups*. A group represents a collection of ambient names; ambient names belong to groups in the same sense that values belong to types. We studied the properties of a new process operator $(\nu G)P$ that lexically scopes groups. Using groups, our type system can impose behavioural constraints like "this ambient crosses only ambients in one set of groups, and only dissolves ambients in another set of groups".

18.1 Related Work on Types

The ambient calculus is related to earlier distributed variants of the pi calculus, some of which have been equipped with type systems. The type system of Amadio [Ama97] prevents a channel from being defined at more than one location. Sewell's system [Sew98] tracks whether communications are local or non-local, so as to allow efficient implementation of local communication. In Riely and Hennessy's calculus [RH98], processes need appropriate permissions to perform actions such as migration; a well-typed process is guaranteed to possess the appropriate permission for any action it attempts. Other work on typing for mobile agents includes a type system by De Nicola, Ferrari, and Pugliese [DFP99] that tracks the access rights an agent enjoys at different localities; type-checking ensures that an agent complies with its access rights.

Our groups are similar to the *sorts* used as static classifications of names in the pi calculus [Mil99]. Our basic system of Section 14 is comparable to Milner's sort system, except that sorts in the pi calculus are mutually recursive; we would have to add a recursion operator to achieve a similar effect. Another difference is that an operator for sort creation does not seem to have been considered in the pi calculus literature. Our operator for group creation can guarantee secrecy properties, as we show in the setting of a typed pi calculus equipped with groups [CGG00b]. Our systems of Sections 15 and 16 depend on groups to constrain the opening and crossing behaviour of processes. We are not aware of any uses of Milner's sorts to control process behaviour beyond controlling the sorts of communicated names.

Apart from Milner's sorts, other static classifications of names occur in derivatives of the pi calculus. We mention two examples. In the type system of Abadi [Aba99] for the spi calculus, names are classified by three static *security levels*—*Public*, *Secret*, and *Any*—to prevent insecure information flows. In the flow analysis of Bodei, Degano, Nielson, and Nielson [BDNN98] for the pi calculus, names are classified by static *channels* and *binders*, again with the purpose of establishing security properties. (Similar flow analyses now exist for the ambient calculus [NNHJ99, HJNN99].) Although there is a similarity between these notions and groups, and indeed to sorts, nothing akin to our (νG) operator appears to have been studied.

There is a connection between groups and the region variables in the work of Tofte and Talpin [TT97] on region-based implementation of the λ-calculus. The store is split into a set of stack-allocated regions, and the type of each stored value is labelled with the region in which the value is stored. The scoping construct *letregion ρ in e* allocates a fresh region, binds it to the region variable ρ, evaluates e, and on completion, deallocates the region bound to ρ. The constructs *letregion ρ in e* and $(\nu G)P$ are similar in that they confer static scopes on the region variable ρ and the group G, respectively. One difference is that in our operational semantics $(\nu G)P$ is simply a scoping construct; it allocates no storage. Another is that scope extrusion laws do not seem to have been explicitly investigated for *letregion*. Still, we can interpret *letregion* in terms of (νG), as is reported elsewhere [DG00].

18.2   Related Work on Ambients

The introduction to this part, Section 10, is extracted from the original article on the ambient calculus [CG00b]; more motivations may be found in another paper [Car99], which develops a graphical metaphor for ambients, the folder calculus.

The rest of this part reports research into type systems for the ambient calculus, some parts of which have been described in conference papers. In [CG99] we have investigated *exchange types*, which subsume standard type systems for processes and functions, but do not impose restrictions on mobility; no groups were present in that system. In [CGG99] we have reported on *immobility* and *locking* annotations, which are basic predicates about mobility, still with no notion of groups; Zimmer [Zim00] proposes inference algorithms for a generalization of this type system. In [CGG00a] we introduce the notion of groups; much of this part of the notes is drawn from that paper.

As well as work on types, there has been work on a variety of other techniques for reasoning about the ambient calculus. In [GC99], we define a form of testing equivalence for the ambient calculus, akin to the testing equivalence we introduced in Part II for the spi calculus; we develop some techniques for proving testing equivalence including a context lemma. Several papers investigate program logics for the ambient calculus; in [CG00a] we introduce a logic with both spatial modalities—for talking about the structure of ambient processes— and temporal modalities—for talking about their evolution over time. A recent paper extends the first with modal operators to express properties of restricted names [CG01]. Two other papers investigate the equivalence induced by the logic [San01] and the complexity of the model checking problem [CDG$^+$01].

Levi and Sangiorgi [LS00] propose a variant of the calculus called Safe Ambients. As well as the original *in*, *out*, and *open* capabilities, they introduce three dual capabilities, written $\overline{in}$, $\overline{out}$, and $\overline{open}$, respectively. To enter a sibling named n, an ambient needs to exercise the *out n* capability, as before, but additionally, the sibling needs to exercise the $\overline{out}\,n$ capability. Similarly, to exit its parent named n, an ambient needs to exercise the *out n* capability, as before, but additionally, the parent needs to exercise the $\overline{out}\,n$ capability. To dissolve an ambient named n, its environment needs to exercise the *open n* capability, as before, but additionally, the ambient itself needs to exercise the $\overline{open}\,n$ capability. The resulting ambient calculus is a little more complicated than the one described here, but the advantages shown by Levi and Sangiorgi are that certain race conditions may be avoided, and in some ways more accurate typings are possible. Bugliese and Castagna [BC01] investigate an extension of Safe Ambients intended to describe security properties; their notion of ambient domain is akin to the notion of group discussed in these notes.

The first implementation of the ambient calculus was a Java applet [Car97]. More recent implementations support mobility between machines distributed on a network; they include an implementation of the original calculus using Jocaml [FLS00], and of Safe Ambients using Java RMI [SV01].

Acknowledgement C.A.R. Hoare and G. Castagna commented on a draft of these notes.

References

[Aba99]   M. Abadi. Secrecy by typing in security protocols. *Journal of the ACM*, 46(5):749–786, September 1999. 289, 323

[ABLP93]   M. Abadi, M. Burrows, B. Lampson, and G. Plotkin. A calculus for access control in distributed systems. *ACM Transactions on Programming Languages and Systems*, 15(4):706–734, 1993. 273

[AF01]   M. Abadi and C. Fournet. Mobile values, new names, and secure communication. In *28th ACM Symposium on Principles of Programming Languages (POPL'01)*, pages 104–115, 2001. 288, 289

[AFG98]   M. Abadi, C. Fournet, and G. Gonthier. Secure communications implementation of channel abstractions. In *13th IEEE Symposium on Logic in Computer Science (LICS'98)*, pages 105–116, 1998. 289

[AG98]   M. Abadi and A. D. Gordon. A bisimulation method for cryptographic protocols. *Nordic Journal of Computing*, 5:267–303, 1998. 289

[AG99]   M. Abadi and A. D. Gordon. A calculus for cryptographic protocols: The spi calculus. *Information and Computation*, 148:1–70, 1999. An extended version with full proofs appears as Digital Equipment Corporation Systems Research Center report No. 149, January 1998. 264, 266

[Ama97]   R. M. Amadio. An asynchronous model of locality, failure, and process mobility. In *COORDINATION 97*, volume 1282 of *Lecture Notes in Computer Science*. Springer, 1997. 293, 323

[AN96]   M. Abadi and R. Needham. Prudent engineering practice for cryptographic protocols. *IEEE Transactions on Software Engineering*, 22(1):6–15, January 1996. 281

[AP94]   R. M. Amadio and S. Prasad. Localities and failures. In *Foundations of Software Technology and Theoretical Computer Science (FST&TCS'94)*, volume 880 of *Lecture Notes in Computer Science*, pages 205–216. Springer, 1994. 317

[AP99]   R. Amadio and S. Prasad. The game of the name in cryptographic tables. In *Advances in Computing Science (ASIAN'99)*, volume 1742 of *Lectures Notes in Computer Science*, pages 5–26. Springer, 1999. 289

[AR00]   M. Abadi and P. Rogaway. Reconciling two views of cryptography. In *Theoretical Computer Science (IFIP TCS 2000)*, volume 1872 of *Lectures Notes in Computer Science*, pages 3–33. Springer, 2000. 273

[BAN89]   M. Burrows, M. Abadi, and R. M. Needham. A logic of authentication. *Proceedings of the Royal Society of London A*, 426:233–271, 1989. 270, 272, 273, 274

[BB90]   G. Berry and G. Boudol. The chemical abstract machine. In *17th ACM Symposium on Principles of Programming Languages (POPL'90)*, pages 81–94, 1990. 284

[BC01]   M. Bugliesi and G. Castagna. Secure safe ambients. In *28th ACM Symposium on Principles of Programming Languages (POPL'01)*, pages 222–235, 2001. 324

[BDNN98]   C. Bodei, P. Degano, F. Nielson, and H. Nielson. Control flow analysis for the π-calculus. In *CONCUR'98: Concurrency Theory*, volume 1466 of *Lecture Notes in Computer Science*, pages 84–98. Springer, 1998. 323

[BN95]   M. Boreale and R. De Nicola. Testing equivalence for mobile processes. *Information and Computation*, 120(2):279–303, August 1995. 272, 286

[BNP99]   M. Boreale, R. De Nicola, and R. Pugliese. Proof techniques for cryptographic processes. In *14th IEEE Symposium on Logic in Computer Science*, pages 157–166, 1999. 289

[Box98]   D. Box. *Essential COM*. Addison-Wesley, 1998. 263

[BR95]   M. Bellare and P. Rogaway. Provably secure session key distribution: The three party case. In *27th ACM Symposium on Theory of Computing*, 1995. 273

[BV01]   C. Bryce and J. Vitek. The JavaSeal mobile agent kernel. *Agent Systems Journal*, 2001. To appear. A preliminary version appears in the proceedings of the *3rd International Symposium on Mobile Agents (MA/ASA'99)*, 1999. 266

[Car95]   L. Cardelli. A language with distributed scope. *Computing Systems*, 8(1):27–59, January 1995. 265, 292

[Car97]   L. Cardelli. Mobile ambient synchronization. SRC Technical Note 1997–013, Digital Equipment Corporation Systems Research Center, July 1997. 325

[Car99]   L. Cardelli. Abstractions for mobile computation. In C. Jensen and J. Vitek, editors, *Secure Internet Programming: Issues in Distributed and Mobile Object Systems*, volume 1603 of *Lecture Notes in Computer Science*, pages 51–94. Springer, 1999. 265, 324

[CDG⁺01]   W. Charatonik, S. Dal Zilio, A. D. Gordon, S. Mukhopadhyay, and J.-M. Talbot. The complexity of model checking mobile ambients. In *Foundations of Software Science and Computation Structures (FoSSaCS'01)*, Lecture Notes in Computer Science. Springer, 2001. To appear. 324

[CG89]   N. Carriero and D. Gelernter. Linda in context. *Communications of the ACM*, 32(4):444–458, 1989. 292

[CG99]   L. Cardelli and A. D. Gordon. Types for mobile ambients. In *26th ACM Symposium on Principles of Programming Languages (POPL'99)*, pages 79–92, January 1999. 266, 298, 317, 324

[CG00a]   L. Cardelli and A. D. Gordon. Anytime, anywhere: Modal logics for mobile ambients. In *27th ACM Symposium on Principles of Programming Languages (POPL'00)*, pages 365–377, 2000. 324

[CG00b]   L. Cardelli and A. D. Gordon. Mobile ambients. *Theoretical Computer Science*, 240:177–213, 2000. 265, 266, 294, 297, 324

[CG01]   L. Cardelli and A. D. Gordon. Logical properties of name restriction. In *Typed Lambda Calculi and Applications (TLCA'01)*, Lecture Notes in Computer Science. Springer, 2001. To appear. 324

[CGG99]   L. Cardelli, G. Ghelli, and A. D. Gordon. Mobility types for mobile ambients. In *26th International Colloquium on Automata, Languages and Programming (ICALP'99)*, volume 1644 of *Lecture Notes in Computer Science*, pages 230–239. Springer, 1999. 322, 324

[CGG00a] L. Cardelli, G. Ghelli, and A. D. Gordon. Ambient groups and mobility types. In *Theoretical Computer Science (IFIP TCS 2000)*, volume 1872 of *Lecture Notes in Computer Science*, pages 333–347. Springer, 2000. 266, 324

[CGG00b] L. Cardelli, G. Ghelli, and A. D. Gordon. Group creation and secrecy. In C. Palamidessi, editor, *CONCUR 2000—Concurrency Theory*, volume 1877 of *Lecture Notes in Computer Science*, pages 365–379. Springer, 2000. 323

[CGZ95]   N. Carriero, D. Gelernter, and L. Zuck. Bauhaus linda. In P. Ciancarini, O. Nierstrasz, and A. Yonezawa, editors, *Object-Based Models and Languages for Concurrent Systems*, volume 924 of *Lecture Notes in Computer Science*, pages 66–76. Springer, 1995. 292

[CH88]   T. Coquand and G. Huet. The calculus of constructions. *Information and Computation*, 76(2/3):95–120, February/March 1988. 297

[Dam96]   M. Dam. Model checking mobile processes. *Information and Computation*, 129(1):35–51, 1996. 272

[Dam98]   M. Dam. Proving trust in systems of second-order processes. In *31st Hawaii International Conference on System Sciences*, volume VII, pages 255–264, 1998. 272

[DES77]   Data encryption standard. Fed. Inform. Processing Standards Pub. 46, National Bureau of Standards, Washington DC, January 1977. 274

[DFP99]   R. De Nicola, G. Ferrari, and R. Pugliese. Types as specifications of access policies. In *Secure Internet Programming 1999*, volume 1603 of *Lecture Notes in Computer Science*, pages 117–146. Springer, 1999. 323

[DG00]   S. Dal Zilio and A. D. Gordon. Region analysis and a π-calculus with groups. In *Mathematical Foundations of Computer Science 2000 (MFCS2000)*, volume 1893 of *Lectures Notes in Computer Science*, pages 1–21. Springer, 2000. 324

[DH76]   W. Diffie and M. Hellman. New directions in cryptography. *IEEE Transactions on Information Theory*, IT-22(6):644–654, November 1976. 287

[DH84]   R. De Nicola and M. C. B. Hennessy. Testing equivalences for processes. *Theoretical Computer Science*, 34:83–133, 1984. 286

[DS81]   D. E. Denning and G. M. Sacco. Timestamps in key distribution protocols. *Communications of the ACM*, 24(8):533–536, 1981. 264

[DY83]   D. Dolev and A. C. Yao. On the security of public key protocols. *IEEE Transactions on Information Theory*, IT-29(2):198–208, 1983. 273

[FG94]   R. Focardi and R. Gorrieri. A classification of security properties for process algebra. *Journal of Computer Security*, 3(1):5–33, 1994. 273

[FG96]   C. Fournet and G. Gonthier. The reflexive CHAM and the Join-calculus. In *23rd ACM Symposium on Principles of Programming Languages (POPL'96)*, pages 372–385, 1996. 264, 266, 293

[FGL+96] C. Fournet, G. Gonthier, J.-J. Lévy, L. Maranget, and D. Rémy. A calculus of mobile agents. In *CONCUR'96: Concurrency Theory*, volume 1119 of *Lecture Notes in Computer Science*, pages 406–421. Springer, 1996. 266, 293

[FLS00]   C. Fournet, J.-J. Lévy, and A. Schmitt. An asynchronous, distributed implementation of mobile ambients. In *Theoretical Computer Science (IFIP TCS 2000)*, volume 1872 of *Lecture Notes in Computer Science*. Springer, 2000. 266, 325

[GC99]   A. D. Gordon and L. Cardelli. Equational properties of mobile ambi-
            ents. In *Foundations of Software Science and Computation Structures
            (FoSSaCS'99)*, volume 1578 of *Lecture Notes in Computer Science*, pages
            212–226. Springer, 1999. An extended version appears as Microsoft Re-
            search Technical Report MSR–TR–99–11, April 1999. 324

[GJ01]   A. D. Gordon and A. Jeffrey. Authenticity by typing for security protocols.
            Submitted for publication. Available at *http://research.microsoft.com/
            ~adg/Publications*, 2001. 289

[GJS96]   J. Gosling, B. Joy, and G. Steele. *The Java language specification.*
            Addison-Wesley, 1996. 292

[GM95]   J. Gray and J. McLean. Using temporal logic to specify and verify cryp-
            tographic protocols (progress report). In *Proceedings of the 8th IEEE
            Computer Security Foundations Workshop*, pages 108–116, 1995. 273

[GS01]   A. D. Gordon and D. Syme. Typing a multi-language intermediate
            code. In *28th ACM Symposium on Principles of Programming Languages
            (POPL'01)*, pages 248–260, 2001. 297

[HJNN99]   R. R. Hansen, J. G. Jensen, F. Nielson, and H. R. Nielson. Abstract inter-
            pretation of mobile ambients. In *Static Analysis Symposium (SAS'99)*, vol-
            ume 1694 of *Lecture Notes in Computer Science*, pages 134–148. Springer,
            1999. 323

[Hoa85]   C. A. R. Hoare. *Communicating Sequential Processes.* Prentice-Hall In-
            ternational, 1985. 263

[IK01]   A. Igarashi and N. Kobayashi. A generic type system for the pi calculus.
            In *28th ACM Symposium on Principles of Programming Languages*, pages
            128–141, 2001. 272

[Kem89]   R. Kemmerer. Analyzing encryption protocols using formal verifica-
            tion techniques. *IEEE Journal on Selected Areas in Communications*,
            7(4):448–457, 1989. 273

[LABW92]   B. Lampson, M. Abadi, M. Burrows, and E. Wobber. Authentication in
            distributed systems: Theory and practice. *ACM Transactions on Com-
            puter Systems*, 10(4):265–310, November 1992. 273

[Lie93]   A. Liebl. Authentication in distributed systems: A bibliography. *ACM
            Operating Systems Review*, 27(4):31–41, 1993. 272

[LMMS98]   P. Lincoln, J. Mitchell, M. Mitchell, and A. Scedrov. A probabilistic
            poly-time framework for protocol analysis. In *Fifth ACM Conference on
            Computer and Communications Security*, pages 112–121, 1998. 273

[Low96]   G. Lowe. Breaking and fixing the Needham-Schroeder public-key protocol
            using CSP and FDR. In T. Margaria and B. Steffen, editors, *Tools and Al-
            gorithms for the Construction and Analysis of Systems (TACAS'96)*, vol-
            ume 1055 of *Lectures Notes in Computer Science*, pages 147–166. Springer,
            1996. 264, 273

[LS00]   F. Levi and D. Sangiorgi. Controlling interference in ambients. In *27th
            ACM Symposium on Principles of Programming Languages (POPL'00)*,
            pages 352–364, 2000. 324

[LY97]   T. Lindholm and F. Yellin. *The Java Virtual Machine Specification.*
            Addison-Wesley, 1997. 297

[Mao96]   W. Mao. On two proposals for on-line bankcard payments using open
            networks: Problems and solutions. In *IEEE Symposium on Security and
            Privacy*, pages 201–210, 1996. 289

[MCF87]   J. K. Millen, S. C. Clark, and S. B. Freedman. The interrogator: Proto-
           col security analysis. *IEEE Transactions on Software Engineering*, SE–
           13(2):274–288, 1987. 273

[Mea92]   C. Meadows. Applying formal methods to the analysis of a key manage-
           ment protocol. *Journal of Computer Security*, 1(1):5–36, 1992. 273

[Mil89]   R. Milner. *Communication and Concurrency*. Prentice-Hall International,
           1989. 263

[Mil92]   R. Milner. Functions as processes. *Mathematical Structures in Computer
           Science*, 2:119–141, 1992. 283

[Mil99]   R. Milner. *Communicating and Mobile Systems: the π-Calculus*. Cam-
           bridge University Press, 1999. 263, 272, 298, 318, 323

[MPW92]   R. Milner, J. Parrow, and D. Walker. A calculus of mobile processes, parts
           I and II. *Information and Computation*, pages 1–40 and 41–77, 1992. 263,
           272

[MPW93]   R. Milner, J. Parrow, and D. Walker. Modal logics for mobile processes.
           Theoretical Computer Science, 114:149–171, 1993. 272

[MS92]   R. Milner and D. Sangiorgi. Barbed bisimulation. In *19th International
           Colloquium on Automata, Languages and Programming (ICALP'92)*, vol-
           ume 623 of *Lecture Notes in Computer Science*. Springer, 1992. 272

[Nee89]   R. M. Needham. Names. In S. Mullender, editor, *Distributed Systems*,
           pages 89–101. Addison-Wesley, 1989. 263

[NFP97]   R. De Nicola, G.-L. Ferrari, and R. Pugliese. Locality based linda: pro-
           gramming with explicit localities. In *Proceedings TAPSOFT'97*, volume
           1214 of *Lecture Notes in Computer Science*, pages 712–726. Springer, 1997.
           293

[NNHJ99]   F. Nielson, H. R. Nielson, R. R. Hansen, and J. G. Jensen. Validating
           firewalls in mobile ambients. In *CONCUR'99: Concurrency Theory*, vol-
           ume 1664 of *Lecture Notes in Computer Science*, pages 463–477. Springer,
           1999. 323

[NS78]   R. M. Needham and M. D. Schroeder. Using encryption for authentication
           in large networks of computers. *Communications of the ACM*, 21(12):993–
           999, 1978. 264, 272

[Ode00]   M. Odersky. Functional nets. In *European Symposium on Programming
           (ESOP 2000)*, volume 1782 of *Lecture Notes in Computer Science*, pages
           1–25. Springer, 2000. 264

[PS96]   B. Pierce and D. Sangiorgi. Typing and subtyping for mobile processes.
           Mathematical Structures in Computer Science, 6(5):409–454, 1996. 272

[PT00]   B. C. Pierce and D. N. Turner. Pict: A programming language based on
           the pi-calculus. In G. Plotkin, C. Stirling, and M. Tofte, editors, *Proof,
           Language and Interaction: Essays in Honour of Robin Milner*. MIT Press,
           2000. 264

[RH98]   J. Riely and M. Hennessy. A typed language for distributed mobile pro-
           cesses. In *25th ACM Symposium on Principles of Programming Languages
           (POPL'98)*, pages 378–390, 1998. 292, 317, 323

[RSA78]   R. L. Rivest, A. Shamir, and L. Adleman. A method for obtaining digital
           signatures and public-key cryptosystems. *Communications of the ACM*,
           21(2):120–126, February 1978. 287

[San01]   D. Sangiorgi. Extensionality and intensionality of the ambient log-
           ics. In *28th ACM Symposium on Principles of Programming Languages
           (POPL'01)*, pages 4–13, 2001. 324

[Sch96a]   S. Schneider. Security properties and CSP. In *IEEE Symposium on Security and Privacy*, pages 174–187, 1996. 273

[Sch96b]   B. Schneier. *Applied Cryptography: Protocols, Algorithms, and Source Code in C*. John Wiley & Sons, Inc., second edition, 1996. 286

[Sew98]   P. Sewell. Global/local subtyping and capability inference for a distributed π-calculus. In *25th International Colloquium on Automata, Languages and Programming (ICALP'98)*, volume 1443 of *Lecture Notes in Computer Science*, pages 695–706. Springer, 1998. 292, 317, 323

[SV01]   D. Sangiorgi and A. Valente. A distributed abstract machine for Safe Ambients. Available from the authors, 2001. 325

[SW01]   D. Sangiorgi and D. Walker. *The π-calculus: a Theory of Mobile Processes*. Cambridge University Press, 2001. 263, 272

[TT97]   M. Tofte and J.-P. Talpin. Region-based memory management. *Information and Computation*, 132(2):109–176, 1997. 323

[VC99]   J. Vitek and G. Castagna. Seal: A framework for secure mobile computations. In *Internet Programming Languages*, volume 1686 of *Lecture Notes in Computer Science*, pages 47–77. Springer, 1999. 266

[Whi96]   J. E. White. Mobile agents. In J. Bradshaw, editor, *Software Agents*. AAAI Press/The MIT Press, 1996. 265, 292

[WL93]   T. Y. C. Woo and S. S. Lam. A semantic model for authentication protocols. In *IEEE Symposium on Security and Privacy*, pages 178–194, 1993. 289

[Zim00]   P. Zimmer. Subtyping and typing algorithms for mobile ambients. In *Foundations of Software Science and Computation Structures (FoSSaCS'00)*, volume 1784 of *Lecture Notes in Computer Science*, pages 375–390. Springer, 2000. 300, 312, 324

Classification of Security Properties*
(Part I: Information Flow)

Riccardo Focardi[1] and Roberto Gorrieri[2]

[1] Dipartimento di Informatica, Università Ca'Foscari di Venezia
focardi@dsi.unive.it
[2] Dipartimento di Scienze dell'informazione, Università di Bologna
gorrieri@cs.unibo.it

Abstract. In the recent years, many formalizations of security properties have been proposed, most of which are based on different underlying models and are consequently difficult to compare. A classification of security properties is thus of interest for understanding the relationships among different definitions and for evaluating the relative merits. In this paper, many non-interference-like properties proposed for computer security are classified and compared in a unifying framework. The resulting taxonomy is evaluated through some case studies of access control in computer systems. The approach has been mechanized, resulting in the tool CoSeC. Various extensions (e.g., the application to cryptographic protocol analysis) and open problems are discussed.

This paper mainly follows [21] and covers the first part of the course "Classification of Security Properties" given by Roberto Gorrieri and Riccardo Focardi at FOSAD'00 school.

1 Introduction

The wide spread of distributed systems, where resources and data are shared among users located almost everywhere in the world, has enormously increased the interest in security issues. In this context, it is likely that a user gets some (possibly) malicious programs from an untrusted source on the net and executes them inside its own system with unpredictable results. Moreover, it could be the case that a system completely secure inside, results to be insecure when performing critical activities such as electronic commerce or home banking, due to a "weak" mechanism for remote connections. It is important to precisely define security properties in order to have formal statements of the correctness of a security mechanism. As a consequence, in the recent years there have been a number of proposals of formal definitions of security properties (see, for instance, [1,2,8,11,12,17,21,30,44,45,51,53,59,60]).

* This work has been partially supported by MURST projects TOSCA, "Certificazione automatica di programmi mediante interpretazione astratta" and "Interpretazione astratta, type systems e analisi control-flow", and also partially supported by Microsoft Research Europe.

R. Focardi and R. Gorrieri (Eds.): FOSAD 2000, LNCS 2171, pp. 331–396, 2001.

In this paper we deal with a particular class of security properties, called *information flow properties*, which aim at controlling the way information may flow among different entities. They have been first proposed as a means to ensure confidentiality, in particular to verify if access control policies are sufficient to guarantee the secrecy of (possibly classified) information. Indeed, although access control is a well studied technique for system security, it is not trivial to find an access control policy which guarantees that no information leak is possible. One of the main problems is to limit, and possibly to avoid, damages produced by malicious programs, called *Trojan Horses*, which try to leak secret information.

For example, consider a classic *Discretionary Access Control* security (DAC for short), where every *subject* (i.e., an active agent such as a user), decides the access properties of its *objects* (i.e., passive agents such as files). The file management in Unix is a classic example of DAC. Indeed it allows users to decide the access rights on their files. This flexibility may facilitate security leakages. As an example, if a user A executes a Trojan Horse program, this can directly modify the access properties of A's objects making, e.g., all A's data visible to every other user. In this respect, we can say that the DAC approach gives no guarantees against "internal" attacks.

A different approach to this problem is the *Mandatory Access Control* (MAC for short), where some access rules are imposed by the system. Even if we have executed a Trojan Horse program, its action will be limited since it is not allowed to change MAC rules. An example of MAC is *Multilevel Security* [5]: every object is bound to a security level, and so is every subject; information can flow from a certain object to a certain subject only if the level of the subject is greater than the level of the object. So a Trojan Horse, which operates at a certain level, has in principle no way to *downgrade* information, and its action is restricted to that level. This policy can be implemented through two access rules: *No Read Up* (a subject cannot read data from an upper level object) and *No Write Down* (a subject cannot write data in a lower level object).

However, even if we adopt the less flexible MAC approach, this could be insufficient to stop the action of a Trojan Horse. Indeed, it could be possible to transmit information indirectly using system side effects. For example, if two levels – 'high' and 'low' – share some finite storage resource (e.g., a hard disk), it may be possible to transmit data from level 'high' to level 'low' by exploiting the 'resource full' error message. For a high level transmitter, it is sufficient to alternatively fill or empty the resource in order to transmit a '1' or a '0' datum. Simultaneously, the low level receiver tries to write on the resource, decoding every error message as a '1' and every successful write as a '0'. It is clear that such indirect transmissions, called *covert channels*, do not violate the two multilevel access rules (see Figure 1). Therefore it is often necessary to integrate a MAC discipline with a covert channel analysis (see, e.g., [63]).

The existence of covert channels has led to the more general approach of information flow security, mentioned above. The idea is to try to directly control the whole flow of information, rather than the accesses of subjects to objects [36]. By imposing some information flow rules, it is possible to indifferently control

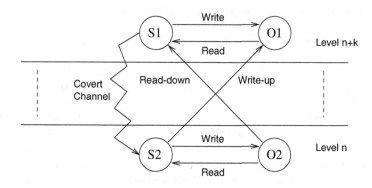

Fig. 1. Information flows in multilevel security

direct and indirect leakages, as, in this perspective, they both become "unwanted information flows".

In the literature, there are many different security definitions reminiscent of the information flow idea, each based on some system model (see, e.g., [36,64,41,48,49,62,7]). In [24] we have compared and classified them, leading to our proposed notion of *Bisimulation Non Deducibility on Compositions* (*BNDC*, for short). We will present *BNDC* starting by the idea of Non Interference [36]. Through a running example and a comparison with other existing approaches, we will try to convince the reader that such a property can effectively detect unwanted information flows in systems, both direct and indirect.

We now describe the topics of the next sections. Section 2 presents the *Security Process Algebra* (SPA, for short) language. All the properties we will present and apply to the analysis of systems and protocols are based on such a language. SPA is an extension of CCS [50] – a language proposed to specify concurrent systems. The basic building blocks are the atomic activities, simply called *actions*; unlike CCS, in SPA actions belong to two different levels of confidentiality, thus allowing the specification of multilevel (actually, two-level) systems. As for CCS, the model used to describe the operational semantics of SPA is the *labelled transition system* model [43], where the states are the terms of the algebra. In order to express that certain states are indistinguishable for an external observer, semantic equivalences over terms/states are defined such that two terms are observationally indistinguishable iff they are equivalent. As explained below, the information flow security properties we introduce are all based on these notions of observable behaviours.

Section 3 is about such properties, that capture the existence of information flows among groups of users. We will see that these properties are all of the following algebraic form. Let E be an SPA process term, let X be a security property, let $\approx$ be a semantic equivalence among process terms and let $\mathcal{C}_X$ and $\mathcal{D}_X$ be two SPA contexts[1] for property X. Then, we can say:

$$E \text{ is } X\text{-secure if and only if } \mathcal{C}_X[E] \approx \mathcal{D}_X[E].$$

where the contexts $\mathcal{C}_X$ and $\mathcal{D}_X$ are such that only (part of) the low behaviour of E becomes observable; hence, the behavioural equivalence compares these, possibly different, low behaviours of E.

A first obvious consequence is that the security properties become parametric w.r.t. the chosen notion of equivalence: if an equivalence $\approx_1$ is finer than $\approx_2$ then each security property based on $\approx_1$ is satisfied by a subset of the processes satisfying the corresponding security property based on $\approx_2$. A second, less obvious consequence is that such information flow properties are not safety properties, i.e. properties that can be specified as sets of acceptable behaviours. Indeed, by defining a property of this form for E as an equivalence problem $- \mathcal{C}_X[E] \approx \mathcal{D}_X[E] -$ on suitable contexts, we are actually stating that if some behaviour can occur, then it must be the case that also some other related behaviour must be possible; such a property cannot be expressed simply as a set of acceptable behaviour.

We analyze which kinds of flows are detectable by the various properties through the running example of an access monitor. In particular, we try to show that certain properties are not appropriate to deal with some kinds of information flows and so it is necessary to strengthen them by choosing a finer equivalence notion or, if this is not enough, by following a different approach.

In Section 4 we present a tool called *Compositional Security Checker* (CoSeC, for short) which can be used to check automatically (finite state) SPA specifications against some information flow security properties. We exploit the algebraic definition style. Indeed, checking the X-security of E is reduced to the "standard" problem of checking semantic equivalence between two terms having E as a sub-term. The CoSeC tool has the same modular architecture as Concurrency Workbench (CW for short) [14], from which some modules have been imported, and others modified. The tool is equipped with a parser, which transforms an SPA specification into a parse-tree; then, for the parsed specification CoSeC builds the labelled transition system following the operational rules defined in Plotkin' SOS style [54]. When a user wants to check if an SPA process E is X-secure, CoSeC first provides operational semantic descriptions to the terms $\mathcal{C}_X[E]$ and $\mathcal{D}_X[E]$ in the form of two LTSs; then verifies the semantic equivalence of $\mathcal{C}_X[E]$ and $\mathcal{D}_X[E]$ using their LTS representations. An interesting feature of CoSeC is the exploitation of the compositionality of some security properties in order to avoid, in some cases, the exponential state explosion due to the parallel composition operator.

---

[1] An SPA context $\mathcal{G}$ is an SPA term "with a hole". E.g., $\mathcal{G}[-] = F + -$. The insertion of E in the context $\mathcal{G}$, written as $\mathcal{G}[E]$, has the effect of filling the hole with E. In the example, $\mathcal{G}[E] = F + E$. Subscript X simply means that $\mathcal{C}_X$ and $\mathcal{D}_X$ are two particular contexts for property X, i.e., it is used to give a name to contexts for property X.

Finally, in Section 5 we give some concluding remarks and discuss some open problems.

2   SPA and Value-Passing

In this Section we present the language that will be used to specify and analyze security properties over concurrent systems. We first present the "pure" version of the language. Then we show how to extend it with value-passing. Finally, we present an example of value-passing agent specification. It will be our running example for the next sections.

2.1   The Language

The *Security Process Algebra* (SPA for short) [24,26] is a slight extension of Milner's CCS [50], where the set of visible actions is partitioned into high level actions and low level ones in order to specify multilevel systems. [2]

SPA syntax is based on the same elements as CCS. In order to obtain a partition of the visible actions into two levels, we consider two sets Act_H and Act_L of high and low level actions which are closed with respect to function $\bar{\cdot}$ (i.e., $\overline{Act_H} = Act_H$, $\overline{Act_L} = Act_L$); moreover they form a covering of $\mathcal{L}$ and they are disjoint (i.e., $Act_H \cup Act_L = \mathcal{L}$, $Act_H \cap Act_L = \emptyset$). Let Act be the set $Act_H \cup Act_L \cup \{\tau\}$, where τ is a special unobservable, internal action. The syntax of SPA *agents* (or *processes*) is defined as follows:

$$E ::= \underline{0} \mid \mu.E \mid E + E \mid E|E \mid E \backslash\backslash L \mid E[f] \mid Z$$

where μ ranges over Act, $L \subseteq \mathcal{L}$ and $f : Act \rightarrow Act$ is such that $f(\bar{\alpha}) = \overline{f(\alpha)}$, $f(\tau) = \tau$. Moreover, for every constant Z there must be the corresponding definition: $Z \stackrel{\text{def}}{=} E$, and E must be *guarded* on constants. This means that the recursive substitution of all the non prefixed (i.e., not appearing in a context $\mu.E'$) constants in E with their definitions terminates after a finite number of steps. In other words, there exists a term obtainable by constant substitutions from E where all the possible initial actions are explicitly represented (through the prefix operator $\mu.E$). For instance, agent $A \stackrel{\text{def}}{=} B$ with $B \stackrel{\text{def}}{=} A$ is not guarded on constants. On the contrary, if B is defined as $a.A$, then B is guarded on constants. This condition will be useful when we will do automatic checks over SPA terms. As a matter of fact, it basically avoids infinite constant substitution loops.

Intuitively, we have that $\underline{0}$ is the empty process, which cannot do any action; $\mu.E$ can do an action μ and then behaves like E; $E_1 + E_2$ can alternatively

---

[2] Actually, only two-level systems can be specified; note that this is not a real limitation because it is always possible to deal with the multilevel case by grouping – in several ways – the various levels in two clusters.

choose [3] to behave like E_1 or E_2 ; $E_1|E_2$ is the parallel composition of E_1 and E_2, where the executions of the two systems are interleaved, possibly synchronized on complementary input/output actions, producing an internal τ; $E \backslash\backslash L$ can execute all the actions E is able to do, provided that they do not belong to L; if E can execute action μ, then $E[f]$ performs $f(\mu)$.

The only other difference from CCS is the restriction operator $\backslash\backslash$; as we said above, $E \backslash\backslash L$ can execute all the actions E is able to do, provided that they do not belong to L. In CCS the corresponding operator $\backslash$ requires that the actions do not belong to $L \cup \bar{L}$. We will show in a moment that it is easy to define the standard restriction operator of CCS using this new restriction. The reason why we introduce this slight modification is that it is necessary to define an additional input restriction operator which will be useful in characterizing some security properties in an algebraic style. After that we will have no further use for the $\backslash\backslash$ operator. We define the CCS restriction and the input restriction operators as follows:

$$E \backslash L \overset{\text{def}}{=} E \backslash\backslash L \cup \bar{L}$$

$$E \backslash_I L \overset{\text{def}}{=} E \backslash\backslash L \cap I$$

$E \backslash L$ is the CCS restriction operator, while $E \backslash_I L$ requires that the actions of E do not belong to $L \cap I$

For the definition of security properties we also need the hiding operator of CSP [39] which can be defined as a relabelling as follows:

$$E/L \overset{\text{def}}{=} E[f_L] \text{ where } f_L(x) = \begin{cases} x \text{ if } x \notin L \\ \tau \text{ if } x \in L \end{cases}$$

E/L turns all the actions in L into internal τ's.

Let $\mathcal{E}$ be the set of SPA agents, ranged over by E and F. Let $\mathcal{L}(E)$ denote the *sort* of E, i.e., the set of the (possibly executable) actions occurring syntactically in E. The sets of high level agents and low level ones are defined as $\mathcal{E}_H \overset{\text{def}}{=} \{E \in \mathcal{E} \mid \mathcal{L}(E) \subseteq Act_H \cup \{\tau\}\}$ and $\mathcal{E}_L \overset{\text{def}}{=} \{E \in \mathcal{E} \mid \mathcal{L}(E) \subseteq Act_L \cup \{\tau\}\}$, respectively. From a security point of view, processes in $\mathcal{E}_H$ and in $\mathcal{E}_L$ are secure by isolation, as all the actions they perform are bound to one particular level (high or low, respectively). More interesting is the case of processes in $\mathcal{E}_H \cup \mathcal{E}_L \subset \mathcal{E}$, i.e., of those processes that execute both high level and low level actions, allowing for communications between the two levels, hence possibly introducing unwanted information flows.

2.2   Operational Semantics and Equivalences

The operational semantics of SPA is the LTS $(\mathcal{E}, Act, \rightarrow)$, where the states are the terms of the algebra and the transition relation $\rightarrow \subseteq \mathcal{E} \times Act \times \mathcal{E}$ is defined as for

---

[3] For notational convenience, we use sometimes the $\sum$ operator (indexed on a set) to represent a general n-ary (or even infinitary) sum operator.

Table 1. The operational rules for SPA

Prefix	$$\dfrac{-}{\mu.E \xrightarrow{\mu} E}$$
Sum	$$\dfrac{E_1 \xrightarrow{\mu} E_1'}{E_1 + E_2 \xrightarrow{\mu} E_1'} \qquad \dfrac{E_2 \xrightarrow{\mu} E_2'}{E_1 + E_2 \xrightarrow{\mu} E_2'}$$
Parallel	$$\dfrac{E_1 \xrightarrow{\mu} E_1'}{E_1|E_2 \xrightarrow{\mu} E_1'|E_2} \qquad \dfrac{E_2 \xrightarrow{\mu} E_2'}{E_1|E_2 \xrightarrow{\mu} E_1|E_2'} \qquad \dfrac{E_1 \xrightarrow{\alpha} E_1' \ \ E_2 \xrightarrow{\bar{\alpha}} E_2'}{E_1|E_2 \xrightarrow{\tau} E_1'|E_2'}$$
Restriction	$$\dfrac{E \xrightarrow{\mu} E'}{E \backslash\!\backslash L \xrightarrow{\mu} E' \backslash\!\backslash L} \ \text{ if } \mu \notin L$$
Relabelling	$$\dfrac{E \xrightarrow{\mu} E'}{E[f] \xrightarrow{f(\mu)} E'[f]}$$
Constant	$$\dfrac{E \xrightarrow{\mu} E'}{A \xrightarrow{\mu} E'} \ \text{ if } A \stackrel{\text{def}}{=} E$$

CCS by structural induction as the least relation generated by the axioms and inference rules reported in Table 1. The operational semantics for an agent E is the subpart of the SPA LTS reachable from the initial state E. We denote with $\mathcal{E}_{FS}$ the set of all the SPA agents with a finite LTS as operational semantics. Table 2 shows some simple examples of SPA terms with their corresponding LTSs. Now we introduce the idea of observable behaviour: two systems should have the same semantics if and only if they cannot be distinguished by an external observer. To obtain this we define an equivalence relation over states/terms of the SPA LTS, equating two processes when they are indistinguishable. In this way the semantics of a term becomes an equivalence class of terms.

It is possible to define various equivalences of this kind, according to the different assumptions on the power of observers. We recall three of them. The first one is the classic definition of *trace equivalence*, according to which two agents are equivalent if they have the same execution traces. The second one discriminates agents also according to the nondeterministic structure of their LTSs. This equivalence is based on the concept of *bisimulation* [50]. The last one, introduced for the CSP language [39], is able to observe which actions are not executable after a certain trace (*failure* sets), thus detecting possible deadlocks.

Since we want to focus only on observable actions, we need a transition relation which does not take care of internal τ moves. This can be defined as follows:

Definition 1. *The expression $E \stackrel{\alpha}{\Longrightarrow} E'$ is a shorthand for $E(\stackrel{\tau}{\rightarrow})^* E_1 \stackrel{\alpha}{\rightarrow} E_2(\stackrel{\tau}{\rightarrow})^*$ E', where $(\stackrel{\tau}{\rightarrow})^*$ denotes a (possibly empty) sequence of τ labelled transitions. Let*

Table 2. Some simple SPA terms

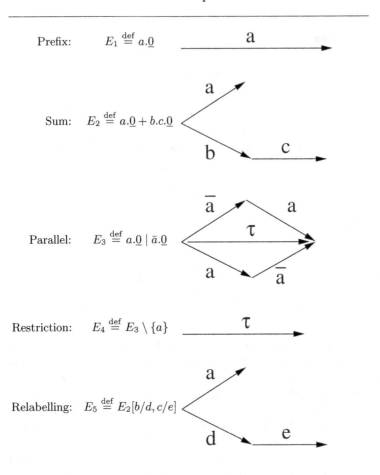

$\gamma = \alpha_1 \ldots \alpha_n \in \mathcal{L}^*$ *be a sequence of actions; then* $E \overset{\gamma}{\Longrightarrow} E'$ *if and only if there exist* $E_1, E_2, \ldots, E_{n-1} \in \mathcal{E}$ *such that* $E \overset{\alpha_1}{\Longrightarrow} E_1 \overset{\alpha_2}{\Longrightarrow} \cdots \overset{\alpha_{n-1}}{\Longrightarrow} E_{n-1} \overset{\alpha_n}{\Longrightarrow} E'.$ *For the empty sequence* $\langle\rangle$ *we have that* $E \overset{\langle\rangle}{\Longrightarrow} E'$ *stands for* $E(\overset{\tau}{\rightarrow})^* E'.$ *We say that* E' *is* reachable *from* E *when* $\exists \gamma : E \overset{\gamma}{\Longrightarrow} E'$ *and we write* $E \Longrightarrow E'.$ ∎

Trace Equivalence We define trace equivalence as follows:

Definition 2. *For any* $E \in \mathcal{E}$ *the set* $T(E)$ *of* traces *associated with* E *is defined as follows:* $T(E) = \{\gamma \in \mathcal{L}^* \mid \exists E' : E \overset{\gamma}{\Longrightarrow} E'\}.$ E *and* F *are* trace equivalent *(notation* $E \approx_T F$*) if and only if* $T(E) = T(F).$ ∎

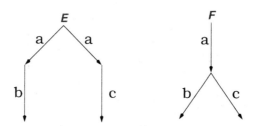

Fig. 2. Systems not observationally equivalent

Observational Equivalence Bisimulation is based on an idea of mutual step-by-step simulation, i.e., when E executes a certain action moving to E', F must be able to simulate this single step by executing the same action and moving to an agent F' which is again bisimilar to E' (this is because it must be able to simulate every successive step of E'), and vice-versa.

A weak bisimulation is a bisimulation which does not care about internal τ actions. So, when F simulates an action of E, it can also execute some τ actions before or after that action.

In the following, $E \stackrel{\hat{\mu}}{\Longrightarrow} E'$ stands for $E \stackrel{\mu}{\Longrightarrow} E'$ if $\mu \in \mathcal{L}$, and for $E (\stackrel{\tau}{\rightarrow})^* E'$ if $\mu = \tau$ (note that $(\stackrel{\tau}{\rightarrow})^*$ means "zero or more τ labelled transitions" while $\stackrel{\tau}{\Longrightarrow}$ requires at least one τ labelled transition).

Definition 3. *A relation $R \subseteq \mathcal{E} \times \mathcal{E}$ is a weak bisimulation if $(E, F) \in R$ implies, for all $\mu \in Act$,*

- *whenever $E \stackrel{\mu}{\longrightarrow} E'$, then there exists $F' \in \mathcal{E}$ such that $F \stackrel{\hat{\mu}}{\Longrightarrow} F'$ and $(E', F') \in R$;*
- *conversely, whenever $F \stackrel{\mu}{\longrightarrow} F'$, then there exists $E' \in \mathcal{E}$ such that $E \stackrel{\hat{\mu}}{\Longrightarrow} E'$ and $(E', F') \in R$.*

Two SPA agents $E, F \in \mathcal{E}$ are observationally equivalent, notation $E \approx_B F$, if there exists a weak bisimulation containing the pair (E, F). ∎

In [50] it is proved that $\approx_B$ is an equivalence relation. Moreover, it is easy to see that $E \approx_B F$ implies $E \approx_T F$; indeed, if $E \approx_B F$ then F must be able to simulate every sequence of visible actions executed by E, i.e., every trace of E; since the simulation corresponds to the execution of the actions interleaved with some τ's, then every trace of E is also a trace for F. Symmetrically, E must be able to simulate every sequence of F. So $E \approx_T F$.

In Figure 2 there is an example of two trace-equivalent systems which are not observationally equivalent. In fact both E and F can execute the three traces a, ab and ac. However, it is not possible for E to simulate step-by-step process F. In particular, F executes a and moves to a state where it can execute both b and c. Process E can simulate this first step of F but, after this, it cannot simulate F anymore since it is in a state where it can execute only b or c.

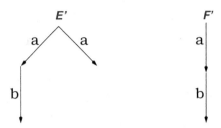

Fig. 3. Observational equivalence detects deadlocks

This ability of observing the branching structures of systems makes $\approx_B$ able to detect potential deadlocks. If we consider $E' \stackrel{\text{def}}{=} E \setminus \{c\}$ and $F' \stackrel{\text{def}}{=} F \setminus \{c\}$ (see Figure 3) we have that E' and F' are still trace equivalent but not observationally equivalent. Indeed, system E' can reach a deadlock state after the execution of action a. On the other hand, F' is not able to simulate this move since after a it can always execute b.

We conclude this section about bisimulation by introducing the notion of weak bisimulation up to $\approx_B$. It will be very useful when proving that two agents are observation equivalent. Indeed, we see that in order to ensure $P \approx_B Q$ it is sufficient that (P, Q) is in some weak bisimulation up to $\approx_B$.

Definition 4. *A relation* $S \subseteq \mathcal{E} \times \mathcal{E}$ *is a* weak bisimulation up to $\approx_B$ *if* $(E, F) \in S$ *implies, for all* $\mu \in Act$,

- *whenever* $E \stackrel{\mu}{\Longrightarrow} E'$, *then there exists* $F' \in \mathcal{E}$ *such that* $F \stackrel{\hat{\mu}}{\Longrightarrow} F'$ *and* $E' \approx_B S \approx_B F'$;
- *conversely, whenever* $F \stackrel{\mu}{\Longrightarrow} F'$, *then there exists* $E' \in \mathcal{E}$ *such that* $E \stackrel{\hat{\mu}}{\Longrightarrow} E'$ *and* $E' \approx_B S \approx_B F'$.

where $\approx_B S \approx_B$ *is the composition of binary relations, so that* $E' \approx_B S \approx_B F'$ *means that for some* E'' *and* F'' *we have* $E' \approx_B E''$, $(E'', F'') \in S$, $F' \approx_B F''$. ∎

In [50] it is proven the following result:

Proposition 1. *If S is a bisimulation up to $\approx_B$ then $S \subseteq \approx_B$.*

Hence, to prove $P \approx_B Q$, we only have to find a bisimulation up to $\approx_B$ which contains (P, Q). This is one of the proof techniques we will often adopt in the following.

Failure/Testing Equivalence The failure semantics [9], introduced for the CSP language, is a refinement of the trace semantics where it is possible to observe which actions are not executable after a certain trace. In particular, a system is characterized by the so-called failures set, i.e., a set of pairs (s, X)

where s is a trace and X is a set of actions. For each pair (s, X), the system must be able, by executing trace s, to reach a state where every action in X cannot be executed.[4] For instance, consider again agents E' and F' of Figure 3. As we said above, E' can stop after the execution of a and, consequently, E' can refuse to execute action b after the execution of a. So E' has the pair $(a, \{b\})$ in its failure set. System F' is always able to execute b after the execution of a. So F' does not have $(a, \{b\})$ in the failure set, hence it is not failure equivalent to E'. We deduce that also failure semantics is able to detect deadlocks. Moreover, also systems E and F of Figure 2 are not failure equivalent.

A different characterization of failure equivalence (called *testing equivalence*) has been given in [52]. It is based on the idea of tests. We can see a test T as any SPA process which can execute a particular *success* action $\omega \notin \mathcal{L}$. A test T is applied to a system E using the parallel composition operator $|$. A test T *may be satisfied* by system E if and only if system $(E|T) \setminus \mathcal{L}$ can execute ω. Note that in system $(E|T) \setminus \mathcal{L}$ we force the synchronization of E with test T.

Definition 5. *E may T if and only if $(E|T) \setminus \mathcal{L} \overset{\omega}{\Longrightarrow} (E'|T') \setminus \mathcal{L}$* ∎

A maximal computation of $(E|T) \setminus \mathcal{L}$ is a sequence $(E|T) \setminus \mathcal{L} = ET_0 \overset{\tau}{\to} ET_1 \overset{\tau}{\to} \ldots \overset{\tau}{\to} ET_n \overset{\tau}{\to} \ldots$ which can be finite or infinite; if it is finite the last term must have no outgoing transitions. A test T *must be satisfied* by E if and only if every maximal computation of $(E|T) \setminus \mathcal{L}$ contains a state ET_i which can execute ω.

Definition 6. *E must T if and only if for all maximal computations of $ET_0 = (E|T) \setminus \mathcal{L}, \exists i$ such that $ET_i \overset{\omega}{\to} ET'_i$* ∎

Now we can define testing equivalence as follows:

Definition 7. *Two systems E and F are testing equivalent, $E \approx_{test} F$, if and only if*

i) E may $T \Leftrightarrow F$ may T
ii) E must $T \Leftrightarrow F$ must T

for every test T. ∎

It is easy to see that the first condition holds if and only if $E \approx_T F$. In fact, if E may satisfy T, then E is able to execute the trace which moves T to the state where it can execute ω.[5] It is not difficult to see that the second condition corresponds to failure equivalence. The basic idea is that if E fails to execute a certain action a after a trace γ, we can detect this with a test T which executes the complementary actions of γ followed by $\bar{a}$, and then executes ω. In fact, for that T we have that E must T.

---

[4] Indeed, there is a condition on the traces s in pairs (s, X). It is required that during any execution of s no infinite internal computation sequences are possible. We will analyze this aspect more in detail in the following.

[5] We could have more than one trace or more than one ω. However if a system may satisfy a test T, then it may satisfy also a test T' with only one ω and only one trace to it. T' corresponds to one of the traces executed by the system in order to satisfy the test T.

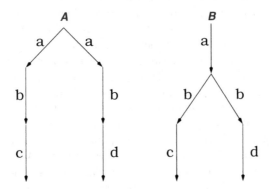

Fig. 4. Systems testing equivalent but not observationally equivalent

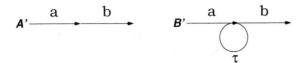

Fig. 5. Systems observationally equivalent but not testing equivalent

We have seen that both $\approx_B$ and $\approx_{test}$ are stronger than $\approx_T$, since they basically observe something of the branching structure of the LTSs. However we have said nothing about the relation between these two equivalences. The reason is that they are incomparable, i.e., no one of them implies the other. Indeed, we have that $\approx_B$ is in most cases more sensitive than $\approx_{test}$ to the branching structure of the agents. We can see this in the simple example of Figure 4. It shows that $\approx_B$ does not permit to "shift" the non-deterministic choice even if the first actions executed after the branch are exactly the same (b, in this case).

On the other hand $\approx_{test}$ is more discriminating with respect to divergent behaviour, i.e., infinite sequences of internal τ actions. Indeed, a divergence may "ruin" a test by generating unexpected maximal computations. As an example, see Figure 5 where the divergence after a in process B' determines that $B' \not{must} \bar{a}.\bar{b}.\omega.\underline{0}$ while A' $must$ $\bar{a}.\bar{b}.\omega.\underline{0}$. This happens because, after the execution of a, the process could diverge never reaching the ω success action. This aspect will be analyzed more in detail in the next chapters, when we will try to use $\approx_{test}$ in the specification of security properties.

We conclude this section presenting a class of finite state agents. This will be useful in the automatic verification of security properties. This class of agents consists of the so-called *nets of automata*:

$$p ::= \underline{0} \mid \mu.p \mid p + p \mid Z$$
$$E ::= p \mid E|E \mid E \setminus L \mid E \setminus_I L \mid E/L \mid E[f]$$

where for every constant Z there must be the corresponding definition $Z \stackrel{\text{def}}{=} p$ (with p guarded on constants). It is easy to prove that every agent of this form is finite state. However, this condition is not necessary, in the sense that other agents not belonging to the class of nets of automata are finite state as well. For instance, consider $B \stackrel{\text{def}}{=} a.\underline{0} + D \setminus \{i\}$ with $D \stackrel{\text{def}}{=} i.(o.\underline{0}|D)$. It can execute only an action a and then it stops, so it is clearly finite state. However note that it does not conform to the syntax of nets of automata since there is a parallel operator underneath a sum.

2.3   Value-Passing SPA

In this section we briefly present a value-passing extension of "pure" SPA (VSPA, for short). All the examples contained in this paper will use this value passing calculus, because it leads to more readable specifications than those written in pure SPA. Here we present a very simple example of a value-passing agent showing how it can be translated into a pure SPA agent. Then we define the VSPA syntax and we sketch the semantics by translating a generic VSPA agent into its corresponding SPA agent.

As an example, consider the following buffer cell [50]:

$$C \stackrel{\text{def}}{=} in(x).C'(x)$$
$$C'(x) \stackrel{\text{def}}{=} \overline{out}(x).C$$

where x is a variable that can assume values in $\mathbf{N}$ (we usually write $x \in \mathbf{N}$). C reads a natural number n through action in and stores it in variable x. Then this value is passed to agent C' which can give n as output through action out moving again to C. So C represents a buffer which may hold a single data item. If we assume that in is a low level action and out a high level action, then C is a system exhibiting a legitimate direct information flow from low to high. On the contrary, if in is high and out is low, then C is an insecure system, downgrading information from high to low.

Now we show how C can be translated into an SPA agent. The parametrized constant C' becomes a family of constants C'_v one for each value $v \in \mathbf{N}$. Similarly $\overline{out}(x)$ becomes a family $\overline{out}_v$ of prefixes. So the single definition for C' becomes the following family of definitions:

$$C'_v \stackrel{\text{def}}{=} \overline{out}_v.C \quad (v \in \mathbf{N})$$

Now consider the prefix $in(x)$. To reflect the fact that it can accept any input value, binding variable x, we translate it into $\sum_{v \in \mathbf{N}} in_v$. So the definition becomes:

$$C \stackrel{\text{def}}{=} \sum_{v \in \mathbf{N}} in_v.C'_v$$

VSPA is very similar to the value-passing CCS introduced in [50]. The main difference is that in VSPA we can have more than one parameter for actions and parameters are multi-sorted.

The syntax of VSPA agents is defined as follows:

$$E ::= \underline{0} \mid a(x_1, \ldots, x_n).E \mid \bar{a}(e_1, \ldots, e_n).E \mid \tau.E \mid E + E \mid E|E \mid$$
$$\mid E \setminus L \mid E \setminus_I L \mid E/L \mid E[f] \mid A(e'_1, \ldots, e'_n) \mid$$
$$\mid \text{if } b \text{ then } E \mid \text{if } b \text{ then } E \text{ else } E$$

where the variables $x_1, \ldots, x_n$, the value expressions $e_1, \ldots, e_n$ and $e'_1, \ldots, e'_n$ must be consistent with the arity of the action a and constant A, respectively (the arity specifies the sorts of the parameters), and b is a boolean expression. The arity of actions and constants is given by function ari. This function returns a tuple of sets (called *Sorts*) that represent the ranges of the parameters for the specific action or constant considered. For example, $ari(a) = (S_1, \ldots, S_n)$ means that action a has n parameters with ranges $S_1, \ldots, S_n$, respectively.

It is also necessary to define constants as follows: $A(x_1, \ldots, x_m) \stackrel{\text{def}}{=} E$ where E is a VSPA agent which may contain no free variables except $x_1, \ldots, x_m$, which must be distinct. As in [50] the semantics of the value-passing calculus is given as a translation into the pure calculus. The translations rests upon the idea that a single label a of VSPA, with n parameters with sorts $S_1 \ldots S_n$, becomes the set of labels $\{a_{v_1 \ldots v_n} : v_i \in S_i, \forall i \in [1, n]\}$ in SPA. We consider only agents without free variables because if an agent has a free variable then it becomes a family of agents, one for each value of the variable. The translation can be given recursively on the structure of agents. Note that, since we have no free variable all the value and boolean expressions can be calculated; we will write $\hat{b}$ and $\hat{e}$ for the value obtained by evaluating a boolean expression b and a value expression e respectively.

We will use the notation $E\{a/b\}$ to represent agent E with all the occurrences of b substituted by a. We will also use $\mathcal{E}^+$ to denote the set of VSPA agents. For each agent $E \in \mathcal{E}^+$ without free variables, its translation $[\![E]\!]$ is given in Table 3 where $ari(a) = S_1 \ldots S_n$; $\hat{L} = \{l_{v_1, \ldots, v_n} : l \in L, ari(l) = S_1 \ldots S_n, v_i \in S_i, \forall i \in [1, n]\}$ is the set of the translations of actions in L and $\hat{f}(l_{v_1, \ldots, v_n}) = f(l)_{v_1, \ldots, v_n}$ is the translation of relabelling function f. Furthermore, the single definition $A(x_1, \ldots, x_m) \stackrel{\text{def}}{=} E$ with $ari(A) = S_1 \ldots S_m$, is translated to the set of equations:

$$\{A_{v_1, \ldots, v_m} = [\![E\{v_1/x_1, \ldots, v_m/x_m\}]\!]; v_i \in S_i \forall i \in [1, m]\}$$

Note that we do not partition the set of actions into two levels; we directly refer to the partition in the pure calculus. In this way it is possible for a certain

Table 3. Translation of VSPA to SPA

$E \in \mathcal{E}^+$	$[\![E]\!] \in \mathcal{E}$
$\underline{0}$	$\underline{0}$
$a(x_1, \ldots, x_n).E$	$\sum_{i \in [1,n], v_i \in S_i} a_{v_1, \ldots, v_n}.[\![E\{v_1/x_1, \ldots v_n/x_n\}]\!]$
$\bar{a}(e_1, \ldots, e_n).E$	$\bar{a}_{\widehat{e_1}, \ldots, \widehat{e_n}}.[\![E]\!]$
$\tau.E$	$\tau.[\![E]\!]$
$E_1 + E_2$	$[\![E_1]\!] + [\![E_2]\!]$
$E_1 \vert E_2$	$[\![E_1]\!] \vert [\![E_2]\!]$
$E \setminus L$	$[\![E]\!] \setminus \widehat{L}$
$E \setminus_I L$	$[\![E]\!] \setminus_I \widehat{L}$
E/L	$[\![E]\!]/\widehat{L}$
$E[f]$	$[\![E]\!][\widehat{f}]$
$A(e_1, \ldots, e_n)$	$A_{\widehat{e_1}, \ldots, \widehat{e_n}}$
if b **then** E	$\begin{cases} [\![E]\!] & \text{if } \widehat{b} = True \\ \underline{0} & \text{otherwise} \end{cases}$

action in VSPA to correspond, in the translation, to actions at different levels in SPA. This can be useful if we want a parameter representing the level of a certain action. As an example consider an action $access\_r(l, x)$ with $l \in \{high, low\}$ and $x \in [1, n]$, representing a read request from a user at level l to an object x; we can assign the high level to the actions with $l = high$ and the low level to the others in this way: $access\_r(high, x) \in Act_H$ and $access\_r(low, x) \in Act_L$ for all $x \in [1, n]$. [6]

A VSPA agent is finite state if its corresponding SPA agent is so. Hence, in general, a necessary condition is that every variable can assume values over a finite set only.

2.4   The Access Monitor

Here we give a more complex example of a VSPA agent specification. It is an access monitor which handles read and write requests on two binary variables enforcing the multilevel security policy. We will analyse and modify this example in the next sections in order to assess the merits of the various information flow properties that we will propose.

Example 1. Consider the system in Table 4 where $x, y, z, l \in \{0, 1\}$, $L = \{r, w\}$ and $\forall i \in \{0, 1\}$ we have $r(1, i)$, $w(1, i)$, $access\_r(1, i)$, $val(1, i)$, $val(1, err)$,

---

[6] Note that $access\_r(high, x)$ stands for $access\_r_{high, x}$, with $x \in [1, n]$. Indeed, for the sake of readability, we often write $c(v)$ instead of its translation c_v.

Table 4. The *Access_Monitor_1* System

$$Access\_Monitor\_1 \stackrel{\text{def}}{=} (Monitor \mid Object(1,0) \mid Object(0,0)) \setminus L$$

$$Monitor \stackrel{\text{def}}{=} access\_r(l,x).$$

(**if** $x \leq l$ **then**

$$r(x,y).\overline{val}(l,y).Monitor$$

else

$$\overline{val}(l,err).Monitor)$$

$+$

$$access\_w(l,x).write(l,z).$$

(**if** $x \geq l$ **then**

$$\overline{w}(x,z).Monitor$$

else

$$Monitor)$$

$$Object(x,y) \stackrel{\text{def}}{=} \overline{r}(x,y).Object(x,y) + w(x,z).Object(x,z)$$

$access\_w(1,i), write(1,i) \in Act_H$ and all the other actions are low level ones. Note that in *Access_Monitor_1* every variable can assume values over a finite set only. When we translate it into SPA, we obtain a net of automata, hence *Access_Monitor_1* is a finite state agent

Figure 6 represents process *Access_Monitor_1* that handles read and write requests from high and low level users on two binary objects: a high level variable and a low level one. It achieves *no read up* and *no write down* access control rules allowing a high level user to read from both objects and write only on the high one; conversely, a low level user is allowed to write on both objects and read only from the low one. Users interact with the monitor through the following access actions: $access\_r(l,x), access\_w(l,x), write(l,z)$ where l is the user level ($l = 0$ low, $l = 1$ high), x is the object ($x = 0$ low, $x = 1$ high) and z is the binary value to be written.

As an example, consider $access\_r(0,1)$ which represents a low level user ($l = 0$) read request from the high level object ($x = 1$), and $access\_w(1,0)$ followed by $write(1,0)$ which represents a high level user ($l = 1$) write request of value 0 ($z = 0$) on the low object ($x = 0$). Read results are returned to users through the output actions $val(l,y)$. This can be also an error in case of a read-up request. Note that if a high level user tries to write on the low object – through $access\_w(1,0)$ followed by $write(1,z)$ – such a request is not executed and no error message is returned.

In order to understand how the system works, let us consider the following transitions sequence representing the writing of value 1 in the low level object,

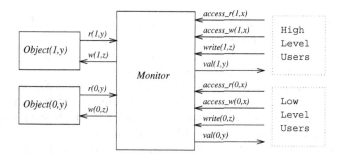

Fig. 6. The Access Monitor for Example 1

performed by the low level user:

$(Monitor \mid Object(1,0) \mid Object(0,0)) \setminus L$

$\xrightarrow{access\_w(0,0)} (write(0,z).\overline{w}(0,z).Monitor \mid Object(1,0) \mid Object(0,0)) \setminus L$

$\xrightarrow{write(0,1)} (\overline{w}(0,1).Monitor \mid Object(1,0) \mid Object(0,0)) \setminus L$

$\xrightarrow{\tau} (Monitor \mid Object(1,0) \mid Object(0,1)) \setminus L$

The trace corresponding to this sequence of transitions is

$$access\_w(0,0).write(0,1)$$

and so we can write:

$(Monitor \mid Object(1,0) \mid Object(0,0)) \setminus L$

$\xRightarrow{access\_w(0,0).write(0,1)} (Monitor \mid Object(1,0) \mid Object(0,1)) \setminus L$

Note that, after the execution of the trace, the low level object contains value 1.

$Access\_Monitor\_1$ is a value passing specification of an access monitor. Its translation into CoSeC syntax for pure SPA is reported in Table 12 of Section 4.4. As an example, here we provide the translation of $Object(x,y)$ into the pure calculus by means of the following four constant definitions:

$$Object_{00} \stackrel{\text{def}}{=} \overline{r}_{00}.Object_{00} + w_{00}.Object_{00} + w_{01}.Object_{01}$$

$$Object_{01} \stackrel{\text{def}}{=} \overline{r}_{01}.Object_{01} + w_{00}.Object_{00} + w_{01}.Object_{01}$$

$$Object_{10} \stackrel{\text{def}}{=} \overline{r}_{10}.Object_{10} + w_{10}.Object_{10} + w_{11}.Object_{11}$$

$$Object_{11} \stackrel{\text{def}}{=} \overline{r}_{11}.Object_{11} + w_{10}.Object_{10} + w_{11}.Object_{11}$$

Note that we have, for every possible value of the pair (x,y), one different process $Object_{xy}$. ∎

3   Information Flow Properties

In this Section we present some Information Flow properties. The common intuition behind all these properties is strictly related to the classic notion of *Non Interference* (NI, for short) [36], i.e., the low level users should not be able to deduce anything about high level users' activity.

As already mentioned earlier in this chapter, processes in $\mathcal{E}_H$ or $\mathcal{E}_L$ are secure by isolation, as they are confined to work in one single confidentiality level. The really interesting processes are those built with both high level and low level actions, as they may show unwanted information flows.

In the first three sections we present properties based on different equivalence notions. We start with the weakest and most intuitive one: trace equivalence. Then, we see that it is necessary to move to finer equivalence notions in order to detect possible high level deadlocks that can compromise the security of the system. For this reason, in the second section we base our security properties on failure and testing equivalences [9,52], which have been designed specifically to detect deadlocks. However, we discover that the failure/testing setting is not ideal for our purposes because of the way it deals with (potential) divergences. This leads us, in the third section, to prefer to base our security properties on the notion of weak bisimulation. In the fourth section we show that deadlocks due to high level activity are indeed dangerous and cannot be ignored. In section 3.5 we compare our security properties with other proposals in the literature which are also based on Process Algebras.

Part of the material contained in this section has been published in [24], [26], [21], [23], [22], [18].

3.1   Properties Based on Trace Equivalence

We start with *Non-deterministic Non Interference* (*NNI*, for short) [24,26], which is a natural generalization to non-deterministic systems of NI (assuming two user groups only). The basic idea of NI is that the high level does not interfere with the low level if the effects of high level inputs are not visible by a low level user. This idea can be rephrased on the LTS model as follows. We consider every trace γ of the system containing high level inputs. Then, we look if there exists another trace γ' with the same subsequence of low level actions and without high inputs. A low level user, which can only observe low level actions, is not able to distinguish γ and γ'. As both γ and γ' are legal traces, we can conclude that the possible execution of the high level inputs in γ has no effect on the low level view of the system.

As for NI, we can define this property by using some functions which manipulates sequences of actions. In particular, it is sufficient to consider the function $low : \mathcal{L}^* \longrightarrow Act_L^*$ which takes a trace γ and removes all the high level actions from it, i.e., returns the low level subsequence of γ. Moreover we use the function $highinput : \mathcal{L}^* \longrightarrow (Act_H \cap I)^*$ which extracts from a trace the subsequence composed of all the high level inputs.

Definition 8. *(NNI: Non-deterministic Non Interference)*
$E \in NNI$ if and only if $\forall \gamma \in T(E), \exists \delta \in T(E)$ such that

(i) $low(\gamma) = low(\delta)$
(ii) $highinput(\delta) = \langle \rangle$

where $\langle \rangle$ denotes the empty sequence. ∎

This may be expressed algebraically as:

Proposition 2. $E \in NNI \iff (E \setminus_I Act_H)/Act_H \approx_T E/Act_H$.

PROOF. ($\Rightarrow$) It is enough to show that if E is *NNI* then $T(E/Act_H) \subseteq T((E \setminus_I Act_H)/Act_H)$, because the opposite inclusion simply derives from $T(E \setminus_I Act_H) \subseteq T(E)$. Let $\gamma \in T(E/Act_H)$; then, by definition of / operator, $\exists \gamma' \in T(E)$ such that $low(\gamma') = \gamma$. Since $E \in NNI$ then $\exists \delta \in T(E)$ such that $low(\gamma') = low(\delta)$ and $highinput(\delta) = \langle \rangle$. Hence $\delta \in T(E \setminus_I Act_H)$ and $\delta' = low(\delta) \in T((E \setminus_I Act_H)/Act_H)$. Since $\gamma = low(\gamma') = low(\delta) = \delta'$, then $\gamma = \delta'$ and thus $\gamma \in T((E \setminus_I Act_H)/Act_H)$.
($\Leftarrow$) Let $\gamma \in T(E)$. Then $\exists \delta \in T(E \setminus_I Act_H)$ such that $low(\gamma) = low(\delta)$. Since $\delta \in T(E \setminus_I Act_H)$ then $highinput(\delta) = \langle \rangle$ and $\delta \in T(E)$. ∎

As a matter of fact, in E/Act_H all the high level actions are hidden, hence giving the low level view of the system; $E \setminus_I Act_H$ instead prevents traces from containing high level inputs. So, if the two terms are equivalent, then for every trace with high level inputs we can find another trace without such actions but with the same subsequence of low level actions.

   In the following we will consider this algebraic characterization as the definition of *NNI*. Indeed, all the other properties we present below in this section are defined using this compact algebraic style. An interesting advantage of this style is that it reduces the check of a security property to the "standard" and well studied problem of checking the semantic equivalence of two LTSs.

   It is possible to prove that *Access_Monitor_1* of Example 1 is *NNI*. In fact, the next example shows that *NNI* is able to detect whether the multilevel access control rules are implemented correctly in the monitor.

Example 2. Consider the modified monitor [7] in Table 5 which does not control write accesses: Now it is possible for a high level user to write in the low level object (action $access\_w(1,0)$ followed by $write(1,z)$) so the system is not secure. We have that *NNI* is able to detect this kind of direct flow. *Access_Monitor_2* can execute the following trace:

$$\gamma = access\_w(1,0).write(1,1).access\_r(0,0).\overline{val}(0,1)$$

In γ we have two accesses to the monitor: first a high level user modifies the value of the low object writing down value 1, and then the low user reads value 1 from the object. If we purge γ of high level actions, we obtain the sequence

$$\gamma' = access\_r(0,0).\overline{val}(0,1)$$

---

[7] In the following, if an agent is not specified (e.g. *Object(x,y)*) we mean that it has not been modified with respect to the previous versions of the Access Monitor.

Table 5. The *Access_Monitor_2* System

$Access\_Monitor\_2 \overset{\text{def}}{=} (Monitor\_2 \mid Object(1,0) \mid Object(0,0)) \setminus L$

$Monitor\_2 \overset{\text{def}}{=} access\_r(l,x).$

        (**if** $x \leq l$ **then**

                $r(x,y).\overline{val}(l,y).Monitor\_2$

        else

                $\overline{val}(l,err).Monitor\_2)$

        $+$

        $access\_w(l,x).write(l,z).\overline{w}(x,z).Monitor\_2$

---

representing the reading by a low level user of value 1 from the low object. This trace is not a legal trace for *Access_Monitor_2* since the low object is initialized to value 0. Moreover, it is not possible to obtain a trace for *Access_Monitor_2* by adding to γ' only high level outputs, because all the high level outputs in *Access_Monitor_2* are prefixed by high level inputs. Hence γ' is not even a trace for $(Access\_Monitor\_2 \setminus_I Act_H)/Act_H$. In other words, it is not possible to find a trace γ'' of *Access_Monitor_2* with the same low level actions of γ and without high level inputs.

Since γ' is a trace for agent *Access_Monitor_2*/Act_H but it is not a trace for agent $(Access\_Monitor\_2 \setminus_I Act_H)/Act_H$, we conclude that *Access_Monitor_2* is not *NNI*. ∎

The example above shows that *NNI* reveals if something is wrong in the access policy we are implementing. Indeed, it is quite intuitive that if some access rule is missing then there will be a particular execution where some classified information is disclosed to low level users (otherwise such a rule would be useless). This will certainly modify the low level view of the system making it not *NNI* for sure.

However, the next example shows that *NNI* is not adequate to deal with synchronous communications and, consequently, it is too weak for SPA agents.

Example 3. Consider *Access_Monitor_1*, and suppose that we want to add a high level output signal which informs high level users about write operations of low level users in the high level object. This could be useful to know the integrity of high level information. We obtain the VSPA agent of Table 6 with the new *written_up* action and where $\forall i \in \{0,1\}$, $written\_up(i) \in Act_H$.

It is possible to prove that *Access_Monitor_3* is *NNI*. However, consider the following trace of *Access_Monitor_3*:

$$\gamma = access\_w(0,1).write(0,0).\overline{written\_up}(0).access\_w(0,1).write(0,0)$$

Table 6. The *Access_Monitor_3* System

$Access\_Monitor\_3 \overset{\text{def}}{=} (Monitor\_3 \mid Object(1,0) \mid Object(0,0)) \setminus L$

$Monitor\_3 \overset{\text{def}}{=} access\_r(l,x).$

(**if** $x \leq l$ **then**

$\quad r(x,y).\overline{val}(l,y).Monitor\_3$

else

$\quad \overline{val}(l,err).Monitor\_3)$

$+$

$access\_w(l,x).write(l,z).$

(**if** $x = l$ **then**

$\quad \overline{w}(x,z).Monitor\_3$

else

$\quad$ **if** $x > l$ **then**

$\qquad \overline{w}(x,z).\overline{written\_up}(z).Monitor\_3$

$\quad$ **else**

$\qquad Monitor\_3)$

where a low level user writes two times value 0 into the high level object. If we purge γ of high level actions (i.e. of *written_up*) we obtain the following sequence:

$$\gamma' = access\_w(0,1).write(0,0).access\_w(0,1).write(0,0)$$

that cannot be a trace for *Access_Monitor_3*, because after every low level write operation there must be an action *written_up*.

So, if a low level user succeeds in executing the two write requests, then (s)he will know that some high level user has "accepted" the high level output $\overline{written\_up}$ (because of synchronous communications). In other words, a high level user can interfere with a low level one accepting or not the high level output $\overline{written\_up}$. *NNI* is not able to detect this, because it verifies only the high level input interferences over low level actions. In fact, since γ is a trace of *Access_Monitor_3*, then γ' is a trace for both *Access_Monitor_3*/Act_H and $(Access\_Monitor\_3 \setminus_I Act_H)/Act_H$. ∎

The example above shows that synchronous communications induce a symmetry over inputs and outputs. For this reason, we define a symmetric form of *NNI*. It requires that, for every trace γ, the sequence γ', obtained from γ by deleting all the high level actions, is still a trace. This property is called *Strong NNI* (*SNNI* for short).

Definition 9. $E \in SNNI \Leftrightarrow E/Act_H \approx_T E \setminus Act_H$.   ∎

We have that $Access\_Monitor\_3$ is not $SNNI$ since γ' is a trace for the agent $Access\_Monitor\_3/Act_H$ and γ' is not a trace for $Access\_Monitor\_3 \setminus Act_H$. The reason why the name "*Strong NNI*" has been chosen is a consequence of the following result:

Proposition 3. $SNNI \subset NNI$.

PROOF. If $E \in SNNI$ then $E/Act_H \approx_T E \setminus Act_H$. Since $T(E \setminus Act_H) \subseteq T((E \setminus_I Act_H)/Act_H)$ and $T((E \setminus_I Act_H)/Act_H) \subseteq T(E/Act_H)$ then $E \in NNI$. The inclusion is strict because $E = \bar{h}.l.0$ is NNI but not $SNNI$.   ∎

It is thus possible to prove that $Access\_Monitor\_1$ of Example 1 is also $SNNI$.

$SNNI$ seems to be quite satisfactory in a trace equivalence setting. Unfortunately, in the following example, we will see that trace equivalence – as the basic equivalence for security properties – is too weak; in particular, it is not able to detect deadlocks due to high level activities, that influence the security of a system.

Example 4. Suppose we have a high level action h_stop which explicitly stops the monitor. Obviously, in such a case there is a possible deadlock caused by a high level activity. In particular, consider the system in Table 7 where $h\_stop \in$

Table 7. The $Access\_Monitor\_4$ System

$$Access\_Monitor\_4 \stackrel{\text{def}}{=} (Monitor\_4 \mid Object(1,0) \mid Object(0,0)) \setminus L$$

$$Monitor\_4 \stackrel{\text{def}}{=} access\_r(l,x).$$
$$(\text{ if } x \leq l \text{ then}$$
$$r(x,y).\overline{val}(l,y).Monitor\_4$$
$$\textbf{else}$$
$$\overline{val}(l,err).Monitor\_4)$$
$$+$$
$$access\_w(l,x).write(l,z).$$
$$(\text{ if } x \geq l \text{ then}$$
$$\overline{w}(x,z).Monitor\_4$$
$$\textbf{else}$$
$$Monitor\_4)$$
$$+$$
$$h\_stop.\underline{0}$$

Act_H. It is possible to prove that it is $SNNI$. This is because trace equivalence is not able to detect deadlocks and h_stop does not modify the low traces of the system. It could seem that a deadlock caused by a high level activity is not really interfering with any low level users, since a low level user, trying to make an access to the monitor, is not able to conclude that the monitor is blocked. However such a user can obviously deduce that the system is not blocked every time it accepts some access requests or gives some outputs. In the case of $Access\_Monitor\_4$, a low level user will never be able to conclude that h_stop has been executed; nonetheless, at every interaction with the system, the user will know that $Access\_Monitor\_4$ is not blocked and so that h_stop has not been executed yet. In section 3.4 we will show how the subtle information flow caused by a potential deadlock can be exploited in order to construct an information channel from high level to low level.   ■

In order to detect this kind of flows, it is necessary to use some notion of equivalence which is able to detect deadlocks. Note that by simply changing the equivalence notion in the definition of $SNNI$ we obtain a security property which inherits all the observation power of the new equivalence notion. So, for detecting deadlocks, one obvious possibility could be the failure/testing setting [9,52], that has been designed for this purpose.

3.2 Detecting High Level Deadlocks through Failure/Testing Equivalences

Consider the version of $SNNI$ based on testing equivalence:

Definition 10. *(testing SNNI)* $E \in TSNNI \iff E/Act_H \approx_{test} E \setminus Act_H$ ■

We have that $Access\_Monitor\_4 \notin TSNNI$. In fact it is sufficient to consider the test $T \overset{\text{def}}{=} \overline{access\_r}(0,0).\omega.\underline{0}$ which is able to detect the deadlock introduced by action h_stop. In particular, we have that:

$$Access\_Monitor\_4 \setminus Act_H \ must \ T$$

$$Access\_Monitor\_4/Act_H \ m\slashed{u}st \ T$$

Intuitively, when we hide h_stop in $Access\_Monitor\_4/Act_H$ we obtain an internal transition to a deadlock state. If the system moves to that state before the execution of $access\_r(0,0)$ the test will not be satisfied.

So, it seems that $TSNNI$ is exactly the deadlock-sensitive extension of $SNNI$ we were looking for. However, in the following we want to show that for systems with some high level loops or with τ loops, $TSNNI$ is not interesting and is not able to detect security flaws. This is caused by the way testing equivalence deals with divergences (infinite sequences of τ actions). In fact, it is possible to prove that if E is divergent, then the (failure) condition (ii) of $\approx_{test}$ is verified if and only if also F is divergent. In the failure setting, when we have a divergent state we can observe the behaviour of a process only before reaching that state. All the actions after a divergence cannot be observed. In section 2.2, we have seen that $A' \overset{\text{def}}{=} a.b.0$ is not testing equivalent to $B' \overset{\text{def}}{=} a.B''$ with $B'' \overset{\text{def}}{=} \tau.B'' + b.0$.

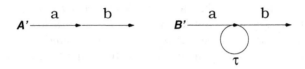

Fig. 7. Divergence makes A and B non testing equivalent

The only difference between A' and B' is the divergence after the execution of a in B' (see Figure 7).

Now, consider a system E with some high level loops and without divergences. When we hide high level actions in *TSNNI* with operation E/Act_H, we obtain some τ loops and so E/Act_H is divergent. As we said above, this will be failure equivalent to $E \setminus Act_H$ only if $E \setminus Act_H$ is divergent as well. However since E is without divergences, $E \setminus Act_H$ cannot have divergences too. We conclude that this kind of systems cannot be *TSNNI* no matter what the interactions between high and low level actions are. Note that every recursive high level system (with no low level actions and so secure by definition) is of this kind. All the access monitors we have seen so far have this feature as well.

Moreover we have an even worse situation if we consider a divergent process D, as also $D \setminus Act_H$ and D/Act_H are divergent. So for these two processes (ii) is verified. This means that for divergent processes $\approx_{test}$ becomes equal to $\approx_T$. Hence *TSNNI* becomes equal to *SNNI* and, in general, all the properties based on testing equivalence become equal to the corresponding ones based on trace equivalence. Now, we present an example of a divergent *TSNNI* process which, nonetheless, contains some high level deadlocks.

Example 5. Consider again agent *Access_Monitor_4*. We want to add a backup feature which is able to make a copy of the values stored in objects periodically. Obviously, there should be also a recovery procedure, but we do not model this in order to simplify as much as possible the example. We have a first process which represents the backup timer and sends periodically a signal in order to obtain a backup. It is an abstraction of a clock, since in SPA it is not possible to handle time directly.

$$Backup\_timer \stackrel{\text{def}}{=} \overline{backup}.Backup\_timer$$

Then we slightly modify the *Monitor* process by inserting two actions which suspend its execution until the backup is finished.

$$Monitor\_B \stackrel{\text{def}}{=} \ldots$$

$$\text{the same as in } Access\_Monitor\_4$$

$$\ldots$$

$$+ \; start\_backup.end\_backup.Monitor$$

The backup process is enabled by the timer, then it stops the monitor, reads the values of variables, stores them into two additional objects ($Object(2, y)$ and $Object(3, y)$) and resumes the monitor:

$$Backup \stackrel{\text{def}}{=} \overline{backup}.$$
$$\overline{start\_backup}.$$
$$r(0, y).r(1, z).$$
$$\overline{w}(2, y).\overline{w}(3, z).$$
$$\overline{end\_backup}.$$
$$Backup$$

The access monitor with backup is given by the following system:

$$Access\_Monitor\_B \stackrel{\text{def}}{=} (Monitor\_B \mid Backup\_timer \mid Backup \mid Object(0, 0) \mid$$
$$\mid Object(1, 0) \mid Object(2, 0) \mid Object(3, 0)) \setminus L$$

where $L = \{r, w, start\_backup, end\_backup, backup\}$. As a result, the backup procedure of the system is something internal, i.e., an external user can see nothing of the backup task. This makes the system divergent. In fact, if the variable values are unchanged, then the backup procedure is a τ loop that moves the system to the same state where it started the backup. For weak bisimulation this is not a problem and we can analyze this new system as well. In particular, we can check with the CoSeC tool (presented in Section 4) that $Access\_Monitor\_B$ is observationally equivalent to $Access\_Monitor\_4$. This is enough to prove (Theorem 5) that every security analysis made on $Access\_Monitor\_4$ is valid also for $Access\_Monitor\_B$. In particular, $Access\_Monitor\_B$ is not secure because of the potential high level deadlock we have explicitly added in $Access\_Monitor\_4$.

On the other hand, if we try to analyze this system with some testing equivalence based property, we have an inaccurate result. Indeed $Access\_Monitor\_B$, differently from $Access\_Monitor\_4$, is $TSNNI$. This happens because process $Access\_Monitor\_B$ is divergent and so processes $Access\_Monitor\_B/Act_H$ and $(Access\_Monitor\_B|\Pi) \setminus Act_H$ ($\forall \Pi \in \mathcal{E}_H$) are divergent as well. Thus they are failure equivalent and, since $Access\_Monitor\_B$ is $SNNI$ they are also trace (and so testing) equivalent. ∎

There is also an interesting, practical difference between bisimulation and failure/testing. On the one hand, it is possible to check bisimulation (observational equivalence) in polynomial time [42]. On the other hand, we have that the problem of establishing language equivalence of nondeterministic finite automata is reducible in polynomial time to the problem of checking any of the testing, failure, and trace equivalences. Such a problem has been proved to be PSPACE-complete [61]. The consequence is that all these problems are PSPACE-complete as well.

Moreover it is interesting to observe that failure/testing equivalences are not known to be decidable on infinite state systems. On the other hand, there are some interesting results on the decidability of weak bisimulation over some classes of infinite state systems, e.g. totally normed Basic Process Algebras (BPA) [38].[8] For instance it is possible to define a BPA agent representing an unbounded queue.

All these arguments have convinced us to adopt bisimulation and observational equivalence as the default semantic equivalence for our properties.

In the next section we move to weak bisimulation and observational equivalence. As we have seen, these notions are able to detect deadlocks as well. Moreover they give a *fair* interpretation of divergence, i.e., they assume that a τ loop will be executed an arbitrary, yet finite, number of times. In this way they can observe system behaviour also after divergences.

3.3   Properties Based on Observational Equivalence

We introduce the bisimulation-based security properties *BNNI* and *BSNNI*, by substituting $\approx_B$ for $\approx_T$ in their SPA-based definitions.

Definition 11. *(Bisimulation NNI, SNNI)*

(i) $E \in BNNI \iff E/Act_H \approx_B (E \setminus_I Act_H)/Act_H$
(ii) $E \in BSNNI \iff E/Act_H \approx_B E \setminus Act_H$ ∎

As expected, it can be proved that each of these new properties is properly finer than its corresponding trace-based one.

Proposition 4. *The following hold:*

(i) $BNNI \subset NNI$,
(ii) $BSNNI \subset SNNI$,

PROOF. It immediately follows from the fact that $E \approx_B F$ implies $E \approx_T F$. The inclusions are proper because $E = \tau.l.0 + \tau.h.l.0$ is such that $E \in NNI, SNNI$ and $E \notin BNNI, BSNNI$.   ∎

Consider again *Access_Monitor_4* containing the *h_stop* event. It is neither *BSNNI* nor *BNNI*, as observational equivalence is able to detect deadlocks. In particular, *Access_Monitor_4/Act_H* can move to $\underline{0}$ through an internal action τ, while *Access_Monitor_4 \ Act_H* is not able to reach (in zero or more τ steps) a state equivalent to $\underline{0}$.

Now we want to show that *BSNNI* and *BNNI* are still not able to detect some potential deadlocks due to high level activities. This will induce us to propose another property based on a different intuition. Let us consider *Access_Monitor_1*. We can prove that such a system is *BSNNI* as well as *BNNI*. However, the following two dangerous situations are possible: (i) a high level user makes a read

---

[8] BPA [6] are basically the transition systems associated with Greibach normal form (GNF) context-free grammars in which only left-most derivations are permitted. In order to obtain an LTS an action is associated with every rule.

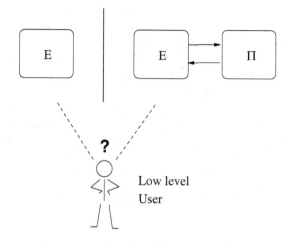

Fig. 8. BNDC intuition

request without accepting the corresponding output from the monitor (remember that communications in SPA are synchronous) and (*ii*) a high level user makes a write request and does not send the value to be written. In both cases we have a deadlock due to a high level activity that *BNNI* and *BSNNI* are not able to reveal. To solve this problem, we are going to present a stronger property, called *Bisimulation-based Non Deducibility on Compositions* (*BNDC*, for short). It is simply based on the idea of checking the system against all high level potential interactions. A system E is *BNDC* if for every high level process Π a low level user cannot distinguish E from $(E|\Pi) \setminus Act_H$. In other words, a system E is *BNDC* if what a low level user sees of the system is not modified by composing any high level process Π to E (see Figure 8).

Definition 12. *E is BNDC iff* $\forall \Pi \in \mathcal{E}_H$, $E/Act_H \approx_B (E \mid \Pi) \setminus Act_H$. ∎

Example 6. We want to show that *Access_Monitor_1* is not *BNDC*. Consider $\Pi = \overline{access\_r}(1,1).\underline{0}$. System $(Access\_Monitor\_1 \mid \Pi) \setminus Act_H$ will be blocked immediately after the execution of the read request by Π, moving to the following deadlock state:

$$((\overline{val}(1,0).Monitor \mid Object(0,0) \mid Object(1,0)) \setminus L \mid 0) \setminus Act_H$$

This happens because Π executes a read request and does not wait for the corresponding return value (action *val*). We conclude that Π can interfere with low level users. Since there are no possible deadlocks in $Access\_Monitor\_1/Act_H$, we find out that $(Access\_Monitor\_1|\Pi)\setminus Act_H \not\approx_B Access\_Monitor\_1/Act_H$ and so *Access_Monitor_1* is not *BNDC*.

Moreover, there is another potential source of deadlock when a high level user makes a write request and does not send the value to be written. In particular, the

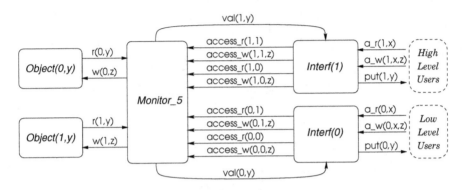

Fig. 9. The *BNDC Access_Monitor_5*

high level user $\Pi' = \overline{access\_w}(1,0).\underline{0}$ will block system $(Access\_Monitor\_1|\Pi') \setminus Act_H$ immediately after the execution of the write request by Π', moving the system to the following deadlock state:

$$(((write(1,0).\overline{w}(1,0).Monitor + write(1,1).\overline{w}(1,1).Monitor) \mid Object(0,0) \mid \\ \mid Object(1,0)) \setminus L \mid 0) \setminus Act_H$$

Again, we have $(Access\_Monitor\_1|\Pi') \setminus Act_H \not\approx_B Access\_Monitor\_1/Act_H$. In order to obtain a *BNDC* access monitor, we modify the monitor by adding an interface for each level which temporarily stores the output value of the monitor (passing it later to the users and thus making communication asynchronous) and that guarantees mutual exclusion within the same level; moreover, we use an atomic action for write request and value sending. Note that, because of the interface, actions *access_r*, *access_w* and *val* become *a_r*, *a_w* and *put*, respectively. The resulting system is reported in Table 8 (see also Figure 9).

In such a system we have that $k \in \{0,1,err\}$, $L = \{r, w\}$, $N = \{val, access\_r, access\_w\}$ and $a\_r(1,x)$, $a\_w(1,x)$, $put(1,y) \in Act_H$ $\forall x \in \{0,1\}$ and $\forall y \in \{0,1,err\}$, while the same actions with 0 as first parameter belong to Act_L. It is possible to verify that *Access_Monitor_5* is *BNDC* using the automatically checkable property we are going to present. Table 9 summarizes the properties satisfied by the different versions of the access monitor. ■

The next theorem shows that the bisimulation-based properties are related in a different way with respect to the corresponding ones. Indeed, we have that *BNDC* is stronger than *BNNI* and *BSNNI*. Moreover *BSNNI* $\not\subset$ *BNNI* while for trace equivalence we had that *SNNI* $\subset$ *NNI*. *BSNNI*

Theorem 1.

(i) *BNNI* $\not\subseteq$ *BSNNI* and *BSNNI* $\not\subseteq$ *BNNI*.
(ii) *BNDC* $\subset$ *BSNNI* $\cap$ *BNNI*.

Table 8. The *Access_Monitor_5* System

$Access\_Monitor\_5 \overset{\text{def}}{=} (AM \mid Interf) \setminus N$

$\quad AM \overset{\text{def}}{=} (Monitor\_5 \mid Object(1,0) \mid Object(0,0)) \setminus L$

$\quad Monitor\_5 \overset{\text{def}}{=} access\_r(l,x).$

$\qquad\qquad (\textbf{ if } x \leq l \textbf{ then}$

$\qquad\qquad\qquad r(x,y).\overline{val}(l,y).Monitor\_5$

$\qquad\qquad \textbf{else}$

$\qquad\qquad\qquad \overline{val}(l,err).Monitor\_5)$

$\qquad\qquad +$

$\qquad\qquad access\_w(l,x,z).$

$\qquad\qquad (\textbf{ if } x \geq l \textbf{ then}$

$\qquad\qquad\qquad \overline{w}(x,z).Monitor\_5$

$\qquad\qquad \textbf{else}$

$\qquad\qquad\qquad Monitor\_5)$

$\quad Interf \overset{\text{def}}{=} Interf(0) \mid Interf(1)$

$\quad Interf(l) \overset{\text{def}}{=} a\_r(l,x).\overline{access\_r}(l,x).val(l,k).\overline{put}(l,k).Interf(l)$

$\qquad\qquad +$

$\qquad\qquad a\_w(l,x,z).\overline{access\_w}(l,x,z).Interf(l)$

PROOF. (*i*) Let us consider the following agent $E = l.\overline{h}.l.h.l.0 + l.l.l.0 + l.l.0$; we have that $E \in BNNI$ and $E \notin BSNNI$. Let us now consider the agent $F = l.\overline{h}.l.h.l.0 + l.l.l.0 + l.0$; we have that $F \in BSNNI$ and $F \notin BNNI$.

(*ii*) To show that $BNDC \subseteq BSNNI$, consider $\Pi' = 0$ (the empty process). Then, by $BNDC$ definition, we have that $E/Act_H \approx_B (E \mid 0) \setminus Act_H$ and so $E/Act_H \approx_B E \setminus Act_H$.

To show that $BNDC \subseteq BNNI$, consider $\Pi'' = \sum_{i \in Act_H \cap I} i.\Pi''$ (the process which accepts all the high inputs) then, by $BNDC$ definition, we have that $E/Act_H \approx_B (E \mid \Pi'') \setminus Act_H$. Now it is sufficient to note that $(E \mid \Pi'') \setminus Act_H \approx_B (E \setminus_I Act_H)/Act_H$.

In order to show that the inclusion is strict we need a system which is both $BSNNI$ and $BNNI$, and which is not $BNDC$. Such a system is $E = l.h.l.h.l.0 + l.l.l.\underline{0} + l.\underline{0}$. It is easy to see that it is $BSNNI$ and $BNNI$. Moreover if we consider $\Pi''' = \overline{h}.\underline{0}$ we obtain that $(E \mid \Pi''') \setminus Act_H \approx_B l.l.\underline{0} + l.l.l.\underline{0} + l.\underline{0} \not\approx_B E$. ∎

We need another simple result before we can draw a diagram of the relations among all the properties we have seen up to now.

Proposition 5. $BNNI \not\subseteq SNNI$.

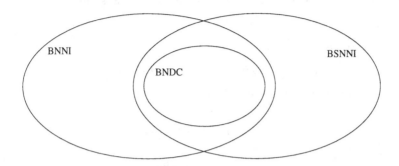

Fig. 10. The inclusion diagram for bisimulation-based properties

PROOF. It is sufficient to consider agent $E = \bar{h}.l.0$ which is *BNNI* but not *SNNI*. ∎

Figure 10 summarizes the relations among the bisimulation-based properties presented so far.

It is now interesting to study the trace equivalence version of *BNDC* called *NDC*. Indeed it could improve the *SNNI* property which is still our better proposal for the trace equivalence setting (no detection of deadlocks). Surprisingly, we find out that such property is exactly equal to *SNNI*.

Theorem 2. $NDC = SNNI$.

PROOF. We first prove that if $E \in NDC$ then $E \in SNNI$. By hypothesis, $E/Act_H \approx_T (E|0) \setminus Act_H$ for the specific $\Pi = 0$. Since $(E|0) \setminus Act_H \approx_T E \setminus Act_H$ then we have $E/Act_H \approx_T E \setminus Act_H$.

Now we want to prove that if $E \in SNNI$ then $E \in NDC$. By hypothesis, $E/Act_H \approx_T E \setminus Act_H$. Since $T(E \setminus Act_H) \subseteq T((E|\Pi) \setminus Act_H)$ then we have $T(E/Act_H) \subseteq T((E|\Pi) \setminus Act_H)$. Observe also that the reverse inclusion holds, in fact, if E and Π synchronize on a certain high action, then E/Act_H can always "hide" it. Hence $E/Act_H \approx_T ((E|\Pi) \setminus H)/Act_H$. ∎

Table 9. Properties satisfied by the different versions of the access monitor

Ver.	Description	*NNI*	*SNNI*	*BNNI*	*BSNNI*	*BNDC*
1	Multilevel rules	X	X	X	X	
2	Without write control					
3	With high signal for integrity	X				
4	With explicit high level deadlock	X	X			
5	With buffers and atomic write	X	X	X	X	X

This, in a sense, confirms that the intuition behind *SNNI* (and so NI) is good at least in a trace equivalence model. Indeed, in such a model the fact that we check the system against every high level process is useless. It is sufficient to statically check if the hiding of high level actions corresponds to the restriction of such actions. This points out a critical point: *BNDC* is difficult to use in practice, because of the universal quantification on high level processes. It would be desirable to have an alternative formulation of *BNDC* which avoids universal quantification, exploiting local information only as for the trace-equivalence case; even if Martinelli has shown that *BNDC* is decidable over finite state processes [47], a solution to this problem is still to be found. In the same work, Martinelli also shows a negative fact regarding the verification of *BNDC*: it is not compositional, i.e., if two systems are *BNDC* their composition may be not so. This does not permit us to reduce the *BNDC*-security of a big system to the *BNDC*-security of its simpler subsystems and forces us to always prove *BNDC* over the whole system.

For these reasons, here we propose a sufficient condition for *BNDC*, namely the *SBSNNI* property, which exploits local information only and moreover is compositional (i.e., if two systems are *SBSNNI* their composition is *SBSNNI* too).

Definition 13. *(SBSNNI: Strong BSNNI)*
A system $E \in SBSNNI$ if and only if for all E' reachable from E we have $E' \in BSNNI$. ∎

SBSNNI is easily verifiable, as *BSNNI* is so; moreover, we can use it in order to check that a system is *BNDC* because of the following result.

Proposition 6. $SBSNNI \subset BNDC$

PROOF. Let E be a system and Π a high level process. Let R be a relation defined as follows: $(E' \setminus Act_H, (E' \mid \Pi') \setminus Act_H) \in R$, for all E', Π' such that $E \Rightarrow E'$ and $\Pi \Rightarrow \Pi'$. We want to prove that if E is *SBSNNI* then R is a weak bisimulation up to $\approx_B$ (see [50]). There is only one non trivial case: $(E' \mid \Pi') \setminus Act_H \xrightarrow{\tau} (E'' \mid \Pi'') \setminus Act_H$. As there exists $h \in Act_H$ such that $E' \xrightarrow{h} E''$, then $E'/Act_H \xrightarrow{\tau} E''/Act_H$. By hypothesis, $E' \in BSNNI$ hence we have $E'/Act_H \approx_B E' \setminus Act_H$ and so there exists an agent E''' such that $E' \setminus Act_H \overset{\hat{\tau}}{\Longrightarrow} E''' \setminus Act_H$ and $E''' \setminus Act_H \approx_B E''/Act_H$. By hypothesis, $E'' \in BSNNI$ hence we also have that $E''/Act_H \approx_B E'' \setminus Act_H$ and so $E''' \setminus Act_H \approx_B E'' \setminus Act_H$. Since $(E'' \setminus Act_H, (E'' \mid \Pi'') \setminus Act_H) \in R$ and $E''' \setminus Act_H \approx_B E'' \setminus Act_H$ then R is a bisimulation up to $\approx_B$.

Now we have that $E \setminus Act_H \approx_B (E \mid \Pi) \setminus Act_H$ for all $\Pi \in \mathcal{E}_H$. Since $E \in BSNNI$, then $E/Act_H \approx_B E \setminus Act_H$. Therefore $E/Act_H \approx_B (E \mid \Pi) \setminus Act_H$. This means that $E \in BNDC$.

The inclusion is strict because agent $E = l.h.l.0 + l.0 + l.l.0$ is *BNDC* but not *SBSNNI*. ∎

The next theorem states that *SBSNNI* is *compositional*, i.e., preserved by the parallel and the restriction operators. This is useful in the automatic check of this property because it allows to check it directly on the subsystems thus reducing the exponential explosion of the states due to all possible interleavings of parallel systems. We will study this in details in the next section. Similar results of compositionality hold for *NNI* and *SNNI* [24].

Theorem 3. *The following hold:*

(i) $E, F \in SBSNNI \Longrightarrow (E|F) \in SBSNNI$
(ii) $E \in SBSNNI, L \subseteq \mathcal{L} \Longrightarrow E \setminus L \in SBSNNI$

PROOF. We need the following:

Lemma 1. $(E|F)/Act_H \approx_B E/Act_H|F/Act_H$.

PROOF. Consider the following relation: $((E'|F')/Act_H, E'/Act_H|F'/Act_H) \in R$ if and only if $E \Rightarrow E'$ and $F \Rightarrow F'$. It is easy to prove that R is a bisimulation. Indeed the only non trivial case is the synchronization $(E'|F')/Act_H \overset{\tau}{\rightarrow} (E''|F'')/Act_H$ which is simulated by $E'/Act_H|F'/Act_H \overset{\tau.\tau}{\rightarrow} E''/Act_H|F''/Act_H$. ∎

Now we can prove the Theorem.

(i) Consider the relation $((E'|F') \setminus Act_H, E' \setminus Act_H|F' \setminus Act_H) \in R$ for all E', F' such that $E \Rightarrow E'$ and $F \Rightarrow F'$. If we prove that R is a weak bisimulation up to $\approx_B$ then, by hypothesis and Lemma 1, we obtain the thesis. We consider the only non trivial case: $(E'|F') \setminus Act_H \overset{\tau}{\rightarrow} (E''|F'') \setminus Act_H$ with $E' \overset{h}{\rightarrow} E''$ and $F' \overset{\bar{h}}{\rightarrow} F''$. Since $E'/Act_H \overset{\tau}{\rightarrow} E''/Act_H$ and, by hypothesis, $E' \in BSNNI$, we have that $\exists E'''$ such that $E' \setminus Act_H \overset{\hat{\tau}}{\Longrightarrow} E''' \setminus Act_H$ and $E''/Act_H \approx_B E'''\setminus Act_H$; finally, by hypothesis, $E'' \in BSNNI$, hence we obtain $E'''\setminus Act_H \approx_B E'' \setminus Act_H$. Repeating the same procedure for F' we have $\exists E''', F'''$ such that $E' \setminus Act_H|F' \setminus Act_H \overset{\hat{\tau}}{\Longrightarrow} E''' \setminus Act_H|F''' \setminus Act_H \approx_B E'' \setminus Act_H|F'' \setminus Act_H$. Since $((E''|F'') \setminus Act_H, E'' \setminus Act_H| F'' \setminus Act_H) \in R$, then R is a bisimulation up to $\approx_B$.

(ii) Consider the following relation $((E'/Act_H) \setminus L, (E' \setminus L)/Act_H) \in R$, for all E' such that $E \Rightarrow E'$ and for all $L \subseteq \mathcal{L}$. If we prove that R is a bisimulation up to $\approx_B$ then, by applying hypothesis and observing that $(E' \setminus L) \setminus Act_H \approx_B (E'\setminus Act_H)\setminus L$, we obtain the thesis. The only non trivial case is $(E'/Act_H)\setminus L \overset{\tau}{\rightarrow} (E''/Act_H) \setminus L$ with $E' \overset{h}{\rightarrow} E''$ and $h \in Act_H$. By hypothesis, $E' \in BSNNI$ hence we have that $(E'/Act_H) \setminus L \approx_B (E' \setminus Act_H) \setminus L$ and so $\exists E'''$ such that $(E' \setminus Act_H)\setminus L \overset{\hat{\tau}}{\Longrightarrow} (E'''\setminus Act_H)\setminus L \approx_B (E'''/Act_H)\setminus L$ and $(E''' \setminus Act_H)\setminus L \approx_B (E''/Act_H) \setminus L$. Obviously, we also have that $(E' \setminus L)\setminus Act_H \overset{\hat{\tau}}{\Longrightarrow} (E'''\setminus L) \setminus Act_H$ and so $(E'\setminus L)/Act_H \overset{\hat{\tau}}{\Longrightarrow} (E'''\setminus L)/Act_H$. We briefly summarize the proof: we had the synchronization $(E'/Act_H) \setminus L \overset{\tau}{\rightarrow} (E''/Act_H) \setminus L$ and we proved that there exists E''' such that $(E' \setminus L)/Act_H \overset{\hat{\tau}}{\Longrightarrow} (E''' \setminus L)/Act_H$ and $(E'''/Act_H) \setminus L \approx_B (E''/Act_H) \setminus L$. Since $((E'''/Act_H) \setminus L, (E''' \setminus L)/Act_H) \in R$ then R is a weak bisimulation up to $\approx_B$. ∎

It is worthwhile noticing that *SBSNNI* was not the first sufficient condition proposed for *BNDC*. In [24] we introduced a property stronger than *SBSNNI*, but nevertheless quite intuitive, called *Strong BNDC* (*SBNDC*). This property just requires that before and after every high step, the system appears to be the same, from a low level perspective. More formally we have the following definition.

Definition 14. *(SBNDC: Strong BNDC)*
A system $E \in SBNDC$ if and only if $\forall E'$ reachable from E and $\forall E''$ such that $E' \xrightarrow{h} E''$ for $h \in Act_H$, then $E' \setminus Act_H \approx_B E'' \setminus Act_H$

We now prove that *SBNDC* is strictly stronger than *SBSNNI*. To this purpose, we need the following Lemma

Lemma 2. $E \in BNDC \Leftrightarrow E \setminus Act_H \approx_B (E|\Pi) \setminus Act_H$ for all $\Pi \in \mathcal{E}_H$.

PROOF. It follows immediately from Theorem 1.*(ii)* and Definition 12.   ∎

Proposition 7. $SBNDC \subset SBSNNI$.

PROOF. Let E be a system and Π a high level process. Let R be a relation defined as follows: $(E' \setminus Act_H, (E' \mid \Pi') \setminus Act_H) \in R$, for all E', Π' such that $E \Rightarrow E'$ and $\Pi \Rightarrow \Pi'$. We want to prove that if E is *SBNDC* then R is a bisimulation up to $\approx_B$ (see [50]). There is only one interesting case: $(E' \mid \Pi') \setminus Act_H \xrightarrow{\tau} (E'' \mid \Pi'') \setminus Act_H$. As there exists $h \in Act_H$ such that $E' \xrightarrow{h} E''$, then $E'' \setminus Act_H \approx_B E' \setminus Act_H$; since $(E'' \setminus Act_H, (E'' \mid \Pi'') \setminus Act_H) \in R$, then $(E'' \mid \Pi'') \setminus Act_H \approx_B E' \setminus Act_H$. So $E' \setminus Act_H \approx_B (E' \mid \Pi) \setminus Act_H$ (i.e., $E' \in BNDC$), for all E' reachable from E. As *BNDC* is stronger than *BSNNI* (Theorem 1.*(ii)*), we obtain the thesis. The inclusion is strict because agent $E = \tau.l.0 + l.l.0 + h.l.0$ is *SBSNNI* but not *SBNDC*.   ∎

As for *SBSNNI*, we have a compositionality theorem:

Theorem 4. *The following hold:*

(i) $E, F \in SBNDC \implies (E|F) \in SBNDC$,
(ii) $E \in SBNDC \Rightarrow E \setminus S \in SBNDC$, if $S \subseteq \mathcal{L}$.
(iii) $E, F \in SBNDC \implies (E\|F) \in SBNDC$

PROOF. (i) It must be proved that $\forall E', F' : E \Rightarrow E', F \Rightarrow F', \forall E'', F'' : (E' \mid F') \xrightarrow{h} (E'' \mid F'')$ with $h \in Act_H$, the following holds: $(E' \mid F') \setminus Act_h \approx_B (E'' \mid F'') \setminus Act_H$. Let R be the relation defined as follows: $((\tilde{E} \mid \tilde{F}) \setminus Act_H, (\tilde{E}' \mid \tilde{F}') \setminus Act_H) \in R, \forall \tilde{E}, \tilde{E}', \tilde{F}, \tilde{F}'$ such that $E \Rightarrow \tilde{E}, E \Rightarrow \tilde{E}', F \Rightarrow \tilde{F}, F \Rightarrow \tilde{F}'$ and $\tilde{E} \setminus Act_H \approx_B \tilde{E}' \setminus Act_H, \tilde{F} \setminus Act_h \approx_B \tilde{F}' \setminus Act_H$. It can be easily proved that R is a weak bisimulation (under the hypothesis $E, F \in SBNDC$); there is only one interesting case: $(\tilde{E} \mid \tilde{F}) \setminus Act_H \xrightarrow{\tau} (\tilde{E}'' \mid \tilde{F}'') \setminus Act_H$. Thus we have that $\tilde{E} \setminus Act_H \approx_B \tilde{E}'' \setminus Act_H$ and $\tilde{F} \setminus Act_H \approx_B \tilde{F}'' \setminus Act_H$ and so $((\tilde{E}'' \mid \tilde{F}'') \setminus Act_H, (\tilde{E}' \mid \tilde{F}') \setminus Act_H) \in R$.

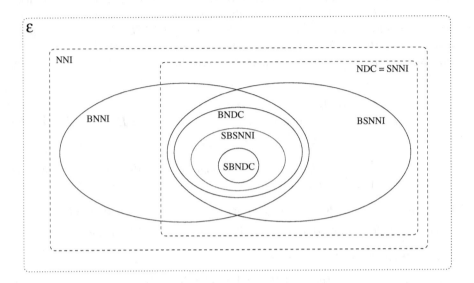

Fig. 11. The inclusion diagram for trace-based and bisimulation-based properties

(*ii*) Observe that $(E'\backslash S)\backslash Act_H \approx_B (E''\backslash S)\backslash Act_H$ if and only if $(E'\backslash Act_H)\backslash S \approx_B (E'' \backslash Act_H) \backslash S$. As $\approx_B$ is a congruence for restriction [50] the thesis follows trivially.
(*iii*) Trivial from (*i*) and (*ii*). ∎

Figure 11 summarizes the relations among all the trace-based and bisimulation-based properties we have presented.

We end this section with a remark. In the automatic verification of properties, it can be very useful to work on a *reduced* system, i.e., a system equivalent to the original one, but with a smaller number of states. In fact, the tool we will present in the next section provides a procedure that minimizes the number of states, thus reducing a lot the time spent in the verification. In order to see if this proof strategy can be used also in our case, we need to prove that if a system E is *BNDC*, then any other observation equivalent system F is *BNDC* too. Indeed, the theorem below shows that this is the case, also for all the other security properties we have discussed in this section.

Theorem 5. *If* $E \approx_B F$, *then* $E \in X \Leftrightarrow F \in X$, *where* X *can be NNI, SNNI, NDC, BNNI, BSNNI, BNDC, SBSNNI, SBNDC.*

PROOF. It derives from the definition of the security properties, observing that trace and bisimulation equivalences are congruences with respect to $\_\backslash L$ and $\_|\_$ operators of CCS [50]. It is possible to prove that they are also congruence with with respect to $\_\backslash_I L$ and $\_/L$ operators of SPA. For trace equivalence the proof is trivial. In the following we prove the closure of weak bisimulation equivalence

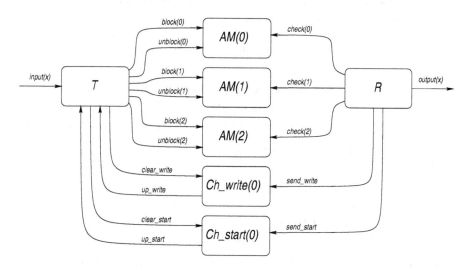

Fig. 12. The *Channel* process, a one-bit channel obtained by three processes with high level deadlocks

w.r.t. $\_\backslash_I L$ and leave to the reader the other similar case of $\_/L$. Let $E \approx_B F$; we want to prove that $E \backslash_I L \approx_B F \backslash_I L$. Consider a bisimulation R such that $(E, F) \in R$; then define the relation P as follows: $(E' \backslash_I L, F' \backslash_I L) \in P$ if and only if $(E', F') \in R$. P is a bisimulation too, in fact if $E' \backslash_I L \xrightarrow{\mu} E'' \backslash_I L$ then $\mu \notin L \cap I$ and $E' \xrightarrow{\mu} E''$. So $\exists F''$ such that $F' \xRightarrow{\hat{\mu}} F''$; since $\mu \notin L \cap I$ then $F' \backslash_I L \xRightarrow{\hat{\mu}} F'' \backslash_I L$ (and vice versa for $F' \backslash_I L \xrightarrow{\mu} F'' \backslash_I L$). ∎

3.4   Building Channels by Exploiting Deadlocks

In Example 6 we have seen that *Access_Monitor_1* is not *BNDC* because of potential high level deadlocks. We said that a deadlock due to high level activity is visible from low level users, hence it gives some information about high level actions, and cannot be allowed. However, one could doubt that a high level deadlock is really dangerous and, in particular, that it can be exploited to transmit information from high to low. We demonstrate that it is indeed the case by simply showing that it is possible to build a 1-bit channel from high to low level using systems which contain high level deadlocks. In particular we obtain a 1-bit channel with some initial noise (before the beginning of the transmission), using three processes with high level deadlocks composed with other secure systems.

Of the two high level deadlocks of process *Access_Monitor_1* we only exploit the one due to write requests. So the following method can be applied also to systems with only one high level deadlock. Process *Channel* is reported in Table 10 where $n \in \{0, 1, 2\}$, $x, y \in \{0, 1\}$; {*block, unblock, up_write, up_start, input,*

Table 10. The *Channel* process which exploits deadlocks

$$Channel \overset{\text{def}}{=} (Ch\_write(0) \mid Ch\_start(0) \mid AM(0) \mid AM(1) \mid AM(2) \mid$$
$$\mid R \mid T) \setminus N$$

$$AM(n) \overset{\text{def}}{=} Access\_Monitor\_1[check(n)/access\_r(0,0),$$
$$block(n)/access\_w(1,1),$$
$$unblock(n)/write(1,0)] \setminus \{access\_r, access\_w, write, val\}$$

$$Ch\_write(x) \overset{\text{def}}{=} send\_write.Ch\_write(1)$$
$$+$$
$$clear\_write.Ch\_write(0)$$
$$+$$
if $x = 1$ **then**
$$\overline{up\_write}.Ch\_write(0)$$

$$Ch\_start(0) \overset{\text{def}}{=} Ch\_write(0)[send\_start/send\_write, up\_start/up\_write,$$
$$clear\_start/clear\_write]$$

$$R \overset{\text{def}}{=} \overline{send\_write}.R$$
$$+$$
$$\overline{check}(2).\overline{send\_start}.$$
$$(\overline{check}(0).\overline{output}(0).R$$
$$+$$
$$\overline{check}(1).\overline{output}(1).R)$$

$$T \overset{\text{def}}{=} \overline{block}(2).\overline{clear\_write}.up\_write.\overline{block}(0).\overline{block}(1).T1$$

$$T1 \overset{\text{def}}{=} \overline{clear\_start}.unblock(2).up\_start.\overline{block}(2).\overline{clear\_write}.$$
$$input(y).\overline{unblock}(y).up\_write.\overline{block}(y).T1$$

$clear\_write$, $clear\_start\} \subseteq Act_H$; $N = \{check, block, unblock, send\_write,$ up_write, $clear\_write$, $send\_start$, up_start, $clear\_start\}$.

Channel (see Figure 12) is the composition of three instances of Access Monitor ($AM(0)$,$AM(1)$ and $AM(2)$), two channels from low to high level ($Ch\_write(0)$ and $Ch\_start(0)$), a transmitter and a receiver (T and R). In particular $AM(n)$ is an instance of *Access_Monitor_1* where we call $check(n)$ the reading request of low level users in low object, it is used to check if $AM(n)$ is in a deadlock state; $block(n)$ is a writing request by a high level user, it is used to block $AM(n)$; finally $unblock(n)$ is a write action and is used to unblock $AM(n)$ which was previously blocked with $block(n)$. $Ch\_write(x)$ moves to $Ch\_write(1)$ every time a $send\_write$ is executed by the receiver. $Ch\_write(1)$ can give to T the $\overline{up\_write}$ signal; it also ignores all the $send\_write$ signals. Moreover, when

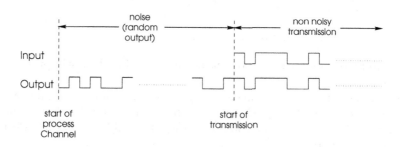

Fig. 13. Noise in *Channel* and *C*

clear_write is executed by the transmitter this resets the process to $Ch\_write(0)$. So if R executes $\overline{send\_write}$ and after this, T executes $\overline{clear\_write}$ and up_write, then T will be blocked. $Ch\_start(0)$ is equal to $Ch\_write(0)$ with appropriate action relabeling.

R and T use the monitor $AM(2)$ for synchronization and $AM(0)$, $AM(1)$ for transmission. In particular T blocks $AM(2)$ and then it waits for a write enable signal (up_write). Afterward it blocks also monitors $AM(0)$ and $AM(1)$ moving to $T1$ which is the writing loop; $T1$ unblocks monitor $AM(2)$—which is the signal for R to start receiving the bit—and waits for a start writing signal (up_start). Then it blocks $AM(2)$ again, reads the high level value y, unblocks monitor $AM(y)$ (transmitting the value y) and waits for a write enable signal. When it receives such a signal, it blocks again monitor $AM(y)$ and moves to $T1$ in order to transmit another bit.

R can always send a writing enable signal moving again to R. Moreover it can check if $AM(2)$ is blocked. If such a monitor is not blocked (by T) it sends a start writing signal and checks if $AM(0)$ and $AM(1)$ are blocked. If it discovers that $AM(t)$, with $t = 0$ or $t = 1$, is not blocked, then it gives as output $\overline{output}(t)$. Finally it moves again to R in order to receive the next bit.

Note that if R executes $\overline{check}(2)$ before T has blocked monitor $AM(2)$ then R will give a non-deterministic output $\overline{output}(x)$. In fact T and R will synchronize and start transmitting the 1-bit messages as soon as T will execute $\overline{block}(2)$ blocking $AM(2)$. So we have some random output before the beginning of the transmission. It is possible to automatically check that

$$Channel \approx_B C$$

where

$$C \stackrel{\text{def}}{=} \tau.C'$$
$$+ \tau.($$
$$\tau.(\tau.\overline{output}(0).C' + \tau.\overline{output}(1).C')$$
$$+ \tau.(\overline{output}(0).C + \tau.\overline{output}(0).C')$$

$$+ \tau.(\overline{output}(1).C + \tau.\overline{output}(1).C')$$
$$)$$
$$C' \overset{\text{def}}{=} input(x).\overline{output}(x).C'$$

This automatic check can be done using the CoSeC tool we will present in the next section.

C can move to a 1-bit channel C' or can give some non-deterministic output (initial noise before the synchronization between T and R). Note that after moving to C' (the channel is ready to transmit) it will behave as a perfect 1-bit channel (see Figure 13).

3.5   Comparison with Related Work

The use of process algebras to formalize information flow security properties is not new. In [57] it is possible to find a definition of Non Interference given on CSP [39]. It looks like *SNNI* with some side conditions on acceptable low level actions. This definition is recalled in [4], where a comparison with another information flow property is reported.

More recent results based on the CSP model are contained in [56], where the authors introduce some information flow security properties based on the notion of *deterministic views* and show how to automatically verify them using the CSP model checker FDR [55].

The most interesting property is *lazy security* (*L-Sec*) which, however, requires the absence of non-determinism in the low view of the system (i.e., when hiding high actions through interleaving) and for this reason we think it could be too restrictive in a concurrent environment. For example, all the low non-deterministic systems – such as $E = l.\bar{l}_1 + l.\bar{l}_2$ – are considered not secure. In this section we compare those properties with ours using a failure-equivalence version of *BNDC*, called *FNDC* (see also [18] for more details). The main result is that *BNDC* restricted to the class of low-deterministic and non-divergent processes is equal to *L-Sec*.

Here we give a definition of failure equivalence which does not correspond completely to the original one [39]. Indeed, it does not consider possible divergences but this is not a problem since our comparison will focus on the class of non-divergent processes. We prefer this definition because it is very simple and is implied by $\approx_B$.

We need some simple additional notations. We write $E \overset{\mu}{\nrightarrow}$ to indicate that $\nexists E'$ such that $E \overset{\mu}{\Longrightarrow} E'$ and $E \overset{K}{\nrightarrow}$ with $K \subseteq \mathcal{L}$ stands for $\forall \mu \in K, E \overset{\mu}{\nrightarrow}$.

Definition 15. *If $\gamma \in T(E)$ and if, after executing γ, E can refuse all the actions in set $X \subseteq \mathcal{L}$, then we say that the pair (γ, X) is a failure of the process E. Formally we have that:*

$$failures(E) \overset{\text{def}}{=} \{(\gamma, X) \subseteq \mathcal{L}^* \times \mathbb{P}(\mathcal{L}) \mid \exists E' \text{ such that}$$
$$E \overset{\gamma}{\Longrightarrow} E' \text{ and } E' \overset{X}{\nrightarrow}\}$$

When failures(E) = failures(F) we write $E \approx_F F$ (failure equivalence).   ∎

We identify a process E with its failure set. So if $(\gamma, X) \in$ *failures*(E) we write $(\gamma, X) \in E$. Note that $\gamma \in T(E)$ if and only if $(\gamma, \emptyset) \in E$. So $E \approx_F F$ implies $E \approx_T F$.

We also have that $E \approx_B F$ implies $E \approx_F F$:

Proposition 8. $E \approx_B F$ *implies* $E \approx_F F$.

PROOF. Consider $E \approx_B F$ and $(\gamma, X) \in E$. We want to prove that $(\gamma, X) \in F$. Since $(\gamma, X) \in E$ we have that $\exists E'$ such that $E \stackrel{\gamma}{\Longrightarrow} E'$ and $E' \stackrel{X}{\not\Longrightarrow}$. By definition of $\approx_B$ we know that since $E \stackrel{\gamma}{\Longrightarrow} E'$ then $F \stackrel{\gamma}{\Longrightarrow} F'$ and $E' \approx_B F'$ (it is sufficient to simulate every step of the execution $E \stackrel{\gamma}{\Longrightarrow} E'$). Suppose by contradiction that $\exists \mu \in X$ such that $F' \stackrel{\mu}{\Longrightarrow} F''$. Then, by definition of $\approx_B$ and since $E' \approx_B F'$, we obtain that $E' \stackrel{\mu}{\Longrightarrow} E''$ but this is not possible since $E' \stackrel{X}{\not\Longrightarrow}$. We obtain that $F' \stackrel{X}{\not\Longrightarrow}$ and so $(\gamma, X) \in F$. The symmetric case can be done for every $(\gamma, X) \in F$ which must belong also to E.   ∎

Lazy Security We now report the *lazy security* property [56] and we show that it can only deal with low-deterministic processes, i.e., processes which have a deterministic behaviour with respect to low level actions. Here we do not consider the *eager security* property (introduced in [56] to deal with output actions) since it supposes that high level actions happen instantaneously while in SPA, which has synchronous communications, both input and output actions can be delayed by users. We start with a formal definition of determinism.

Definition 16. E *is deterministic ($E \in$ Det) if and only if whenever $\gamma a \in$ traces(E) then $(\gamma, \{a\}) \notin E$.*   ∎

So a process is deterministic if after every trace γ it cannot both accept and refuse a certain action a. We give another characterization for determinism. A system E is deterministic if and only if whenever it can move to two different processes E' and E'' executing a certain trace γ, such processes are failure equivalent.

Proposition 9. $E \in$ Det *if and only if for all $\gamma \in$ traces(E) we have that $E \stackrel{\gamma}{\Longrightarrow} E'$, $E \stackrel{\gamma}{\Longrightarrow} E''$ implies $E' \approx_F E''$.*

PROOF. ($\Rightarrow$) Let $E \in Det$, $E \stackrel{\gamma}{\Longrightarrow} E'$, $E \stackrel{\gamma}{\Longrightarrow} E''$ and $(\delta, K) \in E'$. We want to prove that $(\delta, K) \in E''$. Since $E \stackrel{\gamma}{\Longrightarrow} E'$, we have that $(\gamma\delta, K) \in E$. By $E \in Det$ we obtain that $\forall a \in K, \gamma\delta a$ is not a trace for E. We also have that δ is a trace for E''; in fact, if E'' can execute only a prefix of δ, i.e. $E'' \stackrel{\alpha}{\Longrightarrow} E'''$ with $\delta = \alpha b \beta$, we have that E can execute trace $\gamma\alpha b$ (through E') and can refuse b after $\gamma\alpha$ (through E'') contradicting the determinism hypothesis. Now, since $\forall a \in K, \gamma\delta a \notin traces(E)$, we also have that $\forall a \in K, \delta a \notin traces(E'')$ and so $(\delta, K) \in E''$.
($\Leftarrow$) Trivial.   ∎

Corollary 1. *If $E \overset{\gamma}{\Longrightarrow} E'$ and $E \in Det$ then $E' \in Det$.*

PROOF. We have to prove that $E' \overset{\delta}{\Longrightarrow} E''$ and $E' \overset{\delta}{\Longrightarrow} E'''$ implies $E'' \approx_F E'''$. Consider $E \overset{\gamma\delta}{\Longrightarrow} E''$ and $E \overset{\gamma\delta}{\Longrightarrow} E'''$ then by $E \in Det$ we have that $E'' \approx_F E'''$. ∎

In the following we denote with $E|||F$ the interleaving without communication between agents E and F. It can be expressed in SPA as $(E[A/\mathcal{L}(E)] \mid F[B/\mathcal{L}(F)])[\mathcal{L}(E)/A, \mathcal{L}(F)/B]$ where $A, B \subseteq \mathcal{L}, A \cap B = \emptyset$ and $A/\mathcal{L}(E)$ is a bijective function which maps all the actions executable by E into actions of A, with $\mathcal{L}(E)/A$ as inverse (the same holds for $B/\mathcal{L}(F)$ and $\mathcal{L}(F)/B$). This expression means that the actions in E and F are first relabelled using the two disjoint sets A and B, then interleaved (no communication is possible) and finally renamed to their original labels.

Recall that a process is *divergent* if it can execute an infinite sequence of internal actions τ. As an example consider the agent $A \overset{\text{def}}{=} \tau.A + b.\underline{0}$ which can execute an arbitrary number of τ actions. We define *Nondiv* as the set of all the non-divergent processes.

We can now present the *lazy security* property [56]. This property implies that the obscuring of high level actions by interleaving does not introduce any non-determinism. The obscuring of high level actions of process E by interleaving is obtained considering process $E|||RUN_H$ where $RUN_H \overset{\text{def}}{=} \sum_{h \in Act_H} h.RUN_H$. In such a process an outside observer is not able to tell if a certain high level action comes from E or from RUN_H.

L-Sec also requires that $E|||RUN_H$ is non-divergent. [9] This is equivalent to requiring that E is non-divergent, because RUN_H is non-divergent and the $|||$ operator does not allow synchronizations (which could generate new τ actions).

Definition 17. $E \in L\text{-}Sec \Leftrightarrow E|||RUN_H \in Det \cap Nondiv$. ∎

In the following we want to show that *L-Sec* can only analyze systems which are *low-deterministic*, i.e., where after any low level trace γ no low level action l can be both accepted and refused. The low-determinism requirement is not strictly necessary to avoid information flows from high to low level. So, in some cases, *L-Sec* is too strong. As an example consider the following non-deterministic system without high level actions: $E \overset{\text{def}}{=} l.l'.\underline{0} + l.l''.\underline{0}$. It is obviously secure but it is not low-deterministic and so it is not *L-Sec*. Formally we have that:

Definition 18. *E is low-deterministic ($E \in Lowdet$) iff $E \setminus Act_H \in Det$.* ∎

The following holds:

Theorem 6. $L\text{-}Sec \subseteq Lowdet$.

---

[9] Note that in [56] the non-divergence requirement is inside the deterministic one. This is because the authors use the failure-divergence semantics [10]. In this work we use the failure equivalence which does not deal with divergences. So, in order to obtain exactly the *L-Sec* property, we require the non-divergence condition explicitly.

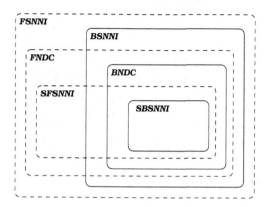

Fig. 14. Failure based and bisimulation based properties

PROOF. Let $E \in L\text{-}Sec$. Consider a trace γa of $E \setminus Act_H$ and suppose that $(\gamma, \{a\}) \in E \setminus Act_H$. So there exists E' such that $E \setminus Act_H \overset{\gamma}{\Longrightarrow} E' \setminus Act_H$ and such that $E' \setminus Act_H \overset{a}{\not\Longrightarrow}$. Since RUN_H cannot execute the low level action a then we have that $E' |||RUN_H \overset{a}{\not\Longrightarrow}$ and so $(\gamma, \{a\}) \in E |||RUN_H$ because $E |||RUN_H \overset{\gamma}{\Longrightarrow} E' |||RUN_H$. Since γa is a trace for $E \setminus Act_H$ then it is also a trace for $E |||RUN_H$ and we obtain that $E |||RUN_H$ is not deterministic, contradicting the hypothesis. So $(\gamma, \{a\}) \notin E \setminus Act_H$ and $E \in Lowdet$. ∎

Failure Non Deducibility on Compositions Now we define the failure based security properties by simply substituting $\approx_B$ with $\approx_F$ in all the bisimulation based properties previously defined.

Definition 19. *(Failure based properties)*

(i) $E \in FNDC \Leftrightarrow E/Act_H \approx_F (E \mid \Pi) \setminus Act_H$, *for all* $\Pi \in \mathcal{E}_H$;
(ii) $E \in FSNNI \Leftrightarrow E/Act_H \approx_F E \setminus Act_H$;
(iii) $E \in SFSNNI \Leftrightarrow \forall E'$ *such that* $\exists \gamma : E \overset{\gamma}{\Longrightarrow} E'$ *we have* $E' \in FSNNI$. ∎

Since bisimulation equivalence is stronger than failure equivalence, it can be proved that each of these new property is weaker then its corresponding bisimulation based one. E.g. $BNDC \subset FNDC$. Moreover we prove that some of the inclusion results we have for bisimulation based properties can be extended also to these new properties.

Theorem 7. $SFSNNI \subset FNDC \subset FSNNI$.

PROOF. $(SFSNNI \subset FNDC)$ Let E be a $SFSNNI$ process. We have to prove that $(E|\Pi) \setminus Act_H \approx_F E/Act_H$ for every high level process Π.
We first prove that $(\gamma, K) \in (E|\Pi) \setminus Act_H$ implies $(\gamma, K) \in E/Act_H$. Consider $(\gamma, K) \in (E|\Pi) \setminus Act_H$, then $\exists E', \Pi'$ such that $(E|\Pi) \setminus Act_H \overset{\gamma}{\Longrightarrow} (E'|\Pi') \setminus$

$Act_H \overset{K}{\not\Rightarrow}$. Hence $E' \backslash Act_H \overset{K}{\not\Rightarrow}$ because $traces(E' \backslash Act_H) \subseteq traces((E'|\Pi') \backslash Act_H)$.

Now, since $E \in SFSNNI$ then $E' \backslash Act_H \approx_F E'/Act_H$; hence $E'/Act_H \overset{K}{\not\Rightarrow}$. Note that $E/Act_H \overset{\gamma}{\Longrightarrow} E'/Act_H$, hence $(\gamma, K) \in E/Act_H$.

We now prove that $(\gamma, K) \in E/Act_H$ implies $(\gamma, K) \in (E|\Pi) \backslash Act_H$. Consider $(\gamma, K) \in E/Act_H$. By hypothesis we have that $(\gamma, K) \in E \backslash Act_H$ and so $\exists E'$ such that $E \backslash Act_H \overset{\gamma}{\Longrightarrow} E' \backslash Act_H \overset{K}{\not\Rightarrow}$. Since $E \in SFSNNI$ then $E'/Act_H \overset{K}{\not\Rightarrow}$. Hence we also have that $(E'|\Pi) \backslash Act_H \overset{K}{\not\Rightarrow}$ because $traces((E'|\Pi) \backslash Act_H) \subseteq traces(E'/Act_H)$. Since we have that $E \backslash Act_H \overset{\gamma}{\Longrightarrow} E' \backslash Act_H$ then $(E|\Pi) \backslash Act_H \overset{\gamma}{\Longrightarrow} (E'|\Pi) \backslash Act_H$ and so $(\gamma, K) \in (E|\Pi) \backslash Act_H$.

The inclusion is strict because agent $E \overset{def}{=} l.h.l.\underline{0} + l.\underline{0} + l.l.\underline{0}$ is FNDC but not SFSNNI.

(FNDC $\subset$ FSNNI) It is sufficient to consider $\Pi = \underline{0}$. We have that $(E|\underline{0}) \backslash Act_H \approx_F E \backslash Act_H$ and so, since $(E|\underline{0}) \backslash Act_H \approx_F E/Act_H$ we have $E/Act_H \approx_F E \backslash Act_H$.

The inclusion is strict because agent $E \overset{def}{=} l.h.l.h'.l.\underline{0} + l.\underline{0} + l.l.l.\underline{0}$ is FSNNI but not FNDC. ∎

Figure 14 summarizes the inclusions among the presented security properties. It can be drawn using the previous inclusion results and the following remarks: $BNDC \not\subseteq SFSNNI$, in fact agent $l.h.l.\underline{0} + l.\underline{0} + l.l.\underline{0}$ is BNDC but not SFSNNI; we also have that $BSNNI \not\subseteq FNDC$ because of agent $h.l.h'.l.\underline{0} + l.l.\underline{0}$; finally $SFSNNI \not\subseteq BSNNI$ because of agent $h.l.(l'.\underline{0} + l''.\underline{0}) + l.l'.\underline{0} + l.l''.\underline{0}$.

The next theorem shows that under the low-determinism assumption the properties SFSNNI and FNDC collapse into the same one. We need the following Lemma.

Lemma 3. If $E, \tilde{E} \in Det$, $E \overset{\gamma}{\Longrightarrow} E'$, $\tilde{E} \overset{\gamma}{\Longrightarrow} \tilde{E}'$ and $E \approx_F \tilde{E}$ then $E' \approx_F \tilde{E}'$.

PROOF. We prove that if $(\delta, K) \in E'$ then $(\delta, K) \in \tilde{E}'$. Let $(\delta, K) \in E'$. Then $(\gamma\delta, K) \in E$ and by $E \approx_F \tilde{E}$ we obtain that $(\gamma\delta, K) \in \tilde{E}$. So $\exists \tilde{E}'', \tilde{E}'''$ such that $\tilde{E} \overset{\gamma}{\Longrightarrow} \tilde{E}'' \overset{\delta}{\Longrightarrow} \tilde{E}''' \overset{K}{\not\Rightarrow}$, hence $(\delta, K) \in \tilde{E}''$. Since $\tilde{E} \in Det$ then by Proposition 9 and hypothesis we have that $\tilde{E}'' \approx_F \tilde{E}'$ and so $(\delta, K) \in \tilde{E}'$. We can prove in the same way that if $(\delta, K) \in \tilde{E}'$ then $(\delta, K) \in E'$. So $E' \approx_F \tilde{E}'$ ∎

Theorem 8. $FNDC \cap Lowdet \subseteq SFSNNI$.

PROOF. Since $FNDC \subset FSNNI$ and $E \in FNDC$, we have that $E \backslash Act_H \approx_F E/Act_H$. By $E \in Lowdet$ we obtain $E/Act_H \in Det$. Now consider $E \overset{\gamma}{\Longrightarrow} E'$. We have to prove that $E'/Act_H \approx_F E' \backslash Act_H$. Let Π' be the high level process which executes exactly the complement of the high level projection of γ, i.e. the complement of the subsequence of γ composed by all the high level actions in γ. If γ' is the low level projection of γ we have that $(E|\Pi') \backslash Act_H \overset{\gamma'}{\Longrightarrow} (E'|\underline{0}) \backslash Act_H \approx_F E' \backslash Act_H$. Since $E \overset{\gamma}{\Longrightarrow} E'$ then $E/Act_H \overset{\gamma'}{\Longrightarrow} E'/Act_H$. By hypothesis we have that $(E|\Pi') \backslash Act_H \approx_F E/Act_H$. Since $E/Act_H \in Det$ then, by Lemma 3, we have that $E'/Act_H \approx_F (E'|\underline{0}) \backslash Act_H \approx_F E' \backslash Act_H$. ∎

Corollary 2. *FNDC* $\cap$ *Lowdet* = *SFSNNI* $\cap$ *Lowdet*.

PROOF. Trivial by Theorems 8 and 7.   ∎

Comparison We now show that under the low-determinism and the non-divergence assumption the *BNDC* property is equal to *L-Sec*. We start proving this result for *FNDC*.

Theorem 9. *L-Sec* $\subseteq$ *SFSNNI*.

PROOF. Let $E \in$ *L-Sec*. Then we have to prove that if $E \stackrel{\gamma}{\Longrightarrow} E'$ then $E' \setminus Act_H \approx_F E'/Act_H$. We first prove that if $(\delta, K) \in E'/Act_H$ then $(\delta, K) \in E' \setminus Act_H$. Consider $(\delta, K) \in E'/Act_H$. Then we have that $\exists E''$ such that $E'/Act_H \stackrel{\delta}{\Longrightarrow} E''/Act_H \stackrel{K}{\not\Longrightarrow}$.

Now we want to prove that δ is a trace also for $E' \setminus Act_H$. Let $\delta = \delta_1\delta_2 \ldots \delta_n$ and consider the execution $E'/Act_H \stackrel{\delta_1}{\Longrightarrow} E_1'/Act_H \stackrel{\delta_2}{\Longrightarrow} \ldots \stackrel{\delta_n}{\Longrightarrow} E''/Act_H$. Suppose that δ_i is the first action in δ that $E' \setminus Act_H$ is not able to execute. In other words we have that

$$E' \setminus Act_H \stackrel{\delta_1}{\Longrightarrow} E_1' \setminus Act_H \stackrel{\delta_2}{\Longrightarrow} \ldots \stackrel{\delta_{i-1}}{\Longrightarrow} E_{i-1}' \setminus Act_H \stackrel{\delta_i}{\not\Longrightarrow}$$

This means that in order to execute δ_i, process E_{i-1}'/Act_H executes some hidden high level actions $h_1 \ldots h_k$. So $E_{i-1}' \stackrel{h_1 \ldots h_k \delta_i}{\Longrightarrow} E_i'$. If we execute such high level actions with RUN_H we obtain that $E|||RUN_H \stackrel{\gamma\delta_1 \ldots \delta_{i-1}h_1 \ldots h_k}{\Longrightarrow} E_{i-1}'|||RUN_H$. Since $E_{i-1}' \setminus Act_H \stackrel{\delta_i}{\not\Longrightarrow}$ and $\delta_i \in Act_L$ then we obtain that $(\gamma\delta_1 \ldots \delta_{i-1}h_1 \ldots h_k, \{\delta_i\}) \in E|||RUN_H$. Moreover, if we execute actions $h_1 \ldots h_k$ with E_{i-1}' we have that $E|||RUN_H \stackrel{\gamma\delta_1 \ldots \delta_{i-1}h_1 \ldots h_k \delta_i}{\Longrightarrow} E_i'|||RUN_H$ and so $\gamma\delta_1 \ldots \delta_{i-1}h_1 \ldots h_k \delta_i$ is a trace for $E|||RUN_H$. This means that $E|||RUN_H \notin Det$ hence $E \notin$ *L-Sec*. We obtain a contradiction, so no δ_i can be refused by $E' \setminus Act_H$ and δ is a trace for such process. So we have that $E' \setminus Act_H \stackrel{\delta}{\Longrightarrow} E''' \setminus Act_H$.

Now we want to prove that $(\delta, K) \in E' \setminus Act_H$. Let $E' \setminus Act_H \stackrel{\delta}{\Longrightarrow} E''' \setminus Act_H$ and suppose that $E''' \setminus Act_H$ can execute a certain action $a \in K \cap Act_L$ (the actions in $K \cap Act_H$ cannot be executed by such process) then $\gamma\delta a$ is a trace for $E|||RUN_H$. Now consider the sequence δ' obtained by adding to δ all the high level action executed by E' in order to reach E'' in the transition $E'/Act_H \stackrel{\delta}{\Longrightarrow} E''/Act_H$; i.e. $E' \stackrel{\delta'}{\Longrightarrow} E''$. Then we will have that $E'|||RUN_H \stackrel{\delta'}{\Longrightarrow} E''|||RUN_H$ and since $E''/Act_H \stackrel{K}{\not\Longrightarrow}$ then $E''|||RUN_H \stackrel{a}{\not\Longrightarrow}$ and so $(\gamma\delta', \{a\}) \in E|||RUN_H$. Now if $\gamma\delta a$ is a trace for $E|||RUN_H$ then also $\gamma\delta'a$ is, and so, again, we obtain that $E|||RUN_H \notin Det$ and $E \notin$ *L-Sec*. Hence $E''' \setminus Act_H \stackrel{a}{\not\Longrightarrow}$ for every $a \in K$ and so $(\delta, K) \in E' \setminus Act_H$.

Now we prove that if $(\delta, K) \in E' \setminus Act_H$ then $(\delta, K) \in E'/Act_H$. Suppose $(\delta, K) \in E' \setminus Act_H$. Then we have that $\exists E''$ such that $E' \setminus Act_H \stackrel{\delta}{\Longrightarrow} E'' \setminus Act_H \stackrel{K}{\not\Longrightarrow}$.

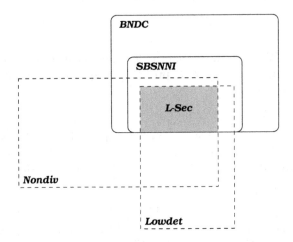

Fig. 15. Relations among properties

Hence also $E'/Act_H \stackrel{\delta}{\Longrightarrow} E''/Act_H$. Suppose that E''/Act_H can execute a certain $a \in K \cap Act_L$ then consider δ' obtained by adding to δ all the high level actions executed by E' before a in the transition $E'/Act_H \stackrel{\delta}{\Longrightarrow} E''/Act_H \stackrel{a}{\Longrightarrow} E'''/Act_H$, i.e., such that $\delta' a$ is a trace for E'. We have that $\gamma \delta' a$ is a trace for $E|||RUN_H$. Now, $(\delta, \{a\}) \in E' \setminus Act_H$ with $a \in Act_L$ and so $(\delta, \{a\}) \in E'|||RUN_H$ which implies that $(\delta', \{a\}) \in E'|||RUN_H$ and finally $(\gamma \delta', \{a\}) \in E|||RUN_H$. This contradict the fact that $E \in$ L-Sec and so $E''/Act_H \stackrel{a}{\not\Longrightarrow}, \forall a \in K$. Hence $(\delta, K) \in E'/Act_H$. ∎

Theorem 10. *SFSNNI* ∩ *Lowdet* ∩ *Nondiv* ⊆ *L-Sec.*

PROOF. Let $E \in$ *SFSNNI* ∩ *Lowdet* ∩ *Nondiv* and γa be a trace for process $E|||RUN_H$. We want to prove that $(\gamma, \{a\}) \notin E|||RUN_H$. It trivially holds if $a \in Act_H$ because in such a case it can always be executed by RUN_H. So let $a \in Act_L$. Suppose $E|||RUN_H \stackrel{\gamma}{\Longrightarrow} E'|||RUN_H \stackrel{a}{\not\Longrightarrow}$ and consider the sequence γ' obtained removing all the high level actions from γ. Then $E/Act_H \stackrel{\gamma'}{\Longrightarrow} E'/Act_H$ and by hypothesis $E'/Act_H \approx_F E' \setminus Act_H$. Since $E'|||RUN_H \stackrel{a}{\not\Longrightarrow}$ then $E' \setminus Act_H \stackrel{a}{\not\Longrightarrow}$ and so $E'/Act_H \stackrel{a}{\not\Longrightarrow}$ and $(\gamma', \{a\}) \in E/Act_H$. Since $E \in$ *SFSNNI* we obtain that $(\gamma', \{a\}) \in E \setminus Act_H$. Now γa is a trace for $E|||RUN_H$ and so $\gamma' a$ must be a trace for E/Act_H this means that $\gamma' a$ is also a trace for $E \setminus Act_H$. Since $E \in$ *Lowdet* then $E \setminus Act_H$ is deterministic. However we found that $\gamma' a$ is a trace for $E \setminus Act_H$ and $(\gamma', \{a\}) \in E \setminus Act_H$ obtaining a contradiction. So $E'|||RUN_H$ cannot refuse a and $(\gamma, \{a\}) \notin E|||RUN_H$. Hence $E|||RUN_H \in$ *Det* and since $E \in$ *Nondiv* we also have that $E|||RUN_H \in$ *Nondiv* ∎

Corollary 3. *SFSNNI ∩ Lowdet ∩ Nondiv = L-Sec.*

PROOF. By Theorems 6 and 9 and by Definition 17 we find that L-Sec ⊆ *SFSNNI ∩ Lowdet ∩ Nondiv*. Finally by Theorem 10 we obtain the thesis. ∎

Note that by Corollary 2 we also have that *FNDC ∩ Lowdet ∩ Nondiv = L-Sec*. Now we show that this result also holds for *SBSNNI* and *BNDC*. We first prove that for deterministic processes $\approx_F$ becomes equal to $\approx_B$.

Proposition 10. $E \in Det, E \approx_F F \Longrightarrow E \approx_B F$.

PROOF. If $E \in Det$ and $E \approx_F F$ we also have that $F \in Det$. Now it is sufficient to consider the relation $R \subseteq \mathcal{E} \times \mathcal{E}$ defined as follows: $(E', E'') \in R$ if and only if $\exists \gamma : E \stackrel{\gamma}{\Longrightarrow} E', E \stackrel{\gamma}{\Longrightarrow} E''$. It is easy to show that R is a weak bisimulation. ∎

Finally, the following holds.

Theorem 11. *BNDC ∩ Lowdet ∩ Nondiv = SBSNNI ∩ Lowdet ∩ Nondiv = L-Sec.*

PROOF. (*SBSNNI∩Lowdet∩Nondiv = L-Sec*). We have that *SBSNNI∩Lowdet∩ Nondiv ⊆ SFSNNI ∩ Lowdet ∩ Nondiv* because *SBSNNI ⊂ SFSNNI*. So by Theorem 10 *SBSNNI ∩ Lowdet ∩ Nondiv ⊆ L-Sec*.
Now we prove that *L-Sec ⊆ SBSNNI ∩ Lowdet ∩ Nondiv*. If $E \in$ *L-Sec* then by Corollary 3 we have that $E \in$ *SFSNNI ∩ Lowdet ∩ Nondiv*. So $\forall E'$ such that $\exists \gamma : E \stackrel{\gamma}{\Longrightarrow} E'$ we have $E' \setminus Act_H \approx_F E'/Act_H$ with $E \setminus Act_H \in Det$. In particular we also have that $E \setminus Act_H \approx_F E/Act_H$ and since $E \setminus Act_H \in Det$, we obtain that $E/Act_H \in Det$. Note that $E/Act_H \stackrel{\gamma'}{\Longrightarrow} E'/Act_H$ where γ' is the sequence obtained removing all the high level actions from γ. Hence, by Corollary 1, $E'/Act_H \in Det$. Finally, by Proposition 10 we obtain that $E' \setminus Act_H \approx_B E'/Act_H$.
(*BNDC∩Lowdet∩Nondiv = SBSNNI∩Lowdet∩Nondiv*) Trivial by *SBSNNI ⊂ BNDC ⊂ FNDC* and since *SBSNNI ∩ Lowdet ∩ Nondiv = L-Sec = FNDC ∩ Lowdet ∩ Nondiv*. ∎

Figure 15 summarizes the relations among various properties and conditions. We have shown that *BNDC* and *SBSNNI* are equal to *L-Sec* when dealing with low-deterministic and non-divergent processes. In the next section we will introduce the CoSeC tool which is able to automatically check the *SBSNNI* property over finite state agents. This implies that for low-deterministic, non-divergent and finite-state processes it is possible to use the CoSeC in order to verify also the *L-Sec* property. In [56] it is shown how to use the FDR tool [55] to check the *L-Sec* property. It would be interesting to compare the performance of FDR and CoSeC for the verification of such a property.

We also want to point out that *SBSNNI ∩ Lowdet* can extend in a *fair* manner the *L-Sec* property to divergent processes. *L-Sec* assumes that processes cannot diverge. The semantics used by authors to define *L-Sec* is the failure-divergence one [10]. Failure-divergence semantics gives a so-called *catastrophic* interpretation of divergences, since in the presence of divergences a process may

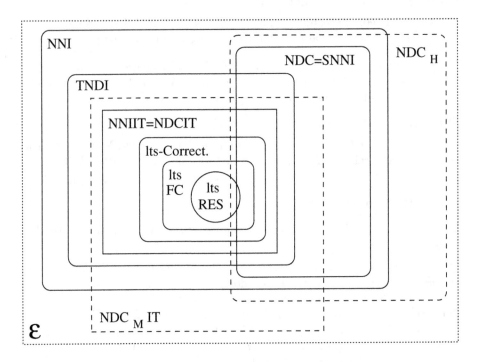

Fig. 16. The inclusion diagram for trace-based security properties

show any behaviour. We have already seen this problem when we used testing equivalence for the definition of our properties. On the other hand bisimulation gives a *fair* interpretation of divergences by assuming that an infinite loop of internal actions will be taken a finite number of times, i.e., soon or later we will exit from the loop. This is useful, for example, if we want to model a fair communication media, where a τ-loop represents the unbounded but finite losses of messages. The property *SBSNNI* $\cap$ *Lowdet* can be seen as an extension of *L-Sec* which gives a fair interpretation of divergences.

A good reference about modelling NI in CSP can be found in this volume [58]. In such a paper, a new notion based on power bisimulation is also proposed. We intend to compare it with our bisimulation-based properties with the aim making our classification as much complete as possible.

3.6 Other Security Properties

In [24] we have compared our properties with a number of existing proposal. Here we just report the diagram (Figure 16) of the relations among such properties and we give the bibliographic references to them. In particular, TNDI derives from *Non Deducibility on Inputs* [62], lts-Correctability comes from *Correctability* [41], lts-FC is *Forward-Correctability* [41], lts-RES is a version of *Restrictiveness* [48].

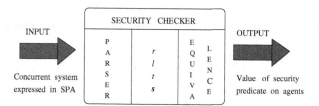

Fig. 17. Structure of the CoSeC

Moreover NNIIT is *NNI* where we require that systems are *input total*. This means that in every state the system must be able to accept every possible input by the environment. The aim of this (quite restrictive) condition is to prevent users from deducing anything about the state of the system, even if they observe the inputs the system accepts. All the properties included in NNIIT requires this condition over input actions. NDCIT is *NDC* with input totality. Finally NDC_H and $NDC_M IT$ are parametric versions of *NDC* where the high level user can exploit only the actions in sets H and M to communicate with the system. Table 11 reports all the needed counterexamples which differentiate the properties. For more details, please refer to [24].

4   The Compositional Security Checker

In this Section we briefly describe the CoSeC structure and architecture. Before giving this description, we want to informally justify why the theory developed so far should be equipped with a tool. First of all, we need a tool to practically check the examples; even for small problems, the state space grows quite beyond our human ability to manage it. A tool is also useful to help intuition on what flaws these security properties really capture; only through the tool we can analyze easily a large number of examples, and refine our understanding of the security properties and of the tractability of validating them. Finally, a tool gives an idea of which kind of verification techniques engineers should become acquainted with in the future to certify their products (e.g., security protocols). As we will show in the next sections, the CoSeC tool has been obtained by modifying the Concurrency Workbench [14]. Part of the material contained in this Section has been published in [26,32,25].

4.1   Input-Output and Architecture

The inputs of CoSeC are concurrent systems expressed as SPA agents. The outputs are answers to questions like: "does this system satisfy that specific security property ?". The structure of CoSeC is described in Figure 17. In detail, the tool is able:

Table 11. The inclusion table for trace-based security properties

	NNI	NDC SNNI	TNDI	lts-RES	lts-cor.	lts-FC	NDC$_H$	NNIIT NDCIT	NDC$_M$IT
NNI	$=$	**8**	2	2	2	2	9	10	10
NDC SNNI	$\subset$	$=$	**2**	2	2	2	$\subset$	**10**	10
TNDI	$\subset$	1	$=$	3	3	3	9	**10**	10
lts-RES	$\subset$	1	$\subset$	$=$	$\subset$	$\subset$	**9**	$\subset$	$\subset$
lts-cor.	$\subset$	1	$\subset$	6	$=$	6	9	$\subset$	$\subset$
lts-FC	$\subset$	1	$\subset$	5	$\subset$	$=$	9	$\subset$	$\subset$
NDC$_H$	**7**	7	7	7	7	7	$=$	10	10
NNIIT NDCIT	$\subset$	1	$\subset$	3	**3**	3	9	$=$	$\subset$
NDC$_M$IT	**4**	4	4	4	4	4	3	4	$=$

Let $T[x, y]$ be the table element contained in row x and column y. If $T[x,y] \in \{=, \subset\}$ then $xT[x,y]y$. If $T[x,y] = n$ then the agent n below is in x and is not in y. In the following Π_0 represents the Input-Total empty agent: $\Pi_0 = \sum_{i \in I} i.\Pi_0$.

1) $Z = \sum_{i \in I} i.Z + \bar{h}.Z'$ and $Z' = \sum_{i \in I} i.Z' + \bar{l}.\Pi_0$
2) $h.l.0 + l.0 + l'.0$
3) $Z = \sum_{i \in I} i.Z + \bar{h}.(\Pi_0 + \bar{l}.\Pi_0)$
4) $Z = \sum_{i \in I} i.Z + h.(\Pi_0 + \bar{l}.\Pi_0)$ with $h \notin M \cup \bar{M}$
5) $Z = \sum_{i \in I} i.Z + \bar{l}.\Pi_0 + h.\Pi_0$
6) $Z = \sum_{i \in I} i.Z + \bar{h}.Z' + \bar{h}'.Z''$ and $Z' = \Pi_0 + h.Z' + \bar{l}.\Pi_0$ and
   $Z'' = \sum_{i \in I \setminus \{h\}} i.Z'' + h.\Pi_0 + \bar{l}.\Pi_0$
7) $h.l.0$ with $h \notin H \cup \bar{H}$
8) $\bar{h}.l.0$
9) $Z = \sum_{i \in I} i.Z + \bar{h}.Z'$ and $Z' = \sum_{i \in I} i.Z' + \bar{l}.\Pi_0$ with $\bar{h} \in H \cup \bar{H}$
10) 0

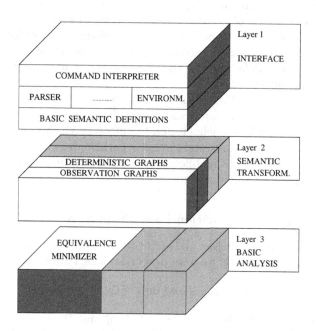

Layer 1

INTERFACE

COMMAND INTERPRETER

PARSER   ....   ENVIRONM.

BASIC SEMANTIC DEFINITIONS

Layer 2

SEMANTIC
TRANSFORM.

DETERMINISTIC GRAPHS
OBSERVATION GRAPHS

EQUIVALENCE
MINIMIZER

Layer 3

BASIC
ANALYSIS

Fig. 18. CoSeC architecture

- to parse SPA agents, saving them in suitable environments as parse trees;
- to give a semantics to these parse trees, building the corresponding rooted labelled transition systems (RLTS for short); this phase terminates only if the SPA term generates a finite LTS.
- to check if an agent satisfies a certain security property; the routine implemented for this purpose verifies the equivalence of two particular agents modeled as RLTS. In this way, future changes to the language will not compromise the validity of the core of the tool.

The CoSeC has the same general architecture of the CW [14]. In its implementation we have decided to exploit the characteristic of versatility and extensibility of CW. In particular CoSeC maintains the strongly modular architecture of CW.

Figure 18 shows the architecture of CoSeC. The modules of the system have been partitioned in three main layers: interface layer, semantic layer, analysis layer. In the interface layer we have the command interpreter. It allows us to define the agents and the set of high level actions; it also allows to invoke the security predicates and the utility functions on the behaviour of an agent. Then we have a parser which recognizes the SPA syntax of agents and stores them as parse trees in appropriate environments. The partition of the set of visible actions in the sets of high and low level actions has been obtained by defining the set of high level actions; by default, all the other possible actions are considered at low level. Then we have defined a function that, according to the operational semantic rule of SPA, provides all possible transitions for an agent. This function allows the construction of the LTS associated with an agent.

In the semantic layer, CoSeC uses two transformation routines to translate LTSs into deterministic and observation graphs [10] respectively. Since they both refer to processes modeled as LTSs, they have been imported from CW in CoSeC without any modification.

In the analysis layer, CoSeC uses a routine of equivalence and one of minimization that belong to the analysis layer of CW. These are a slight modification of the algorithm by Kanellakis and Smolka [42] which finds a bisimulation between the roots of two finite state LTSs by partitioning their states. It is interesting to note that a simple modification of this algorithm can be used to obtain the minimization of a finite state LTS.

4.2   Checking the Information Flow Properties

Here we describe in details how the verification of Information Flow Properties proceeds. As we said before, we have properties which are in the following form:

$$E \text{ is } X\text{-secure if and only if } \mathcal{C}_X[E] \approx \mathcal{D}_X[E].$$

We have seen for *SNNI* that $\mathcal{C}_X[-] = - \setminus Act_H$ and $\mathcal{D}_X[-] = -/Act_H$. Hence, checking the X-security of E is reduced to the "standard" problem of checking semantic equivalence between two terms having E as a sub-term.

In the following we briefly explain how the system works in evaluating security predicates *NNI, SNNI, NDC, BNNI, BSNNI, SBSNNI*, and we discuss about their computational complexity. CoSeC computes the value of these predicates over finite state agents (i.e. agents possessing a finite state LTS), based on the definitions given in Section 3 that we report below in CoSeC syntax (for ease of parsing, in CoSeC the hiding and input restriction operators are represented by ! and ?, respectively.):

$$E \in NNI \Leftrightarrow E!Act_H \approx_T (E?Act_H)!Act_H$$
$$E \in SNNI \equiv NDC \Leftrightarrow E!Act_H \approx_T E \setminus Act_H$$
$$E \in BNNI \Leftrightarrow E!Act_H \approx_B (E?Act_H)!Act_H$$
$$E \in BSNNI \Leftrightarrow E!Act_H \approx_B E \setminus Act_H$$
$$E \in SBSNNI \Leftrightarrow E' \in BSNNI, \ \forall E' \text{ reachable from } E$$

As for CW, the inner computation of the CoSeC follows three main phases.

Phase a) (the same for all predicates) CoSeC builds the RLTSs of the two agents of which it wants to compute the equivalence. For example in the case of NNI, CoSeC computes the transition graph for $(E?Act_H)!Act_H$ and $E!Act_H$. In

---

[10] An observation graphs [14] is obtained by obscuring the precise amount of internal computation. In particular the edges of the LTS are modified in order to reflect the $\leadsto$ relation defined as: $n \overset{\epsilon}{\leadsto} n'$ iff $n \overset{\tau}{\Longrightarrow} n'$ and $n \overset{a}{\leadsto} n'$ iff $n \overset{a}{\Longrightarrow} n'$.

this phase we do not have any particular problem with complexity, except for the intrinsic exponential explosion in the number of states of the RLTS due to parallel composition.

Phase b) (This is split into two depending on the semantics requested by the security predicate)

> **b1:** (for predicates *NNI, SNNI, NDC*) The two RLTSs obtained in Phase a) are transformed into deterministic graphs following the classic subset construction (see e.g. [40]). This algorithm has exponential complexity since it is theoretically possible, in the deterministic graph, to have a node for every subset of nodes in the original graph. However, experience shows that very often the number of obtained nodes is less than the number of nodes of the beginning graph because of the collapsing of the τ-transitions.

> **b2:** (for predicates *BNNI* and *BSNNI*) The two RLTSs obtained in Phase a) are transformed into observation graphs using the classic algorithms for the product of two relations and the reflexive transitive closure of a relation. This transformation has a $O(n^3)$ complexity, in which n is the number of nodes in the original graph.

Phase c) (For all predicates) The general equivalence algorithm [42] is applied to the graphs obtained in Phase b). Time and space complexities of this algorithm are $O(k * l)$ and $O(k + l)$ respectively, where l is the number of nodes and k is the number of edges in the two graphs. This is not a limiting factor in the computation of the observational and trace equivalences. In particular, for observational equivalence, in most cases 80% of computation time is due to the routine for reflexive transitive closure of Phase b).

Since *SBSNNI* is verified by testing *BSNNI* over all the n states of the original graph, the resulting complexity will be n times the *BSNNI* complexity.

It is interesting to observe that the exponential explosion of the number of nodes of the transition graphs (Phase a), due to the operator of parallel composition, influences negatively the following phases, but it cannot be avoided because of its intrinsic nature. A solution to this problem for the predicates *NNI, SNNI, NDC* and *SBSNNI* could be based on the exploitation of compositional properties (see Section 4.5 for more details).

4.3   A Sample Session

The style used in specifying SPA agents in CoSeC is the same used for CCS agents in CW. For example the command line [11]

Command: **bi** A $h.'l.'h.A + 'h.'l.A$

---

[11] Here we use the typewriter style for CoSeC messages (such as the prompt "Command:"); the bold style for CoSeC commands and the italic style for the remaining text (such as agents and sets) inserted by users.

defines the agent $A \stackrel{\text{def}}{=} h.\bar{l}.\bar{h}.A + \bar{h}.\bar{l}.A$. As in CW the first letter of agents must be a capital letter and output actions have to be prefixed by $'$.

We assumed that the set of visible actions $\mathcal{L}$ is partitioned in two complete subsets Act_H and Act_L of high and low level actions respectively. With the command:

> Command: **acth** $h\ x$

we specify that $Act_H = \{h,' h, x,' x\}$. In this way we obtain that $h,' h, x,' x$ are considered as high level actions and any other action as low level one.

Now, we can check whether agent A is NNI secure:

> Command: **nni** A
> true

CoSeC tells us that A is NNI secure. Now we can check if agent A is SNNI secure too:

> Command: **snni** A
> false

So A is *NNI* secure but is not *SNNI* secure. If we want to know why such a system is not *SNNI* we can use the *debugging* version of the *SNNI*:

> Command: **d_snni** A
> false
> Agent A!ActH
> can perform action sequence 'l
> which agent A\ActH
> cannot

The tool shows a (low level) trace which distinguishes processes A/Act_H and $A \setminus Act_H$. The trace is $\bar{l}$ which can be executed only by the first one. This can be useful to understand why a process is not secure. Finally the command **quit** causes an exit to the shell.

4.4   An Example: Checking the Access Monitor

In this Section we use CoSeC to automatically check all the versions of the access monitor discussed in Example 6. Since CoSeC works on SPA agents we have to translate all the VSPA specifications into SPA. Consider once more *Access_Monitor_1*. Table 12 reports the translation of *Access_Monitor_1* specification into the CoSeC syntax for SPA. [12] It has been used a new command **basi** which binds a set of actions to an identifier. Moreover, the \ character at the end of a line does not represent the restriction operator, but is the special

---

[12] In the translation, we use values $\{l, h\}$ in place of $\{0, 1\}$ for the levels of users and objects in order to make the SPA specification clearer. As an example $access\_r(1, 0)$ becomes **access_r_hl**.

Table 12. Translation of Access_Monitor_1 to CoSeC syntax for SPA

```
bi  Access_Monitor_1
 (Monitor  |  Object_10  |  Object_h0)~L

bi  Monitor
 access_r_hh.(rh0.'val_h0.Monitor + rh1.'val_h1.Monitor) + \
 access_r_lh.'val_l_err.Monitor + \
 access_r_hl.(rl0.'val_h0.Monitor + rl1.'val_h1.Monitor) + \
 access_r_ll.(rl0.'val_l0.Monitor + rl1.'val_l1.Monitor) + \
 access_w_hh.(write_h0.'wh0.Monitor + write_h1.'wh1.Monitor) + \
 access_w_lh.(write_l0.'wh0.Monitor + write_l1.'wh1.Monitor) + \
 access_w_hl.(write_h0.Monitor + write_h1.Monitor) + \
 access_w_ll.(write_l0.'wl0.Monitor + write_l1.'wl1.Monitor)

bi Object_h0
 'rh0.Object_h0 + wh0.Object_h0 + wh1.Object_h1

bi Object_h1
 'rh1.Object_h1 + wh0.Object_h0 + wh1.Object_h1

bi Object_10
 'rl0.Object_10 + wl0.Object_10 + wl1.Object_11

bi Object_11
 'rl1.Object_11 + wl0.Object_10 + wl1.Object_11

basi L
 rh0  rh1  rl0  rl1  wh0  wh1  wl0  wl1

acth
 rh0 rh1 wh0 wh1 access_r_hh access_r_hl val_h0 val_h1 val_h_err \
 access_w_hh access_w_hl write_h0 write_h1
```

---

character that permits to break in more lines the description of long agents and long action lists.

We can write to a file the contents of Table 12 and load it, in CoSeC, with command **if** <*filename*>. Now we can check that *Access_Monitor_1* satisfies all the security properties except *SBSNNI* using the following command lines:

> Command: **bnni** *Access_Monitor_1*
> true
> Command: **bsnni** *Access_Monitor_1*
> true
> Command: **sbsnni** *Access_Monitor_1*
> false: ('val_h1.Monitor | Object_11 | Object_h1) \ L

Note that when CoSeC fails to verify *SBSNNI* on a process E, it gives as output an agent E' which is reachable from E and is not *BSNNI*.

So we have found that

$$Access\_Monitor\_1 \in BSNNI, BNNI$$

but

$$Access\_Monitor\_1 \notin SBSNNI$$

Since we have that $SBSNNI \subset BNDC \subset BSNNI, BNNI$, we cannot conclude whether $Access\_Monitor\_1$ is $BNDC$ or not. However, using the output state E' of the $SBSNNI$ verification, it is easy to find a high level process Π which can block the monitor. Indeed, in the state given as output by $SBSNNI$, the monitor is waiting for the high level action $'$val_h1; so, if we find a process Π which moves the system to such a state and does not execute the val_h1 action, we will have a high level process able to block the monitor. It is sufficient to consider $\Pi = {}'access\_r\_hh.0$. Agent $(Access\_Monitor\_1|\Pi)\backslash Act_H$ will be blocked immediately after the execution of the read request by Π, moving to the following deadlock state:

$$(({}'\text{val\_h0.Monitor} \mid \text{Object\_10} \mid \text{Object\_h0}) \setminus L \mid 0) \setminus Act_H$$

(this state differs from the one given as output by $SBSNNI$ only for the values stored in objects). It is possible to verify that $Access\_Monitor\_1 \notin BNDC$ by checking that $(Access\_Monitor\_1|\Pi) \setminus Act_H \not\approx_B Access\_Monitor\_1/Act_H$ using the following command:

```
Command: bi   Pi  'access_r_hh.0
Command: eq
Agent: (Access_Monitor_1 | Pi) \ acth
Agent: Access_Monitor_1 ! acth
false
```

As we said in Example 6, such a deadlock is caused by synchronous communications in SPA. Moreover, using the CoSeC output again, we can find out that also the high level process $\Pi' = {}'access\_w\_hl.0$ can block $Access\_Monitor\_1$, because it executes a write request and does not send the corresponding value. Hence, in Example 6 we proposed the modified system $Access\_Monitor\_5$ with an interface for each level and atomic actions for write request and value sending. We finally check that this version of the monitor is $SBSNNI$, hence $BNDC$ too:

```
Command: sbsnni  Access_Monitor_5
true
```

4.5   State Explosion and Compositionality

In this section we show how the parallel composition operator can increase exponentially the number of states of the system, and then how it can slow down the execution speed of security predicate verification. This is basically caused by the fact that we have all the possible interleaving of the actions executed by the parallel processes. In order to avoid this we exploit some results related to the compositionality of the proposed security properties. For some of the properties we have that if two systems are "secure" also their parallel composition is secure. So, the tool has a special feature that decomposes systems in their parallel components and then checks the properties over that components. If both of them

Table 13. Number of states and time spent on a SPARC station 5

agent	B	D	$B\|D\|B$	$B\|D\|D\|B$
state number	3	3	27	81
time spent	<1 sec.	<1 sec.	~11 sec.	~270 sec.

are secure the tool will conclude that also the whole system is secure. Otherwise the check will be performed over the whole system. We prove that this method is correct and that it terminates. Moreover we show some modular versions of the Monitor that can be verified very efficiently with this compositional technique.

We start with a very simple example. Let us define in CoSeC the two agents B, D and the set Act_H of high level actions:

```
Command: bi  B  y.a.b.B + a.b.B
Command: bi  D  'a.'b.(x.D + D)
Command: acth  x  y
```

Let us check now if B and D are *SBSNNI* secure:

```
Command: sbsnni  B
true
Command: sbsnni  D
true
```

We have seen that *SBSNNI* is a compositional property, so the two agents $B|D|B$ and $B|D|D|B$ must also be *SBSNNI* secure. Hence the verification of these two agents could be reduced to the verification of their two basic components B and D only. The time spent in verifying *SBSNNI* directly on $B|D|B$ and $B|D|D|B$ is very long. Using the **size** command of CoSeC, which computes the number of states of an agent, we can fill in Table 13, which points out the exponential increase of the number of states and the consequent increase of the computation time for verification of *SBSNNI*.

CoSeC is able to exploit the compositionality of security properties through an algorithmic scheme we are going to present. For a certain compositional property P this scheme also requires the following condition: if $Z \stackrel{\text{def}}{=} E$ and E is P-secure then also Z is P-secure. This condition is satisfied by all the above presented properties because of Theorem 5.

Definition 20. *(Compositional Algorithm) Let $P \subseteq \mathcal{E}$ be a set of SPA agents such that*

- $E, E' \in P \Longrightarrow E|E' \in P$
- $E \in P, L \subseteq \mathcal{L} \Longrightarrow E \setminus L \in P$
- $E \in P, Z \stackrel{\text{def}}{=} E \Longrightarrow Z \in P$

and let A_P be a decision algorithm which checks if a certain agent $E \in \mathcal{E}_{FS}$ belongs to P; in other words, $A_P(E) = true$ if $E \in P$, $A_P(E) = false$ otherwise. Then we can define a compositional algorithm $A'_P(E)$ in the following way:

1) *if E is of the form $E' \setminus L$, then compute $A'_P(E')$; if $A'_P(E') = true$ then return true, else return the result of $A_P(E)$;*
2) *if E is of the form $E_1|E_2$, then compute $A'_P(E_1)$ and $A'_P(E_2)$; if $A'_P(E_1) = A'_P(E_2) = true$ then return true, else return the result of $A_P(E)$;*
3) *if E is a constant Z with $Z \stackrel{\text{def}}{=} E'$, then return the result of $A'_P(E')$;*
4) *if E is not in any of the three forms above, then return $A_P(E)$.* ∎

The compositional algorithm $A'_P(E)$ works as the given algorithm $A_P(E)$ when the outermost operator of E is neither the restriction operator, nor the parallel one, nor a constant definition. Otherwise, it applies componentwise to the arguments of the outermost operator; if the property does not hold for them, we cannot conclude that the whole system is not secure, and we need to check it with the given algorithm.

Note that the compositional algorithm exploits the assumption that property P is closed with respect to restriction and uses this in step 1. This could seem of little practical use, as the dimension of the state space for, let say, E is often bigger than that of $E \setminus L$. However, parallel composition is often used in the form $(A|B) \setminus L$ in order to force some synchronizations, and so if we want to check P over A and B separately, we must be granted that P is preserved by both parallel and restriction operators.

To obtain the result for $A'_P(F)$, we essentially apply – in a syntax-driven way – the four rules above recursively, obtaining a proof tree having (the value of) $A'_P(F)$ as the root and the various (values of) $A_P(E)$'s on the leaves for the subterms E of F on which the induction cannot be applied anymore. The following theorem justifies the correctness of the compositional algorithm, by proving that the evaluation strategy terminates and gives the same result as the given algorithm $A_P(F)$.

Theorem 12. *Let $F \in \mathcal{E}_{FS}$. If the agent E' occurring in step 1 belongs to $\mathcal{E}_{FS}$ each time the algorithm A'_P executes that step, then $A'_P(F)$ terminates and $A_P(F) = A'_P(F)$.*

PROOF. First we want to prove that, in computing $A'_P(F)$, if the evaluation of the given algorithm A_P is required on an agent E, then E belongs to $\mathcal{E}_{FS}$. The proof is by induction on the proof tree for the evaluation of $A'_P(F)$. The base case is when F can be evaluated by step 4; as – by hypothesis – agent F is finite state, the thesis follows trivially. Instead, if F is of the form $E' \setminus L$, then – by the premise of this theorem – $E' \in \mathcal{E}_{FS}$, and the inductive hypothesis can be applied. In step 2, as $F = E_1|E_2$, we have that $E_1, E_2 \in \mathcal{E}_{FS}$, and the inductive hypothesis can be applied to prove the thesis. Similarly for step 3, as constant Z is finite state if and only if the defining agent E' is so. So, when the algorithm executes $A_P(E)$ in steps 1, 2, 3 or 4, it always terminates because $E \in \mathcal{E}_{FS}$.

To complete the proof concerning termination of the compositional algorithm, we still have to prove that the inductive evaluation, in steps 1, 2 and 3, cannot loop; in other words, that the proof tree for $A'_P(F)$ is finite. While it is obvious for cases 1 and 2 (no term can be a proper subterm of itself in a finite term), the thesis follows in case 3 because of the constant guardedness condition over SPA agents. It guarantees that the recursive substitution of non prefixed constants with their definitions terminates. Hence the computation of $A'_P(F)$ ends.

To prove that the result of the compositional algorithm A'_P is consistent with the one obtained by the given algorithm A_P, we observe that the four rules above guarantee this, using compositionality properties for steps 1 and 2.   ∎

The theorem above requires that – in evaluating $A'_P(E)$ – if E is in the form $E' \setminus L$, then E' must be finite state. In fact, if we consider a finite state system $E \setminus L$ such that $E \notin \mathcal{E}_{FS}$, then $A_P(E \setminus L)$ terminates while $A'_P(E \setminus L)$ possibly do not, because it tries to compute $A_P(E)$ on the non-finite state agent E. The premise of the theorem above trivially holds for agents in the class of *nets of automata*.

The CoSeC command **c_sbsnni** checks the *SBSNNI* property exploiting compositionality. Let us now compare the compositional algorithm w.r.t. the normal one, starting from *Access_Monitor_5*. The normal verification of the *SBSNNI* property on such a system requires a lot of time (about 16 minutes [13] on a SUN5 workstation) because of the above mentioned exponential state explosion due to parallel composition. We could hope to get a better result using the compositional algorithm. Table 14 reports the output of the compositional verification of *Access_Monitor_5* where the symbols [\] and [|] represent steps 1 and 2 of the algorithm, respectively. This table shows that the algorithm fails in the verification of *SBSNNI* over *AM* and then succeeds in checking the system as a whole.[14] Hence, in this case, the compositional technique cannot help reducing the execution time. However, we can modify *AM* in order to obtain a *SBSNNI* system by making (only!) high level communications asynchronous. This can be done adding a high level buffer between the monitor and the interface. The resulting system is reported in Table 15 where $j \in \{0, 1, err, empty\}$, $L = \{r, w, val(1, y)\}$, $N = \{res, access\_r, access\_w\}$ and $res(1, y) \in Act_H, \forall y \in \{0, 1, err, empty\}$, while the same actions with 0 as first parameter belong to Act_L. Note that we have modified the interface so that it is now able to wait until the high buffer is filled by the monitor.

Using the compositional algorithm, system *Access_Monitor_6* can be checked very efficiently; the verification of *SBSNNI* takes about 90 seconds (see Table 16). We can also check that $Access\_Monitor\_5 \approx_B Access\_Monitor\_6$; so, as expected, the introduction of the buffer does not modify the behaviour of the monitor. This verification requires about 2 minutes. Note that, by Theorem 5, we can conclude that also *Access_Monitor_5* is *SBSNNI*, even if a direct check takes (as we said) about 16 minutes.

Access_Monitor_6 represents an example of successful application of the compositional checking; nonetheless, this does not mean that we cannot do bet-

---

[13] This value and all the following are obtained exploiting also the state minimization feature of the tool.

[14] The reason why it fails on *AM* is because *AM* is essentially *Access_Monitor_1* with atomic write operations; hence, it is not *SBSNNI* because of the possible high level deadlock of Example 6 caused by synchronous communications. The interface was indeed introduced in order to make communications asynchronous.

Table 14. Verification of *SBSNNI* on *Access_Monitor_5* with the compositional algorithm

```
Command: c_sbsnni  Access_Monitor_5
[\] Verifying AM | Interf
  [|] Verifying AM
    [\] Verifying Monitor_5 | Object_10 | Object_h0
      [|] Verifying Monitor_5
      [|] Failed!
    [\] Failed!
        Verifying directly (Monitor_5 | Object_10 | Object_h0)\L
  [|] Failed!
[\] Failed!
    Verifying directly (AM | Interf)\K
true
```

Table 15. The *Access_Monitor_6*

$$Access\_Monitor\_6 \overset{\text{def}}{=} (AM\_6 \mid Interf\_6) \setminus N$$

$$AM\_6 \overset{\text{def}}{=} ((Monitor\_5 \mid Object(1,0) \mid Object(0,0)$$
$$\mid hBuf(empty)) \setminus L)[res(0,y)/val(0,y)]$$

$$hBuf(j) \overset{\text{def}}{=} \overline{res}(1,j).hBuf(empty) + val(1,k).hBuf(k)$$

$$Interf\_6 \overset{\text{def}}{=} Interf\_6(0) \mid Interf\_6(1)$$

$$Interf\_6(l) \overset{\text{def}}{=} a\_r(l,x).\overline{access\_r}(l,x).Interf\_6\_reply(l)$$
$$+$$
$$a\_w(l,x,z).\overline{access\_w}(l,x,z).Interf\_6(l)$$

$$Interf\_6\_reply(l) \overset{\text{def}}{=} res(l,y).$$
$$(\text{ if } y = empty \text{ then}$$
$$Interf\_6\_reply(l)$$
$$\text{else}$$
$$\overline{put}(l,y).Interf\_6(l))$$

Table 16. Verification of *SBSNNI* on *Access_Monitor_6* exploiting compositionality

---

```
Command: c_sbsnni Access_Monitor_6
[\] Verifying AM_6 | Interf_6
  [|] Verifying AM_6
  [|] Verifying Interf_6
    [|] Verifying Interf_6_1
    [|] Verifying Interf_6_0
true
```

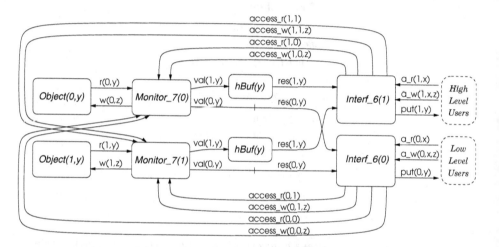

Fig. 19. The Modular *Access_Monitor_7*

ter. Indeed, such a system is not defined in a very modular way and we hope that a more modular definition will lead to a more efficient compositional verification. In fact, suppose we want to add other objects to *Access_Monitor_6*; in such a case, the size of *AM_6* will increase exponentially with respect to the number of added objects. Now we present a rather modular version of the access monitor. The basic idea of this new version (Figure 19) is that every object has a "private" monitor which implements the access functions for such (single) object. To make this, we have decomposed process *Monitor_5* into two different processes, one for each object; then we have composed such processes to their respective objects together with a high level buffer obtaining the *SBSNNI*-secure *Modh* and *Modl* agents. In particular, *Monitor_7(x)* handles the accesses to object x ($x = 0$ low, $x = 1$ high). As in *Access_Monitor_6*, we have an interface which guarantees the exclusive use of the monitor within the same level and is able to read values from the high buffer. The resulting system is reported in Ta-

Table 17. The *Access_Monitor_7*

$Access\_Monitor\_7 \stackrel{\text{def}}{=} (Modh \mid Modl \mid Interf\_6) \setminus L$

$\qquad Modh \stackrel{\text{def}}{=} ((Monitor\_7(1) \mid Object(1,0) \mid hBuf(empty)) \setminus Lh)$
$\qquad\qquad [res(0,y)/val(0,y)]$

$\qquad Modl \stackrel{\text{def}}{=} ((Monitor\_7(0) \mid Object(0,0) \mid hBuf(empty)) \setminus Lh)$
$\qquad\qquad [res(0,y)/val(0,y)]$

$Monitor\_7(x) \stackrel{\text{def}}{=} access\_r(l,x).$

$\qquad$(if $x \leq l$ then

$\qquad\qquad r(x,y).\overline{val}(l,y).Monitor\_7(x)$

$\qquad$**else**

$\qquad\qquad \overline{val}(l,err).Monitor\_7(x))$

$\qquad +$

$\qquad access\_w(l,x,z).$

$\qquad$(if $x \geq l$ then

$\qquad\qquad \overline{w}(x,z).Monitor\_7(x)$

$\qquad$**else**

$\qquad\qquad Monitor\_7(x))$

ble 17 where $L = \{res, access\_r, access\_w\}$ and $Lh = \{r, w, val(1, y)\}$. Table 18 reports the output of the (successful) verification of the *SBSNNI* property for *Access_Monitor_7*. This task takes about 20 seconds on a SUN5 workstation, supporting our claim that a modular definition would help. Moreover, we can also check the new version of the monitor is functionally equivalent to the previous ones: in about 5 minutes, CoSeC is able to check that *Access_Monitor_7* $\approx_B$ *Access_Monitor_5*, and so also *Access_Monitor_7* $\approx_B$ *Access_Monitor_6*.

As a final remark, the compositional verification is more convenient only when building complex systems as parallel composition of simpler ones. For this reason, the tool offers to the user the choice between the normal and the compositional verification algorithms. It is up to the user to choose which one (s)he thinks could go better, or even to make them work in parallel.

5   Conclusion

In this paper we have proposed a formal model for the specification and analysis of information flow properties. We have adopted a particular algebraic style in

Table 18. Verification of *SBSNNI* on *Access_Monitor_7* exploiting compositionality

```
Command: c_sbsnni Access_Monitor_7
[\] Verifying Modh | Modl | Interf_6
  [|] Verifying Modh
  [|] Verifying Modl
  [|] Verifying Interf_6
    [|] Verifying Interf_6_1
    [|] Verifying Interf_6_0
true
```

the definition of such properties. Indeed we have always given properties which are parametric with respect to a notion of semantic equivalence. This is useful since we can change the discriminating power of a property by simply "plugging in" the appropriate equivalence notion. Moreover, in this way we have obtained very compact and simple definitions. We have also seen how this algebraic style can be very profitable when automatically checking the properties. Indeed we can reduce the task of checking a security property to the well studied problem of checking the semantic equivalence of two terms of the language.

We have seen that the main motivation for information flow properties is historically bound to system security, in particular to the detection of direct and indirect information flows inside a system. However we have obtained a very general setting where we can study if a certain class of users, the high level users, can in some way interfere with the low level ones. Indeed we have used this Non-Interference abstraction in order to model the absence of information flow: "if high level users cannot interfere with low level ones then no information flow is possible from high to low level".

We have tried to convince the reader that the properties we have proposed are satisfactory for the detection of information flows inside a system, in particular the *BNDC* property which can also detect flows due to potential high level deadlocks.

In recent papers [28,3], the underlying model has been extended in order to deal with time and probability. Once an appropriate semantics equivalence has been defined in these new models, the *BNDC* property has been shown to naturally handle the new features of the model. In particular, in such models, *BNDC* has been shown to be able to detect timing and probabilistic convert channels, respectively.

Another aspect we are studying is the possibility of defining a criterion for evaluating the quality of information flow properties [33]. We are trying to do this by defining classes of properties which guarantee the impossibility of the construction of some "canonical" channels. We have seen, for example, that using some systems which are not *BNDC* it is possible to obtain a (initially noisy) perfect channel from high to low level. The aim is to classify the information flow properties depending on which kind of channels they effectively rule out.

We have seen that it is possible to automatically check almost all the properties we have presented. Indeed we are still looking for a good (necessary and sufficient) characterization of the *BNDC* property. We have also briefly presented the CoSeC tool. In [47], Martinelli has applied partial model checking techniques to the verification of *BNDC*, leading to the implementation of an automatic verifier [46] which is able to automatically synthetize the possible interfering high-level process.

As we have stated above, the setting we have proposed is quite general. We claim that information flow (or NI) properties could have a number of different applications since they basically capture the possibility for a class of users of modifying the behaviour of another user class. This generality has allowed to apply some variants of our properties to the analysis of cryptographic protocols [15,30,29,31], starting from a general scheme proposed in [34]. This has been the topic of the second part of the course "Classification of Security Properties" at FOSAD'00 school, and we are presently working on a tutorial which will cover it [27].

This application of NI properties to network security is new to our knowledge. The interesting point is that they can be applied to the verification of protocols with different aims, e.g., authentication, secrecy, key-distribution. We have analyzed a number of different protocols, thanks to a new tool interface which permits to specify value-passing protocols and to automatically generate the enemy [15]; this has also allowed to find new anomalies in some cryptographic protocols [16].

In [19,20,11,12], a new definition of entity authentication, which is based on explicit locations of entities, has been proposed. We are presently trying to characterize also this property through information flow. We also intend to carry the *BNDC* theory over more expressive process calculi, like, e.g., pi/spi-calculus [2] and Mobile Ambients [13]. This would allow to compare it with new recent security properties proposed on such calculi and reminiscent of some Non-Interference ideas (see, e.g., [37,35]).

References

1. M. Abadi. "Secrecy by Typing in Security Protocols". *Journal of ACM*, 46(5):749–786, 1999. 331
2. M. Abadi and A. D. Gordon. A calculus for cryptographic protocols: The spi calculus. *Information and Computation*, 148(1):1–70, 1999. 331, 392
3. A. Aldini. "Probabilistic Information Flow in a Process Algebra". To appear in proceedings of CONCUR'01, 2001. 391
4. P. G. Allen. "A Comparison of Non-Interference and Non-Deducibility using CSP". In *Proceedings of the Fourth IEEE Computer Security Foundations Workshop*, pages 43–54, Franconia, New Hampshire, June 1991. 368
5. D. E. Bell and L. J. La Padula. "Secure Computer Systems: Unified Exposition and Multics Interpretation". *ESD-TR-75-306, MITRE MTR-2997*, March 1976. 332

6. J. A. Bergstra and J. W. Klop. "Algebra of Communicating Processes with Abstraction". *Theoretical Computer Science*, 37:77–121, 1985. 356

7. P. Bieber and F. Cuppens. "A Logical View of Secure Dependencies". *Journal of Computer Security*, 1(1):99–129, 1992. 333

8. C. Bodei, P. Degano, F. Nielson, and H. Riis Nielson. "Static Analysis of Processes for No Read-Up and No Write-Down". In *proc. of 2nd FoSSaCS'99*, Amsterdam, March 1999. Springer. 331

9. S. D. Brookes, C. A. R. Hoare, and A. W. Roscoe. "A Theory of Communicating Sequential Processes". *Journal of the Association for Computing Machinery*, 31(3):560–599, July 1984. 340, 348, 353

10. S. D. Brookes and A. W. Roscoe. "An Improved Failures Model for Communicating Processes". In *Proceedings of the Pittsburgh seminar on concurrency*, pages 281–305. Springer-Verlag, LNCS 197, 1985. 370, 375

11. C. Bodei, P. Degano, R. Focardi, and C. Priami. "Authentication via Localized Names". In *Proceedings of CSFW'99*, pages 98–110. IEEE press, 1999. 331, 392

12. C. Bodei, P. Degano, R. Focardi, and C. Priami. "Primitives for Authentication in Process Algebras". Theoretical Computer Science, to appear, 2001. 331, 392

13. L. Cardelli and A. Gordon. "Mobile Ambients". In *proceedings of FoSSaCS'98*, pages 140–155. Springer LNCS 1378, 1998. 392

14. R. Cleaveland, J. Parrow, and B. Steffen. "The Concurrency Workbench: a Semantics Based Tool for the Verification of Concurrent Systems". *ACM Transactions on Programming Languages and Systems*, Vol. 15 No. 1:36–72, January 1993. 334, 377, 379, 380

15. A. Durante, R. Focardi, and R. Gorrieri. "A Compiler for Analysing Cryptographic Protocols Using Non-Interference". *ACM Transactions on Software Engineering and Methodology*, 9(4):489–530, 2000. 392

16. A. Durante, R. Focardi, and R. Gorrieri. "CVS at Work: A Report on New Failures upon Some Cryptographic Protocols". In *proceedings of Mathematical Methods, Models and Architectures for Computer Networks Security*, pages 287–299, St. Petersburg, Russia, May 2001. LNCS 2052. 392

17. N. Durgin, J. Mitchell, and D. Pavlovic. "Protocol composition and correctness". In *proceedings of Workshop on Issues in the Theory of Security (WITS '00)*, University of Geneva, July 2000. 331

18. R. Focardi. "Comparing Two Information Flow Security Properties". In *Proceedings of Ninth IEEE Computer Security Foundation Workshop, (CSFW'96), (M. Merritt Ed.)*, pages 116–122. IEEE press, June 1996. 348, 368

19. R. Focardi. "Located Entity Authentication". Technical Report CS98-5, University of Venice, 1998. 392

20. R. Focardi. "Using Entity Locations for the Analysis of Authentication Protocols". In *Proceedings of Sixth Italian Conference on Theoretical Computer Science (ICTCS'98)*, November 1998. 392

21. R. Focardi. *Analysis and Automatic Detection of Information Flows in Systems and Networks*. PhD thesis, University of Bologna (Italy), 1999. 331, 348

22. R. Focardi and R. Gorrieri. "An Information Flow Security Property for CCS". In *Proceedings of the Second North American Process Algebra Workshop (NAPAW '93)*, TR 93-1369, Cornell (Ithaca), August 1993. 348

23. R. Focardi and R. Gorrieri. "A Taxonomy of Trace-based Security Properties for CCS ". In *Proceedings Seventh IEEE Computer Security Foundation Workshop, (CSFW'94), (Li Gong Ed.)*, pages 126–136, Franconia (NH), June 1994. IEEE Press. 348

24. R. Focardi and R. Gorrieri. "A Classification of Security Properties for Process Algebras". *Journal of Computer Security*, 3(1):5–33, 1994/1995. 333, 335, 348, 362, 363, 376, 377

25. R. Focardi and R. Gorrieri. "Automatic Compositional Verification of Some Security Properties". In *Proceedings of Second International Workshop on Tools and Algorithms for the Construction and Analysis of Systems (TACAS'96)*, pages 167–186, Passau (Germany), March 1996. Springer-Verlag, LNCS 1055. 377

26. R. Focardi and R. Gorrieri. "The Compositional Security Checker: A Tool for the Verification of Information Flow Security Properties". *IEEE Transactions on Software Engineering*, 23(9):550–571, September 1997. 335, 348, 377

27. R. Focardi, R. Gorrieri, and F. Martinelli. "Classification of Security Properties (Part II: Network Security)". Forthcoming. 392

28. R. Focardi, R. Gorrieri, and F. Martinelli. "Information Flow Analysis in a Discrete Time Process Algebra". In *Proceedings of 13th IEEE Computer Security Foundations Workshop (CSFW13), (P.Syverson ed.)*, pages 170–184. IEEE CS Press, July 2000. 391

29. R. Focardi, R. Gorrieri, and F. Martinelli. Message authentication through noninterference. In *Proc. of 8th International Conference in Algebraic Methodology and Software Technology* (AMAST), 2000. 392

30. R. Focardi, R. Gorrieri, and F. Martinelli. "Non Interference for the Analysis of Cryptographic Protocols". In *Proceedings of ICALP'00*, pages 744–755. LNCS 1853, July 2000. 331, 392

31. R. Focardi, R. Gorrieri, and F. Martinelli. Secrecy in security protocols as noninterference. In *Workshop on secure architectures and information flow*, volume 32 of *ENTCS*, 2000. 392

32. R. Focardi, R. Gorrieri, and V. Panini. "The Security Checker: a Semantics-based Tool for the Verification of Security Properties". In *Proceedings Eight IEEE Computer Security Foundation Workshop, (CSFW'95) (Li Gong Ed.)*, pages 60–69, Kenmare (Ireland), June 1995. IEEE Press. 377

33. R. Focardi, R. Gorrieri, and R. Segala. "A New Definition of Multilevel Security". In *proceedings of Workshop on Issues in the Theory of Security (WITS '00)*, University of Geneva, July 2000. 391

34. R. Focardi and F. Martinelli. "A Uniform Approach for the Definition of Security Properties". In *Proceedings of World Congress on Formal Methods (FM'99)*, pages 794–813. Springer, LNCS 1708, 1999. 392

35. C. Fournet and M. Abadi. "Mobile Values, New Names, and Secure Communication". In *Proceedings of the 28th ACM Symposium on Principles of Programming Languages (POPL'01)*, pages 104–115, January 2001. 392

36. J. A. Goguen and J. Meseguer. "Security Policy and Security Models". In *Proceedings of the 1982 Symposium on Security and Privacy*, pages 11–20. IEEE Computer Society Press, April 1982. 332, 333, 348

37. M. Hennessy and J. Riely. "Information Flow vs. Resource Access in the Asynchronous Pi-Calculus". In *proceedings of ICALP*, pages 415–427, 2000. 392

38. Y. Hirshfeld. "Bisimulation Trees and the Decidability of Weak Bisimulations". Technical report, Tel Aviv University, 1996. 356

39. C. A. R. Hoare. *Communicating Sequential Processes*. Prentice-Hall, 1985. 336, 337, 368

40. J. Hopcroft and J. Ullman. *Introduction to Automata Theory, Languages and Computation.*, pages 22–24. Addison-Wesley, 1979. 381

41. D. M. Johnson and F. J. Thayer. "Security and the Composition of Machines". In *Proceedings of the Computer Security Foundations Workshop*, pages 72–89, June 1988. 333, 376

42. P. Kanellakis and S. A. Smolka. "CCS Expressions, Finite State Processes, and Three Problems of Equivalence". *Information & Computation 86*, pages 43–68, May 1990. 355, 380, 381

43. R. Keller. "Formal Verification of Parallel Programs". *Communications of the ACM*, 19 (7):561–572, 1976. 333

44. G. Lowe. "Casper: A Compiler for the Analysis of Security Protocols". *Journal of Computer Security*, 6:53–84, 1998. 331

45. G. Lowe and B. Roscoe. "Using CSP to detect Errors in the TMN Protocol". *IEEE Transactions on Software Engineering*, 23(10):659–669, 1997. 331

46. D. Marchignoli and F. Martinelli. Automatic verification of cryptographic protocols through compositional analysis techniques. In *Proceedings of the International Conference on Tools and Algorithms for the Construction and the Analysis of Systems (TACAS)*, 1999. 392

47. F. Martinelli. "Partial Model Checking and Theorem Proving for Ensuring Security Properties". In *Proceedings of the 11th Computer Security Foundation Workshop, (CSFW'98)*. IEEE press, 1998. 361, 392

48. D. McCullough. "Noninterference and the Composability of Security Properties". In *Proceedings, 1988 IEEE Symposium on Security and Privacy*, pages 177–186. IEEE Computer Society Press, April 1988. 333, 376

49. J. K. Millen. "Hookup Security for Synchronous Machines". In *Proceedings of the Third Computer Security Foundation Workshop III*. IEEE Computer Society Press, 1990. 333

50. R. Milner. *Communication and Concurrency*. Prentice-Hall, 1989. 333, 335, 337, 339, 340, 343, 344, 361, 363, 364

51. J. C. Mitchell, M. Mitchell, and U. Stern. "Automated Analysis of Cryptographic Protocols Using Murϕ". In *Proceedings of the 1997 IEEE Symposium on Research in Security and Privacy*, pages 141–153. IEEE Computer Society Press, 1997. 331

52. R. De Nicola and M. Hennessy. "Testing equivalences for processes". *Theoretical Computer Science*, 34:83–133, 1984. 341, 348, 353

53. L. C. Paulson. "Proving Properties of Security Protocols by Induction". In *10th Computer Security Foundations Workshop*, pages 70–83. IEEE Computer Society Press, 1997. 331

54. G. Plotkin. "A Structural Approach to Operational Semantics". Technical Report DAIMI-FN-19, Aarhus University, 1981. 334

55. A. W. Roscoe. "Model Checking CSP". In A. W. Roscoe (ed) *A Classical Mind*. Prentice Hall, 1994. 368, 375

56. A. W. Roscoe, J. C. P. Woodcock, and L. Wulf. "Non-interference through Determinism". In *Proceeding of European Symposium on Research in Computer Security 1994 (ESORICS'94)*, pages 33–53. Springer-Verlag LNCS 875, 1994. 368, 369, 370, 375

57. P. Y. A. Ryan. "A CSP Formulation of Non-Interference". In *Proceedings of the 1990 Computer Security Foundation Workshop III*, Franconia, 1990. IEEE press. 368

58. P. Y. A. Ryan. "Mathematical Models of Computer Security". In this volume. 376

59. S. Schneider. "Verifying authentication protocols in CSP". *IEEE Transactions on Software Engineering*, 24(9), September 1998. 331

60. G. Smith and D. M. Volpano. "Secure Information Flow in a Multi-Threaded Imperative Language". In *Proc. of POPL*, pages 355–364, 1998. 331
61. L. J. Stockmeyer and A. R. Meyer. "Word problems requiring exponential time". In *Proceedings of the 5th ACM Symposium on Theory of Computing*, pages 1–9, Austin, Texas, 1973. 355
62. D. Sutherland. "A Model of Information". In *Proceedings of the 9th National Computer Security Conference*, pages 175–183. National Bureau of Standards and National Computer Security Center, September 1986. 333, 376
63. C. R. Tsai, V. D. Gligor, and C. S. Chandersekaran. "On the Identification of Covert Storage Channels in Secure Systems". *IEEE Transactions on Software Engineering*, pages 569–580, June 1990. 332
64. J. T. Wittbold and D. M. Johnson. "Information Flow in Nondeterministic Systems". In *Proceedings of the 1990 IEEE Symposium on Research in Security and Privacy*, pages 144–161. IEEE Computer Society Press, 1990. 333

Author Index

Lecture Notes in Computer Science

For information about Vols. 1–2144
please contact your bookseller or Springer-Verlag